Air Fryer Cookl 2022

1000+ Scrumptious and Delicious Recipes To Cook In Air fryer And Enjoy Healthy Meals with Your Loved ones

VERA MORENO

Contents

Chapter 10: Air Fryer Vegan Recipes 166

Chapter 11: Air Fryer Vegetarian Recipes ...196

Introduction

In practically every kitchen, counter space is in short supply. Even if you have a lot of room, it's easy to overcrowd it and fill it with the newest kitchen gadgets. However, you'll want to create a place for an air fryer. In the sense that it bakes and roasts, an air fryer is similar to an oven, but the difference is that its heating elements are only on top and are associated by a large, powerful fan, likely to result in food that is super crispy in no time — and, most importantly, with less oil than the deep-fried counterparts.

Because of the combination of an intense heat source and the size and positioning of the fan, air fryers often heat up rapidly and cook food quickly and evenly. Air fryers are easy and quick to operate and can be used to cook fresh things like steak, chicken, pork chops, fish, and vegetables or heat the frozen items after you learn how they work. Because most meats are already juicy, they don't need any additional oil; season them with some salt and your preferred herbs and spices. Stick to dry spices since less moisture means crispier results. Wait until a final couple of minutes of cooking to brush meats with barbecue sauce or honey. Tater tots, frozen mozzarella sticks, frozen fries, and chicken nuggets are all good options.

Air fryers are also great for making fried chicken, particularly amazing wings. Roasted veggies will be crispy, browned, and properly cooked in the middle, but you'll need the same amount of oil as if you were roasting them in the oven. Anything that can get advantage from high heat, such as cut-in-half potatoes drizzled in olive oil, steaks, chickpeas that can become a super-crunchy snack, chops, and more, is ideal for an air fryer. Air fryer s 'mores are a fantastic party trick, and you can also make bread and cookies. Yes, you may use your air fryer to prepare delectable dishes. This book has 800 tasty and healthful air fryer recipes for you to try. Enjoy!

Chapter 1: What Is an Air Fryer

It is no mystery that the need for nutritious, tasty, and convenient meals is juggled by most people 7 days a week. However, the quickest choices for dinner are always unhealthy and filled with salt and grease. Many consumers struggle to balance delicious, quick, and simple meals as our lives move at significantly higher speeds. The Philips Electronics Corporation presented the world with an appliance that is genuinely like no other to solve the said dilemma: The Air Fryer. This creative piece of machinery solved all aspects of mealtime challenges. Air Fryer is a machine that can fry tasty meals without needing to use cooking oil, making you obese or unhealthy. An amazing aspect of the Air Fryer is that it provides extremely delicious meals by using little cooking oil. The technology behind the fryer eliminates fat and calories, along with the oil usually used to make fried foods. This process prevents their meals and arteries from being coated with cooking oil. Philips is actively updating the Air Fryer, announcing that hot air is the new hot oil, while the original Air Fryer needs minor tweaking and newer versions do not vary profoundly from the 2010 appliances. The engineers behind the Air Fryer allow customers' needs and feedback to guide their product evolution. Adjustments such as increasing motor power, extending the fryer capacity, and making accessory packages customized to cooking areas like baking, grilling, and simultaneously cooking several foods have been the most notable improvements. The organization also listens to advice from professionals such as those at Industry Insider, in addition to the feedback of their client base, who indicate that customers prefer performance, ease of use, versatility, and significant capacity in an Air Fryer. It operates by using superheated air for cooking your meal, which circulates inside its chamber.

A fan causes the hot air to flow within the air fryer and lets the air fryer produce a reaction known as the Maillard effect. The Maillard effect, named after Louis-Camille Maillard, a French chemist, is a chemical reaction characterized by amino acid bonding and sugar reducing effects. Most prominently, this chemical reaction is known to give browned food its distinctive flavor and fragrance. Biscuits, steaks, bread, fried dumplings, and many more are some instances of browned foods. This invention has considered the requirements of people who are conscious about their lifestyle and health. There is up to 80% less fat in the dishes that are fried using the Air Fryer. That's a big reduction in the fat you eat every time you consume oily foods, including French fries, popcorn, and many more. Not only is the equipment limited to preparing dishes, but it also makes desserts like cake, cookies and more. The number of items this machine can prepare is almost infinite. The Air Fryer brilliantly cooks steaks and chops, apart from the foods you could hope to obtain from a machine with the word fryer in the name. Provided you use the specially built separating trays, it will prepare all of your breakfast staples and side dishes. The trays prevent the foods' different tastes from mixing. It also divides the cooking chamber so that each form of food is perfectly cooked. The truth is that the Air Fryer is an outstanding device for baking surprises many customers. While it is less than a decade old, the Air Fryer is already a cornerstone in many homes.

Since the fryer can cook delicious meals, it can replace many other appliances in your kitchen, not just the kinds of foods usually prepared by frying. The Air Fryer makes an outstanding addition to your kitchen as an all-in-one useful device.

Tips and tricks

Given below are the tips and tricks for effective use of Air Fryer:

Use frozen food for crispy results

In an air-fryer, frozen nuggets will get crunchy and golden. The air fryer is a perfect appliance to reheat or prepare frozen food.

You can quickly make cookies in an air fryer

In an air fryer, cookies will thrive; plus, they are easy to prepare.

Use your air fryer for cooking steak

Since air fryers can act as miniature ovens, steak can also be cooked. You will get wonderfully fried steak in the air fryer with a little bit of preparation, helping you to avoid the smoke and fire from the grill.

Cook chicken breasts in the air fryer for juicy results

The air fryer produces a chicken breast much juicier than either the microwave or the stove-top.

You can cook leaner and cleaner bacon in the air fryer

The extra oil falls into a separate reservoir when frying bacon, rendering clean-up a

breeze. To make it a little leaner, fat drips out of the basket, and it's so much less sticky and needs less supervision than most ways of cooking.

If you are running short of time, then switch to air-fried omelets

Air-fryer omelets are the best option if pressed for time one morning. It is possible to do all the preparation work the evening before. They cook in about six minutes.

Air-fried doughnuts are simply tasty

People don't have to fry doughnuts in oil. Doughnuts may be a heavy meal, but they might be a bit lighter if you cook them in an air fryer rather than oil.

Avoid cooking broccoli

Although air-frying yields better Brussels sprouts, it does not work for broccoli. Sadly, they get really dry and dusty, and the feeling is as if you are chewing on sandpaper.

Do not use large roasts or whole chickens

Large roasts or whole chickens just won't cook uniformly in the air fryer, despite the simple issue of whether they'll fit into the air-fryer basket.

Cheese can make it difficult to use an air fryer

You ought to stop sticking cheese in an air fryer as well. An air fryer is not a fryer because there's not the instant outer crust you'd get for, say, anything like a mozzarella stick from extremely deep-frying cheese. You're going to have a cheesy mess in the fryer instead.

Avoid using an air fryer for a burger

Without a bit of compromise, air frying a burger to optimal medium-rare is simply not going to happen.

Do not use fresh greens

Fresh greens are also something you want to stop putting into an air fryer, like spinach or kale.

Avoid over seasoned vegetables and proteins

Another big mistake is over-seasoning the meat and vegetables before putting them in the air fryer. In general, these seasonings could get blown off by the airflow inside an air fryer or fall through the basket when you have a product that seems to have a dry surface with seasonings.

Do not overcrowd the basket of the air fryer

Food, if it's too crowded, won't cook uniformly. You just want to stop overfilling the air-fryer basket, although it's tempting to put all of the ingredients into the air fryer at once in the hope of easily reheating or frying your meal.

Do not forget to pat the proteins dry before putting them in the air fryer

Before putting it in an air fryer, dry the surface of the meat. Another way to prevent soggy food is to ensure that when you begin to fry it, the surface of the food is dry.

Always clean your air fryer properly

You should clean the basket of your air fryer in the sink. Your air fryer needs to be cleaned, particularly if you use it frequently. You'll want to give a thorough wash to all the removable pieces of your air fryer or when you prepare something especially messy.

Always preheat the air fryer

If you forget to preheat your air fryer, you may contribute to undercooked food. A few minutes before putting the food in the air-fryer basket, set the air fryer to the right temperature for optimal cooking.

Do not use it to make fried foods only

To make fast and simple dinners such as pork chops or chicken breasts, cook small roasts and reheat your leftovers, you could use the air fryer as a mini convection oven.

Never forget to rotate the proteins during the cooking process

Not rotating the proteins is another popular air-fryer mistake. Halfway through cooking, tossing your protein will give you a uniformly cooked final dish.

Always move the vegetables around during the frying

When frying them in an air fryer, you may want to move your vegetables around regularly. If you toss them midway through cooking, vegetables can get browned excessively.

Use an air fryer for baking

For baking desserts, air fryers are also excellent. The air fryer is ideal for baking casseroles, doughnuts and even cakes if you are trying to make a delicious homemade dessert.

Do use oil

While you don't require oil to use the air fryer, you shouldn't be afraid to coat those foods a little bit, as it will help make them crispy.

How to look after and clean your air fryer

Gain knowledge about the do's and don'ts of air fryer maintenance before you deep clean your air fryer. Avoid using abrasive sponges, metal utensils, or steel wire brushes to remove the residue and food particles from your air fryer. Your air fryer's nonstick coating may be damaged due to this. Immerse the air fryer in water only if necessary. Because the main unit is an electric appliance, this will cause it to malfunction. If your air fryer emits a bad odor, place half a lemon in the basket and set it aside for 30 minutes before cleaning.

How often should you clean your air fryer

After each use

Wash the basket, tray, & pan with soap and warm water each time you use the air fryer, or put them in the dishwasher. Reassemble after drying all of the pieces.

After every few uses

Wipe off the outside with a damp cloth now and then. You should also look for any oil or residue on the heating coil. Allow the machine to cool before wiping it down with a damp cloth if there is any build-up.

How to clean the air fryer

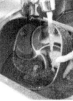

You will need the following:

- Clean, dry cloth
- Damp microfiber cloth or non-abrasive sponge
- Baking Soda
- Dish soap
- Soft-bristle scrub brush

Instructions

- To begin, unplug your air fryer. Allow for 30 minutes of cooking time.
- Remove your baskets & pans from the oven and wash them in hot, soapy water. Allow these pieces to soak in the hot soapy

water for a minimum of 10-minutes before washing with a non-abrasive sponge if any of them have baked-on grease or food. Some pieces may be dishwasher friendly; consult the manual if you want to clean in the dishwasher.

- Wipe out the interior with a damp microfiber cloth or a non-abrasive sponge dampened with dish soap. With a clean moist cloth, wipe away the soap.

- Turn the appliance upside down and clean the heating element with a damp cloth or sponge.

- Make a paste with water and baking soda if there is any baked-on or hard residue on the primary appliance. Using a soft-bristle scrub brush, scrape the paste into the residue and wipe away with a clean cloth.

- Wipe clean the outside using a damp cloth. With a clean damp cloth, wipe away the soap.

- Before reassembling, make sure all removable parts and the main unit are completely dry.

Olive oil and Air fryers

The best are high smoke point (or flashpoint) oils that won't burn at high temperatures. Because the cooking element/coils are close to the foods in air fryer cooking, some oils start smoking at high temperatures, and smoke and burning are common. Using high smoke point oil that doesn't smoke at high temperatures will result in better-tasting foods and fewer smoking problems. Extra virgin olive oil is usually unsuitable for air frying due to its low smoke point, but it can be utilized with its higher smoke point.

Chapter 2: Air Fryer Breakfast and Brunch Recipes

Air Fryer Candied Bacon

Preparation and Cooking Time

23 minutes

Servings

12 persons

Nutritional facts

131 calories ,9g fat ,8g fiber,10g carbs ,3g protein

Ingredients

- One tablespoon butter
- A quarter cup white miso paste
- 6 tablespoons honey or maple syrup
- One tablespoon rice wine vinegar
- Eight ounces thick-cut bacon

Instructions

- Preheat the air fryer to 390 F.
- In a small saucepan, melt the butter over medium heat. Then increase the heat to medium-high and add the miso paste, honey and rice wine vinegar. Stir until all ingredients are fully combined and bring the mixture to a boil. Remove it from the heat and set it aside.
- Place the bacon in the air fryer in a single layer and fry for 3-4 minutes on each side. Using a pastry brush, brush a thin layer of the miso glaze over one side of the bacon and air fry for 1 additional minute. It should be crispy and sticky when it's finished.

Cheesy Breakfast Egg Rolls

Preparation and Cooking Time

40 minutes

Servings

12 persons

Nutritional facts

209 calories ,10g fat ,1g fiber,19g carbs ,10g protein

Ingredients

- A half-pound bulk pork sausage
- A half-cup shredded sharp cheddar cheese
- A half-cup shredded Monterey Jack cheese
- 1/8 teaspoon pepper
- One tablespoon butter
- 12 egg roll wrappers
- One tablespoon chopped green onions
- 4 large eggs
- One tablespoon 2% milk
- 1/4 teaspoon salt
- Cooking spray
- Maple syrup or salsa, optional

Instructions

- In a small nonstick skillet, cook sausage over medium heat until no longer pink, 4-6 minutes, breaking into crumbles; drain. Stir in cheeses and green onions; set aside. Wipe skillet clean.
- Whisk eggs, milk, salt, and pepper in a small bowl until blended. In the same skillet, heat butter over medium heat. Pour in egg mixture; cook and stir until eggs are thickened, and no liquid egg remains. Stir in the sausage mixture.
- Preheat air fryer to 400°. With 1 corner of an egg roll wrapper facing you, place a quarter cup filling just below the center of the wrapper. (Cover the left over wrappers with a damp paper towel until they are ready to use.) Fold the bottom corner over your filling and moisten the wrapper edges with water. Fold side corners toward center overfilling. Roll egg roll up tightly, pressing at the tip to seal. Repeat.
- In batches, arrange egg rolls in a single layer on a greased tray in the air-fryer basket; spritz with cooking spray. Cook until lightly browned, 3-4 minutes. Turn; spritz with cooking spray. Cook until golden brown and crisp, 3-4 minutes longer. If desired, serve with maple syrup or salsa.

Air Fried Banana

Preparation and Cooking Time

8 minutes

Servings

2 persons

Nutritional facts

124 calories ,0.7g fat ,3.1g fiber, 27g carbs ,1.3g protein

Ingredients

- 1 ripe banana cut into 1/2 inch slices
- 1 tbsp. Granola to taste
- 1/4 tsp. cinnamon
- 1/2 tsp. brown sugar
- 1 tbsp. Chopped toasted nuts to taste

Instructions

- Combine the cinnamon & brown sugar in a small bowl and put aside.
- Grease a shallow baking pan lightly. In the pan, place the banana slices. Spray the banana with oil and then sprinkle it with cinnamon sugar. Air fried for 4-5 minutes at 400°F (200°C).
- To serve, sprinkle granola & nuts on top of the banana.

Air Fryer Shortbread Heart Cookies

Preparation and Cooking Time

25 minutes

Servings

2 persons

Nutritional facts

635 calories, 24g fat,1g fiber, 43g carbs ,5g protein

Ingredients

- 250g Plain Flour
- 1tsp Vanilla Essence

- 75g Caster Sugar
- 175g Butter
- Chocolate Buttons

Instructions

- Combine the self-rising flour, butter, and caster sugar in a mixing bowl.
- To make thick breadcrumbs, rub the butter into the flour.
- Knead the dough until it forms a ball and then rolls it with the rolling pin.
- Cut out your favorite shapes with cookie cutters.
- Cook your shortbread in an air fryer using either an air fryer grill plate or an air fryer baking mat. Preheat the oven to 180°C/360°F and set the timer for 10 minutes.
- Allow for some cooling time before serving.

Easy Pizza Pinwheels Air Fryer

Preparation and Cooking Time

30 minutes

Servings

10 persons

Nutritional facts

79 calories, 6g fat,1g fiber, 23g carbs,13g protein

Ingredients

- 2 tablespoons Tomato Paste
- 2 Basil Leaves, finely chopped
- ¼ teaspoon Dried Oregano
- 2 strips of bacon, diced
- Quarter Red Capsicum / Bell Pepper, diced
- 1 cup Shredded Cheddar Cheese
- 1 Puff Pastry Sheet, thawed
- **Instructions**
- Use baking paper to line the basket or trays of your air fryer.
- Place the puff pastry sheet on a clean, flat surface and evenly spread the tomato paste across it.
- Spread the remaining toppings evenly over the puff pastry sheet and then roll it up tightly. Cut into ten even pieces using a sharp knife.
- Place the pinwheels carefully into the paper-lined air fryer basket or trays, leaving some room between each one.
- Top each pinwheel with a sprinkling of cheese. Then cook for 12-15 minutes in an air fryer at 180°C/350°F, or once the cheese is melted, the puff pastry is golden.

Chewy Anzac Biscuits Air Fryer

Preparation and Cooking Time

25 minutes

Servings

15 persons

Nutritional facts

166 calories, 8g fat,1g fiber, 22g carbs, 2g protein

Ingredients

- 1 cup Rolled Oats / Old-Fashioned Oats
- 2 tablespoon Golden Syrup
- ½ teaspoon Bicarb Soda
- 1 cup Plain / All-Purpose Flour
- ⅔ cup Brown Sugar
- ⅔ cup Desiccated / Finely Shredded Coconut

- 125g Butter
- 2 tablespoon Boiling Water

Instructions

- Combine the oats, flour, sugar, and coconut in a mixing basin.
- In a medium saucepan, melt the butter & golden syrup together. Stir for another 2 minutes, just until the butter has completely melted. Combine bicarb and 2 tablespoons of hot water in a saucepan and then pour into it. This is a good thing since the butter will appear foamy, and there's no need to be concerned.
- Stir the wet ingredients into the dry ingredients in the mixing bowl. Take a tablespoon of the mixture & roll it into a ball and then carefully set it in the air fryer basket that has been prepared. To slightly flatten, press down. Continue with the remaining dough, allowing a gap between the biscuits to spread.
- Place the basket in the air fryer and cook for 15 minutes at 140°C / 285°F or golden brown.
- Remove the biscuits from the basket and set them aside to rest for 15 minutes before moving them to a wire rack to cool entirely.

Air Fryer Granola

Preparation and Cooking Time

15 minutes

Servings

4 persons

Nutritional facts

293 calories,17g fat, 4g fiber, 31g carbs, 6g protein

Ingredients

- ½ cup Natural Almonds, roughly chopped
- 2 tablespoon Coconut Oil
- 1 cup Old Fashioned / Rolled Oats
- 1 teaspoon Cinnamon
- Pinch of Salt
- 3 tablespoon Honey
- 1 teaspoon Vanilla Extract

Instructions

- In a mixing bowl, combine all ingredients and stir well to blend.
- Use parchment paper to line the air fryer basket. Pour out the granola mixture and spread it out evenly with a spoon.
- Cook for 10 minutes at 180 degrees Celsius / 350 degrees Fahrenheit, stirring every few minutes. When the mixture is golden brown, the granola is ready.
- Carefully remove the granola from the air fryer basket using the parchment paper's edges and place it on the counter to cool entirely.

Air Fryer Sweet Potato Wedges

Preparation and Cooking Time

30 minutes

Servings

2 persons

Nutritional facts

214 calories, 7g fat, 2g fiber,14g carbs,1g protein

Ingredients

- 2 Sweet Potatoes, skin on, washed & cut into wedges
- 2 tablespoons Olive Oil
- 1 tablespoon Corn Flour / Corn Starch

- 1 tablespoon Paprika
- Salt, to taste

Instructions

- Combine sweet potato wedges, corn flour/starch, paprika, and olive oil in a large mixing bowl. To blend, whisk everything together thoroughly.
- Place wedges in an air fryer basket or rack in a single layer, ensuring they don't touch. Cook for 20-25 minutes at 200°C/390°F, rotating the wedges halfway through. When the wedges are golden and crisp, they're done.
- Transfer to a platter and season liberally with salt. Serve right away.

Air Fryer Crispy Chicken Wings

Preparation and Cooking Time

35 minutes

Servings

4 persons

Nutritional facts

378 calories,11g fat ,1g fiber ,1g carbs ,6g protein

Ingredients

- 500g / 1 lbs. Chicken Wings
- 3 tablespoons butter
  - ¼ cup Frank's Hot Sauce (or more, to taste)
- 1 tablespoon Brown Sugar
- 1 tablespoon Baking Powder
- 1 teaspoon Paprika
- 1 teaspoon Garlic Powder
- Salt and Pepper, to taste
- 1 teaspoon Worcestershire Sauce
- ½ teaspoon Garlic Powder

Instructions

- Dry the wings as much as possible; the less moisture remaining on them, the crispier the skin! Toss the chicken wings with the baking powder, paprika, garlic powder, salt, and pepper in a mixing basin using your hands to ensure they are uniformly covered.
- In the air fryer basket, arrange the wings in a single layer with a little space between each wing.
- Cook at 150°C/300°F for fifteen minutes, then at 200°C/400°F for 10-15 minutes, or until thoroughly cooked. You may confirm this by checking the interior temperature of the wings using a meat thermometer. You can top it with your favorite sauce right away if you're serving it plain.
- In a small saucepan over medium heat, combine the ingredients. Cook stirring periodically until the sauce has slightly thickened and decreased.
- Toss your wings in the buffalo sauce and toss to coat them. Return the wings to the air fryer for another 2 minutes at 200°C to crisp up the sauce. Serve right away.

Air Fryer Pizza Pinwheels with Pineapple

Preparation and Cooking Time

25 minutes

Servings

8 persons

Nutritional facts

201 calories, 3g fat ,1g fiber, 23g carbs ,13g protein

Ingredients

- 1 cup Greek Yogurt
- 2 tablespoon Tinned Pineapple Pieces, finely diced
- 1 cup Shredded Mozzarella / Cheddar Cheese
- 1 ½ cups Self-Raising / Self-Rising Flour, plus more if needed
- 2 tablespoons Tomato Paste
- ¼ Red Capsicum / Bell Pepper, finely diced
- 2 slices Ham or Bacon, diced
- ½ teaspoon Dried Oregano

Instructions

- Use baking paper to line the basket or trays of your air fryer.
- In a mixing basin, combine Greek yogurt and stir well. Stir in one cup of flour until everything is well combined, and add more flour gradually until the dough begins to form a ball.
- Place the dough on a well-floured surface & knead for a minute or two with your hands. If the dough is still sticky, add more flour and knead it some more. It is ready when the dough holds its shape and does not stick to the hands or the surface.
- Roll out the dough into a rectangle, spread tomato paste on top and then top with the remaining ingredients.
- Cut the dough into 8 equal pieces after rolling it up tightly. Place the pinwheels in the paper-lined air fryer basket or trays with care, leaving enough space between each one for them to rise.
- Sprinkle a little cheese on top of each pinwheel and cook for 12-15 minutes in the air fryer, or till the cheese is melted and the dough is golden and cooked through.
- Allow pinwheels to cool on a wire rack.

Air Fryer Quesadillas

Preparation and Cooking Time

10 minutes

Servings

2 persons

Nutritional facts

310 calories, 3g fat, 9g fiber, 21g carbs, 61g protein

Ingredients

- Two flour tortillas
- 4 tablespoon Refried Beans, or more if needed
- Quarter cup Cheese, or more if needed

Instructions

- Place the tortilla on a flat surface. Next, spread refried beans on the tortilla's (half).
- Fold the tortilla in half and sprinkle cheese on top of the beans. Using the remaining tortilla, repeat the process.
- Place the tortillas in the air fryer basket and cook for 8 minutes, flipping halfway, or till the quesadillas are crisp & golden and the cheese is melted. Check on your quesadillas in the very first few minutes of cooking and check whether the tortilla has lifted slightly away from the fillings, push it back down with a spatula.
- If desired, serve with guacamole & sour cream or Greek yogurt right away.

Puffy Dogs

Preparation and Cooking Time

20 minutes

Servings

9 persons

Nutritional facts

257 calories, 5g fat,1g fiber, 9g carbs, 2g protein

Ingredients

- One Frozen Puff Pastry Sheet, thawed
- Nine Mini Hotdogs / Cocktail Frankfurt
- Egg lightly whisked for egg wash

Instructions

- Puff pastry sheets should be cut into nine even squares. Place a tiny hotdog/cocktail Frankfurt horizontally across a square of puff pastry and wrap the puff pastry around the hotdog, seam side down.
- If using, brush pastry with egg wash & sprinkle with optional toppings. Repeat with the rest of the ingredients.
- Preheat the air fryer to 200°C/390°F and cook the fluffy dogs for 7-10 minutes, or when the pastry is puffed & brown. Serve immediately with a dipping sauce of your choice.

Two Ingredient Dough Pretzel Bites

Preparation and Cooking Time

25 minutes

Servings

32 persons

Nutritional facts

35 calories,10g fat,1g fiber,19g carbs, 6g protein

Ingredients

- 1 cup Greek Yogurt
- One and a half cup self-raising / Self-Rising Flour (+ extra for flouring surface etc.)
- Two tablespoons butter, melted
- Pretzel Salt / Flakey Sea Salt, to taste

Instructions

- In a mixing bowl, whisk together one cup of Greek yogurt. Then stir in one cup of flour until everything is well combined.
- At this point, slowly add more flour until the dough comes together and forms a ball. This will usually be between 12 and 34 cups extra, depending on how wet your yogurt was, to begin with.
- Knead your dough ball on a well-floured surface until it is thoroughly mixed. If it's still too sticky, keep adding flour till you reach the desired consistency. The dough should keep its shape and not stick to the work surface.
- Cut the dough into four pieces that are all the same size. Each piece should be rolled into a long rope and then cut into equal bite-sized pieces.
- Arrange the pretzel bites in a single layer in the air fryer basket. If you're using a smaller air frying basket, do them in batches to not overlap and cook evenly. Cook for 7-10 minutes at 180 degrees Celsius / 350 degrees Fahrenheit, stirring the basket every few minutes, till golden brown.
- Brush the bites with melted butter & season with salt and pepper.

Spinach and Feta Pinwheels

Preparation and Cooking Time

30 minutes

Servings

12 persons

Nutritional facts

135 calories,13g fat, 3g fiber,14g carbs, 7g protein

Ingredients

- 1 sheet of Frozen Puff Pastry, defrosted
- 50g of Feta Cheese, crumbled
- 1 teaspoon of Olive Oil
- 2 minced Garlic Cloves
- 200g of Baby Spinach
- 2 tablespoons of Parmesan Cheese, grated
- Salt and Pepper, to taste

Instructions

- In a skillet pan over medium heat, heat the oil. Then you need to sauté for thirty seconds after adding the garlic. Add the spinach and cook until it has wilted. Remove the skillet from the heat, season the spinach with salt and black pepper, and set aside to cool.
- A Puff pastry sheet should be laid out on a clean, flat surface. Cooked spinach, feta cheese, and parmesan cheese are uniformly distributed throughout the puff pastry sheet. Make a tight roll with the puff pastry sheet. Cut the scrolls into 12 pieces with a sharp knife.
- Set the air fryer to 180C / 350F by running it at that temperature for 5 minutes.
- Cook the scrolls for 15 minutes in the air fryer basket, or till golden & cooked through.

Air Fryer Sausages

Preparation and Cooking Time

12 minutes

Servings

5 persons

Nutritional facts

210 calories ,35g fat ,1g fiber ,1g carbs ,16g protein

Ingredients

- Six sausages (Beef, Chicken, Pork etc.)

Instructions

- Preheat the air fryer to 180 degrees Celsius (350 degrees Fahrenheit).
- Prick each sausage two or three times with a knife and then arrange it in an air fryer basket in a single layer. It's fine if they're touching each other.
- Cook for 8 to 12 minutes, flipping halfway through until the sausages are browned & cooked through. Serve right away.

Bang Bang Cauliflower

Preparation and Cooking Time

30 minutes

Servings

2-4 persons

Nutritional facts

216 calories, 7g fat,1g fiber, 24g carbs, 2g protein

Ingredients

- ½ head of Cauliflower, cut into bite-sized florets
- 1 cup Panko Breadcrumbs
- Salt
- 2 tablespoon Mayonnaise
- 2 tablespoons Sweet Chili Sauce
- 1 teaspoon Sriracha
- Spray Oil

Instructions

- Heat the air fryer to 180 degrees Celsius (350 degrees Fahrenheit).
- In a mixing bowl, combine mayonnaise, sweet chili, and sriracha. On a separate plate, combine panko breadcrumbs and salt. In a mixing bowl, toss the cauliflower florets with the spicy mayonnaise and afterward coat with breadcrumbs. After spraying the cauliflower with oil, place it in the air fryer basket.
- Bake for 20 minutes, until golden and crisp, rotating the cauliflower pieces halfway through.
- Serve with bang bang sauce on the side or in a rice bowl with vegetables.

Air Fryer Apple Cinnamon Rolls No Yeast

Preparation and Cooking Time

25 minutes

Servings

8 persons

Nutritional facts

185 calories ,1g fat ,2g fiber ,35g carbs ,4g protein

Ingredients

- One cup Greek Yogurt
- 1 ½ cups Self-Rising Flour
- 2 tablespoon Unsalted Butter, melted
- Half cup Brown Sugar
- 1 ½ tbsp. Cinnamon
- 1 Apple finely diced

Instructions

- Heat the air fryer to 180°C/350°F by running it at that temperature for 5 minutes.
- In a mixing bowl, combine Greek yogurt and stir well. Stir in one cup of flour until everything is well combined, and add more flour gradually until the dough begins to form a ball.
- Place the dough on a well-floured surface & knead for a minute or two with your hands. If the dough is still sticky, add more flour and knead it some more. It is ready when the dough holds its shape and does not stick to the hands or the surface.
- Roll the dough into a rectangle using a well-floured rolling pin and then brush with butter and sprinkle with brown sugar and cinnamon. Apple slices should be sprinkled on top.
- Cut the dough into eight equal pieces after rolling it up tightly. Spread the pieces out in the air fryer basket, leaving enough room between each one for them to rise. You might have to cook in two batches with a smaller air fryer.
- Cook for 10-15 minutes, or until the dough has turned golden and is thoroughly cooked. Allow cooling completely on a wire rack.

Air Fryer Croutons

Preparation and Cooking Time

10 minutes

Servings

1 person

Nutritional facts

51 calories, 6g fat ,1g fiber ,10g carbs ,2g protein

Ingredients

- 2 slices of Bread
- One tsp. Olive Oil

Instructions

- Set the air fryer to 180C / 350F by running it at that temperature for 5 minutes.
- Make cubes out of your bread slices. Toss the bread pieces in a mixing bowl with the olive oil and mix well with your hands to ensure they are uniformly covered.
- Fill the air fryer basket halfway with bread cubes & spread them out in a single layer. Cook shaking the basket every minute for 3-5 minutes, or until golden and crisp.
- Allow the bread cubes to cool on a platter before using them right away or storing them in an airtight container.

Air-Fried Pizza Bombs

Preparation and Cooking Time

45 minutes

Servings

2 persons

Nutritional facts

305 calories ,10g fat ,1g fiber ,16g carbs ,5g protein

Ingredients

- 3 center-cut bacon slices
- 4 ounces fresh prepared whole-wheat pizza dough
- 3 large eggs, lightly beaten
- 1 ounce 1/3-less-fat cream cheese, softened
- 1 tablespoon chopped fresh chives
- Cooking spray

Instructions

- In a medium skillet over medium heat, cook bacon until crisp, about 10 minutes. Remove the bacon from the pan and crumble it. Cook, frequently stirring, till almost set but still loose, approximately 1 minute, in the bacon drippings in the pan. In a mixing bowl, whisk together the eggs, cream cheese, chives, & crumbled bacon.
- Divide the dough into four equal halves. On a lightly floured board, roll each piece into a 5-inch circle. Fill each dough circle with one-fourth of the egg mixture. Brush the outside edge of the dough with water and then wrap it around the egg mixture to form a purse, pinching the seams together.
- Coat the dough purses in cooking spray and arrange them in a single layer in the air fryer basket. Cook at 350°F for 5 to 6 minutes, or until golden brown.

Air Fryer Breakfast Bombs

Preparation and Cooking Time

19 minutes

Servings

6 persons

Nutritional facts

156 calories ,15g fat ,2g fiber ,26g carbs ,19g protein

Ingredients

- 1 tablespoon extra-virgin olive oil
- 1 can refrigerator Grand Biscuits
- 1/3 cup sharp cheddar cheese, shredded
- 1/2 lb. bulk breakfast sausage
- 3 large eggs, beaten
- 1/4 teaspoon salt
- 1/4 teaspoon pepper
- 1 egg
- 1 tablespoon water

Instructions

- Cut parchment paper to fit your air fryer basket.
- Heat the oil in a medium skillet over medium-high heat. Brown, the sausage, breaking it up into little pieces as it cooks until it is no longer pink. Remove the skillet from the heat, drain it, and put it aside.
- Reduce heat to medium-low in the same skillet. Add the beaten eggs, salt, and pepper to the same pan, and cook until the eggs are barely cooked through. Don't overcook the food. Stir the eggs into the sausage bowl to mix. Allow 5 minutes for the mixture to cool.
- Remove the biscuits from the package & layer them two at a time. Make a 4-inch circle out of each biscuit half. One heaping tablespoon of the egg mixture should be placed in the center of each round, and shredded cheese should be lightly sprinkled on top.
- Fold the edges up and over the filling, pinching to seal the top.
- In a small mixing dish, whisk together the remaining egg & water. Apply the egg wash to all sides of the biscuits with a pastry brush.
- Preheat the Air Fryer to 325°F, as directed by the manufacturer. Place the biscuit bombs in the air fryer basket, seam sides down, on parchment paper.
- Cook for an additional 8 minutes. Continue to heat for another 4 to 6 minutes, or when the biscuits are cooked through, the internal temperature reaches 165°F.
- Because the insides will be hot, remove them from the air fryer and set them aside for 5 minutes before serving.

Air Fryer Biscuit Bombs

Preparation and Cooking Time

45 minutes

Servings

10 persons

Nutritional facts

190 calories ,9g fat ,1g fiber ,2g carbs ,5g protein

Ingredients

- 1 tablespoon vegetable oil
- 1 can (10.2 oz.) refrigerated Pillsbury™ Grands! ™ Flaky Layers Original Biscuits (5 Count)
- 2 oz. sharp Cheddar cheese, cut in ten 1/2-inch cubes
- 1/4 lb. bulk breakfast sausage
- 2 eggs, beaten
- 1/8 teaspoon salt
- 1/8 teaspoon pepper
- 1 egg
- One tablespoon water

Instructions

- Cooking parchment paper is cut into two 8-inch rounds. Place one round in the bottom of the air fryer basket, and cooking spray should be used.
- Heat the oil in a 10-inch nonstick skillet over medium-high heat. Cook sausage in oil for 2 to 5 minutes, until no longer pink, occasionally tossing to crumble; transfer to a medium bowl with a slotted spoon. Reduce to a medium heat setting. Add beaten eggs, salt, and pepper to drippings in skillet; simmer, often turning, till eggs are thickened but still moist. In a mixing dish, whisk together the eggs and sausage. Allow 5 minutes for cooling.
- Separate the dough into five biscuits; each biscuit should be divided into two layers. Each should be pressed into a 4-inch round. One heaping tablespoon of the egg mixture should be spooned into the center of each round. One piece of cheese

should be placed on top. Fold the edges up and over the filling gently; pinch to seal. In a small mixing dish, whisk together the remaining egg & water. Brush the egg wash all over the biscuits.

- In an air fryer basket, place 5 biscuit bombs, seam sides down, on parchment paper. Cooking spray is applied on all sides of the second parchment round. Place the second parchment round on top of the biscuit bombs in the basket and then top with the remaining five biscuit bombs.
- Preheat oven to 325°F and bake for 8 minutes. Remove top parchment round; carefully turn biscuits with tongs and place in a single layer in the basket. Cook for another 4 to 6 minutes, or until well cooked (at least 165°F).

Air Fryer Breakfast Taquitos

Preparation and Cooking Time

30 minutes

Servings

20 persons

Nutritional facts

80 calories ,8g fat ,2g fiber ,13g carbs ,8g protein

Ingredients

- ½ pound ground breakfast sausage
- 1 tablespoon olive oil
- Quarter cup sour cream for dipping
- 3 large eggs, whisked
- ¾ cup Monterrey Jack cheese, shredded
- ¼ cup salsa
- 20 wonton wrappers
- ¼ cup salsa, for dipping

Instructions

- Heat the air fryer to 370°F & put a nonstick cooking spray into the basket.
- Brown the sausage in a medium skillet over medium-high heat.
- Reduce the heat to medium-low & add the whisked eggs. Continue cooking until done (about 3-5 minutes).
- Add the cheese & salsa to the sausage and eggs. To blend, stir everything together.
- Equally, divide the sausage and egg mixture among each wonton wrapper (about 1 tablespoon each).
- Roll each wrapper up (leaving the ends open) & place it in a single layer in the air fryer basket. You may need to work in batches depending on the size of your air fryer.
- Brush the taquitos' tops with the oil. Cook for 5 minutes at 370°F in an air fryer. Turn the taquitos over and continue to air fry for another five minutes.
- Remove the air fryer basket from the oven & serve with sour cream & additional salsa for dipping.

Air Fryer Breakfast Tacos

Preparation and Cooking Time

30 minutes

Servings

4 persons

Nutritional facts

432 calories ,15g fat ,4g fiber ,26g carbs ,19g protein

Ingredients

- Nonstick cooking spray for the molds
- 2 tablespoons mayonnaise
- 1 tablespoon hot sauce

- 4 large eggs
- Kosher salt
- Four 6-inch corn tortillas
- 1 cup shredded Mexican blend cheese
- 1 tomato, seeded and diced
- 1 avocado, cubed

Instructions

- Apply oil to the cavities of mold. Push the mold to one side in the basket of air fryer to make place for a second mold.
- Whisk together the eggs in a cup until no white streaks remain. Add 1/2 teaspoon salt and pepper to taste. Slowly pour the eggs into the mold's cavities, dividing them equally.
- Stack the corn tortillas, wrap them in a damp paper towel, and microwave on high for about 1 minute, or until warm and flexible. Fold one tortilla in half gently and press the folded edge into one hole of a second ice cube stick mold, being careful not to break the tortilla. It's now in the shape of a firm taco shell. Carry on with the other tortillas in the same manner.
- Transfer the mold to the air fryer basket next to the mold with the eggs and divide the cheese evenly among the shells, tapping it down equally into the bottoms.
- Preheat the air fryer to 300°F and bake for 12 minutes. The cheese in the taco shells should be melted before transferring the form to a work surface.
- Lift each portion of the egg from the mold gently to check if it's set.
- Transfer the mold to your work area if there is no liquid egg on the bottom.
- Cook for one additional minute if there is a liquid egg on the bottom.
- In a small mixing dish, combine the mayonnaise and spicy sauce.
- Allow 1 minute for the taco shells & eggs to cool enough to handle before removing them from the molds. The taco shells & eggs should be removed from the molds. Place the eggs and top with tomatoes, avocado, and spicy mayonnaise in taco shells.

Air Fryer Breakfast Bake

Preparation and Cooking Time

45 minutes

Servings

2 persons

Nutritional facts

282 calories ,4g fat ,3g fiber ,14g carbs ,9 protein

Ingredients

- 4 eggs
- 1 1/2 cups Baby Spinach
- 1/4 cup shredded cheddar cheese
- 2 tablespoons 1% low-fat milk
- 1/2teaspoon kosher salt
- 1 teaspoon hot sauce
- 1 slice whole-grain bread, torn into pieces
- Half cup diced bell pepper
- 2 tablespoons shredded cheddar cheese

Instructions

- Preheat the air fryer to 250°F. Set aside a 6-inch soufflé dish sprayed with nonstick cooking spray.

- Whisk together the milk, eggs, salt, and spicy sauce in a medium mixing bowl.
- Combine the bread, spinach, bell pepper and 14 cups of cheese in a mixing bowl.
- Fill the casserole dish with egg mixture and place in air fryer basket.
- The cooking time is 20 minutes. Cook for another 5 minutes, or until the eggs are set, and the edges are golden brown. Pause the machine, and sprinkle with the remaining cheese.
- Remove from the fryer basket with care and set aside 10 minutes before serving.

Air Fryer Breakfast Casserole

Preparation and Cooking Time

45 minutes

Servings

4 persons

Nutritional facts

234 calories ,43g fat ,2g fiber ,9g carbs ,32 protein

Ingredients

- 8 large eggs
- 2 handfuls baby spinach or kale
- 1/2 cup Parmesan cheese shredded
- 1/2 cup milk any
- 15 brown mushrooms thinly sliced
- 1 large red bell pepper thinly sliced
- 1/3 cup red onion thinly sliced
- 1/2 tsp. salt divided
- Ground black pepper to taste

Instructions

- Vegetables should be chopped, and cheese should be grated.
- Preheat the air fryer for 5 minutes at 400 degrees F.
- Line the air fryer basket with parchment paper, making sure it is properly spaced in the center to contain the egg mixture on all sides. Trim any protruding corners.
- Mushrooms, bell pepper, red onion, and 1/4 teaspoon salt and pepper are added to the pan. Shake and stir once during the 15-minute air fry.
- Meanwhile, whisk together eggs, milk, 1/2 teaspoon salt, and pepper in a medium mixing bowl.
- Remove the basket from the air fryer and mix in the spinach with a tiny spatula until it is slightly wilted and uniformly distributed.
- Sprinkle with Parmesan cheese & pour the egg mixture over it carefully. Bake for 20 minutes at 300 degrees F, or until a toothpick inserted in the center comes out clean.
- Serve hot or cold after being cut into eight slices with a serrated knife.

Air Fryer Bacon and Egg Toast

Preparation and Cooking Time

10 minutes

Servings

1 person

Nutritional facts

256 calories ,16g fat ,0.2g fiber ,6g carbs ,11g protein

Ingredients

- Butter (if desired)

- 1 slice of bread
- 1 slice of bacon
- 1 egg
- Salt & pepper to taste

Instructions

- Place a slice of bread in the air fryer after buttering it. Place a slice of bacon on the bread and wrap it around it. In the center, crack an egg.
- Close the air fryer & cook at 340 degrees for 9 minutes, or until done to your liking. Then season with salt and pepper to taste.

Air Fryer French toast

Preparation and Cooking Time

12 minutes

Servings

2 persons

Nutritional facts

472 calories ,2g fat ,3g fiber ,6 carbs ,14g protein

Ingredients

- 3 large eggs
- ⅛ teaspoon salt
- 3 slices of thick-sliced brioche bread
- Oil for spraying
- ¼ cup of heavy cream
- 2 tbsp. of light brown sugar
- ½ teaspoon of vanilla extract
- ½ teaspoon of ground cinnamon

Instructions

- Preheat the air fryer to a temperature of 380°F.
- Whisk together the heavy cream, vanilla essence, eggs, ground cinnamon, light brown sugar, and salt in a large bowl.
- Allow 10 seconds for each side of the bread slices to soak in the egg mixture.
- Spray the inside of the air fryer basket with some oil and place the air fryer slices inside. Close and cook for 4 minutes at 380°F & then open and carefully flip the bread slices and cook for another 3 minutes.
- Remove from the oven, serve, and enjoy.

Air-Fryer Ham & Cheese Breakfast Bundles

Preparation and Cooking Time

45 minutes

Servings

4 persons

Nutritional facts

301 calories ,24g fat ,0g fiber ,10g carbs ,12g protein

Ingredients

- 5 sheets phyllo dough (14x9 inches)
- 1/8 teaspoon pepper
- 1/4 cup chopped fully cooked ham
- 1/4 cup shredded provolone cheese
- 1/4 cup butter, melted
- 2 ounces' cream cheese, cut into 4 pieces
- 4 large eggs
- 1/8 teaspoon salt
- Two teaspoons seasoned bread crumbs

- 2 teaspoons minced chives

Instructions

- Preheat the air fryer to 325 degrees F. Brush 1 sheet of phyllo dough with butter on a work surface. Brush four more phyllo sheets on top, brushing each layer.
- Cut layered sheets in half crosswise, then lengthwise.
- Each stack should be placed in a buttered 4-ounce ramekin. Fill each with a cream cheese slice. Break one egg into each cup with care. Use salt and pepper to taste; top with ham, cheese, bread crumbs, and chives. Pinch the phyllo together above the filling to seal it and form bundles.
- Brush the remaining butter over the ramekins on the tray in the air-fryer basket. Cook for 10-12 minutes, or until golden brown.

Air Fryer French Toast Pockets – Raspberry & Cream

Preparation and Cooking Time

12 minutes

Servings

1 person

Nutritional facts

243 calories ,22g fat ,2g fiber ,65g carbs ,16g protein

Ingredients

- Two slices of soft bread
- 1 tablespoon raspberry jam
- One tablespoon cream cheese softened
- 1 large egg
- One tbsp. milk

Instructions

- Place a spoonful of raspberry jam in the middle of one slice of bread as well as a tablespoon of cream cheese in the middle of the other. Spread the jam & cream cheese evenly across the top, but not the edges.
- Use a sandwich sealer to seal the jam and cream cheese slices together.
- Whisk the egg and milk together in a small dish.
- Preheat the air fryer for 2 minutes at 380°F.
- Using cooking spray, coat the air fryer basket. Cook 5 minutes at 380°F in an air fryer after dipping the sealed sandwich in the egg mixture. Flip the sandwich over and cook for another 2 minutes.

Air Fryer Breakfast Flautas

Preparation and Cooking Time

40 minutes

Servings

4 persons

Nutritional facts

443 calories ,24g fat ,2g fiber ,51g carbs ,36g protein

Ingredients

- 1 Tbsp. butter
- 1 tsp. chili powder
- ½ cup cotija cheese (or crumbled feta)
- 2 small avocados
- ½ cup sour cream
- 1 lime, juiced
- 8 fajita size tortillas
- 4 oz. cream cheese, softened

- 8 slices cooked bacon
- 8 eggs, beaten
- ½ tsp. salt
- ¼ tsp. pepper
- 1 ½ tsp. cumin
- ½ cup shredded Mexican cheese
- ½ tsp. salt
  - ¼ tsp. pepper

Instructions

- Melt the butter in a large skillet over medium heat. Scramble the eggs for 3-4 minutes, or until just cooked. Then season with salt, pepper, cumin, and chili powder after removing from the heat.
- Cream cheese should be spread along the center of each tortilla. One piece of
- bacon should be placed on top of the cream cheese, followed by scrambled eggs & shredded cheese.
- Tortillas should be tightly rolled.
- Place four tortillas, seam side down, on top of the baking rack in the low position in the bowl.
- Set the temperature to 400°F and bake for 10-12 minutes, or until the tortillas are crispy.
- Remove the tortillas and continue the process with the remaining tortillas.
- Meanwhile, combine all avocado crème ingredients & blend on low-medium speed till smooth.
- Top the flautas with avocado crème and cotija cheese.

Air Fryer Baby Breakfast Potatoes

Preparation and Cooking Time

25 minutes

Servings

4 persons

Nutritional facts

203 calories ,9g fat ,2g fiber ,30g carbs ,4g protein

Ingredients

- 1 ½ pound mini red potatoes, halved
- ½ teaspoon onion powder
- ½ teaspoon smoked paprika
- ½ teaspoon dried parsley
- ¼ teaspoon cayenne pepper
- Optional Garnish
- 2 Tablespoons olive oil
- 1 teaspoon salt
- ½ teaspoon pepper
- ½ teaspoon granulated garlic
- scallions, flakey salt, oregano

Instructions

- Mix the potatoes, olive oil, and spices in a large mixing bowl. Toss thoroughly.
- Fill the air fryer basket with enough potatoes to cover the bottom, but not too many. You may need to do this in several batches depending on the size of your air fryer.
- Cook for about ten min at 400°F.
- Rotate the potatoes in the basket by shaking them. Cook for another 8-10 minutes, or when the potatoes are golden brown and soft.

Roasted Potatoes with Bacon

Preparation and Cooking Time

30 minutes

Servings

4 persons

Nutritional facts

96 calories ,7g fat ,3g fiber ,22g carbs ,5g protein

Ingredients

- 1/2 lb. small gold potatoes skin on, quartered
- 4 slices bacon cut into large chunks
- 1/2 lb. small red potatoes skin on, quartered
- 1 Tbs. vegetable oil
- 1-2 tsp. of Montreal steak seasoning
- shredded cheddar and chopped scallions as a garnish, if desired

Instructions

- Stir the potatoes with the oil in a large mixing bowl & then season with the seasoning blend and toss again.
- Move the seasoned potatoes to the air fryer rack and air fry for 6-8 minutes at 400 degrees F. Place the bacon slices on top of the potatoes and air fry for 5 minutes.
- Toss the potatoes and bacon together with two big spoons; air fry for 5 minutes more, or when the potatoes are fork-tender as well as the bacon is crisp. Serve right away.

Air Fryer Frozen Breakfast Burritos

Preparation and Cooking Time

15 minutes

Servings

1 person

Nutritional facts

43 calories ,9g fat ,5g fiber ,40g carbs ,9g protein

Ingredients

- One frozen breakfast burrito

Instructions

- The frozen burrito is to be put into the air fryer basket. Cook at 350F for 15 minutes.

Air Fryer Breakfast Cups

Preparation and Cooking Time

30 minutes

Servings

8 persons

Nutritional facts

403 calories ,21g fat ,1g fiber ,23g carbs ,4g protein

Ingredients

- 1/4 cup ground breakfast sausage 2 ounces
- 2 tablespoons nutritional yeast
- 2 tablespoons coconut milk
- 1/4 cup potato
- Quarter cup onion
- 1/4 cup kale
- 6 large eggs
- non-stick cooking spray
- salt & pepper

Instructions

- Line the air fryer basket with foil for easy cleanup. Put silicone baking cups in a single layer in the fryer basket. Using nonstick cooking spray, coat the cups.
- Pour a quarter cup of the egg mixture into each cup carefully. Preheat the air fryer to 300 degrees F and "fry" the egg for 10 to 12 minutes, or until it is fully cooked. Allow at least five min for the cups to cool before removing them from the baking cups.

Ninja Foodi Breakfast Casserole

Preparation and Cooking Time

45 minutes

Servings

8 persons

Nutritional facts

350 calories ,12g fat ,0g fiber ,3g carbs ,15g protein

Ingredients

- 8 eggs
- 1 1/2 tsp. salt
- 1 tsp. black pepper
- 1-pound pork sausage - jimmy dean
- One and a half cups whole milk or heavy cream
- 1 30 oz. frozen shredded hash browns
- 2 cups cheddar cheese
- 1/4 tsp. garlic powder

Instructions

- Toss the uncooked ground sausage into the pot.
- Press Sauté and cook for 6-8 minutes, or until sausage is browned.
- Mix in the frozen hash browns thoroughly.
- Mix in 1 cup of cheese.
- Whisk together the eggs, heavy cream, and spices in a separate basin. Fill the pot with the egg mixture.
- Set the Foodi to Air Crisp at 350 degrees F for 30 minutes after closing the Air Crisp lid.
- After 25 minutes, check to see if the eggs are fully cooked. Eggs may need an extra 10 minutes to finish cooking.
- Close the lid and sprinkle the remaining one cup of cheese on top of the casserole.
- The cheese will melt as a result of the heat.
- Serve immediately

Air Fryer Breakfast Sandwiches

Preparation and Cooking Time

25 minutes

Servings

4 persons

Nutritional facts

405 calories ,10g fat ,2g fiber ,29g carbs ,13g protein

Ingredients

- 4 breakfast sausage patties
- 4 bagel thins or English muffins
- 4 eggs
- kosher salt, pepper
- 1 Tbsp. butter
- 4 slices cheese of choice

Instructions

- In the air fryer basket, place the breakfast sausage patties. Preheat the air fryer to 390 degrees Fahrenheit and cook for 15 minutes. Remove the sausage from the pan and place it on paper towels to absorb excess fat.
- In a mixing bowl, whisk the eggs with kosher salt and pepper. Melt the butter in a medium-sized skillet over low heat. Once the butter has melted, pour in the beaten eggs in a single layer. Cook for 2 - 3 minutes before flipping and cooking for another 1 to 2 minutes. Cut the egg into four equal pieces after removing it from the pan.
- Place the bottom half of the bagel or English muffin in the air fryer basket. Top each with a sausage patty, a cooked egg, and a piece of cheese.
- On each sandwich, place the top of the bagel or English muffin. Preheat the air fryer to 390°F for 4–5 minutes.

Air Fryer Breakfast Puffed Egg Tarts

Preparation and Cooking Time

26 minutes

Servings

4 persons

Nutritional facts

398 calories ,31g fat ,0.9g fiber ,27g carbs ,14g protein

Ingredients

- All-purpose flour
- One sheet frozen puff pastry half a 17.3-oz/490 g package, thawed
- 3/4 cup shredded cheese
- Four large eggs
- One tbsp. minced fresh parsley or chives optional

Instructions

- Unfold the pastry sheet on a gently floured surface. Cut each piece into four squares.
- Two squares should be placed in the air fryer basket, spacing apart. You need to air-fry for 10 minutes or until golden brown pastry.
- To form an indentation, open the basket and press down the centers of each square with a metal spoon. Three tbsp. (45 ml) cheese should be sprinkled into each indentation. Then crack an egg into each pastry's center.
- You need to cook for 7 to 11 minutes in the air fryer or until eggs are done to your liking. Allow cooling for 5 minutes on a wire rack set over waxed paper. If preferred, top with half of the parsley.
- Continue with the other pastry squares, cheese, eggs, and parsley.

Air Fryer Nashville-Style Hot Chicken and Waffles

Preparation and Cooking Time

1 hour 50 minutes

Servings

4 persons

Nutritional facts

763 calories ,27g fat ,3g fiber ,91g carbs ,41g protein

Ingredients

- 1-pound chicken thighs bone-in skin on
- 1 teaspoon paprika
- 3 teaspoons baking powder

- 1 teaspoon cinnamon
- 2 eggs
- salt and black pepper to taste
- 1 cup milk of choice optional to use buttermilk
- ½ teaspoon cayenne pepper
- ½ teaspoon chili powder
- ½ cup all-purpose flour or gluten-free (if needed)
- 1 teaspoon garlic powder
- 2 tablespoons maple syrup
- 1 cup milk of choice
- cooking spray
- 2 tablespoons butter
- 1 teaspoon chili powder
- 2 teaspoons thyme
- 1.5 cups all-purpose flour or gluten-free (if needed)
- ½ cup maple syrup

Instructions

- Marinate or brine the chicken for at least 60 minutes, but better overnight, in salt, pepper, and milk. Preheat the air fryer to 375°F.
- In a medium-sized mixing bowl, combine flour and spices and then coat a piece of chicken in the flour mixture on all sides.
- Cook the chicken for 25-30 minutes in the air fryer basket, flipping halfway through.
- In a large mixing basin, whisk all the waffle ingredients until smooth.
- Preheat the waffle machine and spray it with cooking spray once it's ready. In the waffle maker, pour about 1/4-1/3 cup of waffle mix and cook until gently browned on both sides. Continue until you've used up all of the mixes.
- In a small saucepan, add the butter, maple syrup, and spices and cook on low until the butter has melted, stirring constantly. Turn the heat off.
- Serve 1-two waffles with one to two pieces of chicken on top, and drizzle with maple butter sauce.

Air Fryer Bagels

Preparation and Cooking Time

15minutes

Servings

8 persons

Nutritional facts

166 calories ,2g fat ,1g fiber ,27g carbs ,10g protein

Ingredients

- Two cups unbleached all-purpose flour plus more for dusting work surface
- 1 tablespoon baking powder
- One teaspoon kosher salt
- 2 cups plain nonfat Greek yogurt
- One egg beaten

Instructions

- Measure and combine the flour, baking powder, and salt in a mixing bowl. To combine the ingredients, whisk them together.
- After that, whisk in the Greek yogurt with a rubber spatula until everything is well mixed. Form a ball out of the dough and place it on a floured surface.
- Cut the dough into eight equal pieces. Roll each piece into an 8-10-inch rope and squeeze the sides together to produce a bagel

shape. Brush the bagel with an egg wash and top with your favorite bagel toppings.
- Preheat the air fryer to 350 degrees Fahrenheit. Bagels should be air-fried for 10 to12 minutes or till golden.
- Allow for 5 minutes of cooling before slicing.

Air Fryer Frittata Omelet

Preparation and Cooking Time

25minutes

Servings

2 persons

Nutritional facts

214 calories ,27g fat ,0.4g fiber ,2g carbs ,31g protein

Ingredients

- 4 eggs
- Half cup shredded cheese
- Quarter cup finely chopped vegetables, for example, white or green onion, bell pepper, broccoli
- 1/8 tsp. salt
- One eighth tsp. pepper

Instructions

- Apply cooking spray on the bottom and sides of the baking dish to fit inside the air fryer. In the air fryer basket, place the baking dish.
- Combine the eggs, vegetables, salt, pepper, and 1/4 cup shredded cheese in a mixing bowl.
- Fill the baking dish halfway with the egg mixture. On top, strew the leftover 1/4 cup of shredded cheese.
- In an air fryer, cook the frittata for 20 minutes at 360°F, or until set.

Homemade Cajun Breakfast Sausage

Preparation and Cooking Time

45minutes

Servings

12-14 persons

Nutritional facts

126 calories ,4.4g fat ,0.8 fiber ,11g carbs ,11g protein

Ingredients

- 1.5 lbs. of ground sausage (chicken sausage or lean pork
- 1/4 tsp. or to taste Sea Salt: black pepper each
- Chopped sage (optional)
- 2 tsp. brown sugar, maple syrup for paleo option or coconut palm sugar
- 3 tsp. of minced garlic
- Herbs to garnish optional
- 1 tsp. of chili flakes
- Fresh thyme of 2 tsp. fresh leaves only
- 1 tsp. of onion powder
- 1/2 tsp. of each paprika and cayenne
- Tabasco 2 tbsp. of plus extra for serving

Instructions

- In a large mixing bowl, place the ground sausage. Check to see if it's chilled. Add any other spices or herbs you'd like. With your hands, combine everything. To make it less hot, omit the Tabasco sauce.
- Patties should be 3 to 3 1/2 inches wide and 1 to 1.5 inches thick.

When air fried, they will shrink.

- Place patties on a baking tray coated with parchment paper to prevent sticking.
- At a time, place 4 to 5 patties in the air fryer.
- You need to air fryer at 370F for 20 minutes on the chicken setting. Halfway through cooking, remove the tray and flip the patties, and the cooking will resume once you replace the tray in the oven.
- When the timer goes off, remove the sausage from the air fryers. Cover and place on a clean platter.
- Repeat with the remaining patties.
- Serve with additional Tabasco sauce or your preferred sauce.

Air-Fryer Egg and Ham Pockets

Preparation and Cooking Time

25minutes

Servings

2 persons

Nutritional facts

326 calories ,12g fat ,2g fiber ,39g carbs ,12g protein

Ingredients

- One large egg
- two teaspoons of 2% milk
- two teaspoons of butter
- One ounce of chopped and thinly sliced deli ham
- 2 tablespoons of shredded cheddar cheese
- One tube of refrigerated crescent rolls

Instructions

- Preheat air fryer to 300°. In a small bowl, combine milk and egg. In a skillet, heat the butter. Add the egg mixture; cook and stir over low to medium heat until the eggs are completely set. Remove from the heat. Fold in cheese and ham.
- Separate crescent dough into 2 rectangles. Seal perforations; spoon half the filling down the center of each rectangle. Fold dough over filling; pinch to seal. Place in a single layer on a greased tray in the air-fryer basket. Cook until golden brown, 8-10 minutes.

Air Fryer Breakfast Potatoes

Preparation and Cooking Time

20 minutes

Servings

2 persons

Nutritional facts

245 calories ,7g fat ,13g fiber ,67g carbs ,13g protein

Ingredients

- 3 cups red potatoes chopped into half-inch cubes
- 1/4 tsp. herbs thyme
- 1/4 cup bell pepper finely diced
- 1 tbsp. olive oil
- 1/2 tsp. kosher salt divided
- 1/4 tsp. paprika
- 1/4 tsp. garlic powder
- 1/4 cup onion finely diced
- 2 scallions for garnish if desired

Instructions

- If required, preheat the air fryer to 400 degrees.

- Meanwhile, combine the potatoes, olive oil, half the salt, and all the paprika, garlic powder, and herbs in a mixing bowl.
- Shake the potatoes in the air fryer basket to ensure they're properly spread. Set the timer for fifteen minutes and then hit the start button.
- After 5 minutes, give it another shake.
- Meanwhile, return the potatoes to the bowl and insert the peppers, onions, and remaining salt. Stir it up to coat the onions and peppers in the leftover potato spice and olive oil.
- Take the basket out 5 minutes before the potatoes are done cooking, add the peppers and onions on top, and cook until the timer turns off.
- Taste the potatoes after pouring them into a serving bowl. If required, season with extra salt and pepper.

Air Fryer Frozen Hash Brown Patties

Preparation and Cooking Time

8 minutes

Servings

4 persons

Nutritional facts

144 calories ,9g fat ,1g fiber ,0.7g carbs ,14.1g protein

Ingredients

- Four frozen hash brown patties

Instructions

- Preheat the air fryer to 400 degrees.
- Put hash brown patties on the inside of your air fryer in one layer, and cook for 8 to 10 minutes, flipping halfway through.
- Take out the hash browns from the air fryer. Let them cool for 2 minutes. Then enjoy.

Sausage Patties in the Air Fryer

Preparation and Cooking Time

6 minutes

Servings

8 persons

Nutritional facts

144 calories ,9g fat ,1g fiber ,0.7g carbs ,14.1g protein

Ingredients

- Eight raw sausage breakfast patties

Instructions

- Heat the air fryer to 370 degrees F.
- Put the raw sausage patties in one layer into the air fryer.
- It should be cooked for 6-8 minutes, till they reach 160 degrees F.

Air Fryer Jelly Donuts

Preparation and Cooking Time

15 minutes

Servings

8 persons

Nutritional facts

380 calories ,21g fat ,2g fiber ,34g carbs ,4g protein

Ingredients

- 1 package Pillsbury Grands
- Half cup seedless raspberry jelly
- 1 tablespoon butter, melted

- Half cup sugar

Instructions

- Preheat the air fryer to 320 degrees Fahrenheit.
- Cook the Grand Rolls in a single layer in the air fryer for 5-6 minutes, or until golden brown.
- Remove the rolls from the air fryer & place them on a plate to cool.
- Sugar should be placed in a broad bowl with a level bottom.
- Brush the donut with butter on all sides, and then roll it in sugar to cover it completely. Finish with the remaining donuts.
- Pipe 1-two tbsp. of raspberry jelly into each donut with a large cake tip.
- Enjoy right now or store for up to three days.

Air Fryer Scrambled Eggs

Preparation and Cooking Time

12 minutes

Servings

2 persons

Nutritional facts

126 calories ,4.4g fat ,1g fiber ,0.3g carbs ,6g protein

Ingredients

- 1/3 tablespoon unsalted butter
- Two eggs
- 1/8 cup cheddar cheese
- 2 tablespoons milk
- salt and pepper to taste

Instructions

- Put butter in an air fryer-safe pan, and air fry it.
- Cook for about 2 minutes at 300 degrees till the butter has melted.
- Combine the eggs and milk in a mixing bowl, and then season with salt and pepper to taste.
- Place eggs in a pan and cook at 300 degrees F for 3 minutes and then stir them about by pushing them to the inside of the pan.
- Cook for another 2 minutes before adding the cheddar cheese and whisking the eggs once more.
- Cook for another 2 minutes.
- Remove the pan from the air fryer & serve right away.

Air Fryer Turkey Bacon

Preparation and Cooking Time

6 minutes

Servings

4 persons

Nutritional facts

60 calories ,3g fat ,0g fiber ,0.5g carbs ,3g protein

Ingredients

- Eight slices of turkey bacon (cured or uncured)

Instructions

- Heat the air fryer to 400 degrees F.
- Put the turkey bacon in the air fryer and cook for 5-6 minutes. Cook uncured bacon for around 8-9 minutes. Flip the bacon halfway through cooking.
- Take out the turkey bacon from the air fryer. Enjoy

Quick and Easy Ube Glazed Air Fryer Donuts Recipe

Preparation and Cooking Time

11 minutes

Servings

8 persons

Nutritional facts

349 calories ,6g fat ,0.2g fiber ,27g carbs ,4g protein

Ingredients

- 1 cup powdered sugar
- ¼ teaspoon vanilla extract
- 2 tablespoons milk
- ½ teaspoon ube extract
- 1 can (16.3 ounces) Grands! ™ Flaky Layers Biscuits

Instructions

- Preheat the air fryer to 350 degrees Fahrenheit.
- Mix powdered sugar, milk, ube extract, & vanilla extract in a small bowl. Whisk everything together until it's completely smooth.
- Put biscuits on a cutting board after opening the biscuit can. Cut out the center hole of the donuts with one inch round cookie cutter. The donut holes can be kept to air fry as well.
- Spray the air fryer's basket with nonstick cooking spray. Place donuts in a basket with enough space between them. It's best to avoid stacking these while they're cooking.
- Open the drawer and flip the donuts over when the 3 minutes are up. Close the drawer and continue to air fry for an additional 2-3 minutes.
- Remove the donuts from the air fryer and set them aside to cool. Then dip the donut in the ube glaze and set it aside to cool entirely on a wire cooling rack set over a cookie sheet to catch any drips. Enjoy.

Crispy Air Fryer Breakfast Potatoes

Preparation and Cooking Time

30 minutes

Servings

4 persons

Nutritional facts

212 calories ,7g fat ,13g fiber ,67g carbs ,13g protein

Ingredients

- 3-4 russet potatoes
- 1/2 tsp. onion powder
- 1/2 tsp. sweet paprika
- 2-3 tbsp. olive oil
- 1 tsp. salt
- 1 tsp. garlic powder
- cooking spray

Instructions

- Peel the potatoes and chop them into 1-inch pieces.
- Toss the potatoes in olive oil and spice, ensuring they're all uniformly coated.
- Spray the air fryer basket with nonstick spray before adding the potatoes.
- You need to air fryer for twenty minutes at 400°F, shaking at least once halfway through.
- When done, serve right away.

Strawberry Turnovers

Preparation and Cooking Time

27 minutes

Servings

4 persons

Nutritional facts

257calories ,14g fat ,1g fiber ,34g carbs ,3g protein

Ingredients

- 1 can Crescent Dough Sheets 1 large or 2 small sheets
- One 20-oz Can strawberry pie filling
- 1 Large Egg beaten
- Two tsp. Water

Instructions

- Gently beat the egg with the water in a small bowl and leave aside.
- Cut the thawed puff pastry sheet(s) into 8 rectangles after unrolling.
- Fill 1 end of each rectangle with about 2 teaspoons of filling.
- Brush the egg wash around the filling on the three edges of the pastry.
- To seal the rectangle, fold the other end over the filling & press all three corners with a fork, poke a few holes in the top of each turnover.
- Brush the egg wash on the tops of the turnovers.
- Put the turnovers in the air fryer basket after spraying them with nonstick spray or lining it with parchment paper.
- Preheat the air fryer to 320 degrees Fahrenheit and cook for 17 minutes. Any turnovers which didn't quite fit in the basket should be placed on a parchment-lined baking sheet and refrigerated until ready to bake.
- Place the baked turnovers on a cooling rack after removing them from the fryer.

Low-Carb Air Fryer Bacon and Egg Cups

Preparation and Cooking Time

20 minutes

Servings

6 persons

Nutritional facts

115 calories ,9g fat ,1.2g fiber ,2g carbs ,8g protein

Ingredients

- Three slices bacon, sliced in half
- 6 large eggs
- One bunch green onions, optional
- salt and pepper, optional

Instructions

- In the air fryer basket, place 6 baking cups. Using nonstick frying spray, coat the pan.
- Bacon slices are used to line the cups. Crack an egg into every other cup with care. If desired, season with salt and pepper.
- Preheat the air fryer to 330 degrees & cook for ten minutes until the eggs are set. Take out from the air fryer with care and serve with preferred toppings.

Low-Carb Vegetable Egg Bake

Preparation and Cooking Time

35 minutes

Servings

8 persons

Nutritional facts

89 calories ,20g fat ,1.8g fiber ,8g carbs ,22g protein

Ingredients

- 8 large eggs
- 1/3 cup tomato, chopped
- One third cup zucchini, sliced
- Quarter cup coconut milk, from can
- 1/2 cup spinach, chopped
- Quarter tsp. sea salt
- 1/4 tsp. ground pepper

Instructions

- Heat the oven to 350 degrees Fahrenheit. Set aside a baking dish that has been sprayed with nonstick cooking spray.
- In a large mixing bowl, whisk together the eggs. Combine the tomato, coconut milk, spinach, zucchini, and salt and pepper in a large mixing bowl. Combine all of the ingredients.
- Bake for about 25 minutes, or until eggs are fully cooked but not over-cooked.

Air Fryer Pineapple Cream Cheese Wontons

Preparation and Cooking Time

22 minutes

Servings

10 persons

Nutritional facts

121 calories ,19g fat ,1g fiber ,3g carbs ,3g protein

Ingredients

- 8 oz. cream cheese, softened
- 30 wonton wrappers
- 2 tbsp. olive oil
- 1/4 cup crushed pineapple, drained
- 1/4 cup green onion, diced

Instructions

- Combine the cream cheese, crushed pineapple, and green onions in a medium mixing bowl.
- Fill the center of the wonton wrapper with a spoonful of filling. Using a brush, wet all of the sides. To make a pocket, pinch the two sides together. Next, pinch the other two sides together.
- Brush the outsides of the wontons lightly with olive oil before placing them in the air fryer basket. You may need to cook in batches to avoid overcrowding the basket.
- Preheat oven to 300°F & cook for 7 to 9 minutes.

Air Fryer Mozzarella Sticks

Preparation and Cooking Time

2 hours 24 minutes

Servings

6 persons

Nutritional facts

276 calories ,20g fat ,1g fiber ,20g carbs ,22g protein

Ingredients

- 16 oz. mozzarella block cheese
- 1/4 cup all-purpose flour
- 2 large eggs
- 3 tbsp. nonfat milk
- 1 cup plain breadcrumbs

Instructions

- Create 3 by 1/2-inch cheese sticks.
- In a mixing bowl, add the bread crumbs. In a mixing bowl, insert flour. In a mixing bowl, combine the egg and milk.
- Flour, egg, and bread crumbs are used to coat cheese sticks.
- Place the breaded sticks on a cookie sheet and spread them out flat.
- Freeze for 2 hours or till completely solid.
- Preheat the air fryer to 390° F for around 5 minutes. Using nonstick cooking spray, coat the basket. Remove the basket from the air fryer before spraying.
- Fill the fryer basket with small batches of breaded sticks. Do not overcrowd the area.
- Cook for 2 minutes at 390°F. Cook for another two minutes after flipping the mozzarella sticks.

Vanilla Bean Air Fryer Doughnuts

Preparation and Cooking Time

30 minutes

Servings

3 persons

Nutritional facts

189 calories ,8g fat ,1g fiber ,39g carbs ,5g protein

Ingredients

- Twelve ounces' fresh sea scallops, defrosted
- 2 tbsp. olive oil
- Half tsp. sea salt
- 1/2 tsp. ground black pepper
- Half tsp. garlic powder
- 1/2 tsp. onion powder
- Quarter cup traditional bread crumbs
- One tsp. Old Bay seasoning

Instructions

- In a large mixing bowl or resealable bag, pour the olive oil. Add the scallops and coat them completely.
- Mix the salt, pepper, garlic, and onion powder in a second bowl or bag. Toss the scallops in the seasonings after removing them from the olive oil.
- In a third bowl or bag, mix bread crumbs & Old Bay seasoning. Toss the scallops with the bread crumb mixture to coat them.
- Remove the air fryer basket and coat it lightly with nonstick cooking spray. In the basket, arrange the scallops in a beautiful pattern. Scallops may need to be cooked in two batches to avoid overcrowding.
- Preheat oven to 400°F and bake for 12 minutes. If the scallops are larger, cook for up to 15 minutes or until they reach an internal temperature of 145°F.

Easy Air Fryer Parmesan Zucchini Chips

Preparation and Cooking Time

25 minutes

Servings

6 persons

Nutritional facts

88 calories ,7g fat ,3g fiber ,39g carbs ,13g protein

Ingredients

- 3 small zucchini
- 1/8 tsp. sea salt

- 1/4 tsp. ground pepper
- 2 tbsp. olive oil
- 1/2 cup traditional bread crumbs
- 2 tbsp. grated parmesan cheese
- 1 tsp. garlic powder

Instructions

- Slice the zucchini into 1/4" thick slices. Place in a large mixing bowl.
- Drizzle olive oil over the zucchini & toss to coat well.
- Combine bread crumbs, parmesan cheese, pepper, salt, and garlic powder in a separate large mixing bowl. Mix all of the ingredients.
- Coat the zucchini slices in the bread crumb mixture. Continue until all of the zucchini has been coated.
- Place zucchini slices in the air fryer basket in small batches.
- Preheat the air fryer to 400°F and cook for 5 minutes. Cook for another 5 to 7 minutes, till the zucchini, is crisp.

Tasty Donuts

Preparation and Cooking Time

2 hour 40 minutes

Servings

6 persons

Nutritional facts

349 calories ,12g fat ,0g fiber ,34g carbs ,2g protein

Ingredients

- Half cup milk, 100-110 F
- 1 teaspoon vanilla bean paste
- 2 cups all-purpose flour
- 1 cup powdered sugar
- 2 ¼ teaspoons instant yeast (.25-ounce packet)
- Quarter cup granulated sugar
- 1 egg
- 2 tablespoons vegetable oil
- 3 tablespoons heavy cream
- 1 teaspoon vanilla bean paste

Instructions

- In the bowl of a stand mixer fitted with the dough hook attachment, combine the milk, yeast, and sugar (or into a large bowl mixing by hand). Mix until everything is well blended.
- Mix the egg, vegetable oil, & vanilla bean paste until thoroughly combined.
- With the mixer on low speed, gently add the flour. Continue kneading at low speed for another 5 minutes or till the dough is smooth & slightly tacky.
- Place the dough in an oiled bowl, cover with plastic wrap, and let aside for one hour to rise.
- Roll out the dough to a thickness of 12" on a lightly floured board. Cut 3-inch doughnuts with a doughnut cutter. Set the doughnuts to rise for another hour on a silicone or parchment-lined sheet pan.
- Spray the air fryer basket with nonstick cooking spray. Air fry for 7-8 minutes in batches a few at a time, at 365 F, or when they're a deep golden brown. Repeat with remaining dough and put on a cooling rack.
- Mix the powdered sugar, heavy cream, & vanilla bean paste.
- Dip the doughnuts in the icing and lay them aside to set on a wire rack.

Air Fryer Baked Apples

Preparation and Cooking Time

25 minutes

Servings

2 persons

Nutritional facts

220 calories ,0.1g fat ,1g fiber ,18g carbs ,0g protein

Ingredients

- 2 medium apples
- 2 tablespoons (25 grams) brown sugar or coconut sugar
- 2 tablespoons (28 grams) unsalted butter or coconut oil, melted and cooled (coconut oil for vegan)
- 2 tablespoons (15 grams) pecans optional
- 1/2 cup (46 grams) rolled oats (if gluten-free, use GF oats)
- 2 tablespoons (15 grams) all-purpose flour, white whole wheat flour or for GF, use 2 tablespoons (18 grams) Bob's Red Mill 1-to-1 Gluten-free Baking Mix
- 3/4 teaspoon ground cinnamon
- pinch of salt

Instructions

- If the air fryer is large enough to accommodate whole apples, you can cut and fill them the same way you would in the oven. If your air fryer can't fit a whole apple, cut it in half, as well as remove the core and stem. Make sure they're the right size for your air fryer and, if necessary, cut more away.
- Some toppings will splatter, so prepare your air fryer accordingly.
- Preheat the air fryer to 325 degrees Fahrenheit (162 degrees Celsius).
- Combine everything except the apples and raisins in a small mixing bowl.
- In the center of each apple, place ½ tablespoon of raisins. To prevent the raisins from burning, place them between the crumble and the apples.
- To keep the crumble from blowing around in the air fryer, divide it among the 4 apple halves and press it down over the raisins to compact it.
- With crumble topping side on the upper side place them in the air fryer very gently.
- Then cook for about 15-18 minutes, or until the vegetables are softened. The apples should have softened slightly but not become mushy, and the crumble mixture should have begun to brown. As they sit, they'll soften a little more.

Easy and Delicious Air Fryer Bagels

Preparation and Cooking Time

25 minutes

Servings

2 persons

Nutritional facts

160 calories ,10g fat ,1g fiber ,6g carbs ,9g protein

Ingredients

- Half cup self-rising flour
- 5.3 oz. plain Greek yogurt, I use the personal size Chobani containers
- Quarter tsp. salt
- 1 egg white, beaten

Instructions

- Combine flour and salt in a large mixing bowl. Using a fork, stir in the yogurt till a rough, crumbly mixture forms.
- On a floured surface, place the dough. Knead until the dough is no longer sticky but still slightly tacky. The dough should be divided in half.
- Roll out each piece into a 1" thick rope and tie the ends together to make a bagel. Brush the beaten egg whites all over the cake. At this point, you can add whatever seasonings you choose.
- Using nonstick cooking spray, lightly coat the air fryer basket. Take the basket out of the air fryer to spray it; do not spray directly into the air fryer. Place the bagels in the basket with some space between them.
- Preheat oven to 280°F and bake bagels for 15 minutes. Remove the bagels from the basket and set them aside to cool for about fifteen minutes on a cooling rack.

Air Fryer Cheesy Baked Eggs

Preparation and Cooking Time

20 minutes

Servings

2 persons

Nutritional facts

240 calories ,2g fat ,1g fiber ,38g carbs ,5g protein

Ingredients

- 4 large Eggs
- Two ounces Smoked gouda, chopped
- Kosher salt and pepper to taste
- Everything bagel seasoning

Instructions

- Using cooking spray, coat the interior of each ramekin. Insert two eggs in each ramekin, followed by 1 ounce of minced Gouda. Then season with salt and pepper to taste. On top of each ramekin, sprinkle everything bagel seasoning (as much as you like).
- In the air fryer basket, place each ramekin. Cook for 16 minutes at 400°F or till eggs are fully cooked.

Air Fryer Brussels Sprouts & Potato Hash

Preparation and Cooking Time

55 minutes

Servings

4 persons

Nutritional facts

251 calories ,7g fat ,1g fiber ,8g carbs ,3g protein

Ingredients

- 2 cups Brussels sprouts
- 2 tbsp. avocado oil
- 1/2 tsp. salt
- 1 small to medium red onion
- 2 cups baby red potatoes
- 1/2 tsp. black pepper

Instructions

- Preheat the air fryer to 375°F (190°C). Using a knife or fork, poke a few holes in a sheet of parchment paper and place it in the air fryer basket. Toss the potatoes into the basket in an equal layer. Half of the oil should be sprayed or drizzled on and then seasoned gently with salt and pepper.
- Cook for 10 minutes, rotating once halfway through if using pre-boiled potatoes. Cook for 22 to 25 minutes, rotating every 7-8 minutes if using raw potatoes.

- Add the Brussels sprouts and onions to the air fryer after the potatoes have started to crisp up, spray or drizzle the remaining oil over the veggies, & cook for another 6 minutes, stirring or shaking halfway through.
- Then season with salt and pepper to taste. Distribute the hash between four plates. Add the avocado & eggs (or other protein of choice) if serving as a complete meal, and enjoy.

Air Fryer Cinnamon Rolls

Preparation and Cooking Time

2 hours 35 minutes

Servings

2 persons

Nutritional facts

230 calories ,4g fat ,0.5g fiber ,33g carbs ,5g protein

Ingredients

- ¾ cup warm milk, 100-110°F
- 3 cups of all-purpose flour, some extra for dusting
- 4 Tablespoons of unsalted butter
- ¾ cup of powdered sugar
- 1 teaspoon of vanilla extract
- ¾ teaspoon of salt
- 1 ½ Tablespoon of ground cinnamon
- ¼ cup of unsalted butter
- 2 ¼ teaspoons of active yeast
- ¼ cup of granulated sugar
- 1 egg and 1 egg yolk, room temperature
- ¼ cup of unsalted butter, melted
- 4 ounces of cream cheese at room temperature

Instructions

- In a mixing bowl, pour warm milk and add yeast. Allow settling for 5 minutes after stirring. Whisk the eggs, sugar, & melted butter until thoroughly incorporated in a large mixing bowl. Stir in the flour and salt till a dough forms.
- Attach a dough hook to a stand mixer & mix on medium till dough forms into a ball and does not stick to the bowl. If the mixture is too sticky, add extra flour. If you're using your hands to knead the dough, knead it on a floured surface for ten minutes until it's no longer sticky.
- In a well-oiled bowl, place the dough ball. Wrap in plastic wrap and a warm towel to keep warm. Allow the dough to double in size by setting the bowl on the counter for an hour and a half.
- Divide the dough into two parts. Place one part of the dough on a floured board and roll out with a rolling pin until it's about a square foot in size.
- Rub room temperature butter all over the dough, leaving a little border all around it. In a separate bowl, mix the cinnamon & sugar for the filling & sprinkle on top of buttered dough. With your hands, carefully press it into the dough.
- Cut the dough into inch-and-a-half broad strips with a sharp knife or pizza cutter. Roll the strips into a spiral, each one building on the previous one. Place dough wheel in air fryer basket-compatible spring mold pan. Let the dough rest in the pan for 15 minutes after covering it with a cloth.
- Cook for twenty minutes at 350°F in an air fryer. In the meantime, prepare the next dough part into a cinnamon roll, which you will cook once the first one has been completed in the air fryer.
- When the food is done frying, remove it from the air fryer and set it aside to cool before removing it from the pan.
- Mix the frosting ingredients in a medium mixing bowl and beat until smooth. Enjoy the cinnamon roll with frosting on top.

Air Fryer Pop-Tarts

Preparation and Cooking Time

19 minutes

Servings

1 person

Nutritional facts

219 calories ,5g fat ,1g fiber ,38g carbs ,2g protein

Ingredients

- Pre-Made Pie Crust
- Vanilla Icing
- Sprinkles
- Grape Jelly
- 1 Egg

Instructions

- Cut out three-inch rectangles from the rolled-out pie crust.
- Half of the rectangles should have a teaspoon of grape jelly in the center.
- Put a rectangle on top of the jelly rectangles and use a fork to press the sides together.
- Each rectangle should be egg-washed.
- Preheat the air fryer to 375°F and cook for 5-8 minutes. Keep an eye on these since they cook quickly.
- Remove the cakes from the air fryer and smother them in icing.

Best Air Fryer Blueberry Bread

Preparation and Cooking Time

35 minutes

Servings

15 slices

Nutritional facts

140 calories ,8g fat ,1g fiber ,4g carbs ,17g protein

Ingredients

- 1 cup of milk
- 3 eggs
- 1.5 cups of frozen blueberries
- 3 cups of Bisquick
- ¼ cup of protein powder

Instructions

- All of the ingredients should be mixed properly.
- Put into a loaf pan.
- Then air fry at 350 degrees F for thirty minutes.

Pumpkin Spice Donuts

Preparation and Cooking Time

30 minutes

Servings

8 persons

Nutritional facts

380 calories ,14g fat ,1g fiber ,57g carbs ,4g protein

Ingredients

- 16-ounce of jumbo flaky biscuit dough
- 1 tbsp. of pumpkin spice
- 6 tbsp. of butter melted
- 1/2 cup of granulated sugar
- Half tbsp. of cinnamon

Instructions

- Begin by dividing the biscuits into eight parts.
- Flatten the biscuits using your hands.
- Cut a circle in the middle of the dough using a small shot glass.
- Apply a thin layer of olive oil to the bottom of air fryer.
- Preheat the air fryer to 350°F and fry the donuts for three minutes before removing the basket and flipping them. Cook for an additional 3 minutes.
- While the donuts are air-frying, melt the butter in a shallow dish & combine the sugar, pumpkin spice, and cinnamon in a separate bowl.
- Take the donuts out of the oven as soon as they're done.
- Then dip the buttered donuts into the coating, flip them over, and repeat the process.
- Finally, place the donuts on a wire rack to cool.
- Allow cooling before eating.

Easy Air Fryer Roasted Potatoes

Preparation and Cooking Time

25 minutes

Servings

4 persons

Nutritional facts

68 calories ,2g fat ,1g fiber ,55g carbs ,6g protein

Ingredients

- 2 large sweet potatoes, cut into small cubes
- 1 teaspoon sea salt
- 1 teaspoon ground black pepper
- 2 slices bacon, cut into small pieces
- 2 tablespoons olive oil
- One tbsp. smoked paprika
- 1 teaspoon dried dill weed

Instructions

- Preheat your air fryer to 400°F (200 degrees C).
- Combine the sweet potato, bacon, olive oil, paprika, salt, pepper, & dill. Place the mixture in the air fryer that has been warmed. Preheat oven to 350°F and bake for 12 - 18 minutes. After 10 minutes, check and stir, then every four minutes till crispy and golden.

Air-Fried Cinnamon and Sugar Doughnuts

Preparation and Cooking Time

14 minutes

Servings

9 persons

Nutritional facts

276 calories ,15g fat ,0.5g fiber ,37g carbs ,3g protein

Ingredients

- ½ cup white sugar
- 1 teaspoon salt
- ½ cup sour cream
- ⅓ cup white sugar
- 2 ½ tablespoons butter, at room temperature
- 2 large egg yolks
- 2 ¼ cups all-purpose flour
- 1 ½ teaspoons baking powder

- 1 teaspoon cinnamon
- Two tbsp. butter, melted, or as needed

Instructions

- In a mixing bowl, combine ½ cup white butter and sugar until crumbly. Stir in the egg yolks until completely mixed.
- Sift together the flour, baking powder, and salt in a separate basin. One-third of the flour mixture and half of the sour cream should be added to the sugar and egg mixture. Combine the remaining flour & sour cream in a mixing bowl. Keep the dough refrigerated till ready to use.
- In a bowl, combine 1/3 cup sugar & cinnamon.
- Roll out the dough to a thickness of 1/2 inch on a lightly floured work surface. To make doughnut shapes, cut nine large circles in the dough and a little circle out of the middle of each large round.
- Preheat your air fryer to 350°F (175 degrees C).
- Brush both sides of the doughnuts with 1/2 of the melted butter.
- Place half doughnuts in the air fryer basket and cook for 8 minutes. Cooked donuts are brushed with melted butter and then dipped in the cinnamon-sugar mixture. Carry on with the rest of the doughnuts in the same manner.

Easy, Crispy, and Perfect Air Fryer Bacon

Preparation and Cooking Time

10 minutes

Servings

2 persons

Nutritional facts

75 calories ,18g fat ,2g fiber ,10g carbs ,45g protein

Ingredients

- Six slices Bacon

Instructions

- Use parchment paper to line the air fryer basket. The parchment paper will absorb the grease, preventing the air fryer from smoking. On top of the paper, place the bacon.
- On top of the bacon, some air fryer brands may require a trivet. If you have an older or louder air fryer, you would need a trivet to keep the bacon from falling out.
- Cook the bacon at 380 degrees F for 10 minutes.
- Cook for an extra 10 minutes if necessary to achieve the optimum level of crunch.

Air Fryer Bacon and Egg Bite Cups

Preparation and Cooking Time

25 minutes

Servings

8 persons

Nutritional facts

119 calories ,3g fat ,1g fiber ,1g carbs ,3g protein

Ingredients

- 6 large eggs
- ¼ cup shredded mozzarella cheese
- 3 slices of cooked and crumbled bacon
- ¼ cup chopped red peppers
- ¼ cup chopped onions
- ¼ cup chopped fresh spinach
- 2 tablespoons of heavy whipping cream or milk (any is fine)
- Salt and pepper to taste

- ¼ cup chopped green peppers
- ½ cup shredded cheddar cheese

Instructions

- In a large mixing bowl, put the eggs.
- Add the cream and season with salt and pepper to taste. To combine the ingredients, whisk them together.
- Green peppers, red peppers, onions, spinach, cheeses, and bacon should be sprinkled on top.
- To combine the ingredients, whisk them together.
- Fill each silicone mold halfway with the egg mixture. Half of the remaining vegetables should be sprinkled on top.
- Cook the egg bites cups at 300 degrees F for 12-15 minutes. The eggs are done when the toothpick inserted in the center comes out clean.

Air Fryer Sausage

Preparation and Cooking Time

20 minutes

Servings

5 persons

Nutritional facts

260 calories, 3g fat ,1g fiber ,33g carbs ,2g protein

Ingredients

- Five raw and uncooked sausage links

Instructions

- Use parchment paper to line the air fryer basket. The parchment paper will absorb the grease, preventing the air fryer from smoking. On top of the paper, place the sausage.
- Preheat the oven to 360°F and cook for 15 minutes. Cook for a further 5 minutes after opening and flipping, or till the sausage reaches an internal temperature of 160 degrees F.
- Allow cooling before serving.

Whole 30, Paleo Crispy Browns

Preparation and Cooking Time

50 minutes

Servings

4 persons

Nutritional facts

134 calories, 3g fat,1g fiber ,11g carbs ,4g protein

Ingredients

- 4 sweet potatoes peeled
- 1 teaspoon paprika
- 2 garlic cloves minced
- 1 teaspoon cinnamon
- salt and pepper to taste
- 2 teaspoons olive oil

Instructions

- Using the biggest holes on a cheese grater, shred the sweet potatoes.
- In a bowl of cold water, place the sweet potatoes. Allow 20-25 minutes for the sweet potatoes to soak. The starch from the sweet potatoes can be removed by soaking them in cold water. This gives them a crispy texture.
- Using a paper towel, completely dry the potatoes after draining the water.
- In a dry bowl, place the potatoes. Toss in the olive oil, garlic, paprika, and season to taste with salt and pepper. To combine the ingredients, stir them together.
- In the air fryer, place the potatoes.
- Preheat oven to 400°F and bake for 10 minutes.
- Shake the potatoes in the air fryer. Cook for a total of ten minutes more.
- Allow cooling before serving.

Easy Air Fryer Cherry Turnovers

Preparation and Cooking Time

25 minutes

Servings

8 persons

Nutritional facts

244 calories,2g fat ,0.5g fiber ,22g carbs ,4g protein

Ingredients

- 17 oz. package puff pastry 4 sheets
- 2 tablespoons water
- 10 oz. can of cherry pie filling
- 1 egg beaten
- cooking oil

Instructions

- On a flat surface, place the pastry sheets.
- Fold both sheets of puff pastry dough in half. Cut each sheet into four squares, for a total of eight squares.
- To make an egg wash, whisk the egg and water in a small bowl.
- Brush the egg wash along the edges of each square with a cooking brush or your fingers.
- One to one and a half tbsp. cherry pie filling should be placed in the center of each square sheet. Don't stuff the pastry too much.
- Fold the dough in half diagonally to form a triangle and seal it. To seal the turnovers, use the back of a fork to press lines into the open edges.
- Make three slits in the top of the crust to allow the turnovers to breathe.
- Brush the egg wash over the top of each turnover.
- Spritz the turnovers with cooking oil and place them in the air fryer basket. Make sure the turnovers don't touch and aren't stacked. If necessary, cook in batches.
- Then air fry for 8 minutes at 370 degrees.
- Allow 2-3 minutes for the pastries to cool before removing them from the air fryer. This will prevent them from sticking.

Air Fried Blueberry Muffins

Preparation and Cooking Time

25 minutes

Servings

12 persons

Nutritional facts

121 calories ,5g fat ,1g fiber ,31g carbs ,2g protein

Ingredients

- 1 1/2 cups all-purpose or white whole wheat flour
- 1/2 teaspoon cinnamon
- 1/2 teaspoon salt
- 1 cup milk
- 1/4 cup melted unsalted butter (at room temperature)

- 2 teaspoons vanilla
- 1 cup blueberries
- 3/4 cup old-fashioned oats (oatmeal)
- 1/2 cup brown sweetener
- 1 tablespoon baking powder
- 2 eggs (at room temperature)

Instructions

- Mix the rolled oats, flour, salt, brown sweetener, cinnamon, and baking powder in a large mixing bowl.
- Then mix.
- Whisk the eggs, milk, vanilla, and butter in a separate bowl. Using a silicone spoon, combine the ingredients.
- In a mixing bowl, combine the wet ingredients with the dry ingredients. Stir.
- Add the blueberries as well as stir to combine.
- Fill twelve silicone muffin cups halfway with batter and place them in the air fryer. It's up to you whether or not you want to oil the liners. Muffins don't usually stick together.
- Preheat the air fryer to 350°F. Because each model cooks differently, keep a close eye on the muffins to ensure they get the right amount of time in the oven. The muffins will take 11-15 minutes to bake. If a toothpick inserted in the center of a muffin comes out clean, the muffins are done baking.

Air Fryer Loaded Hash Browns

Preparation and Cooking Time

50 minutes

Servings

4 persons

Nutritional facts

246 calories,4g fat ,1g fiber ,12g carbs ,3g protein

Ingredients

- 3 russet potatoes
- Quarter cup chopped onions
- 2 garlic cloves chopped
- 1 teaspoon paprika
- 1/4 cup chopped green peppers
- Quarter cup chopped red peppers
- salt and pepper to taste
- 2 teaspoons olive oil

Instructions

- Grate the potatoes.
- Soak the potatoes in cold water and dry them with a paper towel. Mix garlic, paprika, olive oil, and salt and pepper. To combine the ingredients, stir them together.
- Put the potatoes in the air fryer and cook for ten minutes at 400 degrees F.
- Add the peppers and onions, chopped. Cook for another ten minutes.
- Leave to cool before serving.

Air Fryer Homemade Strawberry Pop-Tarts

Preparation and Cooking Time

25 minutes

Servings

6 persons

Nutritional facts

274 calories,2g fat ,1g fiber ,4g carbs, 1g protein

Ingredients

- 2 refrigerated pie crusts
- 1/2 cup plain, non-fat vanilla Greek yogurt
- 1 oz. cream cheese
- 1 teaspoon cornstarch
- 1/3 cup low-sugar strawberry preserves
- cooking oil
- 1 tablespoon sweetener
- 1 teaspoon sugar sprinkles

Instructions

- Place the pie crust on a flat surface to work with.
- Slice the two pie crusts into six rectangles with a knife or pizza cutter. Because you'll fold them over to close the pop tart, they should be pretty long.
- In a mixing bowl, mix the preserves and cornstarch.
- A spoonful of preserves should be added to the crust. Place the preserves on the crust's top layer.
- To close the pop tarts, fold them in half.
- Make imprints with a fork down the edges of each pop tart to form vertical and horizontal lines.
- In the Air Fryer, place the pop tarts. If necessary, cook in batches rather than stacking. Cooking oil is sprayed over the surface.
- Cook for 10 minutes at 370 degrees F. After 8 minutes, check on the Pop-Tarts to make sure they aren't too crisp for the taste.
- Mix the Greek yogurt, cream cheese, & sweetener in a mixing bowl.
- Remove the Pop-Tarts from the Air Fryer after they have cooled. This is critical. They may break if you do not allow them to cool.
- Take the pop tarts out of the Air Fryer and set them aside. Finish with a dollop of frosting on each. Sprinkle sugar sprinkles around the pop tarts.

Quick and Easy Air Fryer Grilled Cheese

Preparation and Cooking Time

12 minutes

Servings

2 persons

Nutritional facts

486 calories,2g fat ,1g fiber ,11g carbs ,2g protein

Ingredients

- 4 slices of bread
- 5-6 slices cooked bacon Optional
- 1 tablespoon butter melted
- 2 slices mild cheddar cheese
- 2 slices mozzarella cheese

Instructions

- Microwave the butter for 10-15 seconds to soften it.
- On one side of each slice of bread, spread the butter.
- Put a slice of buttered bread in the air fryer basket (butter side down).
- Fill the rest of the air fryer with the remaining ingredients in the following order: a slice of cheddar cheese, a slice of fried bacon, a slice of mozzarella cheese, and the second slice of bread on top (butter side up).
- If your air fryer is really loud, you'll probably need to add a layer rack or trivet to keep the sandwich from flying.
- Preheat the oven to 370°F and cook for 4 minutes.

- Open the air fryer. Toss the sandwich over. Cook for another 3 minutes.
- Remove and serve.

Sweet Potatoes with cooked bacon

Preparation and Cooking Time

30 minutes

Servings

4 persons

Nutritional facts

208 calories,3g fat ,1g fiber ,22g carbs ,4g protein

Ingredients

- Two medium sweet potatoes
- Two tsp. olive oil
- Four eggs
  - 1/4 c. whole milk
- salt and pepper
- Four slices of cooked bacon
- Two green onions, sliced

Instructions

- Wash the sweet potatoes and add 3-4 cuts to the potatoes. Microwave for 6-8 minutes, depending on their size, until soft.
- Using an oven mitt, slice the potatoes in half lengthwise. Scoop out the potato flesh, leaving 1/4 inch around the edges. Save the scooped sweet potato for another use.
- Brush the potato skins with olive oil and sprinkle with sea salt. Arrange the skins in your Air Fryer basket and cook at 400° F (or the highest available temp) for 10 minutes.
- Meanwhile, add the milk, eggs, salt and pepper to a non-stick skillet. Cook the mixture over medium heat, constantly stirring, until there are no visible liquid eggs.
- Top each cooked potato skin with 1/4 of the scrambled eggs and 1 slice of crumbled bacon. Cover with shredded cheese and cook for 3 minutes, or until the cheese is melted.
- Serve topped with green onion.

Air Fryer Breakfast Cookies

Preparation and Cooking Time

30 minutes

Servings

1 dozen

Nutritional facts

212 calories,8g fat ,2g fiber ,10g carbs ,5g protein

Ingredients

- One cup mashed ripe bananas (about 2 medium)
- A half-cup chunky peanut butter
- A half-cup honey
- One teaspoon vanilla extract
- One cup old-fashioned oats
- A half-cup whole wheat flour
- A quarter cup nonfat dry milk powder
- two teaspoons ground cinnamon
- A half teaspoon of salt
- 1/4 teaspoon baking soda
- One cup dried cranberries or raisins

Instructions

- Preheat air fryer to 300° F. Beat banana, peanut butter, honey and vanilla until blended. In another bowl, add flour, oats, milk powder, salt cinnamon, and baking soda; gradually beat into the banana mixture. Add in dried cranberries.
- In batches, drop dough by 1/4 cupful's.
- Cook until lightly browned, 6-8 minutes. Cool in the basket for 1 minute. Remove to wire racks.
- Serve warm or at room temperature.
- Freeze cookies in freezer containers, separating layers with waxed paper. To use, thaw before serving or, if desired, reheat in a preheated 300° air fryer until warmed, about 1 minute.

Air Fryer Breakfast Frittata

Preparation and Cooking Time

35 minutes

Servings

2 persons

Nutritional facts

380 calories,3g fat ,1g fiber ,2g carbs ,1g protein

Ingredients

- Quarter pound breakfast sausage fully cooked and crumbled
- One pinch of cayenne pepper (Optional)
- cooking spray
- Four eggs, lightly beaten
- half cup shredded Cheddar-Monterey Jack cheese blend
- Two tablespoons red bell pepper, diced
- One green onion, chopped

Instructions

- Mix well in small bowl eggs, cheddar cheese, sausage, cayenne, bell pepper and onion.
- Heat the air fryer to about 360 degrees F.
- Next, a nonstick cake pan of 6x2-inch is sprayed with cooking spray.
- Put the egg mixture in the cake pan.
- Then cook it in the air for eighteen to twenty minutes until the frittata is set.

Ninja Foodi Low-Carb Breakfast Casserole Air Fryer

Preparation and Cooking Time

45 minutes

Servings

8 persons

Nutritional facts

182 calories,3g fat, 1g fiber ,2g carbs ,1g protein

Ingredients

- One teaspoon Fennel Seed
- One-pound Ground Sausage
- A quarter cup Diced White Onion
- A half-cup Shredded Colby Jack Cheese
- 1 Diced Green Bell Pepper
- 8 Whole Eggs, Beaten
- A half teaspoon Garlic Salt

Instructions

- Use the sauté feature to brown the sausage in the foodi pot if you use the Ninja Foodi. You can use a skillet to do this using an air-fryer.

- Insert the onion and pepper and simmer until the vegetables are soft and the sausage is cooked, along with the ground sausage.
- Spray an 8.75 inches pan and the air fryer with the cooking spray.
- Place the mixture of ground sausages on the bottom of the pan.
- Cover with cheese uniformly.
  - Pour the beaten eggs uniformly over the sausage and cheese.
- Over the eggs, add fennel seed and garlic salt uniformly.
- In Ninja Foodi, put the rack in the low position and place the pan on top.
- Set at 390 degrees F for 15 minutes on Air Crisp.
- If you are using an air fryer, put the dish straight into the air fryer's basket and cook at 390 degrees F for 15 minutes.
- Remove and serve wisely.

Air Fryer Donuts

Preparation and Cooking Time

15 minutes

Servings

8 persons

Nutritional facts

316 calories,4g fat ,1g fiber ,6g carbs ,1g protein

Ingredients

- Half cup granulated white sugar
- Two teaspoons ground cinnamon
- 4 Tablespoons butter melted
- 16 oz. refrigerated flaky jumbo biscuits
- olive or coconut oil spray

Instructions

- Combine in a small bowl sugar and cinnamon; set aside.
- The biscuits are withdrawn from the can, divided and placed on a flat surface. To cut holes out of the middle of each biscuit, use a 1-inch round biscuit cutter (or similarly-sized bottle cap).
- Cover the air fryer basket lightly with olive or coconut oil spray. Do not use a non-stick spray like Pam, as the coating on the basket may be damaged.
- Put four donuts in a single layer in the air fryer's basket. Ensure that they are not touching.
- Then air fry for five minutes at 360 degrees and lightly brown.
- The donuts are to be removed from Air Fryer. Then dip them in melted butter. Next, roll them in cinnamon sugar to coat.
- Serve immediately.

Vegan Bacon-Wrapped Breakfast Burritos

Preparation and Cooking Time

55 minutes

Servings

4 persons

Nutritional facts

184 calories ,7gfat ,2g fiber ,21g carbs ,2g protein

Ingredients

- Two tablespoons cashew butter
- Two to three tablespoons of tamari
- One to Two tablespoons liquid smoke
- 1 small tree broccoli, sautéed

- 6-8 stalks fresh asparagus
- handful spinach, kale, other greens
- One to Two tablespoons water
- 4 pieces of rice paper
- 2 servings Vegan Egg scramble
- One-third cup of roasted sweet potato cubes
  - 8 strips of roasted red pepper

Instructions

- Preheat the oven to 350 °F. Line with the parchment the baking dish.
- Whisk the cashew butter, tamari, liquid smoke, and water in a small bowl. And put aside.
- Prepare to assemble rolls for all fillings.
- Rice Paper Hydrating: have a large plate/surface ready for filling/rolling wrapper.
- Keep one rice paper under a water faucet that runs cool water, wetting both sides of the wrapper for just a few seconds. Then it should be removed from the water. While it is still firm, it should be placed on a plate to fill. Subsequently, the rice paper will soften as it sits. However, it will not be too tender to stick to the surface.
- Then it is to be filled by placing ingredients away from the middle. Ensure to leave sides of rice paper-free. Fold in two sides, just like a burrito. Each roll is to be dipped into cashew - liquid smoke mixture. You have to ensure to coat it completely. Then the rolls are to be arranged on a parchment baking sheet.
- Now cook these for eight to ten minutes at 350 °F and till it becomes crisp.

Air Fryer Breakfast Sausage

Preparation and Cooking Time

20 minutes

Servings

8 persons

Nutritional facts

188 calories, 5g fat ,2g fiber ,23g carbs ,2g protein

Ingredients

- One-pound ground pork
- One-pound ground turkey
- Two teaspoons fennel seeds
- Two teaspoons dry rubbed sage
- Two teaspoons garlic powder
- One teaspoon paprika
- One teaspoon sea salt
- One teaspoon dried thyme
- One tablespoon real maple syrup

Instructions

- Start by combining in a wide bowl the pork and turkey together. Mix the rest of the ingredients in a small bowl: fennel, sage, salt, powdered garlic, paprika and thyme. Mix spices into the meat and keep combining until the spices are thoroughly blended.
- Spoon (about 2-3 teaspoons of meat) into balls, then flatten into patties. You would have to do this in two batches.
- Fix the temperature and cook for 10 minutes at 370 degrees F. Remove and repeat the leftover sausage in the air fryer.

Avocado Boats

Preparation and Cooking Time

5 minutes

Servings

2 persons

Nutritional facts

122 calories,2g fat ,1g fiber ,4g carbs ,1.2g protein

Ingredients

- A quarter cup diced red onion
- Two tablespoons chopped fresh cilantro
- 2 plum tomatoes, seeded and diced
- 4 eggs (medium or large recommended)
- 1 tablespoon finely diced jalapeno (optional)
- 1 tablespoon lime juice
- 1/2 teaspoon salt
- A quarter tsp. black pepper
- 2 avocados, halved and pitted

Instructions

- Scoop the avocado pulp out of the skin with a spoon, keeping the shell intact. Dice the avocado and put it in a medium bowl. Combine the tomatoes, onion, cilantro, jalapeno, lime juice, salt, and pepper if needed. Cover and refrigerate the mixture of avocado until ready for use.
- The air fryer is preheated to 350 degrees F.
- Place them on a foil ring to ensure that the avocado shells do not rock while cooking. Simply roll 2 3-inch-wide strips of aluminum foil into rope shapes to make them, and form each into a 3-inch circle. Place each avocado shell on a foil ring in an air fryer basket. Break 1 egg into each shell of avocado and fry for 5 to 7 minutes or until the doneness is achieved.
- Remove from the basket; top with salsa the avocado and serve.

Crispy Bacon in the Air Fryer

Preparation and Cooking Time

10 minutes

Servings

12 persons

Nutritional facts

177 calories,9g fat ,3g fiber ,33g carbs ,11g protein

Ingredients

- One Pound of Bacon

Instructions

- Add bacon uniformly into the air fryer basket. Depending on the size, this can require two batches to cook all the bacon.
- Cook for 5 minutes at 350 degrees F.
- Flip the bacon and cook for an additional five minutes or until the crispiness you prefer.
- Remove the bacon with tongs and put it on a plate lined with paper towels.
- Allow it to cool and serve.

Ninja Foodi - Air Fryer Breakfast Stuffed Peppers

Preparation and Cooking Time

18 minutes

Servings

2 persons

Nutritional facts

164 calories,3g fat ,1g fiber ,12g carbs ,2g protein

Ingredients

- 4 eggs
- One teaspoon olive oil
- 1 bell pepper halved, middle seeds removed
- 1 pinch salt and pepper
- 1 pinch sriracha flakes for a bit of spice, optional

Instructions

- Cut bell peppers in half lengthwise and remove seeds and middle leaving the edges intact like bowls.
- Use your finger to rub a bit of olive oil just on the exposed edges (where it was cut).
- Crack two eggs into each bell pepper half. Sprinkle with desired spices.
- Set them on a trivet inside your Ninja Foodi or directly inside your other brand of the air fryer.
- Close the lid on your air fryer (the one attached to the Ninja Foodi machine).
- Turn the machine on, press the air crisper button at 390 degrees for 13 minutes (times will vary slightly according to how well you like your egg, but this was perfect for us).
- Alternatively, if you'd rather have your bell pepper and egg less brown on the outside, add just one egg to your pepper and set the air fryer to 330 degrees for 15 minutes. (for an over hard egg consistency)

Quick - Hand Held Hot Breakfast Recipe

Preparation and Cooking Time

20 minutes

Servings

8 persons

Nutritional facts

170 calories,2g fat ,1g fiber ,13g carbs ,2g protein

Ingredients

- 5 eggs
- A half-cup sausage crumbles, cooked
- Half cup bacon, cooked
- one box puff pastry sheets
- A half-cup cheddar cheese, shredded

Instructions

- Cook eggs in the form of regular scrambled eggs. If desired, add meat to the egg mixture while you are cooking.
- Spread puff pastry sheets on a cutting board and use a cookie cutter or knife to cut out rectangles, making sure they are all uniform, so they fit together nicely.
- Spoon half of the pastry rectangles with the preferred combination of egg, meat, and cheese.
- Place a pastry rectangle on top of the mixture and press the edges together with a sealing fork.
- Spray with spray oil if a shiny, smooth pastry is desired, but it is optional.
- Place breakfast pockets in the air-fryer basket and cook at 370 degrees for 8-10 minutes.
- Carefully watch and check for desired doneness every 2-3 minutes.

Air Fryer Bacon and Egg Breakfast Biscuit Bombs

Preparation and Cooking Time

50 minutes

Servings

8 persons

Nutritional facts

200 calories,4g fat ,0g fiber ,23g carbs ,3g protein

Ingredients

- 2 eggs, beaten
- A quarter tsp. pepper
- 5 biscuits
- 2 oz. sharp cheddar cheese, cut into ten 3/4-inch cubes
- 1 egg
- 4 slices bacon, cut into 1/2-inch pieces
- 1 tablespoon butter
- One tablespoon water

Instructions

- Cut two 8-inch rounds of parchment paper for cooking. Set one round at the bottom of the basket of the air fryer. Spray with cooking spray.
- In a nonstick 10-inch skillet, cook bacon until crisp over medium-high heat.
- Place on a paper towel; remove from the pan. Wipe the skillet carefully with a paper towel. To the skillet, add butter and melt over medium heat. Add 2 beaten eggs and pepper to the skillet; cook until the eggs are thickened, stirring frequently but still moist. Remove from the heat; add bacon and stir. Cool for five minutes.
- Meanwhile, divide the dough into five biscuits; separate the 2 layers of each biscuit.
- Press into a 4-inch round each. Then spoon 1 onto the center of each round heaping tablespoonful of the egg mixture. Top it with one of the cheese pieces. Fold the edges gently up and over the filling; pinch to seal. Beat the remainder of the egg and water in a small bowl. Brush the biscuits with egg wash on all sides.
- Place 5 biscuit bombs on the parchment in the air fryer basket and seam side down. With cooking spray, spray both sides of the second round of parchment. Top the biscuit bombs in the basket with the second parchment, then top with the remaining 5 biscuit bombs.
- Set to 325 ° F; cook for eight minutes. Re moves the top of the round parchment; use tongs to carefully turn the biscuits and place them in a single layer in the basket. Cook 4 to 6 minutes longer or (at least 165°F) until cooked through.

Air Fryer Breakfast Potatoes

Preparation and Cooking Time

55 minutes

Servings

4 persons

Nutritional facts

145 calories,2g fat ,1g fiber ,14g carbs ,2g protein

Ingredients

- 1 1/2 pounds' potatoes (Little Potato Co. recommended) (diced)
- 1/2 teaspoon salt
- 1/2 teaspoon paprika
- 1/4 onion (chopped)
- 1 green bell pepper (chopped)
- 2 garlic cloves (minced)
- One Tablespoon olive oil
- A quarter tsp. pepper

Instructions

- Wash the potatoes and bell pepper.
- Dice the potatoes and boil them for 30 minutes in water. Pat it dry after 30 minutes.
- Then onion, bell pepper and potatoes are to be chopped. Use minced garlic.
- Apply all the ingredients and mix them in a dish. Put it into an air-fryer.
- Cook in an air fryer for 10 minutes at 390-400 degrees F. Shake the basket and cook for another 10 minutes, then shake the basket again and cook for another 5 minutes, for a total of 25 minutes.
- Serve.

Breakfast Egg Rolls - Air Fryer

Preparation and Cooking Time

25 minutes

Servings

3 persons

Nutritional facts

178 calories,9g fat ,2g fiber ,11g carbs ,2g protein

Ingredients

- Two eggs
- Two tbsp. of milk
- pepper
- salt
- Half cup of shredded cheddar cheese
- 2 sausage patties
- 6 egg roll wrappers
- One tbsp. of olive oil
- water

Instructions

- Cook or replace the sausage in a small skillet according to the packet. It should be removed from the pan and sliced into small pieces.
- Whisk the eggs, sugar, and a pinch of salt and pepper together. Over medium/low heat, add a tsp. of oil or a little pat of butter to a pan. Pour in the mixture of eggs and cook for a few minutes, stirring regularly to produce scrambled eggs. Stir the sausage in. And put aside.
- Place the egg roll wrapper with points that create a diamond shape on a working surface. Then place roughly 1 tbsp. of the cheese on the bottom third of the wrapper. Cover with a mixture of eggs.
- Wet a finger or pastry brush and brush all the sides of the egg roll wrapper, helping it seal.
- The egg roll wrapper should be folded up and over the filling, trying to get it as secure as you can. Then, fold the sides together to make an envelope-looking shape. Place the seam side down and start assembling the remaining rolls.
- Preheat an air fryer for 5 minutes to 400 F.
- Rub rolls with oil or spray them with a misto if you have one. Put in the preheated basket. Set for 8 minutes to 400 F.
- Flip the eggs over after 5 minutes. For another 3 minutes, return the egg rolls to the air fryer.
- Serve and Enjoy.

Air Fryer-Egg in Hole

Preparation and Cooking Time

15 minutes

Servings

1 person

Nutritional facts

130 calories,3g fat, 1g fiber ,10g carbs ,4g protein

Ingredients

- One piece of toast
- One egg
- salt and pepper

Instructions

- Oil the air fryer-safe pan with cooking spray that is non-stick.
- Place your slice of bread in the air fryer pan.
- Create a hole with a cup. Then the bread is to be removed.
- Crack the egg in the hole.
- Then air fry for 6 minutes at 330 degrees F. take a spatula to flip the egg and fry for another three to four minutes.

Air Fryer Sausage Breakfast Casserole

Preparation and Cooking Time

30 minutes

Servings

1 person

Nutritional facts

517 calories, 6g fat,1g fiber ,11g carbs ,3g protein

Ingredients

- One-pound Hash Browns
- One-pound Ground Breakfast Sausage
- 1 Yellow Bell Pepper Diced
- A quarter cup Sweet Onion Diced
- 4 Eggs
- 1 Green Bell Pepper Diced
- 1 Red Bell Pepper Diced

Instructions

- Line with a foil the air fryer's basket.
- On the bottom, put the hash browns.
- Top with uncooked sausage.
- The onions and peppers should be uniformly placed on top.
- Cook for 10 minutes at 355 degrees F.
- Open the air fryer and, if necessary, mix the casserole a little.
- Crack eggs in a bowl, then pour on the casserole top.
- Cook for another ten minutes at 355 degrees F.
- Enjoy with salt and pepper as per your taste.

Low Carb Baked Eggs Recipe

Preparation and Cooking Time

15 minutes

Servings

1 person

Nutritional facts

115 calories,3g fat ,1g fiber ,8g carbs ,2g protein

Ingredients

- 1 large (1 large) egg

- black pepper, to taste
- Cooking Spray for muffin cups or ramekins
- One tablespoon (15 ml) milk or half & half
- 1 tablespoon (15 ml) frozen spinach, thawed (or sautéed fresh spinach)
- One to two teaspoons (5 ml) grated cheese
- salt, to taste

Instructions

- Spray with oil spray inside of the ramekin or silicone muffin cups.
- Add the muffin or ramekin cup with egg, spinach, cream, and cheese.
- Then season with pepper and salt. Gently mix the egg whites with the ingredients without separating the yolk.
- Air Fry for roughly 6-12 minutes at 330 ° F.
- It may need a little longer to cook in a ceramic ramekin. Cook for less time if you like runny yolks. After 5 minutes, keep testing the eggs to ensure that the egg is of your desired texture.

Air Fryer Breakfast Burritos

Preparation and Cooking Time

20 minutes

Servings

6 persons

Nutritional facts

160 calories, 2g fat ,1g fiber, 3g carbs ,2g protein

Ingredients

- 6 medium flour tortillas
- 6 scrambled eggs
- 1/2 lb. ground sausage – browned
- 1/2 bell pepper – minced
- One third cup bacon bits
- 6 medium flour tortillas
- 6 scrambled eggs
- A half-cup shredded cheese
- oil for spraying

Instructions

- Combine scrambled eggs, bell pepper, cooked sausage, bacon bits & cheese in a big bowl. Stir to blend.
- A half-cup of the mixture is spooned into the middle of a flour tortilla.
- Fold the sides and then roll.
- For the remaining ingredients, you have to repeat the same process.
- Put filled burritos in the air fryer's basket & liberally spray with oil.
- Cook for 5 minutes at 330 degrees F.

Air Fryer Breakfast Pizzas with English Muffins

Preparation and Cooking Time

40 minutes

Servings

2 persons

Nutritional facts

429 calories,11g fat ,2g fiber ,8g carbs ,5g protein

Ingredients

- 6 Eggs, Cooked & Scrambled
- Olive Oil Spray
- Fennel Seed (Optional)
- 1 Pound Ground Sausage, Cooked
- A half-cup Shredded Colby Jack Cheese
- 3 English Muffins, Sliced in Half (6 Halves)

Instructions

- First, ensure that eggs and sausage are properly cooked.
- Spray the oil cooking spray into the air fryer's basket.
- You will have to fill it in 2 batches, with each batch containing 3 or more.
- Spray with a light coat of olive oil spray the English muffins. Then top them with cooked sausage and cooked eggs.
- Next, the cheese is added to the top of each one. Moreover, you can also use fennel seed, but it is usually not required.
- Cook for five minutes at 355 degrees F.
- Remove the muffins cautiously and repeat the process for the additional muffins.

Chapter 3: Air Fryer Lunch Recipes

Air Fryer Rotisserie Chicken Taquitos

Preparation and Cooking Time

38 minutes

Servings

15 persons

Nutritional facts

195 calories,5g fat ,1g fiber ,22g carbs ,2g protein

Ingredients

- 2 tsp. vegetable oil
- 1/8 tsp. ground black pepper
- 30 6" corn tortillas
- 2 lb. rotisserie chicken, skin removed and meat shredded
- 1 cup shredded Colby Jack cheese
- 1 small yellow onion, diced
- 1 clove garlic, minced
- 7 oz. can dice green chilies
- 1/8 tsp. salt

Instructions

- In a large skillet, heat the vegetable oil over medium heat. Cook, occasionally stirring, until the onion is tender, about 3-5 minutes. Cook stirring periodically for another minute after adding the garlic.
- Insert salt and pepper, the green chilies, shredded chicken, and shredded cheese. Stir for about 2-3 minutes until the mixture is thoroughly warmed. Remove the pan from the heat.
- You need to warm tortillas in a skillet or the microwave by placing them on a platter. You'll want to reheat the tortillas before rolling them to make them more pliable. Warm a few tortillas at a time to avoid them becoming cold during assembly.
- Roll up each tortilla with approximately 3 tbsp. of the chicken mixture down the center. Continue with the remaining tortillas.
- Remove the air fryer basket and coat it lightly with non - stick cooking spray. Put taquitos in the air fryer, spacing them apart, so they don't contact.
- Cook for 5 minutes at 400°F and then flip and cook for another 2-3 minutes until crisp. Continue until all of the taquitos are cooked.

Air-Fryer Ravioli

Preparation and Cooking Time

30 minutes

Servings

18 pieces

Nutritional facts

40 calories,2g fat ,1g fiber ,21g carbs ,4g protein

Ingredients

- One cup seasoned bread crumbs
- A quarter cup shredded Parmesan cheese
- two teaspoons dried basil
- A half-cup all-purpose flour
- Two large eggs, lightly beaten
- One package (9 ounces) frozen beef ravioli, thawed
- Cooking spray
- Fresh minced basil, optional
- One cup marinara sauce, warmed

Instructions

- Preheat the air fryer to 350 degrees Fahrenheit. Combine bread crumbs, Parmesan cheese, and basil in a small basin. Separate the flour and eggs into small dishes. Coat both sides of ravioli with flour and brush off excess. Dip in the eggs, then in the crumb mixture, patting down to help the coating stick.
- Place ravioli in a thin layer on a greased tray in the air-fryer basket and spritz with cooking spray in batches. Cook for 3-4 minutes, or until golden brown. Spritz with cooking spray and turn. Cook for another 3-4 minutes, or until golden brown. Immediately top with basil and more Parmesan cheese, if desired. Warm marinara sauce is served on the side.

Air-Fryer Crispy Curry Drumsticks

Preparation and Cooking Time

50 minutes

Servings

4 persons

Nutritional facts

180 calories,7g fat ,2g fiber ,17g carbs ,1g protein

Ingredients

- One-pound chicken drumsticks
- A three fourth teaspoon salt, divided
- 2 tablespoons olive oil
- two teaspoons curry powder
- A half teaspoon onion salt
- A half teaspoon garlic powder
- Minced fresh cilantro, optional

Instructions

- In a large bowl, place chicken and enough water to cover. Add 1/2 teaspoon salt; let stand 15 minutes at room temperature. Drain and pat dry.
- Preheat the air fryer to 375° F. In another bowl, mix oil, curry powder, onion salt, garlic powder and remaining 1/4 teaspoon salt; add chicken and toss to coat. Place chicken in a single layer on a tray in an air-fryer basket in batches. Cook until a thermometer inserted in the chicken reads 170°-175° F, 15-17 minutes, turning halfway through. If desired, sprinkle with cilantro.

Popcorn Shrimp Tacos with Cabbage Slaw

Preparation and Cooking Time

30 minutes

Servings

4 persons

Nutritional facts

456 calories,10g fat ,1g fiber ,22g carbs ,3g protein

Ingredients

- Two cups coleslaw mix
- A quarter cup minced fresh cilantro
- Two tablespoons lime juice
- Two tablespoons honey
- A one-fourth teaspoon of salt
- One jalapeno pepper, seeded and minced, optional
- 2 large eggs
- 2 tablespoons 2% milk
- A half-cup all-purpose flour
- A one and a half cup panko bread crumbs
- One tablespoon ground cumin
- One tablespoon garlic powder
- One-pound uncooked shrimp (41-50 per pound), peeled and deveined
- Cooking spray
- 8 corn tortillas (6 inches), warmed
- One medium ripe avocado, peeled and sliced

Instructions

- In a small bowl, combine coleslaw mix, cilantro, lime juice, honey, salt and, if desired, jalapeno; toss to coat. Set aside.
- Preheat the air fryer to 375° F. In a shallow bowl, whisk eggs and milk. Place flour in a separate shallow bowl. In a third shallow bowl, mix panko, cumin and garlic powder. Dip shrimp in flour to coat both sides; shake off excess. Dip in egg mixture, then in panko mixture, patting to help coating adhere.
- In batches, arrange shrimp in a single layer in greased air-fryer basket; spritz with cooking spray. Cook until golden brown, 2-3 minutes. Turn; spritz with cooking spray. Cook until golden brown and shrimp turn pink, 2-3 minutes longer.
- Serve shrimp in tortillas with coleslaw mix and avocado.

Air-Fryer Steak Fajitas

Preparation and Cooking Time

30 minutes

Servings

6 persons

Nutritional facts

309 calories,2g fat ,1g fiber ,14g carbs ,2g protein

Ingredients

- 2 large tomatoes, seeded and chopped
- A half-cup diced red onion
- A quarter cup lime juice
- One large onion, halved and sliced
- 6 whole-wheat tortillas (8 inches), warmed
- Optional: Sliced avocado and lime wedges
- One jalapeno pepper, seeded and minced
- 3 tablespoons minced fresh cilantro
- two teaspoons ground cumin, divided
- 3/4 teaspoon salt, divided
- One beef flank steak (about 1-1/2 pounds)

Instructions

- Put the required ingredients in a small bowl; stir in 1 teaspoon cumin And 1/4 teaspoon salt. Let stand until serving.
- Preheat the air fryer to 400° F. Sprinkle steak with the remaining cumin and salt. Place on a greased tray in the air-fryer basket. Cook until meat reaches desired doneness (for medium-rare, a thermometer should read 135°F; medium, 140°F; medium-well, 145°F), 6-8 minutes per side. Remove from basket and let stand 5 minutes.
- Meanwhile, place onion on a tray in the air-fryer basket. Cook until crisp-tender, 2-3 minutes, stirring once. Slice steak thinly across the grain; serve tortillas with onion and salsa. If desired, serve with avocado and lime wedges.

Air-Fryer Coconut Shrimp

Preparation and Cooking Time

30 minutes

Servings

2 persons

Nutritional facts

423 calories,3g fat ,2g fiber ,30g carbs ,6g protein

Ingredients

- A half-pound uncooked large shrimp
- A half-cup sweetened shredded coconut
- 3 tablespoons panko bread crumbs
- 2 large egg whites
- Dash crushed of red pepper flakes
- A one-eighth teaspoon of salt
- Dash pepper
- Dash Louisiana-style hot sauce
- 3 tablespoons all-purpose flour
- A one third cup apricot preserves
- A half teaspoon of cider vinegar

Instructions

- Preheat the air fryer to 375 degrees Fahrenheit. • Toss coconut with the bread crumbs in a shallow basin. Peel and thinly slice shrimp, leaving tails on. In a small basin, whisk together salt, egg whites, pepper, and spicy sauce. In a third shallow dish, put the flour.
- Lightly coat shrimp in flour and brush off excess. Dip in the egg white mixture, then in the coconut mixture, pressing it down to help it stick.
- Arrange the shrimp in a single layer in the air-fryer basket on a greased tray. Cook for 4 minutes, then flip shrimp and cook for another 4 minutes, or until coconut is lightly golden and shrimp are pink.
- In a small saucepan, mix sauce ingredients; simmer and stir over medium-low heat till preserves are melted. Serve the shrimp with the sauce right away.

Air-Fryer Wasabi Crab Cakes

Preparation and Cooking Time

30 minutes

Servings

24 cakes

Nutritional facts

49 calories,20g fat ,1g fiber ,14g carbs ,2g protein

Ingredients

- One finely chopped sweet red pepper
- One finely chopped celery rib
- 3 green onions, finely chopped
- Two large egg whites
- 3 tablespoons of reduced-fat mayonnaise
- A one-fourth teaspoon of prepared wasabi

- A one-fourth teaspoon of salt
- 1/3 cup plus a half cup dry bread crumbs, divided
- A one and a half lump crabmeat, drained
- Cooking spray
- 1 celery rib, chopped
- A one-third cup reduced-fat mayonnaise
- One green onion, chopped
- One tablespoon sweet pickle relish
- A half teaspoon prepared wasabi
- A one-fourth teaspoon of celery salt

Instructions

- Preheat the air fryer to 375° F. Combine the required ingredients; add 1/3 cup bread crumbs. Gently fold in crab.
- Place remaining bread crumbs in a shallow bowl. Drop heaping tablespoons of crab mixture into crumbs. Gently coat and shape into 3/4-in.-thick patties. Place crab cakes in a single layer on a greased tray in an air-fryer basket in batches. Spritz crab cakes with cooking spray. Cook until golden brown, 8-12 minutes, carefully turning halfway through cooking and spritzing with additional cooking spray.
- Meanwhile, place sauce ingredients in a food processor; pulse 2 or 3 times to blend or achieve desired consistency. Serve crab cakes immediately with dipping sauce.

Air-Fryer Caribbean Wontons

Preparation and Cooking Time

40 minutes

Servings

24 wontons

Nutritional facts

83 calories,1g fat ,2g fiber ,19g carbs ,3g protein

Ingredients

- 4 ounces' cream cheese, softened
- A quarter cup sweetened shredded coconut
- A quarter cup mashed ripe banana
- Two tablespoons chopped walnuts
- 2 tablespoons canned crushed pineapple
- One cup marshmallow creme
- 24 wonton wrappers
- Cooking spray
- One pound fresh strawberries, hulled
- A quarter cup of sugar
- One teaspoon cornstarch
- Confectioners' sugar and ground cinnamon

Instructions

- Preheat your air fryer to 350 degrees Fahrenheit. Whisk the cream cheese in a small mixing bowl until creamy. Combine the banana, coconut, walnuts, and pineapple in a mixing bowl. Combine marshmallow crème and whipped topping in a mixing bowl.
- Hold a wonton wrapper with one tip facing you. Cover the rest of the wrappers with a moist paper towel until ready to use. Fill the middle of the wrapper with two tablespoons of filling. Wet the edges and fold opposing corners together over the filling, pressing to seal. Rep with the rest of the wrappers and filling.
- Spritz wontons with cooking spray and put in a single layer on a prepared tray in the air-fryer basket in batches. Cook for 10-12 minutes, or until golden brown and crisp.

- In the meanwhile, purée the strawberries in a food processor with the lid on. Combine cornstarch and sugar in a small pot. Stir in the pureed strawberries. Bring to a boil, then simmer and stir for 2 minutes, or until the sauce has thickened. Strain the mixture, keeping the sauce; discard the seeds if preferred. Confectioners' sugar and cinnamon are sprinkled over the wontons. Serve with sauce.

Air-Fryer Apple Fritters

Preparation and Cooking Time

18 minutes

Servings

15 persons

Nutritional facts

145 calories, 21g fat ,1g fiber ,7g carbs ,9g protein

Ingredients

- Cooking spray
- One and a half cup all-purpose flour
- A quarter cup of sugar
- two teaspoons baking powder
- One and a half teaspoons ground cinnamon
- A half teaspoon of salt
- 2/3 cup 2% milk
- 2 large eggs, room temperature
- One tablespoon lemon juice
- One and a half teaspoon vanilla extract, divided
- Two medium Honey crisp apples, peeled and chopped
- A quarter cup butter
- One cup confectioners' sugar
- One tablespoon 2% milk

Instructions

- Line air-fryer basket with parchment (cut to fit); spritz with cooking spray. Preheat air fryer to 410 degrees F.
- Combine Sugar, flour, cinnamon, baking powder, and salt in a large bowl. Add eggs, milk, lemon juice and 1 teaspoon vanilla extract; stir just until moistened. Fold in apples.
- Drop dough by 1/4 cupful's 2-in. apart onto an air-fryer basket in batches. Spritz with cooking spray. Cook until golden brown, 5-6 minutes. Turn fritters; continue to air-fry until golden brown, 1-2 minutes.
- Melt butter in a small saucepan over medium-high heat. Carefully cook until butter starts to brown and foam, 5 minutes. Remove from heat; cool slightly. Add milk, confectioners' sugar, and remaining 1/2 teaspoon vanilla extract to the browned butter and whisk until smooth. Drizzle over fritters before serving.

Air-Fryer Keto Meatballs

Preparation and Cooking Time

40 minutes

Servings

4 persons

Nutritional facts

404 calories,1g fat ,5g fiber ,5g carbs ,3g protein

Ingredients

- A half-cup grated Parmesan cheese
- A half-cup shredded mozzarella cheese
- One large egg, lightly beaten
- 2 tablespoons heavy whipping cream

- One garlic clove, minced
- One-pound lean ground beef (90% lean)
- One can (8 ounces) tomato sauce with basil, garlic and oregano
- 2 tablespoons prepared pesto
- A quarter cup heavy whipping cream

Instructions

- Preheat the air fryer to 350° F. In a large bowl, combine the first 5 ingredients. Add beef; mix lightly but thoroughly. Shape into 1-1/2 inch balls. Place a single layer on a greased tray in the air-fryer basket; cook until lightly browned and cooked through, 8-10 minutes.
- Meanwhile, in a small saucepan, mix sauce ingredients; heat through. Serve with meatballs.
- Freeze the meatballs in the freezer containers after they have cooled. Refrigerate until slightly thawed before using. Preheat the air fryer to 350 degrees. Reheat for 3-5 minutes, or until well heated. Make the sauce according to the package directions.

Air-Fryer Taco Twists

Preparation and Cooking Time

35 minutes

Servings

4 persons

Nutritional facts

371 calories,7g fat ,1g fiber ,26g carbs ,34g protein

Ingredients

- 1/3-pound ground beef
- One large onion, chopped
- A two-third cup shredded cheddar cheese
- A one third cup salsa
- 3 tablespoons canned chopped green chilies
- A one fourth teaspoon garlic powder
- A one-fourth teaspoon hot pepper sauce
- A one-eighth teaspoon of salt
- A one eighth teaspoon ground cumin
- One tube (8 ounces) refrigerated crescent rolls

Instructions

- Preheat the air fryer to 300 degrees Fahrenheit. Cook the beef and onion in a large pan over medium heat; drain. Combine the cheese, chilies, salsa, garlic powder, salt, hot pepper sauce, and cumin in a large mixing bowl.
- Unroll the crescent roll dough and cut it into four rectangles, sealing the holes. In the middle of each rectangle, place a half-cup of the meat mixture. Bring four corners to the center and twist them together; squeeze to close. In batches, place a single layer on an oiled tray in the air-fryer basket. Cook for 18-22 minutes, or until golden brown. Serve with toppings of your choice, if preferred

Air-Fryer Potato Chips

Preparation and Cooking Time

45 minutes

Servings

6 persons

Nutritional facts

148 calories,7g fat ,2g fiber ,14g carbs ,10 protein

Ingredients

- Two large potatoes

- cooking spray (Olive oil-flavored)
- A half teaspoon of sea salt
- Minced parsley, optional

Instructions

- Preheat the air fryer to 360 degrees Fahrenheit. Cut potatoes into extremely thin slices using a vegetable peeler. Transfer to a large mixing bowl and cover with cold water. Drain after 15 minutes of soaking. Soak for another 15 minutes with additional cold water.
- Drain potatoes, then set them on towels to dry. Using cooking spray, lightly coat the potatoes and season with salt. In batches, arrange potato slices on a tray in a single layer in a greased air-fryer basket. Cook for 15-17 minutes, tossing and flipping every 5-7 minutes, until crisp and golden brown. Sprinkle with parsley if desired.

Spicy Air Fryer Chicken Tenders

Preparation and Cooking Time

60 minutes

Servings

4 persons

Nutritional facts

160 calories,11g fat ,1.1g fiber ,33g carbs ,7g protein

Ingredients

- 1 1/2 lb. chicken tenders
- Kosher salt
- 1/4 tsp. hot sauce (optional)
- Pinch of kosher salt
- Freshly ground black pepper
- Freshly ground black pepper
- One and a half cup all-purpose flour
- Two and a half cup panko bread crumbs
- 2 eggs
- 1/4 c. of buttermilk
- Cooking spray
- One third cup mayonnaise
- 3 tablespoons honey
- 2 tablespoons. Dijon mustard

Instructions

- Chicken tenders are seasoned with salt and pepper on both sides. In two separate small pans, put bread crumbs and flour. Whisk the eggs and buttermilk together in a third bowl. Dip the chicken in the flour, then the mixture of the eggs, and finally in the bread crumbs, pressing to coat.
- Working in batches, put chicken tenders in the air fryer basket, making sure not to overcrowd them. Spray the chicken tops with cooking spray and roast for 5 minutes at 400 ° F. Flip over the chicken, coat the tops with some more cooking spray, and cook for 5 more minutes. Repeat for the remaining chicken tenders.
- Make the sauce: Whisk together Dijon, mayonnaise, honey and hot sauce, if used, in a small bowl. And use a pinch of salt and a few black pepper cracks to season.
- Serve with honey mustard the chicken tenders.

Bacon-Wrapped Avocado

Preparation and Cooking Time

5 minutes

Servings

24 persons

Nutritional facts

120 calories,10g fat ,0.5g fiber ,12g carbs ,3g protein

Ingredients

- Three avocados
- Twenty-four thin strips of bacon
- A quarter cup ranch dressing for serving

Instructions

- Slice every avocado into eight wedges of equal size. Wrap each wedge with a bacon strip and, if necessary, cut the bacon.
- Working in batches, place in a single layer in an air fryer basket. Cook for 8 minutes at 400 °F until the bacon is fried and crispy.
- Serve warm along with the ranch.

Antipasto Egg Rolls

Preparation and Cooking Time

30 minutes

Servings

12 persons

Nutritional facts

280 calories,5g fat ,1g fiber ,5g carbs ,2g protein

Ingredients

- Twelve egg roll wrappers
- Twelve slices provolone
- 1 cup shredded mozzarella
- 1 cup sliced Pepperoncini
- Twelve slices of deli ham
- 36 slices pepperoni
- 1/4 cup freshly grated Parmesan
- Italian dressing, for serving

Instructions

- Put an egg roll wrapper in a diamond shape place on a clean. Then it is topped with one 3 slices of pepperoni, a slice of ham and a large pinch of both pepperoni and mozzarella. Now the bottom half is to be folded up. Then tightly fold in sides. Roll gently. Then seal the fold with a few drops of water.
- Working in batches, Cook egg rolls for 12 minutes at 390° F or golden. Do not forget to flip halfway.

Cauliflower Tots

Preparation and Cooking Time

30 minutes

Servings

6 persons

Nutritional facts

340 calories,4g fat ,1g fiber ,16g carbs ,4g protein

Ingredients

- 1 cup shredded cheddar
- Half cup ketchup
- 2 tablespoons. Sriracha
- 1 cup freshly grated Parmesan
- 2/3 cup panko breadcrumbs
- 2 tablespoons. freshly chopped chives
- Cooking spray
- 4 cup cauliflower florets, steamed (about 1/2 large cauliflower)
- 1 large egg, lightly beaten

- Kosher salt
- Freshly ground black pepper

Instructions

- Process steamed cauliflower in a food processor till riced. Put riced cauliflower on a clean kitchen towel. Then squeeze to drain water.
- Move cauliflower to a big bowl with panko, egg, cheddar, Parmesan and chives. Now mix till combined. Season with pepper and salt as per the requirement.
- Using your hands, one tablespoon mixture is spooned and rolled into a tater-tot shape. Working in batches, these have to be arranged in a single layer in the air fryer basket.
- Then cook for ten minutes at 375° F or until tots turn golden.
- Prepare spicy ketchup by combining ketchup and Sriracha in a small serving bowl. Stir well to mix.
- Enjoy warm cauliflower tots along with spicy ketchup.

Cheesy Beef Empanadas

Preparation and Cooking Time

2 hours

Servings

15 persons

Nutritional facts

456 calories, 6g fat ,2g fiber ,17g carbs ,3g protein

Ingredients

- Half cup cold butter, cut into cubes
- 3/4 cup water
- 1 large egg
- 1 tablespoon extra-virgin olive oil
- 1 yellow onion, chopped
- 2 cloves garlic, minced
- 3 cup all-purpose flour, plus more for surface
- 1 tsp. kosher salt
- 1 tsp. baking powder
- 1 lb. ground beef
- 1 tablespoon tomato paste
- 1 tsp. oregano
- 1 tsp. cumin
- Egg wash for brushing
- Freshly chopped cilantro for garnish
- Sour cream, for serving
- A half teaspoon. Of paprika
- black pepper to taste
- Half cup chopped tomatoes
- Half cup chopped pickled jalapeños
- 1 1/4 cup shredded Cheddar
- 1 1/4 cup Shredded Monterey Jack

Instructions

- Whisk the flour, salt, and baking powder together in a big bowl. Use your hands or a pastry cutter to cut the butter into the flour until pea-sized. Add the water and egg and combine until it forms a dough. Turn the dough on a lightly floured surface and knead for around 5 minutes, until smooth.
- Wrap up and refrigerate for at least 1 hour in plastic wrap.
- Heat oil in a skillet over medium heat. Add the onion & cook until soft, about 5 minutes, then add garlic and cook for 1 more minute, until fragrant. Add the ground beef and cook for 5

minutes, breaking the meat with a wooden spoon until it is no longer pink. Fat is to be drained.

- Return the pan to medium heat and stir in the beef with the tomato paste. Season with salt and pepper and add oregano, cumin, and paprika. Add the tomatoes and jalapeños and cook for about 3 minutes, until hot. Remove from heat and allow it to cool slightly.
  Put the dough on a lightly floured surface and divide it in half. Cut out rounds using a 4.5" round cookie cutter." Repeat with the dough that remains.
- Lightly moisten the outer edge of a dough round with water and put around two tablespoons of cheddar and Monterey filling in the middle and top. Fold dough in half over the filling. Crimp the edges together with a fork. Then brush them with egg wash. Repeat with the leftover filling and dough.
- Put the empanadas in parchment-paper-lined Air Fryer basket to ensure they do not touch, and cook for 10 minutes in batches at 400 ° F.
- It is to be garnished with cilantro. Finally, serve with some sour cream.

Homemade Cannoli

Preparation and Cooking Time

3 hours

Servings

20 persons

Nutritional facts

160 calories,3g fat ,1g fiber ,14g carbs ,7g protein

Ingredients

- Half cup powdered sugar, divided
- 3/4 cup heavy cream
- 6 tablespoons. white wine
- 1 large egg
- 1 egg white for brushing
- Vegetable oil for frying
- 1 tsp. pure vanilla extract
- 1 tsp. orange zest
- 1/4 tsp. kosher salt
- Half cup mini chocolate chips, for garnish
- Two cups all-purpose flour, plus more for surface
- 1 (16-oz.) container ricotta
- Half cup mascarpone cheese
- 1/4 cup granulated sugar
- 1 tsp. kosher salt
- A half teaspoon. cinnamon
- 4 tablespoons. cold butter, cut into cubes

Instructions

- Drain the ricotta by placing a fine-mesh strainer over a wide bowl. Let it drain for at least an hour in the refrigerator and up to overnight.
- Using a hand mixer, mix heavy cream and a quarter cup of powdered sugar in a large bowl until stiff peaks appear.
- Combine ricotta, mascarpone, and a quarter of a cup of powdered sugar, salt, vanilla and orange zest in another large bowl. Fold the whipped cream into it. Refrigerate for at least 1 hour until ready to fill with cannoli.
- Whisk the flour, sugar, salt, and cinnamon together in a big bowl. Using your hands or pastry cutter, cut butter into the flour mixture until pea-sized. Add the wine and egg and combine until it forms a dough. To make the dough come together, knead a few times in the bowl. Pat into a flat circle,

cover and refrigerate for at least 1 hour and up to overnight in plastic wrap.

- Divide the dough into halves on a lightly floured surface. Roll to 1/8" thick. To cut out dough, use a 4 circle cookie cutter. Repeat with the dough that remains. To cut a few extra circles, re-roll the scraps.
- Wrap cannoli molds and brush egg whites around the dough to join to seal together.
- Working in batches, put molds in air fryer baskets and cook for 12 minutes or golden at 350 ° F.
- Remove twist shells gently from molds when cool enough to handle or use a kitchen towel to hold them.
- The pipe is filled into shells and then dipped into mini chocolate chips.
- Put filling in a pastry bag. It should be fitted with an open star tip. The filling is to be piped into shells. Next, dip ends in mini chocolate chips and enjoy.

Twice Air Fryer Baked Potatoes

Preparation and Cooking Time

2 hours

Servings

6 persons

Nutritional facts

179 calories,11g fat ,1g fiber ,20g carbs ,3g protein

Ingredients

- Kosher salt
- Half cup (1 stick) butter, softened
- Half cup milk
- Half cup sour cream
- 1 Half cup shredded Cheddar, divided
- 2 green onions, thinly sliced, plus more for garnish
- 6 large russet potatoes, scrubbed clean
- 1 tablespoon extra-virgin olive oil
- Freshly ground black pepper

Instructions

- Pat potatoes with paper towels fully dry. With a fork, poke the potatoes all over, brush them with oil & sprinkle with salt. Acting in batches, put the potatoes in an air fryer basket and cook for 40 minutes at 400 ° F. Place it on a big baking sheet and allow it to cool until cool enough to treat.
- Cutting length-wise cut a thin layer off the top of each potato. Scoop out each potato, leaving a 1/2" border. Place the insides of it in a big bowl. Keep the tops of the potatoes and roast them as a snack on the tray!
- Add sour cream, butter and milk and smash until butter is melted and potatoes are almost smooth, but with some chunks, to bowl with potatoes. Insert 1 cup of the green onions and cheese and stir until combined. With salt and pepper, season.
- Cover the baked potatoes with potato mixture and put them back in the air fryer basket. Top with half a cup of cheddar left. Cook for 5 minutes at 400 °F until the cheese is melted and crispy outside.
  - Garnish before serving with more green onions.

Air Fryer Steak

Preparation and Cooking Time

45 minutes

Servings

2 persons

Nutritional facts

460 calories,21g fat ,2g fiber ,39g carbs ,4g protein

Ingredients

- Two teaspoons freshly chopped parsley
- Kosher salt
- Freshly ground black pepper
- 1 tsp. freshly chopped chives
- 1 tsp. freshly chopped thyme
- 1 tsp. freshly chopped rosemary
- 4 tablespoons butter, softened
- 2 cloves garlic, minced
- 1 (2 lb.) bone-in rib eye

Instructions

- Combine the butter and spices in a shallow bowl. Place it in the middle of the plastic piece middle and roll it into a log. Twist ends together. It should be refrigerated for twenty minutes' till hardened.
- Season the steak with salt and pepper on both sides.
- Put the steak in the air fryer basket and cook at 400 ° F for twelve to fourteen minutes, for medium, based on steak thickness, flipping halfway through.
- Top steak with herb butter slice.

Air Fryer Brownies

Preparation and Cooking Time

35 minutes

Servings

2 persons

Nutritional facts

195 calories ,7g fat ,3g fiber ,22g carbs ,3g protein

Ingredients

- Half cup granulated sugar
- One third cup cocoa powder
- 1/4 cup butter, melted and cooled slightly
- 1 large egg
- 1/4 cup all-purpose flour
- 1/4 tsp. baking powder
- Pinch kosher salt

Instructions

- Grease a 6-inch diameter cake pan with cooking spray. Whisk in a medium bowl to mix sugar, salt, chocolate powder, flour and baking powder.
- Whisk the melted butter and egg in a small bowl until mixed. To dry ingredients, add wet ingredients and stir till combined.
- Move brownie batter to the prepared cake pan as well as the smooth top. Cook for 16-18 minutes in the air fryer at 350 ° F. Before slicing, let cool for 10 minutes.

Spicy Chicken Taquitos

Preparation and Cooking Time

45 minutes

Servings

12 persons

Nutritional facts

160 calories, 9g fat, 1g fiber ,23g carbs ,4g protein

Ingredients

- 1 tsp. cumin

- 1 tsp. chili powder
- Kosher salt
- Cooking spray
- 3 cups shredded cooked chicken
- 1 (8-oz.) block cream cheese, softened
- Freshly ground black pepper
- 1 chipotle in adobo sauce, chopped, plus 1 tablespoon sauce
- 12 small corn tortillas
- One and a Half cup shredded cheddar
- One and a Half cup shredded Pepper Jack
- Pico de Gallo, for serving
- 1 clove garlic
- Juice of lime
- Kosher salt
- Freshly ground black pepper
- Crumbled queso fresco for serving
- For the avocado cream sauce
- 1 large avocado, pitted
- Half cup sour cream
- 1/4 cup packed cilantro leaves

Instructions

- Combine the chicken, cream cheese, chipotle, sauce, cumin, and chili powder in a large bowl. With salt and pepper, season.
- Place the tortillas on a secure microwave plate and cover them with a wet paper towel. Microwave for 30 seconds or before more pliable and wet.
- Spread on one end of the tortilla about a quarter cup of filling, then scatter a little cheddar and pepper jack next to the filling. Tightly roll-up. Repeat with the filling and cheese.
- Place in the air fryer basket, seam side down, and cook for 7 minutes at 400 ° F.
- Serve with salsa, pico de gallo, and queso fresco with avocado cream.
- Mix the cilantro, avocado, sour cream, garlic and lime juice in a food processor. With salt and pepper, season. Pour into a bowl, press directly over the top with plastic wrap, and refrigerate until ready to use.

Air Fryer Pizza

Preparation and Cooking Time

10 minutes

Servings

2 persons

Nutritional facts

345 calories,15g fat, 3g fiber ,16g carbs ,6g protein

Ingredients

- 2 (8-oz.) packages pizza dough
- 1 tablespoon extra-virgin olive oil, divided
- Freshly ground black pepper
- 1/2 (8-oz.) mozzarella ball, cut into Quarter" slices
- Basil leaves for serving
- One-third cup crushed tomatoes
- 1 clove garlic, minced
- A half teaspoon. oregano
- Kosher salt

Instructions

- Gently flatten the dough ball with your hands up to about 8" in diameter on a smooth, floured surface (or smaller than the air fryer's basket). Repeat it with the second ball of dough. Brush both with olive oil and pass one to your air fryer's basket, oil side up.
- Stir to mix crushed tomatoes, garlic, then oregano, and season with salt and pepper in a medium bowl. On the middle of the rolled-out pizza dough, spoon half the tomato mixture, then spread into an even layer, leaving ½" bare outer crust.
- Apply half the slices of mozzarella to the pie. Air fry for 10 to 12 minutes at 400 ° F, or until the crust is golden and the cheese is melted.
- Using 2 sets of tongs, remove the first pizza from the air fryer basket and garnish it with basil leaves. Prepare and cook the second pizza, garnish and serve.

Special Air Fryer Donuts

Preparation and Cooking Time

2 hours 40 minutes

Servings

6 persons

Nutritional facts

160 calories,7g fat ,3g fiber ,22g carbs ,4g protein

Ingredients

- Cooking spray
- 2 tablespoons ground cinnamon
- 2 tablespoons melted butter
- Half cup milk
- 1/4 cup plus 1 tsp. granulated sugar, divided
- 1 (0.25-oz.) packet or 2 1/4 tsp. active-dry yeast
- 1 large egg
- 1 tsp. pure vanilla extract
- For the vanilla glaze
- 1 cup powdered sugar
- Two cups all-purpose flour
- A half teaspoon. kosher salt
- 4 tablespoons. butter, melted
- 2 oz. milk
- A half teaspoon. pure vanilla extract
- 3/4 cup powdered sugar
- 1/4 cup unsweetened cocoa powder
- 3 tablespoons milk
- Half cup granulated sugar

Instructions

- Grease a large bowl with cooking oil spray. Add milk into a small, microwave-safe bowl or glass measuring cup. Microwave for 40 seconds until lukewarm. Insert a teaspoon of sugar and stir to dissolve. Then sprinkle with the yeast and leave to rest for around 8 minutes until frothy.
- Whisk the flour and salt together in a medium bowl. Whisk the remaining quarter of a cup of sugar, butter, egg, and vanilla together in a large bowl. Pour in the yeast mixture, blend to combine, and add to the dry ingredients, stirring until shaggy dough shapes with a wooden spoon.
- Switch to a floured surface and knead until elastic and just slightly tacky, adding a teaspoon of more flour at a time, about 5 minutes if required. Place the dough in an oiled bowl and cover it with a clean dish towel. Let the dough rise for around 1 hour in a warm place until it has doubled in size.

- Cover a large baking sheet with parchment paper and gently grease it. Punch down the dough, then move it onto a finely floured work surface and stretch it out into a rectangle that is ½ inch thick.
- Punch the doughnuts out with a doughnut cutter or 3 inch and 1-inch biscuit cutters. Knead some scraps together and punch more doughnuts or holes out. Put doughnuts and holes on baking sheets, cover with a dish towel, and let rise again for an additional 40 minutes to 1 hour.
- Grease the air fryer basket with cooking spray and insert 2 doughnuts and 2 doughnut holes at a time to ensure the doughnuts do not touch. Cook until deeply golden at 375 ° F for 6 minutes. Put on the cooling rack and repeat for the remaining dough.
- Dip doughnuts in glaze. Return to the rack for cooling and let sit before serving for 5 minutes.
- Whisk the powdered sugar, milk, and vanilla together in a medium bowl until smooth.
- Combine the powdered sugar, chocolate powder, and milk in a medium bowl.
- Whisk together cinnamon and sugar in a big shallow cup. Brush doughnuts with melted butter as well as toss in cinnamon sugar.

Air Fryer Salmon

Preparation and Cooking Time

15 minutes

Servings

2 persons

Nutritional facts

177calories,8g fat ,1g fiber ,18g carbs ,2g protein

Ingredients

- Freshly ground black pepper
- Two teaspoons. extra-virgin olive oil
- 2 tablespoons whole-grain mustard
- 1 tablespoon packed brown sugar
- 1 clove garlic, minced
- 2 (6-oz.) salmon fillets
- Kosher salt
- A half teaspoon. thyme leaves

Instructions

- Season salmon with salt and pepper all over. Whisk the sugar, oil, mustard, garlic and thyme together in a small dish. Spread atop the salmon.
- Arrange salmon in a basket of the air fryer. Set the air fryer to 400 degrees F. Now cook for 10 minutes.

Air Fryer Brussels sprouts Chips

Preparation and Cooking Time

25 minutes

Servings

2-3 persons

Nutritional facts

205 calories,9g fat ,2g fiber ,22g carbs ,2g protein

Ingredients

- 2 tablespoons freshly grated Parmesan, plus more for garnish
- 1 tsp. garlic powder
- Kosher salt
- 1/2 lb. Brussels sprouts, thinly sliced

- 1 tablespoon extra-virgin olive oil
- Freshly ground black pepper
  - Caesar dressing, for dipping

Instructions

- Toss the Brussels sprouts with garlic powder, oil and parmesan in a large bowl. Then season with salt and pepper. Arrange in the air fryer in an even layer.
- Bake for 8 minutes at 350°F, toss, and bake for 8 more minutes, until crisp and golden.
- For dipping, it can be garnished with more Parmesan. Then serve with Caesar dressing.

Air Fryer Cheeseburger

Preparation and Cooking Time

30 minutes

Servings

4 persons

Nutritional facts

521 calories,6g fat ,1g fiber ,18g carbs ,5g protein

Ingredients

- 1 tablespoon low-sodium soy sauce
- Kosher salt
- Sliced tomatoes
- Thinly sliced red onion
- Freshly ground black pepper
- 4 slices American cheese
- 4 hamburger buns
- 1 lb. ground beef
- 2 cloves garlic, minced
- Mayonnaise
- Lettuce

Instructions

- Combine the soy sauce, beef and garlic in a large bowl. Shape and flatten into 4-inch circle 4 patties. With salt and pepper, season both sides.
- Put 2 patties in an air fryer and cook for four minutes per side, on average, at 375 °F. Remove and cover with a slice of cheese quickly. Repeat with 2 patties left.
- Layer mayo on hamburger buns and then finish with tomatoes, lettuce, patties and onions.

Air Fryer Blooming Onion

Preparation and Cooking Time

45 minutes

Servings

4 persons

Nutritional facts

160 calories,20g fat ,2g fiber ,30g carbs ,4g protein

Ingredients

- 1 large yellow onion
- A half teaspoon. garlic powder
- 1/4 tsp. dried oregano
- Kosher salt
- 3 large eggs
- 1 cup breadcrumbs
- Two teaspoons. paprika

- One tsp. garlic powder
- One tsp. onion powder
- One tsp. kosher salt
- 3 tablespoons. extra-virgin olive oil
- 2/3 cup mayonnaise
- 2 tablespoons. ketchup
- One tsp. horseradish
- A half teaspoon. Paprika

Instructions

- Cut the onion stem off and arrange the onion on the flat side. Cut an inch from the root into 12 to 16 sections, being careful not to cut all the way. To remove petals, turn over and softly pull sections of onion out.
- Whisk the eggs and 1 tablespoon of water together in a shallow bowl. Whisk the breadcrumbs and spices together in another small bowl. Dip the onion into the egg wash, dredge it in the breadcrumb paste, and cover it completely with a spoon. Sprinkle the onion with some oil.
- Place in the air fryer basket and cook at 375 ° F until the onion is tender, 20 to 25 minutes all the way through. Drizzle as needed with more oil.
- Meanwhile, make a sauce: stir together horseradish, mayonnaise, ketchup, paprika, garlic powder and dried oregano in a medium bowl, with salt, season.
- For dipping, serve the onion with sauce.

Air Fryer Potatoes

Preparation and Cooking Time

25 minutes

Servings

4 persons

Nutritional facts

160 calories,11g fat ,1g fiber ,31g carbs ,3g protein

Ingredients

- 1-pound baby potatoes, halved
- 1 tablespoon extra-virgin olive oil
- One tsp. garlic powder
- One tsp. Italian seasoning
- One tsp. Cajun seasoning (optional)
- Kosher salt
- Freshly ground black pepper
- Lemon wedge, for serving
- Freshly chopped parsley for garnish

Instructions

- Toss potatoes with Cajun seasoning, Italian seasoning, and oil and garlic powder in a large bowl. With salt and pepper, season.
- Place the potatoes in an air fryer basket and cook for 10 minutes at 400 ° F. Shake the basket, stir the potatoes, and cook for another 8 to 10 minutes until the potatoes are golden and soft.
- Squeeze the lemon juice over the fried potatoes and garnish it before serving with parsley.

Air Fryer Fish

Preparation and Cooking Time

30 minutes

Servings

2 persons

Nutritional facts

160 calories,20g fat ,3g fiber ,21g carbs ,2g protein

Ingredients

- 1 lb. cod, cut into 4 strips
- 1 large egg, beaten
- Two cups panko bread crumbs
- 1 tsp. Old Bay seasoning
- Lemon wedges, for serving
- Kosher salt
- Freshly ground black pepper
- Half cup all-purpose flour
- Tartar sauce, for serving

Instructions

- Dry and season the fish with salt and pepper on both sides.
- Place in three shallow bowls the flour, egg, and panko. To mix, add Old Bay to panko & toss. Acting one at a time, cover the fish with the flour, then with the egg, and then with the panko, and press to coat.
- Working in batches, put fish in the air fryer basket and cook for 10 to 12 minutes at 400 ° F, softly tossing halfway through or until the fish is golden and comfortably flakes with a fork.
- Serve with tartar sauce and lemon wedges.

Air Fryer Chicken Breast

Preparation and Cooking Time

30 minutes

Servings

2 persons

Nutritional facts

257 calories,9g fat ,2g fiber ,22g carbs ,4g protein

Ingredients

- One large egg, beaten
- 1/4 cup all-purpose flour
- 3/4 cup panko bread crumbs
- One-third cup freshly grated Parmesan
- Two teaspoons. lemon zest
- 1 tsp. dried oregano
- A half teaspoon. cayenne pepper
- Kosher salt
- Freshly ground black pepper
- Two boneless skinless chicken breasts

Instructions

- Place in two separate shallow bowls, the eggs and starch. Combine the oregano, panko, parmesan, lemon zest and cayenne in the third shallow bowl. With salt and pepper, season.
- Dip the chicken into the flour, then the eggs, and then the panko paste, pressing to cover, one at a time.
- Put in the air-fryer basket and cook for 10 minutes at 375 °F. Flip the chicken and cook for another five minutes until the chicken is golden and cooked through.

Air Fryer Pork Chops

Preparation and Cooking Time

20 minutes

Servings

4 persons

Nutritional facts

488 calories,12g fat ,1g fiber ,16g carbs ,2g protein

Ingredients

- 4 boneless pork chops
- 1 tsp. kosher salt
- 1 tsp. paprika
- 1 tsp. garlic powder
- 1 tsp. onion powder
- 2 tablespoons. extra-virgin olive oil
- Half cup freshly grated Parmesan
- A half teaspoon. freshly ground black pepper

Instructions

- Pat-dry pork chops with paper towels. Cover the two sides with oil. Combine the parmesan and spices in a medium bowl. Coat the pork chops with Parmesan paste on both sides.
- Place pork chops in an air-fryer basket and cook for 9 minutes at 375 ° F, flipping midway through.

Air Fryer Rotisserie Chicken

Preparation and Cooking Time

1 hour 10 minutes

Servings

6 persons

Nutritional facts

260 calories,5g fat ,2g fiber ,19g carbs ,3g protein

Ingredients

- 1 (3-lb) chicken, cut into 8 pieces
- Two teaspoons.
- 2 tablespoons dried oregano
- Two teaspoons garlic powder
- Two teaspoons onion powder
- 1 tsp. smoked paprika
- Kosher salt
- Freshly ground black pepper
- 1 tablespoon dried thyme
- 1/4 tsp. cayenne

Instructions

- Season the chicken pieces with salt and pepper all over. Whisk the herbs and spices together in a medium bowl and then brush the spice mix over the chicken bits.
- Insert dark pieces of meat into the air fryer basket and cook 10 minutes at 350 ° F. Then flip and cook ten minutes more. Repeat for chicken breasts. However, reduce the time per side to eight minutes. To ensure the chicken is cooked through, each piece should reach 165 ° F using a meat thermometer.

Best-Ever Mozzarella Sticks

Preparation and Cooking Time

2 hours 25 minutes

Servings

6 persons

Nutritional facts

230 calories,9g fat ,2g fiber ,21g carbs ,4g protein

Ingredients

- 6 mozzarella sticks
- 2 large eggs, well-beaten
- 3 tablespoons all-purpose flour
- One cup panko bread crumbs

- Kosher salt
- Freshly cracked black pepper
- Warm marinara, for serving

Instructions

- Freeze sticks of mozzarella until completely frozen for at least 2 hours.
- Establish a breading station after 3 hours: Put panko, eggs, and flour in three Different shallow bowls. With salt and pepper, season the panko generously.
- Frozen mozzarella sticks are covered in flour, then soaked in eggs, then panko, back in the egg, finally back in the panko.
- Arrange frozen sticks of breaded mozzarella in an even layer in the air fryer's basket. Cook for 6 minutes at 400 ° F, or until the exterior is golden and crisp and melted in the middle.
- It can be served with warm marinara sauce.

Air Fryer Garlic Herb Turkey Breast

Preparation and Cooking Time

1 hour

Servings

6 persons

Nutritional facts

286 calories,8g fat ,4g fiber ,20g carbs ,2g protein

Ingredients

- 2 pounds' turkey breast, skin on
- Kosher salt
- Freshly ground black pepper
- 1 tsp. freshly chopped thyme
- 4 tablespoons. butter, melted
- 3 cloves garlic, minced
- 1 tsp. freshly chopped rosemary

Instructions

- Dry the turkey breast and season with salt and pepper on both sides.
- Combine the thyme, melted butter, garlic and rosemary in a shallow bowl. Brush the butter all over the breast of the turkey.
- Put in the air fryer basket, skin side up. Now cook for 40 minutes at 375 ° F or until the internal temperature exceeds 160 °F, turning halfway through.
- Allow 5 minutes to rest before slicing.

Chapter 4: Air Fryer Appetizers Recipes

Air Fryer Crispy Crab Rangoon

Preparation and Cooking Time

30 minutes

Servings

7 persons

Nutritional facts

98 calories,11g fat ,2g fiber ,8g carbs ,5g protein

Ingredients

- 4 or 6 oz. cream cheese, softened if you prefer creamy crab Rangoon, use 6 oz.
- 2 garlic cloves, minced
- 1 teaspoon Worcestershire sauce
- 4 or 6 oz. lump crab meat if you prefer your crab Rangoon to have more cream cheese and less crab, use 4 oz. Seafood lovers may want to go for 6 oz.
- 2 green onions, chopped
- 21 wonton wrappers
- salt and pepper to taste
- cooking oil

Instructions

- Heat the cream cheese in the microwave for thirty seconds to soften it.
- Mix the green onions, cream cheese, crab meat, salt, Worcestershire sauce, pepper, & garlic. Stir everything together thoroughly.
- On a work surface, lay out wonton wrappers. Using water, wet each of the wrappers.
- Fill each wrapper with about a spoonful and a half of the filling. Take care not to overfill the container.
- Fold the wrapper diagonally across. Then, with the two opposite corners facing each other, draw them up toward each other. Squeeze the edges of each piece together.
- Spritz the cooking oil into the air fryer basket.
- Fill the air fryer basket halfway with crab Rangoon's. Do not overfill. If necessary, cook in batches.
- Spritz with a little oil.
- Preheat the Air Fryer to 370 degrees Fahrenheit. Cook for ten minutes.
- Open the crab Rangoon and flip it. Cook for another 2-5 minutes, or until they are golden brown & crisp to your liking.
- Take out the crab Rangoon from the air fryer & serve with a dipping sauce of your preference.

Crispy, Homemade Onion Rings

Preparation and Cooking Time

40 minutes

Servings

4 persons

Nutritional facts

305 calories, 2g fat,1g fiber, 3g carbs, 2g protein

Ingredients

- A large Vidalia onion
- 1 teaspoon of smoked paprika
- 1 teaspoon of garlic powder
- Salt and pepper to taste.
- 1 1/2 cup panko breadcrumbs
- 1 cup of buttermilk
- 1 beaten egg
- 1 cup of flour
- cooking oil spray
- 1/2 teaspoon of smoked paprika
- 1/2 teaspoon of oregano
- 1/3 cup of mayo
- 1 1/2 -2 tablespoons of ketchup
- 1-2 tablespoons of creamy horseradish
- salt and pepper to taste

Instructions

- Lightly coat the air fryer basket with cooking oil.
- Peel the onion and cut it into 1/2-inch thick rounds. Onions have a shaky texture. When slicing, take caution and a mandolin if required. Before you slice the onion, try to keep it stable.
- In a basin big enough to dredge the onions, pour the flour. Add garlic powder, smoked paprika, salt, and pepper to the flour to taste.
- Combine the seasoned flour, egg, and buttermilk in a mixing bowl.
- Transfer the panko breadcrumbs to a separate bowl.
- Using your flour and buttermilk mixture, dredge the sliced onions, then coat them in panko breadcrumbs.
- Arrange the onion rings on a serving platter. Freeze the onion rings for about 15 minutes after breading them. This is an optional step; however, it is highly encouraged since it aids in the preservation of the breading.
- In the air fryer, place the onions. They should not be stacked. If necessary, cook in batches.
- Cooking oil should be sprayed on the surface.
- Preheat oven to 370°F and bake for 10-12 minutes.

Air Fryer Bang Fried Shrimp

Preparation and Cooking Time

30 minutes

Servings

4 persons

Nutritional facts

242 calories,3g fat ,1g fiber ,8g carbs ,2g protein

Ingredients

- 1-pound raw shrimp peeled and deveined
- McCormick's Grill Mates Montreal Chicken Seasoning to taste
- salt and pepper to taste

- cooking oil
- 1/3 cup plain, non-fat Greek yogurt
- One egg white 3 tbsp.
- Half cup all-purpose flour
- 3/4 cup panko bread crumbs
- 1 tsp. paprika
- 2 tbsp. Sriracha
- 1/4 cup sweet chili sauce

Instructions

- Preheat the Air Fryer to 400 degrees Fahrenheit.
- Using the seasonings, season the shrimp.
- Combine the flour, egg whites, & panko bread crumbs.
- Set up a kitchen area. The shrimp should be first inserted in flour, then egg whites, and finally panko bread crumbs.
- You don't have to soak the shrimp in the egg whites while dipping them. Apply a light dab of flour on the shrimp, ensuring that most flour remains on the shrimp. The egg white should stick to the panko crumbs.
- Cooking oil should be sprayed on the shrimp.
- In the Air Fryer basket, place the shrimp. It should be cooked for four minutes. Flip the shrimp to the other side after opening the basket. Cook for another 4 minutes, or until crisp.

Easy Air Fryer Fifteen Minute Crab Cakes

Preparation and Cooking Time

15 minutes

Servings

4 persons

Nutritional facts

160 calories, 6g fat ,1g fiber ,11g carbs ,3g protein

Ingredients

- Cooking oil
- ¼ cup green peppers diced
- 1 medium egg
- ¼ cup mayo
- 8 ounces of jumbo lump crab meat
- 1 tablespoon Old Bay Seasoning
- 1/3 cup breadcrumbs
- ¼ cup red peppers diced
- ½ lemon juice
- 1 teaspoon flour

Instructions

- Cooking oil should be sprayed into the air fryer basket.
- Except for the flour, combine all ingredients in a large mixing bowl.
- Make 4 patties out of the mixture. Dust each of the patties with a little flour.
- In the Air Fryer, place the crab cakes. Cooking oil should be sprayed on the crab cakes.
- Cook at 370 degrees F for 10 minutes.
- Allow cooling before serving.

Crispy Air Fryer Fried Chicken Wings

Preparation and Cooking Time

30 minutes

Servings

4 persons

Nutritional facts

470 calories, 3g fat, 1g fiber ,10g carbs ,4g protein

Ingredients

- 2 pounds' chicken wings drumettes (flats and drums)
- 1 tablespoon baking powder
- cooking oil spray
- McCormick's Grill Mates Montreal Chicken Seasoning to taste
- salt and pepper to taste

Instructions

- Using paper towels, completely dry the chicken.
- Put the chicken wings in a big bowl or a plastic bag that can be sealed.
- Season the chicken with salt and pepper to taste and chicken seasoning. Sprinkle the baking powder on top and make sure it's equally distributed.
- The chicken wings should be placed on a parchment-paper-lined baking sheet. Cooking oil should be sprayed over the top of the chicken.
- Preheat the oven to 320°F and air fry for fifteen minutes.
- Flip the chicken over in the air fryer. Cooking oil should be sprayed on this side of the chicken.
- Cook for a further 8 to 10 minutes at 400 degrees F, or until the chicken is crisp to your liking. A meat thermometer should be used to check the internal temperature of the chicken. Ensure the chicken reaches a temperature of 165 degrees F on the inside. Use a meat thermometer to check the temperature of the meat.
- Leave to cool before serving.

Fifteen Minute Air Fryer Three Cheese Stuffed Mushrooms

Preparation and Cooking Time

15 minutes

Servings

5 persons

Nutritional facts

116 calories, 9g fat ,2g fiber ,11g carbs ,2g protein

Ingredients

- 8 oz. fresh mushrooms
- 1/8 cup shredded white cheddar cheese
- 1 teaspoon Worcestershire sauce
- 2 garlic cloves Minced
- 4 oz. cream cheese
- ¼ cup shredded parmesan cheese
- 1/8 cup shredded sharp cheddar cheese
- salt and pepper to taste

Instructions

- Cut the stem out of the mushroom to prepare it for stuffing. First, chop off the stem
- and then make a circular cut around the stem area. Continue to cut until you have removed excess mushroom.
  - Place the cream cheese in the microwave for 15 seconds to soften.
  - Combine the cream cheese, shredded cheeses, salt, pepper, garlic, and Worcestershire sauce in a medium bowl. Stir to combine.
  - Stuff the mushrooms with the cheese mixture.

- Place the mushrooms in the Air Fryer for 8 minutes at 370 degrees F.
- Allow the mushrooms to cool before serving.

Easy Crispy Crunchy Sweet Potato Fries

Preparation and Cooking Time

1 hour 30 minutes

Servings

6 persons

Nutritional facts

94 calories, 2g fat ,1g fiber ,14g carbs ,2g protein

Ingredients

- 2 large sweet potatoes peeled and cut lengthwise; mine weighed about a couple of pounds' total
- 2 teaspoons garlic powder
- salt and pepper to taste
- 1 1/2 tablespoons cornstarch
- 2 teaspoons paprika
- 1 tablespoon olive oil

Instructions

- Place the sliced sweet potatoes in a large bowl with cold water. Allow the sweet potatoes to soak in the water for an hour.
- Remove the sweet potatoes from water and dry them completely. Sprinkle the cornstarch throughout.
- Sprinkle in the paprika, garlic powder, salt and pepper.
- Place the fries in the air fryer basket and spray with olive oil. Do not overcrowd the basket. Cook in batches if necessary. If you see white spots of cornstarch on the fries, spray the area with olive oil.
- Adjust the temperature to 380 degrees F and cook for 23-25 minutes. Set a timer for 10 minutes and stop and shake the basket at the 10-minute mark (once). Use your judgment. If you like crispy fries, cook them longer and check on them.
- Cool before serving.

Thai Chili Fried Chicken Wings

Preparation and Cooking Time

30 minutes

Servings

2 persons

Nutritional facts

202 calories,4g fat ,0g fiber ,23g carbs ,3g protein

Ingredients

- 1-pound chicken wings drummettes (party wings)
- 3 tablespoons soy sauce
- 1 tablespoon sesame oil
- 3 garlic cloves minced
- 1 tablespoon fresh lime juice
- 1 teaspoon ginger grated
- 1 teaspoon rice wine vinegar
- 1 tablespoon Sriracha
- 1/2 cup flour
- McCormicks Grill Mates Chicken Seasoning to taste
- 2 green onions finely chopped
- sesame seeds optional garnish
- cooking spray
- 1 teaspoon raw honey

Instructions

- Cooking oil should be sprayed into the air fryer basket.
- In a bowl dredge the chicken, combine the flour and seasoning.
- Dry the chicken with a paper towel. Using the seasoned flour, coat each chicken wing.
- In the air fryer basket, place each wing. Do not stack the items. If necessary, cook in batches. Cooking oil should be sprayed all over the chicken.
- Preheat the oven to 400°F and air fry for 12 minutes.
- Flip the chicken over in the air fryer. Add another 4-5 minutes to the cooking Time.
- Take the chicken out of the air fryer basket and set it aside. Use the Thai chili marinade to glaze each piece of chicken.
- Transfer the chicken to the Air Fryer to finish cooking. Cook for 6-8 minutes, or when the chicken is crisp and reaches 165 degrees F on the inside. Use a meat thermometer to check the temperature of the meat.
- Green onions & sesame seeds go on top.

Easy Air Fryer Homemade Crispy French Fries

Preparation and Cooking Time

30 minutes

Servings

4 persons

Nutritional facts

162 calories,2g fat ,1g fiber ,13g carbs ,2g protein

Ingredients

- 1 pound large russet potatoes peeled and cut lengthwise
- One tbsp. olive oil
- salt to taste

Instructions

- Place the sliced potatoes in a large bowl with cold water.
- Allow the potatoes to soak in the water for at least 30 minutes, preferably an hour.
- Drain the water from the bowl. Dry the fries completely with paper towels.
- Coat the fries with olive oil. You can toss them in a large bowl or spread the fries onto a flat surface and coat them. Sprinkle with the salt, pepper, and optional seasoning salt.
- Add half of the fries to the Air Fryer basket. Adjust the temperature to 380 degrees F and cook for 15-20 minutes. Set a timer for 10 minutes and stop and shake the basket at the 10-minute mark (once).
- Use your judgment. If the fries need to be crisper, allow them to cook for additional time. If the fries look crisp before 15 minutes, remove them. I cooked both of my batches for almost 20 minutes. Also, use your judgment to determine if the fries will need to be cooked in batches. This will vary based on the size of your air fryer. You do not want to overfill the basket.
- When the first half finishes, cook the remaining half (if necessary).
- Cool before serving.

Easy Air Fryer Seasoned Potato Wedges

Preparation and Cooking Time

55 minutes

Servings

5 persons

Nutritional facts

115 calories, 3g fat ,1g fiber ,12g carbs ,2g protein

Ingredients

- 4 russet potatoes
- 1 teaspoon smoked paprika
- salt and pepper to taste
- 1 tablespoon olive oil
- 1/2 tablespoon Herbes de Provence seasoning
- 1 teaspoon garlic powder
- cooking oil spray

Instructions

- Wash and scrub the potatoes well. Cut each potato in half lengthways and then cut the potato on the diagonal to make 8-10 wedges per potato. Try to make sure they are about the same thickness and size.
- Place the sliced potatoes in a large bowl with hot water. This will remove excess starch and help the potatoes crisp. Leave the potatoes in hot water for 20-30 minutes.
- Remove the potatoes from the water and dry them. I used paper towels.
- Add the potatoes to a large, dry bowl. Drizzle the olive oil throughout, and then add the seasonings. Toss with tongs to ensure the potatoes are evenly coated.
- Spray the air fryer basket with cooking oil spray. Add the potato wedges to the basket. Do not overcrowd the basket and cook in batches if needed.
- Cook for 12 minutes at 400 degrees F.
- Open the air fryer and flip the wedges with tongs. Cook for an additional 10-15 minutes and mine were perfectly crisp, around 25 minutes of total cook time.
- Cool before serving.

Easy Garlic Parmesan Chicken Wings

Preparation and Cooking Time

60 minutes

Servings

4 persons

Nutritional facts

374 calories, 9g fat ,3g fiber ,33g carbs ,11g protein

Ingredients

- 1-pound chicken wings (drummettes)
- cooking oil
- 3 garlic cloves minced
- 1/2 tablespoon of McCormick's Grill Mates Chicken Seasoning
- 1/2 cup flour
- 1/2 cup of grated parmesan must be divided into 2 1/4 cup of servings
- pepper and salt to taste
- 1 tablespoon of butter
- 1 tablespoon of olive oil

Instructions

- Place the chicken in a big dish or plastic bag after patting it dry.
- Toss the chicken with the flour, 1/4 cup grated parmesan, chicken seasoning, salt, and pepper. Assemble the chicken and make sure it's completely coated.
- Air fryer parchment paper should be used to line the air fryer basket. Put the chicken on a parchment-paper-lined baking sheet. Using olive oil, spritz the chicken.
- Preheat the oven to 400 degrees F and air fry for fifteen minutes.

- Flip the chicken over in the air fryer. Cooking oil should be sprayed on the chicken. Cook for a further 5 minutes.
- Use medium-high heat for the saucepan. Combine the butter, 1 tbsp. oil, garlic, and 1/4 cup grated parmesan cheese in a mixing bowl.
- Cook for another 2-3 minutes, or when the butter & cheese are completely melted.
- Remove the chicken from the air fryer and spread the garlic parmesan butter on top.
- Place the chicken back in the air fryer. Cook for a further 3-4 minutes at 400 degrees F in the air fryer.
- If desired, garnish with parsley and parmesan cheese.

Easy Honey BBQ Chicken Wings

Preparation and Cooking Time

30 minutes

Servings

5 persons

Nutritional facts

345 calories,2g fat ,1g fiber ,4g carbs ,1.2g protein

Ingredients

- 1-pound chicken roomettes (party wings)
- 1/2 cup BBQ sauce
- Pepper and salt to taste
- 1/4 cup honey
- McCormick's Grill Mates Chicken Seasoning to taste
- 1/4 cup all-purpose flour
- cooking oil

Instructions

- Season the chicken wings with salt and pepper to taste the chicken spice.
- Using flour, coat the chicken.
- Cooking oil should be sprayed into the air fryer basket.
- Fill the basket with the chicken. Cooking oil should be sprayed on both sides. When you spritz the chicken with oil, the floury exterior should disappear.
- Preheat oven to 400°F and bake for 8 minutes. Make sure the air fryer basket isn't too full. If necessary, cook in batches.
- Flip the chicken over in the air fryer. Cook for a further 7 minutes.
- In a bowl or mixing cup, combine the honey and BBQ sauce.
- Place the chicken in a large mixing bowl. Spread the honey BBQ sauce over the entire dish.
- Again put the chicken to the air fryer. Cook for 5 minutes longer at 400 degrees F. Cooking times vary depending on the air fryer brand. Make an informed decision. Cook, occasionally stirring, till the honey barbecue sauce has dried & crisped. Check if the chicken has reached a temperature of about 165 degrees F on the inside. Use a thermometer to check the temperature of the meat.

Buffalo Chicken Hot Wings

Preparation and Cooking Time

35 minutes

Servings

6 persons

Nutritional facts

208 calories, 5g fat ,2g fiber ,23g carbs ,2g protein

Ingredients

- 16 chicken wings
- pepper to taste
- Cooking Oil
- 2 teaspoons of low-sodium soy sauce
- Montreal Grill Mates Chicken Seasoning to taste
- 1 tsp. of garlic powder
- 1/4 cup of Frank's red hot buffalo wing sauce

Instructions

- Over the chicken, drizzle the soy sauce. This will aid in the production of juicy chicken while also adding flavor.
- Season the chicken to taste with chicken seasoning, garlic powder, and pepper.
- In the air fryer, place the chicken.
- Cooking oil should be sprayed all over the chicken.
- Preheat the oven to 400 degrees F & cook the chicken for 5 minutes. Remove the pan from the heat & shake the chicken to assure that all of the pieces are cooked through.
- Place the chicken back in the air fryer. Allow for another five minutes of cooking time for the chicken.
- Take the chicken out of the air fryer and set it aside.
- Brush the buffalo wing sauce over each piece of chicken.
- Place the chicken back in the air fryer. Cook for 7 to 12 minutes, or until the chicken is crisp on the outside and no longer pink on the inside.
- Allow cooling before serving.

Air Fryer Pizza Rolls

Preparation and Cooking Time

32 minutes

Servings

32 persons

Nutritional facts

211 calories, 7g fat ,2g fiber ,21g carbs ,2g protein

Ingredients

- 1 tablespoon olive oil
- salt and pepper to taste
- 64 wonton wrappers
- cooking oil spray
- 2 cups marinara sauce
- 1 cup shredded mozzarella cheese
- 1 cup chopped onions I like to use red onions.
- 1/2-pound ground sausage
- 2 garlic cloves, minced
- 1/2 cup pepperon
- 1 teaspoon Italian Seasoning

Instructions

- Place the olive oil onions in a pan over medium-high heat.
- Cook, occasionally stirring, till the onions are transparent and aromatic, about 2-3 minutes.
- Using a meat chopper, break down the sausage, Italian seasoning, salt, and pepper. Cook the sausage for 3-4 minutes, or until it is no longer pink.
- Combine the garlic, marinara sauce, pepperoni, & mozzarella. Reduce the heat to medium and cook for another 4-5 minutes.

- On a dry cooking surface, line the wonton wrappers. Wet the four corners of each wonton wrapper with water and a frying brush.
- Fill each wrapper to the brim with the filling. Concentrate on packing the filling toward one of the wrapper's edges. It will be easier to seal as a result of this.
- Spray both sides of the rolls with cooking oil spray before placing them in the air fryer. Make sure the basket isn't too full. If you stack the pizza rolls, they will take longer to cook and may not cook at the same rate.
- Preheat the oven to 370°F and air-fry the rolls for 8 minutes. Open the rolls and flip them over. Cook for another 3 to 5 minutes.

Easy Shrimp Egg Rolls

Preparation and Cooking Time

40 minutes

Servings

12 persons

Nutritional facts

219 calories, 4g fat ,1g fiber ,6g carbs ,1g protein

Ingredients

- 1-pound raw shrimp Peeled and deveined and roughly chopped into chunks
- 12-14 egg roll wrappers some egg roll wrap brands are really thin. You may need to double wrap your egg rolls.
- 1 small cup water
- 1 teaspoon fish sauce
- 1 1/2 teaspoons sesame oil
- 1/2 teaspoon ground ginger
- salt and pepper to taste
- 2-3 garlic cloves minced
- 3 cups coleslaw mix
- 1 tablespoon soy sauce or liquid aminos
- 2 green onions chopped
- cooking oil

Instructions

- Cooking oil should be sprayed into the air fryer basket.
- Fill the basket with egg rolls. The basket should not be stacked or crowded. If necessary, cook in batch.
- Spritz the egg rolls' tops with cooking oil.
- Cook for 7 minutes at 400°F in an air fryer.
- Flip the egg rolls in the air fryer. Cook for another 3-5 minutes, or until the potatoes are crisp. Each air fryer brand cooks at a different speed. Keep an eye on the egg rolls to figure out how much time you'll need for your batch.

Air Fryer Beef Taco Egg Rolls

Preparation and Cooking Time

40 minutes

Servings

8 persons

Nutritional facts

348 calories, 3g fat, 1g fiber ,2g carbs ,1g protein

Ingredients

- 1-pound ground beef
- 1 tablespoon chili powder
- 1 teaspoon cumin

- 1 teaspoon smoked paprika
- 8 oz. refried black beans
- 1 cup shredded Mexican cheese
- 1/2 cup whole kernel corn
- cooking oil spray
- 16 egg roll wrappers
- 1/2 cup chopped onion
- 2 garlic cloves minced
- 16 oz. can diced tomatoes and chilies
- salt and pepper to taste

Instructions

- Combine the ground beef, salt, pepper, and taco seasoning in a skillet over medium-high heat. Cook until the steak is browned, cutting it up into smaller pieces as it cooks.
- Add the chopped onions and garlic once the meat has begun to brown. Cook till the onions are aromatic, about 5 minutes.
- Combine the chopped tomatoes & chilies, Mexican cheese, beans, & corn in a large mixing bowl. To ensure that the ingredients are well blended, stir them together.
- On a level table, place the egg roll wrappers. In a bowl of water, dip a cooking brush. Use the wet brush to glaze the edges of each egg roll wrapper. This softens the crust and makes rolling it easier.
- Fill each wrapper with 2 teaspoons of the mixture. Don't stuff too much. You might need to double wrap the egg rolls depending on the kind of egg roll wrappers you choose.
- To close the wrappers, fold them diagonally. Fill the area with the filling and press firmly to keep it in place. As triangles, fold the left and right sides in. To finish, fold the final layer over the top. Wet the area with the cooking brush & secure it in place.
- Cooking oil should be sprayed into the air fryer basket.
- Place the egg rolls in the Air Fryer's basket. Cooking oil should be sprayed on each egg roll.
- Preheat oven to 400°F and bake for 8 minutes. Turn the egg rolls over. Cook for another 4 minutes, or until the bacon is browned and crisp.

Air Fryer Vegetarian Southwestern Egg Rolls with Avocado Ranch

Preparation and Cooking Time

32 minutes

Servings

8 persons

Nutritional facts

265 calories, 3g fat ,1g fiber ,2g carbs ,1g protein

Ingredients

- 1/4 red onion chopped
- 1/2 orange pepper chopped
- 1/4 cup shredded cheese
- 1/4 packet taco seasoning i used trader joe's
- Cooking oil
- A cup of water
- 8 oz. Sour cream
- 8 oz. Low-sodium black beans (drained)
- 1 can diced tomatoes and chilies (drained)
- 1 cup frozen kernel corn
- 2 teaspoons cilantro chopped
- 1/2 lime juice

- 2-3 garlic cloves chopped
- 16 egg roll wrappers
- 1/2 red pepper chopped
- 1/2 yellow pepper chopped
- 1 avocado
- 1/2 packet Hidden Valley Ranch Dip Seasoning

Instructions

- Heat a skillet on medium-high heat. Add the garlic and onions. Cook for 2-3 minutes until fragrant.
- Add all of the peppers to the skillet. Mix well. Cook for 1-2 minutes
- Add the black beans, corn, tomatoes, and cheese. Cook for 2-3 minutes.
- Drizzle the fresh lime juice throughout. Add the cilantro and taco seasoning. Stir.
- Lay the egg roll wrappers on a flat surface. Dip a cooking brush in water. Glaze each egg roll wrapper with the wet brush along the edges. This will soften the crust and make it easier to roll.
- Use 2 egg rolls for each. I chose to double roll the egg rolls to prevent them from leaking. If the brand of egg rolls wrappers you purchased is pretty thick, you may only need one wrapper and no need to double up.
- Load the mixture into each of the wrappers.
- Fold the wrappers diagonally to close. Press firmly on the area with the filling, cup it to secure it in place. Fold in the left and right sides as triangles. Fold the final layer over the top to close. Use the cooking brush to wet the area and secure it in place. Spray each egg roll with cooking oil.
- Load the egg rolls into the pan of the Air Fryer. Spray with cooking oil.
- Cook for 8 minutes at 380 degrees. Flip the egg rolls. Cook for an additional 4 minutes. Cool before serving.
- Peel the avocado and remove the pit. Mash the avocado in a bowl. I like to use a potato masher.
- Add the sour cream and ranch seasoning. Stir well to combine.

Easy Buffalo Shrimp Recipe

Preparation and Cooking Time

20 minutes

Servings

4 persons

Nutritional facts

241 calories, 8g fat ,2g fiber ,10g carbs ,5g protein

Ingredients

- 1-pound raw shrimp Peeled and deveined
- 1-pound raw shrimp Peeled and deveined
- 1 teaspoon of paprika
- salt and pepper to taste
- cooking oil
- 1/4 cup Primal Kitchen Buffalo Sauce
- 1 teaspoon olive oil
- 1 egg Beaten
- 1/2 cup all-purpose flour
- 3/4 cup panko bread crumbs
- 1 teaspoon paprika
- salt and pepper to taste
- 1/4 cup Primal Kitchen Buffalo Sauce

Instructions

- Cooking oil should be sprayed into the air fryer basket.
- Combine the flour, egg, and panko bread crumbs in three separate dishes. In the same bowl as the flour, put the paprika, salt, & pepper to taste.
- Set up a kitchen area. The shrimp should be floured first, then dipped in the egg and the panko bread crumbs.
- In the Air Fryer basket, place the shrimp. Cooking oil should be sprayed on the shrimp. Preheat oven to 400°F and bake for 6 minutes.
- Flip the shrimp to the other side by opening the basket. Cook for an extra 2 minutes without adding the buffalo sauce if you prefer your buffalo shrimp saucy (add it after the shrimp have cooked). If you want the buffalo sauce flavor baked into the shrimp, do so. Take the shrimp out of the basket, toss it in the buffalo sauce, and cook for another 2 minutes in the air fryer.
- Check to see if the shrimp have crisped to your preference and, if necessary, alter the cooking time.
- Preheat the oven to 400 degrees Fahrenheit.
- Follow the above-mentioned breading directions.
- On a sheet pan, place the breaded shrimp. Cooking oil should be sprayed on the shrimp. They will be crisp after 10-15 minutes in the oven.
- Season the shrimp to taste with paprika, salt, and pepper.
- Heat the olive oil & shrimp in a pan over medium-high heat.
- Cook for 2-3 minutes on each side, or until the shrimp is no longer pink.
- Take the shrimp out of the skillet and coat them in buffalo sauce.

Easy Beef Empanadas Recipe

Preparation and Cooking Time

40 minutes

Servings

12 persons

Nutritional facts

261 calories, 7g fat ,3g fiber ,22g carbs ,5g protein

Ingredients

- 12 Goya Empanadas wrappers thawed
- 1/2 teaspoon onion powder
- 1/2 teaspoon garlic powder
- 1/2 teaspoon paprika
- 1 egg
- 2 teaspoons water
- 1/2 tablespoon chili powder
- 1/2 teaspoon cumin
- 1/2-pound ground beef
- 1/2 cup chopped onion
- 2 garlic cloves minced
- 1 cup shredded Mexican Blend cheese shredded
- salt and pepper to taste

Instructions

- Spritz your air fryer basket with oil or use parchment paper to line it.
- In the air fryer basket, place the empanadas.
- Air fry for 8-10 minutes at 350°F or until crisp.

Easy Air Fryer Dessert Empanadas

Preparation and Cooking Time

25 minutes

Servings

12 persons

Nutritional facts

164 calories, 9g fat ,2g fiber ,30g carbs ,4g protein

Ingredients

- 12 empanada wrappers thawed
- 2 teaspoon cornstarch
- 1 teaspoon water
- 2 apples
- 2 tablespoons raw honey
- 1 teaspoon vanilla extract
- 1 tsp. cinnamon
- 1/8 teaspoon nutmeg
- 1 egg beaten
- cooking oil

Instructions

- Preheat a pot to medium-high. Combine the apples, cinnamon, nutmeg, honey, & vanilla in a mixing bowl. Cook, occasionally stirring, for 2-3 minutes, just until the apples are tender.
- In a small bowl, combine the cornstarch and water. Add to the pan and swirl to combine. It should be cooked for30 seconds in the microwave
- Allow at least 5 minutes for the filling to cool before filling the empanada wrappers.
- On a level surface, place the empanada wrappers. In a bowl of water, dip a cooking brush. Use the wet brush to glaze the edges of each empanada wrapper. This softens the crust and makes rolling it easier.
- Fill each with the apple mixture. Fill each empanada with 1 tbsp. of the apple mixture.
- With a spoon, flatten the mixture.
- Bring the empanadas to a close. Create indents in the crust with a fork to seal the empanadas along the edges. Along the edge of each crust, press a fork into it.
- Spritz the cooking oil into the air fryer basket. Fill the Air Fryer basket halfway with empanadas. Empanadas should not be stacked. If necessary, cook in batches.
- Brush the tops of each empanada with the beaten egg using a frying brush (egg wash).
- Preheat the Air Fryer to 400°F. Cook until crisp, about 8-10 minutes.
- Allow cooling before serving.

Easy Air Fryer Beef Jerky

Preparation and Cooking Time

1 day 1 hour 10 minutes

Servings

24 persons

Nutritional facts

46 calories, 24g fat ,2g fiber ,51g carbs ,36g protein

Ingredients

- 1 1/2 pounds' sirloin tip steak
- 1 teaspoon smoked paprika
- 1 teaspoon garlic powder
- One teaspoon onion powder

- 1/3 cup soy sauce
- 1 teaspoon Worcestershire sauce
- 1/2 cup brown sweetener
- 1 teaspoon liquid smoke
- 1/2 teaspoon black pepper

Instructions

- Cut the meat into thin strips about 1/8-inch-thick using a sharp knife. Your jerky will be tender if you slice against the meat's grain.
- In a large mixing bowl, place the steak. Combine all of the marinade ingredients in a
    mixing bowl and stir well.
- Refrigerate for at least 30 minutes and up to 24 hours. The longer you marinate it, the more flavorful it becomes.
- The jerky can be placed in the air fryer in two ways. Bamboo skewers can be used to thread the meat lengthwise through the skewer, allowing the steak to dangle from the skewer. Several slices of beef can be added, but make sure they don't touch. This will aid in distributing the air flow required to dry the beef. Put the skewers along the air fryer's top borders.
- Alternatively, you may just put the meat in the air fryer basket.
- If using an air fryer basket, cook the meat for 2-3 hours at 180 degrees F.
- In all cases, keep an eye on your beef to make sure it gets the desired texture. The jerky will be firm but delicate around 60 minutes with the bamboo stick method. If you want it to be chewy, you'll need to cook it for longer.
- It will become firm and tender in about 2 hours using only the air fryer method, but chewy jerky will need longer.

Air Fryer Tater Tots

Preparation and Cooking Time

45 minutes

Servings

4 persons

Nutritional facts

70 calories, 22g fat ,2g fiber ,65g carbs ,16g protein

Ingredients

- 1 1/2 pounds' russet potatoes
- 1 teaspoon garlic powder
- 1/4 teaspoon thyme
- 2 teaspoons all-purpose flour
- salt and pepper to taste
- cooking oil
- 1 teaspoon smoked paprika

Instructions

- Bring a saucepan or pot 3/4 of the way full of cold water to a boil with a pinch of salt. Add enough water to cover the potatoes.
- Add the potatoes and simmer for 6-12 minutes. You should be able to pierce the potatoes easily on the outside and tell that the inside of the potatoes is still firm.
- Remove the potatoes from the water. Dry and allow them to cool.
- Once cooled, use the large area of a cheese grater to grate the potatoes. Squeeze out any excess water from the potatoes.
- Place the grated potatoes in a bowl with flour and seasonings. Russet potatoes are bland. Be sure to use salt to taste. Stir to combine.
- Use your hands to form tots with the mixture

- Spray both sides of the tots with cooking oil. Place the tots in the air fryer. Air fry for 10 minutes at 400 degrees.
- Open the air fryer and flip the tots. Cook for another 5 minutes to achieve the crispy level.

Easy Air Fryer Kale Chips

Preparation and Cooking Time

15 minutes

Servings

12 persons

Nutritional facts

61 calories,24g fat ,0g fiber ,10g carbs ,12g protein

Ingredients

- 10 oz. fresh kale ribs removed and chopped into large pieces
- One tablespoon olive oil
- salt and pepper to taste
- Quarter cup grated parmesan cheese

Instructions

- Combine the kale and olive oil in a large bowl and sprinkle the salt and pepper to taste throughout.
- Place the kale in the air fryer basket.
- Air-fry the kale at 270 degrees for 5 minutes.
- Open the air fryer and shake the basket. Cook for an additional 2 minutes.
- Open the air fryer and sprinkle the parmesan cheese throughout. Cook for an additional 2 minutes.

Zucchini Chips

Preparation and Cooking Time

25 minutes

Servings

5 persons

Nutritional facts

207 calories, 2g fat ,3g fiber ,6 carbs ,14g protein

Ingredients

- 1 large zucchini
- 1/4 cup of shredded parmesan cheese
- Pepper and salt to taste
- 2 beaten eggs
- 1/2 cup of all-purpose flour
- 1 teaspoon of Italian Seasoning
- 1 teaspoon of Smoked Paprika
- 1 1/2-2 cups of breadcrumbs

Instructions

- Spray your air fryer basket with some cooking oil.
- Add flour, eggs, and breadcrumbs to separate bowls.
- Thinly slice the zucchini into 1/4-inch thick pieces. A mandolin may also be used for fine slicing. To ensure that the zucchini chips fry at the same temperature, make sure they are all approximately the same size.
- Season the flour with salt, pepper, and paprika to taste, then top with grated parmesan.
- Toss the zucchini in flour, egg, and breadcrumbs before placing in the air fryer. To ensure that the breadcrumbs stay, completely cover the chip in the eggs.
- Keep a moist towel nearby because your hands will get sticky.
- Spray the zucchini chips with the cooking oil spray.

- Air Fry for about 5 minutes at 400 degrees.
- Flip the chips. Spray with additional oil and cook for 4-7 minutes at 400 degrees. The zucchini chips will brown by 8 minutes; cook them a little longer if you like them crispy.

Easy Air Fryer Tortilla Chips

Preparation and Cooking Time

11 minutes

Servings

48 persons

Nutritional facts

112 calories,16g fat ,0.2g fiber ,6g carbs ,11g protein

Ingredients

- Six corn tortillas
- Kosher salt to taste
- cooking oil spray

Instructions

- Spray both sides of each tortilla with cooking oil, then rotate the stack and cut again to make 4 pieces.
- Lay the tortillas in 1 stack. Use a knife or pizza cutter and cut the stack in half.
- Then you will cut down the middle again, both horizontally and vertically, to form 8 total chips per layer.
- Sprinkle salt throughout the chips. You can add any additional seasonings if you wish.
- Load the chips into the air fryer. Do not overcrowd the basket. Cook in batches if needed. Overcrowding will lead to some chips that taste stale.
- Air-fry the chips for 6 minutes at 370 degrees.

Easy Air Fryer Sweet Potato Chips

Preparation and Cooking Time

60 minutes

Servings

4 persons

Nutritional facts

94 calories, 43g fat ,2g fiber ,9g carbs ,32 protein

Ingredients

- 2 sweet potatoes
- 2 teaspoons paprika
- 2 teaspoons garlic powder
- 1 teaspoon chives dried or fresh
- 1/4 teaspoon pepper
- 1/2 teaspoon salt
- cooking oil

Instructions

- Microwave the sweet potatoes for 60 seconds to soften.
- Peel the skin off the sweet potatoes and slice them into slices about 1/8ths of an inch thick.
- Soak the sweet potatoes in a large bowl of cold water for 30 minutes.
- Remove the potatoes from water and dry them completely.
- Spritz with oil and then sprinkle the seasonings throughout. Stir to combine.
- Place the sweet potato chips in the air fryer basket. Air -fry the sweet potatoes for 7-8 minutes at 400 degrees.
- Open and shake the basket to move the chips around. Air fry for an additional 7-8 minutes or until crisp.

- You will know the sweet potato chips have finished cooking when they start to crisp and harden at the edges.

Crunchy Homemade Sour Cream and Onion Potato Chips

Preparation and Cooking Time

50 minutes

Servings

4 persons

Nutritional facts

90 calories, 4g fat ,3g fiber ,14g carbs ,9 protein

Ingredients

- 2 large russet potatoes
- 1 tablespoon onion powder
- kosher salt to taste
- cooking oil spray
- 1 1/2 tablespoons buttermilk powder
- 1 teaspoon chives (dried)

Instructions

- Wash and scrub the potatoes. Use a mandolin and cut the potatoes into small slices about 1/10 of an inch thick.
- Add the sliced potatoes to a bowl of cold water. Allow the potatoes to soak for at least 30 minutes.
- Remove the potatoes from the water and dry them thoroughly.
- Spray the air fryer basket with cooking oil.
- Sprinkle the potato slices with salt and add them to the air fryer.
- Cook the potatoes at 400 degrees for 8 minutes.
- Open the air fryer and shake the potatoes. Cook for an additional 7 minutes or until the potatoes are golden brown in the middle and brown along the edges.
- Add the buttermilk powder, onion powder, and chives to a food processor or blender. Blender for 20-30 seconds.
- Remove the chips from the air fryer and toss them in the bowl with the seasonings.
- Allow the chips to cool for 30 minutes.

Air Fryer Blooming Onion Recipe

Preparation and Cooking Time

1 hour 30 minutes

Servings

4 persons

Nutritional facts

219 calories, 15g fat ,4g fiber ,26g carbs ,19g protein

Ingredients

- 1 -1 1/2 cups all-purpose flour
- 2 eggs, beaten
- 1/2 teaspoon smoked paprika
- 1/8 teaspoon garlic powder
- One large sweet onion
- 1/2 cup milk
- cooking oil
- 1/2 cup mayo
- 2 teaspoons ketchup
- 1 tablespoon horseradish
- 1 teaspoon garlic powder
- 1 teaspoon smoked paprika

- salt and pepper to taste
- 1/4 teaspoon oregano
- salt and pepper to taste

Instructions

- Cut off the pointy stem of the onion, leaving the root end intact. Peel the onion and place it cut side down. The root end of the onion should be facing up.
- Starting 1/2 an inch from the root end, cut downward to make 4 evenly spaced cuts. In each section, make 3 additional cuts. There should be 16 cuts in the onion. This recipe includes a video that shows exactly how to cut the onion.
- Turn the onion over and fluff out the "petals."
- Place the flour in a bowl with the garlic powder, paprika, salt and pepper to taste.
- Add the eggs and milk to a separate bowl and stir.
- Put the onion in the flour mixture and dredge it completely.
- Next, dip the onion in the milk and egg batter. Use a spoon or cooking brush to ensure it is fully coated.
- Return the onion to the flour mixture again and cover completely.
- Wrap the onion in foil and freeze for 45 minutes.
- Spray the air fryer basket with cooking oil or use air fryer parchment paper. Unwrap the onion and spray it with cooking oil.
- Cook for 10 minutes at 400 degrees.
- Open the air fryer and spray any white areas with cooking oil. Cook for an additional 10-15 minutes or until crisp.

Easy Crunchy Fried Pickles

Preparation and Cooking Time

35 minutes

Servings

6 persons

Nutritional facts

142 calories, 8g fat ,2g fiber ,13g carbs ,8g protein

Ingredients

- 1/2 tablespoon of dried dill
- 24 oz. of dill pickle slices
- 1/2 teaspoon of garlic powder
- pepper and salt to taste
- 1 3/4 -2 cups of Panko breadcrumbs
- 1 egg
- 3/4 cup of flour
- 3/4 cup of buttermilk
- cooking oil spray

Instructions

- Spray the air fryer basket with cooking oil or use air fryer parchment paper.
- Dry the pickles completely. It will make them easier to bread.
- Add the flour to a bowl large enough to dredge the pickles. Season the flour with dried dill, garlic powder, salt, and pepper to taste.
- Add the buttermilk and egg to the seasoned flour. Beat and then stir to combine.
- Add the panko breadcrumbs to a separate bowl large enough to dredge the pickles.
- Dredge your pickles into the flour buttermilk mixture and then panko breadcrumbs.

- Place the breaded pickles on a plate. After breading the pickles, freeze the pickles for 15 minutes. This is an optional step but highly recommended. It helps keep the breading intact.
- Place the pickles in the air fryer. Do not stack them. Cook in batches if needed.
- Spray the pickles with cooking oil. I use olive oil.
- Cook for 7-10 minutes on 400 degrees flipping after 5 minutes. Each air fryer brand will cook at different speeds.

BBQ Beef Meatballs

Preparation and Cooking Time

25 minutes

Servings

5 persons

Nutritional facts

336 calories, 9g fat ,1g fiber ,2g carbs ,5g protein

Ingredients

- 1 pound of ground chuck beef
- 1 teaspoon of McCormick's Grill Mates Steak Seasoning
- pepper and salt to taste
- An egg
- ¼ cup of shredded cheddar cheese
- 1 teaspoon of Worcestershire sauce
- ½ cup of almond meal
- ½ cup of chopped onions
- 2 garlic cloves
- 1/2 cup of sugar-free BBQ Sauce

Instructions

- Combine the almond meal, ground chuck beef, Worcestershire sauce, onions, cheddar, garlic, egg, and seasonings in a large mixing bowl.
- Combine the materials in a big ball with clean hands.
- Form ten smaller meatballs using a spoon. To avoid contamination, place them on parchment paper.
- Fill the air fryer halfway with meatballs. It is acceptable to stack them.
- Cooking oil can also be sprayed on the air fryer basket.
- Cook the meatballs at 365°F for 8 minutes.
- Flip the meatballs in the air fryer.
- Cook for another 5-8 minutes, just until the meatballs reach a temperature of 165 degrees F on the inside.
- Take out the meatballs from the air fryer & coat with barbecue sauce.

Chapter 5: Air Fryer Side Dish Recipes

Air Fried Vegan Beignets

Preparation and Cooking Time

2 hours 6 minutes

Servings

24 persons

Nutritional facts

102 calories, 8g fat ,4g fiber ,20g carbs ,2g protein

Ingredients

- 1 cup of Whole Earth Sweetener Baking Blend
- 1 cup of coconut milk
- 3 cups unbleached white flour, with a little extra to sprinkle on the cutting board for later
- 3 tablespoons powdered baking blend
- 1 1/2 teaspoons active baking yeast
- Two tablespoons melted coconut oil
- Two tablespoons aquafaba, the drained water from a can of chickpeas
- 1 teaspoon organic corn starch
- 2 teaspoons vanilla

Instructions

- Insert the Whole Earth Baking Blend and corn starch into your mixer and process until smooth and powdery. The cornstarch can prevent clumping, but you should store it if you don't need enough of it in the recipe. (Or, later in the recipe, you can add standard powdered sugar.)
- Heat the coconut milk until it is warm yet cold enough that you can dip your finger in it without burning yourself. You kill the yeast if it's too hot. With the sugar and yeast, add it to the mixer. Let the yeast sit for 10 minutes before it starts to foam.
- Mix coconut oil, aquafaba, and vanilla with the paddle attachment. Then, add a cup of flour at a time.
- If you have one, turn to your dough hook once the flour is added in and the dough comes from the sides of the mixer.
- For about 3 minutes, knead the dough in your mixer. The dough would be wetter in contrast to if you were making a loaf of bread, but without it sitting on your side, you must be able to scrape out the dough & form a ball.
- In a mixing bowl, put the dough, cover it with a clean dishtowel, and let it rise for 1 hour.
- Sprinkle some flour on a large cutting board and pat the dough out into a 1⁄3-inch-thick rectangle. Slice into 24 squares and leave for 30 minutes to proof before cooking them.

- Preheat the air fryer to 390 F. You can insert 3 to 6 beignets at a time, depending on the size of the air fryer.
- Cook on one side for 3 minutes. Flip them over, then cook for 2 more minutes. Since air fryers differ, you need to cook yours for another minute or two for them to get golden brown.
- Sprinkle freely and enjoy the powdered baking mix you made in the beginning.
- When they are all finished, continue cooking in batches.
- Preheat the oven to 350 degrees F. Place the beignets on a parchment paper-lined baking sheet.
- Bake until golden brown or for about 15 minutes. Sprinkle with the powdered baking mix you made initially and eat it liberally.

Sriracha-Honey Chicken Wings

Preparation and Cooking Time

40 minutes

Servings

2 persons

Nutritional facts

197 calories, 11g fat ,1g fiber ,23g carbs ,3g protein

Ingredients

- Two tablespoons sriracha sauce
- One and a half tablespoons soy sauce
- 1 tablespoon butter
- juice of 1/2 lime
- 1 pound of chicken wings, wings cut into drummettes and flats and tips removed
- A quarter cup of honey
- cilantro, chives, or scallions for garnish

Instructions

- The air fryer is preheated to 360 degrees F. To make sure the wings are sufficiently browned, put the chicken wings into the air fryer basket and cook for thirty minutes, turning the chicken around every 7 minutes with tongs.
- Insert the sauce ingredients into a small sauce pan as the wings are frying, and bring to a boil for about three minutes.
- Toss them in a bowl with the sauce when the wings are cooked until thoroughly covered. Then sprinkle with the garnish. Serve immediately.

Air Fryer Cinnamon Apples

Preparation and Cooking Time

20 minutes

Servings

4 persons

Nutritional facts

178 calories, 9g fat ,1g fiber ,22g carbs ,4g protein

Ingredients

- 6 Medium Apples
- 1 Tablespoon Extra-Virgin Avocado Oil
- Air Fryer Oven
- Mandoline
- 1 Tablespoon Cinnamon

Instructions

- Six medium-sized apples are thinly cut using a mandolin (or something similar).
- Toss your sliced apples in oil using the chosen balanced oil. Sprinkle the apples in cinnamon after you've applied the oil.

- Load it into the air fryer and cook at 200c/400F for 15 minutes.
- Adjust the cooking time to four hours and a temperature to 30C/85F if using the air fryer oven.

Air Fryer Buffalo Cauliflower

Preparation and Cooking Time

25 minutes

Servings

4 persons

Nutritional facts

191 calories, 11g fat ,1g fiber ,23g carbs ,3g protein

Ingredients

- 1 head cauliflower
- A quarter tsp. cayenne pepper
- A half-cup Frank's Red Hot Original Cayenne Pepper Sauce or your favorite
- 2 cloves garlic, minced
- A quarter tsp. chili powder
- A quarter tsp. paprika
- 1 cup of all-purpose flour
- 1 teaspoon of vegan chicken bouillon granules
- A quarter tsp. of dried chipotle chili flakes
- 1 cup soy milk
- canola oil spray
- Two tablespoons nondairy butter

Instructions

- Slice the cauliflower into bite-size parts. Rinse the cauliflower pieces and drain them.
- Combine the chili powder, flour, bouillon granules, and cayenne, paprika, and chipotle flakes in a large bowl. Whisk in the milk slowly until a thick batter develops.
- Spray the air fryer basket with canola oil and preheat the air fryer for 10 minutes to 390 °F.
- Throw the cauliflower in the batter while the air fryer is preheating. Move the battered cauliflower to the bowl of an air fryer. Cook it at 390 ° F for 20 minutes. Turn the cauliflower pieces after 10 minutes using tongs (do not be worried if they stick).
- Heat the garlic, butter and hot sauce over medium-high heat in a shallow saucepan after turning the cauliflower. Bring the mixture to a boil, cook, reduce the heat, and cover it.
- Move it to a wide bowl once the cauliflower is baked. Over the cauliflower, pour the sauce and toss gently with tongs. Immediately serve.

Air Fryer 6 Minute Pita Bread Cheese Pizza

Preparation and Cooking Time

35 minutes

Servings

4 persons

Nutritional facts

213 calories,14g fat ,2g fiber ,30g carbs ,2g protein

Ingredients

- One Pita Bread
- One Tablespoon of Pizza Sauce
- One Tablespoon of Yellow or Brown Onion sliced thin
- 1/2 teaspoon of Fresh Garlic minced
- A quarter cup of Mozzarella Cheese
- One drizzle of Extra Virgin Olive Oil
- One Stainless Steel of Short Legged Trivet
- 7 slices of Pepperoni or more
- A quarter cup of Sausage

Instructions

- Use the spoon and swirl pizza sauce on the pita bread. Insert your favorite cheese and toppings. On top of the pizza, apply a little more drizzle of extra virgin olive oil.
- Place a trivet over Pita Bread in the Air Fryer. Cook for 6 minutes at 350 degrees F. Finally, remove the Air Fryer cautiously and cut.

Air fryer plantains recipe

Preparation and Cooking Time

13 minutes

Servings

2 persons

Nutritional facts

130 calories, 8g fat ,1g fiber ,12g carbs ,6g protein

Ingredients

- One ripe plantain - (It should be almost all brown and very soft.)
- One teaspoon neutral oil
- A pinch of salt

Instructions

- Cut the plantain, cutting parts that are around ½" thick.
- Combine the plantain slices, oil, and salt in a medium bowl. Make sure all the pieces are covered in oil.
- Move to your air fryer basket and fry for 8-10 minutes at 400 ° F, shaking after 5 minutes. The plantains are finished when browned on the outside and soft on the inside. Depending on how ripe your plantains are, frying time can vary. Check-in at 8 minutes and, if necessary, add another minute or two to hit the nice, browned outside.

Clean Eating Air Fryer Cheese Sticks Recipe

Preparation and Cooking Time

22 minutes

Servings

6 persons

Nutritional facts

67 calories ,14g fat ,3g fiber ,21g carbs ,4g protein

Ingredients

- Six snack-size cheese sticks (the individual ones you buy for kids)
- A quarter cup grated parmesan cheese
- 1 tsp. Italian Seasoning
- 1 tsp. garlic powder
- 2 large eggs
- A quarter cup whole wheat flour (any type - pastry or white whole wheat work well)
- 1/4 tsp. ground rosemary

Instructions

- Unwrap the sticks of cheese and set them aside.
- With a fork, crack and beat the eggs in a small bowl that is broad enough to match the length of the cheese sticks.
- Blend the flour, cheese and seasonings in another bowl (or plate).

- Roll the sticks of cheese into the egg and then into the batter. Repeat until it is well covered all around the cheese sticks.
- Place them in your air fryer's basket, ensuring they do not touch.
- Cook as directed by your air fryer. The temperature should be 370 F and fry for 6-7 minutes.
- Serve with clean marinara.

Air fried Kale

Preparation and Cooking Time

10 minutes

Servings

2 persons

Nutritional facts

100 calories,12g fat ,2g fiber ,31g carbs ,10g protein

Ingredients

- Four cups loosely packed kale - stemmed
- Two teaspoons olive oil
- pinch of salt
- One to two tablespoons seasoning mix of your choice

Instructions

- Lightly massage the kale in a medium-sized bowl of oil and salt. You're not going here for a kale salad; just a touch of wilting is all right. Dump the coated kale into your air fryer's basket, then.
- Cook for 4-6 minutes at 370 ° F (do not preheat), shake after 2 minutes, check for thickening. Check-in for the last 2 minutes, every minute.
- Toss and eat quickly with the seasoning of choice.

Air Fryer Hard Boiled Eggs

Preparation and Cooking Time

16 minutes

Servings

6 persons

Nutritional facts

77 calories, 14g fat ,2g fiber ,32g carbs ,2g protein

Ingredients

- Six large cold eggs

Instructions

- Within the basket, set up the wire rack. Then put the eggs atop the wire rack. If your air fryer doesn't have a wire rack, position it at the bottom of the air fryer basket.
- Set the time to 250 F and 16 minutes for the timer. After the eggs have finished in the air fryer, take them out and place them in an ice-water bath to stop frying. Peel and enjoy the shells.

Healthy Low Fat Air Fryer French Fries

Preparation and Cooking Time

30 minutes

Servings

4 persons

Nutritional facts

189 calories, 9g fat ,3g fiber ,22g carbs ,2g protein

Ingredients

- Three medium russet potatoes
- Two tablespoons parmesan cheese
- Two tablespoons finely chopped fresh parsley

- One tablespoon olive oil plus more to brush wire basket
- salt

Instructions

- Potatoes are sliced into 1/4" thick fries."
- To extract extra moisture, pat dry using a kitchen towel.
- Insert salt, parmesan cheese, fresh parsley and oil. To coat cheese, herbs, and oil evenly, toss or gently blend.
- Preheat the Air Fryer for 2-3 min at 360 F. Rub some oil gently on the wire basket base.
- Then spread the seasoned fries uniformly on the mesh. Now cook for a total of 20 minutes.
- Using metal tongs, mix the fries gently after 10 minutes of frying.
- Continue to cook for another 5 minutes. Mix the fries again.
- Finally, cook for an extra 5 minutes.
- These fries are eaten warm with ketchup or your favorite sauce.

Air Fryer Avocado Fries

Preparation and Cooking Time

20 minutes

Servings

4 persons

Nutritional facts

51 calories, 20g fat ,1g fiber ,27g carbs ,4g protein

Ingredients

- Half cup of panko breadcrumbs
- Half teaspoon salt
- One Haas avocado - peeled, pitted, and sliced
- aquafaba from one 15 ounces can of white beans or garbanzo beans

Instructions

- Toss the panko and salt together in a shallow bowl. Into another shallow bowl, put the aquafaba.
- In the aquafaba and then in the panko, dredge the avocado slices and obtain a clean, even coating.
- Arrange the slices in your air fryer basket in a single layer. The single layer is important. Air fry at 390F for 10 minutes (do not preheat), shaking well 5 minutes later.
- Serve with your favorite dipping sauce instantly.

Air Fryer Sweet Potato Chips

Preparation and Cooking Time

1 hour 5 minutes

Servings

1 person

Nutritional facts

357 calories, 6g fat ,2g fiber ,21g carbs ,3g protein

Ingredients

- Two Sweet Potatoes thinly sliced
- Pepper and salt to taste
- A quarter cup of Olive Oil
- One teaspoon ground Cinnamon

Instructions

- Cut rather finely the sweet potatoes. And use a mandolin or processor.
- Soak the sweet potato slices for 30 minutes in cold water.

- Drain and pat the slices thoroughly to dry. Repeat several times until it's fully dry. This is a vital step to ensure that the chips are crispy.
- Add the cinnamon, olive oil, salt and pepper to sweet potato slices (if used), ensuring that each slice is covered with oil.
- The air-fry basket is lightly greased.
- Air fried the sweet potatoes at 390F for 15 min in batches, giving the basket a strong shake for cooking every 7 to 8 minutes. Suppose it is still not crisp; fry for an extra 5 minutes.
- Serve warm with ketchup.

Air Fryer Corn Tortilla

Preparation and Cooking Time

10 minutes

Servings

2 persons

Nutritional facts

373 calories,17g fat ,4g fiber ,34g carbs ,7g protein

Ingredients

- 12 corn tortillas
- One tablespoon olive oil
- 2 teaspoons kosher salt
- One tablespoon of McCormick® TASTY Jazzy Spice Blend
- guacamole, for serving

Instructions

- Preheat the fryer to 350°F
- Brush the tortillas gently on both sides with olive oil.
- Sprinkle your tortillas with salt and the Delicious Jazzy Spice Mix on both sides.
- Slice any single tortilla in six wedges.
- Introduce the tortilla wedges in a single layer to the air fryer and 'fry' for 5 minutes or until brown and crispy golden.
- Serve with guacamole.
- Enjoy.

Healthy Air Fried Chicken Tenders

Preparation and Cooking Time

20 minutes

Servings

2 persons

Nutritional facts

375 calories, 9g fat ,1g fiber ,18g carbs ,2g protein

Ingredients

- Twelve ounces of Chicken Breasts
- 1 Egg White
- 1/8 Cup Flour
- Thirty-five grams Panko Bread Crumbs
- Salt and Pepper

Instructions

- Trim the chicken breast and slice into tenders.
- With salt and pepper, season each side.
- Dip chicken tenders into egg whites. Then panko bread crumbs and then into flour.
- Load and spray with olive spray into the air fryer basket.
- It has to be cooked for about ten minutes or until fully cooked at 350 degrees F.

Chapter 6: Air Fryer Dinner Recipes

Air-Fryer Turkey Croquettes

Preparation and Cooking Time

30 minutes

Servings

6 persons

Nutritional facts

322 calories,13g fat ,1g fiber ,21g carbs ,3g protein

Ingredients

- Two cups of mashed potatoes (with added butter and milk)
- A half-cup of grated Parmesan cheese
- A half-cup of shredded Swiss cheese
- 1 shallot
- two teaspoons of minced fresh rosemary
- 1 teaspoon of minced fresh sage
- A half of teaspoon of salt
- 1/4 teaspoon of pepper
- 3 cups of finely chopped cooked turkey
- 1 large egg
- Two tablespoons of water
- quarter cup of panko bread crumbs
- Sour cream
- cooking spray (Butter-flavored)

Instructions

- Preheat the air fryer to 350 degrees Fahrenheit. Combine cheeses, shallot, mashed potatoes, rosemary, salt, sage, and pepper in a large mixing bowl; stir in turkey. Form the burgers into twelve 1-inch thick patties.
- In a small dish, mix together the egg and the water. In a small dish, place the bread crumbs. Dip the croquettes in the egg mixture, then in the bread crumbs, pressing them down to ensure that the coating sticks.
- Arrange croquettes in a thin layer on an oiled tray in the air-fryer basket and spritz with cooking spray in batches. Cook for 4-5 minutes, or until golden brown. Spritz with cooking spray and turn. Cook for 4-5 minutes, or until golden brown. Serve with the sour cream if preferred.

Air-Fryer French Toast Sticks

Preparation and Cooking Time

30 minutes

Servings

18 sticks

Nutritional facts

184 calories per three sticks,15g fat ,1g fiber ,20g carbs ,2g protein

Ingredients

- Six slices of day-old Texas toast
- Four large eggs
- 1 cup whole milk
- Two tablespoons sugar
- One teaspoon vanilla extract
- A one fourth to a half teaspoon ground cinnamon
- One cup crushed cornflakes, optional
- Confectioners' sugar, optional
- Maple syrup

Instructions

- Cut each slice of bread into thirds and put in a 13x9-inch baking dish that hasn't been buttered. Dish. In a large mixing bowl, whisk together the milk, eggs, sugar, vanilla, and cinnamon. Pour over the bread and soak for 2 minutes, rotating halfway through. Coat the bread with cornflakes crumbs on both sides if desired.
- Pour the batter into a prepared 15x10x1-inch baking pan. Freeze for 45 minutes or until firm. Place in the freezer in an airtight container or a resealable freezer bag.
- Preheat the air fryer to 350 degrees Fahrenheit. In the air-fryer basket, place the required number of cookies on a greased tray. 3 minutes in the oven Cook for another 2-3 minutes, or until golden brown. If desired, dust with confectioners' sugar. Serve with a side of syrup.

Garlic-Herb Patty Pan Squash

Preparation and Cooking Time

25 minutes

Servings

4 persons

Nutritional facts

58 calories,5g fat ,1g fiber ,16g carbs ,4g protein

Ingredients

- Five cups of patty pan squash
- One tablespoon olive oil
- 2 garlic cloves, minced
- A half teaspoon of salt
- A one-fourth teaspoon of dried oregano
- A one-fourth teaspoon of dried thyme
- A one-fourth teaspoon of pepper
- 1 tablespoon of minced fresh parsley

Instructions

- Preheat the air fryer to 375° F. Place squash in a large bowl. Mix garlic, oil, salt, thyme, oregano and pepper; drizzle over the squash. Toss to coat. Place squash on a greased tray in the air-fryer basket. Cook until tender, 10-15 minutes, stirring occasionally. Sprinkle with parsley.

Air-Fryer Quinoa Arancini

Preparation and Cooking Time

25 minutes

Servings

3 persons

Nutritional facts

423 calories,11g fat ,2g fiber ,22g carbs ,4g protein

Ingredients

- One package quinoa
- 2 large eggs, beaten, divided
- One cup of seasoned bread crumbs, divided
- A quarter cup of shredded Parmesan cheese
- One tablespoon of olive oil
- 2 tablespoons of minced fresh basil
- A half teaspoon of garlic powder
- A half teaspoon of salt
- 1/8 teaspoon pepper
- Six cubes part-skim mozzarella cheese (3/4 inch each)
- Cooking spray
- Warmed pasta sauce, optional

Instructions

- Preheat the air fryer to 375° F. Prepare quinoa according to package directions. Stir in 1 egg, one and a half cup bread crumbs, Parmesan cheese, oil, basil and seasonings.
- Divide into 6 portions. Shape each portion around a cheese cube to cover completely, forming a ball.
- In separate shallow dishes, place the remaining egg and half cup bread crumbs. Egg-dipped quinoa balls after that, roll it in bread crumbs. In the air-fryer basket, place on a greased tray and sprinkle with cooking spray. Cook for 6-8 minutes, or until golden brown. Serve with pasta sauce if desired.

Air Fryer Chicken Tenders

Preparation and Cooking Time

40 minutes

Servings

4 persons

Nutritional facts

256 calories, 4g fat ,1g fiber ,12g carbs ,2g protein

Ingredients

- A half-cup panko bread crumbs
- A half-cup potato sticks, crushed
- A half-cup crushed cheese crackers
- A quarter cup grated Parmesan cheese
- 2 bacon strips, cooked and crumbled
- two teaspoons minced fresh chives
- A quarter cup butter, melted
- 1 tablespoon sour cream
- 1-pound chicken tenderloins
- Additional sour cream and chives

Instructions

- Preheat the air fryer to 400° F. In a shallow bowl, combine the first 6 ingredients. In another shallow bowl, whisk butter and sour cream. Dip chicken in butter mixture, then in crumb mixture, patting to help coating adhere.
- In batches, arrange chicken in a single layer on a greased tray in the air-fryer basket; spritz with cooking spray. Cook until coating is golden brown and chicken is no longer pink, 7-8 minutes on each side. Serve with additional sour cream and chives.

Air-Fryer General Tso's Cauliflower

Preparation and Cooking Time

45 minutes

Servings

4 persons

Nutritional facts

528 calories, 11g fat ,1g fiber ,21g carbs ,3g protein

Ingredients

- A half-cup all-purpose flour
- A half-cup cornstarch
- One teaspoon salt
- 1 teaspoon baking powder
- A three fourth cup club soda
- 1 medium head cauliflower, cut into 1-inch florets (about 6 cups)
- A quarter cup orange juice
- Three tablespoons sugar
- Three tablespoons soy sauce
- Three tablespoons vegetable broth
- 2 tablespoons rice vinegar
- two teaspoons sesame oil
- two teaspoons cornstarch
- Two tablespoons canola oil
- Two to six dried pasilla or other hot chilies, chopped
- Three green onions, white part minced, green part thinly sliced
- Three garlic cloves, minced
- One teaspoon grated fresh ginger root
- A half teaspoon grated orange zest
- 4 cups hot cooked rice

Instructions

- Preheat air fryer to 400°. Combine flour, cornstarch, salt and baking powder. Stir in club soda just until blended (batter will be thin). Toss florets in batter; transfer to a wire rack set over a baking sheet. Let stand 5 minutes. In batches, place cauliflower on a greased tray in the air-fryer basket. Cook until golden brown and tender, 10-12 minutes.
- Meanwhile, whisk together the first 6 sauce ingredients; whisk in cornstarch until smooth.
- In a large saucepan, heat canola oil over medium-high heat. Add chilies; cook and stir until fragrant, 1-2 minutes. Add the white part of onions, garlic, ginger and orange zest; cook until fragrant, about 1 minute. Stir orange juice mixture; add to saucepan. Bring to a boil; cook and stir until thickened, 2-4 minutes.
- Add cauliflower to sauce; toss to coat. Serve with rice; sprinkle with thinly sliced green onions.

Air-Fryer Beef Wellington Wontons

Preparation and Cooking Time

45 minutes

Servings

42 wontons

Nutritional facts

42 calories per wonton,13g fat ,2g fiber ,31g carbs ,3g protein

Ingredients

- A half-pound of lean ground beef
- One tablespoon of butter

- 1 tablespoon of olive oil
- Two garlic cloves, minced
- One and a half teaspoon of chopped shallot
- 1 cup each chopped baby Portobello chopped fresh shiitake, and white mushrooms
- A quarter cup dry red wine
- 1 tablespoon minced fresh parsley
- A half teaspoon of salt
- A one-fourth teaspoon of pepper
- 1 package (12 ounces) wonton wrappers
- One large egg
- One tablespoon water
- Cooking spray

Instructions

- Preheat air fryer to 325°. In a small skillet, cook beef over medium heat until no longer pink, breaking into crumbles, 4-5 minutes; transfer to a large bowl; in the same skillet, heat butter and olive oil over medium-high heat. Add garlic and shallot; cook for 1 minute. Stir in mushrooms and wine. Cook until mushrooms are tender, 8-10 minutes; add to beef. Stir in salt, parsley, and pepper.
- Fill the center of each wonton wrapper with roughly two tablespoons of filling. Mix the water and the egg together. Using the egg mixture to moisten the wonton edges, fold opposing corners over the filling and press to seal.
- Spritz wontons with cooking spray and put in a single layer on an oiled tray in the air-fryer basket in batches. Cook for 4-5 minutes, or until gently browned. Spritz with cooking spray and turn. Cook for another 4-5 minutes, or until golden brown and crisp. Warm the dish before serving. Option to freeze: Place unbaked wontons on the parchment-lined baking trays and freeze until hard. Return to the freezer in freezer containers. Cook pastries according per package directions.

Nacho Hot Dogs

Preparation and Cooking Time

35 minutes

Servings

6 persons

Nutritional facts

216 calories, 25g fat ,2g fiber ,18g carbs ,2g protein

Ingredients

- 6 hot dogs
- Three cheddar cheese sticks halved lengthwise
- A one and a quarter cup of self-rising flour
- One cup of plain Greek yogurt
- A quarter cup of salsa
- A one fourth teaspoon of chili powder
- 3 tablespoons of chopped seeded jalapeno pepper
- One cup of crushed nacho-flavored tortilla chips,
- sour cream and guacamole optional

Instructions

- Make a slit o each hot dog avoiding cutting through it; place a split cheese stick in the slit.
- Preheat the air fryer to 350 degrees. To make a soft dough, combine yoghurt, flour, chili powder, salsa, jalapenos, and 1/4 cup crumbled tortilla chips in a large mixing basin. Divide dough into sixths on a gently floured surface. Wrap a strip around a cheese-stuffed hot dog and roll into a 15-inch long strip. Rep with the rest of the hot dogs and dough. Coat

them with cooking spray and roll them in the remaining crumbled chips lightly. Spray the air fryer basket with cooking spray and set them in it without touching, providing enough space for them to grow. Cook in batches until the dough is slightly browned and the cheese has melted, about 8-10 minutes. Serve with more sour cream, salsa, and guacamole if preferred.

Chickpea Fritters with the Sweet-Spicy Sauce

Preparation and Cooking Time

25 minutes

Servings

24 fritters

Nutritional facts

34 calories,13g fat ,2g fiber ,26g carbs ,5g protein

Ingredients

- One cup plain yogurt
- 2 tablespoons sugar
- One tablespoon honey
- A half teaspoon of salt
- A half teaspoon of pepper
- A half teaspoon crushed red pepper flakes
- 1 can (15 ounces) chickpeas or garbanzo beans, rinsed and drained
- 1 teaspoon ground cumin
- A half teaspoon of salt
- A half teaspoon garlic powder
- A half teaspoon of ground ginger
- 1 large egg
- A half teaspoon of baking soda
- A half-cup chopped fresh cilantro
- 2 green onions, thinly sliced

Instructions

- Preheat air-fryer to 400°F. Combine the first 6 ingredients; refrigerate until serving.
- Place chickpeas and seasonings in a food processor; process until finely ground. Add egg and baking soda; pulse until blended. Transfer to a bowl; stir in cilantro and green onions.
- In batches, drop rounded tablespoons of bean mixture onto greased tray in the air-fryer basket. Cook until lightly browned, 5-6 minutes. Serve with sauce.

Air-Fryer Crispy Sriracha Spring Rolls

Preparation and Cooking Time

60 minutes

Servings

24 spring rolls

Nutritional facts

127 calories, 3g fat ,0.5g fiber ,10g carbs ,2g protein

Ingredients

- Three cups coleslaw mix (about 7 ounces)
- Three green onions, chopped
- One tablespoon soy sauce
- One teaspoon sesame oil
- 2 tablespoons Sriracha chili sauce
- 24 spring roll wrappers
- Cooking spray

- One-pound boneless skinless chicken breasts
- One teaspoon seasoned salt
- 2 packages (8 ounces each) cream cheese, softened
- Optional: Sweet chili sauce and additional green onions

Instructions

- Preheat air fryer to 360°. Toss the coleslaw mix, soy sauce, green onions, and sesame oil; let them stand while cooking the chicken. Place chicken in a single layer on a greased tray in the air-fryer basket. Cook until a thermometer inserted in the chicken reads 165°, 18-20 minutes. Remove chicken; cool slightly. Finely chop chicken; toss with seasoned salt.
- Increase air-fryer temperature to 400°. Mix cream cheese and Sriracha chili sauce; stir in chicken and coleslaw mixture. With 1 corner of a spring roll wrapper facing you, place about 2 tablespoons of filling just below the center of the wrapper. Fold the bottom corner over your filling; moisten the remaining edges with water. Fold side corners toward center over filling; roll up tightly, pressing the tip to seal. Repeat.
- In batches, arrange spring rolls in a single layer on a greased tray in the air-fryer basket; spritz with cooking spray. Cook until lightly browned, 5-6 minutes. Turn; spritz with cooking spray. Cook until golden brown and crisp, 5-6 minutes longer. If desired, serve with sweet chili sauce and sprinkle with green onions.
- Freeze uncooked spring rolls 1 in. apart in freezer containers, separating layers with waxed paper. To use, cook frozen spring rolls as directed, increasing time as necessary.

Air-Fryer Green Tomato Stacks

Preparation and Cooking Time

35 minutes

Servings

8 persons

Nutritional facts

114 calories, 11g fat ,1g fiber ,18g carbs ,2g protein

Ingredients

- A quarter cup fat-free mayonnaise
- A one-fourth teaspoon grated lime zest
- 2 tablespoons lime juice
- One teaspoon minced fresh thyme or 1/4 teaspoon dried thyme
- A half teaspoon pepper, divided
- A quarter cup all-purpose flour
- 2 large egg whites, lightly beaten
- A three fourth cup cornmeal
- A one-fourth teaspoon of salt
- Two medium green tomatoes
- Two medium red tomatoes
- Cooking spray
- Eight slices of Canadian bacon, warmed

Instructions

- Preheat air fryer to 375°. Mix mayonnaise, lime zest and juice, thyme and 1/4 teaspoon pepper; refrigerate until serving. Place flour in a shallow bowl; place egg whites in a separate shallow bowl. Mix cornmeal, salt, and the remaining 1/4 teaspoon pepper in a third bowl.
- Cut each tomato crosswise into 4 slices. Lightly coat the slices in flour; shake off excess. Dip in the egg whites, and then cornmeal mixture.
- Now place the tomatoes on a greased tray in the air-fryer basket; spritz with cooking spray. Cook until golden brown, 4-

6 minutes. Turn; spritz with cooking spray. Cook until golden brown, 4-6 minutes longer.

- Stack 1 slice of each green tomato, bacon, and red tomato for each serving. Serve with sauce.

Air-Fryer Pretzel-Crusted Catfish

Preparation and Cooking Time

25 minutes

Servings

4 persons

Nutritional facts

466 calories,16g fat ,1g fiber ,21g carbs ,1g protein

Ingredients

- Four catfish fillets
- A half teaspoon of salt
- A half-cup all-purpose flour
- 2 tablespoons of 2% milk
- 4 cups of coarsely crushed honey mustard miniature pretzels
- A half teaspoon of pepper
- Cooking spray
- 2 large eggs
- A one third cup of Dijon mustard
- Lemon slices, optional

Instructions

- Preheat the air fryer to 325 degrees Fahrenheit. Season the catfish with pepper and salt before serving. In a small dish, whisk together the mustard, eggs, and milk. Separate the flour and pretzels into small basins. Coat the fillets in flour, then dip them in the egg mixture before coating them with pretzels.
- Spritz fillets with cooking spray and arrange in a single layer on an oiled tray in the air-fryer basket in batches. Cook for 10-12 minutes, or until the salmon flakes readily with a fork. Serve with the lemon slices if preferred.

Air-Fryer Shrimp Po'Boys

Preparation and Cooking Time

45 minutes

Servings

4 persons

Nutritional facts

716 calories, 11g fat ,1g fiber ,18g carbs ,2g protein

Ingredients

- A half-cup mayonnaise
- One tablespoon Creole mustard
- One tablespoon chopped cornichons or dill pickles
- One tablespoon minced shallot
- One and a half teaspoons lemon juice
- 1/8 teaspoon cayenne pepper
- One cup all-purpose flour
- One teaspoon herbes de Provence
- A half teaspoon of sea salt
- A half teaspoon garlic powder
- A half teaspoon of pepper
- A one fourth teaspoon cayenne pepper
- One large egg
- A half cup2% milk

- One teaspoon hot pepper sauce
- 2 cups sweetened shredded coconut
- One-pound uncooked shrimp (26-30 per pound), peeled and deveined
- Cooking spray
- Four hoagie buns, split
- 2 cups shredded lettuce
- One medium tomato, thinly sliced

Instructions

- For remoulade, in a small bowl, combine the first 6 ingredients. Refrigerate, covered, until serving.
- Preheat air fryer to 375°. Mix flour, herbes de Provence, sea salt, garlic powder, pepper, and cayenne in a shallow bowl. Whisk egg, milk, and hot pepper sauce in a separate shallow bowl. Place coconut in a third shallow bowl. Dip shrimp in flour to coat both sides; shake off excess. Dip in egg mixture, then in coconut, patting to help adhere.
- In batches, arrange shrimp in a single layer on a greased tray in the air-fryer basket; spritz with cooking spray. Cook until coconut is lightly browned and shrimp turn pink, 3-4 minutes on each side.
- Spread cut side of buns with remoulade. Top with shrimp, lettuce and tomato.

Air-Fryer Herb and Cheese-Stuffed Burgers

Preparation and Cooking Time

35 minutes

Servings

4 persons

Nutritional facts

369 calories, 9g fat ,1g fiber ,30g carbs ,4g protein

Ingredients

- Two green onions, thinly sliced
- Two tablespoons minced fresh parsley
- Fourth teaspoons Dijon mustard, divided
- Three tablespoons dry bread crumbs
- Two tablespoons ketchup
- A half teaspoon of salt
- A half teaspoon dried rosemary, crushed
- A one-fourth teaspoon of dried sage leaves
- 1-pound lean ground beef (90% lean)
- Two ounces' cheddar cheese, sliced
- Four hamburger buns, split
- Optional toppings: Lettuce leaves, sliced tomato, mayonnaise and additional ketchup

Instructions

- Preheat air fryer to 375°. Combine green onions, parsley, and two teaspoons of mustard in a small bowl. Mix bread crumbs, ketchup, seasonings, and two teaspoons of mustard in another bowl. Add beef to the bread crumb mixture; mix lightly but thoroughly.
- Shape mixture into 8 thin patties. Place sliced cheese in the center of 4 patties; spoon green onion mixture over cheese. Top with remaining patties, pressing edges together firmly, taking care to seal completely.
- Place burgers in a single layer on a tray in an air-fryer basket in batches. Cook 8 minutes. Flip; cook until a thermometer inserted in the burger reads 160°, 6-8 minutes longer. Serve burgers on buns, with toppings if desired.

Healthy Chicken and Veggies

Preparation and Cooking Time

20 minutes

Servings

4 persons

Nutritional facts

230 calories, 9g fat ,1g fiber ,30g carbs ,4g protein

Ingredients

- 1 zucchini chopped
- One cup bell pepper chopped (any colors you like)
- A half onion chopped
- 2 cloves garlic minced or crushed
- 2 tablespoons olive oil
- A half teaspoon each garlic powder, chili powder, salt, pepper
- One pound of chicken breast, chopped in bite-size pieces
- One cup of broccoli florets
- 1 tablespoon Italian seasoning (or spice blend of choice)

Instructions

- Preheat air fryer to 400F.
- Chop the veggies and chicken into small bite-size pieces and transfer to a large mixing bowl.
- Add the seasoning and oil to the bowl and toss to combine.
- Add the veggies and chicken to the preheated air fryer and cook for about 10 minutes, shaking halfway, or until the chicken and veggies are charred, and chicken is cooked through. If your air fryer is small, you may have to cook them in 2-3 batches.

Healthy Air Fryer Chicken and Broccoli Stir Fry

Preparation and Cooking Time

25 minutes

Servings

4 persons

Nutritional facts

224 calories, 10g fat ,2g fiber ,29g carbs ,2g protein

Ingredients

- One pound (454 g) boneless skinless chicken breast or thighs, cut into 1-inch bites sized pieces
- A one fourth to a half-pound (113-226 g) broccoli, cut into florets (1-2 cups)
- a half medium onion, sliced thick
- 3 Tablespoons (45 ml) olive oil or grape seed oil
- A half teaspoon (2.5 ml) garlic powder
- One Tablespoon (15 ml) of fresh minced ginger
- One Tablespoon (15 ml) low sodium soy sauce, or to taste (use Tamari for Gluten Free)
- One Tablespoon (15 ml) rice vinegar (use distilled white vinegar for Gluten Free)
- One teaspoon (5 ml) sesame oil
- Two teaspoons (10 ml) hot sauce (optional)
- A half teaspoon sea salt, or to taste
- black pepper, to taste
- serve with lemon wedges, optional

Instructions

- Prepare the marinade by combining all of the ingredients in a mixing bowl. In a mixing bowl, whisk together the oil, ginger, garlic powder, soy sauce, rice vinegar, sesame oil, rice vinegar, optional spicy sauce, salt, and pepper.

- Put the chicken in a separate bowl. In a separate bowl, combine the broccoli and onions. Divide the marinade between the two bowls and toss to evenly coat each.

- Place the chicken in the air fryer basket alone. Air fry for 10 minutes at 380°F/195°C. Combine the onions and broccoli with the chicken in a mixing bowl. Continue to Air Fry for another 8-10 minutes at 380°F/195°C, or until the chicken is cooked through. Stir halfway during cooking to ensure that the broccoli is uniformly cooked.

- Season with pepper and salt to taste. Serve warm with a squeeze of fresh lemon juice on top if desired.

Air Fryer Orange Chicken

Preparation and Cooking Time

30 minutes

Servings

4 persons

Nutritional facts

380 calories, 14g fat ,1g fiber ,26g carbs ,2g protein

Ingredients

Ingredients for the chicken

- One and a half pound raw boneless, skinless chicken breast
- 1 large egg, whisked
- Two-third cup cornstarch or potato starch (see blog notes)

Ingredients for the sauce

- A one-third cup freshly squeezed orange juice, from about 2 medium oranges
- 4 garlic cloves, minced
- One tsp. minced ginger
- One tbsp. cornstarch
- Two tbsp. rice wine vinegar
- Two tbsp. oyster sauce
- 3 tbsp. soy sauce or tamari
- A two and a half tbsp. honey
- One tbsp. water
- A one-fourth tsp. red pepper flakes

Instructions

- Preheat air fryer to 375F.
- Cut chicken into 1-inch cubes. Mix with whisked egg until all chicken is coated.
- In a large plastic bag, add the cornstarch. Using tongs, take chicken pieces out of the egg mixture, allowing excess egg to drip off and add to the bag.
- Close the bag and shake chicken pieces around until fully coated by the cornstarch. Remove pieces from the bag and place them on the cutting board that you used to cut up your chicken.
- Liberally coat the side of the chicken facing up with cooking spray. Add the chicken, sprayed side down, to the basket of your air fryer. Now spray the side facing up, so all sides of the chicken are coated.
- Air fry at 375F for 10-15 minutes, or until chicken is slightly browned and cooked through.
- As the chicken cooks, make the sauce in a medium-sized skillet. Whisk sauce ingredients together and cook over medium heat, constantly stirring, until the sauce thickens–about 5 minutes.
- Toss cooked chicken with sauce and serve immediately.

Air Fryer Frozen Mozzarella Sticks

Preparation and Cooking Time

6 minutes

Servings

10 sticks

Nutritional facts

537 calories,22g fat ,1g fiber ,33g carbs ,4g protein

Ingredients

- marinara sauce for dipping
- Ten mozzarella sticks

Instructions

- Heat the air fryer to about 360 degrees Fahrenheit.
- In the air fryer, cook the frozen mozzarella sticks for 6-8 minutes.
- Slightly pinch. They're done when the cheese inside would be soft and the mozzarella stick has a little give to it.
- Take them out of the air fryer and serve with a marinara sauce to dip them in.

Air Fryer Sweet Potato Fries

Preparation and Cooking Time

20 minutes

Servings

4 persons

Nutritional facts

89 calories, 22g fat ,1g fiber ,33g carbs ,4g protein

Ingredients

- Two medium sweet potatoes
- One tablespoon olive oil
- A half teaspoon fine sea salt
- A half teaspoon garlic powder
- A one-fourth teaspoon of paprika

Instructions

- Cut sweet potatoes into 1/2 inch strips to create fries.
- Coat sweet potato fries with olive oil.
- Add the fine sea salt, garlic powder, and paprika and mix to combine seasoning evenly.
- Cook the sweet potato fries at 380 degrees for 15-18 minutes, shaking the basket every 5 minutes.

Air Fryer Dessert Fries

Preparation and Cooking Time

20 minutes

Servings

4 persons

Nutritional facts

110 calories, 9g fat ,1g fiber ,21g carbs ,2g protein

Ingredients

- Two sweet potatoes
- One tablespoon butter, melted
- One teaspoon butter, melted and separated from the above
- 2 tablespoons sugar
- A half teaspoon cinnamon

Instructions

- Preheat your air fryer to 380 degrees.

- Peel and cut the sweet potatoes into skinny fries
- Coat fries with 1 tablespoon of butter.
- Cook fries in the preheated air fryer for 15-18 minutes. They can overlap but should not fill your air fryer more than 1/2 full.
- Remove the sweet potato fries from the air fryer and place them in a bowl.
- Coat with the remaining butter and add in sugar and cinnamon. Mix to coat.
- Enjoy immediately.

Air Fryer Spicy Cauliflower Buffalo

Preparation and Cooking Time

22 minutes

Servings

3-4 persons

Nutritional facts

160 calories, 10g fat ,2g fiber ,31g carbs ,3g protein

Ingredients

- 1 1/2 teaspoon maple syrup
- 2 teaspoons avocado oil
- 2-3 tablespoons nutritional yeast (more for a cheesier flavor; I use 3)
- A quarter tsp. sea salt
- 1 medium head cauliflower, chopped into 1 1/2" florets (approximately 6 cups)
- 2-3 tablespoons Frank's Red Hot Sauce (start with 2 if heat-sensitive)
- 1 tablespoon cornstarch or arrowroot starch

Instructions

- Set the air fryer to 360 degrees F. Add all the ingredients except the cauliflower to a large mixing bowl. Whisk thoroughly to mix. To cover uniformly, apply the cauliflower and flip.
- Apply the cauliflower to the fryer (no need to oil the basket). Cook for twelve to fourteen minutes, shaking halfway through, or until the perfect consistency is reached. Repeat with the remaining cauliflower, except for 9-10 minutes of shortened cooking time. Cauliflower must be kept securely packed for up to 4 days in the refrigerator. To reheat, add 1-2 minutes to the air fryer until hot and slightly crispy.

Air Fryer Oreos

Preparation and Cooking Time

10 minutes

Servings

9 persons

Nutritional facts

77 calories, 18g fat ,1g fiber ,21g carbs ,3g protein

Ingredients

- half cup complete pancake mix
- 9 chocolate sandwich cookies (such as Oreo®)
- 1 tablespoon confectioners' sugar, or to taste
- ⅓ cup water
- cooking spray

Instructions

- Mix the pancake mixture and water until well mixed.
- Line the basket of an air fryer with parchment paper. With nonstick cooking oil, spray parchment paper. In the pancake mixture, dip each cookie and put it in the basket. Make sure they don't touch them; if possible, cook in batches.

- The air fryer is preheated to 400 degrees F (200 degrees C). Add the basket and cook for 5 - 6 minutes; flip and cook 2 to 3 more minutes until golden brown. Sprinkle with confectioner's sugar.

Air Fryer French Fries with Seasoned Salt

Preparation and Cooking Time

50 minutes

Servings

1 person

Nutritional facts

235 calories, 11g fat ,2g fiber ,18g carbs ,2g protein

Ingredients

- 1 Russet potato (I keep the skin on, but you can peel the potato if you prefer.)
- 2 teaspoons chili powder
- ½ teaspoon garlic powder
- 5 sprays olive oil or avocado oil cooking spray, (You may want to use a little more or less depending on the size of your potato)
- Two tablespoons salt
- 1 teaspoon ground cumin
- ½ teaspoon onion powder

Instructions

- Cut the potato into small strips about a quarter of an inch thick.
- Place the potato slices for about 30 minutes in a bowl of water to soak.
- Meanwhile, prepare the seasoned salt by combining the ingredients in a small bowl. Just put it aside.
- Drain the slices of potato and use kitchen towels to dry properly.
- The potato slices should be put in a dry bowl. Spray with about 5 cooking oil sprays. Use your hands to coat them.
- Apply the preferred amount of Seasoned Salt to the potato slices and use your hands to toss to cover.
- Place the potato slices and spread them out as thinly as possible in the basket of your air fryer.
- Cook for 15 to 20 minutes at 390 degrees F (or your model's maximum temperature), flipping midway through until the fries are finely browned and crispy.
- Instantly serve.

Air Fried Sweet Potato Dessert Fries

Preparation and Cooking Time

40 minutes

Servings

4 persons

Nutritional facts

130 calories, 10g fat ,2g fiber ,31g carbs ,8g protein

Ingredients

- Two medium sweet potatoes and yams peeled (see notes for low carb option)
- Optional Two teaspoons melted butter (for coating)
- A quarter cup coconut sugar or raw sugar
- One to Two tablespoons cinnamon
- Optional powdered sugar for dusting (see notes for sugar-free option)
- Dessert Hummus
- Vanilla Greek Yogurt

- Half a tablespoon of coconut oil.
- 1 tablespoon arrowroot starch or cornstarch
- Maple Frosting {vegan}

Instructions

- Peel and wash your sweet potatoes with clean water, then dry.
- Slice peeled sweet potatoes, 1/2 inch deep, lengthwise.
- Toss 1/2 tbsp. of coconut oil and arrowroot starch in your sweet potato slices.
- Place the air fryer at 370F for 18 minutes. Shake for 8-9 minutes halfway through.
- Take the fries from the fryer and put them in a wide bowl. Drizzle on top of the fries with two teaspoons of optional butter. Then mix the sugar and cinnamon and toss the fries once again.
- Place it on a serving plate and sprinkle it with powdered sugar.
- Serve fries with the preferred dipping sauce. Hold the fries wrapped in foil and a fridge to stock. Then reheat to warm again in the oven before serving. You should stay for 2-3 days.

Garlic Herb Turkey Breast Deep Fryer

Preparation and Cooking Time

5 hours 8 minutes

Servings

3 persons

Nutritional facts

179 calories, 9g fat ,3g fiber ,17g carbs ,4g protein

Ingredients

- Guacamole
- 2 teaspoons cumin
- fresh finely chopped cilantro to taste (about One-third cup)
- sea salt & pepper to taste
- 8 tablespoons fine almond flour
- One egg
- One egg white
- One third cup almond flour
- 3 medium ripe avocados
- juice from 1 lime
- One-third cup chopped onion
- Substitute: coconut flour; protein baking powder; tapioca or arrowroot powder
- 90g (One and a half cups gluten-free panko
- Substitute: wheat breadcrumbs, regular panko
- spray olive oil

Instructions

- Combine and mash the guacamole ingredients in a bowl without the almond flour. Add in the almond flour until you have the perfect spice, until the guacamole is dense, like brownie batter. Add additional tablespoons of almond flour to the batter to make it thick as needed. This can leave the guacamole wet and loose; avoid applying too much lime juice. Set the bowl to harden for 1-2 hours in the freezer until it has hardened.
- Line with parchment paper or nonstick foil the baking sheet. Use a spoon to scoop the guacamole out and shape a ball with your hands, about the size of a ping pong ball, and put it on the baking tray. Repeat with the leftover guacamole VERY easily. Use nonstick foil to protect the tray and place it in the freezer for at least 4 hours or overnight.
- Set air fryer to the 390F (199C).
- Eggs are beaten together in a bowl.

- You must work hard, and you will have to do this in batches. To make them get 'sticky,' gently brush a guacamole ball in olive oil, then dip it in almond flour, egg mixture, panko crumbs. Repeat ONLY until you have enough guacamole balls to fill the air fryer's basket, so place the remainder of the balls back in the freezer (without coating).
- Place the coated balls in the air fryer's basket, spray with a little olive oil, and cook for 6 to 8 minutes or until golden brown on the outside. Keep them out of the air fryer if the balls start cracking. Allow them to cool slightly before treating, because as they cool.

Air Fried German Pancakes

Preparation and Cooking Time

13 minutes

Servings

2persons

Nutritional facts

139 calories, 6g fat ,1g fiber ,15g carbs ,3g protein

Ingredients

- Three whole eggs
- Substitutes: reduced-fat milk; coconut milk
- pinch of salt
- Two heaping tablespoons of unsweetened applesauce
- fresh berries
- Greek yogurt
- Swerve confectioner's sugar
- raw cacao nibs (unsweetened)
- Substitutes: oat flour
- 1 cup of whole wheat flour
- 1 cup of almond milk
- maple syrup (optional)

Instructions

- Set the air-fryer to 390F/199C. Place the ramekin or cast iron tray within the air fryer as it heats.
- Add all the batter components to a blender and mix until creamy. Also, add teaspoons of milk along with applesauce to thin it out if the batter appears to be too thick.
- Spray with nonstick baking spray on a cast iron tray or ramekin. Then pour the batter into a serving.
- It is to be air-fried for about 6 to 8 minutes. Don't worry if the top comes out sort of 'hard' to handle. This is the advantage of using the air fryer-it gives a good firm exterior coating/edges to the pancake that softens as it cools.
- Put the leftover batter in an airtight jar in the fridge to keep it fresh every morning.
- Garnish and rejoice.

Air-Fried Popcorn

Preparation and Cooking Time

20 minutes

Servings

2 persons

Nutritional facts

20 calories, 5g fat ,2g fiber ,30g carbs ,2g protein

Ingredients

- Forty grams (3 tablespoons) dried corn kernels (I used white corn)
- spray avocado oil

- Substitutes (preferably oils with a high smoke point): coconut oil; safflower oil; peanut oil
- sea salt & pepper to taste
- Garnish
- Two tablespoons nutritional yeast dried chives

Instructions

- Set the Air Fryer System to (199C).
- Add the kernels to the basket of the fryer and spray gently with a little avocado/coconut oil. To avoid popped popcorn from escaping the basket and floating around in the air fryer, line the tray sides with aluminum foil if necessary.
- Insert the basket. Set 15 minutes. Check it every 3 to 5 minutes to ensure that the kernels do not burn. Once they start popping, keep a close eye on them until the popping sound ceases or 15 minutes have passed.
- Immediately empty the basket and pour the contents into a large bowl. Spray with coconut or avocado oil gently, then sprinkle with garnish.
- Enjoy warm or at room temperature.

Air Fried Patatas Bravas

Preparation and Cooking Time

25 minutes

Servings

4 persons

Nutritional facts

97 calories, 8g fat ,1g fiber ,19g carbs ,3g protein

Ingredients

- 300g red potato, cut into 1-inch chunks
- pinch of sea salt & pepper
- Seasoning
- 1 tablespoon smoked paprika
- 1/2 teaspoon cayenne (optional)
- sea salt & pepper to taste
- Garnish
- dried chives
- 1 tablespoon avocado oil
- Substitutes (preferably oils with a high smoke point): coconut oil; safflower oil; peanut oil
- 1 teaspoon garlic powder
- garlic aioli

Instructions

- Bring a water pot to a boil. Insert the red potatoes and roast for 6 minutes. And use a filter to extract the potatoes from the water quickly and put them on a kitchen towel to cool and pat them dry. After the potatoes have cooled to room temperature (approximately 15 minutes), make sure they are "dry," then add them with avocado oil, garlic powder, sea salt and pepper in a large bowl. Coat the potatoes and add them, ideally in batches, to an air-fryer tray so that the basket does not overcrowd, which can lead to poor frying. Food requires space to breathe.
- Set the air fryer to (199C).
- Add the basket to the air fryer and cook for 15 minutes, then shake the basket after 7 minutes. You should also brush the potatoes gently with avocado oil another time before frying to ensure a good crispy coating.
- Transfer the "fried" potatoes to a bowl and brush lightly with avocado oil. Apply the seasonings, then. Shake the bowl to coat the potatoes, then enjoy with your favorite condiment instantly.

Air Fryer Spicy Chicken Thighs

Preparation and Cooking Time

1 hour 20 minutes

Servings

4 persons

Nutritional facts

160 calories, 11g fat ,2g fiber ,23 carbs ,4g protein

Ingredients

- One-third cup low-sodium soy sauce
- A quarter cup extra-virgin olive oil
- 2 tablespoons. honey
- 2 tablespoons. chili garlic sauce
- 4 bone-in, skin-on chicken thighs (about 2 lb.)
- Thinly sliced green onions for garnish
- Toasted sesame seeds for garnish
- Juice of 1 lime
- 2 cloves garlic, minced
- Two teaspoons. freshly grated ginger

Instructions

- Combine the soy sauce, oil, butter, ginger, chili garlic sauce, lime juice and garlic in a large bowl. Reserve half a cup of marinade. To bowl, add chicken thighs and toss to cover. Cover for at least 30 minutes and refrigerate.
- Take 2 thighs from the marinade and put them in the air fryer basket. Cook for 15 to 20 minutes at 400 ° F before the thighs are cooked to an internal temperature of 165 ° F. Move the thighs to a plate. Repeat for the thighs that remain.
- Meanwhile, bring the reserved marinade to a boil in a shallow saucepan over medium heat. Reduce the heat and cook for 4 to 5 minutes until the sauce thickens slightly.
- Brush the sauce on the thighs and garnish before serving with sesame seeds and green onions.

Air Fryer Fried Chicken

Preparation and Cooking Time

2 hours 10 minutes

Servings

3 persons

Nutritional facts

191 calories, 20g fat ,2g fiber ,31g carbs ,3g protein

Ingredients

- Two pounds' bone-in skin-on chicken pieces (mix of cuts)
- Two cups buttermilk
- Half cup hot sauce
- 3 tsp. kosher salt, divided
- A half teaspoon. freshly ground black pepper
- 1/4 tsp. cayenne pepper
- Two cups all-purpose flour
- 1 tsp. garlic powder
- 1 tsp. onion powder
- A half teaspoon. oregano

Instructions

- Trim the extra fat of chicken and put it in a large bowl. Combine the buttermilk, hot sauce, and two tablespoons of salt in a medium bowl.
- Pour the paste over the chicken, ensuring that all parts are

coated. For at least sixty minutes and up to overnight, cover and refrigerate.

- Combine the flour, the remaining 1 teaspoon of salt and seasonings in a shallow bowl or pie dish. Remove the chicken from the buttermilk and shake off the extra buttermilk, working one at a time. Place in the mixture of flour and turn to coat.
- Place coated chicken in the air fryer basket, running in batches as required to prevent overcrowding the basket. Cook at 400 ° F until the chicken is golden and the internal temperature hits 165 ° F, turning midway through for 20 to 25 minutes.
- Repeat for leftover chicken.

Crispy Air Fryer Bacon
Preparation and Cooking Time

15 minutes

Servings

8 persons

Nutritional facts

160 calories,12g fat ,4g fiber ,30g carbs ,4g protein

Ingredients

- Three quarter pounds thick-cut bacon

Instructions

- Lay bacon in a single layer within the air-fryer basket.
- Set the air fryer to 400 °F and cook for 10 minutes until crispy. (You should search and re-arrange pieces with tongs halfway through.

Air Fryer Cinnamon and Cheese Rolls
Preparation and Cooking Time

30 minutes

Servings

6 persons

Nutritional facts

210 calories ,11g fat ,1g fiber ,20g carbs ,2g protein

Ingredients

- 2 tablespoons. melted butter, plus more for brushing
- One-third cup packed brown sugar
- All-purpose flour, for surface
- 1 (8-oz.) tube refrigerated Crescent rolls
- A half teaspoon. ground cinnamon
- Kosher salt
- 2 oz. cream cheese softened
- Half cup powdered sugar
- 1 tablespoon whole milk, plus more if needed

Instructions

- Make rolls: Line the air fryer's bottom with parchment paper and coat with butter. Combine the butter, brown sugar, cinnamon and a large pinch of salt in a medium bowl until smooth and fluffy.
- Roll out crescent rolls in one piece on a lightly floured board. Pinch the seams and fold them together in half. Roll into a rectangle of 9"-x-7". Spread the mixture of butter over the dough, leaving a 1/4-inch border. Roll up the dough like a jelly roll, starting with a long side, and cut crosswise into 6 pieces.
- Arrange pieces in a prepared air fryer, cut-side up, evenly spaced.
- Set the air fryer to 350 ° F and cook for about 10 minutes until golden.

- Make the glaze: mix the cream cheese, powdered sugar and milk together in a medium bowl. If required, apply a teaspoonful of more milk to the thin glaze.
- Spread the glaze over warm rolls of cinnamon and serve.

Parmesan "Fried" Tortellini
Preparation and Cooking Time

25 minutes

Servings

6 persons

Nutritional facts

156 calories,2g fat ,3g fiber ,10g carbs ,4g protein

Ingredients

- One-third cup freshly grated Parmesan
- 1 tsp. dried oregano
- A half teaspoon. garlic powder
- A half teaspoon. crushed red pepper flakes
- Kosher salt
- Freshly ground black pepper
- 1 c. all-purpose flour
- 2 large eggs
- 1 (nine ounces) package cheese tortellini
- 1 cup Panko breadcrumbs
- Marinara, for serving

Instructions

- Cook tortellini in a big pot of boiling salted water. Then drain.
- Mix the garlic powder, Panko, Parmesan, oregano and red pepper flakes in a shallow bowl. With salt and pepper, season. Beat the eggs in another shallow bowl and add the flour to the third shallow bowl.
- Cover the tortellini in flour, dredge them in eggs, and then mix them in Panko. Continue until they are all covered with tortellini.
- Place in an air fryer and fry for 10 minutes at 370 °F until crispy.
- Serve with marinara as well.

French toast Sticks
Preparation and Cooking Time

35 minutes

Servings

6 persons

Nutritional facts

257 calories, 12g fat ,2g fiber ,25g carbs ,2g protein

Ingredients

- One-third cup of heavy cream
- 2 large eggs
- 6 thick slices of any white loaf or Pullman
- Kosher salt
- 3 tablespoons. of granulated sugar
- One-third cup. whole milk
- 1/4 tsp. of ground cinnamon
- A half teaspoon. Of pure vanilla extract
- Maple syrup, for serving

Instructions

- Beat the cinnamon, eggs, cream, milk, sugar, vanilla, and salt pinch in a big shallow baking dish. Insert the bread and turn a couple of times to coat.

- Arrange French toast in the air fryer basket, working in lots if necessary to prevent overcrowding the basket. Set the air fryer to 375°F and cook for about 8 minutes until golden, flipping halfway through. Drizzle with maple syrup and eat warm toast.

Garlic Parmesan Chicken

Preparation and Cooking Time

35 minutes

Servings

4 persons

Nutritional facts

246 calories, 10g fat ,1.2g fiber ,23g carbs ,2g protein

Ingredients

- 2/3 cup freshly grated Parmesan
- 2 large eggs
- Kosher salt
- Freshly ground black pepper
- 1 cup Panko breadcrumbs
- 1 tsp. garlic powder
- 4 bone-in, skin-on chicken thighs
- 1 tsp. Italian seasoning

Instructions

- With salt and pepper, season the chicken. Whisk the parmesan, panko, garlic powder and Italian seasoning in a shallow bowl. Beat the eggs in yet another shallow bowl.
- Dip the chicken thighs in the egg and then roll until thoroughly covered in the Panko mix.
- Cook at 360 F for about 30 min or until golden.

Air Fryer Fried Pickles

Preparation and Cooking Time

55 minutes

Servings

3 persons

Nutritional facts

160 calories, 10g fat ,1.2g fiber ,23g carbs ,2g protein

Ingredients

- Two cups dill pickle slices
- 1/4 cup freshly grated Parmesan
- 1 tsp. dried oregano
- 1 tsp. garlic powder
- 1 egg, whisked with 1 tablespoon water
- Half cup bread crumbs
- Ranch, for dipping

Instructions

- Pat pickle chips dry using paper towels. Stir the oregano, bread crumbs, and parmesan and garlic powder together in a medium bowl.
- Dredge pickle chips first in the egg and then bread crumb mixture. Working in batches, put a single layer in the air fryer basket. Cook for 10 minutes at 400°F.
  - Serve warm with the ranch.

Chapter 7: Air Fryer Poultry Recipes

Air Fryer Chicken Breast

Preparation and Cooking Time

30 minutes

Servings

2 persons

Nutritional facts

257 calories, 20g fat ,2g fiber ,19g carbs ,2g protein

Ingredients

- One large egg, beaten
- 1/4 cup all-purpose flour
- 3/4 cup panko bread crumbs
- One-third cup freshly grated Parmesan
- Two teaspoons. lemon zest
- 1 tsp. dried oregano
- A half teaspoon. cayenne pepper
- Kosher salt
- Freshly ground black pepper
- Two boneless skinless chicken breasts

Instructions

- Place in two separate shallow bowls, the eggs and starch. Combine the oregano, panko, parmesan, lemon zest and cayenne in the third shallow bowl. With salt and pepper, season.
- Dip the chicken into the flour, then the eggs, and then the panko paste, pressing to cover, one at a time.
- Put in the air-fryer basket and cook for 10 minutes at 375 °F. Flip the chicken and cook for another five minutes until the chicken is golden and cooked through.

Air Fryer Chicken Tenders with Lemon Wedges

Preparation and Cooking Time

35 minutes

Servings

4 persons

Nutritional facts

291 calories, 8g fat ,1g fiber ,25g carbs ,3g protein

Ingredients

- 12 chicken tenders (1 1/4 lbs.)

- 1/2 cup seasoned panko
- olive oil spray
- 2 large eggs, beaten
- 1 teaspoon kosher salt
- black pepper, to taste
- 1/2 cup seasoned breadcrumbs
- lemon wedges, for serving

Instructions

- Season the chicken with salt and pepper.
- In a shallow bowl, crack the egg. Mix the bread crumbs & panko in a second shallow bowl.
- Place the chicken on a big dish or cutting board, dip it in the egg, then into the breadcrumb mixture, shaking off the excess. Liberally coat both sides of the chicken with oil.
- Preheat the air fryer to 400 degrees Fahrenheit.
- Cook the chicken in batches for 5 to 6 minutes on each side, or until cooked through & crispy and golden on the outside. Serve with lemon slices on the side.

Air Fried (breast, thigh, wing, and leg)

Preparation and Cooking Time

35 minutes

Servings

4 persons

Nutritional facts

318 calories ,10g fat ,2g fiber ,34g carbs ,6g protein

Ingredients

- ½ whole chicken cut into separate pieces (breast, thigh, wing, and leg)
- 1 tsp. garlic powder
- 1 tsp. onion powder
- 1 tsp. Italian seasoning
- ½ cup hot sauce
- ½ cup buttermilk
- ¾ cup All-Purpose Flour
- 2 tsp. seasoning salt
- ½ tsp. cayenne pepper
- Oil for spraying Canola or Vegetable

Instructions

- Combine the buttermilk and spicy sauce with the chicken pieces. Put in refrigerator and marinate for 1 to 24 hours.
- In a mixing bowl, combine all-purpose flour, salt, garlic powder, onion powder, Italian seasoning, & cayenne pepper.
- In the Air Fryer basket, place a parchment liner.
- Remove a chicken piece from the buttermilk mixture & coat it completely in flour, shaking off any excess flour. Arrange the chicken pieces in a single layer in the basket.
- Close the Air Fryer basket & set the temperature to 390°F with a 25-minute timer. Start up the Air Fryer.
- Open the air fryer after 13 minutes & spray any flour spots on the chicken. Spray the other side of the chicken with oil, making sure all flour areas are covered. Cook for another 12 minutes in the Air Fryer.
- When the timer goes off, open the Air Fryer and a quick read thermometer to examine the chicken pieces. When the thickest section of the chicken reaches an internal temperature of 165 degrees F, it is done.

The Best Air Fryer Fried Chicken

Preparation and Cooking Time

30 minutes

Servings

4 persons

Nutritional facts

592 calories ,19g fat ,2g fiber ,45g carbs ,8g protein

Ingredients

- 2 lb. bone-in skin-on chicken pieces' mix of cuts
- ½ cup corn starch or replace with more flour
- 1 teaspoon EACH paprika garlic powder, onion powder, salt, pepper
- 1 cup buttermilk
- ¼ cup hot sauce
- 1 teaspoon EACH paprika garlic powder, black pepper, salt
- 1 cup flour
- Oil for spraying chicken Canola, Peanut, Vegetable, or olive oil

Instructions

- Combine buttermilk, spicy sauce, and marinade spices in a large mixing bowl. Toss in the chicken and stir to mix. Cover and marinate in the refrigerator for up to 24 hours, or use right away.
- Preheat the air fryer to 375 degrees Fahrenheit.
- Whisk together the flour, cornstarch, & spices in a medium shallow bowl to make the breading. Drizzle 2-3 tbsp. of the buttermilk batter into the flour mixture and stir with a fork until thoroughly combined.
- Dredge each piece of chicken in the flour mixture & press flour onto the top of the chicken to make a thick crust. Place the chicken in a single layer, without overlapping, in a preheated air fryer. If necessary, you might have to work in batches.
- Using a spray bottle or a brush, liberally coat the chicken in oil. If you don't coat all of the breading in a generous layer of flour, the flour won't cook and form a crispy crust. If there is still raw flour visible during the cooking process, brush it with additional oil. The crunchier the crust, the more oil you use in your apple.
- Start the Air-fryer and set the timer for 30 minutes. Flip the chicken after 15 minutes and lightly coat the other side with oil. Cook for another 10 minutes, or until the chicken is golden brown as well as the internal temperature reaches 165 degrees F. As needed, repeat with the leftover chicken.

Air Fryer Chicken Breasts

Preparation and Cooking Time

25 minutes

Servings

2 persons

Nutritional facts

298 calories ,14g fat ,2g fiber ,31g carbs ,2g protein

Ingredients

- 1-4 Chicken Breast (skinless/boneless)
- 1/4 tsp. Pepper (per breast)
- 2 tsp. Olive Oil
- Quarter tsp. Salt (per breast)
- 1/4 tsp. Garlic Powder (per breast)

Instructions

- Olive oil should be brushed on the chicken breasts.
- Then season with salt, pepper, & garlic powder on one side.

- Place the seasoned side down in the air fryer basket. Season the other side after that.
- Preheat oven to 360°F and bake for 9 minutes. Cook for yet another 9 minutes after flipping the chicken breast. Larger chicken breasts require a longer cooking time, whereas smaller ones require less.
- With an instant-read thermometer, take the temperature in the thickest portion. The temperature should be between 158 and 160 degrees Fahrenheit. If it's below that, close the cover of the air fryer and let the chicken cook for a few minutes in the residual heat. Then double-check it.
- Place it on a platter and cover it loosely with foil, allowing it to rest for five minutes. In the remaining heat, it will continue to cook. After 5 minutes, take the temperature once more. The temperature must be at least 165 degrees Fahrenheit.
- Serve right away.

Air Fryer Fried Chicken

Preparation and Cooking Time

29 minutes

Servings

4 persons

Nutritional facts

327 calories ,10g fat ,1g fiber ,23g carbs ,2g protein

Ingredients

- 1/2 cup all-purpose flour
- 1 teaspoon seasoning salt
- cooking spray if desired
- 1 egg beaten
- 4 small chicken thighs skin on
- 1 1/2 tablespoons Old Bay Seasoning

Instructions

- Heat the Air Fryer to 390 degrees Fahrenheit.
- Combine the flour, salt, and Old Bay in a mixing bowl.
- Dredge the chicken in the flour mixture, then in the egg, and finally in the flour mixture. Shake off any excess flour well. You can lightly spray the chicken with cooking spray at this point if you wish.
- In the bottom of the Air Fryer cooking compartment, place the 4 chicken thighs. Cook for 25 minutes until the chicken achieves an internal temperature of 180 degrees F.
- Serve and enjoy.

Crispy Chicken Breast

Preparation and Cooking Time

20minutes

Servings

4 persons

Nutritional facts

310 calories,16g fat ,1g fiber ,29g carbs ,2g protein

Ingredients

- 2 large boneless chicken breasts sliced into cutlets
- ¼ teaspoon of ground black pepper
- ¼ teaspoon of cayenne pepper
- ½ teaspoon of salt
- ¼ teaspoon of garlic powder
- 1 tablespoon of oil olive oil
- ½ cup of dried bread crumbs

- ½ teaspoon of paprika
- ¼ teaspoon of dried chili powder
- ¼ teaspoon of onion powder

Instructions

- Drizzle oil over the chicken breasts. Make sure they're completely coated.
- Combine the spices with the dried bread crumbs in a small bowl until well blended.
- Place each chicken breast in the air fryer basket after coating it in bread crumbs.
- Air fry for 10-12 minutes at 390°F or 200°C in an air fryer. After the first seven minutes, remove the chicken from the air fryer, flip it over, and cook for another 3 minutes.

Spicy Air Fryer Chicken Breast

Preparation and Cooking Time

25 minutes

Servings

4 persons

Nutritional facts

118 calories ,11g fat ,1g fiber ,21g carbs ,5g protein

Ingredients

- 2 boneless, skinless chicken breasts, cut in half lengthwise to create 4 chicken breasts
- ½ tsp. chili powder
- 1 tsp. Italian seasoning
- ½ tsp. salt
- 1 tbsp. olive oil
- 1 tsp. garlic powder
- 1 tsp. onion powder
- 1 tsp. paprika
- ¼ tsp. pepper

Instructions

- Set aside the chicken breasts after rubbing them with olive oil on all sides.
- Combine the seasoning blend & rub it all over the chicken breasts until they are evenly coated.
- In the air fryer, arrange the chicken breasts in a single layer. Cook for 10 minutes at 380°F, then rotate and cook for another 5-6 minutes, just until the internal temperature reaches 165°F.
- The chicken breasts should be removed from the pan and set aside to rest for 5 minutes before slicing and serving.

Crispy and Juicy Air Fryer Chicken Breast

Preparation and Cooking Time

48 minutes

Servings

2 persons

Nutritional facts

237 calories,12g fat ,1g fiber ,28g carbs ,2g protein

Ingredients

- 2 boneless, skinless chicken breasts
- ½ teaspoon garlic powder
- ½ teaspoon onion powder
- 1/2 teaspoon kosher salt
- 2 teaspoons olive oil
- 1 teaspoon paprika

- ¼ teaspoon black pepper

Instructions

- Cover the chicken breasts with a large sheet of plastic wrap on a chopping board. Lightly pound into an equal thickness with a rolling pin.
- Put the chicken on a plate & season with kosher salt all over. Refrigerate for at least half an hour or up to 1 day, uncovered.
- Remove the chicken from the refrigerator 15 minutes before air frying to allow it to come to room temperature.
- Combine the paprika, garlic powder, onion powder, & black pepper in a small bowl.
- Drizzle the olive oil over the chicken in a large mixing bowl. Over the top, sprinkle the spice mixture. Toss to coat the chicken, making sure the spices are uniformly distributed on both sides.
- Heat the air fryer to 375 degrees F (190 degrees C). Place the chicken in the air fryer with the smooth side down and cook for 6 minutes.
- Remove the air fryer basket and delicately flip the chicken over with tongs. Cook for another 2 to 8 minutes, or until the chicken reaches a 155 to 160 degrees F temperature.
- Transfer the chicken to a serving platter. Cover and set aside for 10 minutes to allow flavors to meld. Cut into slices and eat.

Air Fryer Basic Chicken Breasts

Preparation and Cooking Time

35 minutes

Servings

4 persons

Nutritional facts

260 calories ,11g fat ,2g fiber ,31g carbs ,2g protein

Ingredients

- 2 tablespoons butter, melted
- 1/4 teaspoon smoked paprika
- Quarter teaspoon black pepper
- 1/2 teaspoon salt
- Quarter teaspoon garlic powder
- 4 boneless skinless chicken breasts (6 oz. each)

Instructions

- Combine butter, salt, garlic powder, smoked paprika, and pepper in a small bowl. Brush the butter mixture on both sides of the chicken breasts.
- Place the chicken in the air fryer basket. Preheat oven to 350°F and bake for 15 minutes. Cook for another 5 to 8 minutes, or until the juices run clear when the thickest section of the chicken is cut at 165°F.

Fried Chicken KFC Copycat

Preparation and Cooking Time

12 hours 26 minutes

Servings

3 persons

Nutritional facts

1063 calories, 8g fat ,2g fiber ,17g carbs ,3g protein

Ingredients

- 10 chicken drumsticks or thighs
- Half teaspoon thyme
- One teaspoon dried mustard
- 4 teaspoons paprika

- 2 teaspoon garlic salt
- 1 teaspoon ground ginger
- 1/2 teaspoon basil
- 1/3 teaspoon oregano
- 1 teaspoon celery salt
- Teaspoon black pepper
- 1 cup Buttermilk
- 2 eggs
- 2 cups flour
- 2/3 teaspoon salt
- 3 teaspoons white pepper

Instructions

- Before beginning this dish, soak the chicken legs in buttermilk for 24 hours.
- In one bowl, whisk the eggs; in another, whisk together the flour and spices. The spices should be thoroughly mixed into the flour, and the eggs should be lightly beaten.
- Place a baking sheet on top of an oven-safe cooling rack.
- Remove the chicken from the buttermilk one piece at a time.
- Dredge each chicken leg in flour, then in eggs, and then back in the flour. Put the coated drumstick on a cooling rack and continue with the rest of the chicken.
- Preheat the Air Fryer at 390 degrees F.
- Place a Parchment round in the bottom of the air fryer to keep the chicken from sticking to the bottom.
- In a Ninja Foodie or Air Fryer, arrange the chicken in a single layer, so the pieces don't touch.
- It should be air-fried for thirteen minutes in the air fryer. Toss it over. You can spray with olive oil if any dry patches where the flour is visible. Continue to fry for another 13 minutes. Make sure the interior temperature is 165 degrees F. If not, cook for an additional 5 minutes at a time till done.

Air Fry skin-on Chicken Thighs

Preparation and Cooking Time

30 minutes

Servings

4 persons

Nutritional facts

213 calories, 20g fat ,1g fiber ,38g carbs ,6g protein

Ingredients

- 4 skin-on, chicken thighs (boneless)
- ½ teaspoon of salt
- ½ teaspoon of ground black pepper
- 2 teaspoons of extra-virgin olive oil
- 1 teaspoon of smoked paprika
- ¾ teaspoon of garlic powder

Instructions

- Preheat your air fryer to 400°F (200 degrees C).
- Brush the skin side of each piece of chicken thighs with olive oil after patting them dry with a paper towel. On a platter, arrange chicken thighs in a single layer, skin-side down.
- In a bowl, combine the garlic powder, salt, smoked paprika, and pepper; evenly sprinkle half of the seasoning mixture over the 4 chicken thighs. Turn the thighs over and uniformly coat them with the remaining spice mixture. Place skin-side up chicken thighs in a single layer in the air fryer basket.
- Cook until the chicken is golden brown and the fluids run clear, approximately 18 minutes in a preheated air fryer. At least 165 degrees F should be read on an instant-read thermometer put into the center (74 degrees C).

Juicy Air Fryer Fried Chicken

Preparation and Cooking Time

15 minutes

Servings

4 persons

Nutritional facts

380 calories, 8g fat ,1g fiber ,21g carbs ,2g protein

Ingredients

- 3 cups buttermilk
- 1 teaspoon onion powder
- Olive oil cooking spray
- 2 cups all-purpose flour
- 2 teaspoons paprika
- 6 garlic cloves, crushed and peeled
- Kosher salt and freshly ground black pepper
- 6 bone-in, skin-on chicken thighs (about 2 pounds)
- 6 chicken drumsticks (about 2 pounds)
- 1 teaspoon garlic powder

Instructions

- In a large re-sealable plastic bag or container, mix the buttermilk, garlic, 1 tablespoon salt, and 2 tablespoons pepper. Add the chicken pieces, close the bag, and chill for at least 1 hour or up to overnight, turning it once or twice.
- In a shallow bowl or dish, mix the flour, paprika, garlic powder, onion powder, 1 tbsp. salt, and 1 teaspoon pepper to cook the chicken. To blend, use a fork to stir everything together thoroughly. Toss the flour with 2 tbsp. of the buttermilk mixture from the bag to generate little lumps throughout.
- Remove the chicken from the marinade & set it aside. Preheat a 3.5-quart air fryer to 360 degrees F and coat the basket with olive oil cooking spray.
- Dredge 3 chicken thighs & 3 drumsticks in flour mixture, brushing off excess. Place the pieces' skin-side up in the preheated air-fryer basket without touching. Spray the chicken generously with cooking spray and air fry for about 27 minutes, or when the chicken is cooked, and the crust is crisp and golden. Halfway through, check on the chicken and spray any parts that look floury with extra cooking spray and then flip the drumsticks only.
- Remove the chicken from the air fryer when it is done & season lightly with salt. With the remaining chicken, repeat the dredging then air-frying operation. Before serving, reheat the first batch in an oven at 250 degrees F for 10 minutes.

Healthy Air Fryer Broccoli and Chicken "Stir Fry"

Preparation and Cooking Time

25 minutes

Servings

4 persons ,13g fat ,2g fiber ,31g carbs ,4g protein

Nutritional facts

224 calories

Ingredients

- 1 pound (454 g) boneless skinless chicken breast or thighs, cut into 1-inch bites sized pieces
- 2 teaspoons (10 ml) hot sauce (optional)
- 1/2 teaspoon sea salt, or to taste

- black pepper, to taste
- 1 Tablespoon (15 ml) fresh minced ginger
- 1 Tablespoon (15 ml) low sodium soy sauce, or to taste (use Tamari for Gluten Free)
- 1 Tablespoon (15 ml) rice vinegar (use distilled white vinegar for Gluten Free)
- 1 teaspoon (5 ml) sesame oil
- 1/4-1/2 pound (113-226 g) broccoli, cut into florets (1-2 cups)
- 1/2 medium onion, sliced thick
- 3 Tablespoons (45 ml) olive oil or grape seed oil
- 1/2 teaspoon (2.5 ml) garlic powder
- serve with lemon wedges, optional

Instructions
- Combine the oil, garlic powder, ginger, soy sauce, rice vinegar, sesame oil, optional spicy sauce, salt, and pepper in a large mixing bowl.
- Put the chicken in a separate bowl. In a separate bowl, combine the broccoli and onions. Divide the marinade between the two bowls and toss to coat each evenly.
- Fill the air fryer basket/tray with only the chicken. Then air fry for 10 minutes at 380°F/195°C. Combine the broccoli & onions with the chicken in a mixing bowl. Continue to Air Fry for another 8-10 minutes at 380°F/195°C, just until the chicken is cooked through. Stir halfway during cooking to ensure that the broccoli is uniformly cooked.
- Then season with salt and pepper to taste. Serve warm with a squeeze of fresh lemon juice on top if desired.

Air Fryer Paprika Chicken

Preparation and Cooking Time
25 minutes

Servings
6 persons

Nutritional facts
222 calories ,10g fat ,1g fiber ,28g carbs ,4g protein

Ingredients
- 6 bone-in, skin-on chicken thighs
- 1/2 teaspoon ground onion powder
- 1/2 teaspoon kosher salt
- 2 cloves garlic, minced
- 3 teaspoons ground paprika
- 1 teaspoon ground oregano
- 1/4 teaspoon ground black pepper

Instructions
- Preheat the air fryer for 5 minutes at 380°F. Spray with cooking spray after preheating.
- Mix the garlic, paprika, oregano, onion powder, salt, and pepper in a small bowl until well blended. Add the chicken thighs to a large mixing bowl, followed by the spice mix. Toss the chicken until it is well coated.
- Place the chicken thighs skin-side down in the air fryer and cook for 10 minutes at 380°F.
- Cook for another 10 to 12 minutes with the skin side up on the chicken thighs. When an internal meat thermometer registers 165°F, the chicken is done.

Air Fryer Tandoori Chicken

Preparation and Cooking Time
30 minutes

Servings
3 persons

Nutritional facts
110 calories ,12g fat ,1g fiber ,20g carbs ,2.3g protein

Ingredients
- 6 chicken drumsticks
- ½ teaspoon of ground turmeric
- 1 tablespoon of dried fenugreek leaves Kasoori methi
- 1 tablespoon of lemon juice
- 1 teaspoon of garam masala
- ⅓ cup of plain yogurt
- 1 tablespoon of ginger paste
- 1 tablespoon of garlic paste
- 1 tablespoon of Kashmiri red chili powder
- 1½ teaspoons of kosher salt
- cooking oil spray

Instructions
- Using a paper towel, pat-dry your chicken drumsticks. Pick up one drumstick with two paper towels & pull its skin down from the thickest part of the chicken to the narrow end, removing the skin. Repeat with the rest of the chicken drumsticks. Paper towels will assist you in gripping the skin and effortlessly removing it.
- Make 3-4 slits in each drumstick's thick section.
- Combine the yogurt, ginger, garlic, red chili powder, turmeric, garam masala, & salt in a large mixing bowl. Put the dried fenugreek leaves in the palms of your hands and rub them together gently to smash them. Toss with the chicken. Mix in the lemon juice, then coat the chicken in the marinade.
- Allow for at least 20 minutes of marinating time, or marinate for up to 24 hours in the refrigerator.
- Heat the air fryer to 350 degrees Fahrenheit. Cooking oil should be lightly sprayed on the air fryer basket. Spray the marinated chicken with oil and place it in the basket.
- Air fry for 15 minutes at 350°F. Shake the basket halfway through and lightly oil it.
- Check the internal temperature of the thickest portion once the cooking cycle has finished ensuring it is at 165°F. Continue to cook the chicken for another minute or two for charred markings, but be careful not to overcook it.
- Serve with cilantro mint chutney and fresh lemon wedges. For a wonderful low-carb meal, serve it with the crunchy cucumber salad.

Air-Fryer Southern-Style Chicken

Preparation and Cooking Time
15 minutes

Servings
6 persons

Nutritional facts
410 calories ,17g fat ,1g fiber ,28g carbs ,2g protein

Ingredients
- 2 cups crushed Ritz crackers (about 50)
- 1/4 teaspoon ground cumin
- 1/4 teaspoon rubbed sage
- 1 large egg, beaten

- 1 tablespoon minced fresh parsley
- 1 teaspoon garlic salt
- 1 teaspoon paprika
- 1/2 teaspoon pepper
- 1 broiler/fryer chicken (3 to 4 pounds), cut up
- Cooking spray

Instructions

- Preheat the air fryer to 375 degrees F. Combine the required ingredients in a small bowl. In a separate shallow bowl, crack the egg. Dip the chicken in the egg, then in the cracker mixture, patting it down to help the coating stick. Place chicken in a single layer on a greased tray in the air-fryer basket in batches, spritzed with cooking spray.
- Cook for ten minutes. Cook, turning chicken once more and spritzing with cooking spray, until golden brown and juices running clear, 10-twenty minutes more.

Air Fryer Roast Chicken

Preparation and Cooking Time

35 minutes

Servings

2 persons

Nutritional facts

140 calories, 20g fat ,2g fiber ,31g carbs ,4g protein

Ingredients

- Four-pound whole chicken
- Ingredients for dry rub recipe

Instructions

- Clean chicken & pat dry.
- Sprinkle liberally with a dry rub.
- Spray air fry basket with cooking spray & put the chicken into the basket.
- Roast chicken for 330 degrees Fahrenheit for a minimum of 30 minutes.
- Flip chicken.
- Roast for another 20 minutes at 330 degrees Fahrenheit to get it fully cooked.

Air Fryer Chicken Breast Cutlets

Preparation and Cooking Time

20 minutes

Servings

6 persons

Nutritional facts

363 calories, 21g fat ,3g fiber ,34g carbs ,5g protein

Ingredients

- 1.5 pounds' chicken breast butterflied
- 1/2 tsp. onion powder divided
- 1/2 tsp. pepper divided
- 2 cups panko bread crumbs or make your own
- 1 egg
- 1/2 cup Kodiak Cakes Flapjack Mix
- 1/2 tsp. salt divided
- 3/4 tsp. paprika divided
- Quarter cup parmesan cheese

Instructions

- Preheat the Air Fryer to 390°F before beginning to cook the air fryer chicken breast. Using an olive oil spray, coat the roasting pan.
- Remove any excess fat from the chicken breasts. Butterfly or pound chicken breasts to a thickness of no more than 1/4 inch. This is a crucial step in ensuring that the chicken cooks fully.
- Breadcrumbs & Kodiak cake mix should be separated into two bowls. Spices should be equally distributed among the breadcrumbs & Kodiak cake mix. Toss the breadcrumb bowl with parmesan cheese. Scramble the egg in the third bowl with a fork. Arrange the bowls in the following order: Kodiak Cakes mix, egg, breadcrumbs.
- Dredge the chicken in the pancake mix, then dip it in the eggs and coat it. On all sides, coat with the breadcrumb mixture.
- Cook the chicken in an air fryer basket at 390°F for 4 minutes. Cook for another 2-4 minutes, depending on the thickness of the chicken. The internal temperature of the chicken should be 165 degrees Fahrenheit, which may be checked with a meat thermometer. Cook until it's all done.

Air Fryer Boneless Chicken Breast – Basic and Crispy Breaded Recipe

Preparation and Cooking Time

20 minutes

Servings

2 persons

Nutritional facts

123 calories ,12g fat ,2g fiber ,32g carbs ,4g protein

Ingredients

- 2 boneless skinless chicken breast halves
- 1/4 tsp. freshly ground black pepper
- 1/4 tsp. garlic powder
- 1 TBS extra virgin olive oil
- 1/4 tsp. sea salt
- 1/4 tsp. dried oregano

Instructions

- Combine the oil, salt, pepper, garlic powder, & oregano in a small bowl. Set aside chicken breasts that have been brushed with the oil mixture on both sides.
- Preheat the air fryer for 3 - 4 minutes @ 350°F.
- Place the chicken breasts on the basket in the air fryer. Cook for an additional 8 minutes. Cook for an additional 5 to 7 minutes on the other side, or when the internal temperature reaches 165°F.
- Allow the chicken to rest for at least 3 minutes on a clean cutting board. Using a knife, cut the breasts into 1/2-inch thick slices. Serve with a side dish of your choice. It's a fantastic idea to serve mashed potatoes with sautéed spinach.

Crispy Boneless Chicken Breasts

Preparation and Cooking Time

20 minutes

Servings

2 persons

Nutritional facts

147 calories ,13g fat ,2g fiber ,26g carbs ,6g protein

Ingredients

- 2 boneless skinless chicken breast halves
- 2 tsp. Italian seasoning
- 1/4 tsp. sea salt

- 1 TBS extra virgin olive oil
- 1/3 cup panko breadcrumbs (can be gluten-free)
- 1/4 cup grated parmesan cheese
- 1/4 tsp. freshly ground pepper

Instructions

- Preheat the air fryer for 3 - 4 minutes at 350°F.
- Combine the breadcrumbs, cheese, spices, salt, and pepper in a large mixing bowl or baking dish. Brush the chicken breasts with oil on both sides. Coat each with the breadcrumb mixture, pushing it into the meat to ensure it sticks.
- Place the chicken breasts on the grill plate in the air fryer. Cook for an additional 8 minutes. Cook for another 5 to 7 minutes on the other side.
- Cut the breasts into half-inch-thick slices. Serve with a side dish of your choice.

The Best Mediterranean Air Fryer Chicken

Preparation and Cooking Time

35 minutes

Servings

4 persons

Nutritional facts

278 calories ,9g fat ,1g fiber ,11g carbs ,1g protein

Ingredients

- 4 chicken quarters bone-in skin on
- 1 tablespoon of granulated garlic
- 1/4 teaspoon of crushed red pepper flakes, optional
- 1 tablespoon of ground coriander
- 1 tablespoon of dried oregano
- 1 tablespoon of sumac
- 2 tablespoons vinegar or lemon juice
- 1 teaspoon of salt
- black pepper to taste
- 1 tablespoon of ground cumin
- 1/4 cup of all-purpose flourr

Instructions

- The chicken quarters should be washed and dried fully.
- Place the chicken in a tray with 3-4 slits cut into it.
- Toss with a little lemon juice or vinegar to coat.
- Season the chicken with salt, herbs, and spices before sprinkling it with flour.
- Combine the chicken and toss it together.
- Preheat the air fryer to 400°F and put the seasoned chicken parts in the basket.
- Cook for 20 minutes, then flip and cook for another 8 minutes until the chicken is crispy.
- Serve with tzatziki and salad.

Air Fryer Spicy Chicken Thighs

Preparation and Cooking Time

27 minutes

Servings

4 persons

Nutritional facts

354 calories, 11g fat ,1g fiber ,24g carbs ,2g protein

Ingredients

- 4 bone-in chicken thighs (or 6-8 boneless, skinless chicken thighs)
- ½ teaspoon onion powder
- ½ teaspoon salt
- 1 tablespoon olive oil
- 1 teaspoon paprika
- 1 teaspoon dried oregano
- 1 teaspoon garlic powder
- ⅙ teaspoon pepper

Instructions

- Preheat the air fryer to 400 degrees Fahrenheit for 5 minutes.
- Dry the chicken thighs with a paper towel. Olive oil should be rubbed on them.
- Combine the seasonings in a small bowl: dried oregano, paprika, onion powder, salt, garlic powder, and pepper. Then season chicken thighs with spices.
- In the air fryer, cook the chicken in a single layer. Cook chicken thighs in the air fryer for 12 minutes at about 400° F, skin side down. Cook for 7-12 minutes on the second side, or until the internal temperature reaches 165° F.

30-minute Bang Bang Chicken Recipe in Air Fryer

Preparation and Cooking Time

30 minutes

Servings

4 persons

Nutritional facts

601 calories, 8g fat ,2g fiber ,18g carbs ,3g protein

Ingredients

- 1/2 cup mayonnaise
- 1/2 cup cornstarch
- 1 egg
- 1 teaspoon sriracha sauce or to taste
- salt & pepper to taste
- 2 tablespoons raw honey
- 1/2 tablespoon sriracha sauce or to taste
- 1 cup buttermilk
- 2/3 cup all-purpose flour more if needed
- 1 lb. boneless & skinless chicken breast or chicken thighs - cut into bite-size pieces
- 1 cup Panko bread crumbs
- oil of your choice for greasing air fryer

Instructions

- In a mixing bowl, combine all of the ingredients for the bang-bang chicken sauce. Whisk everything together until it's completely smooth.
- To prepare bang bang chicken in an air fryer, combine buttermilk, flour, corn Starch, egg, sriracha sauce, salt, and pepper in a buttermilk batter. Then mix everything until its smooth.
- Before adding the chicken, grease the Air Fryer with any oil of your choice. Working in batches, coat the chicken pieces with buttermilk batter and breadcrumbs before placing them in the Air Fryer. Cook at 375°F for 8-10 minutes, or till chicken is thoroughly done.
- Once the chicken pieces have been flipped, repeat the process. (Make sure the chicken pieces aren't crammed into the air fryer.)

- Drizzle the sauce over the chicken & serve with leafy greens or Fried Rice with Green Onion and Eggs.

The Best Air Fryer Whole Chicken

Preparation and Cooking Time

50 minutes

Servings

6 persons

Nutritional facts

425 calories, 19g fat, 3g fiber, 10g carbs, 20g protein

Ingredients

- 1 whole chicken
- One tbsp. dry rub
- salt
- cooking spray or olive oil

Instructions

- Preheat the air fryer to 180 degrees Celsius (350 degrees Fahrenheit).
- Dry the chicken with a paper towel. Rub in the dry rub and, if desired, season with salt.
- Coat the air fryer in cooking spray.
- Cook for 30 minutes on one side after adding the chicken.
- Then based on the size of your chicken, flip it and cook for another 15-30 minutes.
- Before serving, make sure the chicken is at least 75 degrees Celsius (165 degrees Fahrenheit)

Easy Air Fryer Chicken and Potatoes Dinner

Preparation and Cooking Time

25 minutes

Servings

4 persons

Nutritional facts

452 calories, 6g fat ,1g fiber ,16g carbs ,2g protein

Ingredients

- 2 ½ teaspoons Italian seasoning
- 2 ½ tablespoons of olive oil
- 2 lbs. of potatoes cut into 1-inch cubes
- 2 teaspoons of smoked paprika
- Garlic salt to taste
- 1 ½ lbs. of chicken breast cut into 1-inch cubes

Instructions

- Preheat the Air Fryer to 380 degrees Fahrenheit (190 degrees Celsius).
- Combine smoked paprika, Italian seasoning, garlic salt, and oil in a small mixing bowl.
- In a mixing dish, combine the cubed potatoes with half of the seasoned oil & toss to coat.
- Toss the cubed chicken in a mixing bowl with half of the seasoned oil and toss to coat.
- Cook for 10 minutes with the potatoes in the air fryer basket, shaking it halfway through.
- Cook for 10 to 12 minutes after mixing in the chicken shake.

Air Fryer Chicken Breast

Preparation and Cooking Time

23 minutes

Servings

2 persons

Nutritional facts

130 calories ,15g fat ,2g fiber ,31g carbs ,4g protein

Ingredients

- 2 boneless, skinless chicken breasts 6-8oz each
- 2 tbsp. of brown sugar
- ½ tsp. of ground black pepper
- 1 tsp. of salt
- 1 tsp. of dry crushed rosemary
- 3 tbsp. of olive oil
- 3 tbsp. of balsamic vinegar
- 2 tbsp. of soy sauce
- 1 tsp. of lemon juice
- ½ tsp. of garlic powder
- ½ tsp. of onion powder

Instructions

- In a shallow baking dish, whisk together all of the ingredients except the chicken.
- Add the chicken and toss it in the mixture until it's completely covered. Allow for at least thirty minutes of marinating time. Two hours is preferable; overnight is ideal.
- Preheat the air fryer for 5 minutes at 360 degrees F.
- Place chicken breasts in the air fryer and cook for 18 minutes at 360 degrees F, flipping after 10 minutes.
- Remove the chicken and set it aside on a cutting board to rest for 5 minutes prior to slicing.

Air Fryer Juicy Southern Fried Chicken

Preparation and Cooking Time

40 minutes

Servings

6 persons

Nutritional facts

380 calories, 8g fat ,1g fiber ,23g carbs ,2g protein

Ingredients

- 2 lbs. chicken
- 1 tablespoon hot sauce
- 2 tablespoons milk or buttermilk
- 1/4 cup water
- 1 teaspoon onion powder
- 1 teaspoon Italian Seasoning
- 1 cup self-rising flour
- 2 teaspoons sea salt
- 1 1/2 teaspoons black pepper
- 1 1/2 teaspoons garlic powder
- 1 1/2 teaspoons paprika
- 1/4 cup cornstarch
- 2 eggs room temperature
- olive oil

Instructions

- Set aside the chicken once it has been washed and dried.

- Combine the seasonings in a mixing bowl.
- Using roughly a tbsp. of the spice mixture, generously coat the chicken.
- Combine flour, cornstarch, and the remaining spice mix in a gallon-size plastic bag.
- Combine eggs, spicy sauce, milk, & water in a large mixing bowl.
- Lightly coat the chicken in the flour mixture, brushing off any excess.
- Put on a tray to allow part of the flour to absorb some of the liquid.
- Use the egg mixture to coat the chicken (shaking off excess).
- Immediately dredge the chicken in the flour mixture and shake off any excess.
- Allow the chicken to rest for about fifteen minutes to absorb some of the flour.
- Use an oil mister or a brush to lightly cover the chicken in olive oil (all over).
- Place the chicken in a greased Air Fryer basket with enough room for air to circulate around it.
- According to the air fryer's instructions, cook, flip halfway and sprinkle lightly with extra oil (if necessary) until no flour is visible, around 18 minutes.
- Remove the chicken and set it aside to rest for around 5 minutes.

Air Fryer Chicken Nuggets

Preparation and Cooking Time

23 minutes

Servings

4 persons

Nutritional facts

299 calories, 9g fat ,5g fiber ,40g carbs ,9g protein

Ingredients

- 1-pound boneless, skinless chicken breasts, cut into 1½-inch pieces (approximately 2 chicken breasts)
- 2 teaspoons garlic, minced
- ¼ cup parsley, finely diced
- ½ teaspoon paprika
- 2 cups panko breading
- 4 tablespoons Challenge Butter, melted
- 2 tablespoons lemon juice
- 2 tablespoons olive oil
- 1 teaspoon salt
- 1 teaspoon garlic powder
- ½ teaspoon onion powder
- ¼ teaspoons salt

Instructions

- Preheat the air fryer to 400 degrees Fahrenheit.
- Mix the chicken, oil, salt, garlic powder, onion powder, & paprika in a large mixing bowl. Toss everything together until it's uniformly coated. Toss in the panko crumbs & toss again to coat.
- Arrange the chicken in a single, equal layer in the air fryer basket.
- Fry the chicken for 8 minutes, flipping halfway through. Place the chicken in a large mixing bowl and put it aside. While you're making the butter sauce coating, tent it with aluminum foil to keep it warm.

- Melt the butter and add lemon juice, garlic, parsley, & salt to a medium mixing bowl. Pour the sauce over the chicken, making sure it is evenly distributed. Return to the air fryer for another 5 minutes of cooking.
- Serve warm with a dipping sauce of your choice.

15 Minute Crispy Air-Fryer Breaded Chicken Breast

Preparation and Cooking Time

16 minutes

Servings

4 persons

Nutritional facts

110 calories, 7g fat ,3g fiber ,22g carbs ,5g protein

Ingredients

- 2 skinless, boneless chicken breasts (about 4–5 ounces each)
- Lemon
- Parsley
- 2 cups seasoned parmesan breadcrumbs – or make your own, see notes below
- 2 large eggs
- Salt and pepper
- Shredded parmesan cheese – for topping
- Red pepper flakes
- Hot sauce

Instructions

- Start with preparing the chicken. After patting the chicken dry with a clean paper towel, cut in half lengthwise. With a sharp kitchen knife, this is simple to accomplish.
- Prepare the coating mix. In a medium shallow bowl, crack the eggs, season with salt and pepper, and whisk lightly till the yolks are broken down as well as the mixture is bright yellow. Pour the breadcrumbs into a separate shallow bowl and season with 1/4 cup shredded parmesan cheese as well as some dried parsley, which is optional but will give the chicken more flavor.
- Coat the chicken breasts. Dredge each piece of chicken in the egg mixture, then in the breadcrumbs, pushing the breadcrumbs into the chicken to cover it completely. On a clean platter, arrange the breaded chicken breasts.
- Cook in an air fryer that has been preheated. Preheat the oven to 390 degrees Fahrenheit. Spray the basket with olive oil spray once it's finished. Spray each piece of chicken liberally as well. Put two pieces of chicken in the air fryer basket at a time. Close the air fryer basket and cook for 11 minutes, rotating the chicken midway through the cooking period. Continue cooking the chicken until it is completely done.
- Cut into slices. After the chicken has rested for a few minutes, season it with salt, pepper, and a squeeze of lemon for added flavor. Serve it with your favorite salad or nutritious side dish.

Crispy Chicken Parmesan

Preparation and Cooking Time

55 minutes

Servings

4 persons

Nutritional facts

427 calories, 9g fat ,2g fiber ,30g carbs ,4g protein

Ingredients

- 4 boneless, skinless chicken breasts (4 ounces each)
- 1 cup whole-wheat panko breadcrumbs

- Cooking spray
- ½ cup reduced-sodium marinara sauce
- ¼ teaspoon salt
- 1 large egg, lightly beaten
- 1 tablespoon water
- ½ cup all-purpose flour
- 1 teaspoon dried Italian seasoning
- 6 ounces' fresh mozzarella cheese, cut into 4 slices
- 2 tablespoons thinly sliced fresh basil

Instructions

- Pound the chicken between two pieces of plastic wrap. It should be pounded to a thickness of 1/2 inch. Season the chicken well with salt. In a shallow bowl, whisk together the egg and the water. Put flour in a separate small bowl; in a third small bowl, put panko. Dredge the chicken in the flour, one breast at a time, shaking off the excess.
- Allow excess to drop off after dipping in the egg wash. Dredge in the panko and press to coat evenly. On a platter, arrange the breaded chicken.
- Line an air fryer basket with foil and spray it with cooking spray. Put 2 breaded chicken breasts in the prepared basket, 1 inch apart; gently cover the tops of the chicken with cooking spray. Cook for 7 minutes at 360°F. Cook for another 7 minutes, or until the chicken is golden brown on both sides. Drizzle two tablespoons of marinara sauce on top of each chicken breast, plus 1/4 teaspoon Italian seasoning, 1 mozzarella slice on top of each. Cook for about 5 minutes, just until the cheese is completely melted, as well as a thermometer put into the thickest part of the chicken reads 165°F. Remove the foil and chicken from the basket; keep warm by covering with another piece of foil. Carry on with the remaining two chicken breasts in the same manner.
- Basil should be evenly distributed over the cooked chicken. Serve immediately.

Juicy and Crispy Air Fryer Whole Chicken

Preparation and Cooking Time

63 minutes

Servings

6 persons

Nutritional facts

355 calories, 22g fat ,2g fiber ,65g carbs ,16g protein

Ingredients

- One 5lb. whole chicken, giblets removed
- Two tablespoons poultry seasoning

Instructions

- Dry the chicken with paper towels on a clean surface. Take out the giblets from the cavity.
- Season the chicken all over with the spice.
- Place the chicken in the air fryer, breast-side down. Preheat oven to 350 degrees Fahrenheit.
- Set the timer for 50 minutes in the air fryer. Cook for another 10 minutes on the opposite side, or until the internal temperature reaches 165 degrees F.
- Remove and set aside for 10 minutes before serving.

Tender Air Fryer Chicken

Preparation and Cooking Time

8 hours 20 minutes

Servings

4 persons

Nutritional facts

380 calories, 22g fat ,2g fiber ,65g carbs ,16g protein

Ingredients

- 1 1/2 tbsp. whole-grain mustard
- 1 1/2 tbsp. canola oil
- 4 bone-in chicken thighs
- 1 tbsp. smoked paprika
- 1 1/2 tsp. dried rosemary
- 1 lemon, zested and juiced
- Kosher salt and freshly ground black pepper

Instructions

- Mix paprika, lemon zest and juice, mustard, rosemary, & oil in a mixing bowl. To blend, stir everything together.
- Toss in the chicken until it is all covered. Refrigerate for four hours, but preferably for 8 to 12 hours after covering.
- Preheat the air fryer for 2-3 minutes @ 400°F. Remove the chicken from the bowl and drain any excess marinade. Put in the air fryer basket, giving an area for air to circulate each item. Cook, flipping halfway through, for about 18 minutes, or until an instant-read thermometer reads 160°F-165°F.
- Cover thighs loosely with aluminum foil and set aside for 5 minutes to complete cooking and absorb juices. Serve with rice or a simple salad as a side dish.

Chef's Special Air Fryer Southern-Fried Chicken

Preparation and Cooking Time

120 minutes

Servings

4 persons

Nutritional facts

432 calories, 24g fat ,0g fiber ,10g carbs ,12g protein

Ingredients

- 2 1/2 teaspoons paprika
- 3/4 cup buttermilk
- 4 boneless skinless chicken breasts (about 1 1/2 lb. total)
- 1 teaspoon salt
- 1 teaspoon garlic powder
- 1 teaspoon onion powder
- 1/2 teaspoon pepper
- 3/4 cup Gold Medal™ All-Purpose Flour
- Cooking spray

Instructions

- Combine the ingredients for the Seasoning Mix in a small bowl.
- Combine buttermilk and 1 tbsp. of the seasoning mix in a small bowl. Crosswise cut the chicken breasts in half and add to the buttermilk mixture. Coat on the other side. Cover and chill for 1 hour.
- Cut an 8-inch round of cooking parchment paper in the meantime. Place in the air fryer basket's bottom, and cooking spray should be used.
- Combine flour and the remaining 1 tbsp. seasoning mix in a shallow bowl. Remove 4 pieces of chicken from marinade and dredge in flour mixture, keeping the remaining chicken refrigerated.
- In an air fryer basket, place the coated chicken on parchment paper.
- Preheat oven to 325°F and bake for 10 minutes. Cook for another 8 to 12 minutes or till chicken is cooked through. Turn

chicken and sprinkle tops with extra cooking spray. Repeat with the remaining chicken, tossing out any leftover marinade & flour mixture.

Gluten free Chicken Breast

Preparation and Cooking Time

25 minutes

Servings

4 persons

Nutritional facts

170 calories, 2g fat ,3g fiber ,6 carbs ,14g protein

Ingredients

- 2 large chicken breasts
- 1/2 tsp. of Cayenne Pepper (optional)
- 1 tsp. of Herbs de Provence, optional
- 1 tsp. of Garlic Powder
- 1/2 tsp. of Sea Salt
- 1/4 tsp. of Ground Black Pepper
- 1/2 tsp. of Red Crushed Pepper (optional)
- 2 tbsp. of olive oil
- 1 cup of dried breadcrumbs
- 1 tsp. of Paprika
- 1 tsp. of Chili Powder
- 1/2 cup of Parmesan Cheese (optional)

Instructions

- In a medium-sized mixing bowl, mix the breadcrumbs and seasonings.
- To get thinner chicken breasts, cut the chicken in half. To make chicken tenders, chop the chicken breast into cutlet-sized pieces.
- Coat the chicken breast in olive oil, then press it into the breadcrumb mixture until it is uniformly coated on both sides.
- Preheat the air fryer for 5 minutes at 400°F.
- In the air fry basket, place the chicken breasts. Assemble the chicken in a single layer, leaving some space between each piece. If necessary, work in batches. Cook each side for 7-8 minutes.
- Slice the chicken in the middle to show white, completely cooked meat to test doneness. Alternatively, insert an instant thermometer into the thickest section of the chicken breasts. If it's done, the temperature should be at least 165°F.)

Crispy Air-Fryer Lemongrass Chicken

Preparation and Cooking Time

40 minutes

Servings

4 persons

Nutritional facts

183 calories, 16g fat ,0.2g fiber ,6g carbs ,11g protein

Ingredients

- 4 chicken Maryland pieces
- 2 lemongrass stalks, bruised, pale part finely chopped
- 3cm piece ginger, peeled, chopped
- 2cm piece galangal, peeled, chopped
- 2 garlic cloves, roughly chopped
- 1 tsp. ground turmeric
- 2 red shallots, chopped

- 1 tsp. sea salt
- 1/3 cup corn flour (cornstarch)
- vegetable oil or olive oil spray
- steamed rice, to serve
- sweet chili sauce, to serve
- 1 tsp. ground cumin

Instructions

- Place the lemongrass, shallots, and salt in a mortar to make the lemongrass paste. Pound to a medium-coarse paste with a pestle. Add the ginger & pound until it forms a paste. Pound in the galangal. Then pound in the garlic until it becomes a paste. Combine the turmeric & cumin in a mixing bowl.
- To separate the leg from the thigh, cut the Marylands in half. Place in a mixing bowl. Toss in the lemongrass paste with tongs to mix. Cover and marinate for 2-3 hours in the fridge.
- Toss the chicken mixture with the corn flour to combine.
- An air fryer's basket should be sprayed with oil. Place the chicken thighs skin-side down in the air fryer (leave enough space between the pieces to allow for air circulation). Cook for half an hour at 200°C/390°F, turning a few times & drizzling with more oil if necessary, till crisp and tender.
- With steamed rice and sweet chili sauce, serve the chicken.

Air Fryer Orange Chicken

Preparation and Cooking Time

30 minutes

Servings

4 persons

Nutritional facts

380 calories, 43g fat ,2g fiber ,9g carbs ,32 protein

Ingredients

- 1.5 lbs. raw boneless, skinless chicken breast
- 2 1/2 tbsp. honey
- 1 tbsp. water
- 1/4 tsp. red pepper flakes
- 1 tsp. minced ginger
- 1 tbsp. cornstarch
- 2 tbsp. rice wine vinegar
- 2 tbsp. oyster sauce
- 1 large egg, whisked
- 2/3 cup cornstarch or potato starch (see blog notes)
- 1/3 cup freshly squeezed orange juice, from about 2 medium oranges
- 4 garlic cloves, minced
- 3 tbsp. soy sauce or tamari

Instructions

- Preheat the air fryer to 375 degrees Fahrenheit.
- Chicken should be cut into 1-inch cubes. Mix in the whisked egg until the chicken is completely coated.
- Place the cornstarch in a big plastic bag. Remove the chicken pieces from the egg mixture with tongs, let excess egg drop off, and place them in the bag.
- Close the bag & shake the chicken pieces until they are completely coated in cornstarch. Remove the pieces from the bag and lay them on the chopping board to cut up the chicken.
- Spray the side of the chicken that faces up liberally with cooking spray. Place the chicken in the air fryer basket, sprayed side down. Spray the chicken on all sides, starting with the side facing up.

- Cook for 10-15 minutes in an air fryer at 375°F, or till chicken is nicely browned & cooked through.
- In a medium-sized skillet, prepare the sauce while the chicken cooks. Whisk together the sauce ingredients and constantly cook over medium heat until the sauce thickens about 5 minutes.
- Serve immediately after tossing the cooked chicken with the sauce.

Air fryer chicken schnitzel

Preparation and Cooking Time

28 minutes

Servings

4 persons

Nutritional facts

443 calories, 4g fat ,3g fiber ,14g carbs ,9 protein

Ingredients

- 4 x 180g chicken breast fillets
- 50g (1/3 cup) plain flour
- Olive oil spray
- 100g (2 cups) panko breadcrumbs
- 20g (1/4 cup) finely grated parmesan cheese
- 1 egg, lightly whisked
- 2 tbsp. milk
- Lemon wedges, to serve

Instructions

- Place a chicken breast between two cling wrap sheets. Pound it out with a mallet or a rolling pin until it is 2cm thick. Repeat with the rest of the chicken.
- In a medium mixing bowl, combine the breadcrumbs and parmesan cheese. In a separate medium dish, whisk together the egg and milk. Season the flour and spread it out on a platter.
- Shake off the excess flour after dipping the chicken in it. Dip in the egg, coat in the breadcrumb mixture, and press down firmly. Place on a serving tray. Refrigerate for 15 minutes after covering.
- Preheat the air fryer for 3 minutes at 200°C. Using an olive oil spray, coat the chicken. Place half of the chicken in the air fryer basket in a single layer. Preheat the oven to 350°F and set the timer for 12 minutes. Cook till golden and cooked through, rotating halfway through. To keep warm, transfer to a platter and cover with foil. Carry on with the rest of the chicken.
- Lemon wedges should be served alongside the schnitzel.

Air Fryer Cilantro Lime Chicken Tenders

Preparation and Cooking Time

22 hours 30 minutes

Servings

10 persons

Nutritional facts

130 calories, 15g fat ,4g fiber ,26g carbs ,19g protein

Ingredients

- 2.5 lbs. chicken tenderloins 1104 g
- 5 frozen cubes garlic or fresh cloves, minced
- 2 tsp. chili powder
- 2 tsp. ground cumin
- ¼ cup lime juice 60 g
- 1 Tbsp. olive oil 15 g
- 1 Tbsp. honey 15 g

- ¼ cup cilantro minced (20 g)
- 1 tsp. onion powder
- ½ tsp. kosher salt
- Kosher salt and pepper to taste

Instructions

- Trim any visible tendon or strange stuff from the tenderloins and put them in a large resealable bag.
- To make the marinade, combine the remaining ingredients. Pour it over the chicken and let it sit for 30 to 2 hours to marinate.
- Preheat the air fryer to 400 degrees Fahrenheit for 2-3 minutes. Sprinkle a healthy pinch of kosher salt, and a couple cracked of pepper on the chicken just before cooking. Put tenderloins in a single layer in the air fryer basket after spraying it with olive oil. Cook for ten minutes or until the internal temperature reaches 165°F. Alternatively, you can grill for 2-3 minutes per side on medium-high heat.

Five Spice Perfect Chicken

Preparation and Cooking Time

15 minutes

Servings

2 persons

Nutritional facts

210 calories ,8g fat ,2g fiber ,13g carbs ,8g protein

Ingredients

- 2 boneless chicken breasts
- 1/2 teaspoon of Italian seasoning
- 1/2 teaspoon of salt
- 2 teaspoons of paprika
- 1/2 teaspoon of smoked paprika
- 1/2 teaspoon of onion powder
- 1 teaspoon of garlic powder
- 1/4 teaspoon of black pepper
- olive oil

Instructions

- Preheat the air fryer to 390 degrees Fahrenheit.
- In a small mixing bowl, mix the smoked paprika, paprika, onion powder, garlic powder, Italian seasoning, salt, & black pepper. Apply olive oil to both sides of the chicken, then season with salt and pepper.
- Cook the chicken breasts in your air fryer at 390° F for about 12 minutes, flipping halfway through.
- Serve the chicken with a salad, couscous, or broccoli after removing it from the air fryer basket.

Tso's Chicken

Preparation and Cooking Time

35 minutes

Servings

4 persons

Nutritional facts

302 calories ,9g fat ,1g fiber ,2g carbs ,5g protein

Ingredients

- 1 large egg
- 7 tablespoons lower-sodium chicken broth
- 1 tablespoon finely chopped fresh ginger
- 1 tablespoon finely chopped garlic

- 2 tablespoons thinly sliced green onion, divided
- 1 teaspoon toasted sesame oil
- 2 tablespoons lower-sodium soy sauce
- 2 tablespoons ketchup
- 2 teaspoons sugar
- 2 teaspoons unseasoned rice vinegar
- 1 1/2 tablespoons canola oil
- 1 pound boneless, skinless chicken thighs, patted dry and cut into1 to 1 1/4-inch chunk
- 1/3 cup plus 2 tsp. cornstarch, divided
- 1/4 teaspoon kosher salt
- 1/4 teaspoon ground white pepper
- 3 to 4 chilies de árbol, chopped and seeds discarded
- 1/2 teaspoon toasted sesame seeds

Instructions

- In a large mixing bowl, beat the egg, add the chicken and coat well. Combine 1/3 cup cornstarch, salt, and pepper in a separate bowl. Transfer the chicken to the cornstarch mixture with a fork, and toss with a spatula to coat each piece.
- Move chicken to fryer basket in batches, leaving a little space between pieces. Preheat the air fryer for 3 minutes at 400°F. Put the battered chicken and simmer for 12 - 18 minutes, shaking halfway through. Allow three to five minutes for drying. Cook for another 1 to 2 minutes if the chicken is still wet on one side.
- Combine the remaining 2 tablespoons of cornstarch, broth, soy sauce, ketchup, sugar, & rice vinegar in a large mixing bowl. Heat the canola oil and chilies in a large skillet over medium heat. When the pan is gently sizzling, insert the garlic and ginger and simmer for 30 seconds, or until fragrant.
- Re-whisk the cornstarch mixture and mix it into the skillet mixture. Raise the temperature to medium-high. Add the chicken when the sauce starts to bubble. Cook, constantly stirring, until the sauce thickens and sticks to the chicken, approximately 1 1/2 minutes. Remove from heat and mix in 1 tbsp. green onion as well as sesame oil. Serve with sesame seeds and the remaining 1 tbsp. green onion on a serving platter.

The Easiest Air Fryer Chicken Breast

Preparation and Cooking Time

21 minutes

Servings

2 persons

Nutritional facts

343 calories, 15g fat ,2g fiber ,26g carbs ,19g protein

Ingredients

- 16 oz. boneless skinless chicken breast (two or three chicken breasts)
- 1 tsp. ground black pepper
- 1 tbsp. 21 Seasoning Salute Trader Joe's (or any other chicken seasoning)
- 1 tsp. salt
- 1 tbsp. avocado oil

Instructions

- Heat the air fryer to 380 degrees Fahrenheit. Season the chicken breasts on all sides with oil and seasoning.
- Place the chicken in the air fryer one at a time, leaving space between them. Cook for 10 minutes in the air fryer.
- Flip the chicken & air fry for another 5-8 minutes or until it reaches 165°F on the inside.

Air Fryer Crispy Chicken Breasts

Preparation and Cooking Time

20 minutes

Servings

4 persons

Nutritional facts

140 calories, 10g fat ,1g fiber ,16g carbs ,5g protein

Ingredients

- 1-pound boneless skinless chicken breasts (about two 8 ounce breasts; 1-inch thick)
- 1 teaspoon poultry seasoning
- 2 teaspoons olive oil
- 1 teaspoon salt

Instructions

- One teaspoon olive oil is to be rubbed into each chicken breast, then poultry seasoning & salt on both sides.
- To allow optimum air circulation, arrange the chicken breasts in a single layer on the air fryer basket and cook for 10 minutes at 360°F. Cook for another 5 minutes, or until the chicken reaches an internal temperature of 165°F.
- To avoid overcooking the chicken, remove it from the air fryer and let it rest for 5 minutes on a cutting board before serving warm. Cooked chicken leftovers can be kept in an airtight container in the refrigerator for up to 3 days.

Air Fryer Chicken Wings Gluten Free

Preparation and Cooking Time

23 minutes

Servings

6 persons

Nutritional facts

156 calories, 22g fat ,2g fiber ,65g carbs ,16g protein

Ingredients

- 1.5-2 pounds' chicken wings
- 2 teaspoons garlic powder
- 2 teaspoons onion powder
- 1/2 teaspoon olive oil
- 2 teaspoons kosher salt
- 1 teaspoon black pepper
- 1 tablespoon smoked paprika
- 1 tablespoon brown sugar
- 1/4 teaspoon cayenne pepper

Instructions

- Preheat your air fryer to 400 degrees F if it requires it.
- Combine the salt, pepper, paprika, onion powder, garlic powder, cayenne, & brown sugar in a small bowl.
- If necessary, remove any excess fat or skin from the chicken wings. Place the chicken wings in a large mixing bowl after lightly patting them dry with a paper towel.
- Toss the chicken wings with the oil and 2 tbsp. of the rub in a large mixing dish. Toss to coat evenly, giving more rub if necessary.
- Spread the wings evenly throughout the basket or tray of the air fryer, making sure they don't overlap. Preheat oven to 400 degrees F and bake for 10 minutes. Remove the chicken wings from the basket or tray, flip them, and air fry for another 8 minutes at 400 degrees F.
- Serve immediately, or stir with sauce before serving if desired.

Air Fryer Chicken Breast (Lemon Garlic)

Preparation and Cooking Time

25 minutes

Servings

3 persons

Nutritional facts

310 calories, 22g fat ,2g fiber ,65g carbs ,16g protein

Ingredients

- 1 1/2 pounds' skinless chicken breasts
- McCormick's Grill Mates Montreal Chicken Seasoning to taste
- 3 tablespoons lemon garlic marinade
- salt and pepper to taste

Instructions

- Combine the lemon garlic marinade and the chicken in a large mixing bowl. Rub the lemon & garlic into the chicken. Both sides should be coated. Season to taste with chicken seasoning, salt, & pepper.
- It's unnecessary to marinate the chicken overnight, and chicken that has been marinated tends to be juicy.
- In the basket, place the chicken breasts, and the chicken should not be stacked.
- Preheat the oven to 360°F and cook for 10 minutes.
- Flip the chicken over in the air fryer. Cook for another 10-12 minutes until the chicken achieves 165 degrees F inside.
- Allow cooling before serving.

Air Fryer Skinless Boneless Chicken Breasts

Preparation and Cooking Time

22 minutes

Servings

4persons

Nutritional facts

146 calories, 24g fat ,0g fiber ,10g carbs ,12g protein

Ingredients

- 1 lb. skinless boneless chicken breasts
- 1/8 tsp. of pepper
- 1/4 tsp. of garlic powder
- 1/2 tbsp. of olive oil
- 3/4 tsp. of salt
- 1/2 tsp. of paprika optional

Instructions

- Drizzle the olive oil over the chicken breasts and season with pepper, salt, garlic powder, and paprika. So that the chicken is equally seasoned, rub the spices and oil all over it.
- Place the chicken breasts in a single layer in the air fryer basket. Cook for 20 minutes at 400 degrees Fahrenheit for thick chicken breasts, flipping halfway during cooking.

Breaded Air Fryer Chicken

Preparation and Cooking Time

25 minutes

Servings

4 persons

Nutritional facts

221 calories, 2g fat ,3g fiber ,6 carbs ,14g protein

Ingredients

- 4 6 ounces' chicken breasts boneless, skinless

- 1/8 teaspoon garlic powder
- Cooking spray
- 1/4 cup breadcrumbs
- 1/4 teaspoon oregano
- 1/8 teaspoon paprika
- Salt and pepper to taste

Instructions

- Preheat the air fryer to 390 degrees Fahrenheit.
- Combine the breadcrumbs, oregano, paprika, and garlic powder in a medium mixing bowl.
- Dredge the chicken in the breadcrumbs mixture after spraying it with frying spray. Remove any extra breading by shaking it off. Carry on with the rest of the chicken.
- Using cooking spray, coat the air fryer pan. Then, if desired, coat the outside of the breaded chicken with cooking spray. Without overcrowding the pan, place the chicken in the air fryer basket. It's possible that you'll have to work in batches.
- Let it cook for five minutes. Turn the chicken and spray it with more cooking spray; cook for another 4-7 minutes, or until golden brown. Their size and thickness determine the length of time it takes to cook your chicken breasts.
- Remove and serve with a side salad, if preferred.

Frozen Chicken Breast in Air Fryer

Preparation and Cooking Time

15 minutes

Servings

2 persons

Nutritional facts

260 calories,

16g fat ,0.2g fiber ,6g carbs ,11g protein

Ingredients

- 2 large chicken breasts frozen, boneless skinless is what was used
- 1/4 tsp. garlic powder
- 1/2 tsp. salt
- 1/4 tsp. pepper
- 1/4 tsp. parsley flakes

Instructions

- In the air fryer basket, place frozen chicken breasts. Evenly distribute the ingredients on top of the two of them.
- Close and bake for 15 minutes at 360 degrees F. Remove them and double-check that they're finished. Allow about 5 minutes of resting time before slicing to keep the juices intact.

Air Fryer Chicken Stuffed with Prosciutto and Fontina

Preparation and Cooking Time

25 minutes

Servings

2 persons

Nutritional facts

277 calories ,43g fat ,2g fiber ,9g carbs ,32 protein

Ingredients

- 2 skinless, boneless chicken breast halves
- 3 sprigs rosemary
- 1 bunch baby arugula
- 1/2 lemon, juiced

- 4 tablespoons unsalted butter
- 2 tablespoons extra-virgin olive oil
- 1 cup Portobello mushrooms, sliced
- 1/2 cup dry white wine
- 4 ounces' fontina cheese, rind removed, cut into 2-inch sticks
- 2 slices prosciutto
- salt, to taste
- freshly ground black pepper, to taste

Instructions

- Place chicken breast halves between wax paper sheets and pound thin with a mallet or rolling pin.
- Wrap one slice of prosciutto around each fontina cheese stick and lay in the center of each flattened chicken breast half. Toothpicks or butcher's twine can be used to secure the chicken around the prosciutto and cheese. Season the chicken rolls with black pepper and salt.
- Then heat two tablespoons of butter and 1 tbsp. oil in a heavy skillet. Brown chicken rolls in a skillet over medium heat for 2 to 3 minutes per side. In the air fryer basket, place the chicken rolls. Preheat the air fryer to 350 degrees F and cook for 7 minutes. Place the chicken rolls on a cutting board and set them aside for 5 minutes. Cut the rolls into 6 slices at an angle.
- Reheat the skillet, add the rest of the butter, mushrooms, wine, & rosemary, season with salt and pepper, and cook for 10 minutes.
- Toss the arugula leaves with the remaining olive oil, lemon juice, salt, & pepper in a large mixing bowl. Arrange the chicken & mushrooms on a bed of dressed arugula to serve.

Air Fryer Chicken Fajitas

Preparation and Cooking Time

28 minutes

Servings

4 persons

Nutritional facts

203 calories ,4g fat ,3g fiber ,14g carbs ,9 protein

Ingredients

- 1 lb. boneless, skinless chicken breast, sliced
- 1 tsp. salt
- 1 tsp. cumin
- 2 bell peppers, sliced
- 1 onion, sliced
- 2 tsp. olive oil
- 2 tsp. chili powder
- 1/2 tsp. black pepper
- 1 pinch cayenne

Instructions

- In a mixing bowl, combine the cut chicken and vegetables.
- Combine the olive oil, chili powder, salt, cumin, pepper, & cayenne pepper in a mixing bowl.
- Toss to combine and then pour the ingredients into an air fryer tray.
- Place the tray in the air fryer & cook for 16-20 minutes at 360°F, stirring and checking halfway through.
- Serve the fajitas in tortillas, over rice, or over a salad with selected toppings once they've completed cooking.

Air Fryer Chicken Legs

Preparation and Cooking Time

25 minutes

Servings

4 persons

Nutritional facts

936 calories,15g fat ,4g fiber ,26g carbs ,19g protein

Ingredients

- 12 chicken legs drumsticks
- 2 teaspoons garlic powder
- 1 1/2 teaspoon onion powder
- 1 1/2 teaspoon each of salt and pepper
- 1 tablespoon chili powder
- 1 Tablespoon oregano
- 3 tablespoons olive oil

Instructions

- In a large mixing bowl, place the chicken.
- Separately, make the spice blend by putting all spices in a smaller bowl.
- Using kitchen towels, pat the chicken dry. Before frying the chicken in the air fryer, make sure it's completely dry.
- Stir the fried chicken with the dry spice mix and toss thoroughly.
- Preheat your air fryer to 400 degrees Fahrenheit.
- On your air fryer basket, arrange the chicken in a single layer.
- You may need to do this in two batches, depending on the size of the air fryer.
- Flip the chicken in the air fryer basket & cook for another 10 minutes (halfway through).
- In all, it should take 20 minutes to thicken and cook with crispy skin.
- If desired, garnish the air fryer chicken legs with lime wedges, avocados, tomatoes, and lime wedges.

Boneless Skinless Chicken Thighs

Preparation and Cooking Time

20 minutes

Servings

6 persons

Nutritional facts

138 calories, 8g fat ,2g fiber ,13g carbs ,8g protein

Ingredients

- 1 ½ pounds boneless skinless chicken thighs (about 6 boneless thighs)
- ½ teaspoon chili powder
- ½ teaspoon black pepper
- 1 teaspoon turmeric
- 1 teaspoon garlic powder
- 1 teaspoon kosher salt
- olive oil spritz

Instructions

- In a small bowl, combine all spices and ingredients. Rub all sides of the chicken.
- Place the chicken in the air fryer, spritz with one spray of olive oil, and cook for 12 minutes at 390°F. Use a fast read thermometer to check the temperature and add another 2-3

minutes if necessary. Cook the chicken until it reaches a temperature of 165 degrees Fahrenheit.

Crispy Air Fryer Popcorn Chicken Recipe

Preparation and Cooking Time

24 minutes

Servings

4 persons

Nutritional facts

445 calories, 9g fat ,1g fiber ,2g carbs ,5g protein

Ingredients

- 2 Large Boneless Skinless Chicken Breasts
- ½ Tbsp. Garlic Powder
- ½ Tsp. Onion Powder
- ¾ Tsp. Chili Powder
- 1 Tsp. Paprika
- 1 Large Egg
- 1 Tsp. Hot Sauce Optional
- ½ Tsp. Sea Salt
- ¾ Tsp. Ground Black Pepper
- ½ Cup All-Purpose Flour Divided
- ¼ Cup Plain Breadcrumbs
- ½ Cup Panko Breadcrumbs
- ½ Cup Milk
- ½ Tsp. Lawry's Seasoned Salt

Instructions

- Preheat the air fryer to 390°F (190°C).
- In a medium-sized mixing bowl, whisk the milk, egg, and spicy sauce (optional) while preheating. You might also season with a bit of salt & pepper for added taste.
- Set aside half of the flour (1/4 cup) in a separate small bowl.
- Stir together the remaining flour, breadcrumbs, panko, and all of the dried spices in a large mixing bowl until evenly distributed.
- Cut the chicken breasts into one-inch cubes, striving to keep each one uniform in size. Begin breading the chicken once it has been cubed.
- Dip the chicken into the flour bowl one at a time, coating all sides. Dredge the same chicken bite in the egg mixture & set aside to drain the excess. Next, coat the chicken in the breadcrumb mixture, pressing down to ensure that the breading sticks well. Put the breaded chicken on a platter and continue breading the popcorn chicken until all of it is breaded.
- When ready to air fry, spray your air fryer basket with olive oil and arrange the chicken in it, making sure none of them touch.
- Close the lid after liberally misting the edges & tops of the popcorn chicken with olive oil.
- Then air fry for 14 minutes at 390 degrees F, flipping halfway through and re-misting with olive oil. Remove the chicken from the air fryer with tongs once it is cooked through and crispy; serve warm with your preferred sauce.

Air Fryer Chicken Nuggets with Dipping Sauce

Preparation and Cooking Time

25 minutes

Servings

5 persons

Nutritional facts

380 calories ,15g fat ,2g fiber ,26g carbs ,19g protein

Ingredients

- 1/2 cup mayonnaise
- 1/4 cup milk
- 3 tablespoons powdered sugar
- 2 tablespoons corn starch
- 2 tablespoons McCormick® Garlic and Onion, Black Pepper and Sea Salt All Purpose Seasoning
- 1/4 cup pickle juice
- 1 egg
- 1-pound boneless skinless chicken breasts, cut into 1-inch chunks
- 3/4 cup flour
- 2 tablespoons barbecue sauce
- 2 tablespoons honey
- 4 teaspoons French's® Classic Yellow Mustard
- 2 teaspoons cider vinegar
- 1 teaspoon McCormick® Garlic and Onion, Black Pepper and Sea Salt All Purpose Seasoning

Instructions

- In a small bowl, combine all of the sauce ingredients. Refrigerate till ready to use, covered.
- In a large mixing bowl, whisk the milk, pickle juice, and egg for the nuggets. Refrigerate for 30 minutes after adding the chicken. Combine flour, powdered sugar, corn starch, and seasoning in a large shallow bowl.
- Remove nuggets from milk mixture in stages, shaking to remove excess liquid. Toss the nuggets in the flour mixture to coat them, and then shake lightly to remove any excess flour. Allow the extra liquid to drain the nuggets before dipping them again in the milk mixture. Return the nuggets to the flour mixture and coat thoroughly. Remove the remaining milk & flour mixtures and toss them Out.
- Use nonstick cooking spray to spray the air fryer basket. Preheat the air fryer for 3 minutes at 380°F. Fill the basket with nuggets in a single layer; do not overcrowd. Using a nonstick cooking spray, lightly coat the pan. Allow 5 minutes of cooking time. Flip the nuggets and spray with nonstick cooking spray one more. Cook for another 5 minutes, or until the chicken is thoroughly cooked and gently browned. Continue with the remaining nuggets. Serve with Dipping Sauce on the side.

Air Fryer Parmesan Crusted Chicken

Preparation and Cooking Time

20 minutes

Servings

4 persons

Nutritional facts

663 calories, 10g fat ,1g fiber ,16g carbs ,5g protein

Ingredients

- 2 Large Chicken breasts
- 1 cup real mayonnaise
- 1 tbsp. garlic powder
- 1 cup Parmesan shredded
- 1 cup panko bread crumbs

Instructions

- Chicken breasts should be cut in half.
- Use a meat hammer to pound each piece.
- Then season with salt.
- On both sides of each piece of chicken, spread mayonnaise.

- Combine the Panko, Parmesan, & garlic powder in a mixing bowl.
- Using the panko/parmesan mixture, coat each piece of chicken.
- Preheat the air fryer to 390°F.
- Put in the air fryer in a single layer.
- Cook for 15 minutes, turning halfway through.

Air Fryer Chicken Breast Tender and Juicy

Preparation and Cooking Time

26 minutes

Servings

8 persons

Nutritional facts

143 calories, 6g fat ,1g fiber ,10g carbs ,2g protein

Ingredients

- 2 lbs. boneless & skinless chicken breasts
- 1 tsp. oregano dried
- 3/4 tsp. salt
- Ground black pepper to taste
- 1 tbsp. oil
- 1 tsp. smoked paprika
- 1 tsp. garlic powder
- 1 tsp. onion powder
- Cooking spray

Instructions

- Preheat the air fryer to 380 degrees Fahrenheit for 5 minutes.
- Meanwhile, put the chicken in a large bowl or dish with the oil and toss to coat.
- Then season with salt and pepper, as well as smoked paprika, garlic powder, onion powder, oregano, and smoked paprika. Toss to coat evenly.
- Open the basket and spray it with cooking spray after the air fryer has finished preheating.
- Close the basket with a single layer of chicken breasts.
- Cook for 16 minutes at 380°F without turning or shaking.
- Ensure the internal read thermometer inserted in the thickest portion of the basket reads at least 150 degrees F.
- To enable the fluids to settle, transfer to a tray, cover with tin foil, and set aside for 5 minutes.
- Slice against the grain & serve with a salad on any side.

Crispy Brown Sugar Air Fryer Chicken Legs

Preparation and Cooking Time

30 minutes

Servings

2 persons

Nutritional facts

537 calories, 1g fat ,2g fiber ,35g carbs ,4g protein

Ingredients

- 8 chicken legs/drumsticks, about 2-2.5 pounds' total
- 1 teaspoon onion powder
- 1 teaspoon ground mustard
- 1 teaspoon smoked paprika
- 2 tablespoons oil (avocado oil or olive oil)
- 1 tablespoon brown sugar
- 1 ½ teaspoon Kosher salt

- 1 teaspoon garlic powder
- ½ teaspoon cumin
- ½ teaspoon black pepper

Instructions

- Each chicken leg should be trimmed of any excess fat and patted dry. Place the chicken legs in a large mixing bowl or re-sealable plastic bag.
- Toss the chicken legs in the oil with tongs to evenly coat each leg.
- Toss the chicken legs in the spice mixture in the bowl or bag until evenly coated.
- Place the chicken on trays or in the basket of your air fryer and air fry for 20 minutes at 400°F. Halfway through the cooking process, rotate the chicken.
- When the chicken is done cooking, it should be golden brown on the outside and have an internal temperature of 165°F.

Air Fryer Huli Huli Chicken

Preparation and Cooking Time

2 hours 33 minutes

Servings

24 persons

Nutritional facts

197 calories ,35g fat ,1g fiber ,1g carbs ,16g protein

Ingredients

- 4-5 pounds' boneless skinless chicken thighs
- 1/2 cup pineapple juice
- 1/2 tsp. ground ginger
- 1 cup brown sugar
- 3/4 cup ketchup
- 1/2 cup soy sauce
- 1 1/2 tsp. minced garlic

Instructions

- To make a marinade, put all ingredients in a medium bowl, except the chicken. Stir everything together thoroughly.
- Place the chicken thighs in a zip-top plastic bag. Pour the marinade into the bag and turn the chicken to coat it.
- Allow chicken to marinate for at least 2 hours in a plastic bag in the refrigerator.
- Preheat the Air Fryer to 360°F.
- Remove the chicken from the bag and discard the rest of the marinade.
- Place chicken in oiled Air Fryer baskets in batches and cook for 10 minutes. Cook for another 8 minutes after carefully turning the chicken over. Check for doneness, and cook for another 2-5 minutes if necessary.

Kevin Dundon's air fryer chicken tenders

Preparation and Cooking Time

20 minutes

Servings

4 persons

Nutritional facts

380 calories, 13g fat ,3g fiber ,14g carbs ,7g protein

Ingredients

- 2 chicken fillets, cut into long strips
- ½tsp ground ginger
- ½tsp garlic powder

- 1tsp mixed dried herbs
- 120ml buttermilk
- 30g panko breadcrumbs
- 60g plain flour
- ½tsp baking powder
- A pinch of chili powder
- 1tsp paprika
- ½tsp celery salt
- Salt and pepper
- Oil spray

Instructions

- Use a sharp knife to cut the chicken breast into small pieces. Combine with the buttermilk in a mixing bowl. Cover with cling film after tossing to ensure the chicken is coated. Refrigerate for 30 minutes to marinate.
- Mix together the flour, breadcrumbs, baking powder, paprika, chili powder, ginger powder, dried herbs, garlic powder, celery salt, and a pinch of salt and pepper in a mixing bowl.
- Heat the air fryer for five minutes at 180 degrees F.
- Remove the chicken strips from the buttermilk as well as cover all sides in the breadcrumb mixture.
- Cook the chicken fingers for 10-12 minutes in the air fryer basket. After four minutes, spray the chicken on one side with more oil spray, then carefully flip it over and spray the other side to help crisp and color. It is done when the chicken is golden brown & crispy and has achieved a core temperature of 67-70 degrees C.

Air Fryer Chicken 65

Preparation and Cooking Time

63 minutes

Servings

4 persons

Nutritional facts

516 calories,11g fat ,2g fiber ,22g carbs ,4g protein

Ingredients

- 1.5 lbs. of boneless chicken thighs
- 1 teaspoon of salt
- 3-4 Indian or Thai green chilies cut lengthwise
- 4 garlic cloves, minced
- ½ teaspoon of ground black pepper
- ½ teaspoon of chaat masala
- 3-4 lemon wedges
- 1 tablespoon of oil
- 3 tablespoons of rice flour
- ½ cup of thick yogurt
- 7-8 curry leaves chopped
- 1 tablespoon of ginger garlic paste
- 1 teaspoon of cumin powder
- 2 tablespoons of Kashmiri chili powder mild
- 1 teaspoon of ground black pepper
- 7-8 curry leaves
- 2 tablespoons of finely chopped cilantro or coriander leaves for garnishing

Instructions

- Prepare the chicken by chopping it into 2-inch pieces.

- In a mixing bowl, combine all of the ingredients for the marinade.
- Coat the chicken pieces in the marinade one at a time to ensure that they are uniformly marinated.
- Allow 30 minutes for the chicken to marinate in the marinade.
- After the chicken has been marinated, cover it thoroughly with rice flour.
- Coat it completely in oil before placing the air frying basket on the trivet. Heat the air fryer to 400 degrees Fahrenheit (200 degrees Celsius) for 3 minutes.
- Put the chicken pieces in a single layer on the air frying basket, being careful not to overcrowd them — you'll need to do this in two batches.
- Allow 7 minutes for the chicken pieces to cook.

Air Fryer Chicken Parm

Preparation and Cooking Time

27 minutes

Servings

4 persons

Nutritional facts

243 calories,10g fat ,1g fiber ,19g carbs ,6g protein

Ingredients

- A cup of your favorite breadcrumbs
- Quarter cup grated Parmesan cheese
- 4 boneless, skinless chicken breast halves, not frozen
- Extra Virgin Olive Oil (EVOO)

Instructions

- Spray your air fryer's basket.
- Combine your breadcrumbs and grated Parm in a shallow dish.
- Drizzle a little extra virgin olive oil over both sides of each chicken breast. Then dredge each piece in the breadcrumb mixture before placing it in the air fryer.
- Close the air fryer drawer and set the temperature to 325 degrees Fahrenheit with a 22-minute timer.
- The chicken is ready to eat when the timer goes off.

Air Fryer Chicken Tenders Recipe –

Preparation and Cooking Time

30 minutes

Servings

3 persons

Nutritional facts

419 calories, 5g fat ,1g fiber ,9g carbs ,2g protein

Ingredients

- 350g (12oz) chicken breast mini fillets
- 1 tsp. oregano
- 1 tsp. dried chili flakes
- 1 tsp. smoked paprika
- 2 eggs
- 30g (4 tbsp.) plain flour (gluten-free)
- garlic-infused oil (ideally in a spray bottle)
- 70g (1/2 cup) breadcrumbs (gluten-free)
- 1 tsp. salt
- 1 tsp. black pepper

Instructions

- Take three bowls. Crack your eggs into one of the bowls and whisk them together until well combined. Add your gluten-free plain flour to the other. Add the breadcrumbs and spices to the last bowl and stir well.
- Place your chicken breast tiny fillets in a bowl of plain flour and dredge them in it.
- Dredge them in the beaten egg bowl after that.
- Finally, coat them in the breadcrumb/spice mixture.
- Heat the air fryer to 200 degrees Celsius (390F). When it is hot, add the coated chicken, making sure they don't touch.
- Spray a little oil over the entire surface to make it a little shiny.
- Cook for 10 to 12 minutes, turning after five minutes and re-spraying with oil (sparingly).
- Serve as a wrap, salad, or sandwich with your preferred dips.

Air Fried Maple Chicken Thighs

Preparation and Cooking Time

1 hour 35 minutes

Servings

4 persons

Nutritional facts

415 calories, 3g fat ,9g fiber ,221g carbs ,61g protein

Ingredients

- 1 cup buttermilk
- ½ cup all-purpose flour
- 1 teaspoon granulated onion
- ¼ teaspoon ground black pepper
- ¼ teaspoon cayenne pepper
- ½ teaspoon granulated garlic
- ¼ cup tapioca flour
- 1 tablespoon salt
- ½ cup maple syrup
- 1 egg
- 1 teaspoon granulated garlic
- 4 skin-on, bone-in chicken thighs
- 1 teaspoon sweet paprika
- ½ teaspoon smoked paprika
- ½ teaspoon honey powder (such as Savory Spice®)

Instructions

- Mix buttermilk, maple syrup, egg, and 1 tsp. granulated garlic in a re-sealable bag. Add the chicken thighs and marinate in the refrigerator for at least 60 minutes or up to overnight.
- In a shallow bowl, whisk together flour, tapioca flour, salt, sweet paprika, smoked paprika, granulated onion, pepper, cayenne pepper, 1/2 tsp. garlic powder, and honey powder.
- Preheat your air fryer to 380°F (190 degrees C).
- Chicken thighs should be drained and the marinade discarded. Dredge the chicken in the flour mixture, shaking off any excess. Cook for 12 minutes with the skin side down in a preheated air fryer. Turn the thighs and cook for another 13 minutes.

Amazing Buttermilk Air Fried Chicken

Preparation and Cooking Time

35 minutes

Servings

4persons

Nutritional facts

435 calories, 3g fat ,1g fiber ,23g carbs ,13g protein

Ingredients

- 1 cup buttermilk
- 1 egg
- ½ teaspoon of paprika
- ½ teaspoon of onion powder
- ¼ teaspoon of oregano
- teaspoon of black pepper
- ½ cup of all-purpose flour
- 2 teaspoons of salt
- 1 ½ teaspoons of brown sugar
- ½ teaspoon of hot sauce
- ⅓ cup of tapioca flour
- ½ teaspoon of garlic
- ⅛ teaspoon of ground black pepper
- 1 teaspoon of garlic powder
- 1 pound of boneless chicken thighs

Instructions

- Add buttermilk and spicy sauce in a small bowl and stir to blend.
- Shake the tapioca flour, garlic salt, and 1/8 tsp. black pepper in a reusable plastic bag.
- In a shallow bowl, beat the egg.
- Add salt, flour, brown sugar, paprika, garlic powder, oregano, onion powder, and 1/4 tsp. of black pepper in a resealable bag.
- Chicken thighs are to be dipped in buttermilk, tapioca, egg, and flour, shaking off excess after each dipping.
- Preheat your air fryer to 380°F. Use parchment paper to line your air fryer basket.
- Place the coated chicken thighs in the air fryer basket in batches and cook for 10 minutes. Turn the chicken thighs and cook for another 10 minutes, or until the chicken is no longer.

Air Fryer Crumbed Chicken Tenderloins

Preparation and Cooking Time

27 minutes

Servings

4 persons

Nutritional facts

253 calories, 11g fat ,1g fiber ,1g carbs ,6g protein

Ingredients

- 1 egg
- 2 tablespoons vegetable oil
- ½ cup dry bread crumbs
- 8 chicken tenderloins

Instructions

- Preheat your air fryer to 350°F (175 degrees C).
- In a small bowl, whisk the egg.
- In a second bowl, combine bread crumbs & oil until the mixture is loose and crumbly.
- After that, dip each of the chicken tenderloins into the egg bowl and shake off any excess egg. Make sure the chicken is evenly and completely covered in the crumb mixture. Place chicken tenderloins in the air fryer basket. Cook for 12 minutes, or until the center is no longer pink. At least 165 degrees F should be read on an instant-read thermometer put into the center (74 degrees C).

Air Fryer Blackened Chicken Breast

Preparation and Cooking Time

40 minutes

Servings

2 persons

Nutritional facts

432 calories, 7g fat ,2g fiber ,14g carbs ,1g protein

Ingredients

- 2 teaspoons of paprika
- ½ teaspoon of black pepper
- ¼ teaspoon of salt
- 1 teaspoon of ground thyme
- 1 teaspoon of cumin
- ½ teaspoon of cayenne pepper
- ½ teaspoon of onion powder
- 2 teaspoons of vegetable oil
- 2 (12 ounces) boneless chicken breast halves

Instructions

- Mix thyme, paprika, cumin, onion powder, cayenne pepper, black pepper, and salt in a mixing bowl. Place the spice mixture on a platter that is flat.
- Coat each chicken breast in oil until it is completely covered. Roll each piece of chicken in the blackening spice mixture, pressing down, so the spice adheres to all sides. Allow sitting for five minutes while the air fryer heats up.
- Preheat an air fryer for 5 minutes at 360 degrees F (175 degrees C).
- Cook for ten minutes with the chicken in the air fryer basket. Cook for another 10 minutes on the other side. Before serving, transfer the chicken to a plate and set aside for 5 minutes to rest.

Air Fryer Sesame Chicken Thighs

Preparation and Cooking Time

55 minutes

Servings

4 persons

Nutritional facts

485 calories,17g fat ,4g fiber ,31g carbs ,6g protein

Ingredients

- 2 tablespoons sesame oil
- 2 pounds' chicken thighs
- 2 tablespoons soy sauce
- 1 tablespoon honey
- 1 tablespoon sriracha sauce
- 1 teaspoon rice vinegar
- 1 green onion, chopped
- 2 tablespoons toasted sesame seeds

Instructions

- Mix sesame oil, soy sauce, honey, sriracha, and vinegar in a large mixing bowl. Stir in the chicken until everything is well combined. Refrigerate for at least 30 minutes after covering.
- Preheat your air fryer to 400°F (200 degrees C). Remove the chicken from the marinade.
- Place them skin-side up chicken thighs in the air fryer basket. It should be cooked for five minutes, and Cook for another 10 minutes on the other side.

- Before serving, transfer the chicken to a plate and set aside for 5 minutes to rest. Serve with green onion & sesame seeds as garnish.

Air Fryer BBQ Cheddar-Stuffed Chicken Breasts

Preparation and Cooking Time

35 minutes

Servings

2 persons

Nutritional facts

379 calories, 8g fat ,1g fiber ,22g carbs ,2g protein

Ingredients

- 3 strips bacon, divided
- 2 (4 ounces) skinless, boneless chicken breasts
- 2 ounces Cheddar cheese, cubed, divided
- ¼ cup barbeque sauce, divided
- salt and ground black pepper to taste

Instructions

- Preheat your air fryer to 380°F (190 degrees C). In the air fryer, cook one strip of bacon for 2 minutes. Cut into small pieces after removing from the air fryer. Preheat the air fryer to 400 degrees F and line the basket with parchment paper (200 degrees C).
- Mix Cheddar cheese, cooked bacon, and 1 tbsp. of barbecue sauce in a mixing bowl.
- Make a 1-inch cut horizontally at the top of each chicken breast with a long, sharp knife to create a small interior pouch. Fill each breast with an equal amount of the bacon-cheese mixture, and wrap the remaining bacon strips around each chicken breast. Coat the leftover barbecue sauce on the chicken breasts and place them in the air fryer basket that has been made.
- Cook for 10 minutes in the air fryer, then turn and cook for another 10 minutes, or until the chicken is no longer pink in the center and the juices run clear. At least 165 degrees F should be read on an instant-read thermometer put into the center (74 degrees C).

Mexican-Style Air Fryer Stuffed Chicken Breasts

Preparation and Cooking Time

30 minutes

Servings

2 persons

Nutritional facts

185 calories, 6g fat ,1g fiber ,23g carbs ,13g protein

Ingredients

- 4 extra-long toothpicks
- ½ onion, sliced into thin strips
- 1 fresh jalapeno pepper, sliced into thin strips
- 2 teaspoons corn oil
- 2 teaspoons Mexican oregano
- salt and ground black pepper to taste
- ½ red bell pepper, sliced into thin strips
- 4 teaspoons chili powder, divided
- 4 teaspoons ground cumin, divided
- 1 skinless, boneless chicken breast
- 2 teaspoons chipotle flakes
- ½ lime, juiced

Instructions

- Fill a small bowl halfway with water and soak toothpicks to prevent them from burning when cooking.
- Combine 2 teaspoons chili powder and 2 tsp. cumin in a small dish.
- Preheat your air fryer to 400°F (200 degrees C).
- Place the chicken breasts on a work surface that is flat. Cut a horizontal slit in the middle of the pie. Using a kitchen mallet or rolling pin, pound each half until it is about 1/4-inch thick.
- Sprinkle the remaining chili powder, cumin, chipotle flakes, oregano, salt, & pepper evenly over each side of the breast. In the center of one breast half, place 1/2 of the bell pepper, onion, and jalapeño. Roll the chicken from the tapering end upward, securing it with two toothpicks. Repeat with the remaining breasts, seasonings, and vegetables, securing with toothpicks. On a shallow dish, roll each roll-up in chili-cumin mixture while drizzling with olive oil until equally coated. (175 degrees C)
- Place the toothpick side up in the air-fryer basket with the roll-ups. Preheat the oven to 350°F and set the timer for 6 minutes.
- Flip the roll-ups. Cook for another 5 minutes in the air fryer, or until the juices flow clear, as well as an instant-read thermometer put into the center, registers at least 165 degrees F (74 degrees C).
- Before serving, drizzle lime juice evenly over the roll-ups.

Air-Fried Buffalo Chicken

Preparation and Cooking Time

36 minutes

Servings

4 persons

Nutritional facts

234 calories, 24g fat, 1g fiber ,43g carbs ,5g protein

Ingredients

- ½ cup plain fat-free Greek yogurt
- 1 tablespoon sweet paprika
- 1 tablespoon garlic pepper seasoning
- ¼ cup egg substitute
- 1 tablespoon hot sauce (such as Frank's®)
- 1 teaspoon hot sauce (such as Frank's®)
- 1 cup panko bread crumbs
- 1 tablespoon cayenne pepper
- 1 pound of boneless chicken breasts, cut into 1-inch strips

Instructions

- Combine Greek yogurt, egg substitute, and 1 tbsp. + 1 teaspoon hot sauce in a mixing dish.
- Combine panko bread crumbs, paprika, garlic powder, and cayenne pepper in a separate bowl.
- Coat chicken strips in panko bread crumb mixture after dipping them in yogurt.
- In an air fryer, place coated chicken strips in a single layer. Then cook for around 8 minutes per side, or until uniformly browned.

Crispy Ranch Air Fryer Nuggets

Preparation and Cooking Time

40 minutes

Servings

4 persons

Nutritional facts

244 calories, 6g fat ,1g fiber ,23g carbs ,13g protein

Ingredients

- 1-pound chicken tenders, cut into 1.5 to 2-inch pieces
- 1 egg, lightly beaten
- 1 cup panko bread crumbs
- 1 (1 ounce) package dry ranch salad dressing mix
- 2 tablespoons flour
- 1 serving olive oil cooking spray

Instructions

- Toss the chicken with the ranch seasoning in a large mixing bowl. Allow for 5-10 minutes of resting time.
- Fill a re-sealable bag halfway with flour. Crack an egg and spread panko bread crumbs on a plate in a small bowl. Preheat the air fryer to 390°F (200 degrees C).
- Toss the chicken in the bag to coat it. Dip the chicken in the egg mixture lightly, allowing excess to drain off. Roll the chicken pieces in panko crumbs, pressing them into the meat.
- Spray the air fryer basket with oil and arrange the chicken pieces inside, ensuring they don't overlap. Using a light mist of cooking spray, lightly coat the chicken.
- It should be cooked for four minutes. Cook for another 4 minutes, or until the chicken pieces are no longer pink on the inside. Serve right away.

Bacon-Wrapped Stuffed Chicken Breasts in the Air Fryer

Preparation and Cooking Time

45 minutes

Servings

3 persons

Nutritional facts

393 calories, 0.7g fat, 3.1g fiber, 27g carbs ,1.3g protein

Ingredients

- 3 breasts half
- 9 slices of bacon
- 12 each wooden toothpicks
- 1 teaspoon of lemon-pepper seasoning, or to taste
- 3 slices of Monterey Jack cheese
- 6 spears of fresh asparagus

Instructions

- If the manufacturer recommends it, heat the air fryer to 350 degrees F.
- Using paper towels, pat the chicken pieces' dry. Slice horizontally across the center using a sharp knife, starting at the thickest section and without cutting all the way through to the other side. Open the two sides like a book and spread them out.
- Both sides should be seasoned with lemon-pepper seasoning. On each chicken breast, put 1 slice of cheese. Place four halves of asparagus spears on top of the cheese. Keep the stuffing inside each roll by rolling the chicken up and over the cheese & asparagus. Wrap three slices of bacon around each chicken breast and attach with wooden toothpicks where the bacon overlaps.
- Put each bacon-wrapped breast and air fry in the air fryer basket for fifteen minutes. Cook for another 15 minutes on the other side. Check for doneness by inserting an instant-read thermometer into the center of the chicken; it should read 165 degrees F. (74 degrees C).

Air Fryer Stuffed Chicken Thighs

Preparation and Cooking Time

1 hour 35 minutes

Servings

6 persons

Nutritional facts

997 calories, 10g fat, 1g fiber, 19g carbs, 10g protein

Ingredients

- 6 ounces' Swiss cheese
- salt and freshly ground black pepper to taste
- 6 slices turkey lunch meat
- 1 cup panko bread crumbs
- 1 tablespoon sazon seasoning (such as Goya(R) sazonador total), divided
- ½ cup flour, divided
- 2 large eggs
- 6 medium boneless skinless chicken thighs
- nonstick cooking spray

Instructions

- Preheat your air fryer to 400°F (200 degrees C).
- Swiss cheese should be cut into six 2 1/2 by 1/2 by 1/2-inch pieces.
- Set up a breading station by putting bread crumbs, 2 teaspoons sazonador spice, and 1 tablespoon flour in one shallow dish, the rest of the flour & sazonador seasoning in another shallow dish, and the eggs in a third shallow dish. Whip the eggs until they are lightly golden and bubbly. Using salt and pepper, season the
- eggs.
- Place one piece of Swiss cheese on top of each piece of turkey meat. Wrap Swiss cheese around luncheon meat.
- Put a turkey-cheese bundle in the center of each opened chicken thigh. Bundles of chicken thighs should be rolled around them. To coat, dip each in the flour mixture and shake off the excess. Shake off excess egg after dipping. Finally, dip the chicken in the bread crumb mixture & press it into the breading.
- Place the chicken bundles in the air fryer seam-side down. Using a nonstick spray, coat the chicken bundles.
- Reduce the temperature of the air fryer to 380°F (193°C) and air fry the chicken for fifteen minutes. Turn the bundles over, coat with nonstick spray, and reduce the temperature of the air fryer to 370 degrees F. (187 degrees C). Cook for an additional 8 minutes in the air fryer until the chicken is cooked through. Serve right away.

Honey-Cajun Thighs

Preparation and Cooking Time

65 minutes

Servings

6 persons

Nutritional facts

248 calories, 9g fat, 8g fiber, 10g carbs, 3g protein

Ingredients

- ½ cup of buttermilk
- 2 ½ teaspoons of Cajun seasoning
- ½ teaspoon of garlic salt
- ½ teaspoon of honey powder
- ¼ teaspoon of ground paprika
- 1 teaspoon of hot sauce

- 1 ½ pound of boneless chicken thighs
- ¼ cup of all-purpose flour
- ⅓ cup of tapioca flour
- ⅛ teaspoon of cayenne pepper
- 4 teaspoons of honey

Instructions

- In a re-sealable plastic bag, mix the buttermilk and spicy sauce. Half an hour later, add the chicken thighs to the marinade.
- In a small mixing bowl, whisk together the tapioca flour, flour, Cajun spice, honey powder, garlic salt, paprika, and cayenne pepper. Remove the thighs from the buttermilk and dredge them in the flour. Excess flour should be shaken away.
- Preheat the air fryer to 360 degrees Fahrenheit (180 degrees Celsius) (175 degrees C).
- Cook for roughly 15 minutes with the chicken thighs in the air fryer basket. Cook for another 10 minutes on the other side, or until the chicken thighs are no longer pink in the center and the juices run clear. At least 165 degrees F should be read on an instant-read thermometer inserted in the center (74 degrees C). Take the chicken thighs out of the air fryer and pour 1 teaspoon honey over each one.

Air Fryer Buttermilk Fried Chicken

Preparation and Cooking Time

4 hours 35 minutes

Servings

6 persons

Nutritional facts

335 calories, 13g fat, 2g fiber, 23g carbs, 2g protein

Ingredients

- 1 ½ pound boneless, skinless chicken thighs
- ½ tablespoon ground black pepper
- 1 cup panko bread crumbs
- 2 cups buttermilk
- 1 cup all-purpose flour
- 1 tablespoon seasoned salt
- 1 serving cooking spray

Instructions

- In a shallow casserole dish, place the chicken thighs. Refrigerate for four hours or overnight after pouring buttermilk over the chicken.
- Preheat your air fryer to 380°F (190 degrees C).
- In a large gallon-sized resealable bag, combine flour, seasoned salt, and pepper. Chicken thighs should be dredged in seasoned flour. Dip in buttermilk again, then coat in panko bread crumbs.
- Use nonstick cooking spray to spray the air fryer basket. Place half of the chicken thighs in the basket, ensuring they don't touch. Using cooking spray, coat the tops of each chicken thigh.
- Cook for 15 minutes in a preheated air fryer. Flip. Re-spray the chicken's tops. Cook for another 10 minutes or until the chicken is no longer pink in the center as well as the juices run clear. At least 165 degrees F should be read on an instant-read thermometer put into the center (74 degrees C). Repeat with the rest of the chicken.

Air Fryer Chicken Katsu with Homemade Katsu Sauce

Preparation and Cooking Time

40 minutes

Servings

4 persons

Nutritional facts

318 calories, 11g fat ,1g fiber ,21g carbs ,2g protein

Ingredients

- ½ cup ketchup
- 1 ½ cups panko bread crumbs
- 1 serving cooking spray
- 1 teaspoon minced garlic
- 1-pound boneless skinless chicken breast, sliced in half horizontally
- 1 pinch salt and ground black pepper to taste
- 2 tablespoons soy sauce
- 1 tablespoon brown sugar
- 1 tablespoon sherry
- 2 teaspoons Worcestershire sauce
- 2 large eggs, beaten

Instructions

- In a mixing bowl, whisk together ketchup, soy sauce, brown sugar, sherry, Worcestershire sauce, & garlic until the sugar has dissolved. Set aside the katsu sauce.
- Preheat your air fryer to 350°F (175 degrees C).
- Place the chicken pieces on a clean work surface in the meantime. It should be seasoned with salt & pepper to taste.
- In a flat dish, beat the eggs. Fill a second flat dish halfway with bread crumbs. Dredge the chicken in the egg, then in the bread crumbs. Dredge the chicken in egg and afterward bread crumbs again, pushing down to ensure the bread crumbs adhere to the chicken.
- Place the chicken pieces in the air fryer basket that has been preheated. Use nonstick cooking spray to coat the tops.
- It should be cooked for ten minutes in the air fryer. Flip the chicken pieces over and spray the tops with nonstick cooking spray using a spatula. Cook for another 8 minutes. Place the chicken on a cutting board & slice it thinly. Serve with katsu sauce on the side.

Keto Lemon-Garlic Chicken Thighs in the Air Fryer

Preparation and Cooking Time

2 hours 35 minutes

Servings

4 persons

Nutritional facts

258 calories, 14g fat ,2g fiber ,31g carbs ,2g protein

Ingredients

- ¼ cup lemon juice
- ¼ teaspoon salt
- ⅛ teaspoon ground black pepper
- 2 tablespoons olive oil
- 1 teaspoon Dijon mustard
- 2 cloves garlic, minced
- 4 skin-on, bone-in chicken thighs
- 4 lemon wedges

Instructions

- Combine the lemon juice, olive oil, Dijon mustard, garlic, salt, & pepper. Set aside the marinade.
- Fill a large resealable plastic bag halfway with chicken thighs. Pour the marinade over the chicken and seal the bag, ensuring sure that all areas of the chicken are covered. Refrigerate for at least two hours.
- Preheat the air fryer to 360°F (180°C) (175 degrees C).
- Using paper towels, pat the chicken dry after removing it from the marinade. Cook the chicken pieces in batches if necessary in the air fryer basket.
- Fry for 22 to 24 minutes or until the chicken is no longer pink at the bone as well as the juices run clear. A thermometer inserted near the bone should read 165 degrees Fahrenheit (74 degrees C). When serving, squeeze a lemon slice over each piece.

Chapter 8: Air Fryer Seafood Recipes

Garlic Butter Salmon-Fresh

Preparation and Cooking Time

15 minutes

Servings

2 persons

Nutritional facts

338 calories, 7g fat ,2g fiber ,21g carbs ,2g protein

Ingredients

- 2 (6-ounce) boneless, skin-on salmon fillets (preferably wild-caught)
- 1 teaspoon fresh Italian parsley, chopped (or 1/4 teaspoon dried)
- 2 tablespoons butter, melted
- 1 teaspoon garlic, minced
- salt and pepper to taste

Instructions

- Preheat your air fryer to 360 degrees Fahrenheit.
- Apply salt and pepper to the fresh salmon, then combine the melted butter, garlic, and parsley in a mixing bowl.
- Brush the salmon fillets with the garlic butter mixture & carefully set them side-by-side in the air fryer, skin side down.
- Then cook for about 10 minutes, or until salmon readily flakes with a knife or fork.

Air Fryer Mahi Mahi

Preparation and Cooking Time

17 minutes

Servings

4 persons

Nutritional facts

467 calories, 3g fat ,1g fiber ,2g carbs ,1g protein

Ingredients

- 1 to 1 1/2 pounds' mahi-mahi fillets
- 1/2 teaspoon of onion powder
- 1/2 teaspoon of salt
- 2 tablespoons of olive oil
- 2 cups of panko breadcrumbs

- 1 teaspoon of paprika
- 1/2 teaspoon of garlic powder
- 1/2 teaspoon of pepper

Instructions

- Preheat the air fryer to 400 degrees Fahrenheit.
- Cook the fillets in a single layer for 13 to 14 minutes or completely cooked. Halfway through cooking, you need to flip the mahi-mahi. If the fish is breaded, spray it with oil once at the start and once halfway through the cooking process.

Air Fryer Cod

Preparation and Cooking Time

20 minutes

Servings

4 persons

Nutritional facts

302 calories, 8g fat ,2g fiber ,10g carbs ,5g protein

Ingredients

- 4 cod loins
- 1 teaspoon dried dill (or 2 tablespoons fresh dill, chopped)
- 4 tablespoons butter, melted
- 6 cloves of garlic, minced
- 2 tablespoons lemon juice (1 lemon)
- 1/2 teaspoon salt

Instructions

- Preheat the air fryer to 370 degrees Fahrenheit.
- Combine the butter, garlic, lemon juice, dill, & salt.
- Place a cod loin in the bowl and coat it well with the sauce. To prevent the garlic from falling off during cooking, lightly push it into the fish. Continue with the remaining cod pieces.
- Place all cod loins in one layer in the air fryer, not touching.
- Cook for ten minutes before removing from the air fryer with care.
- Top the cod with extra lemon juice or butter and serve if preferred.

Air Fryer Shrimp with Pepper and lemon

Preparation and Cooking Time

13 minutes

Servings

4 persons

Nutritional facts

322 calories, 9g fat ,5g fiber ,40g carbs ,9g protein

Ingredients

- 1-pound of medium raw shrimp, peeled and deveined
- 1 teaspoon of black pepper
- 1/2 cup of olive oil
- 2 tablespoons of lemon juice
- 1/2 teaspoon of salt

Instructions

- Preheat the air fryer to 400 degrees Fahrenheit.
- Combine the shrimp, olive oil, lemon juice, salt, & pepper in a Ziploc bag. Combine all of the ingredients with care.
- Put the raw shrimp in one layer inside the air fryer and cover it with parchment paper (if using).

- Cook for eight minutes, shaking the basket halfway through the cooking time. When the shells turn pink and the shrimp is somewhat white but still opaque, the shrimp is done.
- Take out the lemon pepper shrimp from the air fryer, season with salt and pepper, and serve with pasta if preferred.

Air Fryer Tuna Steaks

Preparation and Cooking Time

24 minutes

Servings

2 persons

Nutritional facts

422 calories, 7g fat ,3g fiber ,22g carbs ,5g protein

Ingredients

- 2 (6 ounces) skinless yellowfin tuna steaks
- 1 teaspoon of grated ginger
- 1 teaspoon of sesame oil
- 1/4 cup of soy sauce
- 2 teaspoons of honey
- 1/2 teaspoon of rice vinegar

Instructions

- Take the tuna steaks out of the refrigerator.
- Mix the honey, soy sauce, sesame oil, grated ginger, & rice vinegar in a large mixing bowl.
- Place the tuna steaks in your marinade & leave to marinate in the fridge for about 20-30 minutes, covered.
- Preheat the air fryer to 380 degrees F and cook the tuna steaks for 4 minutes in one layer.
- Allow the tuna steaks to rest for two minutes before slicing and serving. If desired, garnish with sesame seeds and green onions.

Air Fryer Tilapia

Preparation and Cooking Time

15 minutes

Servings

4 persons

Nutritional facts

287 calories, 9g fat ,2g fiber ,30g carbs ,4g protein

Ingredients

- 4 tilapia fillets
- 1/2 teaspoon onion powder
- 1/2 teaspoon salt
- 2 tablespoons olive oil
- 1/2 teaspoon paprika
- 1/2 teaspoon garlic powder
- 1/2 teaspoon black pepper

Instructions

- Preheat the air fryer to 400 degrees Fahrenheit.
- Drizzle olive oil over the tilapia fillets on a big plate.
- Combine the paprika, garlic powder, onion powder, salt, & pepper in a small bowl.
- Season the fillets evenly and then arrange them in a single layer in the air fryer.
- Cook the tilapia fillets for 10 minutes, flipping halfway through.
- Remove the tilapia from the air fryer, season with salt and pepper, and serve with lemon wedges (if desired).

Air Fryer Frozen Fish Sticks

Preparation and Cooking Time

9 minutes

Servings

3 persons

Nutritional facts

274 calories, 24g fat ,2g fiber ,51g carbs ,36g protein

Ingredients

- Dozen frozen fish sticks

Instructions

- Preheat the air fryer to 400 degrees Fahrenheit.
- Put frozen fish sticks in a single layer in the air fryer, ensuring they don't touch.
- Cook for 9 to 10 minutes, flipping halfway through until thoroughly warmed.
- Take it out of the air fryer and eat it.

Air Fryer Crab Cakes

Preparation and Cooking Time

15 minutes

Servings

4 persons

Nutritional facts

158 calories, 22g fat ,2g fiber ,65g carbs ,16g protein

Ingredients

- 8 ounces lump crab meat
- 3 tablespoons breadcrumbs
- 2 teaspoons Old Bay Seasoning
- 1 red bell pepper, de-seeded and chopped
- 3 green onions, chopped
- 3 tablespoons mayonnaise
- 1 teaspoon lemon juice

Instructions

- Preheat the air fryer to 370 degrees Fahrenheit.
- Combine the lump pepper, crab meat, green onions, breadcrumbs, mayonnaise, Old Bay Seasoning, & lemon juice in a large mixing bowl and stir to combine.
- Form four crab patties of even size. There are a lot of liquids in lump crab meat, and you want to retain as much of them as possible.
- Arrange a ring of parchment paper in the bottom of the hot air fryer and carefully place the crab cakes inside.
- In an air fryer, cook your fresh crab cakes for 8-10 minutes, or until the crust is golden brown.
- Remove the crab cakes from the air fryer and serve with your preferred sauce and a squeeze of lemon, if desired.

Air Fryer Frozen Popcorn Shrimp

Preparation and Cooking Time

6 minutes

Servings

2 persons

Nutritional facts

261 calories, 24g fat ,0g fiber ,10g carbs ,12g protein

Ingredients

- Six ounces frozen popcorn shrimp (about 28-30 pieces)

Instructions

- Preheat the air fryer to 400 degrees Fahrenheit.
- Put frozen shrimp in a single layer in the air fryer.
- Cook the popcorn shrimp in the basket for 6 minutes, shaking halfway through.
- Take the shrimp out of the air fryer & serve right away.

Air Fryer Catfish with Spicy Tartar Sauce

Preparation and Cooking Time

25 minutes

Servings

4 persons

Nutritional facts

481 calories, 2g fat ,3g fiber ,6g carbs ,14g protein

Ingredients

- 3/4 cup cornmeal
- 1/2 cup mayonnaise
- 3 teaspoons Cajun seasoning
- 4 catfish fillets
- 1/4 cup dill pickles
- 1 Tablespoon lemon juice
- 1 teaspoon Cajun seasoning

Instructions

- In a gallon zip lock bag, mix the cornmeal & Cajun spices.
- Paper towels are used to dry the catfish fillets. Then, 2 at a time, add them to the bag and shake to coat the fillets in the mixture. Repeat with the remaining fillets until they are all covered.
- In the air fryer basket, place the catfish fillets. Ensure air can circulate the fillets by not stacking them.
- Cook for 15 minutes at 390 degrees F, turning the fillets halfway through.
- Increase the temperature to 400 F and cook for another 5 minutes to brown the fillets well.
- It can be served with lemon wedges & spicy tartar sauce on the side.
- Dill pickles should be chopped into small bits.
- Combine the mayonnaise, dill pickles, lemon juice, and Cajun seasoning.

Air Fryer Crab Stuffed Mushrooms

Preparation and Cooking Time

33 minutes

Servings

28 persons

Nutritional facts

33 calories, 16g fat ,0.2g fiber ,6g carbs ,11g protein

Ingredients

- 2 pounds of Baby Bella Mushrooms
- 1 teaspoon of Oregano
- 1 teaspoon of Hot Sauce
- 8 ounces of Lump Crab
- ½ cup Seasoned Bread Crumbs
- 1 large egg
- Cooking Spray
- 2 teaspoons of Tony Chachere's Salt Blend
- ¼ Red Onion

- 2 Celery Ribs, diced
- ½ cup Parmesan Cheese, shredded, divided

Instructions

- Preheat the Air Fryer or the oven to 400 degrees Fahrenheit.
- Apply cooking spray to the Air Fryer pan or baking sheet. Mushroom stems should be bent. Spray the tops of the mushrooms with olive oil cooking spray. To season the mushrooms, sprinkle Tony Chachere's on them.
- Onion and celery should be diced.
- Combine the celery, onions, crab, egg, breadcrumbs, oregano, 1/2 of the grated Parmesan, and spicy sauce in a mixing bowl.
- Fill each mushroom with the filling and then pile it up a little to make a tiny mound.
- Top with the remaining shredded Parmesan.
- In an Air Fryer, bake for 8-9 minutes.

Shrimp Po Boy Sandwich Recipe

Preparation and Cooking Time

23 minutes

Servings

6 persons

Nutritional facts

397 calories, 43g fat ,2g fiber ,9g carbs ,32 protein

Ingredients

- 1 lb. (453g) large shrimp peeled, deveined, and tails removed
- 4 tablespoon buttermilk
- shredded lettuce
- sliced tomatoes
- 1-2 jalapeños seeded and sliced
- red onion thinly sliced
- 1 cup Panko breadcrumbs
- 1 tablespoon Franks Red Hot Buffalo Ranch seasoning
- 1/2 teaspoon Italian seasoning
- oil for frying
- 1 cup flour
- 1 teaspoon salt
- 1/2 teaspoon chili powder
- 3 eggs
- 6 French bread rolls or hoagie buns
- Remoulade Sauce

Instructions

- Heat the oil in a skillet to 350 degrees Fahrenheit / 176 degrees Celsius.
- Three small bowls should be gathered. Mix the flour, salt, and chili powder in a separate bowl. In a separate bowl, whisk together the egg and buttermilk. Mix the panko, Franks Red Hot Buffalo Ranch seasoning, & Italian seasoning in the last bowl.
- One pound of shrimp should be peeled, devein, and the tails removed.
- You should first coat the shrimp in the flour mixture, then dip in the egg mixture, & lastly, coat with the Panko seasoning.
- Cook the shrimp in the skillet until golden brown, about 1-two minutes per side, or 3-5 minutes if completely submerged in oil. To drain, place on a platter lined with paper towels.
- Heat the air fryer to 360 degrees Fahrenheit (182 degrees Celsius).

- Shake off any excess crumbs, coat half of the shrimp in cooking spray, and place in the air fryer basket.
- Cook for 8 minutes, flipping halfway through, until crispy and golden brown.
- Remove the shrimp from the air fryer and set them aside before continuing with the remaining shrimp.
- Rolls or buns should be cut in half.
- On both pieces of the bread, spread the remoulade sauce.
- Stack the tomato, onion, jalapenos, and lettuce on top of the fried shrimp on the bottom half of the bread.

Air Fryer Furikake Salmon Recipe

Preparation and Cooking Time

15 minutes

Servings

3 persons

Nutritional facts

578 calories, 4g fat ,3g fiber ,14g carbs ,9 protein

Ingredients

- ½ cup mayonnaise
- salt and pepper to taste
- 1 tablespoon shoyu
- 1-pound salmon fillet
- 2 tablespoon furikake

Instructions

- Preheat the air fryer to 400 degrees Fahrenheit.
- Combine mayonnaise and shoyu in a small bowl. Set aside after thoroughly mixing.
- Dry the salmon fillet with a paper towel. Season both sides of the fillet with salt and pepper. If you want to cook with the skin on, place it side down.
- On top of the salmon, spread the mayonnaise-shoyu mixture in a uniform layer. Furikake should be sprinkled on top of the mayonnaise.
- Using nonstick cooking spray, coat the air fryer basket. Put the salmon fillet skin side down into the pan. Cook for 8-10 minutes, or until flaky & cooked through.

Salmon Cooked to Perfection

Preparation and Cooking Time

35 minutes

Servings

2 persons

Nutritional facts

270 calories, 15g fat ,4g fiber ,26g carbs ,19g protein

Ingredients

- 1 lemon
- 1/2 teaspoon pepper
- Two 4-6 oz. salmon filets
- 1 tablespoon olive oil
- 1/2 teaspoon salt
- 1/2 teaspoon Italian seasoning blend

Instructions

- Slice the lemon in half and set it aside. Half of it should be saved for juicing, and the second half should be cut into thin pieces.
- Drizzle olive oil on top of the salmon fillets, skin side down. Half a lemon's juice should be squeezed over the fish.

- Season the fish with salt, pepper, and the Italian seasoning mix. If desired, garnish with lemon slices.
- In the air fryer basket, put the fish skin side down. Cook the salmon for 8-10 minutes at 375 degrees F, or until done.

Air Fryer Cajun Scallops

Preparation and Cooking Time

11 minutes

Servings

2 persons

Nutritional facts

397 calories, 8g fat ,2g fiber ,13g carbs ,8g protein

Ingredients

- 4-6 Sea scallops
- Kosher salt to taste
- Cooking spray
- Cajun seasoning

Instructions

- Preheat the air fryer to 400 degrees Fahrenheit.
- Remove the fresh sea scallops from the fridge and give them a short rinse in cold water. Remove the side muscle and pat it dry with paper towels with your fingers.
- Line the basket with aluminum foil & lightly spray with cooking spray once your air fryer is preheated.
- Season the scallops with kosher salt and Cajun spice all over with a light spritz of frying oil.
- Cook for 3 minutes in the air fryer with all of the scallops. Cook for 3 minutes more on the other side, or till it is opaque & registers at least 130 degrees Fahrenheit internally.
- Serve with pasta, salad, or roasted vegetables as a side dish.

Honey Sriracha Air Fryer Salmon

Preparation and Cooking Time

10 minutes

Servings

2 persons

Nutritional facts

580 calories, 9g fat ,1g fiber ,2g carbs ,5g protein

Ingredients

- 1.5 lbs. salmon
- salt to taste
- 3 tbsp. honey
- 2 tbsp. sriracha
- cooking spray

Instructions

- Combine the sriracha sauce and honey in a small bowl. Mix thoroughly.
- Season the salmon with salt and drizzle it with the honey mixture. Allow 20 minutes for it to get to room temperature.
- Preheat the air fryer to 400 degrees F and cook the salmon for 7 minutes.

Air Fryer Shrimp Fajitas Recipe

Preparation and Cooking Time

14 minutes

Servings

2 persons

Nutritional facts

338 calories,15g fat ,2g fiber ,26g carbs ,19g protein

Ingredients

- 1 pound (450g) raw shrimp thawed
- pico de gallo
- 1 avocado sliced
- 3 small mixed bell peppers sliced
- 1 small yellow onion sliced
- 1 tablespoon vegetable oil divided
- 4 tortillas
- lime crema

Instructions

- Heat the air fryer for 5 minutes at 375°F (190°F).
- Season the vegetables in the meantime. Combine half of the oil & 1/2 of the fajita seasoning in a mixing bowl. Air fry the vegetables for 3 minutes in the Air Fryer basket.
- Season the shrimp with the remaining oil and fajita seasoning while the vegetable fry.
- After 3 minutes, use a spatula to shift the vegetables to one side of the air fryer basket and the shrimp to the other.
- At 375°F (190°F), air fry for 6 minutes, flipping halfway through. Combine all ingredients in a mixing bowl and serve.
- Assemble the fajitas and top with your preferred toppings on tortillas.

10 Minute Air Fryer Salmon

Preparation and Cooking Time

10 minutes

Servings

2 persons

Nutritional facts

380 calories,10g fat ,1g fiber ,16g carbs ,5g protein

Ingredients

- Two salmon fillets, skin on
- olive oil spray
- salt and pepper

Instructions

- Apply olive oil spray to the air fryer.
- Put the salmon fillet into the air fryer. Now gently spray with olive oil spray and season with desired seasonings.
- You need to air fry at 400 degrees F for 8 minutes.

Air Fryer Tuna Patties

Preparation and Cooking Time

30 minutes

Servings

3 persons

Nutritional facts

387 calories, 6g fat ,1g fiber ,10g carbs ,2g protein

Ingredients

- 1 Tablespoon of EVOO
- 2 7- oz. cans albacore tuna fish
- 1/2 cup of panko crumbs
- 2 eggs whisked
- 1/2 cup of panko crumbs
- 1/4 cup of parmesan cheese

- 1 Tablespoon of lime juice
- 1 stalk of celery
- 1/4 cup of fresh parsley chopped
- 3 Tablespoons of parmesan cheese grated
- 1/2 teaspoon of oregano
- 1/4 teaspoon of salt
- 1 Tablespoon of butter
- 1/2 cup of onion chopped
- 1/2 red bell pepper chopped
- 1 teaspoon of minced garlic
- Black pepper to taste
- 1 teaspoon of sriracha
- Nonstick spray

Instructions

- In a skillet, heat the oil and butter over medium-high heat.
- You need to sauté for 5-7 minutes with the onions, red bell pepper, and garlic.
- Drain tuna cans thoroughly. Fill a medium mixing bowl halfway with the mixture. Lime juice should be poured over the tuna.
- Place sautéed vegetables in a mixing bowl.
- Combine celery, parsley, and cheese in a mixing bowl.
- Add oregano, salt, and pepper to taste.
- Add a dash of sriracha for a strong taste.
- Add the panko crumbs and mix well.
- Mix in the eggs till the mixture forms a beautiful Pattie. You could add an extra egg if necessary, but the tuna is usually wet enough that it isn't required.
- Refrigerate for 30-60 minutes, or even overnight, after forming 6 patties. This will make them more manageable.
- Remove from the refrigerator and coat in a panko crumb and parmesan cheese mixture.
- Place back on the plate and spray nonstick spray on tops.
- Place in the air fryer, being careful not to overcrowd it.
- Air fry for 4 minutes at 390 degrees F. Turn patties carefully and coat tops with nonstick spray. Return to the air fryer for another 4 minutes.
- Remove and sprinkle with chopped parsley.

Air Fryer Keto Blackened Salmon

Preparation and Cooking Time

20 minutes

Servings

2 persons

Nutritional facts

498 calories, 1g fat ,2g fiber ,35g carbs ,4g protein

Ingredients

- 1 tablespoon of keta blackened salmon seasoning
- One lb. of salmon, cut into 3 to 4 filets
- 1 tbsp. of olive oil

Instructions

- Preheat your air fryer to 400 degrees Fahrenheit, then prepare the seasoning.
- Using a silicone brush, brush olive oil across both sides of the salmon fillets.
- Use blackened seasoning to season salmon fillets.

- Place the salmon in the air fryer tray skin-side down.Cook for 7-10 minutes, or until done to your liking.

Air Fryer Tilapia with Herbs and Garlic

Preparation and Cooking Time

15 minutes

Servings

2 persons

Nutritional facts

380 calories, 6g fat ,1g fiber ,10g carbs ,2g protein

Ingredients

- 2 fresh tilapia filets, approximately 6 oz. each
- 1 teaspoon minced garlic
- freshly ground pepper to taste
- 2 teaspoons olive oil
- Two teaspoons fresh chives chopped
- 2 teaspoons fresh parsley chopped
- salt to taste

Instructions

- Preheat the air fryer to 400 degrees Fahrenheit.
- Use a paper towel to pat dry fresh tilapia fillets.
- Combine olive oil, chives, parsley, garlic, salt, and pepper in a small bowl.
- Brush the tops of the tilapia fillets with the mixture.
- Brush a little olive oil or cooking spray on the bottom of the basket.
- You need to cook for 8 - 10 minutes or until the fish is no longer transparent and flakes readily with a fork.
- Serve right away.

Air Fryer Coconut Shrimp with Honey Siracha Sauce

Preparation and Cooking Time

20 minutes

Servings

4 persons

Nutritional facts

372 calories, 1g fat ,2g fiber ,35g carbs ,4g protein

Ingredients

- 1 lb. shrimp, XL or Jumbo, shelled and deveined
- ¼ tsp cayenne pepper
- 1 c shredded coconut, sweetened
- ¼ c honey
- 2 large eggs
- ¾ c flour
- ½ tsp garlic powder
- ½ tsp sea salt
- 1 T Siracha
- Juice of ½ a lime

Instructions

- Set aside the air fryer basket after spraying it with spray oil.
- Take three bowls with you. Combine flour, salt, pepper, garlic, and cayenne in a mixing bowl. In a separate bowl, whisk the eggs thoroughly. Last but not least, add the coconut. The flour mixture, eggs, and coconut should be lined up in the following order: flour mixture, eggs, and coconut.

- Each shrimp should be dipped in flour and evenly coated. Dip it into the egg and coat it completely. Finally, put it in the coconut & gently press it onto the shrimp to keep it in place. Put the shrimp in the air fryer basket in a way that they don't touch. If necessary, work in batches.
- Cook for 4 minutes in an air fryer at 350°F before flipping. Cook for another 3-4 minutes, or until golden brown and crispy.
- Before serving, whisk together the sauce ingredients and enjoy.

Crispy Fish Tacos with Lime Crema

Preparation and Cooking Time

40 minutes

Servings

5 persons

Nutritional facts

534 calories, 20g fat, 3g fiber, 20g carbs, 18g protein

Ingredients

- 1 lb. firm white fish such as cod, haddock, Pollock, halibut, or walleye
- 1 tsp. onion powder
- 1 package corn tortillas
- Toppings such as avocado, tomatoes, cabbage, jalapenos, radishes, salsa, or hot sauce optional
- 2 cups of sour cream
- 1 tsp. of cumin
- 1 tsp. of lemon pepper
- 1 tsp. of red chili flakes
- 1 tsp. of kosher salt split
- 1 tsp. of pepper split
- ¾ cup of gluten-free flour blend
- 3 eggs
- 1 cup of gluten-free Panko breadcrumbs
- 1 tsp. of garlic powder
- non-aerosol cooking oil spray
- 1-2 limes zest and juice

Instructions

- If frozen, defrost 1 pound of firm white fish. Dry the fish with paper towels after it has thawed.
- Liberally season with pepper and kosher salt on both sides of the fish.
- Combine 3/4 cup gluten-free flour blend (or ordinary AP flour if not gluten-free). In a separate bowl, crack 3 eggs and whisk them together until well blended. In a third bowl, place 1 cup gluten-free panko breadcrumbs. Then insert onion powder, garlic powder, onion powder, cumin, lemon pepper, and red chili flakes (1 tsp. each) 1/2 teaspoons salt and pepper. Stir until everything is well blended.
- Each fish should be dipped in flour, then eggs, and finally the breadcrumb mixture. Make certain that each piece is completely coated. On a platter, arrange the battered fish and carry on with the rest of the fish. (Ensure that any surplus flour or breadcrumbs are discarded.)
- Turn on the Air Fryer and generously coat both sides of the fish fillets in cooking oil. Place as many fish as comfortably fit in the basket, but don't overcrowd it. Put the basket in the Air Fryer & set the temperature to 370 degrees Fahrenheit with a 6-minute timer. Cook for 6 minutes, remove the basket, flip the fish, and cook for another 6 minutes. Remove the fish and set it aside once it has finished cooking.
- Repeat the process with the remaining fish, spraying the basket each time. Depending on the thickness of the fish and the model

of the Air Fryer, cooking times may vary slightly. On the outside, the fish should be crispy, and on the interior, it should be cooked through but not overcooked.

- In a small bowl, combine 2 cups of sour cream. Using a small grater, zest lime into the sour cream.
- Squeeze the lime juice into the bowl after cutting it in half. Depending on the size of the limes, you may need two.
- Using a tiny whisk or fork, combine everything with a pinch of salt.
- Warm the tortillas and place the crispy fish on top. Serve with lime crema and any other desired toppings.

Air Fryer Fish Fingers

Preparation and Cooking Time

25 minutes

Servings

2 persons

Nutritional facts

99 calories, 35g fat ,1g fiber ,1g carbs ,16g protein

Ingredients

- 1 pound (450 grams) fish fillets patted dry and salted
- 1 cup (50 grams) dried breadcrumbs
- tartar sauce
- ½ cup all-purpose flour
- 1 teaspoon salt divided
- ½ teaspoon ground black pepper divided
- 2 eggs
- lemon wedges

Instructions

- If you're using frozen fresh, make sure it's thoroughly thawed before using it. Salt the fish and set it aside for at least 20-half an hour (up to 1 hour). This will help remove moisture from the fish & make it firmer, resulting in crispy fish sticks. You can also use this time to season the fish before breading it.
- Season the flour and breadcrumbs with salt and pepper, and do the same with the flour. Other seasonings, like garlic powder, onion powder, chili powder, and smoky paprika, are optional, and you can use any aromatics you choose.
- Using flour, dredge the fish & shake off any excess flour. After that, dip it in the egg and coat it in breadcrumbs.
- Place the fish sticks in the Air Fryer basket when they've been properly coated, making sure they don't overlap. You may then lightly spritz them with oil for added crispiness and color. Cook for 10 minutes at 400°F (200°C), flip, & cook for another 5 minutes.
- Remove the fish sticks from the Air Fryer and serve with homemade tartar sauce and a squeeze of fresh lemon juice for added taste.

Bacon-Wrapped Shrimp in the Air Fryer

Preparation and Cooking Time

55 minutes

Servings

8 persons

Nutritional facts

380 calories,13g fat ,3g fiber ,14g carbs ,7g protein

Ingredients

- 24 jumbo raw shrimp deveined with tail on, fresh or thawed from frozen
- 1 -2 cloves minced garlic

- 1 tablespoon finely chopped fresh parsley
- 8 slices bacon cut into thirds
- 1 tablespoon olive oil
- 1 teaspoon paprika

Instructions

- Combine olive oil, paprika, garlic, and parsley in a small bowl.
- If necessary, peel raw shrimp, leave tails on, and add a medium-sized mixing dish.
- Pour the olive oil mixture over the shrimp and toss lightly to coat them.
- Wrap a piece of bacon around the middle of each shrimp and place seam side down on a small baking dish.
- Refrigerate for 30 minutes before serving. (This keeps the bacon from falling apart when cooking.)
- Preheat the air fryer to 400 degrees Fahrenheit.
- Place the shrimp seam side down on the bacon, tightening it if necessary, but avoid overlapping. (Depending on the size of your air fryer, you may need to cook in batches.)
- Then cook for 8–10 minutes, or till bacon is cooked through. If necessary, repeat with the remaining shrimp. Serve right away.

Foil Packet Salmon

Preparation and Cooking Time

25 minutes

Servings

4 persons

Nutritional facts

245 calories, 10g fat ,1g fiber ,19g carbs ,6g protein

Ingredients

- 1 lb. salmon 4-4 oz. fillets
- 1 tsp garlic powder
- ¼ tsp white pepper
- ¼ tsp red pepper flakes optional
- Kosher salt
- ½ tsp ginger powder
- ½ tsp kosher salt
- 4 c green beans defrosted or vegetable of choice
- 4 tbsp. low sodium soy sauce
- 2 tbsp. honey
- 2 tsp sesame seeds plus more to garnish
- Canola oil spray

Instructions

- Combine the soy sauce, honey, canola oil, sesame seeds, garlic, ginger powder, and red pepper flakes (if using) in a mixing bowl.
- On a baking sheet, lay out four 12" x 11" foil sheets. Season the fillets & green beans with salt to taste after spraying them with cooking spray. Between the foil sheets, divide and center the cut green beans. On top of the green beans, place a salmon fillet.
- Pour the sauce over each piece of fish and wrap it tightly in foil.

Air Fryer Blackened Shrimp

Preparation and Cooking Time

15 minutes

Servings

4 persons

Nutritional facts

175 calories, 5g fat ,1g fiber ,9g carbs ,2g protein

Ingredients

- 1-pound large shrimp, peeled and deveined
- Lemon Wedges
- 2 tablespoons olive oil
- 1 tablespoon blackened seasoning
- Favorite Dipping Sauce
- Parsley, chopped

Instructions

- Preheat the air fryer for 5 minutes at 400 degrees F.
- Toss shrimp with olive oil in a mixing bowl, draining any excess on the bottom.
- Toss the shrimp in a bowl with the blackened seasoning.
- When the air fryer basket is hot, lightly butter it.
- Toss in the shrimp.
- Cook for 5-6 minutes at 400 degrees F, shaking halfway through. Cook until the shrimp are pink and curling.
- Remove and serve with dipping sauces of your choice. Optional garnishes include lemon wedges and parsley.

Air Fryer Salmon Patties Gluten Free

Preparation and Cooking Time

50 minutes

Servings

4 persons

Nutritional facts

358 calories, 3g fat ,9g fiber ,221g carbs ,61g protein

Ingredients

- 1 small salmon fillet, skin removed (about 5 ounces)
- 1 tablespoon freshly squeezed lemon juice
- 1/2 teaspoon garlic powder
- 2/3 cup almond flour
- 1 large egg
- 1/2 medium-sized onion, chopped
- 1 tablespoon chopped fresh chives
- 1/2 teaspoon kosher salt
- 1/8 teaspoon ground black pepper

Instructions

- In a food processor, combine all ingredients and cut the salmon fillet into small pieces.
- Process on high until everything is mixed, but there are still small chunks of fish, onion, and chives.
- Refrigerate for 30 minutes after shaping into 4 3-inch diameter patties.
- Using nonstick cooking spray, coat the air fryer basket. Spray the tops of the patties with cooking spray and arrange them in a single layer at the bottom of the basket.
- Cook for 10-12 minutes in an air fryer at 400°F, or till cooked through and crispy on the outside.

Quick and Easy Air Fryer Cod

Preparation and Cooking Time

21 minutes

Servings

6 persons

Nutritional facts

70 calories, 3g fat ,1g fiber ,23g carbs ,13g protein

Ingredients

- 6 pieces of cod about 1 ½ pound
- ½ teaspoon garlic powder
- ⅛ teaspoon salt
- ¼ cup gluten-free flour
- ½ cup plantain flour or use more gluten-free flour
- 2 teaspoons Cajun seasoning or old bay
- 1 teaspoon smoked paprika
- 1 teaspoon light oil for spraying
- pepper to taste

Instructions

- Preheat the air fryer basket to 360 degrees F and spray it with oil.
- In a mixing bowl, combine the spices and whisk to combine.
- Using a paper towel, pat the cod dry after removing it from the package.
- Each fish should be dipped in the flour spice mixture, then turned over and pressed down to cover all sides.
- In the air fryer basket, place the fish. Make sure there is enough room around each piece of fish for air to circulate.
- Cook for 8 minutes before flipping the fish in the air fryer. Cook for another 8 minutes on the other side.
- Serve with a squeeze of lemon.

Air Fryer Honey Teriyaki Salmon Recipe

Preparation and Cooking Time

25 minutes

Servings

2 persons

Nutritional facts

180 calories, 11g fat ,1g fiber ,1g carbs ,6g protein

Ingredients

- 8 tbsp. Less Sodium Teriyaki
- 2 tbsp. extra virgin olive oil
- 3 tbsp. honey
- 2 cubes frozen garlic
- 3 pieces' wild salmon (each cut into 2 pieces)

Instructions

- Whisk everything together to make the marinade.
- Pour over defrosted fish and marinate for 20 minutes.
- Place 3 pieces at a time in the air fryer. Preheat oven to 350°F and bake for 12 minutes, flipping after 6 minutes.

Air Fried and Korean Grilled Shrimp Skewers

Preparation and Cooking Time

11 minutes

Servings

16 persons

Nutritional facts

76 calories, 7g fat ,2g fiber ,14g carbs ,1g protein

- **Ingredients**
- 1 tablespoon olive oil
- 1 teaspoon minced garlic
- Red pepper flakes to taste optional
- 2 tablespoons tamari soy sauce or regular soy

- 2 tablespoons honey
- 2 tablespoons Korean Gochujang
- 1 tablespoon lemon juice
- 2 pounds (907g) peeled and cleaned shrimp, tails still on

Instructions

- Preheat the Air Fryer to 350 degrees Fahrenheit/180 degrees Celsius. Place the shrimp in the Air Fryer without touching the skewers.
- Cook for 5-8 minutes, rotating the skewers halfway through. Start with less time, adding more as needed because air fryer temperatures can vary.

Cheesy Tuna Air Fryer Flautas – Perfect for Cinco de Mayo

Preparation and Cooking Time

20 minutes

Servings

2 persons

Nutritional facts

234 calories, 17g fat ,4g fiber ,31g carbs ,6g protein

Ingredients

- 8 small flour tortillas
- 1/2 tsp cilantro, chopped
- 1/2 cup cheddar cheese, shredded
- 1 can Wild Selections tuna
- 1/8 tsp salt
- 1/8 tsp garlic powder
- 1/8 tsp ancho chili powder
- 1/2 cup guacamole for dipping
- 1/2 cup sour cream for dipping

Instruction

- In a bowl, combine the tuna, salt, garlic powder, ancho chili powder, as well as cilantro.
- Top each tortilla with a sprinkling of shredded cheddar cheese.
- On top of the cheese, spread roughly 1 tablespoon of tuna mixture.
- If desired, top with more cheese.
- Roll them up and fix them with a toothpick to make the tortillas.
- Close the Air Fryer and put one layer in the bottom.
- Cook for 5-7 minutes at 350 degrees F, checking after 4 minutes.
- Remove from Air Fryer when browned & crispy, and set aside to cool for a few minutes.
- Serve with guacamole & sour cream.

Air Fried Salmon with Hoisin Ginger Marinade

Preparation and Cooking Time

13 minutes

Servings

2 persons

Nutritional facts

180 calories, 8g fat ,1g fiber ,22g carbs ,2g protein

Ingredients

- 1 4-6 oz. salmon filet
- 1 tbsp. sesame oil
- 3 tablespoons maple syrup

- 1/3 cup hoisin sauce
- 2 tablespoon ginger paste
- 1 clove garlic minced
- 1 tsp sriracha
- 2 tablespoons soy sauce
- 1 1/2 tablespoons rice wine vinegar

Instructions

- Seal a zip lock bag with the salmon and marinade, then refrigerate. Marinate the salmon for at least 60 minutes and up to 8 hours for the best results.
- After your fish has marinated, top it with everything but the bagel seasoning & pre-heat your air fryer at 400 degrees for 2-3 minutes.
- Put an air fryer parchment paper circle in the bottom of the air fryer. Put the fish on top and return the basket to the air fryer.
- Depending on the size of the salmon, you can cook for 6-8 minutes.

Air Fryer Garlic Shrimp- Ready in 10 Minutes

Preparation and Cooking Time

15 minutes

Servings

4 persons

Nutritional facts

380 calories, 6g fat ,1g fiber ,23g carbs ,13g protein

Ingredients

- 1 Pound Jumbo shrimp, peeled and deveined
- ½ teaspoon Kosher salt
- 1 teaspoon Garlic powder
- 1 Tablespoon avocado oil
- ½ teaspoon Pepper

Instructions

- Place the shrimp, garlic powder, avocado oil, salt, and pepper in a medium mixing bowl. Toss everything together.
- In your Air Fryer, place your shrimp. Preheat oven to 400 degrees Fahrenheit and bake for 10 minutes. There's no need to shake halfway through. For jumbo shrimp, 10 minutes is the ideal cooking time, but if the shrimp are smaller, you'll need to cook them for much less time.

Bang Shrimp

Preparation and Cooking Time

40 minutes

Servings

6 persons

Nutritional facts

415 calories, 24g fat, 1g fiber ,43g carbs ,5g protein

Ingredients

- 1 cup of cornstarch seasoned with pepper and salt
- 2 tablespoons of buttermilk
- 1 tablespoon of sriracha
- 1/3 cup of sweet Thai chili sauce
- ¼ cup of sour cream
- ¼ cup of mayonnaise
- 2 pounds of shrimp, peeled and deveined
- ½ to 1 cup of buttermilk
- Cooking oil spray

- A large egg whisked with 1 teaspoon of water
- Pinch dried dill weed

Instructions

- Season the corn starch with salt and pepper in a wide, shallow bowl.
- Toss the shrimp in the buttermilk in a large mixing bowl to coat them.
- Dredge the shrimp in seasoned cornstarch & arrange it in an air fryer basket in a single layer. The shrimp will need to be cooked in batches.
- Brush with egg wash after spraying with cooking oil.
- Cook for 4 minutes at 450°F or 5 minutes at 400°F, or until golden brown on top. Turn the shrimp over gently, spritz with oil again and then brush with egg wash. On the second side, cook for 4 to 5 minutes, or till browned and crisp. Repeat with the rest of the prawns.
- While the shrimp is cooking, make the sauce. Whisk the sour cream, sweet chili sauce, mayonnaise, sriracha, buttermilk, & dried dill weed in a medium mixing bowl until smooth.
- Serve the shrimp hot, with the sauce drizzled over them.

Air Fryer Shrimp "Boil"

Preparation and Cooking Time

1 hour 5 minutes

Servings

4 persons

Nutritional facts

505 calories, 0.7g fat, 3.1g fiber, 27g carbs,1.3g protein

Ingredients

- 1 pound of baby red potatoes
- 4 tablespoons of olive oil, divided
- 3 teaspoons of seafood seasoning
- ¼ cup of water
- 8 ounces of andouille sausage, sliced
- 1 ear corn
- 1 medium onion, sliced
- 1 pound of raw large shrimp, peeled and deveined
- 1 lemon, cut into wedges

Instructions

- Heat the air fryer to 400 degrees Fahrenheit.
- In a microwave-safe bowl, place the potatoes. You need to microwave on high for five minutes after adding water. Use cold water to rinse the bowl until the potatoes are cool enough to handle.
- In a large mixing bowl, cut the potatoes in half lengthwise. Combine the sausage, corn, & onion in a large mixing bowl. Mix three tablespoons of olive oil and 2 teaspoons of seafood spice. Stir to coat.
- In a separate bowl, combine the shrimp with the remaining 1 tbsp. oil and 1 tsp seafood seasoning; stir to coat.
- Cook for 10 minutes with half of the potato mixture in the air fryer basket. Cook for another five minutes, stirring occasionally. Cook for another 5 minutes until the potatoes are soft, the sausage is cooked through, the shrimp are bright pink on the outside, and the meat is opaque. Repeat with remaining potato mixture and shrimp. Serve with lemon slices on the side.

Air Fryer Healthy White Fish with Garlic & Lemon

Preparation and Cooking Time

17 minutes

Servings

2 persons

Nutritional facts

169 calories, 10g fat, 1g fiber ,19g carbs ,10g protein

Ingredients

- 12 ounces (340 g) tilapia filets, or other white fish (2 filets-6 ounces each)
- fresh cracked black pepper, to taste
- 1/2 teaspoon (2.5 ml) garlic powder
- 1/2 teaspoon (2.5 ml) lemon pepper seasoning
- 1/2 teaspoon (2.5 ml) onion powder, optional
- kosher salt or sea salt, to taste
- fresh chopped parsley
- lemon wedges

Instructions

- Preheat the Air Fryer for 5 minutes at 360 degrees Fahrenheit.
- Thoroughly clean the fish fillets by washing and drying them. After spraying or coating olive oil, season with garlic powder, lemon pepper, onion powder, salt, and pepper. Rep on the other side.
- Place the perforated baking paper into the air fryer's base. Lightly mist the paper.
- Place the fish on top of the paper. Place a couple lemon slices next to the fish.
- Preheat the oven to 360°F and air fried the fish for 6 to 12 minutes, or until flaky. The amount of time depends on the thickness of the fillets, the temperature of the fillets, and personal choice.
- Garnish with toasted lemon wedges and chopped parsley and serve warm.

Air Fryer Frozen Seafood Medley Mix

Preparation and Cooking Time

15 minutes

Servings

2 persons

Nutritional facts

110 calories, 9g fat, 8g fiber, 10g carbs ,3g protein

Ingredients

- One lb. frozen seafood medley
- Salt and pepper to taste

Instructions

- Use a nonstick cooking spray to coat the air fryer basket.
- In the air fryer basket, place the frozen seafood medley. Cook for 15 minutes at 400 degrees Fahrenheit.
- Remove the air fryer basket halfway through the cooking time, season the seafood medley with salt, pepper, and any other seasonings, toss to coat the seafood, return to the air fryer and finish frying.

Air Fryer Fried Shrimp

Preparation and Cooking Time

55 minutes

Servings

4 persons

Nutritional facts

130 calories, 4g fat ,2g fiber ,25g carbs ,3g protein

Ingredients

- Nonstick cooking spray
- 1 tablespoon ketchup
- 1 tablespoon hot sauce
- 1/2 cup mayonnaise
- 2 tablespoons chopped pickled jalapenos
- 2 tablespoons whole-grain mustard
- 1 pound of large shrimp, peeled and deveined
- Kosher salt and freshly ground black pepper
- 1/2 cup of all-purpose
- 2 large eggs
- 1 cup of panko breadcrumbs
- 1 thinly sliced scallion

Instructions

- Set aside a 3.5-quart air fryer basket that has been sprayed with cooking spray. Using paper towels, pat the shrimp dry, then season with some salt and black pepper.
- Combine the flour, 3/4 tsp salt, and a few pinches of pepper in a shallow baking dish. Whisk the eggs with a pinch of salt in a small basin. Place the panko in a third shallow dish. Before putting a shrimp in the beaten eggs, shake off any extra seasoned flour. Dredge in panko and flip to evenly coat. On a rimmed baking sheet, repeat with remaining shrimp.
- Preheat the oven to 385 degrees Fahrenheit. Place part of the shrimp in a layer in the fryer basket, working in batches, and spray gently with extra cooking spray. Cook for about 10 minutes, flipping halfway through, till the shrimp are golden brown & cooked through.
- In a small mixing dish, combine the pickled jalapenos, mayonnaise, mustard, spicy sauce, ketchup, and scallion. Mix everything together until it's smooth. Dip the fried shrimp into the sauce and enjoy.

Air Fryer 'Shrimp Boil' for Two

Preparation and Cooking Time

25 minutes

Servings

2 persons

Nutritional facts

1250 calories, 9g fat ,4g fiber ,36g carbs ,6g protein

Ingredients

- 3 small red potatoes, sliced 1/2 inch rounds
- 14 Oz smoked sausage, cut into 3-inch pieces
- 2 Tbsp. vegetable oil
- 2 ears of corn, cut into thirds
- 1 Lb. easy-peel shrimp, defrosted
- 1 Tbsp. Old Bay Seasoning

Instructions

- Combine all ingredients in a large mixing bowl and sprinkle with oil, Old Bay seasoning, salt, and pepper. Place the basket on the pan and transfer to the air fryer's basket attachment.

- Put in the air fryer and cook on the fish setting for 7 minutes, tossing halfway through.
- Remove with care and serve.

Spicy Cilantro Lime Shrimp

Preparation and Cooking Time

44 minutes

Servings

4 persons

Nutritional facts

355 calories,11g fat ,4g fiber 29g, carbs ,2g protein

Ingredients

- 1-pound raw shrimp, peeled and deveined
- ½ teaspoon red pepper flakes
- ½ cup cilantro, chopped
- Zest from one lime
- ¼ teaspoon cayenne
- 1 teaspoon smoked paprika or chili powder
- ½ teaspoon ground cumin
- 1 teaspoon kosher salt
- ½ cup fresh lime juice
- ¼ cup salted butter, melted
- ¼ cup olive oil, optional
- 2 garlic cloves, minced
- 1 lime, cut into wedges

Instructions

- Put the shrimp in a plastic bag and seal it.
- In a small mixing bowl, combine the lime juice, butter, olive oil (if using), minced garlic, cayenne pepper, smoked paprika or chili powder, cumin, and salt. Close the bag after pouring over the shrimp.
- Refrigerate for at least 30 minutes.
- Remove the shrimp from the pan and set them in a bowl. Put in the air fryer basket after tossing with cilantro. For even cooking, don't pile the shrimp and don't overcrowd the pan. Spray the shrimp with olive oil or nonstick frying spray and season with paprika or chili powder.
- Set the air fryer to 400°F and place the basket inside. Cook for 2 minutes before removing the basket and flipping the shrimp. Spray with oil and sprinkle with paprika or chili powder. Return to the air fryer & cook for 2 minutes more.
- Remove and serve with lime wedges on the salad or Creamy Cilantro Dressing/Dip.

Spicy Creamy Cilantro Lime Dressing

Preparation and Cooking Time

5 minutes

Servings

1 person

Nutritional facts

998 calories, 7g fat ,2g fiber ,17g carbs, 5g protein

Ingredients

- ½ cup sour cream
- ¼ teaspoon kosher salt
- ½ teaspoon granulated sugar
- ¼ cup mayonnaise, (or if making for a dip, use 1/2 cup)
- 1 cup tightly packed cilantro

- 3 tablespoons olive oil
- 2 cloves garlic, minced
- One jalapeño, deseeded and destemmed
- Lime zest from one lime

Instructions

- In a food processor, combine all ingredients except the lime zest and process for 30 seconds; if you want it creamier, process for 1 minute.
- Pour into a serving bowl or pitcher, and then top with zest.
- Serve as a salad dressing or a dip for chips or shrimp.

Air Fryer Garlic Shrimp with Lemon in 15 minutes

Preparation and Cooking Time

15 minutes

Servings

3 persons

Nutritional facts

164 calories, 7g fat ,8g fiber ,20g carbs ,3g protein

Ingredients

- 1 pound (454 g) raw shrimp, peeled deveined,
- Black pepper, to taste
- lemon wedges
- Vegetable oil or spray to coat shrimp
- 1/4 teaspoon (1.25 ml) garlic powder
- Salt, to taste
- minced parsley and chili flakes (optional)

Instructions

- Toss the shrimp in a bowl with the oil or spray to coat. Toss with the garlic powder, salt, and pepper to coat the shrimp evenly.
- Place the shrimp in a single layer in the air fryer basket.
- Air fry the shrimp for 8-14 minutes at 400°F, lightly shaking and flipping midway through cooking. Cooking times will vary based on the size of the shrimp and the brand and model of air fryer used.
- Place shrimp in a bowl and drizzle with lemon juice. Serve immediately with parsley.

Air Fryer Old Bay Scallops

Preparation and Cooking Time

10 minutes

Servings

4 persons

Nutritional facts

186 calories, 5g fat ,3g fiber ,11g carbs ,4g protein

Ingredients

- 1 pound scallops
- Half Tbsp. olive oil
- 1 Tbsp. Old Bay seasoning

Instructions

- Remove the side muscle from each scallop after patting it dry.
- Combine them with olive oil & Old Bay seasoning in a mixing bowl. Toss until everything is equally distributed.
- Place the scallops in the air fryer basket & cook for 5 to 6 minutes at 400 degrees F.
- Serve and enjoy.

Air Fryer Lobster Tails with Lemon Butter

Preparation and Cooking Time

13 minutes

Servings

2 persons

Nutritional facts

449 calories,13g fat ,3g fiber ,22g carbs ,7g protein

Ingredients

- 2 - 6 oz. Lobster Tails, thawed
- Four Tablespoons salted butter, melted
- One Tablespoon Fresh Lemon juice
- Fresh chopped parsley for garnish

Instructions

- Combine melted butter with lemon to make lemon butter. Combine all ingredients and set aside.
- Lobster tails should be rinsed and drained on paper towels. Butterfly lobster tails cut through the shell, remove the meat, and place it back on top.
- Preheat the Air Fryer to 380 degrees Fahrenheit for 5 minutes. Place the prepared lobster tails in the Air Fryer Basket and drizzle with melted lemon butter tablespoon. Close the Air Fryer basket & cook for 8 minutes at 380° F, or until the lobster meat is opaque. Open the air fryer halfway through baking and drizzle with more lemon butter. Continue to bake until the cake is done.
- Remove lobster tails with care, sprinkle with chopped parsley if preferred, and serve. Extra lemon butter should be available for dipping.

Air Fryer Seafood Boil

Preparation and Cooking Time

20 minutes

Servings

1 person

Nutritional facts

777 calories, 12g fat ,1.1g fiber, 10g carbs, 12g protein

Ingredients

- 1 Fresh Corn of Cob, Cut in Half
- Salt
- 1/2-pound fresh shrimp (or frozen)
- 2 Lobster tails, cut in half (fresh or frozen)
- 2 tablespoons butter
- Black Pepper
- Old Bay Seasoning or Cajun

Instructions

- Combine the seafood boil, butter, and seasonings in the Air Fryer Basket.
- Preheat the oven to 400 degrees F and cook for 10 minutes using the air fryer option. During the cooking process, it's important to shake the basket often.

Air Fryer Fish & Chips

Preparation and Cooking Time

15 minutes

Servings

4 persons

Nutritional facts

309 calories, 9g fat ,2g fiber ,25g carbs ,4g protein

Ingredients

- 1 pound of cod fillet, must be cut into strips
- Large egg beaten
- ¼ teaspoon of black pepper
- 2 cups of panko breadcrumbs
- ½ cup of all-purpose flour
- ½ teaspoon of garlic powder
- 2 teaspoons of paprika
- ¼ teaspoon of salt
- Lemon wedges for serving
- Tartar sauce for serving

Instructions

- Combine the flour, garlic powder, paprika, and salt in a small bowl. In a third bowl, whisk together the beaten egg and panko breadcrumbs.
- Using a paper towel, pat the fish dry. Dredge the fish in the flour mixture, then in the egg, and then in the panko breadcrumbs, softly pushing down until the crumbs stick. Apply oil to both sides.
- For the air fryer, cook for 10 to 12 minutes at 400 degrees F, flipping halfway through, until crispy and faintly brown.
- Open the basket and test for doneness with a fork to see whether it easily peels off. If required, return the fish for another 2 minutes.
- If desired, serve immediately with fries & tartar sauce.

Air Fryer Garlic Shrimp – 15 minutes

Preparation and Cooking Time

25 minutes

Servings

3 persons

Nutritional facts

228 calories, 8g fat ,1g fiber ,15g carbs ,2g protein

Ingredients

- 1 pound (454 g) raw shrimp, peeled deveined,
- Black pepper, to taste
- lemon wedges
- Vegetable oil or spray to coat shrimp
- 1/4 teaspoon (1.25 ml) garlic powder
- Salt to taste, minced parsley, and chili flakes (optional)

Instructions

- Toss the shrimp, garlic powder, salt, and pepper in a bowl to equally coat all shrimp. Place the shrimp in a single layer in the air fryer basket.
- Then air fry for 8-14 minutes at 400°F (depending on shrimp size), gently tossing and flipping halfway through.
- Squeeze lemon juice over the cooked shrimp in the bowl. Serve immediately with parsley and chili flakes.

Garlic Parmesan Air Fried Shrimp Recipe

Preparation and Cooking Time

15 minutes

Servings

2 persons

Nutritional facts

151 calories, 6g fat ,2g fiber ,18g carbs ,2g protein

Ingredients

- 1lb shrimp, deveined and peeled (you can leave tails on if desired)
- 6 cloves garlic, diced
- ½ cup grated parmesan cheese
- 1 tbsp. olive oil
- 1 tsp salt
- 1 tsp fresh cracked pepper
- 1 tbsp. lemon juice
- ¼ cup diced cilantro or parsley, to garnish (optional)

Instructions

- Add shrimp to a large mixing bowl and toss with olive oil, lemon juice, salt, pepper, and garlic.
- Refrigerate for one to three hours after wrapping with plastic wrap.
- Toss parmesan cheese with shrimp in a mixing dish to make a "breading" for the shrimp.
- Preheat the air fryer to 350°F.
- Preheat the air fryer to 350 degrees for 10 minutes, and then put the shrimp in the basket and cook.
- When the shrimp is opaque white, and pink, it is ready to eat.

Classic Shrimp with Salad

Preparation and Cooking Time

17 minutes

Servings

6 persons

Nutritional facts

70 calories,15g fat ,2g fiber ,20g carbs ,4g protein

Ingredients

- 2 pounds large cooked shrimp, peeled and deveined
- 1/2 tsp sea salt
- 1-1/2 cups minced celery
- 1/2 cup minced red onion
- 3 TBS minced fresh dill leaves
- 1/2 tsp sea salt
- 2 pounds' large shrimp cooked in the air fryer
- 1 cup good mayonnaise
- 1 TBS dry white wine
- 1/2 tsp Dijon mustard
- 2 TBS extra virgin olive oil
- 2 tsps. fresh lemon juice
- 3 cloves garlic, finely minced
- 1 tsp freshly ground pepper
- 1/2 tsp freshly ground black pepper

Instructions

- Mix the oil, lemon juice, garlic, pepper, & salt in a large mixing bowl. Toss in the shrimp & toss well to coat. Set this aside for a minute or two.
- Heat the air fryer to 350°F for 3 minutes with the timer set to half an hour.
- In the air fryer basket, arrange the shrimp in a single layer. Cook for about 1 1/2 to 3 minutes, just until the shrimp are pink and translucent. Check the texture and doneness of one. Place the cooked shrimp on a serving plate. Continue to air fry the shrimp in batches until they are all done.
- Mix the mayonnaise, wine, & mustard in a large mixing bowl. Combine the celery, onion, dill, salt, & pepper in a large mixing bowl. Stir everything together thoroughly. Toss the cooked

shrimp in the bowl with the dressing & veggies to evenly coat them. Refrigerate for a few hours or overnight, covered.

- Over butter lettuce leaves, serve the shrimp salad.

Coconut Shrimp with Spicy and Sweet Dipping Sauce

Preparation and Cooking Time

17 minutes

Servings

4 persons

Nutritional facts

82 calories, 8g fat ,1g fiber ,17g carbs ,2g protein

Ingredients

- 1/2 cup orange or apricot marmalade
- 1/2 cup unsweetened coconut shreds or flakes
- 1/2 cup panko breadcrumbs or gluten-free chickpea crumbs
- 1 tsp sea salt
- 1/3 cup Thai chili sauce (use sweet chili sauce if preferred)
- 1-pound large raw shrimp, peeled, deveined, and tails left on
- 1/2 cup all-purpose or gluten-free flour blend (or tapioca flour)
- 2 eggs lightly beaten
- 1/4 tsp freshly ground black pepper
- Vegetable oil spray

Instructions

- Combine the Thai chili paste and marmalade in a small bowl.
- Set aside the cleaned shrimp on a paper towels to dry.
- Prepare three shallow bowls. First, put the flour, and the eggs are placed in the second bowl. Add the coconut, breadcrumbs, salt, & pepper.
- Preheat the air fryer for 3 minutes @ 360°F.
- Dip the shrimp in the flour, then in the eggs, and last in the coconut & breadcrumb mixture, in that order. Prepare only enough to fill the air fryer basket in a single layer.
- Apply enough vegetable oil to the fryer basket to cover it thinly.
- In the air fryer basket, arrange the shrimp in a single layer. Using a small spray of oil, lightly coat the shrimp, and it should be cooked for three minutes. Flip the shrimp after 3 minutes and cook for another 3 minutes, just until the coconut is crisp as well as the shrimp is pink. Continue to air-fried the shrimp in batches, adding a little more oil as needed until all of them are done.
- Place the shrimp in a butcher's paper or parchment-lined basket with dipping sauce on the side.

Popcorn Shrimp with Cocktail Sauce

Preparation and Cooking Time

22 minutes

Servings

4 persons

Nutritional facts

99 calories,10g fat ,1g fiber ,21g carbs ,2g protein

Ingredients

- 3/4 cup ketchup
- 1-pound medium shrimp, peeled and deveined
- 1 tsp garlic powder
- 1 tsp onion powder

- 1/2 tsp sea salt
- 1/2 cup all-purpose flour
- 2 eggs, beaten
- 1 TBS milk
- 1-1/2 cups panko breadcrumbs
- 2 TBS prepared horseradish
- 2 TBS fresh lemon juice
- 1/2 tsp hot sauce
- 1/4 tsp sea salt
- 1 tsp garlic powder
- 1 tsp onion powder
- 1/2 tsp sea salt
- Vegetable oil spray

Instructions

- Mix the ketchup, horseradish, lemon juice, spicy sauce, and 1/4 teaspoon salt in a small bowl. Combine all of the ingredients. Chill the bowl by covering it and placing it in the refrigerator.
- Set aside the cleaned shrimp on a paper towels to dry.
- Prepare three shallow bowls. First, put the flour and the eggs and milk in the second bowl. Add the breadcrumbs, garlic powder, onion powder, salt, and pepper to the third bowl.
- Preheat your air fryer for 3 minutes @ 360°F.
- Dip the shrimp in the flour, then in the egg mixture, and last in the seasoned breadcrumbs, in that order. Prepare only enough to fill the air fryer basket in a single layer.
- Apply enough vegetable oil to the fryer basket or crisper plate to cover it thinly.
- In the air fryer basket or on the crisper plate, arrange the shrimp in a single layer. Using a small spray of oil, lightly coat the shrimp, and 3 minutes in the oven. Flip the shrimp after 3 minutes and cook for another 3 minutes until the coconut is crisp and the shrimp is pink. Continue to air-fried the shrimp in batches, adding a little more oil as needed until all of them are done.
- Place the shrimp in a basket lined with parchment or butcher paper. Serve with cocktail sauce.

Crispy Air Fryer Fish

Preparation and Cooking Time

27 minutes

Servings

4 persons

Nutritional facts

90 calories,10g fat ,1.5g fiber ,29g carbs ,3g protein

Ingredients

- 4-6 Whiting Fish fillets cut in half
- 1 ½ tsp salt
- 1 tsp paprika
- ½ tsp garlic powder
- Oil to mist
- ¾ cup very fine cornmeal
- ¼ cup flour
- 2 tsp old bay
- ½ tsp black pepper

Instructions

- Shake together the ingredients for the fish seasoning in a Zip lock bag. You might also use your preferred fish seasoning instead.

- Clean your fish fillets by rinsing them and patting them dry with paper towels.
- Shake the fish fillets in a zip lock bag until they are completely covered in spice.
- Place the fillets on a baking rack to catch any extra flour.
- Put the fillets in the air fryer basket greased on the bottom. Preheat oven to 400°F and bake fillets for 10 minutes.
- Before flipping, open the basket & spray the fish on the side facing up, ensuring that the fish is well coated. Cook for 7 minutes on the other side. Remove the fish and serve.

Air-Fryer Scallops

Preparation and Cooking Time

20 minutes

Servings

2 persons

Nutritional facts

348 calories,11g fat ,1.5g fiber ,19g carbs ,2g protein

Ingredients

- 8 large (1-oz.) sea scallops, cleaned and patted very dry
- 2 tablespoons very finely chopped flat-leaf parsley
- 2 teaspoons capers, very finely chopped
- ¼ teaspoon ground pepper
- ⅛ teaspoon salt
- Cooking spray
- ¼ cup extra-virgin olive oil
- 1 teaspoon finely grated lemon zest
- ½ teaspoon finely chopped garlic

Instructions

- Season scallops with salt and pepper. Spray the air fryer basket with cooking spray. Coat the scallops in cooking spray and place them in the basket. In the fryer, place the basket. Cook the scallops at 400 degrees F for 6 minutes, or till they achieve an internal temperature of 120 degrees F.
- Combine the oil, parsley, capers, lemon zest, and garlic in a small bowl. Drizzle the sauce all over the scallops.

Air Fryer Breaded Shrimp

Preparation and Cooking Time

36 minutes

Servings

6 persons

Nutritional facts

169 calories, 9g fat ,1g fiber ,21g carbs ,2g protein

Ingredients

- 400 grams (about 0.88 lbs.) raw shrimp (approx. 32–34 large shrimp)
- 1 cup panko crumbs
- 1/4 cup whole wheat flour
- 2 large eggs, scrambled
- 2 teaspoons old bay seasoning

Instructions

- Using a paper towel, pat the shrimp dry.
- Fill a small bowl or rimmed plate halfway with flour.
- In a separate bowl, whisk together your eggs.
- In a shallow bowl or rimmed plate, combine the panko crumbs & old bay seasoning.

- Shake off any excess flour after coating the shrimp in a thin layer of flour.
- Allow any excess egg to drip off after dipping each shrimp into the egg.
- Using panko crumbs, coat the shrimp.
- Place the shrimp in the air fryer basket in a single layer and air fry for 6-10 minutes, flipping halfway through.
- Repeat with the rest of the shrimp.

Air Fryer Low Country Boil

Preparation and Cooking Time

25 minutes

Servings

2 persons

Nutritional facts

326 calories,12g fat ,1g fiber ,31g carbs ,4g protein

Ingredients

- 1 cup of dry white wine
- 2 lobster tails
- 1 lemon
- 2 ears corn
- ½ pound of shrimp
- 6 littleneck of clams
- 1 pound of andouille sausage
- 1 tablespoon of shrimp boil seasoning

Instructions

- Set the temperature to 400 degrees F and preheat the air fryer for 5 minutes with wine in the bottom pan.
- Fill air fryer basket with corn, shrimp, clams, & guile sausage, & lobster tails, leaving wine in place in air fryer pan. Put lemon halves on top of lobster tails and squeeze the lemon halves over the seafood mixture. Sprinkle with the shrimp boil seasoning. Preheat the oven to 350 degrees Fahrenheit and steam for ten minutes.

Air Fryer Calamari – Crispy Squid Rings Recipe

Preparation and Cooking Time

21 minutes

Servings

3 persons

Nutritional facts

443 calories, 21g fat ,1g fiber ,23g carbs ,2g protein

Ingredients

- 12 ounces' small frozen calamari rings, thawed, drained well
- 1 lemon for serving
- ½ teaspoon garlic powder
- ¼ teaspoon onion powder
- salt and pepper, to taste
- 12 ounces' broccoli, chopped (340 grams; fresh or frozen)
- seafood dipping sauce (optional)
- 2 russet potatoes, scrubbed and sliced into ½-¾ inch (1.3-1.9 cm) fries (about 24 ounces/680 grams, do not peel)
- 2 tablespoons olive oil
- 1 teaspoon dried dill weed
- ¼ cup spelt flour
- ¼ cup buttermilk

- ½ tablespoon Old Bay seasoning
- cooking oil spray
- ½ teaspoon dried parsley
- 1 tablespoon sesame oil (toasted)

Instructions

- To prepare them in the air fryer, soak the cut potatoes in cool water for 20-30 minutes before patting them dry. In a medium mixing bowl, combine all of the garlic-dill fry's ingredients. On your oil-misted air fryer rack, spread the fries out in a single layer (s). Preheat oven to 390°F (199°C) and bake for 25 minutes. Halfway through the cooking time, flip the fries.
- Drain your calamari well in a colander after thawing. Using a clean paper towel, pat the squid rings dry.
- Combine the buttermilk, spelt flour, & Old Bay. Toss in the thawed & drained calamari rings and toss well to combine.
- To catch drips, mist your air fryer racks with oil and place them on top of paper towels. Arrange the calamari mixture on the racks in a single layer.
- Make sure the drip tray is in position in your air fryer oven. Place the racks in the oven and bake for 10 minutes at 390°F (199°C).
- In the oven, flip the calamari. Bake for another 8 minutes.
- Break any rings clinging together into individual pieces by flipping the calamari again. To continue crisping them up, bake for three more minutes.
- You could also serve them with your preferred seafood dipping sauce.
- Cook the broccoli until warm (if frozen) or tender-crisp on the stovetop or microwave. Drizzle the toasted sesame oil over the broccoli.
- Serve the calamari with fries and broccoli on a plate.

Air Fryer Salmon in 17 Minutes

Preparation and Cooking Time

17 minutes

Servings

2 persons

Nutritional facts

306 calories, 6g fat ,1g fiber ,18g carbs ,2g protein

Ingredients

- 2 salmon fillets about 6 oz. each
- Salt to taste
- 2 tsp rub with love salmon rub (or any other kind you like)
- 1 garlic clove
- 1 Tbsp. Olive oil

Instructions

- Olive oil, crushed garlic, salmon rub, and salt are used to season the salmon fillets (to taste). Combine 1/4 teaspoon salt, 1/4 teaspoon pepper, 1/4 teaspoon thyme, 1 teaspoon smoked paprika, and 1 tsp brown sugar to make your fish rub.
- Line the bottom of the baking sheet with foil if you're using an oven air fryer.
- Preheat the oven to 400 degrees Fahrenheit and bake the salmon for 10-15 minutes. Cooking time is determined by the thickness of the salmon fillet. The longer the salmon takes to air-fry, the thicker it is. Always ensure that the thickest section of the salmon is at least 145 degrees F on the inside.

Air Fried Shrimp with Dill Spread and Creamy Spinach

Preparation and Cooking Time

55 minutes

Servings

3 persons

Nutritional facts

388 calories,10g fat ,1g fiber ,22g carbs ,3g protein

Ingredients

- 4 French-style bread rolls
- Fresh Parsley
- 2 cups of Tempura style breadcrumbs
- 3 tbsp. of Italian seasoning
- ¼ cup of spinach dip
- 2 tbsp. of dill
- 1 tsp of ground mustard seed
- Fresh ground pepper
- 2 Roma tomatoes
- 2 tsp of extra virgin olive oil
- 2 eggs
- 1 cup of flour

Instructions

- Refrigerated shrimp is to be thawed; remove tails from shrimp once thawed.
- Combine tempura-style breadcrumbs and Italian seasoning in a mixing bowl.
- Then toss thawed shrimp in flour, beaten eggs, and a mixture of breadcrumbs.
- Place in an air fryer and cook for 8 minutes at 350°F.
- While the rolls are toasting, combine the dill, ground mustard seed, & spinach dip and spread over the toasted rolls.
- Toss fresh parsley and tomatoes with olive oil, salt, and pepper and serve with fried shrimp on a roll.

Air Fryer Garlic Shrimp w/ Lemon

Preparation and Cooking Time

19 minutes

Servings

3 persons

Nutritional facts

228 calories, 8g fat ,1g fiber ,15g carbs ,2g protein

Ingredients

- 1 pound (454 g) raw shrimp, peeled deveined,
- Black pepper, to taste
- lemon wedges
- Vegetable oil to coat shrimp
- 1/4 teaspoon (1.25 ml) garlic powder
- Salt, to taste
- minced parsley and chili flakes (optional)

Instructions

- Toss the shrimp in a bowl with the oil, garlic powder, salt, and pepper. Assemble the shrimp and make sure they're equally coated.
- Arrange the shrimp in a single layer in the air fryer basket.

- Air fry for 10-14 minutes at 400°F, gently shaking & flipping halfway through. Cooking time will vary depending on shrimp size.
- Place the shrimp in a serving bowl or on a serving plate. Serve the shrimp with a squeeze of lemon and more lemon wedges.

Air Fryer Salmon Almondine

Preparation and Cooking Time

35 minutes

Servings

4 persons

Nutritional facts

247calories, 6g fat ,1g fiber ,11g carbs ,1g protein

Ingredients

- 4 pieces' salmon or 1-pound slab
- ¼ cup sliced almonds
- 1 tablespoon lemon juice
- 2 tablespoons lemon pepper seasoning
- 1 tablespoon butter
- 2 tablespoons chopped green onions optional

Instructions

- Preheat the air fryer to 350 degrees Fahrenheit.
- After patting the fish dry, season it with lemon pepper spice.
- Put the salmon in the air fryer without overcrowding it.
- Preheat oven to 350°F and bake for 12 minutes.
- Put the butter in a small skillet over medium heat while the fish fries.
- Allow the almonds to simmer for about 3 minutes or golden brown.
- Remove the salmon from the air fryer and pour the lemon juice over it.
- Enjoy with a sprinkling of browned almonds & green onions on top.

Air fryer Shrimp

Preparation and Cooking Time

15 minutes

Servings

3 persons

Nutritional facts

152 calories, 4g fat ,0g fiber ,13g carbs ,1g protein

Ingredients

- 1 lb. of jumbo shrimps
- ¼ teaspoon of cinnamon
- ¼ teaspoon of nutmeg
- ¼ teaspoon of allspice
- 2 Tbsp. of oil
- ⅛ teaspoon of Cayenne pepper
- ½ teaspoon of thyme
- ¼ teaspoon of sugar-free brown sugar
- 1 Tablespoon of lemon juice
- 2 - 3 Tablespoons of homemade blend
- ½ teaspoon of onion powder
- ½ teaspoon of garlic powder
- ¼ teaspoon of bouillon
- ⅛ teaspoon of salt

Instructions

- Shrimps should be cleaned and deveined.
- Dry with a paper towel and then toss with lemon juice, oil, and pepper to coat.
- Cook at 400°F / 204°C in the air fryer for ten to fourteen minutes, or until the desired amount of doneness is reached.
- Drain frozen cleaned shrimp in a colander after 30 minutes in a bowl of warm water.
- Using a paper towel, pat the shrimps dry.
- Toss the shrimp in the oil & lemon juice until they are equally coated.
- Toss in the spice mix and toss to coat.
- If you have time, marinate the seasoned shrimp for around 20 minutes.
- In an air fryer basket, place seasoned shrimp. Preheat oven to 400°F / 204°C and bake for 6-8 minutes, or up to ten minutes if you like it crispy.
- Serve as a side dish or with a dipping sauce.

Air Fryer Crispy Ranch Fish - B

Preparation and Cooking Time

15 minutes

Servings

2 persons

Nutritional facts

147 calories, 6g fat ,1g fiber ,18g carbs ,2g protein

Ingredients

- 2 C panko bread crumbs
- 6 cod filets or tilapia
- olive oil spray
- 3 T dry ranch seasoning
- 1 t garlic powder
- 2 egg
- 1 lemon cut into wedges

Instructions

- In a small bowl, combine the required ingredients.
- In a separate bowl, beat the eggs.
- After dipping the fish in the egg, coat it in the bread crumb mixture. Store it in a container with a lid until the day of cooking.
- Preheat the air fryer to 400 degrees Fahrenheit.
- Spray the fish with olive oil spray and place it in the air fryer.
- Then cook for 10 minutes, flipping halfway through (or until fish is flaky). Serve with a wedge of lemon to squeeze over the fish.

Air Fryer Spicy Shrimp

Preparation and Cooking Time

17 minutes

Servings

4 persons

Nutritional facts

380 calories,10g fat ,1g fiber ,31g carbs ,2g protein

Ingredients

- 1 pound large, raw shrimp tail on
- 1/4 tsp. dried oregano
- 1/4 tsp. ground cumin

- 1/2 tsp. kosher salt
- 1/2 tsp. black pepper
- 1/4 tsp. ground cayenne pepper
- 1/4 tsp. dried thyme
- 1 tsp. avocado oil
- 1 tsp. chili powder
- 1/2 tsp. paprika powder
- 1/4 tsp. garlic powder
- 1/4 tsp. ground dried mustard

Instructions

- Thaw raw shrimp on a paper plate with paper towels & dab dry.
- Preheat the air fryer oven for 5 minutes at 400 degrees F.
- Meanwhile, add the spices in a small bowl, including paprika, chili powder, garlic powder, pepper, salt, cayenne, thyme, cumin, oregano, and crushed mustard. To blend, stir everything together.
- Toss the thawed shrimp in the spice combination after drizzling them with the avocado oil.
- Place shrimp in a single layer in a preheated air fryer basket for even frying. If desired, coat the shrimp with cooking spray. Bake for seven minutes in the air fryer. If preferred, but not essential, flip halfway through.

Air Fryer Coconut Shrimp

Preparation and Cooking Time

40 minutes

Servings

6 persons

Nutritional facts

139 calories, 21g fat ,2g fiber ,34g carbs ,4g protein

Ingredients

- ½ cup flour
- 2 tsp. Minced garlic
- ¼ cup lightly packed fresh mint
- ¼ tsp. salt
- 1 cup unsweetened shredded coconut
- 12 oz. deveined, tail-off raw shrimp
- ¼ cup red pepper jelly
- 2 tsp. bottled ginger
- 2 tsp. salt
- 1 tsp. pepper
- 2 eggs, beaten
- ½ cup panko breadcrumbs
- 2 tsp. apple cider vinegar
- ⅛ tsp. pepper

Instructions

- Season the flour with pepper and salt in a shallow dish.
- Place the beaten eggs in a separate shallow dish. Mix the breadcrumbs & coconut in a final shallow dish.
- Toss 1/3 of the shrimp in the flour, then the egg, and finally the coconut mixture in portions. Coat the shrimp on both sides with the coconut mixture. Repeat with the remaining shrimp on a large chopping board.
- Then place 12 shrimp on top of the baking rack in the high position in the bowl.
- Set the grill to 400 degrees Fahrenheit and cook for 6-7 minutes. Repeat with the rest of the prawns.

- Meanwhile, combine all the sauce ingredients in a small food processor bowl and pulse at low speed until the mint is roughly chopped.
- Serve with dipping sauce and hot coconut shrimp.

Air Fryer Fish Sticks

Preparation and Cooking Time

15 minutes

Servings

2 persons

Nutritional facts

117 calories, 10g fat ,1g fiber ,21g carbs ,2g protein

Ingredients

- 4– 6oz filets of thick white fish (halibut, cod)
- Salt and pepper
- ½ cup of olive oil-based mayonnaise
- 2 cups of corn flakes, crushed
- 1/4c cup of flour, whole wheat, white or gluten-free
- 1 egg
- ¼ cup of milk
- Sriracha

Instructions

- Set aside each salmon fillet after being cut lengthwise into sticks.
- In a shallow dish or pie plate, mix crushed cornflakes and flour, along with salt and pepper.
- Whisk together the egg and milk on a separate pie plate.
- Set aside fish sticks that have been dipped in the egg wash and afterward dredge in the corn flake mixture. Continue until all battered.
- Place the fish sticks in the air fryer basket & cook for 8 minutes at 350°F. Turnover and cook for another 3-4 minutes. The fish will flake easily, and the crust will be golden brown.
- Place half cup mayonnaise in a small dish. To taste, add a few drops of sriracha. Serve with fish sticks.

Garlic Herb Salmon

Preparation and Cooking Time

5 minutes

Servings

4 persons

Nutritional facts

78 calories, 5g fat ,1g fiber ,14g carbs ,1g protein

Ingredients

- 3-4 (5-6 oz.) salmon fillets, 1" each
- 2 tsp of garlic herb seasoning
- 1 Tbsp. of olive oil
- Preheat the air fryer to about 390 degrees for 5 minutes.

Instructions

- Brush the frozen fish with melted butter or olive oil. Season the fillets well with McCormick's spice mix.
- In the air fryer, put the skin-side of salmon down.
- Air fry your salmon fillets for 10 to 12 minutes' total. Cook the salmon till it reaches 130-140 degrees F if you prefer it medium. Allow 5 minutes for the salmon to rest before serving.

Air Fryer Spicy and Tender Salmon

Preparation and Cooking Time

15 minutes

Servings

4 persons

Nutritional facts

276 calories, 10g fat ,1g fiber ,21g carbs ,5g protein

Ingredients

- 1 1/2 lb. salmon fillets
- ¾ tsp garlic powder
- ¼ tsp chili powder
- 1 Tbsp. oil
- ¼ tsp salt
- ½ tsp paprika
- ¼ tsp ground black pepper
- ½ tsp Italian seasoning

Instructions

- Spray the air fryer basket with baking spray or use parchment paper to line it.
- To make the seasonings, put all spices in a small bowl.
- Drizzle the salmon fillets with olive oil and season on all sides.
- Bake the prepared salmon fillets for 8-10 minutes at 400°F in the air fryer basket.

Parmesan Crusted Air Fryer Tilapia

Preparation and Cooking Time

15 minutes

Servings

4persons

Nutritional facts

105 calories, 9g fat ,2g fiber ,31g carbs ,2g protein

Ingredients

- 4 (4 oz.) tilapia fillets
- 1/2 tsp pepper
- 1 egg
- 3/4 cup parmesan cheese, finely grated
- 2 tsp Italian seasoning
- 1/4 tsp salt
- Olive oil spray

Instructions

- Preheat the air fryer to 375°F.
- Combine parmesan cheese, Italian seasoning, pepper, and salt in a plastic bag. To combine, shake the bag.
- Whisk the egg in a small shallow bowl.
- Dip each tilapia fillet into the beaten egg one at a time. Place the fish in the bag and shake to evenly coat with breading.
- Cook for 5 minutes after placing the fillets in the fryer basket and spraying them with olive oil.
- Re-spray the tenders with olive oil spray and bake for another 5 to 6 minutes, or till done.

Air Fryer Catfish

Preparation and Cooking Time

30 minutes

Servings

2 persons

Nutritional facts

380 calories, 6g fat ,0.5g fiber ,11g carbs ,2g protein

Ingredients

- 1/2 lb. catfish filets
- 1 tsp. Cajun seasoning
- 1/4 cup of cornmeal
- Cooking spray

Instructions

- Catfish is to be sliced into pieces.
- Catfish is to be dried with a paper towel.
- Put seasoning & cornmeal into a sealable bag. Then insert the catfish pieces, seal, and shake, coating the fish properly.
- The bottom of the air fryer is to be sprayed with cooking spray. Then put in the catfish pieces.
- It should be cooked at 400 degrees F for 8 minutes, then flipped, and cooked for another 8-10 minutes.

Parmesan Crusted White Fish

Preparation and Cooking Time

25 minutes

Servings

2 persons

Nutritional facts

338 calories, 8g fat ,0g fiber ,16g carbs ,3g protein

Ingredients

- 2 tilapia filets or other white fish (about 4-6 ounces for each filet)
- 1/2 teaspoon (2.5 ml) garlic powder
- 1/2 teaspoon (2.5 ml) onion powder
- 1/2 teaspoon (2.5 ml) smoked paprika, or to taste
- 1 Tablespoon (15 ml) olive oil or oil spray
- 1/2 cup (50 g) grated parmesan cheese
- kosher salt, to taste
- black pepper, to taste
- fresh chopped parsley for garnish
- lemon wedges, for serving

Instructions

- Heat the Air Fryer for 5 minutes at 380°F/193°C.
- Set aside the parmesan cheese in a shallow bowl.
- Drizzle olive oil or use an oil spray to coat the fish. Add salt, pepper, garlic powder, onion powder, and paprika to taste. Fish fillets should be pressed into the cheese mixture & coated on both sides.
- The perforated parchment paper should line the air fryer basket or tray. Using an oil spray, lightly coat parchment paper. Arrange the coated fish on the parchment paper. Using an oil spray, lightly coat the tops of the fish fillets.
- Then air fry for 6-12 minutes at 380°F/193°C, just until the fish could be flaked with 'a fork. The length of time it takes to cook the fish depends on its thickness and the type of air fryer you have.
- Serve with lemon wedges and chopped parsley on top.

Air Fried Maine Seafood

Preparation and Cooking Time

25 minutes

Servings

3 persons

Nutritional facts

180 calories, 23g fat ,1g fiber ,40g carbs ,8g protein

Ingredients

- 2 lbs. steamer clams (or other seafood such as shrimp, cod, and scallop)
- 3 tbs. water (to make egg wash)
- 1 tbs. water
- 2 cups all-purpose flour
- 4 cups panko Japanese bread crumbs
- 3 eggs
- Oil sprayer (with healthy oil of your choice)

Instructions

- Soak the clams in cold water for two or three hours before draining and rinsing. In a pot with a tight-fitting lid, bring one inch of water to a simmer. Cover and steam for 7-10 minutes, or until the clams open. Make sure the steamers aren't overcooked.
- Remove the clams from the shell, remove the neck skin, and leave them aside.
- In a small dish, crack eggs and whisk them with water to wash eggs.
- Shake off extra flour after dipping steamers or other shellfish in flour. Coat the steamers with egg wash and afterward gently push them into the panko to completely coat them.
- Cut additional seafood into small pieces, such as fish, and follow the same procedure.
- Preheat the Philips Air Fryer to 350 degrees Fahrenheit. In the bottom of the Air Fryer, pour 1 tablespoon of water. Spray steamers with oil and set in the Air Fryer basket for 7-10 minutes, depending on the size of the steamers or seafood. Remove the chicken from the basket and top with WATCHAREE's pad Thai sauce.
- Then alternatively, heat oil to 375°F in a pan or deep fryer. For 4-5 minutes, fry clams or seafood till golden brown. Paper towels absorb excess liquid and serve with WATCHAREE's pad Thai sauce.

Frozen Fish Sticks in the Air Fryer

Preparation and Cooking Time

15 minutes

Servings

1 person

Nutritional facts

230 calories,15g fat ,2g fiber ,19g carbs ,4g protein

Ingredients

- frozen fish sticks
- spray oil optional, for extra crispy
- One pinch of salt optional

Instructions

- Preheat the air fryer to 400 degrees Fahrenheit (with the empty basket inserted) for about 3 minutes.
- Remove the basket from the oven and stack the frozen fish sticks in a single layer. Sprinkle with salt after spraying with oil. Toss to coat evenly.

- Replace the basket in the air fryer. Cook for 10 minutes, remove the basket after 5 minutes and shake the fish sticks.
- Remove the fish sticks from the basket and serve.

Air Fryer Black Cod with Black Bean Sauce Gluten Free

Preparation and Cooking Time

32 minutes

Servings

2 persons

Nutritional facts

194 calories,12g fat ,2g fiber ,28g carbs ,5g protein

Ingredients

- 1 lb. piece of black cod
- 1 tablespoon of water
- 1 teaspoon of Maggi sauce
- 1/2 teaspoon of sesame oil
- 1 teaspoon of ground black pepper
- chopped cilantro for garnish
- jalapeño slices, for garnish
- 1/2 tablespoon of fermented black beans
- 1 tablespoon of minced garlic
- 1 teaspoon of soy sauce
- 1 teaspoon of granulated sugar
- 1 teaspoon of salt

Instructions

- Combine soy sauce, garlic, salt, sugar, and pepper in a big zip lock bag. To blend, give it a good shake. Place the cod steaks in the zip lock bag, push out the air, and close tightly. To coat the fish, press marinade around it. Place the bag in the fridge for at least 30 minutes to marinate.
- Remove the marinated fish from the bag and equally spread it over the air frying basket. Preheat oven to 350°F and bake for 17 minutes.
- Make the black bean sauce in the meantime. Combine water, fermented black beans, Maggi sauce, & sesame oil in a small bowl. Stir well to ensure an even distribution of ingredients.
- Place the cod in a serving dish after removing it from the air fryer. Garnish with the cilantro & jalapenos before serving (optional). Serve with a dollop of black bean sauce on top of the fish.

Salt & Pepper Air Fryer Calamari Recipe

Preparation and Cooking Time

32 minutes

Servings

3 persons

Nutritional facts

156 calories, 20g fat ,3g fiber ,41g carbs ,2g protein

Ingredients

- 500g squid rings
- 2 tbsp. cracked pepper
- 1 cup plain all-purpose flour
- 2 cups panko breadcrumbs
- 2 tbsp. salt
- 1 egg
- 1 cup buttermilk

Instructions

- In a medium-sized mixing bowl, whisk together the buttermilk and egg.
- Combine breadcrumbs, salt, pepper, and flour in a second bowl.
- Squid rings are dipped in buttermilk and then rolled in breadcrumbs.
- Arrange coated calamari in a single layer along the bottom of the air fryer basket.
- Cook at 200 degrees Celsius (400 degrees Fahrenheit) for 10-12 minutes, or until golden brown.
- Repeat with the remaining calamari rings as needed.
- Serve with a dipping sauce of your choice.

Air Fryer Calamari with Seafood Sauce

Preparation and Cooking Time

15 minutes

Servings

2 persons

Nutritional facts

257 calories, 9g fat ,1g fiber ,16g carbs ,4g protein

Ingredients

- ½ cup of ketchup
- ½ tsp of dried dill (optional)
- cooking oil spray
- ½ cup of milk
- pepper and salt to taste
- 2 tbsp. of lime juice
- 200 g of calamari rings defrosted
- 1 cup of flour
- 1 tbsp. of horseradish
- ½ tsp of Worcestershire sauce or fish sauce
- 1 tsp of lime juice
- ½ tsp of sriracha hot sauce
- 1 tsp of kosher salt plus more for seasoning

Instructions

- Preheat the air fryer to 390 degrees Fahrenheit.
- Combine all of the ingredients in a large mixing bowl.
- Then season to taste with extra salt or spicy sauce if required.
- For 15-20 minutes, marinate calamari rings in the lime juice.
- Combine the salt, flour, and dill in a mixing bowl. Divide the mixture into two bowls.
- Pour the milk into a separate bowl.
- Using a paper towel, pat the tops of the calamari rings dry.
- Toss a third of the calamari in the first bowl of flour at a time, opening up the rings to completely coat them in flour. Gently toss in the milk until evenly covered. Toss in the second bowl of flour after draining through your fingers.
- Place the calamari rings in the air fryer basket and open them up. It's possible that you'll have to do this in batches to avoid overcrowding the rings. Do not mix them up. Cooking oil spray should be used liberally.
- It should be cooked in the air fryer for two minutes or until the top is firm. Flip, coat with cooking spray again, and continue to air fry for another minute or till firm. Then season with salt and pepper.
- Cook the remaining calamari & serve with the seafood sauce.

Air Fryer Fish Recipe (Crispy Air Fryer Tilapia)

Preparation and Cooking Time

25 minutes

Servings

4 persons

Nutritional facts

350 calories,10g fat ,1g fiber ,23g carbs ,2g protein

Ingredients

- 4 Tilapia Fish Fillet, you may use any light fish fillet
- Aluminum Foil, to add as a liner in the air-fryer basket
- 2 Tbsp. Lemon Pepper Seasoning
- 2 Tbsp. Paprika Powder
- 2 Cups Bread Crumbs
- 1 Large Egg
- 1 Tsp Warm Water, to whisk eggs
- Olive Oil Spray, for cooking the fish
- 1 Tsp Dry Garlic Powder
- 1 Tbsp. Salt, use as per taste

Instructions

- Whisk the egg with 1 teaspoon warm water in a large mixing bowl. Set aside for now.
- In a separate large mixing bowl, combine bread crumbs, seasoning ingredients, and stir to combine. Set aside for now.
- As a liner, insert the aluminum foil into the air-fryer basket.
- Use a fork to dip each fish fillet into the whisked egg bowl. Evenly coat both sides of the fish.
- In the bread crumbs bowl, place the egg-coated fish. Evenly coat both sides.
- Remove any excess bread crumbs from the fish fillet and set it on a clean platter.
- Coat all of the fish fillets in the same manner and set them aside.
- Place 1-2 fish fillets in the air-fryer basket.
- Spray the Air-Fryer with olive oil and set it to 350°F for 10 minutes.
- Turn the fish over after 10 minutes and air-fry for another five minutes to brown the other side.
- Remove the fish once it has turned golden brown on all sides and lay it on a clean platter.
- Air-fry the remaining fish fillets in the same manner.
- Serve the fish fillet with Cucumber Avocado Salad after everything is done.

Honey Pecan Shrimp

Preparation and Cooking Time

25 minutes

Servings

4 persons

Nutritional facts

107 calories,16g fat ,4g fiber ,32g carbs ,8g protein

Ingredients

- 1/4 cup cornstarch
- pecans
- 1 pound raw, peeled, and deveined shrimp
- 1/4 cup honey
- 3/4 teaspoon sea salt, divided

- 1/4 teaspoon pepper
- 2 egg whites
- 2/3 cup finely chopped
- 2 tablespoons mayonnaise

Instructions

- Mix the cornstarch, 1/2 tsp salt, and pepper in a small bowl.
- In a separate dish, whisk the egg whites till they are soft and foamy.
- Combine the pecans and the remaining 1/4 teaspoon of sea salt in a third bowl.
- Using paper towels, pat the shrimp dry. Dip the shrimp in the cornstarch, then the egg whites, and finally the pecans, working in small batches until all of the shrimp are pecan-coated.
- Preheat your air fryer to 330 degrees Fahrenheit.
- Spray the air fryer basket with cooking spray and put the coated shrimp inside. Simmer for 5 minutes before tossing in the shrimp and cooking for another 5 minutes.
- Meanwhile, microwave the honey for 30 seconds in a microwave-safe bowl. In a separate bowl, whisk together the mayonnaise and sour cream till smooth and creamy. In a serving bowl, pour the honey sauce. Toss the cooked shrimp in the serving bowl with the dressing while it's still hot. Serve right away.

Bacon-Wrapped Scallops

Preparation and Cooking Time

18 minutes

Servings

4 persons

Nutritional facts

125 calories,10g fat ,2g fiber ,33g carbs ,7g protein

Ingredients

- Sixteen large scallops
- 8 bacon strips
- Half teaspoon black pepper
- 1/4 teaspoon smoked paprika

Instructions

- Using a paper towel, pat the scallops dry. Each bacon strip should be cut in half. Wrap 1 scallop in 1 bacon strip & secure with a toothpick. Carry on with the remaining scallops in the same manner. Season the scallops with salt and pepper, as well as paprika.
- Preheat your air fryer to 350 degrees Fahrenheit.
- Cook the bacon-wrapped scallops in the air fryer basket for 4 minutes, then shake the basket and cook for another 3 minutes, then shake the basket again and cook for another 1 to 3 minutes. The scallops must be cooked through and somewhat firm but not rubbery, and the bacon should be crispy. Serve right away.

Pecan-Crusted Tilapia

Preparation and Cooking Time

13 minutes

Servings

4 persons

Nutritional facts

129 calories,11g fat ,1g fiber ,28g carbs ,5g protein

Ingredients

- 1 pound skinless, boneless tilapia filets
- 1/4 teaspoon paprika

- 2 tablespoons chopped parsley
- 1/4 cup butter, melted
- 1 teaspoon minced fresh or dried rosemary
- 1 cup finely chopped pecans
- 1 teaspoon sea salt
- 1 lemon, cut into wedges

Instructions

- Using paper towels, pat the tilapia fillets dry.
- Pour the melted butter over the fillets and turn them to coat them completely.
- Combine the rosemary, pecans, salt, & paprika in a medium mixing bowl.
- Preheat your air fryer to 350 degrees Fahrenheit.
- Toss the tilapia fillets with the pecan coating in the air fryer basket. Cook for a total of 8 to 10 minutes. When thoroughly cooked, the fish should be firm to the touch & flake easily.
- Take the fish out of the air fryer and set it aside. Serve the fish with lemon wedges and chopped parsley on top.

Maple-Crusted Salmon

Preparation and Cooking Time

43 minutes

Servings

2 persons

Nutritional facts

136 calories,12g fat ,1g fiber ,22g carbs ,2g protein

Ingredients

- 12 ounces' salmon filets
- 1/2 teaspoon sea salt
- 1/2 lemon
- 1/3 cup maple syrup
- 1 teaspoon Worcestershire sauce
- 2 teaspoons Dijon mustard or brown mustard
- 1/2 cup finely chopped walnuts
- 1 tablespoon chopped parsley for garnish

Instructions

- In a shallow baking dish, place the fish. Maple syrup, Worcestershire sauce, & mustard are drizzled on top. Refrigerate for thirty minutes.
- Preheat your air fryer to 350 degrees Fahrenheit.
- Take the salmon out of the marinade and toss it out.
- Sprinkle salt on the chopped nuts and place them on the salmon fillets. Place the salmon in the air fryer basket, skin side down. Cook for 6–8 minutes, or until the salmon flakes easily when tested in the middle.
- Remove the salmon from the pan and arrange it on a serving tray. Squeeze a fresh lemon over the salmon and sprinkle chopped parsley on top. Serve right away.

Beer-Breaded Halibut Fish Tacos

Preparation and Cooking Time

45 minutes

Servings

4 persons

Nutritional facts

280 calories, 20g fat ,2g fiber ,19g carbs ,2g protein

Ingredients

- 1-pound halibut, cut into 1-inch strips
- 1 cup grape tomatoes, quartered
- 1/2 cup chopped cilantro
- 1/4 cup chopped onion
- 1 egg, whisked
- 1/2 cup cornmeal
- 1/4 cup all-purpose flour
- 1-1/4 teaspoons sea salt, divided
- 2 cups shredded cabbage
- 1 lime, juiced and divided
- 1/4 cup Greek yogurt
- 1 cup light beer
- 1 jalapeño, minced and divided
- 1 clove garlic, minced
- 1/4 teaspoon ground cumin
- 1/4 cup mayonnaise
- 8 corn tortillas

Instructions

- Put the fish, the beer, 1 tsp of chopped jalapeno, garlic, and cumin in a shallow baking dish. Refrigerate for half an hour after covering.
- Meanwhile, combine the cornmeal, flour, and 1/2 teaspoon in a medium mixing bowl.
- Combine the shredded cabbage, 1 tbsp. lime juice, Greek yogurt, mayonnaise, and ½ teaspoon salt in a large mixing bowl.
- To prepare the pico de gallo, combine the tomatoes, cilantro, onion, .25 teaspoons salt, the remaining jalapeno, and the remaining lime juice in a small bowl.
- Take the fish out of the fridge and toss out the marinade. Dredge the fish in the whisked egg, then in the cornmeal flour mixture, till all the fish pieces are breaded.
- Preheat your air fryer to 350 degrees Fahrenheit.
- Spray the fish well with cooking spray before placing it in the air fryer basket. Cook for 6 minutes before flipping and shaking the fish and cooking for an additional 4 minutes.
- Heat the tortillas in a heavy skillet over high heat for 1 to 2 minutes while the fish is cooking.
- Put the battered fish on the cooked tortillas & top with slaw & pico de gallo to assemble the tacos. Serve right away.

Chapter 9: Air Fryer Meat Recipes

Air Fryer Steak Tips Recipe

Preparation and Cooking Time

14 minutes

Servings

3 persons

Nutritional facts

526 calories, 25g fat, 1.3g fiber, 9g carbs, 35g protein

Ingredients

- 1.5 lb. steak (Ribeye, New York)
- 1/2 tsp dried onion powder
- 1 tsp Montreal Steak Seasoning
- 1/8 tsp cayenne pepper
- 1 lb. Asparagus, tough ends trimmed
- 1 tsp oil
- 1/4 tsp salt
- 1/2 tsp black pepper, freshly ground
- 1/2 tsp dried garlic powder
- 1/4 tsp salt
- 1/2 tsp oil (optional)

Instructions

- Heat the air fryer to 400 degrees Fahrenheit for 5 minutes.
- Meanwhile, trim any excess fat from the meat & cut it into cubes. Then toss the meat with the marinade ingredients (oil, salt, black pepper, Montreal seasoning, onion and garlic powder, and cayenne pepper) and massage the spices into the meat to evenly coat it.
- If you have some, spray the bottom of the air fryer basket with non - stick cooking spray and spread the prepared meat across it. After 4-6 minutes of cooking the beef steak tips, check for doneness.
- Toss the asparagus with 1/2 teaspoon of oil and 1/4 teaspoon of salt until well-coated.
- Toss the steak bites around and move to one side once they've reached your desired level of browning. Cook for another 3 minutes with the asparagus on the other side of the air fryer basket.
- Transfer the steak tips and asparagus to a serving plate & serve immediately while they are still hot.

Air Fryer Mongolian Beef

Preparation and Cooking Time

20 minutes

Servings

4 persons

Nutritional facts

423 calories, 10g fat, 1.5g fiber, 28g carbs, 16g protein

Ingredients

- 1-pound flank steak
- 2 tablespoons olive oil
- 4 cloves of minced garlic
- 1/2 cup low sodium soy sauce
- 1/2 cup of water
- 1/2 cup of brown sugar
- 1/4 cup of cornstarch
- 1 tablespoon of minced ginger
- 2 green onions, chopped

Instructions

- Place the steak in a large mixing bowl after slicing it into thin strips.
- Toss the steak in the cornstarch to coat it. Set aside for 5 minutes in the cornstarch.
- Preheat the air fryer to 400°F.
- Spritz the steak with oil and place it in the air fryer basket.
- Shake the basket every couple of minutes while air-frying for 8-10 minutes. Halfway through the cooking process, spritz with additional oil.
- Heat the olive oil in a big deep skillet on the stove while the steak is cooking. Cook for 30 seconds in the oil with garlic and ginger.
- Stir together the soy sauce, water, & brown sugar.
- Bring to a boil and simmer, stirring periodically, for 6-7 minutes, or until sauce thickens.
- Carefully pour the cooked meat into the sauce and simmer for another 1-2 minutes, swirling it around.
- Before serving, sprinkle chopped green onions over the top.

Air Fryer Mushrooms and Steak Bites

Preparation and Cooking Time

28 minutes

Servings

3 persons

Nutritional facts

401 calories, 16g fat, 1.5g fiber, 17g carbs, 27g protein

Ingredients

- 1 lb. steaks, cut into 1/2" cubes
- flakey salt, to taste
- fresh cracked black pepper, to taste
- Minced parsley, garnish
- 8 oz. of mushrooms (halved)
- 2 Tablespoons of butter, melted
- 1 teaspoon of Worcestershire sauce
- 1/2 teaspoon of garlic powder, optional
- Chili Flakes, for garnishing - optional

Instructions

- Rinse and pat dry the beef cubes well. Mix the steak cubes & mushrooms in a mixing bowl. Then season with the Worcestershire sauce, optional garlic powder, as well as a generous amount of pepper and salt after coating with melted butter.
- Heat the Air Fryer for 4 minutes at 400°F.
- In the air fryer basket, arrange the steak & mushrooms in a uniform layer. Then air fry for 10 to 18 minutes at 400°F, shaking and flipping the meat and mushrooms twice during the frying phase.
- Examine the steak to evaluate how well it has been cooked. Cook the beef for a further 2-5 minutes if you want it more done.
- Drizzle with optional melted butter or optional chili flakes and garnish with parsley. If desired, season with more salt and pepper.

Steak Bites with the Cowboy Butter

Preparation and Cooking Time

15 minutes

Servings

6 persons

Nutritional facts

299 calories, 7g fat, 1g fiber, 12g carbs, 18g protein

Ingredients

- 1 lb. of steak sirloin
- ½ tsp. of Garlic powder
- ¼ tsp. of Red pepper flakes
- ½ tsp. of Sea salt
- ½ tsp. of black pepper
- cooking spray
- 1 stick of salted butter, melted
- 1 Tbsp. of lemon zest
- 1 Tbsp. of lemon juice
- ½ Tbsp. of Dijon mustard
- ½ tsp. of Worcestershire sauce
- 1 Tbsp. of parsleychopped

Instructions

- Preheat the air fryer to 400 degrees Fahrenheit.
- In a mixing bowl, combine all of the ingredients for the cowboy butter and stir thoroughly.
- Use a paper towel, pat the steak dry. Cut into 1/2-inch cubes and combine with cowboy butter in a mixing bowl. Remove from the bowl with a slotted spoon after thoroughly mixing.
- Reserving some cowboy butter sauce for dipping is a good idea.
- Spray the air fryer tray with cooking spray after covering it with aluminum foil. Evenly distribute the meat on the tray. Make sure the trays aren't too full.
- Then air fry for 10-15 minutes at 400°F, depending on the desired degree of doneness.
- Serve with the remaining cowboy butter sauce and fresh chopped parsley as a garnish.

Air Fryer Roast Beef

Preparation and Cooking Time

60 minutes

Servings

6 persons

Nutritional facts

212 calories, 40g fat, 1g fiber, 5g carbs, 40g protein

Ingredients

- 2 lb. beef roast
- 1 tsp salt
- 1 tbsp. olive oil
- 1 medium onion (optional)
- 2 tsp rosemary and thyme (fresh or dried)

Instructions

- Preheat the air fryer to 390 degrees Fahrenheit (200 degrees Celsius).
- On a plate, combine the sea salt, rosemary, and oil.
- Using paper towels, pat the meat roast dry. Place the beef roast on a platter and turn it to coat the outside with the oil-herb mixture.
- Peel the onion and slice it in half; insert onion halves in the air fryer basket.
- In the air fryer basket, place the beef roast.
- Set the timer for 10 minutes to air fry the steak.
- Change the temperature to 360°F (180°C) when the timer goes off. If your air fryer requires it, flip the beef roast halfway through the cooking period.
- Set the timer for 30 minutes more on the beef. This should result in medium-rare meat. It's advisable to keep an eye on the temperature with a meat thermometer to ensure it's done to your liking. If you prefer it extra well done, cook for 5 minutes.
- Remove the roast beef from the air fryer and set it aside to rest for at least 10 minutes before serving. This allows the meat to finish cooking and absorb the juices.
- Serve the roast beef with roasted or steamed veggies, wholegrain mustard, and gravy.

Air Fryer Roast Beef with Herb Crust

Preparation and Cooking Time

1 hour 15 minutes

Servings

6 persons

Nutritional facts

336 calories, 32g fat, 0.5g fiber, 1g carbs, 33g protein

Ingredients

- 2 lb. beef roast
- 2 teaspoons basil
- 1/2 tablespoon salt
- 1 teaspoon pepper
- 2 teaspoons garlic powder
- 2 teaspoons onion salt
- 2 teaspoons parsley
- 2 teaspoons thyme
- 1 tablespoon olive oil

Instructions

- Heat the air fryer to 390 degrees F for 15 minutes. Mix the garlic powder, onion salt, parsley, thyme, & basil, as well as salt and pepper in a mixing bowl.
- Rub the olive oil all over the roast, and then rub the herb mixture all over it.
- Put the roast in an air fryer that has been preheated. Set a 15-minute timer. Remove the basket after 15 minutes and flip the roast.

- Return the roast to the air fryer and decrease the temperature to 360 degrees F. Cook for a further 1 hour, or until the thermometer registers the desired level of doneness. Allow 15 minutes for the roast to rest before chopping.

Air Fryer Beef Tenderloin

Preparation and Cooking Time

47 minutes

Servings

8 persons

Nutritional facts

235 calories, 15g fat, 0.2g fiber, 1g carbs, 17g protein

Ingredients

- 2 pounds' beef tenderloin, at room temperature
- 1 teaspoon salt
- ½ teaspoon cracked black pepper
- 1 tablespoon vegetable oil
- 1 teaspoon dried oregano

Instructions

- Heat the air fryer to 400 degrees Fahrenheit (200 degrees Celsius). Using paper towels, pat the beef tenderloin dry.
- The tenderloin should be placed on a plate. Drizzle the meat with oil and season with oregano, salt, & pepper. Spices and oil should be rubbed into the meat. Fold the roast in half to fit it into the air fryer basket. Make sure the basket is closed.
- Reduce the heat to 390°F (198 degrees C). Cook for 22 minutes in the air fryer. Reduce the heat to 360 degrees F (182 degrees C). Cook for another 10 minutes. An instant-read thermometer inserted into the center should read 135°F (57°C) for medium.
- Place the tenderloin on a platter after removing it from the basket. Allow resting for at least ten minutes before serving.

Air Fryer Steak

Preparation and Cooking Time

30 minutes

Servings

2 persons

Nutritional facts

448 calories, 49g fat, 1g fiber, 7.5g carbs, 44g protein

Ingredients

- 2 (10 to 12 ounces EACH) sirloin steaks, about one inch thick
- ½ tablespoon paprika, sweet or smoked
- ½ tablespoon freshly ground black pepper
- ½ tablespoon olive oil OR olive oil cooking spray, for the steaks
- 1 tablespoon kosher salt
- One tablespoon garlic powder
- 1 tablespoon onion powder
- 2 teaspoons dried herbs of choice

Instructions

- Preheat the Air Fryer to 400 degrees Fahrenheit. Set aside both steaks after rubbing them with olive oil or spraying them with cooking spray.
- Mix salt, garlic powder, onion powder, paprika, pepper, & dry herbs in a small mixing bowl. Season the steaks with the desired amount of seasoning. Keep any remaining seasoning blend in an airtight container in a cool, dry place.
- Then cook 1 steak for 6 minutes @ 400°F in the Air Fryer basket.

- If you have a larger Air Fryer, you can cook two steaks at once, but make sure they aren't stacked on top of each other. There should be some distance between the two.
- Cook for four to five minutes more on the other side, or until the steak is cooked through.
- Check for doneness with an Instant Read Thermometer; the temperature for RARE steak should be between 125- and 130-degrees Fahrenheit. An internal
- temperature of 135 degrees Fahrenheit is required for Medium-Rare.
- If the steak isn't cooked through, it could be too thick, in which case you should return it to the air fryer and cook it for another minute or two.
- Cook the other steak in the same manner.
- Remove from the air fryer and set aside for 5–8 minutes before slicing. Serve with a pat of butter and minced parsley on top.

Spicy Air Fryer Steak (Cooked to Perfection)

Preparation and Cooking Time

25 minutes

Servings

2 persons

Nutritional facts

576 calories, 41g fat, 2g fiber, 11g carbs, 102g protein

Ingredients

- 2 strip loin steaks (1.25" thick)
- Two tsp salt (plus more to taste)
- 2 tsp black pepper (plus more to taste)
- Two Tbsp. butter (melted)

Instructions

- Season the steaks with pepper and salt, set them on a plate, and refrigerate uncovered for 2-3 days. Every 12 hours or so, flip the chicken and wipe the juices with a paper towel.
- Remove the steaks from the refrigerator 45 minutes before cooking to allow them to get to room temperature.
- Place the steaks on the air fryer rack and brush both sides with melted butter. You need to cook at 410F for medium doneness for fifteen minutes without preheating.
- Cook 1 - 2 minutes less for medium-rare and rare, and 1-2 extra minutes for medium-well and well done, accordingly. If air frying steaks are thicker or thinner than 1.25" thick, the times will have to be adjusted further.
- Remove the steaks from the air fryer, wrap them in foil or wax paper, and set them aside to rest for 10 minutes before serving. Serve with a dollop of compound butter to improve the taste.

Air Fryer Garlic Steak Bites

Preparation and Cooking Time

25 minutes

Servings

4 persons

Nutritional facts

169 calories, 44g fat, 1g fiber, 12g carbs, 100g protein

Ingredients

- 1 pound of New York steak cut into one inch cubes
- 3 cloves of garlic minced
- 1/4 cup of butter melted
- 1/2 teaspoon of thyme
- 2 Tablespoons of olive oil

- 1/2 teaspoon of salt
- 1/4 teaspoon of pepper
- 1 teaspoon of Italian seasoning
- 1/2 teaspoon of rosemary minced
- 1 teaspoon of parsley minced

Instructions

- Put the steak bites, olive oil, salt, pepper, Italian seasoning, and garlic into a medium mixing bowl. Add to the air fryer's basket.
- Cook for 10-12 minutes at 400 degrees F. When the chicken is done, toss it in the garlic herb butter to coat it.

Air Fryer Pork Chops Recipe

Preparation and Cooking Time

15 minutes

Servings

3 persons

Nutritional facts

284 calories, 8g fat, 1g fiber, 4g carbs, 26g protein

Ingredients

- 1 lb. boneless pork chops or 3 pieces, 1/2-inch thick
- 1 tsp onion powder
- 1/4 tsp ground black pepper
- 1 Tbsp. olive oil
- 1/2 tsp salt
- 1 tsp paprika
- 1 tsp garlic powder
- ½ tsp Italian seasoning

Instructions

- Combine the spice ingredients in a mixing dish, including salt, paprika, garlic powder, onion powder, pepper, & Italian seasoning.
- Heat the air fryer for 5 minutes at 380°F.
- Season the pork chops with the seasoning mix after coating them in oil on both sides.
- Air fry the pork chops at 380°F for 10-fifteen minutes, or until they reach 145°F. Halfway through the cooking time, flip the pork chops.

Best Damn Air Fryer Pork Chops

Preparation and Cooking Time

17 minutes

Servings

2 persons

Nutritional facts

249 calories, 16g fat, 1g fiber, 3g carbs, 22g protein

Ingredients

- 2 center-cut, bone-in pork chops, 1 ½ – 2 inches thick
- 1 teaspoon ground mustard
- ½ teaspoon onion powder
- ¼ teaspoon garlic powder
- 2 tablespoons brown sugar
- 1 tablespoon paprika
- 1 ½ teaspoons salt
- 1 ½ teaspoon fresh ground black pepper
- 1–2 tablespoons olive oil

Instructions

- Preheat the air fryer for 5 minutes at 400 degrees F.
- Completely dry the pork chops using a paper towel after rinsing them with cool water.
- Combine all of the dry ingredients in a small mixing bowl.
  - Rub the pork chops in the mixture after coating them in olive oil. It should be rubbed thoroughly and abundantly. For the two pork chops, use virtually all of the rub mixture.
  - Cook pork chops in an air fryer for 12 minutes at 400 degrees F, flipping after 6 minutes.

Air Fryer Roast Lamb

Preparation and Cooking Time

20 minutes

Servings

2 persons

Nutritional facts

181 calories, 45g fat, 3g fiber, 8g carbs, 46g protein

Ingredients

- 10 oz. butterflied lamb leg roast
- 1 tsp thyme, fresh or dried
- 1/2 tsp black pepper
- 1 tbsp. olive oil
- 1 tsp rosemary, fresh or dried

Instructions

- Preheat the air fryer to 360 degrees Fahrenheit (180 degrees Celsius).
- Combine the olive oil, rosemary, and thyme on a platter.
- Dry completely.
- Then air fry the lamb for 15 minutes in an air fryer basket.
- This should provide a medium-rare lamb.
- If you desire it extra well done, cook for additional 3-minute intervals.
- Remove the roast lamb from the air fryer, cover with foil, and set aside 5 minutes before serving.
- the lamb roast and pour it in the herb oil mixture, rotating it to coat it
- To serve, carve against the grain.

The Best Air Fryer Lamb Chops

Preparation and Cooking Time

13 minutes

Servings

4 persons

Nutritional facts

350 calories, 45g fat, 0.4g fiber, 3g carbs, 25g protein

Ingredients

- 2 Tbsp. olive oil
- ½ tsp kosher salt
- ½ tsp garlic powder
- 1 Tbsp. red wine vinegar
- 1 tsp dried rosemary
- ½ tsp dried oregano
- ¼ tsp black pepper

Instructions

- Combine the lamb chops, extra virgin olive oil, red wine vinegar, rosemary, oregano, salt, garlic powder, & black pepper. Cover and chill for 1 hour after rubbing the marinade into the meat.
- Preheat the air fryer to 400°F (200°C).
- Cook the lamb chops in the air fryer basket for 7-10 min, flipping halfway through.
-

Rosemary Garlic Lamb Chops

Preparation and Cooking Time

1 hour 24 minutes

Servings

4 persons

Nutritional facts

427 calories, 37g fat, 1.1g fiber, 5g carbs, 13g protein

Ingredients

- 1.25 lbs. of rack of lamb, about 7-8 chops
- 1 teaspoon of salt, or to taste
- 3 Tablespoons of olive oil
- 2 Tablespoons of chopped fresh rosemary
- 1 teaspoon of garlic powder
- 1/2 teaspoon of black pepper, or to taste

Instructions

- Dry the lamb rack with a towel. If necessary, remove the silver skin from the underside of the ribs.
- Mix olive oil, rosemary, garlic, salt, and pepper in a large bowl. Toss the lamb in the marinade gently to coat it. Cover and set aside to marinate for 1 hour.
- Heat the Air Fryer for 4 minutes at 380°F/195°C. Spray the inside of the air fryer basket/tray with oil spray and arrange the lamb chops in a single layer.
- Air fry for 8 minutes at 380°F/195°C, then turn & air fry for another 3 to 6 minutes, or until done to your liking.

Air Fryer Lamb Chops Gluten Free

Preparation and Cooking Time

32 minutes

Servings

4 persons

Nutritional facts

153 calories, 8g fat, 1g fiber, 18.5g carbs, 13g protein

Ingredients

- 4 Bone-in Lamb chops (1 1/4 to 1 1/2 lbs.)
- 2 tbsp. honey
- 1 tbsp. fresh mint – chopped (extra whole mint leaves for garnishing)
- 2 small shallots, sliced for frying
- 3–4 tbsp. lemon juice (1/2 large lemon, juiced)
- 1 tsp lime zest
- 1 tbsp. balsamic vinegar
- 3/4 tsp ground cumin
- 1/4 tsp chili powder
- 3/4 tsp garlic powder or 2 garlic cloves, minced
- 1/4 tsp kosher salt and pepper each
- 2 tbsp. olive oil

- Sliced lemon for garnishing

Instructions

- Stir together the marinade ingredients in a small mixing bowl.
- Place the lamb chops in a zip lock bag or a glass container to keep them fresh.
- Marinate the lamb for 20-30 minutes at room temperature.
- Preheat the air fryer to 400 degrees Fahrenheit while the lamb is marinating. If your air fryer doesn't have a preheat option, turn it on for 2 minutes.
- In an air fryer, cook marinated lamb chops with chopped shallots for 12-14 minutes, flipping halfway through cooking.
- Cook chops until they achieve a minimum internal temperature of 145°F. Cooking time varies according to the thickness of the lamb and the type of air fryer used. Remove the
- Remove the chops once they've reached your desired level of doneness and lay them aside to rest for about 5 minutes.
- Drizzle the remaining marinade over the lamb chops. Season with salt and pepper to taste.
- If desired, garnish plate with fried shallot, mint, and lemon.

Lamb Chops with Dijon Garlic Marinade

Preparation and Cooking Time

32 minutes

Servings

2 persons

Nutritional facts

380 calories, 26g fat, 2g fiber, 7g carbs, 16g protein

Ingredients

- 2 teaspoons Dijon mustard
- 1 teaspoon cumin powder
- 1 teaspoon cayenne pepper
- 1 teaspoon Italiano spice blend (optional)
- 2 teaspoons olive oil
- 1 teaspoon soy sauce
- 1 teaspoon garlic, minced
- ¼ teaspoon salt
- 8 pieces of lamb chops

Instructions

- In a medium mixing bowl, combine the olive oil, Dijon mustard, garlic, soy sauce, cumin powder, Italiano spice blend (optional), cayenne pepper, & salt for preparing the marinade.
- Pour the marinade over the lamb chops in a Ziploc bag. Seal the bag tightly after pressing out the air. To properly coat the lamb chops, press the marinade around them. Place in the fridge for at least half an hour, or up to overnight, to marinate.
- Place 3 marinated lamb chops on top of the air frying basket on a grill rack and evenly space them out. Cook for 17 minutes at 350 degrees F, turning the lamb chops halfway through to achieve even cooking.
- Leave the lamb chops in the hot air fryer for another five minutes until they're done. This keeps the lamb chops warm while ensuring that they are fully cooked yet still soft.
- To taste, you can season with more salt and cumin.

Air Fryer-Herbed Lamb Chops

Preparation and Cooking Time

15 minutes

Servings

4 persons

Nutritional facts

426 calories, 52g fat, 0.4g fiber, 5g carbs, 16g protein

Ingredients

- 1 teaspoon of rosemary
- 2 tablespoons of olive oil
- 2 tablespoons of lemon juice
- 1 teaspoon of thyme
- 1 teaspoon of oregano
- 1 teaspoon of salt
- 1 teaspoon of coriander
- 1 pound of lamb chops

Instructions

- In a Ziploc bag, combine all ingredients except the lamb chops. Shake well to mix.
- The lamb chops should then be placed in the bag and refrigerated for at least one hour.
- Then, in the air fryer, set the temperature to 200 degrees Celsius (390 degrees Fahrenheit) and cook the lamb chops for 3 minutes, then flip them and cook for another 4 minutes.

Lamb Chops with Garlic Sauce

Preparation and Cooking Time

50 minutes

Servings

4 persons

Nutritional facts

320 calories, 60g fat, 0.3g fiber, 28g carbs, 37g protein

Ingredients

- 1 garlic bulb
- Sea salt
- Freshly ground black pepper
- 3 tablespoons olive oil
- 1 tablespoon fresh oregano, finely chopped
- 8 lamb chops

Instructions

- Preheat the air fryer to 200 degrees Celsius. Place the garlic bulb in the basket after thinly coating it with olive oil. Set the timer for 12 minutes after sliding the basket into the air fryer. Roast the garlic till it is fully cooked.
- Meanwhile, combine the herbs, sea salt, pepper, and olive oil in a mixing bowl. Leave the lamb chops for 5 minutes after coating them with half a tablespoon of herb oil.
- Preheat the air fryer to 200°C and remove the garlic bulb from the basket.
- In the basket, place four lamb chops and slip the basket into the air fryer. Start by setting the timer for 5 minutes. The lamb chops should be beautifully browned after roasting, and they may still be crimson or pink on the inside. Keep them heated on a plate while you roast the rest of the lamb chops.
- Squeeze the garlic cloves over the herb oil with your thumb and index finger. Season with salt and pepper, & stir well.
- Garlic sauce should be served alongside the lamb chops. With couscous and cooked zucchini, this dish is delicious.

Air Fryer Rack of Lamb with Roasted Garlic Aioli

Preparation and Cooking Time

35 minutes

Servings

4 persons

Nutritional facts

411 calories, 20g fat, 1.6g fiber, 30g carbs, 50g protein

Ingredients

- One 8-rib rack of lamb, Frenched (1 1/4 to 1 1/2 pounds)
- 1 large clove garlic, grated
- 1 teaspoon finely chopped fresh thyme
- 6 large cloves garlic (unpeeled)
- 2 tablespoons olive oil
- 1/2 cup mayonnaise
- 1 teaspoon lemon zest plus 2 teaspoons fresh lemon juice
- 1 teaspoon finely chopped fresh rosemary
- 3 tablespoons extra-virgin olive oil
- Kosher salt and freshly ground black pepper
- 1/2 cup grated Parmesan
- 1/3 cup panko breadcrumbs
- Nonstick cooking spray for the air-fryer basket and lamb
- 1 1/2 teaspoons Worcestershire sauce
- Kosher salt and freshly ground black pepper

Instructions

- Allow 30 minutes for the rack of lamb to come to room temperature before cooking.
- Rub 1 tablespoon olive oil on both sides of the rack of lamb, then season with 2 tablespoons salt as well as several grinds of pepper. Place on a large plate and set aside.
- In a large shallow bowl or pie plate, mix the Parmesan, panko, leftover 2 tbsp. oil, grated garlic, thyme, and rosemary. Place the lamb on top and massage the Parmesan mixture into an even layer.
- To make the aioli, spread the unpeeled garlic cloves on aluminum foil and drizzle with olive oil, a bit of salt, and a few grinds of pepper. Fold the foil into a pouch by folding the sides upwards.
- Preheat an air fryer to 375 degrees Fahrenheit and coat the basket with cooking spray. In the basket, place the fat-side up lamb and the garlic pouch. Using cooking spray, coat the top of the lamb. Air-fry the lamb for eighteen minutes for medium-rare, 20 minutes for medium, and 22 minutes for medium-well, or until the crust is crisp & deep golden brown and the flesh reaches desired doneness. (You can sauté the garlic simultaneously as the meat.) Allow the lamb to rest for 10 minutes on a cutting board, covered loosely with foil.
- While you're waiting, carefully open the foil packet. Squeeze the tender garlic cloves into a medium bowl and mash them until smooth with the olive oil from the pouch. Toss in the mayonnaise, lemon zest and juice, and Worcestershire sauce until everything is well combined. It can be seasoned with salt & pepper to taste.
- After the lamb has rested, slice it into individual chops between the bones & serve warm with the aioli.

Air Fried Masala Chops

Preparation and Cooking Time

55 minutes

Servings

4 persons

Nutritional facts

357 calories, 6g fat, 1g fiber, 8g carbs, 16g protein

Ingredients

- Lamb/Goat chops   500 g
- Cumin powder 1 tbsp.
- White vinegar 1 tbsp.
- Kashmiri red chili powder 1-1/2 tbsp.
- Turmeric powder 1 tbsp.
- Gram Masala Powder 1/2 tbsp.
- Salt 1 tsp
- Ginger Garlic paste   2 tbsp.
- Oil 2-3 tbsp.

Instructions

- In a pan/wok, heat 2-3 tablespoons of oil.
- Two tablespoons of ginger garlic paste are to be added. Stir for a few seconds, but don't let it burn.
- Cook until the chops have changed color and any excess meat juices have evaporated.
- Add the remaining ingredients, along with a little water, and whisk for a few seconds.
- Cook for about 25 minutes with 1/2 cup water.
- Dry it on a high heat setting.
- Place these chops in an air fryer & cook for 8-10 minutes at 180°C. Serve with your preferred yogurt dip.

Air Fryer Lamb Rack

Preparation and Cooking Time

20 minutes

Servings

2 persons

Nutritional facts

181 calories, 45g fat, 3g fiber, 8g carbs, 46g protein

Ingredients

- 2 rack of lamb
- 1½ teaspoons dried garlic
- 1 teaspoon dried onion
- 2 tablespoons dried rosemary
- 3 tablespoons olive oil
- 1 tablespoon dried thyme
- Salt
- pepper

Instructions

- Insert the olive oil, rosemary, thyme, garlic, salt, and pepper into a small mixing bowl. To blend, stir everything together.
- Remove any excess fat from the lamb racks. Brush the herb oil mixture over the lamb.
- Before putting the rack of lamb into the Air Fryer using the grill pan, preheat the Air Fryer to 360°F for 3 minutes. You can use parchment paper to line the Air Fryer basket and place the lamb on top.

- Place the meat side down first in the grill pan and turn halfway through to allow the meat and fat to crisp up.
- Cook the rack of lamb for 12 minutes, then use a thermometer to check the internal temperature of the rack of lamb.
- Take the lamb out of the Air Fryer and set it aside. Wrap aluminum foil around the rack of lamb to allow the meat to rest, and allow for a 5-minute rest period.

Garlic Rosemary Lamb Chops

Preparation and Cooking Time

15 minutes

Servings

2 persons

Nutritional facts

616 calories, 14g fat, 1g fiber, 5g carbs, 15g protein

Ingredients

- 4 Lamb Chops
- 2 Tsp of Garlic Puree
- 2 Tsp of Olive Oil
- Rosemary
- Fresh Garlic
- Salt
- Pepper

Instructions

- Put the lamb chops on the grill pan of the air fryer.
- Season the lamb chops on top with pepper and salt and drizzle with olive oil. Then, on top of each one, drizzle a little garlic puree.
- Fill the spaces in the air fryer grill pan with fresh rosemary sprigs and garlic cloves that haven't been peeled.
- Refrigerate the grill pan for an hour to marinate.
- Put your grill pan in the air fryer after an hour and cook for 6 minutes at 180°C/360°F.
- Flip the lamb chops with a spatula after 6 minutes.
- Repeat step #2 on the other side of the lamb chop, omitting the excess olive oil. Cook for 6 minutes on the other side at the same temperature.
- Remove the fresh garlic & rosemary and set aside for a minute or two before serving.

Air Fryer Lamb Chops with Poblano Sauce

Preparation and Cooking Time

30 minutes

Servings

4 persons

Nutritional facts

999 calories, 51g fat, 0.5g fiber, 4g carbs, 31g protein

Ingredients

- 4 pounds' lamb chops American lamb, trimmed to your taste
- 1/2 teaspoon oregano
- 1 tablespoon oil
- 2-pound bag baby potatoes
- 1/2 teaspoon salt
- 1/2 teaspoon pepper
- 1 teaspoon chili powder
- 1/4 teaspoon garlic powder
- 1/2 teaspoon oregano

- 1/2 teaspoon sea salt
- 1/2 teaspoon black pepper
- 1 teaspoon chili powder
- 1/4 teaspoon onion powder
- 2 tablespoons oil
- 1 avocado
- 2/3 cup cilantro
- 3 tablespoons yogurt or sour cream
- 1 tablespoon honey
- 3 poblano peppers charred
- 1 jalapeno pepper charred
- 2 1/2 tablespoons lime juice
- 2 tablespoons olive oil
- 1/2 teaspoon sea salt
- Lime slices
- cilantro

Instructions

- In a large mixing bowl, combine all ingredients and season the potatoes.
- Heat the air fryer to 400 degrees F for two minutes.
- In the air fryer, arrange the potatoes in a single layer and cook for 10 minutes. Remove the air fryer basket from the air fryer and give it a good shake.
- Return the potatoes to the air fryer for an additional 6-10 minutes, depending on their size.
- Sprinkle with cilantro and place on a serving plate when they're done.
- Preheat the air fryer to 400 degrees Fahrenheit.
- Season all sides of the lamb chops with spice and oil. On your air fryer basket, arrange the chops in a single layer.
- Remove the air fryer basket after 8 minutes of air frying.
- Continue air frying the lamb chops for an additional 4-8 minutes, based on how well you like your lamb chops.
- If you cook for 12 minutes total at 400 degrees F, it is considered medium-rare, whereas 14 minutes is considered medium.
- Make the poblano sauce while the lamb chops are cooking.
- In a food processor, combine all ingredients and pulse until smooth.
- Enjoy the air fryer lamb chops with potatoes, poblano sauce, extra hot sauce, and lime wedges.

Air Fryer Spicy Cumin Lamb

Preparation and Cooking Time

20 minutes

Servings

6 persons

Nutritional facts

670 calories, 5g fat, 0.6g fiber, 2g carbs, 6g protein

Ingredients

- 2 Lb. Boneless Lamb Shoulder (Cut into 1-Inch-Thick Piece strips)
- 1 Teaspoons Ground Funnel
- 1 Teaspoon Himalayan Salt
- 1/8 teaspoon Sichuan peppercorns
- Fresh Cilantro for Garnish
- 1 Teaspoon Ground Ginger

- 1 Teaspoon Ground Garlic
- 2 Tablespoons Shaoxing Wine
- 2 Tablespoons Cumin Powder
- 1 Tablespoon Ground Red Chili, Red Pepper Flakes or Cayenne Pepper
- 1 Tablespoon White Sesame Seed
- 1 Teaspoon Cumin Seeds
- Optional ingredients

Instructions

- Combine all of the ground spices and the optional cooking wine in a large mixing bowl. Then you have the option of marinating or not marinating. Marinating the lamb will help to reduce some of the gamey flavors. It is a matter of personal preference whether to marinate or not to marinate.
- To marinate the lamb strips, combine 1/4 of the spice mix with the meat strips and stir well. If you're not going to marinate your lamb strips, toss them thoroughly in a big mixing bowl, and put it in an air fryer basket after that.
- After filling the air basket, air fry for 10-15 minutes at 350°F or golden crispy. To ensure that the lamb pieces are air frying evenly, flip them halfway or give the air basket a thorough shake halfway through. Put it on top of some fresh bedded cilantro once it's finished cooking. On top, sprinkle sesame and cumin seeds. Serve hot for the finest flavor.

Spicy Korean Lamb Chops Air Fried

Preparation and Cooking Time

1hour 25 minutes

Servings

6 persons

Nutritional facts

580 calories, 30g fat, 0.4g fiber, 12g carbs, 24g protein

Ingredients

- 6 1/2 tsp Red pepper powder
- 3 tbsp. rice wine
- 2 ` tbsp. garlic minced
- 1 tsp Ginger minced
- 2 tbsp. Korean red pepper paste
- 2 tbsp. ketchup
- 6 tbsp. Corn syrup
- 2 lbs. Lamb chops
- 1 cup celery diced
- cilantro chopped
- green onions chopped
- 2 tbsp. granulated sugar
- 1 tbsp. curry powder
- 8 1/2 tbsp. soy sauce
- 1/2 tbsp. sesame oil
- 1/2 tbsp. Green plum extract Optional
- 2 cups Water
- 1 cup red wine
- 3 bay leaves
- 1 cup carrots diced
- 2 cups onions diced
- 1/2 tsp cinnamon powder
- 1 tsp sesame seeds
- 1 tsp black pepper

- 1/3 cup Asian pear ground
- 1/3 cup onion powder

Instructions

- Close and seal the Instant Pot inner pot with all ingredients (except cilantro & green onions).
- Set the timer for 20 minutes on High pressure using the Pressure Cook/Manual button.
- Allow for a 10-15-minute natural release before opening the steam release valve to relieve the remaining pressure. Remove the lamb from the pan and set it aside to cool.
- Select Sauté & toggle to High to make the sauce thicker after pressing Cancel. To keep the sauce from burning, keep stirring it regularly as it cooks. Once it has thickened, press Cancel.
- Clean the inner pot and pour the sauce into a bowl.
- By slicing between the bones, separate the lamb chops from the rack. Place lamb chops separately in a single layer on the dehydration rack and then into the air fry basket using a Duo Crisp. In the cooker pot, place the air fry basket. Place the chops on a trivet in the inner pot if using a standard Instant Pot with the Air Fryer Lid. Brush the lamb chops with more sauce.
- Cover the Instant Pot with the air fryer lid. Preheat the oven to 400°F and broil for 5 minutes. Remove lamp chops & set them aside once they are nicely roasted. Repeat till all the lamb chops have been grilled.
- Garnish with cilantro and green onions, if desired.

Roast Lamb Rack with Lemon & Cumin Crust

Preparation and Cooking Time

1 hour 35 minutes

Servings

2 persons

Nutritional facts

567 calories, 52g fat, 1g fiber, 20g carbs, 29g protein

Ingredients

- 800g (1.7 pounds) Frenched rack of lamb
- 1 tsp cumin seeds
- 1 tsp ground cumin
- 1 tsp oil
- Salt & fresh milled black pepper
- 60g (0.13 pound) dry breadcrumbs (sourdough)
- 1 tsp grated garlic (about 2 fat cloves of garlic)
- 1/2 tsp salt
- Grated lemon rind (1/4 lemon)
- 1 egg, beaten

Instructions

- Heat the air fryer to 100°C (212°F).
- The lamb rack is seasoned with salt and freshly ground black pepper.
- Mix dry breadcrumbs, grated garlic, 1/2 teaspoon salt, cumin seeds, crushed cumin, oil, and grated lemon rind in a large mixing bowl.
- A fork is used to beat an egg in a separate big bowl.
- Form a crust by dipping the lamb rack into the egg and coating it in spiced breadcrumbs afterward.
- Slide the coated lamb rack into the Air fryer basket. Set the timer for 25 minutes.
- Increase the temperature to 200 degrees Celsius after 25 minutes and set the timer for another 5 minutes.
- Remove the meat from the air fryer and then let it rest for 10 minutes before serving, covered in aluminum foil.

Air Fryer Lamb Shanks

Preparation and Cooking Time

1 hour 30 minutes

Servings

4 persons

Nutritional facts

348 calories, 16g fat, 1g fiber, 11g carbs, 38g protein

Ingredients

- 4 lamb shanks
- 1 tsp rosemary leaves
- 2 tsp oregano
- 2 tsp olive oil
- 2 tsp garlic, crushed
- 2 tsp salt
- 1/2 tsp pepper
- 250ml (8.5 fl oz.) chicken stock

Instructions

- Heat the air fryer to 200 degrees Celsius (390 degrees Fahrenheit). It will take about five minutes for the temperature to reach the desired level.
- Olive oil, garlic, salt, pepper, rosemary, & oregano are rubbed into the lamb shanks.
- Place in the air fryer for 20 minutes to cook.
- Reduce the temperature of the air fryer to 150°C (300°F) & add the chicken stock. Allow one hour for cooking.
- Halfway through cooking, turn the lamb shanks.
- Serve and have fun.

Air Fryer Lamb Meatballs

Preparation and Cooking Time

17 minutes

Servings

4 persons

Nutritional facts

328 calories, 16g fat, 1g fiber, 16g carbs, 21g protein

Ingredients

- 1 lb. ground lamb
- 1/4 teaspoon ground cinnamon
- 1 teaspoon ground cumin
- 2 teaspoon granulated onion
- 2 Tablespoon fresh parsley
- Salt and pepper

Instructions

- Mix the lamb, cumin, onion, parsley, & cinnamon in a large bowl. Mix well until all of the ingredients are distributed uniformly.
- Make 1 inch balls out of the mixture.
- Cook the lamb meatballs in the air fryer basket for 12-15 minutes at 350°F. Halfway through, give the meatballs a good shake.

Roasted rack of lamb

Preparation and Cooking Time

30 minutes

Servings

4 persons

Nutritional facts

435 calories, 45g fat, 3g fiber, 8g carbs, 46g protein

Ingredients

- 1 garlic clove
- 75 g unsalted macadamia nuts
- 1 tbsp. breadcrumbs (preferably homemade)
- 1 tbsp. chopped fresh rosemary
- 1 tbsp. olive oil
- 800 g rack of lamb
- pepper & salt
- 1 egg

Instructions

- Garlic should be finely chopped. To make garlic oil, combine the olive oil & garlic. Season the rack of lamb with pepper and salt after brushing it with the oil.
- Heat the air fryer to 100 degrees Celsius.
- Place the nuts in a bowl and finely chop them. Combine the breadcrumbs & rosemary in a mixing bowl. In a separate bowl, whisk the egg.
- Dip the lamb into the egg mixture, draining any excess, to coat it. Apply the macadamia crust to the lamb.
- Slide the coated lamb rack into the Air fryer basket and then into the air fryer. Preheat the oven to 350°F and set the timer for 25 minutes. Increase the temperature to 200°C after 25 minutes & set the timer for another five minutes. Remove the meat from the pan and set aside for 10 minutes to rest, covered in aluminum foil.

Lamb Chops with Horseradish Sauce

Preparation and Cooking Time

30 minutes

Servings

2 persons

Nutritional facts

1231 calories, 19g fat, 0.5g fiber, 5g carbs, 15g protein

Ingredients

- 4 lamb loin chops
- vegetable oil spray for cooking
- ½ cup mayonnaise
- 1 tbsp. Dijon mustard
- 2 tbsp. vegetable oil
- 1 clove garlic minced
- ½ tsp kosher salt
- ½ tsp black pepper
- 1 ½ tbsp. prepared horseradish may reduce to 1 tbsp. if desired
- 2 tsp sugar

Instructions

- Brush the lamb chops with the oil, then massage them with the garlic and season with salt and pepper. Allow 30 minutes to marinate at room temperature.
- Mix the mayonnaise, mustard, horseradish, and sugar in a medium mixing bowl. Stir until everything is completely blended. Half of the sauce should be set aside for serving.

- Place the chops in the air fryer basket after spraying it with vegetable oil spray. Preheat the air fryer to 325°F and cook the chops for 10 minutes, flipping halfway through.
- Remove the chops from the air fryer & place them in a mixing bowl with the horseradish sauce. Toss to coat. Re-insert the chops into the air fryer basket. Preheat the air fryer to 400 degrees Fahrenheit for 3 minutes. Check the internal temperature of the meat with a meat thermometer to confirm it has reached 145°F (for medium-rare).
- Serve the chops with the horseradish sauce that has been set aside.

Air-Fryer Lamb Sliders with Apricot Chutney

Preparation and Cooking Time

20 minutes

Servings

2 persons

Nutritional facts

480 calories, 46g fat, 2g fiber, 30g carbs, 28g protein

Ingredients

- 1 American Lamb rack cut into 8 chops or 8 loin chops (approximately 4 ounces each)
- 1 avocado
- 2/3 cup cilantro
- 3 tablespoons of yogurt or sour cream
- 1 tablespoon of honey
- Lime slices
- Cilantro
- 2 tablespoons of oil
- 2-pound bag of baby potatoes
- 1/2 teaspoon of salt
- 1/2 teaspoon of pepper
- 1 teaspoon chili powder
- 1/4 teaspoon garlic powder
- 1/2 teaspoon of sea salt
- 1/2 teaspoon black pepper
- 1 teaspoon chili powder
- 1/4 teaspoon garlic powder
- 1/2 teaspoon oregano
- 1/2 teaspoon of sea salt
- 2 tablespoons oil
- 3 poblano peppers, charred
- 1 jalapeno pepper, charred
- 2 1/2 tablespoons lime juice
- 2 tablespoons olive oil

Instructions

- In a large mixing bowl, combine all ingredients and season the potatoes.
- Heat the air fryer to 400 degrees F for two minutes.
- In the air fryer, arrange the potatoes in a single layer and cook for 10 minutes. Remove the air fryer basket from the air fryer and give it a good shake.
- Return the potatoes to the air fryer for a further 6-10 minutes, depending on their size.
- Sprinkle with cilantro and place on a serving plate when they're done.
- Preheat the air fryer to 400 degrees Fahrenheit.

- Season all sides of the lamb chops with spice and oil. On your air fryer basket, arrange the chops in a single layer.
- Remove the air fryer basket after 8 minutes of air frying.
- Continue air frying the lamb chops for an additional 4-8 minutes, based on how well you like your lamb chops.
- Make the poblano sauce while the lamb chops are cooking.
- In a food processor, combine all ingredients and pulse until smooth.
- Serve the lamb chops from the air fryer with the potatoes, poblano sauce, extra spicy sauce, and lime wedges

Air Fryer Mint Lamb with Toasted Hazelnuts and Peas

Preparation and Cooking Time

40 minutes

Servings

4 persons

Nutritional facts

329 calories, 42g fat, 0.3g fiber, 1g carbs, 28g protein

Ingredients

- 60 gr hazelnuts
- 220 gr frozen peas
- 80 ml water
- 100 ml white wine
- 600 gr shoulder of lamb cut into 3 cm x 1 cm strips
- 1 tbsp. hazelnut oil
- 2 tbsp. fresh mint leaves chopped
- sea salt and freshly-cracked black pepper to taste

Instructions

- Put the hazelnuts in the Air Fryer, cover, and cook for 10 minutes on manual mode at 160°C. Set the hazelnuts aside after removing them from the Air Fryer.
- Combine the lamb strips with the hazelnut oil in a large mixing bowl & season liberally with sea salt & freshly cracked black pepper.
- Place the mint leaves on the handle side of the Air Fryer pan, followed by the seasoned lamb, then the toasted hazelnuts on top.
- Pour the wine & water over the ingredients, close the lid, and add the peas on the other side of the pan.
- Cook for 25 minutes.
- Remove the items from the pan and arrange them on a serving plate once they're done. If desired, top with additional fresh mint leaves.

Roasted Lamb & Lemon Greens

Preparation and Cooking Time

35 minutes

Servings

2 persons

Nutritional facts

395 calories, 28g fat, 3g fiber, 8g carbs, 21g protein

Ingredients

- 300 grams butterflied lamb leg
- 1/2 tsp Black pepper 2.5g
- 200 grams' green beans
- Juice of half a lemon 20ml

- 1 tbsp. olive oil
- 2 tsp rosemary 2g
- 1 tsp dried thyme 1g
- 1 tsp salt 5g
- 2 1/2 tbsp. slivered almonds 20g

Instructions

- Half-fill a small pot with water, and bring to a boil over high heat.
- Preheat the air fryer to 180°C (350°F).
- Rub the rosemary, olive oil, salt, thyme, and pepper into the meat.
- Place the lamb in the air fryer basket and cook for fifteen minutes for medium-rare.
- Cook the beans in boiling water for 3 minutes.
- After 3 minutes, strain the beans and rinse them under cold water to stop them from cooking further.
- Take the lamb out of the air fryer and leave it aside to rest for at least 5 minutes.
- In a mixing dish, combine the beans, lemon juice, and almonds.
- Serve with sliced lamb and beans on the side.

Tender Rack of lamb Gluten Free

Preparation and Cooking Time

30 minutes

Servings

4 persons

Nutritional facts

456 calories, 8g fat, 1g fiber, 18.5g carbs, 13g protein

Ingredients

- 2 racks of lamb
- 1 tablespoon honey
- Freshly ground pepper
- 1 bunch fresh mint
- 2 garlic cloves
- 100 ml extra virgin olive oil
- Kitchen twine

Instructions

- In the chopper of a hand mixer, combine the mint, garlic, oil, and honey. To make a lovely thin mint pesto, puree all ingredients together.
- Make a tiny incision in the lamb racks from the top between the bones, then use kitchen twine to tie the rack into a crown shape. Using the pesto, smear it all over. Set aside a small portion of the pesto.
- Preheat the Air fryer to 200°F and insert the grill pan accessory. Preheat the oven to 200°F and cook the lamb rack for fifteen minutes. Open the air fryer every five minutes to smear another layer of pesto.
- Serve with fresh vegetables and mashed potatoes.

Balsamic Air-Fried Lamb Chops

Preparation and Cooking Time

60 minutes

Servings

4 persons

Nutritional facts

245 calories, 26g fat, 0.4g fiber, 4g carbs, 15g protein

Ingredients

- 1/4 cup of balsamic vinegar
- 4 lamb chops
- salt and freshly ground black pepper
- 2 tablespoons of olive oil
- 1 teaspoon of garlic, crushed
- 1/2 teaspoon of paprika
- 1/2 teaspoon of onion powder

Instructions

- Put the balsamic vinegar, olive oil, garlic, paprika, & onion powder in a resealable bag. Toss with a pinch of salt and pepper.
- After that, insert the lamb and knead it in the marinade, ensuring all sides are covered. Refrigerate for at least two hours.
- Preheat the air fryer to 400 degrees Fahrenheit (200 C).
- Place the marinated lamb chops in the Air Fryer basket after removing them from the re-sealable bag.
- Cook the lamb chops for 15 minutes in the Air Fryer, turning halfway through.
- Place in a serving dish and serve.
- Serve and have fun.

Leg of lamb with Brussels sprouts and potato quenelles

Preparation and Cooking Time

90 minutes

Servings

4 persons

Nutritional facts

980 calories, 13g fat, 1g fiber, 3g carbs, 20g protein

Ingredients

- 1 kg leg of lamb
- 600 g Brussels sprouts
- 4 large potatoes
- A knob of butter
- 2 spoons groundnut oil
- 15 g rosemary
- 15 g lemon thyme
- 1 garlic clove
- Nutme

Instructions

- Score and stud a fine leg of lamb with a couple of large sprigs of rosemary as well as lemon thyme. Using the groundnut oil, smear the leg. Preheat the oven to 150°F & cook the lamb for 1 hour and 15 minutes in the air fryer.
- Potato quenelles are easy to make and maybe made ahead of time and frozen. Using milk, butter, and nutmeg, mash the potatoes & season to taste. Using two spoons, form the quenelles bypassing the mash from one spoon to the other. If you want to create the quenelles ahead of time, bake them at 200 degrees C for 15 minutes, and they only take 8 minutes if you make them from fresh.
- Clean the Brussels sprouts and toss them in a bowl with some honey and neutral oil. Add the sprouts and frozen quenelles to the Air fryer after 75 minutes of cooking. At 200 degrees C, bake the lamb, sprouts, and quenelles together for fifteen minutes. If you're using fresh quenelles, cook them for seven minutes after the Brussels sprouts.

Easy and Quick Tender Lamb Roast

Preparation and Cooking Time

40 minutes

Servings

4 persons

Nutritional facts

630 calories, 45g fat, 3g fiber, 8g carbs, 46g protein

Ingredients

- 1/2 kg Lamb roast (shoulder or any preferred meat, can even be individual cuts)
- 4 tsp crushed garlic
- 4 tsp Dried rosemary
- 2 tbsp. Olive oil
- 4 tsp Onion flakes
- 3 Brushed potatoes, cut into chunks
- 2 cups frozen peas, defrosted in boiling water
- 2 bunches Dutch carrots, trimmed and peeled if preferred
- 1 medium Sweet potato, peeled and cut into chunks
- 2 tbsp. Instant gravy

Instructions

- Preheat the air fryer to 200 degrees Celsius. In a baking dish, combine the Dutch carrots and potato, and the cooking time is 30 minutes.
- Rub the rosemary, garlic, oil, and onion flakes all over the lamb. In a small frying pan, heat the oil and sear the sides until brown. Season the lamb generously. Cover the bottom of the air fryer tray with foil and baking paper. For the sweet potato, simmer the lamb for 15-20 minutes for medium.
- Remove the carrot & potato from the oven and cover with foil to keep warm. Drain the green peas and set them aside. Make the gravy as per the directions on the package. Remove the lamb from the pan and set it aside to rest for 5-10 minutes. Wrap foil around it. Cook the sweet potato for an additional ten minutes.
- Remove the sweet potato from the oven and combine it with the carrots and potatoes. Serve the lamb with the veggies and gravy.

Spicy Lamb Sirloin Steak

Preparation and Cooking Time

55 minutes

Servings

4 persons

Nutritional facts

182 calories, 32g fat, 0.2g fiber, 2g carbs, 38g protein

Ingredients

- 1/2 Onion
- 1 teaspoon Ground Cinnamon
- 1/2 teaspoon Ground Cardamom
- 1/2 - 1 teaspoon Cayenne Pepper
- 4 slices Ginger
- 5 cloves Garlic
- 1 teaspoon Gram Masala
- 1 teaspoon ground fennel
- 1 teaspoon Kosher Salt
- 1-pound of boneless lamb sirloin steaks

Instructions

- Except for the lamb chops, all of the ingredients go into a blender bowl.
- Blend for 3-4 minutes, or until the onion is finely diced and all ingredients are combined.
- In a large mixing bowl, place the lamb chops. Slash the fat and meat with a knife.
- Mix in the spice paste that has been blended.
- Allow the mixture to rest in the refrigerator for half an hour or up to 24 hours.
- Preheat the air fryer to 330°F and set the lamb steaks in a single layer in the air fryer basket, cooking for 15 minutes, flipping halfway through.
- Check the internal temperature of the beef with a meat thermometer to confirm it has reached 150F for medium well and then serve

Spicy Cumin Lamb Skewers

Preparation and Cooking Time

15 minutes

Servings

2 persons

Nutritional facts

256 calories, 5g fat, 1g fiber, 2g carbs, 7g protein

Ingredients

- 1 Tbsp. of red chili flakes
- 1 ¼ lb. of lamb shoulder chops, cut into 1-inch pieces
- 1 Tbsp. of vegetable oil
- 1 Tbsp. of cumin seed
- 2 tsp. of fennel seed
- 1 tsp. of kosher salt
- 2 tsp. of granulated garlic
- 2 tsp. of pale, dry sherry

Instructions

- Coarsely grind the chili flakes, cumin, and fennel in a mortar & pestle grinder. Insert the granulated garlic & kosher salt into the blender and pulse quickly to break the garlic into smaller pieces. Combine all of the ingredients in a large mixing bowl.
- In a small bowl, set aside 1 tablespoon of the spice mixture. Toss the lamb slices with the leftover spice mix, oil, and wine in a large mixing bowl.
- Place the skewers with the seasoned lamb slices in the Air Fryer Oven. Air fry the skewers at 340°F for ten minutes on the Rotisserie setting.
- Sprinkle the reserved spice mix on the skewers when they're almost done cooking and let them continue cooking.
- Take the skewers out of the oven & serve right away.

Roast Lamb & Lemon Greens

Preparation and Cooking Time

35 minutes

Servings

2 persons

Nutritional facts

395 calories, 45g fat, 3g fiber, 8g carbs, 46g protein

Ingredients

- 300 gr butterflied lamb leg
- 1/2 tsp Black pepper 2.5g

- 200 gr green beans
- Juice of half a lemon 20ml
- 1 tbsp. olive oil
- 2 tsp rosemary 2g
- 1 tsp dried thyme 1g
- 1 tsp salt 5g
- 2.5 tbsp. slivered almonds 20

Instructions

- Fill a small saucepan halfway with water, cover, and bring to a boil on the stovetop.
- Heat the air fryer to 180 degrees Celsius.
- Coat the lamb with olive oil, rosemary, thyme, salt, and pepper.
- Place the lamb in an air fryer basket & cook for fifteen minutes for medium-rare; if you prefer well-done meat, heat for longer in 5-minute increments.
- Cook the beans for 3 minutes in boiling water.
- Remove the beans after 3 minutes, drain, and rinse under cold water to stop them from cooking any further.
- Remove the lamb from the air fryer & set it aside for at least 5 minutes to rest.
- Combine the beans, lemon juice, and almonds in a mixing bowl.
- Serve with sliced lamb and a side of beans.

Lamb Roast with Air Fried Potatoes, Carrots and Sweet Potato

Preparation and Cooking Time

45 minutes

Servings

6 persons

Nutritional facts

380 calories, 45g fat, 3g fiber, 8g carbs, 46g protein

Ingredients

- 1.5kg Lamb Leg (any size close will do as long as it fits your Air Fryer)
- 2 large sprigs of Rosemary
- 4 cloves Garlic
- 1kg Red Royale Potatoes
- 2 medium Sweet Potatoes
- 250g Baby Carrots
- 1 cup Peas
- Salt & Pepper

Instructions

- Insert alternate bits of Rosemary & sliced Garlic into the flesh with a small sharp knife every 5 or so centimeters, then season with salt & pepper. Set aside to finish cooking after the vegetables.
- Cut Sweet Potato into chunky wedges, toss with a little oil and salt, and Air Fry for 10 minutes at 200 degrees Celsius in a tray in the base or in the basket. Replace the lid and cook for another 10 minutes, or till done to your preference.
- Wrap carrots in foil with a little butter & salt and bake at 200°C for 30 minutes.
- Break up the remaining Garlic & Rosemary on a 20x20cm foil tray and use as a base for the Lamb to sit on. This piece of steak requires an hour at 160 degrees Celsius, followed by an additional 10 minutes at 200 degrees Celsius to crisp up the top. It is cooked to perfection with an internal temperature of 65 degrees Celsius, just the way we like it.

- Allow it to rest wrapped in foil for fifteen minutes while you reheat the vegetables and peas at 180 degrees C.

Butterflied Leg of Lamb with Parmentier Potatoes

Preparation and Cooking Time

65 minutes

Servings

4 persons

Nutritional facts

461calories, 17g fat, 1g fiber, 13g carbs, 27g protein

Ingredients

- 1kg boned leg of lamb
- Salt, as desired, and freshly ground black pepper to taste
- 2 garlic cloves, peeled and cut into slivers
- Fresh rosemary sprigs
- 1 tbsp. sunflower oil
- 900g potatoes, scrubbed

Instructions

- Tying the lamb into a nice round shape with cooking twine to ensure uniform cooking. Make deep holes in the lambskin with the sharp tip and insert slivers of garlic & rosemary sprigs. Then season with salt and pepper to taste.
- Connect the probe to the unit. Place the cooking pot in the device, add the oil, and close the top. ROAST is the option to choose, and PRESET is the option to choose. Select LAMB and set MED WELL using the arrows to the left of the monitor. To begin preheating, press START/STOP.
- Place in lamb when the unit beeps to indicate that it has preheated. Horizontally insert the probe into the thickest portion of the lamb. Put the lid back on.
- Potatoes should be cut into 2cm cubes, rinsed in water to remove starch, drained, and patted dry.
- After 25 minutes, flip the lamb and season with salt, pepper, and rosemary sprigs. Prepare the potatoes by tossing them in oil and putting the lid back on.
- When the machine beeps to indicate that the cooking is finished, remove the probe from the lamb with oven gloves, then remove the lamb and set it aside to rest for 10 minutes.
- If the potatoes aren't brown enough, select ROAST, set the temperature to 180°C, and cook for 5-10 minutes. To avoid preheating, select PREHEAT. To begin, select START/STOP.
- Potatoes go well with lamb.

Air-Fried Garlic Lamb Chops

Preparation and Cooking Time

18 minutes

Servings

1 person

Nutritional facts

265 calories, 37g fat, 1.1g fiber, 5g carbs, 13g protein

Ingredients

- 2 lamb chops - blade or loin chops
- 1 teaspoon dried rosemary
- 4 garlic cloves
- 2 teaspoons Worcestershire sauce
- 1/2 teaspoon each salt & pepper

Instructions

- Preheat the air fryer to 380 degrees F for 5 minutes.
- Peel and cut garlic cloves while the air fryer is heating.
- Coat all sides of the lamb chops in frying spray. Season lamb chops on both sides with salt and pepper to taste.
- Rub both sides of the lamb chops with rosemary and Worcestershire sauce.
- Place lamb chops in a preheated air fryer and cook for 6–8 minutes per side, based on how rare you prefer them.

Easy Air Fried Lamb Kofta

Preparation and Cooking Time

27 minutes

Servings

6 persons

Nutritional facts

437 calories, 12g fat, 1g fiber, 5g carbs, 14g protein

Ingredients

- 2 lbs. ground lamb (can sub beef)
- 1 tsp paprika
- 3/4 tsp salt
- 1/2 tsp ground cinnamon
- 2 cloves garlic, finely minced or pressed
- 2 tbsp. chopped fresh cilantro or parsley
- 1 tbsp. ground coriander
- 1 tbsp. ground cumin
- 1/2 tsp black pepper

Instructions

- Soak bamboo skewers in water for at least 60 minutes if you plan to use them.
- Mix all ingredients in a large mixing bowl and mix thoroughly with your hands. Make 12 oval-shaped logs, measuring 1 inch broad and 4 inches long. Thread the logs onto the skewers if you're using them.
- Air fry for 10 to 12 minutes at 400 degrees Fahrenheit, or until well browned and the center of the kofta registers at least 135 degrees Fahrenheit for medium. Allow 5 minutes for resting before serving.
- You can either bake the kofta at 375F or grill it over medium heat, flipping it to brown all sides.

Whole 30 Gyro Meatballs

Preparation and Cooking Time

27 minutes

Servings

40 meatballs

Nutritional facts

42 calories, 14g fat, 0.5g fiber, carbs 1g, 22g protein

Ingredients

- 1 lb. ground lamb
- juice of 1 lemon
- 1 1/2 teaspoon sea salt - or Kosher salt
- 1 lb. ground beef - 93/7 suggested
- 1 egg, whisked
- 1 tablespoon dried rosemary
- 1 tablespoon dried dill
- 1 1/2 teaspoon pepper
- nonstick cooking spray

Instructions

- Mix all meatball ingredients in a food processor.
- Make 1 inch balls out of the mixture.
- Using nonstick cooking spray, coat the air fryer basket. Cook the meatballs in an air fryer at 350°F for 7 minutes. Remove the meatballs from the basket and shake them. Return to the pan and cook for another 4 minutes. It's possible that you'll have to perform this in batches.
- Allow for cooling for 2-3 minutes before serving.

Quick and Easy Greek Lamb and Spinach Meatballs with Tzatziki made in Air Fryer

Preparation and Cooking Time

25 minutes

Servings

30 Spinach meatballs

Nutritional facts

230 calories, 26g fat, 3g fiber, 11g carbs, 30g protein

Ingredients

- 1.5 lb. ground lamb
- 1 egg
- 2 tablespoons chopped fresh mint
- 2 teaspoons lemon juice
- 1 teaspoon olive oil
- 1-2 cloves garlic
- 2 tablespoons olive oil
- 1 tablespoon very finely minced fresh oregano
- 1/2 cup finely crumbled feta
- 1/2 teaspoon salt
- 1 cup full-fat plain Greek yogurt
- 1/3 cup diced cucumber
- 2 tablespoons chopped fresh dill
- 2 cups packed chopped spinach
- 2 cloves minced garlic
- 1 cup minced onion
- 1/3 cup chopped pine nuts
- 1/4 teaspoon salt

Instructions

- Heat the oil in a heavy frying pan until it shimmers. Cook occasionally, stirring, until the onions are completely caramelized, about 10 minutes. Simmer for another 2-3 minutes after adding the garlic, then add the spinach & cook for another 4 to 5 minutes, till the spinach is wilted and some of the liquid has evaporated. Remove the pan from the heat.
- Combine the spinach, lamb, feta, pine nuts, oregano, & salt in a large mixing bowl. Mix well until all of the ingredients are uniformly distributed.
- Cook the meatballs in batches in the Air fryer at 325°F for 11 minutes.
- Suppose you don't have an air fryer, heat 3 tablespoons of oil in the same heavy pan you used for the aromatics before adding the meatballs. Cook, rotating once, on medium-high heat till browned and cooked through, about 5-7 minutes per side.
- While the meatballs are cooking, whisk together all of the ingredients for the tzatziki in a small bowl. Serve alongside meatballs.

Air Fryer Lamb Cutlets with Minted Yogurt Sauce

Preparation and Cooking Time

30 minutes

Servings

6-8 persons

Nutritional facts

341 calories, 51g fat, 0.2g fiber, 4g carbs, 31g protein

Ingredients

- 600 grams' lamb cutlets (approx. 8 large cutlets)
- pinch of salt
- pinch of pepper
- ½ cup natural yogurt
- juice of one lemon, reserve half for sauce
- 1 teaspoon dried oregano
- 1 teaspoon minced garlic
- 1 tablespoon olive oil
- handful fresh mint leaves, about 20 leaves
- reserved lemon juice

Instructions

- Mix the lemon juice, oregano, garlic, olive oil, salt, and pepper in a large mixing bowl. Insert the lamb cutlets into the marinade and coat them thoroughly. Allow for 5 minutes of resting time in the fridge or more if you have time.
- Cook the lamb cutlets in the air fryer for 15-20 minutes at 190 degrees Celsius or as directed by the manufacturer.
- In the meantime, make your sauce by blending the natural yogurt, fresh mint, & lemon juice until smooth.
- Serve the lamb with roasted potatoes, steaming seasonal veggies, and a yogurt sauce.

Gyros in the Air Fryer

Preparation and Cooking Time

1 hour 30 minutes

Servings

8 persons

Nutritional facts

180 calories, 14g fat, 0.5g fiber, carbs 1g, 22g protein

Ingredients

- 1 lb. Ground Lamb
- 1 Sweet or Red Onion Diced
- 4 Large Garlic Cloves diced, minced, or pressed
- 1 Tbsp. Salt
- 1/4 tsp Black Pepper
- 2 tsp Oregano
- 1/2 tsp thyme
- 1 tsp Marjoram
- 1 tsp Rosemary
- 1 tsp Cumin
- 1 lb. Ground Lean Hamburger
- 2 pieces Bread (Russian Rye, Potato, White, Wheat) chopped
- 1/4 cup Heavy Cream
- 1 egg
- 2 Tbsp. Fresh Lemon Juice
- 1/2 tsp Crushed Red Peppers

- 1-2 cups Tzatziki Sauce
- 2 cups Frozen Thin Cut Fries Air fried
- 1/4 tsp Salt for fries
- 1/4 tsp Black Pepper for fries
- 2 Tbsp. Olive Oil (Robust Preferred)
- 6 Pita Bread or Flatbread
- Green Lettuce torn into medium pieces
- 3 – 4 Roma Tomatoes 1 Roma tomato per gyro sandwich
- 1/2 Sweet Onion sliced thin
- 1 tsp Granulated Garlic or Garlic powder for fries
- Feta Cheese (optional)

Instructions

- If preparing tzatziki sauce, combine all ingredients in a mixing bowl, cover, and chill.
- Combine the chopped bread, cream, and egg in a large mixing bowl.
- Mix black pepper, salt, oregano, marjoram, thyme, cumin, rosemary, and crushed red peppers.
- Combine the ground beef and lamb in a large mixing bowl, thoroughly combining all ingredients.
- Oil the aluminum foil and transfer the meat mixture to it.
- Make a form out of the meat mixture, which will fit into the air fryer basket.
- Fold the corner of the oiled aluminum foil to one side and wrap it over the sides of the meat.
- Heat the air fryer to 400 degrees Fahrenheit for 5 minutes.
- Carefully place the gyro loaf in the air fryer basket, wrapped in aluminum foil.
- Preheat oven to 300°F and bake for 45 minutes.
- Remove the air fryer basket and carefully remove the gyro loaf from the aluminum foil with tongs and a spatula.
- Discard the aluminum foil that has been folded around the liquids.
- Transfer the gyro loaf to the air fryer after spraying the basket with olive oil.
- Cook for fifteen minutes at 300°F (total time at 300°F: 60 minutes)
- As soon as the middle of the meat reaches 165°F or above, transfer it to a chopping board and tent it with aluminum foil, then set it aside.
- Season frozen fries liberally with salt, pepper, & garlic powder or granulated garlic in an air fryer basket.
- Cook for 15 minutes at 400°F, shaking every 5 minutes to ensure they don't burn.
- Tomatoes should be sliced. Lettuce should be cut into medium pieces
- Hold the hot gyro meat with tongs and transfer it to a dish or cutting board.
- Allow for 10 minutes of resting time after covering the gyro meat with aluminum foil.
- Air Fry frozen thin-cut French fries at 380° F for around 8 minutes, or until golden brown at the ends, and then season with salt.
- Slice the gyro meat as thinly as possible with a sharp or serrated knife.
- For a few minutes, warm pita bread in the air fryer.
- Assemble the gyros: pita bread, lettuce, 3 to 4 tomato slices, sweet onion slices, approximately 3 tablespoons tzatziki sauce, 2-3 slices gyro meat, a small handful of fries, and feta cheese, if using.

Air Fryer Ribs

Preparation and Cooking Time

40 minutes

Servings

2-4 persons

Nutritional facts

299 calories, 37g fat, 1g fiber, 10g carbs, 26g protein

Ingredients

- Ribs
- 1 tablespoon honey
- 1 tablespoon mustard
- 1 tablespoon ketchup
- 2 tablespoons soy sauce
- 1 rack spare or baby back ribs (about 750 g/ 1.7 lb.)
- 1-2 teaspoons vegetable oil
- fine sea salt and black pepper
- ½ teaspoon sweet paprika powder
- Half teaspoon smoked paprika powder
- chili to taste

Instructions

- Half an hour before frying, remove the ribs from the refrigerator. If desired, remove or clip the membrane from the back of the ribs. To fit the ribs in the air fryer basket, cut them into multiple pieces. Use kitchen towels to dry them, massage them with oil and then season generously with pepper and salt.
- Honey, ketchup, soy sauce, mustard, sweet and smoked paprika powder, salt, and pepper are combined in a bowl. If desired, season with chili powder.
- If necessary, heat the air fryer to 190 degrees Celsius/ 380 degrees Fahrenheit (according to its instructions). In the basket, place the pork ribs.
- It should be cooked for twelve minutes. Cook for another 8 minutes on the other side. Cook for an additional 5 minutes, or until the glaze is glossy and sticky and the chicken is cooked through.

Air Fried Indian Lamb Curry Puffs

Preparation and Cooking Time

35 minutes

Servings

15 persons

Nutritional facts

218 calories, 18g fat, 2.4g fiber, 8g carbs, 33g protein

Ingredients

- 1 Biscuit Dough - thawed
- 1 Large Onion - thinly chopped
- Half Cup Peas-Carrots Mix - thawed
- 1 Tbsp. Curry Powder
- 1/4 Tsp Ginger Powder
- 1/8 Tsp Garlic Powder
- 1 Egg - for brushing the empanadas
- 1 Tsp Butter - for egg wash
- 3 Tbsp. Olive Oil
- 1 Cup Lamb Mince
- 2 Tbsp. Hot Sauce
- Salt - as per taste
- Pepper - as per taste

Instructions

- Whisk together the egg and the butter in a small bowl.
- Divide one biscuit dough ball into two equal pieces.
- Roll one of the parts into a disc and hold it in your hand.
- Place 2 tablespoons of lamb filling in the center of the circle.
- To completely seal the disc, fold and pinch the borders on top (to form a half-moon shape).
- Fill the other dough balls with the filling in the same way.
- Arrange all of the lamb curry puffs/lamb hand pies on a baking sheet.
- Brush them with the egg and butter mixture in an even layer.
- Preheat the oven to 350°F and bake the tray for 15-18 minutes, or until golden brown.
- Place the puffs on a serving tray after removing them from the oven.
- Then air fry for 10-11 minutes at 200°C.
- Serve with chutney of choice.

Air-Fried Chicken Shawarma

Preparation and Cooking Time

6 hours 35 minutes

Servings

4 persons

Nutritional facts

856 calories, 11g fat, 2g fiber, 22g carbs, 17g protein

Ingredients

- 2 garlic cloves minced
- ½ teaspoon ground allspice
- ¼ teaspoon turmeric
- 1 clove garlic minced
- ¼ teaspoon ground cumin
- ¼ teaspoon salt
- 2 teaspoons chopped fresh parsley
- 1 cup diced tomatoes
- 1 small English cucumber
- ¼ teaspoon ground cinnamon
- 1 teaspoon salt
- ½ teaspoon freshly ground black pepper
- 1½ pounds boneless chicken breast about 3 chicken breasts
- 4 pieces' naan bread or fresh pita bread
- ½ cup tahini sesame paste
- 1/3 cup warm water
- 2 tablespoons olive oil
- juice of 1 lemon
- 1 teaspoon ground cumin
- 1 teaspoon paprika
- juice from ½ lemon
- 2 tablespoons minced red onion
- salt and freshly ground black pepper
- juice from ½ lemon
- 1 teaspoon red wine vinegar
- 2 teaspoons olive oil
- 2 tablespoons chopped fresh parsley

Instructions

- Whisk together the olive oil, garlic, lemon juice, & spices. Chicken breasts should be cut in half lengthwise. Combine the chicken and the marinade in a zipper-sealable plastic bag. Massage the chicken in the bag to coat it in the marinade on both sides. Marinate the chicken for at least 6 hours and up to overnight in the refrigerator.
- Preheat the air fryer to 380 degrees Fahrenheit.
- Place the marinated chicken breasts in the air fryer basket and air fry for 8 to 10 minutes at 380°F, flipping halfway through the cooking time.
- To make the Tahini Sauce, combine all ingredients in a mixing bowl. Combine the tahini paste, water, lemon juice, garlic, cumin, and salt in a food processor or blender. Combine the ingredients in a food processor and process until smooth and creamy. Add more warm water if the consistency is too thick. Season with salt and pepper, then toss in the chopped parsley.
- Toss the Tomato-Cucumber Salad together. In a mixing bowl, toss together the tomatoes, cucumber, red onion, lemon juice, red wine vinegar, olive oil, & parsley. Season with salt & freshly ground black pepper and toss to mix. Refrigerate the sandwiches until ready to assemble.
- To put the shawarma together. Brush both sides of the naan with oil & heat for 2 minutes on each side in the air fryer at 400°F.
- Use a sharp knife to cut the chicken breast into thin slices. On the warm naan bread, spread a little tahini sauce. Place the cut chicken on the naan bread and top with a spoonful of the tomato-cucumber salad. Drizzle a bit of extra tahini sauce over the top. Wrap the bread around the fillings and roll or fold it up. To hold the shawarma together, wrap foil around half of it. Serve right away.

Air Fryer Seekh Kabab

Preparation and Cooking Time

23 minutes

Servings

8 persons

Nutritional facts

98 calories, 23g fat, 1.3g fiber, 6g carbs, 20g protein

Ingredients

- Chicken mince -1 cup
- salt -1tsp
- Cilantro chopped- 1 tbsp.
- garam masala powder – ½ tsp
- Coriander powder- 1tsp
- turmeric powder- ½ tsp
- Red Onion finely chopped -1 cup
- Egg -1 large
- Ginger Garlic paste - 2 tsp
- Kashmiri red chili powder -1 tsp
- GF starch -1tsp
- Oil to lightly brush the kababs- 2 tsp

Instructions

- In a large mixing bowl, combine the chicken mince. Add the ginger-garlic paste, chopped onions, and salt and pepper to taste.
- The dry spices, turmeric powder, red chili powder, coriander powder, garam masala, and salt are added.
- Now, lightly combine the corn starch.
- In a large mixing bowl, lightly whisk an egg and add it to the mixture.

- Add the cilantro, chopped.
- To make a smooth mixture, lightly combine all of the ingredients.
- Allow at least 12 hours for the mixture to rest in the refrigerator.
- Apply a little oil to your palms and roll the kababs.
  - Put the skewers in the center and lightly roll them again before setting them aside.
- Put the rolled kababs in the parchment paper-lined Air fryer baskets.
- Apply some oil to the brush.
- Cook the kababs for 5 minutes at 180°C/350°F.
- Serve with onions and mint yogurt.

Kofta Kebab in the Air Fryer

Preparation and Cooking Time

20 minutes

Servings

4 persons

Nutritional facts

124 calories, 12g fat, 1g fiber, 5g carbs, 14g protein

Ingredients

- 1-pound ground beef
- 1 teaspoon salt
- 1/2 teaspoon cumin
- 1 teaspoon oregano
- 1/4 cup white onion, grated
- 1/4 cup parsley, finely chopped
- 1 tablespoon mint, finely chopped
- 2 cloves garlic, minced
- 1/2 teaspoon garlic salt
- 1 egg

Instructions

- In a mixing bowl, place the ground beef.
- After that, add the onion and parsley. Stir in the mint, garlic, and salt to mix.
- Cumin, oregano, and garlic salt are added.
- To blend, stir everything together.
- Place the kebabs in the air fryer basket after shaping them with your hands.
- Cook for 20 mins with the air fryer on.
- Serve with tzatziki sauce on the side.

Herb Crusted Lamb Chops

Preparation and Cooking Time

20 minutes

Servings

4 persons

Nutritional facts

280 calories, 52g fat, 0.5g fiber, 5.2g carbs, 16g protein

Ingredients

- 1/4 cup (50 ml) finely chopped fresh parsley leaves
- 3/4 tsp (4 ml) each salt and pepper
- 4 cloves garlic, minced
- 1 tbsp. (15 ml) each finely chopped fresh rosemary and thyme leaves

- 2 tbsp. (30 ml) olive oil
- 1 tbsp. (15 ml) Dijon mustard
- 8 lamb loin chops, about 750 g

Instructions

- Combine the parsley, rosemary, and thyme in a mixing bowl. Combine the oil, mustard, salt, pepper, and garlic; distribute over the chops.
- Press "OK" after selecting the "Sausage/Pork/Lamb" program. Spray the cooking plates lightly with cooking spray. Place the chops on the grill and close the lid once the purple indicator light has stopped flashing.
- Cook until the color of the indicator light changes to the desired doneness level: yellow for rare, orange for medium, and red for well done. Move the chops to a platter and cover with foil to keep them warm. Allow for a 5-minute rest period before serving.

Crispy Breaded Air Fryer Pork Chops

Preparation and Cooking Time

18 minutes

Servings

4 persons

Nutritional facts

347calories, 16g fat, 1g fiber, 3g carbs, 22g protein

Ingredients

- 1-pound boneless pork chops, 1/2-inch thick
- 1 teaspoon onion powder, divided
- 2 large eggs
- splash of water
- 1/3 cup seasoned Italian breadcrumbs
- 1/2 teaspoon kosher salt
- 1/4 teaspoon black pepper
- 1/2 cup all-purpose flour
- 1 teaspoon garlic powder, divided
- 1/3 cup grated parmesan cheese, plus more for garnish
- fresh chopped parsley for garnish

Instructions

- Season both sides of the pork chops with salt & pepper and set aside.
- With three shallow dishes, set up your breading station:
- In the first bowl, combine the flour, 1/2 teaspoon garlic powder, and 1/2 teaspoon onion powder in a mixing bowl.
- In bowl 2, mix the eggs, a splash of water, 1/2 teaspoon garlic powder, and 1/2 teaspoon onion powder until fully combined.
- In a third bowl, combine the breadcrumbs and parmesan cheese.
- Place the pork chops in the flour mixture one by one and coat evenly. Shake off any excess flour and dip into the egg mixture, coating evenly. Allow any excess egg to drip off the pork chop before quickly coating it in the breadcrumb mixture and shaking off any excess.
- Carry on with the remaining pork chops in the same manner.
- Set your air fryer to 400°F for 5 minutes if it needs to be preheated.
- Spray the air fryer basket with cooking spray and arrange two pork chops or as many as you can fit without touching, in the basket. Using cooking spray, coat the tops of the pork chops.
- Air fry for 4 minutes, flip, spray with more cooking spray, and air fry for another 4 minutes, or till an internal temperature of 145°F is reached.

- If preferred, top with parsley and additional grated parmesan cheese.

Breaded Air Fryer Tender Pork Chops

Preparation and Cooking Time

20 minutes

Servings

4 persons

Nutritional facts

394 calories, 16g fat, 1g fiber, 3g carbs, 22g protein

Ingredients

- 4 boneless, center-cut pork chops, 1-inch thick
- 2 eggs
- 1 teaspoon Cajun seasoning
- 1 ½ cups cheese and garlic-flavored croutons
- cooking spray

Instructions

- Heat the air fryer to 390 degrees F (200 degrees C).
- Season both sides of the pork chops with Cajun seasoning on a platter.
- Pulse croutons until finely chopped; transfer to a shallow plate. In a second shallow bowl, lightly beat eggs. Allow the extra egg to drop off pork chops after dipping them in it. Place the chops on a platter and coat them in crouton breading. Coat the chops in cooking spray.
- Apply cooking spray to the air fryer basket and set the chops inside, making sure not to overcrowd the fryer. Determined by the size of the air fryer, you may need to do two batches.
- It should be cooked for five minutes. If there are any dry or powdery patches on the chops, flip them and spritz them again with cooking spray. Cook for another 5 minutes. Continue with the remaining chops.

Air Fryer Pork Roast

Preparation and Cooking Time

1 hour 45 minutes

Servings

6 persons

Nutritional facts

483 calories, 8g fat, 0.4g fiber, 3g carbs, 24g protein

Ingredients

- One pork loin joint
- Two teaspoon salt

Instructions

- The rind should be scored lengthwise. The rind can be difficult to cut through, so take your time and use a sharp knife. Make sure you're only cutting the rind and not the fat & meat underneath.
- Using a paper towel, pat the rind dry and liberally salt it. Make certain to salt the slices you've just made. The pig roast should then be let to rest in the refrigerator, skin side up, for around 24hrs. While it's resting, take a peek at it once or twice and wipe away any moisture that emerges. This will guarantee that the rind completely dries out.
- Preheat the air fryer to 400 degrees Fahrenheit (200 degrees Celsius).
- Place the pork roast skin side up in the air fryer and cook till the internal temperature reaches 145 F / 63 C.
- Take the cooked pork roast out of the air fryer and let aside for 15 minutes before carving and serving.

Air Fryer Pork Belly Bites

Preparation and Cooking Time

40 minutes

Servings

15 persons

Nutritional facts

80 calories, 16g fat, 0.3g fiber, 2g carbs, 14g protein

Ingredients

- 1 1/2 pounds' pork belly, patted dry
- 1 teaspoon garlic powder
- 3 tablespoons canola oil
- 1 tablespoon brown sugar
- 1 teaspoon salt
- 1 teaspoon pepper

Instructions

- Preheat the air fryer to 400 degrees Fahrenheit.
- Cut the pork belly into 1-inch chunks after patting it dry.
- Meanwhile, whisk together the oil, brown sugar, garlic powder, salt, & pepper in a large mixing bowl.
- Insert the pork belly pieces into the oil mixture, ensuring they're all covered.
- In the air fryer basket, arrange the pork belly pieces in a single layer.
- Air fry the pork belly cubes for 18-twenty minutes, shaking and rotating them several times during the process. Please keep in mind that air frying timings are dependent on the size of the pork belly slices and the size of the air fryer.
- Remove the air fryer and serve immediately.

Air Fryer Fried Pork Chops Southern Style

Preparation and Cooking Time

25 minutes

Servings

4 persons

Nutritional facts

173 calories, 19g fat, 0.4g fiber, 5g carbs, 15g protein

Ingredients

- 4 pork chops (bone-in or boneless)
- Seasoning Salt to taste
- pepper to taste
- 3 tbsp. buttermilk
- 1/4 cup all-purpose flour
- 1 Ziploc bag
- cooking oil spray

Instructions

- Dry the pork chops with a paper towel.
- Season the pork chops with salt and pepper to taste.
- Drizzle the pork chops with the buttermilk.
- Combine the pork chops and flour in a Ziploc bag. To fully coat, give it a good shake.
- Allow 30 minutes to marinate. This is an optional step, and this aids in the sticking of the flour to the pork chops.
- In the air fryer, place the pork chops. If necessary, cook in batches.
- Cooking oil should be sprayed on the pork chops.

- Preheat the oven to 380°F and cook the pork chops for fifteen minutes. After 10 minutes, flip the pork chops over to the other side.

Perfect Air Fryer Pork Chops

Preparation and Cooking Time

35 minutes

Servings

4 persons

Nutritional facts

217 calories, 16g fat, 1g fiber, 3g carbs, 22g protein

Ingredients

- 4 thick-cut pork chops
- 1 tsp paprika
- 1 tsp garlic powder
- 1 tsp salt
- 2 tsp sage
- 2 tsp thyme
- 2 tsp oregano
- 1 tsp rosemary
- 1/2 tsp black pepper

Instructions

- Mix the thyme, sage, oregano, paprika, rosemary, garlic powder, salt, & black pepper in a bowl.
- Preheat the Air Fryer to about 360 degrees Fahrenheit.
- While your Air Fryer is heating up, drizzle a little olive oil on the pork chops and afterward sprinkle your herb mixture all over them.
- Make sure the chops don't overlap in the Air Fryer basket.
- Cook for 14-16 minutes at 360 degrees F, flipping halfway through. When pork chops achieve an internal temperature of 145 degrees Fahrenheit, they are done.
- Take the pork chops out of the Air Fryer & cover them loosely with foil. Allow for a 5-minute resting period.

Air Fryer Roast Pork

Preparation and Cooking Time

55 minutes

Servings

6 persons

Nutritional facts

380 calories, 33g fat, 1.7g fiber, 7g carbs, 30g protein

Ingredients

- Two lb. pork roast (pork loin or any other small pork roast)
- One tbsp. olive oil
- 1 tsp kosher salt

Instructions

- Preheat the air fryer oven to 360 degrees Fahrenheit (180 degrees Celsius).
- If the pork roast has a rind, take it off with a sharp knife and check for deep scores all the way through.
- Drizzle the oil all over the meat and massage it in. Apply salt to the skin & rub it in.
- In an air fryer, cook pork roast for 50 minutes.
- When the cooking time is up, check to see if the pork has reached a temperature of 145°F (63°C) in the thickest portion.
- Remove from the air fryer, cover with foil, and set aside 10 minutes before serving.

- If the crackling isn't quite crisp enough at this stage, remove it before resting the pork and return it to the air fryer for another 5-10 minutes.

Air Fried Pork Chops with Brussels Sprouts

Preparation and Cooking Time

25 minutes

Servings

1 person

Nutritional facts

337 calories, 19g fat, 0.4g fiber, 5g carbs, 15g protein

Ingredients

- 8 ounces' bone-in center-cut pork chop
- 1 teaspoon pure maple syrup
- 1 teaspoon Dijon mustard
- Cooking spray
- 1/8 teaspoon kosher salt
- 1/2 teaspoon black pepper, divided
- 1 teaspoon olive oil
- 6 ounces Brussels sprouts, quartered

Instructions

- Spray the pork chop lightly with cooking spray and season with salt and .25 teaspoons pepper. In a medium mixing bowl, whisk the oil, syrup, mustard, and the remaining 1/4 teaspoon pepper; add the Brussels sprouts and toss to coat.
- Place the coated Brussels sprouts on one side of the air fryer basket and the pork chop on the other. Preheat the air fryer to 400°F and cook the pork until golden brown and cooked to your liking, approximately 10 minutes for medium and thirteen minutes for well-done.

Air Fryer Pork Loin

Preparation and Cooking Time

40 minutes

Servings

6 persons

Nutritional facts

405 calories, 12g fat, 3g fiber, 29g carbs, 29g protein

Ingredients

- 3 lbs. pork loin roast
- Half tsp. kosher salt
- Half tsp. poultry seasoning
- Oil spray

Instructions

- Preheat the air fryer to 370 degrees Fahrenheit.
- Remove any excess fat from the pork loin outside.
- Season the pork with salt & poultry seasoning all over.
- Using an oil spray, spritz the area.
- Put the pork roast in the air fryer's basket. Cook for 12-15 min per pound, just until the roast's internal temperature reaches 145-160°F. This should take approximately 40 minutes to cook a 3-pound roast.
- Allow 5 minutes for the pork loin to rest on a cutting board before slicing.

Boneless Pork Chop in the Air Fryer

Preparation and Cooking Time

20 minutes

Servings

2 persons

Nutritional facts

310 calories, 34g fat, 3g fiber, 24g carbs, 19g protein

Ingredients

- 8 oz. boneless pork chops (1.25" thick)
- Two teaspoons Kosher salt and freshly ground black pepper
- pork rub (optional)

Instructions

- Preheat the air fryer to 400°F for 3 to 4 minutes. Season both sides of the pork chops with salt and pepper or a spice rub.
- Cook pork chops for 6 minutes in a hot air fryer.
- Cook flipping halfway through until an instant-read thermometer registers 135°F-145°F, about 5-8 minutes. If it's not heated enough, cook for another 2-3 minutes, checking every 2-3 minutes until it's done.
- Cover chops with aluminum foil and set aside for 5 minutes to absorb juices before slicing and serving.

Garlic Herb Pork Chops Recipe

Preparation and Cooking Time

45 minutes

Servings

6 persons

Nutritional facts

380 calories, 19g fat, 0.4g fiber, 5g carbs, 15g protein

Ingredients

- 2 Boneless Pork Chops
- One Egg
- 1 Cup Plain Bread Crumbs
- Cooking Spray
- 1 tbsp. Garlic Herb Seasoning

Instructions

- Using a beaten egg, coat the pork chop.
- Roll the pork chop in the bread crumbs until it is fully covered.
- Dip in the egg & bread crumbs again.
- Spray pork chops with frying spray and place on air fryer rack.
- Then air fry for 25 minutes at 375°F.
- Flip and continue to air fry for another 5 minutes at 375°F.
- Serve and take pleasure in it.

Air Fryer Pork Chops with Apples

Preparation and Cooking Time

25 minutes

Servings

2 persons

Nutritional facts

584 calories, 16g fat, 1g fiber, 3g carbs, 22g protein

Ingredients

- 1/2 Small Red Cabbage - sliced thick
- 1/2 teaspoon Cumin
- 1/2 teaspoon Paprika
- 1 Apple - sliced thick
- 1 Sweet Onion - sliced thick
- 2 Tablespoons Oil
- Salt/Pepper - to taste
- 2 Boneless Pork Chops (1" thick)

Instructions

- Apply nonstick spray to the air fryer basket.
- Apples, cabbage, and onions should be tossed in one tablespoon oil, 1/4 teaspoon cumin, 1/4 teaspoon paprika, salt, and pepper.
- Coat the pork chops in oil and season with the remaining ingredients, including salt and pepper. Place the chops in the basket of an air fryer.
- Then air fry for 15 minutes at 400°F. Check the temperature, stir in the apples and cabbage, and air fry for another 5 minutes or until desired doneness is reached. Cook until the internal temperature reaches 145oF-160oF.

Juicy Pork Chops

Preparation and Cooking Time

28 minutes

Servings

4 persons

Nutritional facts

543 calories, 5g fat, 1g fiber, 4g carbs, 16g protein

Ingredients

- 4 8 oz. pork loin chops, bone-in
- 1 tsp Salt
- 1/2 tsp black pepper
- 2 eggs
- 2.3 cup grated Parmesan
- 2/3 cup Panko bread crumbs
- 1 1/2 tsp Paprika
- 1 1/2 tsp onion powder
- 1 clove garlic
- 1 tsp olive oil spray

Instructions

- To begin, grate 2/3 cup parmesan cheese into a large mixing bowl. Then insert two-third cup panko-style bread crumbs, 1 1/2 teaspoons paprika, 1 1/2 teaspoons onion powder, 1 teaspoon salt, and 1/2 teaspoon black pepper.
- Set it aside after thoroughly mixing it.
- Add 2 big eggs and 1 garlic clove in a separate bowl, grated. Beat the eggs for about a minute with a whisk.
- After patting the pork dry, coat it in the egg coating. Make sure the cut is completely covered.
- Allow the excess egg to drip off before immediately incorporating it into the Panko-Parmesan mixture. Use the breading to coat the top, bottom, & sides of each pork chop.
- Preheat your air fryer basket to 400 degrees Fahrenheit now. Spread nonstick spray on the bottom of the air fryer basket and place 2 pork chops in at a time once it's preheated. Cook for around 10 minutes after spraying the tops of the pork chops.
- Cook for another 8 to 10 minutes after flipping the pork chops. Depending on the thickness of the pork chops, cooking time may vary. To ensure that the meat is correctly cooked, use a meat thermometer to check the internal temperature. Now serve it with your preferred gravy.

Air Fryer Pork Steaks

Preparation and Cooking Time

8 minutes

Servings

4 persons

Nutritional facts

680 calories, 37g fat, 1.6g fiber, 30g carbs, 36g protein

Ingredients

- 2 pork butt steaks
- 1 tablespoon Stubb's BBQ Rub
- additional BBQ sauce for coating after cooking (optional)
- 1/2 cup BBQ sauce of choice

Instructions

- Preheat the air fryer to 400 degrees Fahrenheit.
- After properly coating the pork steaks with BBQ dry rub, baste both sides with BBQ sauce.
- Cook the pork steaks in one layer in the air fryer for eight to nine minutes, or until the internal temperature reaches 145 degrees.
- Take them out of the air fryer and set them aside for at least 3 minutes before cutting. If desired, baste with more BBQ sauce before serving.

Air Fryer Pork Chops & Broccoli

Preparation and Cooking Time

15 minutes

Servings

2 persons

Nutritional facts

421 calories, 39g fat, 2.3g fiber, 25g carbs, 57g protein

Ingredients

- 2 5-ounce bone-in pork chops
- 1 teaspoon salt, divided
- 2 cups broccoli florets
- 1 tablespoon olive oil, divided
- 1/2 teaspoon paprika
- 1/2 teaspoon onion powder
- 1/2 teaspoon garlic powder
- 2 cloves garlic, minced

Instructions

- Preheat the air fryer to 350 degrees Fahrenheit, as directed by the manufacturer. Using a nonstick spray, coat the basket.
- Using 1/2 tablespoon of oil, brush the meat with it.
- On both sides, season the pork chops with paprika, onion powder, garlic powder, & 1/2 teaspoon salt.
- Cook the pork chops for 5 minutes in the air fryer basket.
- Toss the broccoli, garlic, remaining 1/2 teaspoon salt, and remaining oil in a bowl to coat while the pork chops are frying.
- Flip the pork chops carefully in the air fryer.
- Transfer to the air fryer with the broccoli in the basket.
- Cook for another 5 minutes, stirring halfway through.
- Remove the meal from the air fryer with care and serve.

Air Fryer Bacon Wrapped Pork Tenderloin

Preparation and Cooking Time

30 minutes

Servings

6 persons

Nutritional facts

153 calories, 23g fat, 3.2g fiber, 30g carbs, 31g protein

Ingredients

- 1/2 teaspoon kosher salt
- 1 pork tenderloin, about 1 1/2 lbs.
- 6 center-cut strips of bacon
- 1/4 teaspoon ground black pepper
- cooking string

Instructions

- Pork should be seasoned with pepper and salt. Place the bacon on a chopping board and cut it to fit the tenderloin.
- Cut 2 bacon strips in half (they don't require the entire strip because the ends are thinner). Place two halves next to each other, then four full strips, and finally two halves.
- Place the tenderloin on top of the bacon with care. Starting with a long side, tightly roll up the pork jelly-roll. Tie the roast with kitchen string at 2-inch intervals, each around 12-inches long.
- To fit in the air fryer, carefully cut the tenderloin in half.
- Fry the tenderloin for 20 minutes at 400 degrees F, flipping halfway, till an instant-read thermometer inserted in the center reads 145-150 degrees F. Allow 5 minutes for the pork to rest before slicing. Cut into 12 pieces.

Air Fryer Pork Tenderloin

Preparation and Cooking Time

35 minutes

Servings

2 persons

Nutritional facts

281 calories, 13g fat, 1.1g fiber, 12g carbs, 41g protein

Ingredients

- 1 pork tenderloin (about one pound)
- 3/4 tsp coarse sea salt
- 2 tbsp. Dijon mustard
- 1 tbsp. brown sugar
- 1/2 tsp coarse ground black pepper

Instructions

- Combine Dijon mustard, brown sugar, sea salt, & black pepper. Brush the marinade over the top of the pork tenderloin using a basting brush - you want a thick, even layer of marinade.
- Preheat the air fryer to 350 degrees Fahrenheit. Put the pork tenderloin in the air fryer basket and coat it with spray oil. Preheat the oven to 350°F and bake the pork for 22-25 minutes. Use an electronic thermometer to check the interior temperature; when it reaches 145F-150F, the pork is done.
- Remove the pork from the air fryer and set aside to rest for 5-10 minutes on a cutting board before slicing into rounds.

Air Fryer Pork Chops and Crispy Garlic Broccoli

Preparation and Cooking Time

20 minutes

Servings

4 persons

Nutritional facts

352 calories, 39g fat, 2.3g fiber, 25g carbs, 57g protein

Ingredients

- 4 pork chops
- 1 teaspoon garlic powder
- 1 teaspoon salt
- 3 tablespoons of avocado oil
- 1 teaspoon of paprika
- 1 teaspoon of onion powder
- 1/2 teaspoon of black pepper
- 1 medium broccoli head
- 2 garlic cloves minced

Instructions

- Mix paprika, black pepper, onion powder, garlic powder, and salt in a small bowl.
- Season the pork chops on both sides with the spice mix after drizzling them with oil.
- Preheat the Air Fryer to 350 degrees Fahrenheit/180 degrees Celsius, then place the pork chops in the basket and cook for 10 minutes. Halfway through, flip it over. Increase the cooking time to 16 minutes if the pork chops are thicker. The internal temperature of perfectly cooked pork chops should be 145 degrees Fahrenheit.
- In the meantime, chop the broccoli into small florets & place in a mixing dish. Toss in the remaining seasoning mix, garlic, and oil/butter to coat.
- Cook for 7 minutes at 400F with the broccoli in the air fryer basket. Halfway through you need to flip.
- Top the pork chops with a dab of flavorful butter before serving.

Air Fryer Pork Bites with Mushrooms

Preparation and Cooking Time

30 minutes

Servings

4 persons

Nutritional facts

241 calories, 24g fat, 1.2g fiber, 8g carbs, 29g protein

Ingredients

- 1 lb. (454 g) pork chops or pork belly, rinsed & patted dry
- 1/2 teaspoon (2.5 ml) garlic powder
- salt, to taste
- 8 oz. (227 g) mushrooms (cleaned, washed, and halved)
- 2 Tablespoons (30 ml) butter, melted (or olive oil)
- 1 teaspoon (5 ml) Worcestershire sauce or soy sauce
- black pepper, to taste

Instructions

- Preheat the Air Fryer for 4 minutes at 400°F. This will provide a lovely sear on pork.
- Combine the pork chops and mushrooms in a bowl and cut them into 3/4" pieces. Season the pork and mushrooms with Worcestershire sauce, garlic powder, salt, and pepper after coating them in melted butter or oil. In the air fryer basket, arrange the pork & mushrooms in a uniform layer.
- Air fry for 10-18 minutes at 400°F, shaking and flipping the pork belly twice during the cooking phase.
- Check the pork chop bites to verify if they are cooked through. Cook for an additional 2-5 minutes if you want it more done.
- If desired, season with more salt and pepper. Serve immediately while still heated. The pork bites will become hard if they become cold.

Pecan Crusted Pork Chops

Preparation and Cooking Time

22 minutes

Servings

2 persons

Nutritional facts

360 calories, 19g fat, 0.4g fiber, 5g carbs, 15g protein

Ingredients

- 1 cup of pecan pieces
- 1/4 teaspoon of sea salt, plus more to taste
- 1 large egg
- 1 teaspoon of Dijon mustard, plus more for serving
- 1/3 cup of arrowroot
- 2 teaspoons of Italian seasoning
- 1 teaspoon of onion powder
- 1 teaspoon of garlic powder
- 1 tablespoon of water
- 2 garlic cloves, crushed
- 6 medium-sized boneless pork chops

Instructions

- Preheat the oven to 400 degrees Fahrenheit.
- In a medium mixing bowl, combine arrowroot starch, pecans, Italian seasoning, garlic powder, onion powder, and sea salt.
- Whisk together the Dijon mustard, egg, water, & garlic in a separate bowl.
- To prepare the pork chops, coat them in the egg mixture first, then transfer them to the bowl with the pecan mixture to coat all sides. Continue with the remaining pork chops. In the air fryer basket, place three pork chops.
- Cook for 6 minutes on one side, then flip and cook for another 6 minutes. Place on a platter and set aside.
- Continue with the remaining pork chops.
- Serve with additional Dijon mustard on the side (if using).

Air Fryer Buffalo Pork Chops {KETO + WHOLE30}

Preparation and Cooking Time

17 minutes

Servings

4 persons

Nutritional facts

240 calories, 19g fat, 0.4g fiber, 5g carbs, 15g protein

Ingredients

- 4 boneless pork chops, 1 1/2 inch thick
- 1 tablespoon garlic powder
- 1/2 tablespoon onion powder

- 2 tablespoons olive oil
- 1 tablespoon kosher salt
- 1 teaspoon cayenne pepper
- 1 teaspoon black pepper
- 2 tablespoons paprika
- 2 tablespoons nutritional yeast

Instructions

- Preheat the air fryer for 5 minutes at 400 degrees.
- Use a meat tenderizer or a fork to poke holes in both sides of each pork chop.
- Combine all of the buffalo seasoning ingredients in a small bowl.
- Coat the pork chops in olive oil and liberally massage in the mixture.
- Cook pork chops in an air fryer for 12 minutes at 400 degrees F, flipping after 6 minutes. The internal temperature ought to be between 155 and 160 degrees Fahrenheit.

Air Fryer BBQ Pork Tenderloin

Preparation and Cooking Time

20 minutes

Servings

2 persons

Nutritional facts

290 calories, 13g fat, 1.1g fiber, 12g carbs, 41g protein

Ingredients

- 285 grams Pork Tenderloin
- Quarter cup BBQ Sauce
- One tsp Olive Oil

Instructions

- After patting the pork tenderloin dry, dice it.
- Toss the pork tenderloin in a bowl with olive oil & barbecue sauce.
- Place the pork tenderloin in the air fryer basket, neither overlapping nor overcrowding it.
- Cook for fifteen minutes at 375°F in an air fryer (190C.

Air Fryer Pork Chops without Breading

Preparation and Cooking Time

20 minutes

Servings

2 persons

Nutritional facts

370 calories, 12g fat, 3g fiber, 9g carbs, 29g protein

Ingredients

- 2 Bone-in center cut pork chops
- salt and pepper to taste
- 1/2 tsp dried thyme
- olive oil or olive oil spray

Instructions

- Sprinkle the pork chops with pepper, salt, & thyme before serving.
- To coat generously, rub with olive oil or spray generously with olive oil spray.
- Allow 5 minutes for the mixture to set.
- Preheat the Ninja Foodi XL Air Fryer to 400°F and air fry the chicken.

- Cook pork chops to an internal temperature of 165°F on an air frying rack, flipping once throughout cooking for 12 minutes.

Pork Chops with Garlic Sage Rub

Preparation and Cooking Time

37 minutes

Servings

4 persons

Nutritional facts

288 calories, 29g fat, 2.1g fiber, 23g carbs, 28g protein

Ingredients

- 2 tablespoons pure olive oil
- 2 teaspoons kosher salt
- ½ teaspoon freshly ground black pepper
- 1 tablespoon dried sage
- 1 tablespoon apple cider vinegar
- 2 teaspoons minced garlic
- 4 bone-in ribeye pork chops (each about 1-inch thick)

Instructions

- Combine the oil, sage, vinegar, garlic, salt, & pepper. Apply the herb mixture to both sides of the pork chops. Allow 15 minutes for cooling.
- Preheat the air fryer to 400 degrees Fahrenheit.
- Arrange the pork chops in the air fryer basket to not overlap. These should be cooked for six minutes. Turn the pork chop using tongs. Cook for another 6 minutes, or till an instant-read thermometer inserted horizontally in the center of the chop reads 140 degrees Fahrenheit. Remove the chops from the air fryer and set them aside for 5 minutes. The internal temperature should increase by 5 degrees to 145 degrees Fahrenheit.

Air Fryer Ginger Pork Skewers

Preparation and Cooking Time

50 minutes

Servings

3 persons

Nutritional facts

213 calories, 5g fat, 0.6g fiber, 8g carbs, 12g protein

Ingredients

- 1 lb. pork shoulder
- 1 1/2 tablespoons honey (or more to taste)
- 1 1/2 tablespoons rice vinegar
- 1 1/2 teaspoons toasted sesame oil
- 1 oz. of ginger crushed
- 1/2 tablespoon of crushed garlic
- 4 1/2 tablespoons of soy sauce
- 8 skewers
- cucumber sticks (to serve)

Instructions

- Pork should be thinly sliced, about 1/4-inch thick. Pound it briefly with a pestle or meat mallet to tenderize the pork. Place in a mixing bowl.
- Combine the garlic, ginger, soy sauce, rice vinegar, honey, and sesame oil in a small bowl. Taste and adapt to your personal preferences. Two-thirds of marinade should be poured over the pork, and the remaining should be reserved to baste the pork during cooking.

- Mix the pork with marinade and set it aside to marinate for about 25-30 minutes at room temperature. Thread onto skewers after that.
- Preheat the air fryer to 350°F (180°C) according to the manufacturer's instructions. Cook for 5-6 minutes after placing the skewers in the basket. Then, open the air fryer & baste both sides of the pork skewers with the remaining marinade, and cook for another 2-3 minutes until the meat is fully cooked.
- Alternatively, you can roast the skewers on the grill (or in a grill pan) until fully done for several minutes, before grilling, lightly oil the grates and baste the pork with the saved marinade.
- Serve with cucumber sticks (and rice, if desired) on the side.

Crispy Air Fryer Pork Chops

Preparation and Cooking Time

21 minutes

Servings

4 persons

Nutritional facts

380 calories, 5g fat, 1g fiber, 4g carbs, 16g protein

Ingredients

- 4 thick-cut pork chops
- 1/4 cup finely grated Parmesan cheese
- 3/4 teaspoon garlic powder
- Salt
- Pepper
- 1/2 cup flour
- 1 egg
- 3/4 cup panko bread crumbs
- 1/2 teaspoon dried basil
- Quarter teaspoon oregano

Instructions

- Preheat the air fryer to 375 degrees Fahrenheit, as directed by the manufacturer.
- Remove any excess fat from the pork chops. Season generously with Kosher salt and black pepper on both sides.
- In a separate bowl, whisk together the flour, the egg, and the Panko, Parmesan cheese, garlic powder, basil, & oregano. Lightly whisk the eggs in a small mixing bowl and combine the Panko mixture.
- Both sides of the pork chops should be floured first, then dipped in the egg, and finally in the panko mixture. Spray them lightly with cooking spray.
- Place as many as will fit in the air fryer without touching. Cook for 7 minutes before flipping. Cook for another 6 minutes, or till an instant-read thermometer reads 140-145 degrees Fahrenheit.
- Allow 3 minutes for the meat to rest before serving.

Air Fryer Pork Chops with Parmesan

Preparation and Cooking Time

20 minutes

Servings

6 persons

Nutritional facts

328 calories, 12g fat, 0.2g fiber, 2g carbs, 30g protein

Ingredients

- 6 Boneless Pork Chops about 1/2 inch thick
- Salt, Pepper, and Garlic Powder to taste

- 1 Egg
- 1 Cup Pork Rind Crumbs about 2 ounces
- 3/4 cup Parmesan Cheese grated
- 2 Tablespoons Heavy Whipping Cream

Instructions

- If necessary, preheat the air fryer to 350 degrees F.
- Salt, pepper, and garlic powder to season on both sides of each pork chop.
- Whisk the heavy whipping cream & egg in a shallow bowl until smooth.
- Mix the pork rind crumbs & grated parmesan in a separate bowl and stir well to combine.
- Each pork chop should be dipped in the egg mixture and then coated with the parmesan mixture.
- Cook the pork chops in the air fryer for 15-twenty minutes on a rack, or until they reach an internal temperature of 145 degrees F. Halfway through cooking, flip the pork chops.

Air Fryer Pork Milanese with Arugula Salad

Preparation and Cooking Time

25 minutes

Servings

2 persons

Nutritional facts

326 calories, 7g fat, 2.2g fiber, 25g carbs, 29g protein

Ingredients

- 2 boneless pork chops, about 3/4 inch thick
- 2 eggs
- 1/8 teaspoon ground black pepper
- 1/8 teaspoon kosher salt
- 1/3 cup breadcrumbs
- 1/3 cup grated Parmesan cheese
- 1/8 teaspoon ground black pepper
- Cooking Spray
- 1/2 cup all-purpose flour
- 1/4 teaspoon ground black pepper
- 1/4 teaspoon onion powder
- 1/4 teaspoon garlic powder
- 1/8 teaspoon kosher salt
- 1 1/2 tablespoon lemon juice
- Salt and Pepper
- 2 cups arugula
- 1/2 cup grape tomatoes, halved
- 1/4 cup shaved Parmesan cheese
- 1 1/2 tablespoons olive oil

Instructions

- Prepare the stations with three shallow bowls or three plates. Combine the flour, garlic powder, onion powder, salt, & pepper in one bowl. Then beat the eggs with pepper and salt in the second. Combine the breadcrumbs, grated parmesan, salt, & pepper in the third bowl.
- After patting the pork chops dry, bread them. To begin, cover the pork chops in flour & shake off any excess. Then dip it in the egg wash to coat it evenly. Finally, dredge the chicken in the breadcrumbs, making sure to coat all sides.
- Coat the breaded pork chops in cooking spray and place them in the air fryer basket. Spray the tops of the pork chops lightly with cooking spray and air fry for 10-13 minutes, or till they

reach 145-150 degrees F. Allow 3 minutes for the pork chops to rest before serving. It's fine if the pork is light pink in the center.

- Stir together the lemon juice, olive oil, and a pinch of salt and pepper in the bowl where you'll mix the salad.
- Toss the arugula, half tomatoes, & shaved parmesan with the dressing until well combined.

Air Fryer Sweet and Sour Pork

Preparation and Cooking Time

23 minutes

Servings

4 persons

Nutritional facts

333 calories, 12g fat, 3.2g fiber, 22g carbs, 36g protein

Ingredients

- 1/3 cup all-purpose flour
- 2 tablespoons brown sugar
- ¼ cup orange juice
- 1 tablespoon soy sauce
- 1 clove garlic minced
- 1 cup cubed pineapple
- 1 egg
- 2 tablespoons milk
- ¾ pound boneless pork cut into 1-inch cubes
- vegetable or canola oil
- 1½ cups large chunks of red and green peppers
- ½ cup ketchup
- 1/3 cup cornstarch
- 2 teaspoons Chinese 5-spice powder
- 1 teaspoon salt
- freshly ground black pepper
- 2 tablespoons rice wine vinegar or apple cider vinegar
- chopped scallions

Instructions

- With two bowls, set up a dredging station. Mix the flour, cornstarch, Chinese 5-spice powder, salt, and pepper in a large mixing bowl. In a separate bowl, whisk together the egg and milk. Dredge the pork cubes in flour first, then in the egg wash, and then back into the flour to cover all sides. Vegetable or canola oil should be sprayed on the breaded pork cubes.
- Preheat the air fryer to 400 degrees Fahrenheit.
- Toss the pepper chunks with a little oil & air-fry for 5 minutes at 4000F, shaking the basket halfway through.
- Begin making the sauce while peppers are cooking. In a medium saucepan, mix the ketchup, rice wine vinegar, brown sugar, orange juice, soy sauce, & garlic and bring to a boil on the stovetop. Reduce the heat to low and continue to cook for 5 minutes. Add the peppers, along with the pineapple pieces, to the pot once they've completed air-frying. Cook for another 2 minutes in the sauce with the peppers and pineapple. Remove and keep warm.
- Place the dredging pork cubes in the air fryer basket and air fry for 6 minutes at 400°F, shaking the basket to turn the cubes over for the last minute of cooking.
- When ready to serve, stir the cooked pork with the pineapples, peppers, and sauce. Garnish with chopped scallions and serve over white rice.

Cajun Air Fryer Pork Chops

Preparation and Cooking Time

15 minutes

Servings

4 persons

Nutritional facts

391 calories, 12g fat, 0.2g fiber, 2g carbs, 30g protein

Ingredients

- 4 thick-cut pork chops
- One tbsp. Cajun/Creole seasoning
- Two Tbsp. olive oil

Instructions

- Olive oil should be brushed on both sides of each pork chop.
- Then, season both sides of each pork chop using the Cajun seasoning.
- Place the ingredients in the air fryer basket. You may need to cook in two batches depending on the size of the basket and pork chops.
- Then air fry for 10 minutes at 375°F, flipping halfway during cooking. The internal temperature should be at least 145 degrees Fahrenheit.
- Remove and serve right away.

Crispy Air Fryer Breaded Pork Chops

Preparation and Cooking Time

22 minutes

Servings

4 persons

Nutritional facts

301 calories, 19g fat, 0.4g fiber, 15g carbs, 18g protein

Ingredients

- 4 pork chops, boneless, 5 ounces each
- 1 cup Italian flavored bread crumbs
- salt and pepper, to taste
- 1 egg
- olive oil spray

Instructions

- Preheat the air fryer to 400 degrees Fahrenheit. Using olive oil spray, coat the air fryer basket. Make the cutlets ahead of time.
- In a mixing bowl, whisk the egg and season with salt and pepper to taste.
- Add Italian-flavored bread crumbs to a separate bowl.
- After dipping the chops in the egg wash with seasoned bread crumbs after dipping the chops.
- Put the seasoned pork chop in the air fryer basket that has been prepared. Using an olive oil spray, spritz the area. Continue with the remaining parts.
- Cook the pork chops for 6 minutes before flipping them. Cook for another 6 minutes after spraying with olive oil spray. Pork should be cooked to a temperature of 145°F on the inside.
- Serve with a wide assortment of side dishes.

Air Fryer Breaded Pork Chops

Preparation and Cooking Time

20 minutes

Servings

4 persons

Nutritional facts

351 calories, 19g fat, 1g fiber, 18g carbs, 25g protein

Ingredients

- 4 (4) Bone-in center-cut pork chops, about 24 oz. (1/2" thick)
- 4 teaspoons paprika
- 2 teaspoons dried parsley
- 1/2 teaspoon garlic powder
- non-fat cooking spray, like Pam cooking spray
- 1 egg, beaten
- 1/4 cup water
- 1 cup Panko breadcrumbs
- 1/2 cup All-purpose flour, optional
- 1/2 teaspoon salt
- 1/2 teaspoon black pepper
- 1/4 – 1/2 teaspoon cayenne pepper, more or less to taste
- 1/4 teaspoon dry mustard

Instructions

- Chops should be completely fat-free. Rinse with water to get rid of any bone fragments.
- Whisk together the egg and water in a shallow dish or baking pan. Combine Panko bread crumbs & seasonings in a shallow bowl or baking pan.
- If using the optional flour dredging, place the flour in a third pan.
- If you're going to use the optional flour step, lightly coat the chop with flour first. Remove any excess flour by shaking it off. This step aids in the adhesion of the egg wash on the pork chop. Skip to the following step if you aren't using flour.
- Turn the chops in the egg wash mixture to moisten all sides. Next, cover both sides of the chops with the crumb mixture.
- In an Air Fryer pan, place the chops. Using nonstick cooking spray, lightly coat the pan. If necessary, add a wire rack to make a second tier of pork chops. Close the drawer and place it in the fryer.
- Preheat the oven to 380 degrees Fahrenheit and set the timer for 12 minutes. Halfway through the cooking time, turn the chops and lightly spray with cooking spray. Continue to cook after closing the drawer. When the internal temperature hits 145 degrees F and the center is no longer pink; the chops are done.
- Allow 3 minutes for the chops to rest before serving.

Air Fryer Boneless Pork Chops

Preparation and Cooking Time

15 minutes

Servings

4 persons

Nutritional facts

192 calories, 34g fat, 3g fiber, 24g carbs, 19g protein

Ingredients

- 1 lb. boneless pork chops
- 1/4 tsp garlic powder
- 1/4 tsp paprika optional
- 3/4 tsp salt
- 1/8 tsp pepper
- 1/2 tbsp. olive oil

Instructions

- Place pork chops in a bowl, drizzle with olive oil, and season with salt, pepper, garlic powder, and paprika on both sides. Rub the pork chops with your hands to evenly season them.
- Place seasoned pork chops in a single layer in the air fryer basket. Preheat the oven to 400°F and cook the pork chops for 12 minutes, flipping halfway through.

Italian Pork Chops for Two

Preparation and Cooking Time

35 minutes

Servings

2 persons

Nutritional facts

330 calories, 16g fat, 0.8g fiber, 3g carbs, 52g protein

Ingredients

- 2 tablespoons all-purpose flour
- 1/4 cup Progresso™ Panko Italian style crispy bread crumbs
- 3 tablespoons grated Parmesan cheese
- 1 egg
- 1/4 teaspoon salt
- 2 boneless pork loin chops, 3/4-inch-thick (4 to 5 oz. each)

Instructions

- The cooking parchment paper should be cut into an 8-inch round. Place in the air fryer basket's bottom.
- Place flour in a small bowl. In a separate shallow bowl, whisk together the egg and salt. Combine bread crumbs and Parmesan cheese in a third shallow dish. Coat the pork in flour, then dip it in the egg mixture and coat it in the bread crumb mixture, pressing it down to adhere.
- In an air fryer basket, put pork chops on parchment paper. Preheat oven to 325°F and bake for 10 minutes. Cook for another 8 to 12 minutes, or until the pork chops are no longer pink in the center (at least 145°F). Serve right away.

Air Fryer Juicy Pork Chops

Preparation and Cooking Time

20 minutes

Servings

3 persons

Nutritional facts

290 calories, 5g fat, 1g fiber, 4g carbs, 16g protein

Ingredients

- 3 (6 ounce-170g) pork chops, rinsed & patted dry
- Fresh black pepper, to taste
- garlic powder, to taste
- 2 teaspoons grape seed, avocado, or olive oil
- Kosher salt, to taste
- smoked paprika, to taste

Instructions

- Using grape seed oil, coat the pork chops. Salt, pepper, garlic powder, & smoked paprika are used to season the pork chops.
- In the Air Fryer basket, place the seasoned pork chops. Air fry the pork chops for 10-14 minutes at 380°F (194°C), flipping halfway through.
- Check for doneness & cook a little longer if necessary.
- Serve with your preferred side dishes while still warm.

Roast pork loin with crackling

Preparation and Cooking Time

45 minutes

Servings

2 persons

Nutritional facts

310 calories, 24g fat, 1.5g fiber, 7g carbs, 37g protein

Ingredients

- 1 kg pork loin
- 1 garlic clove (peeled and roughly chopped)
- 2 tsp salt flakes
- 1 tsp ground fennel seeds
- 2 tsp white vinegar
- 1 tbsp. olive oil (plus more for rind)
- 1 tbsp. sage, thyme, or rosemary (finely chopped)
- 1/2 tsp ground black pepper

Instructions

- Using a paper towel, pat the meat dry. Score the skin in long parallel cuts approximately 5mm apart with a small sharp knife, careful not to cut into the meat. Vinegar should be applied to the skin. Refrigerate uncovered for 60 minutes or overnight if time allows.
- Mix the oil, herbs, garlic, 1 tsp salt, fennel, and
- pepper in a mixing bowl. Rub the meat all over, but not the skin. Cut a large enough piece of foil to wrap the pork in. Place the pork skin side up in the center. Apply oil to the skin & rub in the leftover salt. Wrap the foil around the meat but leave the skin exposed.
- Place the pork on the air-fryer tray in the Crisp 'N Bake Toaster Oven's middle tier. The drip tray should be placed on the bottom shelf. Air-fry the crackling for 30 minutes, or until golden and crisp all over. For consistent browning, rotate the air-fryer tray during cooking.
- Set the Crisp 'N Bake Toaster Oven's roast/bake function to 190°C/375°F and the temperature to 190°C/375°F. Roast for sixty minutes or when the pork is thoroughly done. Insert a meat thermometer into the thickest portion of the meat to check for doneness. The temperature should be at least 63°C/145°F. Otherwise, use a skewer to penetrate the meat. The pork is likely done if the juices run clear.
- Rest the pork roast for 15 minutes on a cutting board. Remove the crackling & cut into strips to serve. Carve the meat into slices across the grain.

Air Fryer Pork Chops Recipe with Rub

Preparation and Cooking Time

17 minutes

Servings

4 persons

Nutritional facts

445 calories, 9g fat, 1.5g fiber, 8g carbs, 41g protein

Ingredients

- 2-4 boneless pork chops (1 1/2 lb. for 4 chops)
- Two tablespoons plus pork rub
- 1 Tbsp. olive oil

Instructions

- Olive oil should be brushed on both sides of the pork chops. For 4 boneless pork chops, you'll need roughly 1 tablespoon plus olive oil.

- Season the pork chops on both sides with the pork rub seasoning. To help the seasoning attach to the pork chops, press the rub gently into the meat.
- Spray the aluminum air fryer basket with cooking spray to make cleanup easier. Do not use a non-stick spray like Pam if it is already non-stick.
- In the air fryer basket, place 2-4 boneless pork chops.
- Preheat the oven to 400 degrees Fahrenheit and cook for 12 minutes.
- Cook the pork chops in the air fryer for approximately seven minutes on one side.
- Cook for another 5 minutes, or when the internal temperature reaches 145 degrees Fahrenheit.
- Suppose you're using an air fryer for baking 4 pork chops, making sure you flip & rotate the pan halfway through to ensure even frying. That is, the pork chops that were in the front for the first 7 minutes should not only be flipped but should also be moved to the back of the pan to finish cooking.
- Allow for at least 5 minutes of resting time before serving. It's critical!

Air Fried Bone-in Pork Chops

Preparation and Cooking Time

27 minutes

Servings

4 persons

Nutritional facts

346 calories, 5g fat, 1g fiber, 4g carbs, 16g protein

Ingredients

- 4 Bone-in pork chops
- Salt and Pepper to taste
- 1/2 tsp garlic and herb seasoning
- 2 Tbsp. olive oil

Instructions

- Preheat the air fryer to 380 degrees Fahrenheit | 180 degrees Celsius.
- Brush the pork chops on both sides with olive oil.
- Then season with salt, pepper, & seasonings.
- Then cook for 15 minutes at 380°F | 180°C.
- Depending on the size & thickness of the chops, flip and cook for another 5-10 minutes.
- Cook pork chops to a minimum of 145 degrees Fahrenheit. Use a meat thermometer because air fryer cooking times vary depending on the type.

Air Fryer Pork Kebabs

Preparation and Cooking Time

35 minutes

Servings

4 persons

Nutritional facts

430 calories, 16g fat, 0.7g fiber, 25g carbs, 31g protein

Ingredients

- One pork tenderloin (about 1 lb./450 g), trimmed (see cook's tips)
- 2 tbsp. (30 mL) vegetable oil
- One tbsp. (15 mL) Rotisserie Seasoning
- One baby arugula
- ripe avocado, cut into cubes

- One large ripe mango
- One large red bell pepper
- ¼ cup (60 mL) orange juice
- tbsp. (30 mL) honey
- ¼ red onion, thinly sliced
- ½ cup (125 ml) canned black beans, drained and rinsed

Instructions

- Using a knife, cut the tenderloin into sixteen pieces. Then the mango and bell pepper should be cut into sixteen pieces of one-inch thickness each.
- In a small mixing bowl, combine the marinade ingredients.
- Stir the pork, mango, bell pepper, and 1/4 cup (60 ml) of the marinade together in a large mixing bowl to coat.
- On each of the Deluxe Air Fryer Skewers, thread 2 pieces of pork, 2 pieces of mango, and 2 pieces of bell pepper.
- Place the completed skewers in the Deluxe Air Fryer & cook on "ROTISSERIE" for 10–12 minutes, just until the pork reaches 145°F (63°C).
- Mix the arugula, avocado, onion, & black beans. Just before serving, toss with 2 tbsp. (30 mL) marinade. Drizzle the remaining marinade over the kebabs.

Boneless Air Fryer Pork Chops

Preparation and Cooking Time

19 minutes

Servings

3 persons

Nutritional facts

298 calories, 34g fat, 3g fiber, 24g carbs, 19g protein

Ingredients

- 1/2 cup flour
- 1 tbsp. paprika
- 3 pork chops
- 1/4 cup powder or grated parmesan cheese
- 1 tbsp. garlic powder
- cooking spray

Instructions

- In a zip lock bag, mix the flour, cheese, garlic powder, & paprika powder and shake to combine.
- Pork chops should be added at this point. To fully coat, give it a good shake.
- Using a small amount of cooking spray, lightly coat your air fryer basket.
- Place the pork chops in your basket and bake for 14-20 minutes at 350 degrees.
- Remove the pan & check the internal temperature; if it reaches 71°C (160°F), it's ready. Allow for five minutes before slicing and serving.
- Serve with a side dish of your choice.

Tender Air Fryer Pork Roast

Preparation and Cooking Time

60 minutes

Servings

4 persons

Nutritional facts

322 calories, 24g fat, 1.5g fiber, 7g carbs, 37g protein

Ingredients

- pork roast, about 2 to 5 pounds
- Two to three tablespoons olive oil
- Two to three tablespoons Brown Sugar Bourbon Rub

Instructions

- Start with rubbing olive oil all over the pork roast, then rub the seasoning mix all over it, making sure it's on front and back.
- Place the seasoned roast in the air fryer basket, set the temperature to 350°F, and cook for 40-50 minutes on the air fryer setting.

Air Fryer Steak with Garlic-Herb Butter

Preparation and Cooking Time

30 minutes

Servings

2 persons

Nutritional facts

380 calories, 32g fat, 0.2g fiber, 2g carbs, 37g protein

Ingredients

- One 1-pound of sirloin steak
- 1 tablespoon of finely chopped fresh chives
- Kosher salt
- 1 clove garlic, finely grated
- 4 tablespoons of unsalted butter
- freshly ground black pepper
- 1 tablespoon of finely chopped fresh parsley
- 1/4 teaspoon of crushed red pepper flakes

Instructions

- Allow 30 minutes for the steak to come to room temperature before cooking.
- Preheat an air fryer to 400 degrees F with a 3.5-quart capacity. Season the steak with a liberal pinch of salt and a few grinds of black pepper on both sides. Cook the steak in the air fryer basket until done to your liking, around ten minutes for medium-rare, twelve minutes for medium, and 14 minutes for medium-well. Allow the steak to rest for about 10 minutes on a cutting board.
- Meanwhile, combine the parsley, butter, garlic, chives, and crushed red pepper in a small mixing bowl. Cut the meat into 1/4-inch thick slices against the grain, and finish with a dollop of garlic-herb butter.

Air Fryer Asian Beef & Veggies

Preparation and Cooking Time

18 minutes

Servings

4 persons

Nutritional facts

289 calories, 23g fat, 5g fiber, 23g carbs, 25g protein

Ingredients

- 1 lb. sirloin steak cut into strips
- 2 tablespoons grated ginger do not sub dry ground ginger
- 1/4 teaspoon red chili flakes
- 1/2 cup soy sauce
- 2 tablespoons cornstarch (or arrowroot powder)
- 1/2 medium yellow onion, sliced
- 1 medium red pepper, sliced into strips
- 3 cloves garlic, minced
- 1/4 cup rice vinegar

- 1/4 cup water
- 1 tsp sesame oil
- 1/3 cup brown sugar
- 1 teaspoon Chinese 5 spice optional

Instructions

- Fill a gallon zip bag halfway with all of the ingredients. Make sure all of the ingredients are mixed.
- Label and store for up to 4 months in the freezer.
- Refrigerate the zip bag overnight to thaw.
- Remove the steak & vegetables with tongs and place them in the Air Fryer. Remove the marinade and toss it out.
- Preheat the Air Fryer to 400 degrees Fahrenheit and set the timer for 8 minutes. Halfway through, shake the basket.
- Serve with rice with sesame seeds & scallions as a garnish.

Steak Bites and Crispy Potatoes Recipe

Preparation and Cooking Time

36 minutes

Servings

6 persons

Nutritional facts

353 calories, 21g fat, 0.2g fiber, 15g carbs, 25g protein

Ingredients

- 1-pound Ribeye Steak, cut to 3/4" cubes
- 2 Tablespoons Butter
- 1 clove garlic, grated on a zester
- 1 Pound Mini Red Potatoes, cut in half
- 2 Tablespoon Olive Oil
- 2 Tablespoons Steak Seasoning Salt (Lawrys)
- 1 teaspoon parsley

Instructions

- Preheat the Air Fryer to 390 degrees Fahrenheit.
- Cut the meat into 3/4" cubes and mix it with 1 tablespoon olive oil before seasoning it with salt.
- In a microwave-safe dish, combine the butter & grated garlic.
- Bring a pot of water to a boil, then blanch the potatoes for 7 minutes, or until they are only partially cooked.
- Drain the water and combine it with the remaining tablespoon of olive oil in a mixing bowl.
- Spray the bottom of the air fryer with spray oil shortly before adding the steak and potatoes to keep the meat from sticking.
- Place the meat on top first, then the potatoes. Cook for ten minutes, shaking every 5 minutes throughout that time. If you prefer your meat rare, take it from the pan and set it aside for 10 minutes while the potatoes finish cooking.
- Leave the steak in for around 14 minutes if you want it to finish medium.
- Using a thermometer to measure the temperature of the meat is the best way to ensure that it reaches the desired temperature.
- Pull the meat & potatoes out of the oven and set them aside to rest for 5 minutes. Put the butter/garlic dish in the microwave for thirty seconds to melt while the meat is resting.
- Plate the meat once it has rested for at least an hour and a half. Drizzle a little butter over the top, and serve with a sprinkling of fresh parsley on top.

Air Fryer Ginger Sesame Beef with Green Beans

Preparation and Cooking Time

50 minutes

Servings

4 persons

Nutritional facts

360 calories, 23g fat, 0.9g fiber, 16g carbs, 22g protein

Ingredients

- Tbsp. lite rice vinegar
- 1 Tbsp. ginger, grated
- 1 Tbsp. garlic powder
- 2 Tbsp. vegetable oil
- 1 tsp. Red chili flakes
- ½ lbs. Skirt Steak, sliced into ¼ in. slices
- ¾ cup low sodium soy sauce
- Tbsp. brown sugar
- 2 Tbsp. sesame oil
- 2 Tbsp. sesame seeds, divided
- 1 lb. fresh green beans, trimmed and washed
- 1 carrot, grated

Instructions

- Preheat the air fryer to 400°F, as directed by the manufacturer.
- Using cooking spray, coat the inside of the air fryer basket. Begin with preparing the green beans. Cook for 8-12 minutes, flipping halfway through, till crispy and slightly golden. Remove the air fryer's cooked green beans. Remove and keep warm.
- Next, lay the beef in the air fryer, being cautious not to overcrowd the basket and, if required, frying in batches. Cook each batch for 8-10 minutes, flipping halfway through. Cook until the outside of the beef is browned and no longer pink, and the internal temperature reaches a minimum of 145°F. Take the beef out of the air fryer.

Perfect Air Fryer Steak with Garlic Herb Butter

Preparation and Cooking Time

32 minutes

Servings

2 persons

Nutritional facts

683 calories, 32g fat, 0.2g fiber, 2g carbs, 37g protein

Ingredients

- 2 8 oz. Ribeye steak
- 2 Tbsp. fresh parsley chopped
- 2 tsp garlic minced
- 1 tsp Worcestershire Sauce
- salt
- freshly cracked black pepper
- olive oil
- 1 stick unsalted butter softened
- 1/2 tsp salt

Instructions

- Garlic Butter is made by properly combining butter, parsley garlic, Worcestershire sauce, & salt.
- Roll the dough into a log using parchment paper. Keep it refrigerated until you're ready to use it.

- Remove the steak from the fridge and set it aside for 20 minutes to come to room temperature. Season the steak with salt & freshly cracked black pepper after rubbing a little olive oil on both sides.
- Apply a small amount of oil to the Air Fryer basket and rub it in. Preheat the Air Fryer to 400°F (200°C). Place steaks in the air fryer when warmed & cook for twelve minutes, flipping halfway through. * Remove from air fryer and set aside for 5 minutes. It should be topped with Garlic butter.

Perfect Air Fryer Steak

Preparation and Cooking Time

17 minutes

Servings

2 persons

Nutritional facts

350 calories, 37g fat, 1.6g fiber, 20g carbs, 36g protein

Ingredients

- 2 sirloin steaks
- Two to three tbsp. steak seasoning
- Spray oil or cooking fat of choice

Instructions

- To begin, pat the steak dry and set it aside to come to room temperature.
- You can season liberally with salt and pepper after lightly spraying oil over the meat.
- Place the steaks in the air fryer basket after spraying or coating the bottom with oil. The steaks can contact or be "smooshed" together in the basket.
- Cook for 6 minutes at 400 degrees F, then flip the steaks & cook for another 6 minutes. Add another 2-3 minutes if you really want your steak to be more well-done. Allow to cool before serving.

Air Fryer Corned Beef

Preparation and Cooking Time

1 hour 15 minutes

Servings

1 person

Nutritional facts

171 calories, 29g fat, 2.8g fiber, 9g carbs, 25g protein

Ingredients

- Corned Beef, 3-4 pounds
- Half Cup Brown Sugar
- Quarter Cup Dijon Mustard
- 1 tbsp. Apple Cider Vinegar

Instructions

- Combine the brown sugar, Dijon mustard, and apple cider vinegar in a mixing bowl.
- Wrap the corned beef in aluminum foil and baste it with glaze.
- Then air fry for 1 hour at 360 degrees F.
- Unwrap the aluminum foil, baste it again, and wrap it loosely.
- Then air fry for 40 minutes at 360 degrees F.
- Remove the foil and baste once more. Leave the foil partially open. Then air fry for 10 minutes at 400 degrees F.

Air Fryer Ground Beef

Preparation and Cooking Time

10 minutes

Servings

6 persons

Nutritional facts

134 calories, 36g fat, 3g fiber, 26g carbs, 42g protein

Ingredients

- One and a half-pound ground beef
- 1/2 tsp. pepper
- 1 tsp. salt
- 1/2 tsp. garlic powder

Instructions

- Place the ground beef in the air fryer basket.
- Salt, pepper, & garlic powder is used to season the beef. With a wooden spoon, stir it around a little.
- Cook for 5 minutes in an air fryer at 400°F. Mix it up a little.
- Cook for another 3-5 minutes, or until the chicken is cooked through and thus no longer pink.
- Using a wooden spoon, crumble the beef. Remove the basket & discard any remaining fat or liquid.

Air Fryer Beef Kabobs

Preparation and Cooking Time

38 minutes

Servings

4 persons

Nutritional facts

382 calories, 23g fat, 1.3g fiber, 6g carbs, 20g protein

Ingredients

- 1.5 pounds' sirloin steak cut into 1-inch chunks
- 1 tablespoon lemon juice
- 1/2 teaspoon
- 1/2 teaspoon
- 1 large bell pepper color of choice
- 1 large red onion or onion of choice
- 4 tablespoons olive oil
- 2 cloves garlic minced
- salt and pepper pinch

Instructions

- Combine the steak and marinade ingredients in a large mixing bowl and mix well. Refrigerate for half an hour or up to 24 hours after covering.
- Heat the air fryer to 400 degrees Fahrenheit when ready to cook. Using skewers, thread the beef, pepper, & onion.
- Place the skewers in the preheated air fryer and cook for 10 minutes, turning halfway through, until the outsides are charred and the insides are soft.

Air Fryer Ground Beef Wellington

Preparation and Cooking Time

1 hour 5 minutes

Servings

5 persons

Nutritional facts

670 calories, 28g fat, 2g fiber, 30g carbs, 32g protein

Ingredients

- 2 eggs beaten
- 1 tablespoon of cream
- 3 tablespoons of butter
- 1 small onion chopped fine
- 4 cloves garlic minced
- 1 ½ pounds of ground beef
- 4 tablespoons of saltine crackers, crushed
- 2 tablespoons of dried parsley fresh
- 1 teaspoon salt
- 8 ounces of baby Bella mushrooms
- salt and pepper, to taste
- ½ cup of red wine
- 1 teaspoon of basil fresh
- mozzarella cheese optional
- 2 sheets puff pastry

Instructions

- Preheat the Air Fryer to 375°F.
- Combine the marinade ingredients in a large mixing bowl.
- Melt the butter in a big saucepan. Toss in the mushrooms and minced onion.
- Cook until the mushrooms sweat and the onions are transparent, about 10 minutes over medium-high heat.
- Reduce the heat to medium-low and stir in the garlic, red wine, & basil.
- Increase the heat to high and cook till the liquid has also been reduced. Remove the pan from the heat. Cool.
- Layout the pastry sheets on a lightly floured surface. Each sheet should be cut into four squares.
- Distribute the mushroom mixture evenly across each square. It should be topped with a thin layer of mozzarella cheese.
- Then put half cup beef mixture on top.
- Pinch the edges together and pull the corners up over the meat.
- Cut small slits in the tops and brush with beaten egg or cream. If you've cut through the pastry, now is the time to re-seal it.
- Bake for 30 minutes, seam sides down, or till golden brown & meat is cooked through. Do not forget to check it after around 20 minutes.

Air Fryer Satay Beef Recipe

Preparation and Cooking Time

43 minutes

Servings

2 persons

Nutritional facts

582 calories, 27g fat, 2g fiber, 19g carbs, 40g protein

Ingredients

- 1-pound of beef flank steak
- 1 tablespoon of Minced Garlic
- 1 tablespoon of Sugar
- 1 teaspoon of Sriracha Sauce
- 1 teaspoon of Ground Coriander
- Two tablespoons of Oil
- 1 tablespoon of Fish Sauce
- 1 tablespoon of Soy Sauce

- 1 tablespoon of Minced Ginger
- 1/2 cup of chopped cilantro divided
- 1/4 cup of chopped roasted peanuts

Instructions

- Place the beef strips in a large mixing bowl or a zip lock bag.
- Toss the meat with the fish sauce, oil, soy sauce, ginger, Sriracha, garlic, sugar, coriander, & 1/4 cup cilantro. Refrigerate for half an hour or up to 24 hours after marinating.
- Put the beef strips in basket of your air fryer with tongs, arranging them side by side and avoiding overlap.
- Preheat your air fryer to 400°F and cook for 8 minutes, flipping halfway through.
- Transfer the meat to a serving platter and garnish with the remaining ¼ cup chopped cilantro & chopped roasted peanuts.
- Serve with a dollop of Easy Peanut Sauce on the side.

Air Fryer Sticky Asian Beef

Preparation and Cooking Time

30 minutes

Servings

6 persons

Nutritional facts

236 calories, 23g fat, 5g fiber, 23g carbs, 25g protein

Ingredients

- 1 Tbsp. coconut oil
- 1/2 tsp. ground ginger
- 1/2 Tbsp. minced garlic
- 1 tsp. red pepper flakes
- Sesame seeds for garnishment
- rice or cauliflower rice
- 1 lb. sirloin steak – thinly sliced
- 1/4 cup arrowroot starch
- 1/4 tsp. salt
- 2 red peppers – sliced
- 1/2 cup liquid aminos
- 1/2 cup water
- 3/4 cup brown sugar
- 1/4 tsp. pepper

Instructions

- Melt the coconut oil in a skillet over medium heat before adding the sliced red peppers. Reduce heat to low once the meat is tender.
- Mix liquid aminos, water, brown sugar, ginger, minced garlic, & red pepper flakes in a saucepan and stir to combine. Bring to a boil, then reduce to low heat and simmer for 10 minutes. While you're preparing the steak, let the sauce simmer. If the sauce is still thin and runny after 10 minutes, add ½ teaspoon arrowroot starch and combine. Reduce to a low heat setting and cook till ready to use.
- Begin preparing the steak while the sauce & peppers are simmering. Slice the sirloin steak thinly. Toss the vegetables with the arrowroot starch, salt, & pepper to coat.
- In the air fryer basket, place the steak. It's fine if some of the parts overlap.
- Cook for ten minutes in an air fryer at 400 degrees F. Toss the steak with a fork after opening the basket. Then heat for an additional five minutes, just until the steak is crispy and cooked to your liking.

- Remove the air fryer basket & transfer the cooked steak to the pan with the red peppers after the steak is done. Stir in the thickened sauce to cover everything.
- Serve with rice, cauliflower rice, or as a stand-alone dish. If desired, sprinkle with sesame seeds.

Steak Bites and Mushrooms

Preparation and Cooking Time

1 hour 20 minutes

Servings

2 persons

Nutritional facts

230 calories, 20g fat, 2g fiber, 10g carbs, 25g protein

Ingredients

- 1 teaspoon kosher salt
- 2 Tablespoons avocado oil
- 8 oz. Baby Bella Mushrooms, sliced
- ½ teaspoon garlic powder
- ¼ teaspoon black pepper
- 2 Tablespoons Worcestershire Sauce
- 1-pound Top Sirloin steak, cut into 1.5 inch cubes

Instructions

- In a large mixing bowl, combine all of the marinade ingredients.
- Toss the steak cubes and cut mushrooms with the marinade in a mixing bowl to
- coat.
- Allow 1 hour for the steak & mushrooms to marinade.
- Preheat the Air Fryer to 400 degrees Fahrenheit for 5 minutes.
- Spray the inside of the air fryer with cooking spray before adding the steak and mushrooms to the air fryer basket.
- Cook the steak & mushrooms for 5 minutes at 400°F on the Air Fryer. Shake the steak & mushrooms in the basket to ensure consistent cooking. Cook for an additional 5 minutes.
- Use an internal meat thermometer to check the temperature of the steak. If the steak is not done to your liking, cook in 3-minute increments until a thermometer inserted in the center of 1 steak bite registers the appropriate temperature.

Air fryer beef and broccoli

Preparation and Cooking Time

1 hour 15 minutes

Servings

3 persons

Nutritional facts

263 calories, 29g fat, 2g fiber, 20g carbs, 37g protein

Ingredients

- 1/2 lb. Round steak
- 2 tbsp. sesame oil
- 1 teaspoon minced ginger
- 1 lb. broccoli florets
- 1/3 cup oyster sauce
- 2 tbsp. soy sauce
- 1 teaspoon minced garlic

Instructions

- In a medium bowl, combine all ingredients and marinate for at least 1 hour.

- Fill the air fryer basket with the ingredients. You can put the ingredients in a dedicated air fryer pan if you want the dish to be saucy. Preheat oven to 350°F and bake for 12-15 minutes. Shake a few times.
- Serve with rice or as is. Serve with chopped scallions & sesame seeds as a garnish.

Air Fryer Beef Jerky

Preparation and Cooking Time

28 hours

Servings

8 persons

Nutritional facts

69 calories, 9g fat, 0.3g fiber, 10g carbs, 9g protein

Ingredients

- 12 ounces' top sirloin beef
- 1 tablespoon turbinado sugar
- 1 tablespoon chili paste
- 1 garlic clove, minced
- 1-inch piece fresh ginger root, peeled and grated
- 2 tablespoons reduced-sodium soy sauce
- 1 tablespoon rice vinegar

Instructions

- Thinly slice the meat with a sharp knife & put it in a resealable bag.
- Whisk the garlic, ginger, soy sauce, sugar chili paste, and rice vinegar in a mixing bowl.
- Place the marinade in a bag, seal it, and refrigerate for at least 4 hours or up to 24 hours.
- Remove the pieces of beef from the marinade and pat them dry with a paper towel when ready to cook.
- Preheat the air fryer to 160 degrees Fahrenheit. Cook for 3 to 4 hours with the steak in the basket. Check the jerky for doneness regularly. Allow for complete cooling before storing in an airtight container.

Air Fryer Taquitos with Beef

Preparation and Cooking Time

30 minutes

Servings

8 persons

Nutritional facts

66 calories, 13g fat, 5g fiber, 38g carbs, 29g protein

Ingredients

- 2 teaspoons extra virgin olive oil
- 1/4 cup shredded cheese optional
- 1/3 cup plain Greek yogurt optional
- 1/3 cup guacamole optional
- 1 cup chopped bell peppers
- 1 teaspoon dried oregano
- 1/2 teaspoon ground cumin
- 1/4 teaspoon cayenne pepper
- 1/4 teaspoon salt
- 1/3 cup chopped onion
- 1 teaspoon minced garlic
- 8 oz. lean Ground Beef
- 8 oz. finely chopped mushrooms

- 8-10 each whole wheat tortillas
- 1/3 cup salsa optional

Instructions

- Begin by sautéing garlic and onions for 3 to 4 minutes in oil. Continue to simmer over medium heat on the stovetop with the ground beef, mushrooms, bell peppers, & seasonings. Sauté until the beef has browned and reached an internal temperature of 160°F (or for about 10minutes.)
- Place the ground beef mixture in the center of the tortillas with a slotted spoon. Allow about 1 inch on all sides for the tortilla to roll into a taquito shape. Cheese should be sprinkled on top.
- Fill the tortillas with the meat mixture until all of them are full. Then carefully fold the tortilla up, ensuring the opposite side is tucked under the center. Spray the air fryer basket lightly with an olive oil mist, then place the rolled taquitos in the air fryer basket & cook for 7 minutes at 370 degrees F.
- Remove the taquitos when golden brown and set aside to cool for 2 to 3 minutes before serving. Depending on the size of the air fryer basket, continue to cook the remaining taquitos.
- Toppings such as plain Greek yogurt, guacamole, or salsa can be added as desired.

Air Fryer Beef Tenderloin Roast

Preparation and Cooking Time

45 minutes

Servings

6 persons

Nutritional facts

354 calories, 15g fat, 0.2g fiber, 1g carbs, 17g protein

Ingredients

- 1.5 lb. Beef tenderloin
- 1 tsp. sea salt
- 2 Tbs. extra virgin olive oil
- 3 garlic cloves pressed
- 1/4 tsp. pepper

Instructions

- To ensure that your tenderloin will fit in your Air Fryer basket, cut it down to size.
- One tbsp. of EVOO is rubbed on each side of the tenderloin. Then season with salt, pepper, and garlic.
- Preheat oven to 325°F and bake for 30-45 minutes, or until internal temperature reaches 145°F for medium.
- Allow for 5 minutes of resting time before slicing and serving.

Air Fryer Hamburgers

Preparation and Cooking Time

14 minutes

Servings

4 persons

Nutritional facts

380 calories, 11g fat, 1.1g fiber, 5g carbs, 15g protein

Ingredients

- One and half-pound ground beef preferably ground chuck 80/20 or leaner
- Salt black pepper, and onion powder, to taste

Instructions

- Preheat the air fryer to 360°F.
- Shape the beef into patties by dividing it into 6-ounce portions. To ensure consistent cooking, make a hole in the center.

- Then season with salt, black pepper, & onion powder on both sides.
- If desired, coat the air fryer basket with nonstick cooking spray. In the air fryer basket, place the patties.
- Before turning the burgers, let them cook for another 10 minutes. Cook for another 2 to 4 minutes, depending on how you want it.

Air Fryer Beef Chips

Preparation and Cooking Time

1 hour 6 minutes

Servings

2 persons

Nutritional facts

290 calories, 9g fat, 0.1g fiber, 8g carbs, 21g protein

Ingredients

- 1/2 lb. Thinly Sliced Beef we recommend leaner cuts like sirloin or round
- Quarter tsp salt
- 1/4 tsp Black Pepper
- Quarter tsp Garlic Powder

Instructions

- Gather all of the necessary ingredients.
- Add salt, black pepper, and garlic powder in a small mixing bowl and stir well to make the seasoning.
- Season both sides of the beef slices and lay them flat.
- Single stack the beef slices in the air frying tray (each slice must be single stacked) and air fry for 45-60 minutes at 200F. Allow beef slices to cool for five minutes before serving. Note that the time will vary substantially depending on the thickness.

Bacon Wrapped Beef Tenderloin

Preparation and Cooking Time

25 minutes

Servings

4 persons

Nutritional facts

390 calories, 21g fat, 2g fiber, 23g carbs, 10g protein

Ingredients

- Four 5 ounces' bacon-wrapped beef tenderloins
- Salt and pepper for seasoning

Instructions

- Season the tenderloins on both sides with pepper and salt. Tenderloins should be placed in a bowl.
- Set the temperature to 425°F & cook the tenderloins for 16-20 minutes, flipping halfway through.
- Remove the tenderloins from the pan and set them aside to rest on a chopping board for about 5-10 minutes.
- Serve tenderloins with the steak sauce as well as a steamed vegetable of your choice.

Air Fryer Jalapeño Beef Poppers with Honey Lime Cream Sauce

Preparation and Cooking Time

43 minutes

Servings

4 persons

Nutritional facts

480 calories, 25g fat, 2g fiber, 20g carbs, 15g protein

Ingredients

- 1 pound Certified Angus Beef ® ground chuck, 80% lean
- 1/2 teaspoon whole mustard seeds
- 8 ounces' sour cream
- 1/2 cup plain bread crumbs
- 1/2 cup panko bread crumbs
- Juice and zest of 1 lime
- 2 tablespoons honey
- 2 tablespoons minced cilantro
- 1/4 cup all-purpose flour
- 6 ounces shredded cheddar cheese
- 3 jalapeños, seeded and minced
- 1 1/2 teaspoons salt
- 1 1/2 teaspoons freshly ground black pepper
- 2 eggs
- Spray oil for cooking

Instructions

- Combine the ground chuck, cheese, jalapenos, salt, pepper, and mustard seeds in a large mixing bowl. Refrigerate 24 football-shaped balls (about 1 ounce each), portioned by hand.
- Prepare the dipping sauce. Set aside a small bowl containing sour cream, lime juice, zest, honey, & cilantro.
- Eggs should be cracked and whisked before being placed on a shallow plate. In a second shallow dish, combine bread crumbs.
- Preheat the air fryer to 400 degrees Fahrenheit. Then put rolls of 6 to 8 poppers at a time in flour, brushing off excess before rolling in egg mixture. Transfer to a plate and wrap in bread crumbs; repeat with the remaining poppers, then spray with frying oil.
- Working in batches of 6 to 8, air fry each popper for 4 minutes, then flip and air fry for another 4 minutes. Then warm on a sheet pan in a low-heat oven. Honey Lime Cream Sauce is served alongside for dipping.

Beef Taquitos

Preparation and Cooking Time

40 minutes

Servings

16 persons

Nutritional facts

187 calories, 13g fat, 5g fiber, 38g carbs, 29g protein

Ingredients

- 1 pound 90% lean ground beef
- 1 ½ cups grated sharp cheddar cheese
- 16 tortillas – fajita size flour, 6-inch corn, or 50/50 blend corn for gluten-free
- avocado oil nonstick cooking spray must be non-propellant
- ½ cup diced yellow onion
- 1 tablespoon taco seasoning mix homemade
- 4 ounces can dice green chilies drained
- Optional for serving –salsa, sour cream, pico de gallo, salsa, guacamole, shredded lettuce

Instructions

- Heat the air fryer to 400 degrees F for 5 minutes. Preheat the oven to 200 degrees F and set a foil-lined baking sheet in the oven to keep the cooked taquitos warm while you cook the next batch.

- The tortillas are already lightly coated in oil, which should keep them from sticking to the air fryer basket. Place the taquitos in the basket, seam side down, in one layer. It is fine if they touch, but they shouldn't be packed or crammed together too tightly. Then cook for 6–8 minutes, or until desired crispiness is achieved.
- To keep the taquitos warm, place them on a baking sheet in the oven. Continue with the remaining taquitos. Following batches may cook more quickly, so keep an eye on them.
- Serve over a bed of shredded lettuce with optional toppings on top, or serve with toppings on the side.

Air Fryer Top Round Roast

Preparation and Cooking Time

1 hour 3 minutes

Servings

4 persons

Nutritional facts

2146 calories, 25g fat, 0.3g fiber, 3g carbs, 99g protein

Ingredients

- 3-pound Beef Top Round Roast
- 1/4 cup beef broth
- 16 ounces' mini potatoes
- 1/2 tsp salt
- 1/4 tsp pepper
- 16 ounces' baby carrots

Instructions

- Prepare the roast by brushing it lightly with olive oil and seasoning it on both sides with salt and pepper.
- Preheat the oven to 400 degrees, place the roast in the basket and cook for 25-28 minutes.
- Toss the carrots and potatoes with olive oil, salt, and pepper while the roast is cooking. Allow to rest until the top of the roast is done.
- Turn the roast over, baste with beef broth, and add the prepared carrots and potatoes after the first 25-28 minutes have passed. Return the basket to the air fryer and cook for another 18-20 minutes at 400 degrees F.
- The potatoes and carrots should be soft, and the roast should be 145 degrees F on the inside. Allow 5-10 minutes for the roast to rest before serving.

Air Fryer Beef and Bean Chimichangas

Preparation and Cooking Time

20 minutes

Servings

8 persons

Nutritional facts

380 calories, 36g fat, 8g fiber, 33g carbs, 40g protein

Ingredients

- 1 can (16 oz.) refried beans
- 2-3 cups Mexican blend cheese
- 1 lb. ground beef, browned
- 2 cans (7.75 oz.) El Pato Mexican tomato sauce
- 8 burrito-sized flour tortillas

Instructions

- Preheat the air fryer to 400°F.

- Combine browned ground beef & 1 can of El Pato tomato sauce in a medium mixing bowl. Microwave on high for 2-3 minutes, or until thoroughly warmed.
- Combine refried beans & 1/4 cup shredded cheese in a separate microwave-safe bowl. Microwave for 2-3 minutes on high or until warm.
- Layer a scoop of refried beans, a scoop of ground beef mixture, & shredded cheese on each tortilla. Fold in the sides of the tortilla and wrap it up.
- In the air fryer basket, arrange the chimichangas in a single layer. Cook for 10 minutes, flipping once, after lightly spraying olive oil.
- More shredded cheese and El Pato tomato sauce should be drizzled over the chimichangas. If preferred, serve with sour cream on top.

Air Fryer Beef Ribs – Quick and Delicious

Preparation and Cooking Time

32 minutes

Servings

3 persons

Nutritional facts

3200 calories, 37g fat, 1g fiber, 10g carbs, 26g protein

Ingredients

- Beef Ribs (3 oz. for 400 Calories)
- 1 tbsp. Sea Salt to taste
- 1-2 tbsp. Light Olive Oil
- 1/4 cup Brown Sugar
- 1/4 cup Paprika
- 1 tbsp. Black Pepper
- 1.5 lbs. Beef Ribs half rack
- 1-2 tbsp. Light Olive Oil
- 2 tbsp. Garlic salt
- 1 tbsp. Black Pepper
- 1 tbsp. Salt
- 1/2 cup Black Pepper
- 1/4 cup Sea Salt
- 2 tbsp. Sweet Paprika
- 2 tbsp. Garlic Powder
- 1 tbsp. Garlic Powder
- 1 tbsp. Onion Powder
- 1 tbsp. Chili Powder
- 1-2 tbsp. Light Olive Oil
- 2 tbsp. Onion Powder
- 1 tbsp. Cumin optional

Instructions

- Make your preferred rib rub.
- Rub the ribs with a mixture of olive oil.
- Then cook for 10 minutes in an air fryer at 400° F | 205° C.
- Reduce heat to 325° F | 162° C and cook ribs for up to 20 minutes. Keep the beef ribs between 190°F | 88°C & 203°F | 95°C using a meat thermometer.

Air Fryer Steak Fajitas

Preparation and Cooking Time

2 hour 26 minutes

Servings

4 persons

Nutritional facts

380 calories, 17g fat, 4.5g fiber, 32g carbs, 20g protein

Ingredients

- 1 1/2 pounds' flank OR sirloin steak
- 2 tablespoons olive oil divided
- salt and pepper to taste
- flour tortillas
- 3 tablespoons olive oil
- 2 tablespoons honey
- 1/4 cup soy sauce
- 1 medium red onion sliced
- 1 small green pepper
- 1/2 small red bell pepper
- 1/2 small orange OR yellow bell pepper
- 1 whole lime juiced
- cheese
- salsa
- 3 cloves garlic rough chopped
- 1/2 teaspoon black pepper
- guacamole
- sour cream

Instructions

- In a zip-top bag, combine the marinated ingredients and then add the meat (whole). Refrigerate for at least two hours and up to 8 hours after sealing.
- Remove the steak from the fridge & drain the marinade when ready to cook. After blotting it dry with paper towels and allowing it to come to room temperature, slice it into strips.
- The onions & peppers should be cut into similar-sized pieces. One tablespoon olive oil is drizzled over the top, season to taste with salt and pepper, then toss to coat.
- Heat the air fryer to 400 degrees for 3 minutes. Cook the peppers & onions in the air fryer basket for 8-10 minutes, pausing midway to give them a good shake, then transfer to a bowl and put aside.
- Toss the steak strips in the leftover tablespoon of olive oil, season with salt, and toss to coat.
- Cook the steak strips in the air fryer for 6-8 minutes, or until done to your liking. Return the vegetables to the air fryer for 60 seconds to reheat before serving.

Easy Air Fryer Beef Taquitos

Preparation and Cooking Time

30 minutes

Servings

14 persons

Nutritional facts

217 calories, 13g fat, 5g fiber, 38g carbs, 29g protein

Ingredients

- 1-pound ground beef 80/20 preferred
- 1 teaspoon garlic powder
- 3/4 teaspoon cumin
- 1/4 teaspoon ground pepper
- 14 medium-sized corn and flour blend tortilla or 100% flour tortillas
- 1 1/2 cups Mexican blend shredded cheese

- 1 teaspoon kosher salt
- 1 teaspoon oregano
- Oil spray

Instructions

- Preheat the air fryer for 10 minutes at 350 degrees Fahrenheit.
- Season the ground beef with salt, pepper, oregano, garlic powder, and cumin. Mix thoroughly.
- Spread the beef filling evenly throughout the tortilla, ensuring that it reaches the edges. Toss in the cheese and roll up tightly. Toothpicks are used to secure the ends.
- Spray the taquitos on all sides with oil.
- In the air fryer basket, arrange the taquitos in a single layer, toothpick side down.
- Then air fry the taquitos for about 8 minutes, or until golden brown and crispy.
- Remove and serve with your favorite dip or salsa.

Crispy Beef and Broccoli Stir-Fry

Preparation and Cooking Time

1 hour 20 minutes

Servings

4 persons

Nutritional facts

430 calories, 29g fat, 2g fiber, 20g carbs, 37g protein

Ingredients

- 2 tbsp. Avocado oil, divided
- 3 tbsp. Granular Sweetener
- 1 tbsp. Minced Garlic
- 2 tsp Ginger paste
- 1 ½ lb. Thinly Sliced Steak, 1-inch pieces
- 4 cups Broccoli Florets
- ½ cup Soy Sauce (use coconut aminos for gluten-free)
- Quarter tsp Crushed red pepper
- ⅛ tsp xanthan gum
- Half tsp sesame seeds

Instructions

- To marinate the beef, combine it with ginger, soy sauce, avocado oil, garlic, and granular sweetener in a large mixing bowl or storage bag. Allow 1 hour in the refrigerator to marinate.
- Remove the steak from the marinade and set it in the air fryer basket, retaining the marinade.
- Preheat the oven to 320 degrees Fahrenheit & set the timer for twenty minutes.
- After 10 minutes, shake the fryer basket and add the broccoli and pepper.
- Bring the marinade to a boil in a skillet over medium heat, then reduce to low heat. Allow thickening by stirring in the xanthan gum.
- When the timer on the air fryer goes off, rapidly empty the fryer basket onto the skillet and toss. Sesame seeds can be sprinkled on top, and serve right away.

Air Fryer Steak with Roasted Potatoes

Preparation and Cooking Time

40 minutes

Servings

1 person

Nutritional facts

392 calories, 21g fat, 0.2g fiber, 15g carbs, 25g protein

Ingredients

- 1/2 lb. Strip Loin
- 1 tsp Italian herbs
- 1 tsp Pepper (ground)
- 4 small Potatoes (chopped)
- 1 1/2 tbsp. Olive oil
- 1 tsp Cayenne pepper
- 1 tsp Salt

Instructions

- Combine potatoes, olive oil, cayenne pepper, Italian herbs, & salt in a medium mixing bowl. Evenly combine the ingredients.
- Preheat the air fryer to 360 degrees Fahrenheit for 5 minutes.
- Fill the air fryer basket halfway with potatoes.
- It should be cooked for fifteen minutes. Halfway through, toss the potatoes. Set aside once cooked.
- Both sides of the steak should be rubbed with oil, salt, and pepper.
- In the air fryer basket, place the steak. Cook for 8 - 15 minutes at 400°F, depending on how you like your steak.
- Allow 10 minutes for the steak to rest once it has been cooked. It can be served with roasted potatoes.

One-Pot Cheesy Beef and Rice Casserole

Preparation and Cooking Time

60 minutes

Servings

8 persons

Nutritional facts

480 calories, 20g fat, 5g fiber, 26g carbs, 25g protein

Ingredients

- 1 lb. of ground beef
- 1 cup of frozen peas
- 10.75 oz. of condensed cream of mushroom
- 1 1/4 cup of beef broth
- 1 cup of long-grain rice (uncooked)
- 1 cup of chopped carrots
- 1 1/2 cups shredded Cheddar cheese

Instructions

- Fill the Instant Pot halfway with ground beef. Select the SAUTE function, change to HIGH, then press START.
- Select CANCEL after browning the meat till no pink remains. Fat should be drained. Cover loosely with foil the browned meat in a shallow dish.
- De-glaze by scraping the brown pieces from the bottom of the pot with a wooden spoon after adding broth.
- Stir in the rice that has been washed.
- Then add the veggies, cooked beef, and soup to the pot. Stirring is not allowed. Place the Pressure Cooking Lid on top of the pressure cooker.
- Select the PRESSURE COOK function from the display panel. Set the timer for 15 minutes and then press START.
- Allow 10 minutes for the pressure to naturally release once the timer has expired, then quickly release the remaining pressure.
- Stir to blend the ingredients, then level the top and sprinkle with cheese uniformly.
- Then secure the >strong>Air Fryer Lid by selecting CANCEL.

- Select the BROIL function from the display panel. Set the temperature to 400 degrees Fahrenheit and the timer to 5 minutes, then press START.
- Remove the lid & set it on the protecting pad once the cheese has melted and begun to brown. Serve hot, scooped into individual bowls.

Air Fryer Roast Beef (Instant Pot Vortex and Omni)

Preparation and Cooking Time

45 minutes

Servings

6 persons

Nutritional facts

443 calories, 40g fat, 1g fiber, 5g carbs, 40g protein

Ingredients

- 2.5-pound of Beef Roast
- Seasoning to taste
- One tbsp. of olive oil

Instructions

- Make the roast more compact by tying it.
- Olive oil should be rubbed all over the roast.
- Season with salt and pepper as desired
- Put the roast on a rotisserie, a tray, or an air fryer basket.
- For medium-rare beef, air fry at 360°F for around 15 minutes per pound.
- Allow 5 minutes for the roast to rest before serving.

Air Fryer Steak Kabobs

Preparation and Cooking Time

15 minutes

Servings

4 persons

Nutritional facts

179 calories, 37g fat, 1.6g fiber, 20g carbs, 36g protein

Ingredients

- 15 oz. steak
- olive oil
- 1 red bell pepper
- 1 green bell pepper
- 1 red onion
- 2 Tbsp. soy sauce

Instructions

- Preheat the Air Fryer to 400 degrees Fahrenheit (200 degrees Celsius). Use a nonstick spray like olive oil or avocado oil to coat the Air Fryer basket.
- While cutting up the vegetable, cube the steak into bite-sized pieces & marinate them in the soy sauce.
- Cut the onion and bell peppers into bite-size pieces.
- Using a skewer, alternately add the steak, onion, & peppers, repeat until the skewer is empty.
- In the prepared Air Fryer basket, arrange the steak skewers in a single layer. Cook for 10 minutes at 400 degrees Fahrenheit, rotating the skewers after five minutes.
- Serve alone, with a dipping sauce, or with a side dish of your choice.

Air Fryer BBQ Beef Jerky

Preparation and Cooking Time

2 hour 35 minutes

Servings

2 persons

Nutritional facts

191 calories, 9g fat, 0.3g fiber, 10g carbs, 9g protein

Ingredients

- Beef Steak 10 ounce
- 1 tablespoon Garlic, Powder
- 1 teaspoon Cumin, Ground
- Gourmet Collection Smoked Paprika by Mccormick
- 2 tsp Tamari Sauce
- 1-½ tablespoon Maple Flavored Syrup by Lakanto
- 1-½ tablespoon Tomato Sauce
- 1 teaspoon Mustard Powder

Instructions

- Slice the beef & place it in a mixing bowl, making sure they are all of the same sizes. Drizzle the syrup, tomato sauce, and tamari sauce over the top. Then season with the dried seasonings. Mix well with your hands, fully coating the meat in the seasonings & liquids. To marinate, cover and chill for 1 hour.
- Take the meat out of the fridge. Shake off any extra liquid from the beef strips before placing them in a single layer in the air fryer basket. In the air fryer, place the basket. Set the timer for 90 minutes and heat the air fryer to 180 degrees Fahrenheit.
- Remove the air fryer basket from the. The texture of the beef ought to be firm but still soft. Then cook for another half an hour or till the desired consistency is attained.

Teriyaki Air Fryer Beef Jerky

Preparation and Cooking Time

1 day 2 hours 6 minutes

Servings

4 persons

Nutritional facts

456 calories, 9g fat, 1g fiber, 10g carbs, 9g protein

Ingredients

- 1 sirloin steak
- 1 tsp ground ginger
- 1 tsp sesame seeds
- ½ tsp red pepper flakes
- 3 tbsp. soy sauce
- 1 tbsp. sesame oil
- 1 tbsp. minced garlic

Instructions

- Slice the sirloin against the grain into extremely thin strips using a sharp knife. Then, combine the remaining ingredients in a mixing bowl and stir with the steak.
- Marinate the steak for 24 hours, turning it a few times to ensure evenly coated.
- Cook for 2 hours, flipping every 30 minutes, using the "dehydrate mode" at 180 degrees in the air fryer.

Air Fryer Jerk Steak w/ Compound Butter

Preparation and Cooking Time

14 minutes

Servings

1 person

Nutritional facts

707 calories, 44g fat, 1.8g fiber, 6g carbs, 28g protein

Ingredients

- 8 oz. ribeye steak
- Half tbsp. jerk spice
- 1 tbsp. compound butter
- One tbsp. olive oil

Instructions

- Olive oil should be brushed on the steak. Rub jerk seasoning on the steak.
- Preheat the air fryer to 400°F.
- Fry the steak for 10-fifteen minutes, flipping halfway through.
- Remove the steak from the pan and set it aside to rest for 5-10 minutes. It should be topped with butter and then served.

Air Fryer Shredded Beef Chimichanga Recipe

Preparation and Cooking Time

30 minutes

Servings

1 person

Nutritional facts

547 calories, 8g fat, 0.2g fiber, 15g carbs, 20g protein

Ingredients

- Prepared Mexican shredded beef
- Chopped tomatoes
- Sour Cream
- Flour tortillas
- Olive or avocado oil

Instructions

- Shredded beef is pan-fried to remove some of the moisture from the meat.
- To soften the tortillas, put them in a skillet over medium heat.
- Place a tortilla on a tray and fill it with 3/4 cup shredded beef. Spread the meat evenly across the tortilla, leaving several inches around the edge.
- Begin folding horizontally, rolling the tortilla into a burrito by folding in the outside of the tortilla (horizontal sides).
- Lightly cover all sides of the burrito with a pastry brush dipped in oil.
- Then in the air fryer, place seam side down.
- Start the air fryer. Then heat for 10 minutes at 375°F, then flip chimichangas & air fry for another 6-10 minutes.
- Place the chimichanga on a serving platter and top with tomatoes, crema, or any other ingredients you choose.

Air Fryer-Beef Stir Fry with Homemade Marinade

Preparation and Cooking Time

25 minutes

Servings

2 persons

Nutritional facts

349 calories, 14g fat, 5g fiber, 32g carbs, 30g protein

Ingredients

- 1-pound beef sirloin
- 1/2 cup of onion, cut into strips
- 1/2 cup of red onion, cut into strips
- 1/4 cup hoisin sauce
- 2 teaspoons minced garlic
- 1 1/2 pounds broccoli florets
- 1 red pepper
- 1 green pepper
- 1 yellow pepper
- 1/4 cup of water
- 1 teaspoon of sesame oil
- 1 tablespoon of soy sauce
- 1 teaspoon of ground ginger

Instructions

- In a mixing bowl, combine all the sauce (marinate) ingredients, then add the meat.
- After that, put it in the fridge for about twenty minutes.
- Add one tbsp. of stir fryer oil to the vegetables and toss to combine.
- Cook the vegetables in the air fryer basket for around 5 minutes at 200°F.
- Then, using your air fryer, combine all vegetables and ensure that they are softened rather than firm. Add another 2 minutes if they haven't softened.
- Remove the veggies to a bowl, then put the pork in the air fryer basket and cook for 4 minutes at 360 degrees F. Check & flip them, and if they aren't done, cook for another 2 minutes.

Bone-in Ribeye Steak

Preparation and Cooking Time

14 minutes

Servings

2 persons

Nutritional facts

323 calories, 27g fat, 0.1g fiber, 1g carbs, 25g protein

Ingredients

- 2-3 tablespoons of butter softened
- 1 bone-in ribeye
- pinch of Kosher salt
- 2 teaspoons of freshly chopped parsley
- 1 teaspoon of chives
- 1 teaspoon of thyme
- Freshly ground black pepper

Instructions

- Mix butter and herbs in a small bowl. Cover and chill for about 15 minutes, or until firm. You could make a log out of it by wrapping it in wax paper or plastic wrap.
- Season both sides of the steak with pepper and salt.
- Cook the steak in the air fryer basket for 12 - 18 minutes, depending on the thickness of the meat and how rare or do you want it, rotating halfway through.
- Place a piece or two of herb butter on top of the steak to serve. Serve with salad or vegetables.

Air Fryer Steak Tips with Peppers, Onions & Mushrooms

Preparation and Cooking Time

30 minutes

Servings

3 persons

Nutritional facts

480 calories, 29g fat, 1.9g fiber, 13g carbs, 41g protein

Ingredients

- 16 oz. ribeye or another type of steak, cut into cubes
- 2 tablespoons of butter melted
- 1 clove of garlic, crushed
- 8 oz. mushrooms, quartered
- 1 cup of bell peppers, chopped
- 1/4 cup onion sliced
- fresh parsley to garnish (optional)

Instructions

- The first step is to slice the meat into bite-sized pieces, and you'll also need to chop up the vegetables.
- Microwave the butter for about 15 seconds, then combine with the crushed garlic.
- Combine the meat, veggies, garlic butter, salt, and black pepper in a large mixing bowl.
- If using an air fryer, spray the basket with cooking spray & evenly distribute the steak and vegetables. Cook for 10 minutes at 400°F, then stir well enough and cook for another 5-10 minutes, depending on how you prefer your steak.
- Preheat a cast iron or other heavy-bottomed skillet using a skillet over medium-high heat. Pour the vegetables and meat mixture into the pan and spread it out evenly. To get a beautiful sear, let them undisturbed for 5 minutes. After that, combine everything and simmer for another 5 minutes. Continue doing this for another 20 minutes until the meat is cooked thoroughly.
- Before serving, if desired, garnish with chopped fresh parsley.

Air Fryer Marinated Steak

Preparation and Cooking Time

1 hour 20 minutes

Servings

6 persons

Nutritional facts

556 calories, 16g fat, 0.5g fiber, 4g carbs, 21g protein

Ingredients

- 1 Tbsp. Salt
- 1 Tbsp. Ground Cumin
- 1 Tbsp. Ground Black Pepper
- 1 cup Soy Sauce
- 2 Tbsp. Smoked Paprika
- 2 Tbsp. Onion Powder
- 2 Tbsp. Garlic Powder
- 2 Tbsp. Dried Oregano
- 1/2 tsp Liquid Smoke
- 6 Boneless Ribeye Steak
- Half cup Fresh Chives, chopped

Instructions

- Combine 3 teaspoon salt, 2 tablespoons smoked paprika, 2 tablespoon onion powder, 2 tablespoon garlic powder, 2 tablespoons dried oregano, 1 tablespoon ground cumin, and 1 tablespoon ground black pepper in a mixing bowl (1 tablespoon).
- Rub all sides of the Boneless Ribeye Steak (6) with the rub & gently press down. Put everything in a zip lock bag.
- Combine the Soy Sauce (1 cup) & Liquid Smoke (½ tsp) in a zipper bag until well blended. Close the bag and coat the steak with the marinade. Refrigerate for at least 1 hour before serving.
- Preheat the air fryer to 400 degrees F (200 degrees C) with the grill plate inside for 5 minutes.
- Cook the steak for 6 minutes on each side in the air fryer, flipping once.
- Allow for a few minutes of rest before serving. It should be topped with Fresh Chives (1/2 cup).

Keto Air Fryer Burgers

Preparation and Cooking Time

15 minutes

Servings

4 persons

Nutritional facts

293 calories, 14g fat, 0.4g fiber, 3g carbs, 20g protein

Ingredients

- 1-pound ground beef 80/20 is best
- 1/2 tsp salt
- 1 tsp garlic powder
- 1 tsp onion powder
- 1/4 tsp pepper

Instructions

- Preheat the air fryer to 360 degrees Fahrenheit.
- In a mixing bowl, combine all ingredients and shape the meat mixture into four patties. To make an indent, press your thumb into the middle of the top of each burger.
- Air fry the burgers for six minutes, then flip and cook for another 2-3 minutes, or until they're done to your liking.
- Top with cheese and return to the air fryer for 30 seconds just until the cheese has melted (optional)
- Serve and have fun.

Air Fryer Meatloaf

Preparation and Cooking Time

45 minutes

Servings

8 persons

Nutritional facts

380 calories, 17g fat, 2g fiber, 24g carbs, 33g protein

Ingredients

- 1-pound ground turkey
- 2 teaspoon steak seasoning
- 1 teaspoon meatloaf seasoning (optional)
- 1 cup oats
- 1 tablespoon olive oil
- 1-pound lean ground beef
- 2 tablespoons steak sauce

- 2 teaspoon onion powder
- 2 teaspoon garlic powder
- Parchment paper
- 1/2 cup ketchup
- chopped parsley for garnish if desired

Instructions

- In a large mixing bowl, combine everything else in the recipe, EXCEPT the ketchup and parsley.
- The finest tool for mixing meatloaf is your hands.
- Mix everything up thoroughly.
- Cut a sheet of parchment to fit the air fryer basket.
- Place the meatloaf in the air fryer basket after shaping it on parchment paper.
- Cook for 30-40 minutes in an air fryer at 375°F or until done. When the internal temperature of the meatloaf hits 160 degrees F, it is ready. Using an instant-read thermometer in the center of the meatloaf is the best way to determine this.
- Allow 10 minutes for cooling before slicing.
- Add 1/2 cup ketchup on top and garnish with parsley when the meatloaf is cool.

Chapter 10: Air Fryer Vegan Recipes

Eggplant Bites with Italian Herbs

Preparation and Cooking Time

15 minutes

Servings

2 persons

Nutritional facts

80 calories, 3g fat, 1.7g fiber, 10g carbs, 3g protein

Ingredients

- 1 medium to large eggplant cut into 1-inch cubes, skin on
- 1/2 tsp dried oregano
- 1/2 tsp sea salt
- 2 TBS extra virgin olive oil
- 1/2 tsp garlic powder
- 1/2 tsp dried basil
- 1/4 tsp freshly ground pepper

Instructions

- Combine the eggplant, olive oil, garlic powder, basil, oregano, salt, pepper, & pepper flakes in a large mixing bowl.
- Preheat the air fryer to 390 degrees Fahrenheit.
- Place the eggplant in the crisper basket or fryer basket. It should be cooked for five minutes. To rotate the eggplant, shake the bucket or drawer. Cook for another 3 to 5 minutes, or until the eggplant has softened and browned.
- Serve with your meal right away.

Air Fryer Sweet Potato Fries

Preparation and Cooking Time

19 minutes

Servings

2 persons

Nutritional facts

98 calories, 7g fat, 4g fiber, 28g carbs, 3g protein

Ingredients

- 1 large sweet potato, washed and patted dry
- 1/4 tsp freshly ground pepper (optional)
- More salt for serving
- 2 tsp grape seed oil or other mild vegetable oil
- 1/2 tsp coarse sea salt
- Ketchup for serving

Instructions

- Preheat the air fryer for 3 to 5 minutes at 375°F.
- Remove the sweet potato's sharp ends. Cut it in half down the middle. Place the potato halves with the broader ends facing down. Cut the potato into 3/8-inch thick planks from top to bottom. Cut the planks into 3/8-inch thick rectangular fries on the cutting board.
- Pour the oil over the fries and place them in a bowl. Use Salt & pepper to taste. Toss to coat evenly.
- Place the fries in a single layer in the air fryer basket. It's possible that you'll have to perform this in two batches. It should be cooked for six minutes. Cook for another 6 minutes after shaking the bucket. To see if a fry is tender, take a bite. Continue to shake for a few more minutes, just until the fries are just how you like them. Season the sweet potato fries with salt and pepper, if preferred, on a serving plate. Serve with ketchup while still warm.

Easy Air Fryer French Fries

Preparation and Cooking Time

23 minutes

Servings

2 persons

Nutritional facts

145 calories, 10g fat, 2g fiber, 25g carbs, 5g protein

Ingredients

- 2 large Russet potatoes
- 1 TBS coconut oil or grape seed oil
- Cold filtered water
- Juice of 1/4 lemon
- 2 tsp sea salt

Instructions

- Wash the potatoes thoroughly. Remove the skins. Cut the potatoes' ends off to make them more evenly shaped. One side of the potatoes should be thinly sliced to sit flat on the cutting surface. Potatoes should be cut into 3/8 inch by 3/8 inch rectangular sticks.
- Put the potatoes in a mixing bowl. To prevent discoloration, cover with water and add lemon juice. Set aside the bowl for 30 minutes.
- Heat the air fryer to 375 degrees Fahrenheit.
- Remove the potatoes from the water and blot dry using paper towels. Also, dry the bowl. Return the potatoes to the bowl. Drizzle the oil over the potatoes & season with 1 teaspoon of salt. Toss to coat evenly.
- Put the potatoes on the crisper plate or in the air fryer basket. Cook for 12-15 minutes, tossing every 6 minutes, or until golden, crispy, and done. Check one to see if it's cooked all the way through.
- Cooked fries should be seasoned with leftover sea salt. With ketchup or one of the dipping sauces, serve the fries.

Easy Air Fryer Asparagus

Preparation and Cooking Time

15 minutes

Servings

4 persons

Nutritional facts

380 calories, 4g fat, 2g fiber, 7g carbs, 4g protein

Ingredients

- 1 bunch of asparagus spears (approximately 1 pound)

- 1/2 tsp sea salt
- 1 TBS extra virgin olive oil
- 1/2 tsp freshly ground black pepper

Instructions

- Under cool running water, wash the asparagus spears. Using paper towels, absorb any excess liquid. With a sharp knife, cut off the thick woody ends of each stem. You could also snap them off at the point where the white and green parts meet. The ends should be discarded.
- Heat the air fryer to 375 degrees Fahrenheit.
- Put the spears on a plate and drizzle with olive oil evenly. Season with salt and pepper to taste.
- In the basket or plate of the air fryer, arrange the spears in a single layer. Set a 10-minute timer. Cook for 3 minutes, rotating the asparagus in the bucket with a shake. Cook for 4 minutes for thin spears and ten minutes for thick spears.
- Arrange the asparagus on a serving plate.

How to Air Fry Any Vegetable

Preparation and Cooking Time

30 minutes

Servings

2 persons

Nutritional facts

104 calories, 4g fat, 2g fiber, 8g carbs, 3g protein

Ingredients

- Cauliflower, Crucifers broccoli, Brussels sprouts
- beets, Root Vegetable carrots, potato, parsnip
- acorn, Winter Squash butternut, pumpkin
- Soft Veggies like tomato, bell pepper
- asparagus
- Any of the veggies from above

Instructions

- For Tender Veggies: Preheat the air fryer to 375°F (190 C). Prepare the vegetables by cutting them to the desired size and sprinkling them with oil if desired. Cook for 10 to 15 minutes in your air fryer, shaking the air fryer pan once or twice during cooking to ensure even cooking.
- For Firm Veggies: Preheat the air fryer to 375°F (190 C). Prepare the vegetables by chopping them to the desired size (smaller pieces' cook faster). Drizzle with oil if desired, and place in an air fryer. Cook for 30 minutes, shaking the air fryer pan multiple times to ensure even cooking.
- For Frozen Veggies: Determine if your vegetable is tender or hard, and then add a few minutes to the cooking time to account for the vegetables having to thaw during the cooking procedure. To ensure that your vegetables are perfectly roasted, leave plenty of space between them.

Air Fryer Frozen Onion Rings

Preparation and Cooking Time

4 minutes

Servings

2 persons

Nutritional facts

303 calories, 35g fat, 3g fiber, 38g carbs, 14g protein

Ingredients

- Six ounces of frozen onion rings (about 1/2 a bag of Alexia onion rings)

Instructions

- Preheat the oven to 350 degrees Fahrenheit for approximately 3 minutes.
- Stack onion rings in the air fryer if required.
- Cook for 4 minutes in the air fryer, shaking the basket halfway through.
- Take it out of the air fryer and eat it right away.

Roasted Air Fryer Carrots

Preparation and Cooking Time

20 minutes

Servings

4 persons

Nutritional facts

50 calories, 6g fat, 3g fiber, 19g carbs, 1g protein

Ingredients

- 16 ounces of carrots
- One teaspoon oil
- salt and pepper (to taste)

Instructions

- Carrots should be peeled and sliced into 2-inch slices. To make all of the pieces the same size, cut any larger pieces in half.
- Preheat the air fryer to 360°F.
- Toss the carrots in 1 teaspoon of olive oil.
- Cook carrots for 15-18 minutes in an air fryer, shaking every few minutes.
- The tenderness of carrots can be determined using a fork. When it effortlessly glides through the carrot, it's done.
- Season with salt and pepper, then shake the basket to coat it.
- Serve and enjoy right away.

Air Fryer Roasted Vegetables

Preparation and Cooking Time

25 minutes

Servings

4 persons

Nutritional facts

207 calories, 6g fat, 1g fiber, 7g carbs, 4g protein

Ingredients

- 1 medium sweet potato
- 1 medium red onion
- 3 tablespoons olive oil (or avocado oil)
- 1 medium potato
- 1 cup chopped butternut squash (yellow squash or pumpkin)
- 1 medium carrot
- 1/2 head broccoli
- 1 teaspoon kosher salt
- 1 teaspoon seasoning (optional)

Instructions

- The potatoes, sweet potatoes, & squash should all be washed and peeled. Cut into 1-2 inch chunks and soak for at least 10 minutes in a dish of cold water.
- The remaining vegetables should be washed and peeled before slicing into 1-2 inch slices.
- Preheat the air fryer to 360 degrees Fahrenheit (180 degrees Celsius).
- Drain and pat all of the vegetables dry once they've been soaked.

- Combine the olive oil, salt, and seasoning in a large mixing bowl. Toss in the firm veggies to coat them in the seasoning.
- Place firm vegetables and air fry in an air fryer basket for five minutes.
- Add the soft veggies to the oil/seasoning mixture and toss to coat while the firm vegetables are air frying.
- After five minutes, give the air fryer basket a gentle shake to redistribute the vegetables, then top with the soft vegetables.
- Shake the basket every five minutes until the vegetables are soft and golden brown, around 10-15 minutes.

Marinated Air Fryer Vegetables

Preparation and Cooking Time

25 minutes

Servings

4 persons

Nutritional facts

200 calories, 4g fat, 2g fiber, 8g carbs, 3g protein

Ingredients

- 2 green zucchini cut into ½ inch pieces
- ½ tsp dried oregano
- ¼ tsp garlic powder
- A few drops of liquid smoke optional
- 4 Tbsp. Olive Oil
- 2 Tbsp. Balsamic Vinegar
- 1 Tbsp. Honey
- 1 ½ tsp salt
- ½ tsp dried thyme
- 1 yellow squash cut into ½ inch pieces
- 4 oz. button mushrooms cut in half
- 1 red onion cut into ½ inch pieces
- 1 red bell pepper cut into ½ inch pieces
- salt to taste

Instructions

- In a large mixing bowl, stir together the marinade ingredients. Put chopped vegetables in a mixing dish and toss until they are completely covered.
- Allow 20-30 minutes for the vegetables to marinade.
- Place marinated vegetables in an air fryer basket and cook for 15-18 minutes at 400 degrees Fahrenheit, stirring every 5 minutes, till tender. Then season with salt to taste.

Air Fryer Baked Sweet Potato

Preparation and Cooking Time

40 minutes

Servings

2 persons

Nutritional facts

75 calories, 7g fat, 4g fiber, 28g carbs, 3g protein

Ingredients

- 2 small sweet potatoes, scrubbed and dried
- 1 teaspoon oil
- Quarter teaspoon salt

Instructions

- Preheat your air fryer to 400 degrees Fahrenheit.
- Poke holes in the skin of the sweet potatoes with a fork.

- Then completely coat sweet potato skins with oil and salt.
- Place the potatoes in the air fryer and cook for 35 to 40 minutes, or until a caramelization around the fork holes appears, and the sweet potato is effortlessly pierced with a fork.
- Cut in half, set aside to chill until barely warm, and then eat.

Air Fryer Sautéed Onions

Preparation and Cooking Time

15 minutes

Servings

2 persons

Nutritional facts

83 calories, 20g fat, 2g fiber, 18g carbs, 10g protein

Ingredients

- 1 onion
- One tablespoon oil
- a small pinch of sugar

Instructions

- The onion should be cut into long slices.
- Heat the oil for 1 minute at 300 degrees F in an air fryer pan.
- Put onion slices in the pan and toss them around to coat them in oil evenly.
- Cook onions for 5 minutes at 300 degrees F, stirring halfway through.
- Cook for another 7 to 10 minutes, stirring every 2-3 minutes, after adding a little sprinkle of sugar to the onions.
- Remove the pan from the air fryer and serve immediately.

Air Fryer Mushrooms with Balsamic Vinegar

Preparation and Cooking Time

13 minutes

Servings

3 persons

Nutritional facts

33 calories, 11g fat, 3g fiber, 24g carbs, 13g protein

Ingredients

- 8 oz. mushrooms
- 1/4 teaspoon black pepper
- 1 teaspoon avocado oil
- 1/2 teaspoon granulated garlic
- 1-2 teaspoons balsamic vinegar optional
- 1/4 teaspoon salt
- 1 teaspoon parsley fresh, chopped

Instructions

- Because the mushrooms will shrink, cut them into large bite-size pieces.
- Pour the oil over the mushrooms in a mixing bowl.
- Toss the mushrooms with the garlic, salt, and pepper to coat, and then arrange them on the air fryer rack, leaving space between them for even air frying.
- Then air-fry the mushrooms for 8 to 10 minutes at 375 degrees F. They should be tossed once after 4-5 minutes.
- Before serving, put the mushrooms in a bowl and combine with freshly chopped parsley & balsamic vinegar.

Air Fryer Veggies

Preparation and Cooking Time

20 minutes

Servings

6 persons

Nutritional facts

50 calories, 6g fat, 1g fiber, 7g carbs, 4g protein

Ingredients

- 3 cups of mixed vegetables (broccoli, cauliflower, squash, beets, carrots, etc.)
- One tablespoon olive oil
- Half teaspoon kosher salt

Instructions

- Put the vegetables in a bowl. Then toss to coat with the oil & salt.
- Put the vegetables in your air fryer basket.
- Cook for fifteen to twenty minutes on 375F degrees F.

Instant Pot Vortex Air Fryer Vegetables

Preparation and Cooking Time

23 minutes

Servings

4 persons

Nutritional facts

147 calories, 4g fat, 2g fiber, 8g carbs, 3g protein

Ingredients

- 1 cup broccoli
- 1 cup carrots
- 1 cup cauliflower
- 1 Tablespoon Olive oil or oil of choice

Instructions

- Toss the vegetables with the oil in a mixing bowl.
- Toss in the seasonings.
- Place the veggies in the air fryer basket.
- It should be cooked at 380°F for 18 minutes or golden brown.
- Remove the basket with care using the removal tool, serve, & enjoy.

Air Fryer Frozen Broccoli, Carrots, and Cauliflower

Preparation and Cooking Time

15 minutes

Servings

3 persons

Nutritional facts

70 calories, 25g fat, 5g fiber, 27g carbs, 15g protein

Ingredients

- 3 cups of frozen mixed carrots, broccoli, and cauliflower
- 1/2 tsp of nutritional yeast (optional)
- 1/2 tsp of sea salt
- 1 TBS of extra virgin olive oil
- 1 tsp of Italian seasoning blend (or oregano, basil, rosemary, and thyme)
- 1/4 tsp of freshly cracked pepper

Instructions

- Preheat the air fryer for 5 minutes at 375°F.

- In a large mixing bowl, combine the frozen vegetables. Toss the veggies in olive oil to coat them. Toss the vegetables again with herbs, salt, pepper, & nutritional yeast.
- Place the vegetables in an even layer on the air fryer's basket. It should be cooked for five5 minutes. Rotate the vegetables or shake the bucket. Cook for another 4 to 6 minutes, or until the veggies are soft and the sauce has thickened to a warm consistency. Taste one to see if it's done.
- On a serving tray, arrange the cooked vegetables. Before serving, sprinkle with extra nutritional yeast.

Roasted Asparagus (Vegan)

Preparation and Cooking Time

15 minutes

Servings

4 persons

Nutritional facts

352 calories, 4g fat, 2g fiber, 7g carbs, 4g protein

Ingredients

- 1-pound fresh asparagus, ends trimmed
- salt, to taste
- 1-2 teaspoons olive oil
- black pepper, to taste

Instructions

- Asparagus should be washed and trimmed. Then season asparagus with pepper and salt after dipping them in olive oil. If you want, add more spices. Cover them with oil to prevent the asparagus tips from burning or drying out too quickly.
- Air fry and turn asparagus halfway through cooking at 380°F for 7-ten minutes, depending on thickness.
- Allow it to cool somewhat before checking seasoning and tenderness. If preferred, cook for a further minute or two and season with additional salt and pepper.

Air Fryer Frozen Vegetables (No mushier frozen broccoli!)

Preparation and Cooking Time

25 minutes

Servings

4 persons

Nutritional facts

128 calories, 15g fat, 3g fiber, 12g carbs, 12g protein

Ingredients

- 1 lb. of frozen cauliflower (454 grams; do not thaw)
- 3 tablespoons of avocado oil
- 1 teaspoon of Trader Joe's Everything
- cooking oil spray of choice
- 1 lb. of frozen broccoli
- 3 tablespoons of avocado oil
- 1 teaspoon Trader Joe's Everything
- cooking oil spray of choice
- 12 ounces of frozen Brussels sprouts (340 grams; do not thaw)
- 2 tablespoons of avocado oil
- 1 teaspoon of Trader Joe's Everything
- cooking oil spray of choice
- 1 lb. frozen whole leaf spinach (454 grams; do not thaw)
- 3 tablespoons avocado oil
- 1 teaspoon Trader Joe's

- cooking oil spray of choice
- 12 ounces frozen okra, chopped (340 grams; do not thaw)
- 2 tablespoons avocado oil
- 1 teaspoon Trader Joe's
- cooking oil spray of choice
- 10 ounces of frozen butternut squash, chopped small (283 grams; do not thaw)
- 2 tablespoons avocado oil
- 1 teaspoon of Trader Joe's Everything
- cooking oil spray of choice
- 1 lb. of frozen zucchini, sliced
- 3 tablespoons of avocado oil
- 1 teaspoon of Trader Joe's Everything
- cooking oil spray of choice

Instructions

- If some frozen broccoli pieces are too large, cut them into smaller pieces. Using the cooking spray, lightly spritz the air fryer baking racks.
- Drizzle the oil over the frozen broccoli and season with salt and pepper. To make sure it's evenly distributed, give it a good stir.
- Arrange the broccoli on the racks in a single layer.
- Make sure the drip tray is in position in your air fryer oven. Place the racks in the oven and bake for 12 minutes at 400°F (200°C).
- Stack the trays in the oven in a different order. Bake for another 8 minutes.
- If some frozen cauliflower pieces are too large, cut them into smaller pieces. Using the cooking spray, lightly spritz your air fryer baking racks.
- Drizzle the oil over the frozen cauliflower and season with salt and pepper. To make sure it's evenly distributed, give it a good stir.
- Arrange the cauliflower on the racks in a single layer.
- Make sure the drip tray is in position in your air fryer oven. Place the racks in the oven and bake for 12 minutes at 400°F (200°C).
- Stack the trays in the oven in a different order. Bake for another 8 minutes.
- Using the cooking spray, lightly spritz the air fryer baking racks.
- Drizzle the oil over the frozen Brussels sprouts and season with salt and pepper. To make sure it's evenly distributed, give it a good stir.
- Arrange the Brussels sprouts on the racks in a single layer.
- Make sure the drip tray is in position in your air fryer oven. Place the racks in the oven and bake for 10 minutes at 400°F (200°C).
- Stack the trays in the oven in a different order. Bake for another 8 minutes.
- Using the cooking spray, lightly spritz your air fryer baking racks.
- Drizzle the oil over the frozen spinach and season with salt and pepper. To make sure it's evenly distributed, give it a good stir.
- Place the spinach on the air fryer racks and spread it out evenly. For a crispier spinach side dish, break apart the frozen clumps.
- Make sure the drip tray is in position in your air fryer oven. Place the racks in the oven and bake for 10 minutes at 400°F (200°C).
- The spinach pieces should be flipped and stirred. Stack the trays in the oven in a different order. Bake for another 10 minutes.
- Using the cooking spray, lightly spritz the air fryer baking racks.

- Drizzle the oil over the frozen okra and season with salt and pepper. To make sure it's evenly distributed, give it a good stir.
- Arrange the okra on the racks in a single layer.
- Make sure the drip tray is in position in your air fryer oven. Place the racks in the oven and bake for 12 minutes at 400°F (200°C).
- Stack the trays in the oven in a different order. Bake for another 8 minutes.
- Using the cooking spray, lightly spritz your air fryer baking racks.
- Drizzle the oil over the frozen winter squash and season with salt and pepper. To make sure it's evenly distributed, give it a good stir.
- Arrange the butternut squash in a single layer on the air fryer racks.
- Make sure the drip tray is in position in your air fryer oven. Place the rack in the oven's top rack and roast for 20 minutes at 400°F (200°C), tossing and rotating the squash after 12 minutes.
- Using the cooking spray, lightly spritz the air fryer baking racks.
- Drizzle the oil over the frozen zucchini and season with salt and pepper. To make sure it's evenly distributed, give it a good stir.
- On the racks, arrange the zucchini in a single layer.
- Make sure the drip tray is in position in your air fryer oven. Place the racks in the oven and bake for 12 minutes at 400°F (200°C).
- Flip the zucchini and move the trays in the oven to a new position. Bake for another 10 minutes.
- Change the trays' positions in the oven one more time. Zucchini should be roasted for three minutes at 400°F (200°C).

Air Fryer Roasted Vegetables Recipe That Compliments Your Dish

Preparation and Cooking Time

25 minutes

Servings

4 persons

Nutritional facts

100 calories, 4g fat, 2g fiber, 7g carbs, 4g protein

Ingredients

- 2 bell peppers
- 2 tablespoons extra virgin olive oil
- 1 teaspoon salt
- 1 red onion
- ½ zucchini
- 1 cup button mushrooms
- ½ teaspoon black pepper

Instructions

- Bell peppers, red onion, zucchini, and button mushrooms should be washed, dried, and chopped into bite-size pieces.
- Combine the veggies, extra virgin olive oil, salt, and black pepper in a large mixing bowl. Mix everything until it's completely combined.
- Use parchment paper to line the air fryer tray.
- Put the vegetables in the tray and bake for 15 minutes at 350 degrees F, flipping halfway through. When the cycle is complete, carefully lift the lid and transfer the vegetables to a serving plate.

Fried Vegetable Sticks

Preparation and Cooking Time

17 minutes

Servings

4 persons

Nutritional facts

264 calories, 5g fat, 1g fiber, 4g carbs, 2g protein

Ingredients

- 6 parsnips
- 1/4 cup water
- salt
- 1/4 cup almond flour
- 1/4 cup olive oil

Instructions

- Peel and cut the parsnips into 1/2" x 3" slices.
- Combine the almond flour, water, olive oil, and salt in a large mixing bowl.
- Stir the parsnips into the mixture until they are well coated.
- Heat the Philips Air fryer for 3 minutes @ 390°F.
- Toss in the parsnips.
- Preheat oven to 350°F and bake for 10 - 15 minutes.
- Take it out of the Air fryer and eat it.

Easy Air Fryer Fajita Veggies with Quick Fajita Sauce

Preparation and Cooking Time

25 minutes

Servings

4 persons

Nutritional facts

861 calories, 3g fat, 2g fiber, 8g carbs, 7g protein

Ingredients

- 1 large White Onion sliced into 1/2-inch-thick slices vertically
- 1 canned Chipotle pepper from the can of chipotle peppers in adobo sauce
- 1/4 cup Olive Oil or use regular cooking oil
- 1 tbsp. Cumin powder
- 1 tsp Garlic powder
- 1 medium Green Bell Pepper sliced into 1/2-inch-thick slices vertically
- 1 medium Red Bell Pepper sliced into 1/2-inch-thick slices vertically
- 2 large Portobello Mushrooms sliced into 1/2-inch-thick slices vertically
- 3 tbsp. Adobo Sauce from the can of chipotle peppers in adobo sauce
- 1 tsp Salt
- 3 tbsp. Lime Juice may use lemon juice too

Instructions

- Preheat the air fryer to 390 degrees Fahrenheit for around 5 minutes. Then Using a spray bottle, coat the air fryer basket in oil. Place the marinated vegetables in the basket. They will be stacked on top of one another. Air fry the vegetables for 12-15 minutes, or until slightly crunchy. After 7-8 minutes, gently toss them in between to ensure even frying.

- If you want crispier vegetables, air-fry them longer. However, extended air frying may cause the vegetables to become dry. So be cautious.
- The Air Fryer Fajita Veggies are ready to serve with your preferred toppings and warm tortillas.

Air Fryer Balsamic Roasted Vegetables

Preparation and Cooking Time

35 minutes

Servings

2 persons

Nutritional facts

280 calories, 7g fat, 10g fiber, 19g carbs, 8g protein

Ingredients

- 4 tablespoons olive oil
- 1/2 teaspoon pepper
- 6 ounces' grape tomatoes
- 1 yellow squash, sliced
- 4 tablespoons balsamic vinegar
- 2 tablespoons brown sugar
- 3 tablespoons soy sauce
- 1 tablespoon Dijon mustard
- 1 zucchini, sliced
- 8 ounces' mushrooms, halved
- Eight ounces' fresh asparagus (If the ends are tough, break them off and discard)

Instructions

- Mix olive oil, balsamic vinegar, brown sugar, soy sauce, Dijon mustard, & pepper in a large mixing bowl.
- Toss in the vegetables, covering them completely.
- Allow 30 minutes for the vegetables to marinade in the refrigerator.
- Cook for 8 minutes at 400 degrees Fahrenheit in an air fryer basket sprayed with olive oil.
- Cook for another five minutes, or until vegetables are soft, stirring or shaking occasionally.

Roasted winter vegetables

Preparation and Cooking Time

20 minutes

Servings

6 persons

Nutritional facts

280 calories, 6g fat, 9g fiber, 28g carbs, 5g protein

Ingredients

- 300 g parsnips
- 300 g 'butternut squash.'
- 1 tbsp. fresh thyme needles
- 1 tbsp. olive oil
- 300 g celeriac
- 2 red onions
- pepper & salt

Instructions

- Preheat the air fryer to 200 degrees Celsius.
- Parsnips, celeriac, and onions should all be peeled. Parsnips and celeriac should be cut into 2 cm cubes, while onions should

- be cut into wedges. Remove the seeds from the 'butternut squash' and chop it into cubes.
- Combine the sliced vegetables, thyme, and olive oil in a mixing bowl. Then season with salt and pepper to taste.
- Put the vegetables in the basket and place them inside the Air fryer. Set the timer for twenty minutes & roast the vegetables until they are nicely browned and cooked. During the roasting process, stir the vegetables once.

Air Fryer Cauliflower with Parsley

Preparation and Cooking Time

15 minutes

Servings

4 persons

Nutritional facts

99 calories, 2g fat, 1.2g fiber, 9g carbs, 5g protein

Ingredients

- 1 large head cauliflower cut into bite-sized florets
- ½ tsp. Salt
- ¼ tsp. black pepper
- 2 Tbsp. oil olive or avocado
- ¼ tsp. garlic powder
- ¼ tsp. paprika
- Parsley optional

Instructions

- Preheat the air fryer to 370 degrees Fahrenheit for at least 3 minutes.
- Combine the oil, garlic powder, paprika, salt, & pepper.
- Stir in the cauliflower florets until they are thoroughly coated in the sauce.
- Cook for 10 to 12 minutes with the cauliflower in the air fryer basket, tossing halfway through.
- Sprinkle paprika & finely chopped parsley on top of the cauliflower.

Air Fryer Veggie Tots

Preparation and Cooking Time

12 minutes

Servings

20 tots

Nutritional facts

197 calories, 18g fat, 7g fiber, 21g carbs, 6g protein

Ingredients

- 1 cup sweet potato (baked in the oven until soft and skin removed)
- ½ tsp paprika
- ¼ tsp salt
- ¼ tsp pepper
- 1 ½ cups kale
- 1 egg
- ½ cup rice crumbs
- ½ tsp garlic powder
- 2 tsp olive oil

Instructions

- In the air fryer, spray or sprinkle 1/2 tsp olive oil. In the air fryer, place the tots. To keep them crispy, don't stack them on top of each other. Cook at 400 degrees F for 10-15 minutes after spraying or drizzling 1 teaspoon olive oil over the top of the tots. If necessary, repeat the process.
- In a food processor, pulse the kale into small flakes.
- With a fork, mash the cooked sweet potato. Allow the sweet potato to cool completely if you just cooked it. Combine the kale, egg, rice crumbs, and spices in a mixing bowl.
- With a 1 tablespoon scoop, make "tot-like" forms or small circular shapes. They don't need to be flawless!
- Half tsp olive oil should be sprayed or drizzled into the air fryer. In the air fryer, place the tots. To keep them crispy, don't stack them on top of each other. One tsp olive oil, sprayed or drizzled over the top of the tots, and air fry for 10-15 minutes at 400 degrees F. Determined by the size of the air fryer, you may need to repeat the process.
- Serve with a dipping sauce on the side.

Tender and Spicy Air fryer vegetable kebab

Preparation and Cooking Time

20 minutes

Servings

3 persons

Nutritional facts

81 calories, 4g fat, 1g fiber, 9g carbs, 13g protein

Ingredients

- 2 bell peppers
- 1/2 onion
- salt and pepper to taste
- 1 eggplant
- 1 zucchini
- 6-inch skewers

Instructions

- Before using wooden skewers, soak them in the water bath for 15 minutes.
- All of the vegetables should be cut into 1-inch pieces. Put them on skewers & season with salt and pepper.
- Preheat the air fryer to 390 degrees Fahrenheit, then add the skewers & cook for 10 minutes.

Air Fryer Zoodles

Preparation and Cooking Time

35 minutes

Servings

2 persons

Nutritional facts

259 calories, 21g fat, 6g fiber, 18g carbs, 12g protein

Ingredients

- 1 Tbsp. olive oil
- Two large zucchinis, spiralized
- ½ tsp. salt

Instructions

- Put zucchini noodles in a colander & season generously with salt until they are completely covered. Allow 10 minutes for the zoodles to absorb any extra water. Squeeze out as much water as possible from the zoodles using a tea towel.
- Toss zoodles with oil & salt in a large mixing bowl. Put in the drum and cover with the lid. Place in the bowl.
- Set the air fryer to 425°F and cook for 20 minutes.
- Serve with your preferred pasta sauce on top.

Veg Cutlet Recipe (Air Fryer Recipe + No Breadcrumbs)

Preparation and Cooking Time

55 minutes

Servings

20 pieces

Nutritional facts

130 calories, 4g fat, 5g fiber, 20g carbs, 7g protein

Ingredients

- 2 cups Sweet Potatoes (Boiled, Peeled and Mashed) 1 cup is 250 ml
- 1 tsp of Kashmiri Red chili powder
- 1 & 1/2 tsp of Gram Masala Powder
- 1/2 tsp of Turmeric Powder
- 1/4 tsp of Chaat Masala Powder
- 1/2 cup of Quick Cooking Oats
- 1 tbsp. of Ginger Paste
- 1 & 1/2 tbsp. of Oil for Cooking cutlets
- Salt to taste
- 3/4 cup of Carrot (finely grated)
- 1/2 cup of Sweet Corn (steamed)
- 1/2 cup of Capsicum (finely chopped)
- 1/3 cup of Green Peas (Steamed)
- 2 to 3 tbsp. of Coriander Leaves (finely chopped)
- 1/2 tsp of Amchur Powder

Instructions

- Boil and mash sweet potatoes, simmer peas, sweet steam corn, shredded carrots, and finely diced capsicum in a large mixing bowl.
- Combine all spices, ginger paste, fast cooking oats, and salt to taste in a large mixing bowl.
- Add the coriander leaves, finely chopped.
- Combine all of the ingredients.
- Divide the cutlet mixture into equal portions & shape them into "oval" shapes. Then heat the Air Fryer to 200°C for 5 minutes after the cutlets have been shaped.
- Place 12 cutlets on a baking sheet, brush or spritz with oil, and bake for fifteen minutes at 200°C.
- After 8 - 10 minutes of cooking, turn them over, repeat the spraying or brushing process, and air fry them until golden brown. Serve with your preferred side dish.

Ranch-Flavored Veggie Chips in an Air Fryer

Preparation and Cooking Time

15 minutes

Servings

2 persons

Nutritional facts

380 calories, 6g fat, 2g fiber, 8g carbs, 3g protein

Ingredients

- 1/2 medium zucchini
- 1/4 tsp salt
- Freshly ground black pepper
- 1/2 medium sweet potato
- 1 small beet
- 1 tsp olive oil
- 2 tsp ranch seasoning

Instructions

- Thinly slice the zucchini, sweet potato, and beet into 1/4-inch thick rounds with a knife or a mandolin.
- Drizzle olive oil over the veggie slices in a medium mixing bowl, season with salt and pepper, & toss to coat.
- Preheat the air fryer to 360°F and arrange the vegetable slices in a single layer in the fryer basket. Cook for approximately 15 minutes, flipping halfway through.
- Remove from the air fryer, place in a bowl, and top with ranch dressing. Toss to evenly coat, then store in an airtight container.

Air Fryer Veggie Chips

Preparation and Cooking Time

30 minutes

Servings

4 persons

Nutritional facts

430 calories, 3g fat, 1.5g fiber, 7g carbs, 2.5g protein

Ingredients

- 1 Zucchini
- 1/2 tsp Pepper
- 1 tsp Salt
- 1 Red Beet peeled
- 1 large Carrot
- 1 Sweet Potato peeled
- 1 tsp Italian Seasoning
- Pinch of Cumin

Instructions

- Using a mandolin, thinly slice the vegetables to about 1/4-inch thickness.
- Place in a single layer in an air fryer set to 356°F.
- Cook for 15-18 minutes, flipping halfway.
- Toss the vegetable chips with the seasoning and serve.

Healthy Air Fryer Veggie Fries Recipe

Preparation and Cooking Time

43 minutes

Servings

4 persons

Nutritional facts

60 calories, 12g fat, 0.5g fiber, 5g carbs, 4g protein

Ingredients

- One large buttercup or butternut squash
- Two Tbsp. of olive oil
- avocado oil, melted lard, melted tallow, melted coconut oil, or melted butter
- salt

Instructions

- Using a vegetable peeler, peel the squash. Remove the seeds and cut them in half. Slice the flesh into 1/2-inch thick sticks.
- Combine the squash sticks, oil, and a pinch of salt in a large mixing bowl.
- Heat the air fryer for 3 minutes at 390 degrees F.
- In the air fryer, place the squash sticks and any excess fat.
- Cook for twenty minutes, pausing halfway through to stir.

- Serve right away with a pinch of salt.

Healthy Air Fryer Asparagus

Preparation and Cooking Time

10 minutes

Servings

4 persons

Nutritional facts

45 calories, 4g fat, 2g fiber, 7g carbs, 4g protein

Ingredients

- 1-pound fresh asparagus, ends trimmed
- salt, to taste
- Oil spray or olive oil
- black pepper, to taste

Instructions

- Season the asparagus with salt and pepper after coating it with oil spray or olive oil. Arrange the asparagus in the air fryer basket in an even layer. Ensure the asparagus tips are well-coated, so they don't burn or dry out. It's preferable to season everything before putting it in the air fryer basket. When there is too much salt in the air fryer baskets, the coating will break down.
- Based on thickness, shake and turn asparagus halfway through cooking at 380°F for 7 to 10 minutes.
- Serve after tasting for seasoning and tenderness.

Air Fryer Seasoned Asparagus

Preparation and Cooking Time

12 minutes

Servings

4 persons

Nutritional facts

32 calories, 4g fat, 2g fiber, 7g carbs, 4g protein

Ingredients

- 1 Bunch Asparagus
- Garlic Salt
- Olive Oil Cooking Spray

Instructions

- Begin by cutting the asparagus stems to around 2 inches long.
- Place the asparagus in the air fryer basket.
- Using an olive oil spray and a pinch of garlic salt, lightly coat the chicken.
- Cook for 5 minutes at 390°F.
- Check and turn the asparagus.
- Cook for another 5 minutes.

Air Fryer Vegetable Kabobs

Preparation and Cooking Time

13 minutes

Servings

6 persons

Nutritional facts

25 calories, 7g fat, 2g fiber, 8g carbs, 1.3g protein

Ingredients

- 1 cup (75g) button mushrooms
- 1/2 bell pepper sliced
- 1 small onion cut into chunks (or 3-4 small shallots, halved)
- 1 cup (200g) grape tomatoes or cherry tomatoes
- 1 small zucchini cut into chunks
- 1/2 tsp ground cumin
- Salt to taste

Instructions

- Before using, soak skewers in water for at least 10 to 15 minutes.
- Preheat the air fryer to 390 degrees Fahrenheit (198 degrees Celsius).
- Vegetables should be threaded onto the skewers.
- Place the skewers in the air fryer, ensuring they don't touch. You might have to cut the ends of the skewers to fit if your air fryer basket is small.
- Cook for a total of 10 minutes, turning halfway through. Start with less time and add more as needed because air fryer temperatures vary.
- Serve the vegetable kabobs on a platter.

15-Minutes Air Fryer Brussel Sprouts

Preparation and Cooking Time

15 minutes

Servings

4 persons

Nutritional facts

31 calories, 4g fat, 5g fiber, 13g carbs, 6g protein

Ingredients

- 3 c halved Brussel sprouts
- ¼ t salt
- 1 T olive oil
- ¼ t pepper

Instructions

- Put Brussels sprouts in olive and salt/pepper.
- Put into air fryer basket.
- Cook in the air fryer at 400 degrees F for 12 minutes.

Asian-Style Air Fryer Green Beans

Preparation and Cooking Time

10 minutes

Servings

4 persons

Nutritional facts

62 calories, 4g fat, 3g fiber, 7g carbs, 2g protein

Ingredients

- 1 lb. green beans, washed and trimmed
- 1 teaspoon garlic salt
- 2 teaspoons sesame oil
- pepper to taste

Instructions

- Preheat the air fryer to 400 degrees Fahrenheit.
- Toss the trimmed green beans with the sesame oil, garlic salt, & pepper in a bowl to cover evenly.
- Green beans should be cooked for 5-7 minutes in a preheated air fryer, shaking the basket halfway through. Use a fork to test for softness to see if the green beans are done.
- Take the green beans out of the air fryer & eat them.

Air Fryer Roasted Vegetables

Preparation and Cooking Time

25 minutes

Servings

4 persons

Nutritional facts

156 calories, 7g fat, 10g fiber, 19g carbs, 8g protein

Ingredients

- 1/2 lb. Brussels Sprouts any vegetables based on preference! (you can add green squash, bell peppers, broccoli, and more!)
- Salt & Ground Black Pepper – to taste
- 3 tbsp. Olive Oil / Avocado Oil / Grape seed Oil Enough to coat the vegetables / Toss in it
- 1 Carrot Sliced or Chopped any vegetables based on preference!
- 1 Onion- Chopped bite-sized any vegetables based on preference!
- 1 package Mushrooms (button, portobello, etc.) Any kind based on preference!
- 4 cloves Garlic – Minced
- 4 tbsp. Balsamic Vinegar Enough to coat the vegetables / Toss in it (More or less based on the preference of taste)
- 1 tsp Garlic Powder (optional)
- 2 tsp Sugar (optional)

Instructions

- Cook for 20 minutes in an air fryer at 400 degrees F, just until the vegetables are cooked & roasted to your preference. Toss it around every 5 to 10 minutes to ensure it isn't burning.
- You may wish to add a little additional balsamic vinegar halfway through the cooking process.
- After that, taste it and add extra garlic powder, salt, pepper, sugar, or balsamic vinegar as desired.

Air Fryer Vegetable Fries

Preparation and Cooking Time

37 minutes

Servings

4 persons

Nutritional facts

103 calories, 12g fat, 0.5g fiber, 5g carbs, 4g protein

Ingredients

- 2 Medium Carrots
- 1.5 Tsp Extra Virgin Olive Oil
- 2 Tsp Oregano
- 2 Tsp Thyme
- 1 Medium Zucchini
- 200 g Butternut Squash
- 200 g Sweet Potato
- Salt & Pepper

Instructions

- Prepare your vegetables by slicing and dicing them. Any vegetables that require peeling should be washed quickly after peeling.
- Combine the vegetables, spices, & extra virgin olive oil in a mixing bowl.
- Cook for twenty minutes at 180°C/360°F in an air fryer basket.
- Cook for another 12 minutes at the same temperature after shaking the air fryer veggies.

- Serve with a dipping sauce of your choice.

How to Make Crispy Chickpeas in an Air Fryer

Preparation and Cooking Time

25 minutes

Servings

1 person

Nutritional facts

119 calories, 2g fat, 6g fiber, 23g carbs, 7g protein

Ingredients

- 1 15oz can chickpeas, rinsed and drained
- ¼ teaspoon sea salt
- 2 teaspoons of oil
- Optional: paprika, garlic powder, onion powder, or za'atar seasoning

Instructions

- Preheat your air fryer to 450 degrees Fahrenheit. Gently blot the chickpeas dry with a paper towel.
- Toss the chickpeas with the oil and seasoning in a large mixing bowl.
- Cook for 10 minutes in the air fryer, remove the basket and shake to toss the chickpeas.
- Cook for another 5-10 minutes, or until crispy.

Air Fryer Special Broccoli

Preparation and Cooking Time

10 minutes

Servings

1 person

Nutritional facts

89 calories, 5g fat, 2g fiber, 6g carbs, 2g protein

Ingredients

- 3 cups broccoli florets, chopped into 1" pieces
- 1/4 teaspoon onion powder
- 2 teaspoons olive oil (or olive oil spray)
- 1/4 teaspoon garlic powder
- Salt to taste

Instructions

- Preheat your air fryer to 390 degrees Fahrenheit.
- Combine the broccoli, oil, garlic powder, & onion powder in a mixing bowl. Alternatively, spray the broccoli with olive oil spray before seasoning. Then season with salt to taste.
- Cook until the broccoli is browned, about 4-5 minutes.

Air Fryer Veggie Chip Medley

Preparation and Cooking Time

1 hour 15 minutes

Servings

4 persons

Nutritional facts

180 calories, 14g fat, 4g fiber, 8g carbs, 4g protein

Ingredients

- 1 sweet potato (about 4 ounces), scrubbed
- 1 purple potato (about 4 ounces), scrubbed
- 2 tablespoons olive oil
- Kosher salt and freshly ground black pepper

- 1 red beet (about 6 ounces), scrubbed
- 1 golden beet (about 6 ounces), scrubbed

Instructions

- On a mandolin, thinly slice both potatoes to about 1/16-inch-thick pieces. Move to a medium bowl and rinse with cold water until virtually all-white starch has been removed and the water is clear. Then dry well with a few paper towels. Also, dry the bowl.
- Return the dry potatoes to the bowl and mix with 1 tablespoon of oil, 1/2 teaspoon salt, and a few grinds of pepper to coat evenly.
- Preheat an air fryer to 320 degrees F with a 3.5-quart capacity. It's fine if there are two layers of potatoes at the bottom of the basket. Cook till the potatoes are golden brown and crisp around the edges, 20 to 25 minutes, stirring with tongs every 5 minutes to ensure even cooking. Remove a few slices to a bowl & continue air frying the remaining parts if you find a few slices are completed cooked and completely crisp before others.
- Meanwhile, finely slice both beets on the mandolin to about 1/16-inch thickness. Toss with the remaining 1 tbsp. oil, 1/2 teaspoon salt, and a few grinds of pepper in a medium mixing bowl until evenly covered.
- Raise the temperature of the air fryer to 320 degrees F. It's fine if there are two layers of beets at the bottom of the basket. Cook till the beets are darker around the edges & crisp, about 30 minutes, flipping every 5 minutes to ensure even cooking. Remove a few slices to a bowl & continue air frying the remaining parts if you find a few slices are completed cooked and completely crisp before others.
- In a large mixing bowl, add the beet and potato chips, season with a touch of salt, and toss to mix. Serve right away, chill, and keep for up to 2 days in an airtight container.

Air Fryer Vegetable "Stir-Fry"

Preparation and Cooking Time

12 minutes

Servings

2 persons

Nutritional facts

200 calories, 2g fat, 1.8g fiber, 7g carbs, 4g protein

Ingredients

- 50 grams extra firm tofu, cut into strips (about 1 cup)
- 1 teaspoon Italian seasoning
- 1/2 teaspoon sesame oil (or olive oil)
- 1/4 teaspoon soy sauce
- 4 stalks asparagus, ends trimmed and cut in half
- 4 Brussels sprouts, halved
- 3 brown mushrooms, sliced
- 2 cloves garlic, minced
- salt and pepper, to taste
- roasted white sesame seeds (for garnish)

Instructions

- Toss all of the ingredients together in a large mixing bowl.
- Transfer to an air fryer basket and air fry for 7-8 minutes at 350 degrees F. Halfway through, give the basket a good shake.
- Remove from the air fryer basket, top with roasted white sesame seeds, and serve with rice on the side.

Crispy Air Fryer Gluten-Free Vegan Potato Latkes

Preparation and Cooking Time

10 minutes

Servings

12 persons

Nutritional facts

158 calories, 30g fat, 3g fiber, 24g carbs, 6g protein

Ingredients

- 2 ½ Cups Peeled, Shredded White Potato
- ½ Tsp Smoked Paprika (optional)
- ¼ Tsp Black Pepper (optional)
- ½ Cup Minced Sweet Onion
- 3 TB Arrowroot Starch
- Prepared Bob's Red Mill Egg Replacement
- Applesauce (to serve)

Instructions

- Preheat the air fryer to 350 degrees Fahrenheit.
- Combine the potato, onion, starch, & prepared egg in a large mixing bowl. If used, season with spices.
- Form a thick flattened disc with about 2 teaspoons of the ingredients.
- Place in the air fryer and continue to cook. Keep the latkes equally spaced in the air fryer basket to ensure proper browning.
- Air fry the latkes for five minutes, then flip them and continue to air fry for another 3 minutes, or till golden brown & crisp.

Air Fryer Roasted Potatoes

Preparation and Cooking Time

15 minutes

Servings

6 persons

Nutritional facts

147 calories, 7g fat, 4g fiber, 28g carbs, 3g protein

Ingredients

- 2 lbs. red potatoes
- 1/2 tsp salt
- 2 tbsp. olive oil or avocado oil
- 1/4 tsp pepper

Instructions

- Preheat the air fryer to 375 degrees Fahrenheit.
- Wash the potatoes & cut them into bite-sized slices, about 1/2-inch-thick, while the air fryer heats up.
- In a big colander, place the cut potatoes and run them under cold water for around five minutes, turning them a few times.
- Place the potatoes on a few sheets of paper towels to absorb any excess moisture. Using a couple more paper towels, pat them dry until they're completely dry.
- Place the potatoes in a mixing bowl. To coat, toss with the oil & seasonings.
- Pour the potatoes into a hot air fryer and roast for 20 minutes, shaking or turning the basket halfway through.

Frozen onion rings and zucchini

Preparation and Cooking Time

4 minutes

Servings

2 persons

Nutritional facts

303 calories, 15g fat, 3g fiber, 20g carbs, 14g protein

Ingredients

- Six ounces of frozen onion rings
- Salt and pepper
- Zucchini

Instructions

- Heat oven to 350 degrees for around 3 minutes.
- Sprinkle salt and pepper on onion rings and zucchini in the air fryer.
- Cook for 4 minutes and enjoy.

Mexican Air Fryer Sweet Potatoes

Preparation and Cooking Time

20 minutes

Servings

4 persons

Nutritional facts

125 calories, 7g fat, 4g fiber, 28g carbs, 3g protein

Ingredients

- 2 large sweet potatoes
- 2 tablespoons olive oil
- 2 teaspoons lime juice
- 1 tablespoon chili powder
- 1 teaspoon cumin

Instructions

- Sweet potatoes should be peeled and diced into 1-inch pieces.
- Mix sweet potatoes with oil in a mixing bowl.
- Mix in the chili powder and cumin until well combined.
- Mix in the lime juice thoroughly once more.
- Cook for 15-twenty minutes, shaking the basket every 7 to 8 minutes, at 380 degrees F in an air fryer. Sweet potatoes are done when soft enough to be pierced with a fork.
- Enjoy right away or keep refrigerated for up to five days.

Air Fryer Vegetables

Preparation and Cooking Time

22 minutes

Servings

4 persons

Nutritional facts

158 calories, 7g fat, 10g fiber, 19g carbs, 8g protein

Ingredients

- 1 Zucchini
- 1 tsp garlic granules
- 1 tsp Herb de Provence
- Pepper and salt
- 2 Bell peppers
- 1 small head of broccoli
- 1 medium red onion
- 1 tsp smoked paprika
- One and a half tbsp. olive oil
- 2 tbsp. Lemon juice

Instructions

- Wash the vegetables, remove the seeds from the bell peppers, and slice the remaining vegetables into equal halves.

- Add the smoked paprika, garlic granules, Herb de Provence, salt and pepper, olive oil, and lemon juice to a large bowl and stir to blend. Allow 15 to 30 minutes for marinating.
- Heat the air fryer for 3 minutes at 200°C/400°F.
- Fill the air fryer basket halfway with marinated vegetables and spread them out. Cook for about 10-15 minutes, shaking your air fryer basket until the vegetables are soft, crunchy, and roasted to perfection.
- Serve and have fun.

Honey Cinnamon Butternut Squash

Preparation and Cooking Time

25 minutes

Servings

4 persons

Nutritional facts

118 calories, 11g fat, 3g fiber, 23g carbs, 4g protein

Ingredients

- 1 butternut squash, cut into 1-inch chunks
- 1/2 teaspoon of ground cinnamon
- 1/4 teaspoon of fine sea salt
- 2 tablespoons of olive oil
- 2 tablespoons of honey
- 1 teaspoon of honey (for drizzling)

Instructions

- Preheat the air fryer for about five minutes at 400 degrees F.
- Combine the cubed butternut squash, honey, olive oil, ground cinnamon, & sea salt.
- Cook for about 14-16 minutes until the butternut squash mixture is cooked (do not fill more than halfway).
- Place in a serving dish & drizzle with more honey.
- Enjoy right away.

Air-Fryer Roasted Veggies

Preparation and Cooking Time

30 minutes

Servings

4 persons

Nutritional facts

37 calories, 7g fat, 10g fiber, 19g carbs, 8g protein

Ingredients

- ½ cup diced zucchini
- ½ cup diced sweet red pepper
- 2 teaspoons vegetable oil
- ¼ teaspoon salt
- ¼ teaspoon ground black pepper
- ½ cup diced summer squash
- ½ cup diced mushrooms
- ½ cup diced cauliflower
- ½ cup diced asparagus
- 1/4 teaspoon seasoning, or more to taste

Instructions

- Heat the air fryer to 360 degrees Fahrenheit (180 degrees Celsius).
- In a mixing bowl, combine the vegetables, oil, salt, pepper, and any additional seasonings. Toss to coat and then place in the frying basket.

- Cook for ten minutes, stirring after five minutes.

Roasted Spaghetti Squash with Herbs and Garlic

Preparation and Cooking Time

35 minutes

Servings

4 persons

Nutritional facts

176 calories,10g fat, 0.2g fiber, 21g carbs, 2g protein

Ingredients

- 1 medium spaghetti squash
- 1/4 tsp of dried basil
- 1/4 tsp of sea salt
- 2 TBS of extra virgin olive oil
- 1 small clove of garlic, minced
- 1/2 tsp of dried oregano
- 1/4 tsp of freshly ground black pepper

Instructions

- Heat the air fryer to 360°F for 5 minutes.
- Mix the olive oil, garlic, & seasonings in a small mixing bowl.
- Squash should be cut in half lengthwise. Scoop out all of the seeds and toss them out or preserve them to roast later. Coat the squash halves' flesh with the olive oil mixture. Ensure that all inner surfaces are covered.
- Place the squash halves in the basket of the preheated air fryer, skin side down. Cook for 25 to 30 minutes, or until the flesh can be scraped with a fork, after closing the bucket or door.
- Allow the squash to cool on a cutting board or in a big bowl until it is ready to handle. While it's cooling, you can make extra toppings.
- Hold the squash half in one hand while scraping the flesh with a fork once it has cooled. It should be somewhat al-dente and resemble capellini pasta noodles.
- Serve plain or with additional toppings.

Spiced Air Fryer Zucchini and Chickpeas over Brown Rice

Preparation and Cooking Time

15 minutes

Servings

2 persons

Nutritional facts

180 calories, 5g fat, 3.9g fiber, 17g carbs, 5g protein

Ingredients

- 2 cups fresh zucchini, diced into 3/4 to 1-inch pieces
- 1/2 tsp dried oregano
- Pinch or 2 of cayenne pepper (optional)
- 1-1/2 TBS minced fresh herbs (cilantro, mint, or parsley)
- Drizzle of extra virgin olive oil to finish the dish
- 1/2 tsp lemon or lime zest
- 1/4 tsp sea salt (more if needed)
- 1/8 tsp garlic powder
- Sea salt
- 3/4 cup canned chickpeas, drained and rinsed
- 2-1/2 tsp extra virgin olive oil
- 1-1/2 tsp curry powder

- 1 cup cooked brown rice or whole-grain rice medley

Instructions

- In a mixing bowl lined with paper towels, place the diced zucchini. Allow sitting for 10 minutes after lightly seasoning with sea salt.
- Using paper towels, blot the zucchini & chickpeas dry. Combine the chickpeas and zucchini in a mixing bowl. Toss in the zucchini & beans with olive oil to coat them. Combine the curry powder, oregano, salt, garlic, & cayenne pepper in a mixing bowl. To coat evenly, mix everything.
- Heat the air fryer for 3 to 5 minutes at 390°F.
- Set the timer for 4 minutes in the air fryer basket with the zucchini and beans. Shake the bucket every 4 minutes to mix the vegetables. Set the timer for 4 minutes more. Brown the zucchini and make the chickpeas slightly crispy. If necessary, continue to cook, checking every minute.
- Fill a serving bowl halfway with rice. Serve the rice with the roasted zucchini & chickpeas, fresh herbs, and a drizzle of good olive oil on top.
- Served as a side dish with a roast or an entrée rice bowl with diced avocado and roasted red peppers/cherry tomato slices.

Easy Air Fryer Green Beans

Preparation and Cooking Time

12 minutes

Servings

2 persons

Nutritional facts

78 calories, 4g fat, 3g fiber, 7g carbs, 2g protein

Ingredients

- 1/2 pound fresh green beans
- 1/4 tsp freshly ground black pepper
- 2 tsp extra virgin olive oil
- 1/4 tsp sea salt
- Salt and pepper for serving

Instructions

- Green beans should be rinsed in cold water and drained on paper towels. Remove the stems from the beans.
- Preheat the air fryer to 390°F and wait 3 minutes.
- In a bowl, combine the dried & trimmed beans. Toss the beans with oil, salt, & pepper to coat them.
- Fill the fryer basket or crisper plate with as many green beans as fit in a single layer. The beans should be cooked for three minutes to cook the beans to rotate the beans, shake the bucket. Cook for another 3 minutes, or until the beans are cooked. Continue to boil for another 2 to 4 minutes, shaking the bucket occasionally, till the beans are cooked to your liking. If desired, season with salt and pepper and serve warm or as a green bean salad.

Asian Style Air Fryer Green Beans

Preparation and Cooking Time

10 minutes

Servings

2 persons

Nutritional facts

80 calories, 4g fat, 3g fiber, 7g carbs, 2g protein

Ingredients

- 1/2-pound haricot verts (French green beans)
- 1/4 tsp freshly ground pepper

- 1/4 tsp garlic powder
- Juice of 1/4 fresh lime
- 2 tsp toasted sesame oil
- 2 tsp coconut aminos
- 1/2 tsp ground ginger
- 1/4 tsp kosher salt
- Sesame seeds for garnish

Instructions

- Green beans should be rinsed in cold water and drained on paper towels. Remove the stems from the beans. In a bowl, combine the beans.
- Mix the oil, coconut aminos, ginger, salt, pepper, & garlic in a small bowl. Toss the beans in the sauce to coat them.
- Preheat the air fryer to 390°F and wait 3 minutes.
- Fill the fryer basket or crisper plate with as many green beans as fit in a single layer. 3 minutes to cook the beans to rotate the beans, shake the bucket. Cook for another 3 minutes, or until the beans are cooked. Cook till the beans are as soft as you want them to be.
- On a serving plate, arrange the green beans. Serve the beans with a squeeze of lemon juice and a sprinkle of sesame seeds.

Air fried Acorn Squash Crescents

Preparation and Cooking Time

25 minutes

Servings

3 persons

Nutritional facts

110 calories, 6g fat, 3g fiber, 36g carbs, 2g protein

Ingredients

- 1 acorn squash
- 1/2 tsp sea salt
- 1-1/2 TBS avocado oil
- 1 tsp dried thyme leaves
- 1/2 tsp onion powder
- 1/4 tsp freshly ground pepper

Instructions

- Cut the acorn squash in half and remove the stem and root end. Squash should be cut in half lengthwise. Remove the seeds & strings with a spoon and throw them away. Slice the squash in half lengthwise again with the cut side down. Each quarter should be cut into 1/2-inch thick crescents.
- Heat the air fryer for 3 minutes at 370°F.
- Put the crescents in a bowl in the meantime. Combine the oil, thyme, onion powder, salt, & pepper in a mixing bowl. Toss everything together to coat the squash evenly.
- Put the squash in the crisper plate or fryer basket. Cook for five minutes, then give the bucket a good shake. Cook for yet another 5 minutes before shaking one more. Finish cooking for another 5 minutes or until the flesh is softened and cooked through.
- Serve immediately on a serving plate.

Stuffed and Roasted Acorn Squash Halves

Preparation and Cooking Time

35 minutes

Servings

2 persons

Nutritional facts

167 calories, 6g fat, 3g fiber, 36g carbs, 2g protein

Ingredients

- 1 large acorn squash
- 1 TBS of dried cranberries or raisins
- 1 TBS of toasted walnuts, chopped
- freshly ground pepper and Sea salt to taste
- 1 tsp of dried oregano
- 1/2 of a crisp apple, diced
- 1/2 cup of cooked brown rice
- 2 TBS of extra virgin olive oil (divided)
- 2 Italian sausage links (approximately 8 ounces)
- 1 small onion, diced
- 2 cloves garlic, minced

Instructions

- Each squash should be cut in half lengthwise. Remove the seeds & strings with a spoon and throw them away. Two teaspoons of olive oil should be brushed on the cut faces of the squash halves, and it should be seasoned with salt & pepper to taste.
- Place the halves in the air fryer basket, cut side down. Preheat the fryer to 390°F. Cook the squash for 10-12 minutes, or until it has softened slightly. While the squash roasts, prepare the stuffing.
- Then warm 1 teaspoon of the oil in a large skillet over medium-high heat. Cook until the ground meat from the sausages is browned, breaking it up with a spoon as it cooks. Place the cooked sausage on a platter and set aside. Wipe the pan down with a paper towel after discarding the fat.
- Reduce the heat in the pan to medium. In the same pan, add 3 additional teaspoons of oil. Add the onion & cook for 3 to 5 minutes, or until transparent and aromatic. Cook for another 30 to 60 seconds, until the garlic is fragrant, before adding the garlic & oregano to the pan.
- Toss in the diced apple and sausage meat to the pan. Stir in the other ingredients and cook for another 2 minutes. Combine the rice, cranberries, & walnuts in a mixing bowl. To blend, whisk everything together thoroughly. To taste, season with salt and pepper.
- Take the squash halves out of the air fryer and set them aside. Turn them over and spoon equal quantities of stuffing into each bowl. Return the squash to the air fryer and cook for 5 to 7 minutes more, just until the stuffing is warm & golden brown on top. The squash's edges will begin to brown & curl.
- Serve the stuffed squash halves as a main meal with a salad.

Air Fryer Roasted Chickpea Recipe

Preparation and Cooking Time

15 minutes

Servings

4 persons

Nutritional facts

120 calories, 2g fat, 6g fiber, 23g carbs, 7g protein

Ingredients

- 1 (15.5 ounces) can of chickpeas
- One tbsp. extra virgin olive oil or grapeseed oil for sweet blends
- Seasoning blend or tamari

Instructions

- In a colander, drain the chickpeas. Remove the pan juices or cooking liquid by rinsing under cold water. To dry the chickpeas, place them on paper towels.
- Preheat your air fryer for 3 minutes at 390°F.

- Prepare the seasoning blend or tamari mix in a small mixing dish or glass jar.
- Fill a bowl halfway with chickpeas. Coat with oil and toss to coat. Toss the chickpeas with 1/2 of the seasoning mixture & toss again to coat evenly.
- In the air fryer basket, place the seasoned chickpeas. When the chickpeas are done roasting, set the bowl aside to reuse. Shake the bucket to distribute them evenly. Cook approximately 5 minutes with the air fryer closed. Shake the bucket again to flip the chickpeas and cook for another 5 to 7 minutes, or until crispy.
- Transfer the hot, roasted chickpeas to the bowl from the air fryer. Toss the warm chickpeas with the remaining seasoning and toss to coat.

Easy, Crispy Air Fryer Brussels Sprouts

Preparation and Cooking Time
20 minutes

Servings
2 persons

Nutritional facts
97 calories. 4g fat, 5g fiber, 13g carbs, 6g protein

Ingredients
- 8 ounces of fresh Brussels sprouts
- One tbsp. extra virgin olive oil
- 1/2 tsp sea salt
- Half tsp freshly ground black pepper

Instructions
- Drain the Brussels sprouts in a strainer or on paper towels after rinsing them under cold water.
- Preheat the air fryer to 350 degrees Fahrenheit.
- Dry the Brussels sprouts with a paper towel. Remove the stem ends and quarter or cut them into bite-size pieces. In a bowl, toss the Brussels sprouts with olive oil. Then season with salt & pepper to taste.
- Put the Brussels sprouts in the air fryer's basket or crisper plate. Preheat the oven to 350°F and set the timer for 12 minutes. Shake the bucket after 5 minutes to rotate them. Check the tenderness of the sprouts with a fork after 8 minutes. The outer leaves must be browned and crisp, and the interior should be cooked through. If necessary, heat for another 2 to 4 minutes, being careful not to burn the sprouts.
- If desired, season with extra salt and pepper. Serve as a snack or a side dish right away.

Air Fryer Brussels Sprouts with Pancetta and Balsamic

Preparation and Cooking Time
22 minutes

Servings
2 persons

Nutritional facts
80 calories, 8g fat, 3g fiber, 11g carbs, 5g protein

Ingredients
- 8 ounces of fresh Brussels sprouts
- 1-1/2 tsp balsamic vinegar
- 1/4 tsp sea salt
- 3 ounces' pancetta, diced
- 2-1/2 tsp extra virgin olive oil
- 1/4 tsp freshly ground black pepper

Instructions
- Drain the Brussels sprouts in a strainer or on paper towels after rinsing them under cold water. Stir together the oil, vinegar, salt, & pepper in a small bowl.
- Preheat the air fryer to 350 degrees Fahrenheit.
- Dry the Brussels sprouts with a paper towel. Remove the stem ends and quarter or cut them into bite-size pieces. In a bowl, toss the Brussels sprouts. If you didn't buy pre-diced pancetta, cut the slab into little cubes, about 3/8 inches in diameter. Combine the pancetta and sprouts in a mixing bowl. Toss everything in the oil mixture to coat it evenly.
- Put the Brussels sprouts & pancetta in the air fryer's basket or crisper plate. Preheat the oven to 350°F and set the timer for 12 minutes. Shake the bucket after 5 minutes to rotate everything. Check the tenderness of the sprouts with a fork after 8 minutes. The outer leaves must be browned and crisp, and the interior should be cooked through. If necessary, heat for another 2 to 4 minutes, being careful not to burn the sprouts.
- If preferred, season with additional salt, pepper, and a little drop of balsamic.

Air Fryer Ginger and Dill Roasted Carrots

Preparation and Cooking Time
15 minutes

Servings
4 persons

Nutritional facts
124 calories, 6g fat, 3g fiber, 19g carbs, 1g protein

Ingredients
- 6 whole medium carrots, washed and trimmed
- 1/2 tsp sea salt
- 1/2 tsp freshly ground pepper
- 1 TBS extra virgin olive oil
- 1 tsp dried dill
- 1/2 tsp ground ginger
- 2 lime wedges for serving

Instructions
- Preheat the air fryer for 3 minutes at 390°F.
- Cut the carrots into one-and-a-half-inch thick pieces diagonally.
- Combine the oil, dill, ginger, salt, & pepper in a large mixing bowl. Toss the carrot pieces in the bowl to evenly coat them.
- Set a timer for 10 minutes and place the prepared carrots in a single layer in the air fryer basket. Carrots should be cooked for 4 minutes. To rotate the carrots, stir them. Cook for another 4 minutes, then test with a fork to see if the potatoes are soft. If the texture isn't just right, cook for a couple of minutes more.
- Squeeze lemon juice over the carrots and place them in a serving bowl. These can be served with curried cauliflower bites.

Crispy Air Fryer Kale Chips (Vegan)

Preparation and Cooking Time
15 minutes

Servings
2 persons

Nutritional facts
102 calories, 3g fat, 1.5g fiber, 7g carbs, 2.5g protein

Ingredients
- 1 bunch fresh kale, washed and dried

- One and a half tbsp. extra virgin olive oil
- 1/4 tsp sea salt
- Quarter tsp of seasoning blend of your choice

Instructions

- After washing the kale, pat it dry with paper towels or spin it in a salad spinner. Remove the leaves from the inner stems. The stems can be discarded or used to make soup broth. Use a sharp knife to cut the leaves into 3" pieces. Place in a mixing bowl.
- Heat the air fryer for 5 minutes at 375°F.
- Toss the greens with olive oil to coat them. Toss in the seasonings and toss again to distribute them evenly. Insert a full teaspoon of nutritional yeast if using.
- Dress the kale and place them in the fryer basket. Arrange them in an even layer. If you have a rack insert, you can use it to keep the greens from flying around. Then air fry for two minutes after closing the bucket. You can cook in two batches if the air fryer is on the smaller side.
- Shake the bucket or turn the chips over after 2 minutes. Close the fryer and cook for another 2 to 3 minutes, just until the chips are dry & crispy.
- Put the chips on a serving platter & serve immediately once they have finished cooking.

Air Fryer Dehydrated Sweet Banana Chips

Preparation and Cooking Time

7 hours 10 minutes

Servings

4 persons

Nutritional facts

380 calories, 1g fat, 3g fiber, 25g carbs, 2g protein

Ingredients

- 2 ripe & firm bananas
- Two tsp fresh lemon juice
- Pinch of sea salt (optional)

Instructions

- Peel the bananas & cut them into 1/4-inch thick pieces diagonally. Put the slices in a bowl with the lemon juice and toss to coat. If used, season with salt. The lemon juice will aid in the preservation of the bananas' color.
- Place half of the banana slices in a single layer on the air fryer's crisper plate or basket. Fill the wire rack with the remaining banana slices in a single layer above the first layer of bananas.
- Preheat the air fryer to 135 degrees Fahrenheit & set the timer for 8 hours. After 6 hours, check on the bananas. You can either stop dehydrating at this stage if you want your chips to be a little chewy, or keep going until they're absolutely dry and crisp.
- These can be enjoyed as a snack or added to granola.

Air Fryer Tostones – Plantain Chips

Preparation and Cooking Time

15 minutes

Servings

2 persons

Nutritional facts

256 calories, 6g fat, 1g fiber, 14g carbs, 1g protein

Ingredients

- 1 large green plantain
- 1 cup water (optional)
- 3 TBS extra virgin olive oil, divided
- 2 tsp kosher or coarse sea salt

Instructions

- To be safe, preheat the Air fryer for 3 minutes at 390°F and then set the timer for half an hour.
- Plantain ends should be trimmed. Make a vertical slit in the skin of the plantain on two sides, just down to the flesh. Remove the skin and throw it away. Plantains should be cut into 1" thick slices. Brush half of the olive oil on both sides of the pieces.
- Put the slices in the crisper plate or the frying basket.
- These should be cooked for five minutes.
- Place the cooked plantain pieces on a chopping board that has been cleaned. Gently break each one into 1/4-inch-thick rounds with the flat side of a meat mallet or a tostone press.
- Speedily dip the rounds in the water & drain on a paper towel for softer tostones. For crunchier tostones, skip this step.
- Brush the remaining olive oil on both sides of the plantain chips. Return them to the air fryer & cook for another 4 minutes. Turn the chips over again and heat for another 3 minutes, or until golden brown and crunchy on the outside.
- Place the tostones on a platter & season both sides with salt. Tostones can be served with blackened tilapia & mango salsa or as a snack with guacamole for dipping.

Sweet Plantain Bites

Preparation and Cooking Time

20 minutes

Servings

2 persons

Nutritional facts

148 calories, 6g fat, 1g fiber, 14g carbs, 1g protein

Ingredients

- 2 ripe plantains
- 1 tsp of coarse salt
- 2 tablespoons of melted coconut oil, divided
- 1/4 tsp of ground cinnamon

Instructions

- To be safe, preheat the Air fryer for 3 minutes at 380°F and set the timer for half an hour.
- Plantain ends should be trimmed. Make a vertical slit in the skin of the plantain on two sides, just down to the flesh. Remove the skin and throw it away. Plantains should be cut into 1" thick slices. Put the plantain chunks in a bowl and drizzle 1 tablespoon of coconut oil over them. Toss to coat evenly.
- Put the bites in the crisper plate or the frying basket. Cook for an additional 8 minutes.
- Flip the plantains in the air fryer. Cover the bits with the remaining tablespoon of coconut oil. Cook for a further 7 minutes, or till golden brown and tender.
- Butcher's paper should be used to line a serving bowl. While the plantains are still warm, toss them in the bowl with the salt & cinnamon, being sure to get some on each bite.
- Plantains can be served as a side dish with marinated pork chops & vegetables or as a dessert with napkins.

Quick and Easy Air Fryer Carrots

Preparation and Cooking Time

15 minutes

Servings

4 persons

Nutritional facts

80 calories, 6g fat, 3g fiber, 19g carbs, 1g protein

Ingredients

- 6 whole medium carrots, washed and trimmed
- Half tsp sea salt
- One tbsp. extra virgin olive oil
- 1/2 tsp freshly ground pepper

Instructions

- Preheat the air fryer for 3 minutes at 390°F.
- Carrots should be cut in half through the middle. Both halves should be cut in half lengthwise. Cut the thicker sections in half lengthwise once more. You will get planks or sticks will be the result. Cut the carrots into bite-sized pieces.
- Place the carrots in a large mixing bowl and drizzle with olive oil. Then season to taste with salt and pepper, then toss to coat evenly.
- Set a timer for 10 minutes and place the oiled and seasoned carrots in a single layer in the air fryer basket. Carrots should be cooked for 4 minutes. To rotate the carrots, shake the bucket or stir them. Cook for another 4 minutes, then test with a fork to see if the potatoes are soft. If the texture isn't just right, cook for two more minutes.
- On a serving platter, arrange the carrots. Serve right away with your main dish. Make the meatloaf ahead of time and keep it warm while the carrots roast.

Air Fryer Roasted Cauliflower

Preparation and Cooking Time

15 minutes

Servings

4 persons

Nutritional facts

98 calories, 2g fat, 1.2g fiber, 9g carbs, 5g protein

Ingredients

- 1 medium Cauliflower, cut into florets
- 1 teaspoon Onion Powder
- 2 tablespoons Olive Oil
- 1 teaspoon Garlic Powder
- Salt and Pepper, to taste

Instructions

- Drizzle olive oil over cauliflower florets in a large mixing bowl. Toss in the garlic powder, onion powder, salt, and pepper until well combined.
- Place the cauliflower in the air fryer basket in a single layer, ensuring it doesn't overlap. Cook for 7-10 minutes at 180°C/350°F, shaking the basket every few minutes, till the cauliflower is cooked through and golden brown around the edges.

Crunchy Roasted Peas Air Fryer

Preparation and Cooking Time

25 minutes

Servings

1 person

Nutritional facts

87 calories, 5g fat, 3g fiber, 12g carbs, 4g protein

Ingredients

- One cup Frozen Peas
- 1 teaspoon Olive Oil
- One teaspoon Garlic Powder
- Salt, to taste

Instructions

- Peas should be defrosted before being dried with a paper towel. Combine them in a mixing bowl with olive oil, garlic powder, and salt.
- Pour peas into the air fryer basket & cook for 15 minutes at 180°C / 350°F. To achieve consistent cooking, shake the basket every few minutes and check on your peas frequently. When they're nice and crispy, they're done.

Air Fryer Potato Wedges

Preparation and Cooking Time

25 minutes

Servings

2 persons

Nutritional facts

226 calories, 17g fat, 6g fiber, 25g carbs, 10g protein

Ingredients

- 2 Potatoes
- 1 tablespoon Olive Oil
- 1 teaspoon Paprika
- ½ teaspoon Garlic Powder
- Salt, to taste

Instructions

- Heat the air fryer to 200 degrees Celsius (390 degrees Fahrenheit).
- Place potatoes on a chopping board after properly washing them (no need to peel them). Each potato should be cut in half lengthwise and then in half again lengthwise. Next, cut each piece in half lengthwise once more. Each potato should yield eight wedges of similar thickness and length.
- Combine the potato wedges, oil, paprika, and garlic powder in a large mixing bowl. In the air fryer basket or tray, arrange wedges in a single layer, leaving space between them.
- Cook for 20 minutes, or till golden and crisp, flipping halfway through. Serve immediately with a pinch of salt.

Air Fryer Crispy Potatoes

Preparation and Cooking Time

25 minutes

Servings

2 persons

Nutritional facts

181 calories, 17g fat, 6g fiber, 25g carbs, 10g protein

Ingredients

- 2 Roasting Potatoes, skin on & diced
- 1 teaspoon of Paprika
- ½ teaspoon of Cayenne Pepper
- ½ Red Capsicum or Bell Pepper, diced
- ½ Brown or Yellow Onion, diced
- 1 tablespoon of Olive Oil
- 1 teaspoon of Garlic Powder
- Salt, to taste

Instructions

- Heat the air fryer to 200 degrees Celsius (390 degrees Fahrenheit).
- Combine potatoes, paprika, garlic powder, cayenne pepper, and olive oil in a large mixing bowl.

- Fill the air fryer basket halfway with potatoes and cook for fifteen minutes, shaking the basket every few minutes.
- In the meantime, mash the bell pepper & onion together in the same mixing bowl as the potatoes.
- Place the bell peppers and onions on top of the potatoes in the air fryer basket and cook for a further five minutes, shaking the basket halfway through. At this stage, the potatoes ought to be crisp and golden, but if they aren't, simmer for a few minutes longer.
- Season with salt and pepper and serve right away.

Crispy Air Fryer Chickpeas

Preparation and Cooking Time

20 minutes

Servings

1 person

Nutritional facts

180 calories, 2g fat, 6g fiber, 23g carbs, 7g protein

Ingredients

- 400g of Canned Chickpeas
- ½ teaspoon of Paprika
- ⅛ teaspoon of Cayenne Pepper
- 1 tablespoon of Olive Oil
- ¼ teaspoon of Garlic Powder
- ¼ teaspoon of Onion Power
- ¼ teaspoon of Cumin
- ¼ teaspoon of Salt

Instructions

- Heat your air fryer to 200°C/390°F.
- Using paper towels, dry a can of chickpeas after draining and rinsing them. It's fine if some of the skins come off in the process; don't fret about removing them all at once.
- Mix the chickpeas, oil, spices, and salt together in a mixing bowl.
- Then cook for around fifteen minutes, or until the seasoned chickpeas are lovely and crispy. To ensure that they all cook evenly, shake the basket every few minutes. From the ten-minute mark onward, keep an eye on them because you don't want them to overcook, and each air fryer is different.
- Serve right away, or cool completely before pouring onto a dish and storing it in an airtight container at room temperature.

Air Fryer Sweet & Salty Kale Chips

Preparation and Cooking Time

8 minutes

Servings

2 persons

Nutritional facts

121 calories, 3g fat, 1.5g fiber, 7g carbs, 2.5g protein

Ingredients

- Half bunch of Kale (2 cups of kale leaves, stems removed)
- 1 tablespoon Olive Oil
- Two tbsp. Maple Syrup

Instructions

- Preheat the air fryer to 180°C/350°F by using the preheat setting or operating it at that temperature for 5 minutes.
- Kale should be well washed and dried. Remove the stems from the kale leaves and cut the leaves into chip-sized pieces.

- In a bowl, combine the kale leaves with the olive oil as well as massage the oil into the kale, helping to ensure that every piece is well covered. After that, add the maple syrup & repeat the process. Then season with a pinch of salt and pepper.
- Place the kale leaves in the air fryer basket that has been warmed. Slide the basket into the air fryer & cook for 2-3 minutes at 180C / 350F, shaking the basket every minute. When the kale is crispy & slightly golden brown, it's ready. Cooking should be done with caution because it can easily burn.
- Take the chips out of the air fryer basket & eat them right away.

Air Fryer Frozen French Fries

Preparation and Cooking Time

20 minutes

Servings

2 persons

Nutritional facts

419 calories, 17g fat, 6g fiber, 25g carbs, 10g protein

Ingredients

- Five hundred grams frozen French Fries (or less)
- Salt, to taste

Instructions

- Heat your air fryer to 200°C/390°F by using the preheat setting or running it at that temperature for 5 minutes.
- Fry for fifteen minutes, just until the fries are crispy and brown, shaking the basket every five minutes to ensure the fries cook evenly. Serve hot with your preferred sauce and a pinch of salt.

Air Fryer Roasted Almonds

Preparation and Cooking Time

10 minutes

Servings

1 person

Nutritional facts

103 calories, 2g fat, 3g fiber, 7g carbs, 7g protein

Ingredients

- One cup Plain Almonds

Instructions

- Heat the air fryer for 2 minutes at 180°C/350°F.
- Cook for five minutes with the almonds in a single layer in the basket. Give the basket a good shake as well as continue cooking until they're done, monitoring every minute.
- Transfer to a bowl to cool completely. Store them in a container once they've cooled.

Vegan Air Fryer Breakfast Potatoes

Preparation and Cooking Time

40 minutes

Servings

8 persons

Nutritional facts

165 calories, 7g fat, 4g fiber, 28g carbs, 3g protein

Ingredients

- 3 lb. potatoes, diced
- 15 oz. mushrooms, diced
- 1 ½ cups or 1-14 oz. can black beans, drained
- 2 bell peppers, any color, diced
- 1 onion, diced

- Spinach and avocado for serving

Instructions

- Place the potatoes in the air fryer basket. Cook for 20 minutes at 400°F (205°C), shaking the basket frequently.
- Cook for another 10 to 15 minutes until the potatoes are tender or crispy, depending on your preference.

Popcorn Tofu

Preparation and Cooking Time

27 minutes

Servings

4 persons

Nutritional facts

261 calories, 11g fat, 5g fiber, 25g carbs, 7g protein

Ingredients

- 14 oz. extra firm tofu in water drained and pressed
- 1 Tablespoon Dijon mustard
- 2 teaspoon garlic powder
- ¾ cup unsweetened dairy-free milk more if needed
- 1.5 cup panko bread crumbs gluten-free if needed
- 2 teaspoon onion powder
- ½ teaspoon salt
- ½ cup quinoa flour
- ½ cup cornmeal
- 3 Tablespoons nutritional yeast
- 2 Tablespoons Better Than Bouillon Vegetarian No Chicken Base
- ½ teaspoon pepper

Instructions

- Fill the air fryer basket with as many nuggets as it will hold. You'll have to do this in several batches because you don't want the basket to become too crowded. Preheat the air fryer to 350°F and cook for 12 minutes. Halfway through, you need to give the basket a good shake.

Healthy Vegan Onion Rings

Preparation and Cooking Time

40 minutes

Servings

6 persons

Nutritional facts

63 calories, 10g fat, 2g fiber, 10g carbs, 4g protein

Ingredients

- 2–3 Yellow Onions
- 1/4 tsp of Turmeric
- 1/2 cup of Flour
- 2/3 cup of Unsweetened Plant Milk
- 1/2 tsp of Paprika
- 1/2 tsp of Salt

Instructions

- Preheat the oven to 400°F and bake the onion rings for 8-10 minutes. To avoid overloading the basket, fry the Onion Rings in many batches. Serve hot.

Vegan Crunch wrap

Preparation and Cooking Time

13 minutes

Servings

1 person

Nutritional facts

519 calories, 5g fat, 1.7g fiber, 15g carbs, 11g protein

Ingredients

- 1 regular size gluten-free tortilla
- 2-3 iceberg lettuce leaves
- 2 tablespoons of guacamole
- 2 tablespoons of refried pinto beans
- 2 tablespoons of grated vegan cheese
- A small corn tortilla
- 2-3 tablespoons of salsa

Instructions

- The oven should be heated to 325 °F.
- Assemble Each crunch wrap is to be assembled by placing first large regular tortilla, beans or meat, grated cheese, small corn tortilla, salsa, whole iceberg lettuce leaves, guacamole, or avocado slices.
- The Taco Crunch Wrap should be cooked for 6 minutes at 350°F.
- It should be baked at 325 °F for 5-8 minutes, till warmed through as well as slightly crispy.
- It should be served with dairy-free sour cream and guacamole for dipping.

Smoky Air Fryer Chickpeas

Preparation and Cooking Time

23 minutes

Servings

3 persons

Nutritional facts

165 calories, 2g fat, 6g fiber, 23g carbs, 7g protein

Ingredients

- 1 15 oz. can of chickpeas
- ½ teaspoon of granulated garlic
- ¼ teaspoon of granulated onion
- ½ teaspoon of sea salt, more to taste
- 1 tablespoon of sunflower oil
- 2 tablespoons of lemon juice
- ¾ teaspoon of smoked paprika
- ½ teaspoon of ground cumin
- ⅛ teaspoon of cayenne pepper

Instructions

- Air Fryer should be set to 390 ° F.
- Put the chickpeas in the basket & fry for fifteen minutes till dry. The basket should be shaken once at the midway mark.
- You can make the seasoning during the cooking process. Insert the lemon, oil, and all seasonings into a medium bowl, and stir to combine well.
- The fried chickpeas should be carefully added to the bowl of seasonings. Whisk to combine well.
- Transfer the seasoned chickpeas to the air fryer basket and set to 360 ° F. They should be cooked for 2-3 minutes till desired crispiness is achieved. The basket should be shaken once at the midway mark.
- Add and adjust seasoning if needed. Allow to cool completely before storing.

Small Batch Brownies in the Air Fryer

Preparation and Cooking Time

30 minutes

Servings

4 persons

Nutritional facts

225.30 calories, 6g fat, 2g fiber, 20g carbs, 3g protein

Ingredients

- ½ cup of whole wheat pastry flour
- ¼ cup of cocoa powder
- 1 tablespoon of ground flax seeds
- ¼ teaspoon of salt
- ¼ cup of non-dairy milk
- ¼ cup of aquafaba
- ½ teaspoon of vanilla extract
- ½ cup of vegan sugar
- ¼ cup of chopped walnuts, pecans, hazelnuts, mini vegan chocolate chips, shredded coconut

Instructions

- In one bowl, combine the dry ingredients. Then, in a large measuring cup, combine the wet ingredients. Combine the wet and dry ingredients and stir well.
- Mix in the mix-in(s) of choice once more.
- Preheat the air fryer to 350 degrees Fahrenheit. To keep a 5-inch cake or pie round pan fully oil-free, spray it with oil or line it with parchment paper.
- In the fryer basket, place the pan. The cooking time is 20 minutes. If the middle isn't well set or a knife inserted in the center doesn't come out clean, cook for another 5 minutes and repeat. The time will vary according to the size of the pan and the type of air fryer you have.

Portobello Mushroom Pizzas with Hummus

Preparation and Cooking Time

50 minutes

Servings

4 persons

Nutritional facts

83 calories, 12g fat, 2g fiber, 22g carbs, 12g protein

Ingredients

- 2 cups of finely chopped potatoes
- 1/4 teaspoon of sea salt
- 1/8 teaspoon of ground black pepper
- 1 teaspoon of extra-virgin olive oil
- 1 clove of garlic
- 4 cups of coarsely chopped kale
- 1/8 cup of almond milk
- Vegetable oil

Instructions

- In a big saucepan of boiling water, place the potatoes. Then cook for about 30 minutes, or until the vegetables are soft.
- Heat the oil in a large skillet over medium-high heat. Sauté the garlic until it turns golden brown. Now you need to sauté for 2 - 3 minutes with the kale. Place in a large mixing bowl.
- Drain the potatoes and place them in a medium mixing bowl. Mash the potatoes with a fork or a potato masher after adding the milk, salt, & pepper. Combine the potatoes and the cooked kale in a large mixing bowl. Heat the air fryer for 5 minutes at 390°F.
- Make 1-inch nuggets out of the potato & kale mixture. Spritz the vegetable oil into the air fryer basket. Put the nuggets in the air fryer & cook for 12 to 15 minutes, shaking after 6 minutes, until golden brown.

Vegan pulled pork in the air fryer

Preparation and Cooking Time

21 minutes

Servings

2 persons

Nutritional facts

136 calories, 9g fat, 0.1g fiber, 8g carbs, 18g protein

Ingredients

- 1 cup warm water
- One teaspoon vegetarian Better Than Bouillon no chicken base
- 1 cup Soy Curls
- Quarter cup BBQ sauce plus more for drizzling

Instructions

- Soak Soy Curls in water and bouillon for 10 minutes in a bowl. Drain them in a mesh sieve, squeezing out as much water as possible.
- Transfer them to a bowl and shred the hydrated Curls by hand, as if you were shredding string cheese.
- At 400 degrees, air-fry the Soy Curls for three minutes.
- Remove them from the air fryer, return them to the bowl, and whisk in ¼ cup of BBQ sauce. Make sure to coat all of the curls evenly.
- Return the air fryer to its original position. At 400 degrees, air fry for 5 minutes, pausing twice to shake the pan.

Tofu and Red Potato

Preparation and Cooking Time

35 minutes

Servings

3 persons

Nutritional facts

400 calories, 11g fat, 4g fiber, 29g carbs, 11g protein

Ingredients

- 1 block tofu - chopped into 1" pieces
- ½ teaspoon onion powder
- ½ cup chopped onion
- 2 ½ cups chopped red potato - 1" cubes, 2-3 potatoes
- 1 tablespoon olive oil
- 2 tablespoons soy sauce
- ½ teaspoon garlic powder
- 4 cups broccoli florets
- 1 tablespoon olive oil
- 1 teaspoon turmeric

Instructions

- Toss the tofu, soy sauce, olive oil, turmeric, garlic powder, onion powder, & onion in a medium mixing bowl. Allow to marinade for a while.
- Toss the potatoes in the olive oil in a separate small bowl and air fry at 400F for fifteen minutes, shaking once around seven to eight minutes into frying.

- Shake the potatoes one more before adding the tofu and storing any remaining marinade. Start the air fryer while the tofu & potatoes cook at 370 degrees for another 15 minutes.
- Toss the broccoli in the reserved marinade while the tofu is cooking. Add a little more soy sauce if it isn't enough to cover the broccoli completely. Add the broccoli to the air fryer 5 minutes before the end of the cooking time.

Air Fryer Fries - Oil-Free and Vegan

Preparation and Cooking Time

36 minutes

Servings

3 persons

Nutritional facts

63 calories, 8 g fat, 6g fiber, 25g carbs, 10g protein

Ingredients

- 3 medium red potatoes
- ¼ tsp paprika
- ¼ tsp basil
- 1 tsp garlic powder
- 1 tsp onion powder
- ¼ tsp chili powder
- salt to taste

Instructions

- The potatoes should be peeled and rinsed.
- Fries are made by slicing the potatoes.
- Toss the fries with the rest of the ingredients in a large mixing bowl.
- Place the fries in the basket of your air fryer. Cook for 25-30 minutes at 400°F, stirring every five to ten minutes.
- Serve with ketchup or gravy or nacho cheese sauce.

Oats with Vegan Bread

Preparation and Cooking Time

9 minutes

Servings

10-12 persons

Nutritional facts

77 calories, 3g fat, 1.1g fiber, 25g carbs, 4g protein

Ingredients

- 1 cup (99g) rolled oats
- 8 pieces of whole-grain vegan bread, regular or cinnamon raisin
- ¾ cup nondairy milk (plain or vanilla)
- 1 cup (113g) pecans or nut of your choice
- 2 tablespoons (12g) ground flax seed
- 1 teaspoon (2g) ground cinnamon
- maple syrup, for serving

Instructions

- To make the topping, pulse the oats, almonds, flax seed, and cinnamon in a food processor until they resemble bread crumbs. Make sure not to over-blend. Fill a shallow pan with enough sauce to dip the bread slices in.
- In a second container, pour the nondairy milk, soak one or two pieces of bread for about 15 seconds, then turn and soak the other side. You don't want it to become mushy if you leave it too long.

- Fill the air fryer basket with the amount that will fit without overlapping. Cook for 3 minutes at 350 degrees, then flip the bread & cook for another 3 minutes.
- Continue until all of the bread has been coated and cooked.
- Serve with maple syrup on top.

Za'atar with Kale

Preparation and Cooking Time

25 minutes

Servings

4 persons

Nutritional facts

81 calories, 3g fat, 1.5g fiber, 7g carbs, 2.5g protein

Ingredients

- 1 large bunch kale, de-stemmed, washed and spun - torn into bite-size pieces
- 1 tbsp. olive oil
- 1-2 tbsp. za'atar seasoning
- ½ - 1 tsp sea salt

Instructions

- Drizzle olive oil over cleaned and dry kale in a large mixing dish.
- Lightly massage the olive oil into the kale with your hands until evenly coated.
- Mix in the seasonings thoroughly.
- Put kale in the air fryer's basket set to 170 degrees C in batches. When the edges of the chips are brown but not scorched, they are ready.
- If you don't have an air fryer, you may bake these on a parchment-lined baking dish at 170 degrees C in your oven. In a preheated oven, it should take about 10-15 minutes.

Potatoes with Mushrooms

Preparation and Cooking Time

35 minutes

Servings

4 persons

Nutritional facts

378 calories, 7g fat, 4g fiber, 28g carbs, 3g protein

Ingredients

- 4 medium Idaho russet potatoes cut in half, then into planks
- ¼ tsp granulated garlic
- ¼ tsp ground black pepper
- 15 ml olive oil
- ½ cup (118 ml) water
- 8 g tapioca starch
- 225 g chopped mushrooms
- 10 ml soy sauce
- 6 cups (1.4 L) boiling water for soaking the potatoes
- 2 tsp (10 ml) olive oil (or use aquafaba)
- 3 g Cajun seasoning blend
- ½ tsp smoked paprika
- ½ tsp salt
- 10 ml vegan Worcestershire sauce

Instructions

- In a heatproof bowl or saucepan, place the cut fries. Bring the water to a boil before pouring it over the fries to cover them completely.

- Allow 15 minutes for the potatoes to soak in the boiling water before straining into a strainer over the sink. Toss the fries in the oil (or aquafaba), Cajun seasoning, paprika, salt, garlic, and black pepper once they're mostly dry.
- Place the potato mixture in the air fryer basket & cook for 5 minutes at 350°F (177°C). After that, shake the basket & cook for another 5 minutes.
- Cook for 5 minutes at 390°F (200°C), then shake the basket & cook for another 5 minutes.
- In a large skillet over medium heat, heat 1 tablespoon olive oil while the potatoes are cooking. When the pan is hot, add the mushrooms & cook until they release their juices. Cook for another 2 minutes after adding the soy sauce & Worcestershire sauce.
- Whisk in the tapioca starch after adding the water. Increase the heat to medium-high and continue to cook until the sauce thickens.

Ravioli with Marinara

Preparation and Cooking Time

23 minutes

Servings

4 persons

Nutritional facts

150 calories, 19g fat, 4g fiber, 29g carbs, 11g protein

Ingredients

- ½ cup of panko bread crumbs
- Pinch salt & pepper
- ¼ cup of aquafaba liquid
- 8 ounces of vegan ravioli
- 2 teaspoons of nutritional yeast flakes
- 1 teaspoon of dried basil
- 1 teaspoon of dried oregano
- 1 teaspoon of garlic powder
- Spritz cooking spray
- ½ cup of marinara for dipping

Instructions

- Panko bread crumbs, dried basil, garlic powder, nutritional yeast flakes, dried oregano, salt, & pepper are combined on a dish.
- Place aquafaba in a separate small bowl.
- Dredge ravioli in bread crumb mixture after dipping in aquafaba and shaking off excess liquid. Make sure the ravioli is completely covered. In the air fryer basket, place the ravioli. Continue breading the ravioli until they are all breaded. In the air fryer, be cautious not to overlap the ravioli too much so that they brown evenly.
- Using frying spray, coat the ravioli.
- Preheat the air fryer to 390°F.They should be cooked for6 minutes in the air fryer. Then carefully turn ravioli to the other side. Then air fry for another 2 minutes.
- Remove the ravioli from the air fryer & serve immediately with a warm marinara sauce for dipping.

Yummy Rolls

Preparation and Cooking Time

30 minutes

Servings

14 persons

Nutritional facts

327 calories, 20g fat, 0.4g fiber, 3g carbs, 9g protein

Ingredients

- 1 (20 ounces) can jackfruit, drained
- 6-7 thin slices vegan Swiss cheese, optional / omitted for oil-free
- 2 large dill pickles, chopped
- ⅓ cup oil-free Vegan Thousand Island Dressing, plus more for dipping
- 1 small sweet onion, peeled and diced
- 2 cloves garlic, peeled and minced
- 12-14 vegan wonton wrappers (rice paper wraps for gluten-free)

Instructions

- Shred the jackfruit using forks. Set aside to marinate in Vegan Thousand Island Dressing.
- Sauté onion and garlic in a little water in a saucepan over medium heat until softened and transparent. Remove from the heat and stir in the jackfruit mixture.
- Make a diamond shape with a wrap. In the bottom corner, place 2 teaspoons of the jackfruit mixture. If using, top with a one-half piece of cheese and one tablespoon minced pickles.
- Pickle juice should be delicately brushed on each roll.
- It should be air-fried without oil at 350°F in the oil-free air fryer. Arrange the items in a single layer. It should be cooked for five minutes. Remove the rolls and shake the basket. Return to the air fryer for 3 more minutes, or until golden brown and crisp.
- Preheat the oven to 350 degrees Fahrenheit. Arrange the rolls in a single layer on a parchment-lined baking sheet. Preheat oven to 350°F and bake for 7 minutes. Remove the pan from the oven and turn it over. Return to the oven for another 5 to 7 minutes, or till golden brown and crisp.
- It can be served warm with a dollop of Vegan Thousand Island Dressing on top.

Vegan pulled pork

Preparation and Cooking Time

21 minutes

Servings

2 persons

Nutritional facts

136 calories, 9g fat, 0.1g fiber, 8g carbs, 18g protein

Ingredients

- 1 cup warm water
- 1 cup Soy Curls
- 1 teaspoon vegetarian Better Than Bouillon no chicken base
- ¼ cup BBQ sauce plus more for drizzling

Instructions

- The Soy Curls should be air-fried for 3 minutes at 400 degrees F.
- Remove them from the air fryer, return them to the bowl, and whisk in 1/4 cup of BBQ sauce. Make sure to coat all of the curls evenly.
- Return the air fryer to its original position. At 400 degrees F, air fry for 5 minutes, pausing twice to shake the pan.

Air Fryer Peanut Butter Banana Dessert Bites

Preparation and Cooking Time

21 minutes

Servings

12 persons

Nutritional facts

179 calories, 2g fat, 1.2g fiber, 10g carbs, 2g protein

Ingredients

- 12 Won Ton Wrappers
- Half cup Peanut Butter
- 1 large Banana (sliced)
- One to two tsp Vegetable Oil (or Coconut, Avocado Oil)
- Oil Mister

Instructions

- Slice the banana and toss it in a bowl of water with a squeeze of lemon juice (to keep from browning).
- In the center of the Won Ton Wrapper, put one banana slice and 1 tsp of peanut butter. Brush water along the Won Ton Wrapper's edges. Squeeze the opposite corners together. Fold and squeeze the remaining opposing edges.
- Place in an Air Fryer Basket that has been properly prepared. Oil should be sprayed liberally.
- Preheat the oven to 380°F and cook for 6 minutes.
- It should be served with a scoop of Vanilla Ice Cream as well as a cinnamon-sugar sprinkling.

Tofu Rancheros with Little Face Salsa and Veggies

Preparation and Cooking Time

4 minutes

Servings

4 persons

Nutritional facts

468 calories, 29g fat, 6g fiber, 24g carbs, 29g protein

Ingredients

- 1/2 teaspoon of smoked paprika
- 1/4 teaspoon of salt, or to taste
- 1 15.5 ounces can of organic black beans
- 20 container of High Protein Tofu
- 1 teaspoon of ground cumin powder
- 1 teaspoon of ground chili powder
- 1/4 cup of Little Face Big Taste Jalapeno Cilantro Salsa
- 1/3 cup of grated carrot
- 1/3 cup of grated zucchini
- 1/3 cup of grated yellow squash
- 1/8 teaspoon of salt
- pinch black pepper
- 1/8 to 1/4 teaspoon of liquid smoke
- 1/8 teaspoon of jalapeno powder
- 1/8 teaspoon of cumin powder
- 4 large flour
- 1 cup of shredded vegan cheese

Instructions

- Combine the tofu cubes, cumin, chili powder, smoked paprika, & salt in a mixing bowl.
- Unless your model doesn't require it, preheat the air fryer to 390°. Add the coated tofu to the air fryer basket once it's hot.
- Set the timer for 5 minutes and shake or mix the tofu when it's done. Continue for another 5 minutes.
- In a small mixing bowl, combine all of the ingredients.

- Preheat the oven to 350 degrees F and place 2 tortillas on a baking sheet. Then a quarter cup of vegan cheese is sprinkled (or smeared) on top of each tortilla. Next
- 1/4 of the salsa beans should be placed in the center of the tortilla & baked for 15 minutes. The beans will be warm, and the tortilla will be crunchy.
- Add the Spiced Crusted Tofu, shredded veggie topping, chopped tomatoes, or any extra veggies you'd like to pile on, such as avocado or shredded lettuce, once everything is warm.
- Finish with a generous tablespoon of Little Face Salsa.

Air Fried Spicy Cauliflower Stir-Fry

Preparation and Cooking Time

30 minutes

Servings

4 persons

Nutritional facts

93 calories, 2g fat, 1.2g fiber, 9g carbs, 5g protein

Ingredients

- 1 head cauliflower cut into florets
- 1 tablespoon rice vinegar
- ½ teaspoon coconut sugar
- ¾ cup onion white, thinly sliced
- 5 cloves garlic finely sliced
- 1 ½ tablespoons tamari or gluten-free tamari
- 1 tablespoon Sriracha or other favorite hot sauce
- 2 scallions for garnish

Instructions

- In the air fryer, place the cauliflower.
- Preheat the oven to 350 degrees Fahrenheit. Cook for ten minutes.
- In the air fryer basket, stir in the sliced onion and simmer for another 10 minutes.
- Stir in the garlic and simmer for another 5 minutes.
- Combine rice vinegar, soy sauce, coconut sugar, salt, Sriracha, and pepper in a small bowl.
- Stir the mixture into the cauliflower. Cook for another 5 minutes.
- To serve, scatter-sliced scallions on top as a garnish.

Air Fried Pickles

Preparation and Cooking Time

40 minutes

Servings

4 persons

Nutritional facts

43 calories, 1g fat, 1g fiber, 16g carbs, 3g protein

Ingredients

- 10 oz. Tofu
- 1 tsp Red Wine Vinegar
- 1/2 tsp Kosher Salt
- 10 Dill Pickle Spears
- 1 cup Unsweetened Almond Milk
- 1 tbsp. Lemon Juice
- 1 tbsp. Cornmeal
- 1 tbsp. Nutritional Yeast
- 1 tsp Garlic Powder

- 1 tsp Onion Powder
- 1 cup Flour
- 2 tbsp. Cornstarch
- 1/4 cup Prepared Horseradish
- 2 tbsp. Unsweetened Almond Milk
- 1 tbsp. Lemon Juice
- 1 tbsp. Dijon Mustard
- 1 cup Panko Breadcrumbs
- 1/2 tsp Kosher Salt
- 1/4 tsp Black Pepper
  - 1 dash Cayenne

Instructions

- Drain the tofu and combine it with the remaining sauce ingredients in a blender. Blend until the mixture is smooth and creamy.
- Allow chilling in the fridge while you prepare the pickles.
- If you haven't already done so, cut pickles into spears.
- Use paper towels to dry the spread gently. One neat method is to roll them into a bundle by laying them along a length of multiple paper towels. Allow drying while you prepare the breading and batter.
- In a medium-sized mixing bowl, combine flour and cornstarch. To make 'buttermilk,' combine almond milk & lemon juice. To make a thick batter, combine the wet and dry ingredients.
- Set aside the batter in a flat, square baking dish.
- Combine the Panko, garlic powder, cornmeal, nutritional yeast, onion powder, salt, & pepper in a medium-sized mixing bowl.
- Place the breading in a second flat, square baking dish.
- Dip a pickle into the batter very gently. To make sure the pickle is completely covered, use a fork. Allow excess to drop off before moving to the breading.
- Cover the battered pickles with your breading mixture with a spoon.
- Transfer to an air fryer basket or a baking sheet coated with parchment paper. Cook the pickles in small batches so they don't touch.
- Air fry for 15-20 minutes at 390°F. Because some air fryers are more powerful than others, check them occasionally to make sure they're browning nicely.

Air Fried Buttermilk Tofu

Preparation and Cooking Time

35 minutes

Servings

2 persons

Nutritional facts

43 calories, 9g fat, 1.7g fiber, 6g carbs, 8g protein

Ingredients

- 8 oz. block of firm or medium-firm tofu, cut lengthwise into 4 slices (no need to press it)
- 1 tsp salt
- 1/2 tsp pepper
- One and a half cups AP flour
- 1/4 red onion, sliced thinly
- 2 cups of red and green cabbage
- 1 jalapeno, sliced thinly
- bread and butter pickles
- hamburger buns

- Earth Balance, for toasting the buns
- 1/3 cup cornstarch
- 1 TB garlic powder
- 1 TB onion powder
- 1 TB salt
- 1 TB paprika
- 2 tsp cayenne
- 1 cup soymilk, with 2 tsp apple cider vinegar whisked in
- 2 TB Follow Your Heart Vegan Egg powder, blended with 1/2 cup ice cold water
- 2 TB bourbon
- 1 TB hot sauce
- 1/2 cup vegan mayo
- 1 TB to 1/4 cup sambal, depending on how spicy you like it

Instructions

- Place the tofu slabs into a rimmed baking sheet on a wire rack. Allow for an hour of resting or chilling after seasoning both sides with salt and pepper.
- In a medium-sized mixing bowl, mix all of the dry ingredients.
- In a separate medium-sized mixing bowl, mix all of the wet ingredients.
- Coat the tofu evenly in the dry mixture, tapping off any excess and returning it to the wire rack one piece at a time.
- Then three tbsp. wet mixture is to be poured into the dry mixture and mixed with your hands.
- Dunk the tofu in the wet mixture one piece at a time, then firmly pack the moistened flour mixture around it.
- Place the battered tofu back on the wire rack in the refrigerator for at least 30 minutes to chill.
- Spray the tofu slabs uniformly with cooking spray before frying. Cook for 10 minutes at 400 degrees F in an air fryer, flipping the slabs halfway through the cooking time. Spray any parts that appear to be dry with a little more spray & cook for an additional minute or two if necessary to produce a rich golden color throughout.
- Spread a little vegan butter on each side of the buns and toast until crispy in a cast iron pan over medium heat. You may also toast the buns in the air fryer for a few minutes at 350 degrees F, but keep an eye on them, so they don't get too crispy.
- Serve with the red onion, cabbage, jalapeno, pickles, and sambal mayo on the side.

Air Fryer Fruit Crumble

Preparation and Cooking Time

4 minutes

Servings

2 persons

Nutritional facts

310 calories, 24g fat, 5g fiber, 30g carbs, 7g protein

Ingredients

- 1 medium apple, finely diced
- 2 tablespoons sugar
- 1/2 teaspoon ground cinnamon
- 1/2 cup frozen blueberries, strawberries, or peaches
- 1/4 cup plus 1 tablespoon brown rice flour
- 2 tablespoons nondairy butter

Instructions

- Heat the air fryer for 5 minutes at 350°F. In an air fryer-safe baking pan or ramekin, mix the apple & frozen blueberries.

- Mix the flour, sugar, cinnamon, & butter in a small mixing bowl. Using a spoon, smear the flour mixture all over the fruit. To cover any exposed fruit, sprinkle a little additional flour on top. Cook for 15 minutes at 350°F.

Air Fryer Roasted Brussels Sprouts Recipe

Preparation and Cooking Time

18 minutes

Servings

4 persons

Nutritional facts

79 calories, 4g fat, 5g fiber, 13g carbs, 6g protein

Ingredients

- One pound Brussels sprouts (cleaned and trimmed)
- ½ tsp. dried thyme
- One tsp. dried parsley
- 1 tsp. garlic powder
- Quarter tsp. salt
- 2 tsp. oil

Instructions

- Toss all ingredients together in a medium to a large mixing bowl to evenly coat the Brussels sprouts.
- Close the air fryer and pour them into the food basket.
- Preheat the oven to 390 degrees Fahrenheit.
- Allow cooling slightly before serving.

Rosemary Roasted Potatoes

Preparation and Cooking Time

25 minutes

Servings

4 persons

Nutritional facts

212.58 calories, 7g fat, 4g fiber, 28g carbs, 3g protein

Ingredients

- 4 cups Baby New Potatoes, cut into 4 pieces each
- 1 teaspoon Ground Black Pepper
- 1 tablespoon fresh lime or lemon juice
- 3 tablespoons Vegetable Oil
- 2 teaspoons dried rosemary, minced
- 1 tablespoon Minced Garlic
- 1 teaspoon Kosher Salt
- 1/4 cup Chopped Parsley

Instructions

- Combine potatoes, oil, rosemary, garlic, salt, & pepper in a large mixing bowl. Mix thoroughly.
- Cook the seasoned potatoes in the air fryer basket for 15 minutes at 400°F. Check to see if the potatoes are fully cooked.
- Serve the potatoes with a squeeze of lemon juice & chopped parsley.

Vegan air fryer hush puppies

Preparation and Cooking Time

50 minutes

Servings

4 persons

Nutritional facts

175 calories, 3g fat, 0.5g fiber, 11g carbs, 2g protein

Ingredients

- ½ cup cornmeal
- ½ teaspoon salt
- Quarter cup soy milk
- ¼ cup water
- 2 tablespoons olive oil
- ½ cup white wheat flour
- 2 teaspoons baking powder
- 1 teaspoon onion powder
- 1 teaspoon garlic powder
- 1 tablespoon flax meal
- 1 tablespoon vegan sugar

Instructions

- Combine the cornmeal, flour, baking powder, onion powder, garlic powder, & salt in a large mixing bowl.
- Mix the other ingredients until you have a thick mixture in the bowl.
- For 20 minutes, put the bowl in the freezer. To get all of the batter cooked, you'll probably need to do two batches. In between rounds of cooking, place the bowl in the refrigerator.
- Cut a piece of parchment paper to fit within your air fryer basket. To make rounded batter balls, use a tbsp. or a cookie scoop. Place the balls on the parchment paper, about 1/2" between them.
- Then air fry for 10 minutes at 400°F.

Air Fryer Beets

Preparation and Cooking Time

30 minutes

Servings

3 persons

Nutritional facts

66 calories, 6g fat, 1g fiber, 7g carbs, 4g protein

Ingredients

- Three Beets
- ¾ tablespoon Oil I use avocado or olive oil
- Quarter teaspoon Kosher Salt
- ⅛ teaspoon Black Pepper freshly cracked, adjust to taste

Instructions

- Fill the air fryer basket halfway with seasoned beets and spread them out in a single layer. Preheat the air fryer to 380 degrees Fahrenheit.
- For the optimum texture, air fried for 17-20 minutes. Then halfway through, you need to shake the basket.
- Then serve roasted beets as is or in a salad. Add some parsley, either chopped or dried.

Ultra Crispy Air Fryer Chickpeas

Preparation and Cooking Time

20 minutes

Servings

3 persons

Nutritional facts

251 calories, 2g fat, 6g fiber, 23g carbs, 7g protein

Ingredients

- 19 oz. can of chickpeas (drained and rinsed)

- ¼ teaspoon onion powder
- ½ teaspoon paprika
- 1 tablespoon olive oil
- ⅛ teaspoon salt
- ¼ teaspoon garlic powder
  - ¼ teaspoon cayenne (optional)

Instructions

- Preheat the air fryer to 390 degrees Fahrenheit (200 degrees Celsius).
- Chickpeas should be drained and rinsed. Toss with a little olive oil and a pinch of salt & pepper.
- Fill the air fryer basket with the entire batch of chickpeas. Cook for 12 to15 minutes, shaking a few times.
- Remove chickpeas from the air fryer when done to your liking, taste, and season with salt & pepper to taste.
- Keep in an airtight container.

Cheesy Potato Wedges

Preparation and Cooking Time

31 minutes

Servings

4 persons

Nutritional facts

220 calories, 17g fat, 6g fiber, 25g carbs, 10g protein

Ingredients

- 1 lb. fingerling potatoes
- ½ cup raw cashews
- ½ teaspoon ground turmeric
- ½ teaspoon paprika
- 2 tablespoon nutritional yeast
- 1 teaspoon extra virgin olive oil
- 1 teaspoon kosher salt
- 1 teaspoon ground black pepper
- ½ teaspoon garlic powder
- 1 teaspoon fresh lemon juice
- 2 tablespoons cup water may need up to ¼ cup

Instructions

- Heat the air fryer for 3 minutes at 400°F. The potatoes should be washed. Transfer the potatoes to a large mixing bowl after cutting them half lengthwise. Toss the potatoes with oil, salt, pepper, & garlic powder. Toss to coat evenly. Place the potatoes in the air fryer to cook. Cook for sixteen minutes, shaking the pan halfway through.
- Mix the turmeric, nutritional yeast, cashews, paprika, & lemon juice. Blend on low for a few minutes, then gradually increase the speed & add water as needed.
- Place the cooked potatoes in an air fryer-safe pan or on parchment paper to cool. Over the potato wedges, drizzle the cheese sauce. Cook for a further 2 minutes at 400°F in the air fryer.

Avocado Egg Rolls

Preparation and Cooking Time

45 minutes

Servings

5 persons

Nutritional facts

380 calories, 23g fat, 5g fiber, 23g carbs, 12g protein

Ingredients

- 10 egg roll wrappers
- oil for frying
- 4 tablespoons sriracha
- 2 tablespoons white sugar
- 3 ripe avocados, peeled and pitted
- 1 Roma tomato, diced
- 1/2 teaspoon table salt
- 1/4 teaspoon ground black pepper
- 1 tablespoon rice vinegar
- 1 tablespoon toasted sesame oil

Instructions

- In a mixing bowl, mash the avocados until they're chunky, then add the tomato, salt, & black pepper.
- Set up a small bowl of water and egg roll wrappers with should be laid out with their corners facing you. On the bottom half of each wrapper, spread the avocado filling. Working with one wrapper at a time, moisten the edges with your finger, fold up the nearest corner over the filling, fold over the sides, and roll-up. To seal the final fold, dab it with a little extra water. Carry on with the remaining wrappers in the same manner.
- Place a big pot over medium heat with enough oil to cover the bottom 2 inches. Add egg rolls in batches of 3-5 based on the size of the pot after the oil temperature reaches 350 F. Cook for roughly 3 minutes till golden brown. To drain, place on a platter lined with paper towels.
- On the bias, halve each egg roll. In a small mixing bowl, thoroughly combine all sauce ingredients. Serve with avocado egg rolls sliced in half.

Vegan Cheese Samboosa

Preparation and Cooking Time

42 minutes

Servings

15-20 persons

Nutritional facts

140 calories, 18g fat, 4g fiber, 22g carbs, 5g protein

Ingredients

- ½ cup of raw cashews (pre-boiled for 10 minutes)
- 1¼ cup of water
- 1 package of samosa pastry sheets
- 1 tbsp. olive oil
- 3 tbsp. of nutritional yeast
- 3 tbsp. + 2 tsp of Tapioca starch
- ¾ tsp sea salt
- 1 tsp apple cider vinegar
- ½ cup water

Instructions

- In a blender, combine all of the cheese ingredients & blend on high till smooth.
- Pour the mixed mixture into a small saucepan over medium heat, then whisk constantly with a wooden spoon or spatula while cooking. As you stir, little clumps will form, and after about five minutes, your mixture should have turned into one big gooey ball of cheese. To ensure that everything is firm, cook for a further thirty seconds to one minute.
- Allow it to cool in the fridge for at least half an hour before handling in a glass container.

- To assemble, arrange a samosa pastry sheet vertically on a cutting board or plate and use a pastry brush to provide a thin wash of water to help the edges hold together better.
- Add about 1-2 tablespoons of the cheese mixture to the far right corner and then fold the dough over the filling in a triangular shape using the bottom right "point." Then fold the top right tip of the triangle horizontally, alternating the previous two procedures until you have a triangle-shaped parcel with the last flap sealed.
- Continue until all samosa sheets are used up.

Kale and Potatoes with almond milk

Preparation and Cooking Time

53 minutes

Servings

4 persons

Nutritional facts

333 calories, 16g fat, 5g fiber, 23g carbs, 9g protein

Ingredients

- 2 cups of finely chopped potatoes
- 1 teaspoon of extra-virgin olive oil
- 1 clove garlic minced
- 4 cups of coarsely chopped kale
- 1/8 cup of almond milk
- 1/4 teaspoon of sea salt
- 1/8 teaspoon of ground black pepper
- Vegetable oil spray as needed

Instructions

- In a big saucepan of boiling water, place the potatoes. Then cook for about 30 minutes, or until the vegetables are soft.
- Heat the oil in a large skillet over medium-high heat. Sauté the garlic until it turns golden brown. You need to sauté for two or three minutes with the kale. Place in a large mixing bowl.
- Drain the potatoes and place them in a medium mixing bowl. Mash the potatoes with a fork or a potato masher after adding the milk, salt, & pepper. Combine the potatoes and the cooked kale in a large mixing bowl. Heat the air fryer for 5 minutes at 390°F.
- Make 1-inch nuggets out of the potato & kale mixture. Spritz the vegetable oil into the air fryer basket. Put the nuggets in the air fryer & cook for 12 to 15 minutes, shaking after 6 minutes, until golden brown.

Meatless Monday Air Fryer Thai Veggie Bites

Preparation and Cooking Time

25 minutes

Servings

16 persons

Nutritional facts

117 calories, 2g fat, 0.2g fiber, 2g carbs, 3g protein

Ingredients

- 1 Large Broccoli
- 1 Large Onion peeled and diced
- 1 Small Courgette
- 1 Tbsp. Olive Oil
- 1 Tbsp. Thai Green Curry Paste
- 1 Tbsp. Coriander
- 1 Tbsp. Mixed Spice
- 2 Leeks cleaned and thinly sliced

- 1 Can Coconut Milk
- 50 g Plain Flour
- 1 cm Cube Ginger peeled and grated
- 1 Tbsp. Garlic Puree
- 1 Large Cauliflower
- 6 Large Carrots
- Handful Garden Peas
- ½ Cauliflower made into cauliflower rice
- 1 Tsp Cumin
- Salt & Pepper

Instructions

- Cook the onion in a wok with garlic, ginger, & olive oil till the onion is slightly colored.
- Cook your veggies (excluding the courgette and leek) in a steamer for twenty minutes or till they are nearly cooked while the onion is cooking.
- Cook for another 5 minutes on medium heat with the courgette, leek, and curry paste in your wok.
- After thoroughly mixing in the coconut milk and the remaining seasonings, add the cauliflower rice.
- Stir in the other ingredients and cook for another 10 minutes.
- Add the cooked vegetables after 10 minutes of simmering as well as the sauce has decreased by half. Mix thoroughly, and you'll have a delicious base for the veggie bites.
- Allow cooling in the refrigerator for an hour.
- After an hour, cut the meat into bite-size pieces and fry in the Air Fryer. Cook at 180°C for 10 minutes before serving with a cooling dip.

Air Fryer Vegan Cornbread

Preparation and Cooking Time

16 minutes

Servings

18 persons

Nutritional facts

157 calories, 14g fat, 3g fiber, 27g carbs, 6g protein

Ingredients

- 1 ¼ cup all-purpose flour
- 1 ¼ cup unsweetened almond milk
- ⅓ cup applesauce (or oil)
- 1 cup yellow corn meal
- ⅓ cup granulated sugar (or coconut sugar, maple syrup)
- 1 teaspoon salt
- 1 tablespoon baking powder
- ⅓ cup frozen corn kernels (optional)

Instructions

- Combine all dry ingredients in a medium mixing bowl.
- Toss in the almond milk, applesauce (or oil), and frozen corn kernels with a spoon until thoroughly combined.
- Fill each silicone muffin cups two-thirds full, then carefully put it in an air fryer basket.
- Bake muffins in an air fryer for 9-11 minutes at 400 degrees F.
- As needed, repeat with the second batch.
- Serve with Vegan Spicy Charro Beans in the Crockpot, Instant Pot Red Beans and Rice, or Lazy Vegan Chili.

Zucchini Corn Fritters

Preparation and Cooking Time

22 minutes

Servings

4 persons

Nutritional facts

118 calories, 8g fat, 0.7g fiber, 15g carbs, 4g protein

Ingredients

- 2 medium zucchini
- 1-2 tsp olive oil
- salt and pepper
- 1 cup corn kernels
- 1 medium potato cooked
- 2 tbsp. chickpea flour
- 2-3 garlic finely minced
- Yogurt tahini sauce or Ketchup

Instructions

- Using a grater or a food processor, grate the zucchini. Mix shredded zucchini with a pinch of salt in a mixing bowl and set aside 10-15 minutes. Then, using clean hands or cheese cloth, squeeze out any extra water from the zucchini.
- Mash the cooked potato as well.
- Mix potato, zucchini, corn, garlic, chickpea flour, salt, & pepper.
- Take about 2 tbsp. of batter, shape it into a patty, and set it on parchment paper.
- Apply a light coat of oil. Preheat the Air Fryer to 360 degrees Fahrenheit.
- Put the fritters on Air Fryer mesh, ensuring they don't touch. Cook for 8 minutes.
- Then flip the fritters & cook for another 3-four minutes, or till well done or the desired color is achieved.
- Serve with yogurt tahini sauce or ketchup while still warm.

Air Fryer Tofu Satay

Preparation and Cooking Time

40 minutes

Servings

4 persons

Nutritional facts

163 calories, 23g fat, 2.5 fiber, 20g carbs, 13g protein

Ingredients

- 2 tablespoons soy sauce
- 2 cloves of garlic
- 1 block tofu
- juice of 1 fresh lime
- 1 tablespoon maple syrup
- 2 teaspoons fresh ginger - no need to peel, coarsely chopped
- 1 teaspoon sriracha sauce
- 1 batch 5-Minute Peanut Butter Sauce - Use the full 6 tablespoons of water that the recipe calls for

Instructions

- In a blender or food processor, purée the soy sauce, lime juice, maple syrup, ginger, sriracha, & garlic until smooth.
- Marinate the tofu strips in the marinade for 15 to 30 minutes. Soak six bamboo skewers with enough water to cover them while the tofu marinate.

- When the marinating time is over, cut the skewers in half with a wire cutter to get 6 half-sized skewers. These half-skewers will fit into the air fryer basket instead of a whole bamboo skewer. Remove any splinters from the cut skewers before skewering 1 tofu strip onto each little stick. Make sure you're sticking the UNCUT side of your tofu through the hole.
- In your air fryer, place the small tofu skewers. Cook for 15 minutes at 370°F without shaking. If you haven't already, make the 5-Minute Peanut Butter Sauce while the tofu cooks.
- You're ready to eat when the air fryer beeps.

Vegan Air Fryer Meatballs

Preparation and Cooking Time

54 minutes

Servings

4 persons

Nutritional facts

174 calories, 1g fat, 0.1g fiber, 6g carbs, 2g protein

Ingredients

- 1 cup shiitake mushrooms (dry)
- Salt and ground black pepper to taste
- 2 tablespoon parsley (chopped, optional)
- ½ teaspoon red pepper flakes
- ½ teaspoon smoked paprika
- 2 teaspoons dry sage
- ½ cup walnuts
- 4 cloves garlic (chopped)
- 2 cups chickpeas (canned or cooked. Strained of all liquid)
- 1 teaspoon ground cumin
- 1 tablespoon tamari

Instructions

- Place the mushrooms in a bowl & cover with 2 cups boiling water. After 30 minutes of steeping, drain the mushrooms. Save the mushroom stock.
  - Shred the mushrooms until they are finely shredded but not pasty in a food processor. If the stems are still tough after soaking, discard them and only utilize the mushroom tips.
  - Process the walnuts until broken down into small pieces but not pulverized.
  - Add the other ingredients, including the chickpeas, garlic, cumin, smoked paprika, red pepper flakes, sage, soy sauce/tamari/Worcestershire sauce, and salt and pepper to taste.
  - Process the ingredients a couple of times to break down the chickpeas. If the ball comes apart after being formed, continue to process the mixture.
  - Remove the blade from the bowl of the food processor. Make 24 meatballs in a large mixing bowl.
  - In the air fryer basket, place the meatballs. To provide an adequate area for air to flow around the meatballs, do this in two batches of twelve meatballs each.
  - Using a frying spray or a brush, coat the meatballs with oil. You can skip this step if you want to make them fully oil-free.
  - Preheat the air fryer to 375°F and cook the meatballs in it for 14 minutes. Open & rotate the balls halfway through cooking to ensure even cooking.

Air Fryer Vegan Rolled Tacos

Preparation and Cooking Time

30 minutes

Servings

8 persons

Nutritional facts

131 calories, 9g fat, 3.1g fiber, 23g carbs, 3g protein

Ingredients

- 1 large avocado or 2 small ones
- 8 corn tortillas
- olive oil
- salt & pepper to taste
- 1 15-ounce can vegan refried beans
- ½ -1 tablespoon taco seasoning
- hot sauce

Instructions

- Place the avocado in a mixing bowl and season with salt and pepper. Set aside after mashing with a fork.
- In a mixing bowl, add the re-fried beans & taco seasoning. If necessary, taste and adjust taco seasoning.
- To keep your tortillas warm, heat them over an open flame and wrap them in a clean dish towel.
- Brush one side of each tortilla with olive oil and afterward flip it over, one at a time. In the center, place a small amount of avocado, a large scoop of beans, as well as a drizzle of hot sauce. Roll the tortilla up from one end and set it seam side down on a platter or cutting board. Repeat with the rest of the ingredients.
- Put the rolled tacos seam side down in the air fryer. Cook for 10 minutes at 380 degrees F, flipping halfway through. You may need to make these in batches based on the size of your air fryer. While the second batch cooks, keep the finished wrapped tacos warm on a platter covered with a clean kitchen towel.
- Serve with your preferred taco toppings on rolled tacos.

Savory Potato Patties

Preparation and Cooking Time

25 minutes

Servings

4 persons

Nutritional facts

73 calories, 13g fat, 0.8g fiber, 8g carbs, 7g protein

Ingredients

- 2/3 cup dry instant potatoes
- 1/4-1/2 teaspoon (0.25) Cayenne Pepper
- 1/2 teaspoon cumin seeds
- 1/4 teaspoon Ground Cumin
- 1/2 teaspoon Kosher Salt
- 1/4 cup (Frozen Peas and Carrots, defrosted
- 2 tablespoons chopped cilantro
- 1 tablespoon Oil
- 1/2 teaspoon Turmeric
- 2/3 cup hot water

Instructions

- Combine all ingredients in a medium mixing bowl. Cover and set aside for 10 minutes to allow the flavors to meld. Mix thoroughly.
- Using a spray bottle, coat the air fryer basket in oil.
- Make twelve round and flat patties with even edges with your hands. Directly into the air fryer basket, place patties. Preheat the air fryer to 400 degrees Fahrenheit for 10 minutes. After 5

minutes, brush the patties with vegetable oil and complete cooking.

Air Fryer Falafel

Preparation and Cooking Time

20 minutes

Servings

15 persons

Nutritional facts

82 calories, 1.1g fat, 3g fiber, 10g carbs, 3g protein

Ingredients

We have listed below the ingredients that would be required by you for cooking this healthy and tasty food in the air fryer:

- 2 cans (14-ounce) organic no salt added chickpeas, rinsed, drained well & patted dry
- 1/3 cup of fresh cilantro
- 1 tsp of ground coriander
- 3/4 tsp of salt
- black pepper
- 2 tbsp. of superfine blanched almond flour
- 1 tsp of baking soda
- 3 tbsp. of nutritional yeast
- 1 tsp of smoked paprika
- 2 tsp of ground cumin
- 1 roughly chopped small red onion
- 3 garlic cloves
- 2 tbsp. of fresh lemon juice
- 1/3 cup of fresh parsley

Instructions

- Combine the drained chickpeas, onion, and garlic in a food processor. Pulse the chickpeas for about 30 seconds or until they are largely smooth.
- Combine the lemon juice, parsley, coriander, nutritional yeast, paprika, cumin, ground coriander, salt, and pepper in a large mixing bowl. Blend till smooth and combine once more. The flour & baking soda is then added.
- Take a tablespoon of the mixture and roll it into a ball or shape it into patties. Repeat with the rest of the mixture. Refrigerate the patties for half an hour to firm up.
- Lightly coat each falafel with avocado oil spray when ready to cook. Put patties in a single layer in the air fryer basket in batches. Preheat the air fryer at 375 degrees Fahrenheit and cook for 12-13 minutes, flipping halfway through.
- It's best served hot, but it'll keep in an airtight container for up to 3 months in the fridge or freezer.

Vegan Cabbage Fritters

Preparation and Cooking Time

25 minutes

Servings

16 persons

Nutritional facts

60 calories, 8g fat, 0.7g fiber, 15g carbs, 4g protein

Ingredients

- ¼ cabbage head, chopped finely
- 2 tbsp. vegetable oil
- ⅓ cup water
- 1 tsp garlic powder

- 2 tsp red chili powder
- 1 tsp salt
- ⅓ red onion, medium, chopped finely
- 1 jalapeno, chopped finely - optional
- 1 cup chickpea flour
- ¼ cup rice flour, for crispiness (optional)
- 1 tsp turmeric

Instructions

- Preheat the air fryer to 380°F.
- Combine the onions, chopped cabbage, flour, jalapenos, spices, and oil in a mixing bowl.
- Stir thoroughly and then fold in the water to make a rough batter.
- Form a fritter out of a scoop of batter the size of a tiny lemon and lay on a lined baking sheet, about 2 inches apart, if using an oven. If using an air fryer, evenly distribute the ingredients in the air fryer basket.
- Place the fritters in the air fryer or oven when it's ready. Bake for 15 minutes in the oven, then flip and bake for another ten minutes. Bake for 15 to 20 minutes till golden brown if using an air fryer.
- For a wonderful snack, serve hot with ketchup and/or mint chutney.

Chapter 11: Air Fryer Vegetarian Recipes

Eggplant Caponata

Preparation and Cooking Time

35 minutes

Servings

4 persons

Nutritional facts

97 calories, 4g fat ,2g fiber ,25g carbs ,3g protein

Ingredients

- 1 lb. air-fried eggplant, approximately 2 solid cups
- 1 red bell pepper, seeds removed and diced
- 1/2 cup pitted green and black olives, chopped
- 1/4 cup capers
- 1/2 tsp sea salt
- 2 TBS extra virgin olive oil
- 1 onion, chopped
- 3 cloves garlic, minced
- 1 (15 ounces) can diced tomatoes
- 1/4 tsp freshly ground black pepper
- 1 small loaf of Italian bread, sliced and toasted

Instructions

- Put the olive oil, onions, and garlic into a medium sauté pan over medium heat. Cook for 3 to 5 minutes, or until barely transparent and fragrant. Cook for another 5 minutes, or until the red bell peppers are softened. Cook for another 5 minutes after adding the diced tomatoes.
- Combine the cooked eggplant, chopped olives, & capers in a mixing bowl. Cook for another 5 minutes. Then season with salt and pepper to taste.
- Serve with toasted bread slices as a chunky dip or warm salad.

Eggplant Pizza Rounds

Preparation and Cooking Time

25 minutes

Servings

4 persons

Nutritional facts

130 calories, 9g fat ,4g fiber ,36g carbs ,6g protein

Ingredients

- 1 eggplant

- 1 tsp of dried Italian seasoning blend
- Olive oil spray
- 1 cup of homemade pizza sauce
- 1 tsp of sea salt
- 1/3 cup of all-purpose flour
- 2 whole eggs, beaten
- 1/2 cup of panko bread crumbs
- 1/3 cup of shredded mozzarella cheese
- 3 TBS of grated parmesan cheese

Instructions

- Use a knife to cut the eggplant into 1/2-inch thick circles. Set aside for 10 minutes after seasoning the slices on both sides with salt.
- Put the flour, beaten eggs, & bread crumbs in three shallow bowls. Toss the bread crumbs with the Italian seasoning and mix well. Mix the mozzarella & parmesan cheeses in a fourth bowl and set aside.
- Heat the air fryer to 360 degrees Fahrenheit.
- Dip the eggplant slices in the flour in groups of 4 to 6 slices each. Remove any excess flour by shaking it off. To coat, dip each in the eggs, then in the bread crumb mixture.
- Using a spray bottle, coat the air fryer basket in oil. In the fryer basket, place the breaded eggplant slices. Apply a little coat of oil on the rounds. Then cook for about 8 minutes, or until the outside is golden and crispy. Open the air fryer & spread a dollop of marinara sauce over each slice of fried eggplant. Cover the sauce with the cheese mixture. Then cook for 1 to 2 minutes, or until the cheese is barely melted.
- Serve as a snack right away while cooking the remaining eggplant slices.

Breaded Pickle Spears

Preparation and Cooking Time

18 minutes

Servings

2 persons

Nutritional facts

80 calories, 11g fat ,4g fiber 29g, carbs ,2g protein

Ingredients

- 4 dill pickles, cut into spears
- 1 tsp of dried oregano
- 1/4 tsp of coarse salt
- 1/2 cup of all-purpose flour
- 1 whole egg + 1 TBS water
- 1/3 cup of bread crumbs
- 2 TBS of cornmeal
- 1/4 tsp of freshly ground pepper
- Olive oil spray

Instructions

- Set aside the pickle spears after draining them on paper towels.
- Prepare three shallow bowls. In the first, put the flour. In the second, mix the egg and the water. In the third bowl, combine the bread crumbs, cornmeal, oregano, salt, & pepper using a fork to blend.
- Remove basket from the air fryer & spray it with olive oil. Preheat the air fryer to 390 degrees Fahrenheit.
- Coat the pickles with flour, egg, and bread crumbs in batches. In the basket, arrange them in a single layer. Apply a little coat

of oil on them. Place these in the air fryer and cook for 6 to 10 minutes, just until the coating is golden brown and crispy.

- Serve immediately with a dipping sauce and napkins.

Air Fryer Pickle Chips

Preparation and Cooking Time

18 minutes

Servings

2 persons

Nutritional facts

280 calories, 7g fat ,2g fiber ,17g carbs, 5g protein

Ingredients

- 2 cups of dill pickle slices
- 1/8 tsp of cayenne pepper
- 1 whole egg
- 1/2 cup of whole buttermilk
- 1 cup of panko bread crumbs
- 1/2 cup of all-purpose flour
- 1/2 tsp of paprika
- 1/4 tsp of garlic powder
- 1/4 tsp of black pepper
- 1/4 tsp of sea salt
- 2 TBS of extra virgin olive oil

Instructions

- The pickle chips should be kept aside after draining.
- Prepare three shallow bowls. Toss together the flour, garlic powder, paprika, pepper, and cayenne in the first bowl. In the second bowl, mix the egg and buttermilk. After that, whisk a quarter cup of flour mixture with the egg and buttermilk until smooth. In the third bowl, combine the salt, bread crumbs, & olive oil, and toss thoroughly with a fork to cover the breadcrumbs in oil.
- Remove basket from the air fryer. Heat the air fryer to 390 degrees Fahrenheit.
- Coat the pickles with flour, egg batter, and bread crumbs in batches. In the basket, arrange them in a single layer. Place these in the air fryer and cook for 6 to 10 minutes, just until the coating is golden brown & crunchy.

Roasted Broccoli in an Air Fryer

Preparation and Cooking Time

17 minutes

Servings

4 persons

Nutritional facts

278 calories, 7g fat ,8g fiber ,20g carbs ,3g protein

Ingredients

- 4 cups broccoli florets, cut to the same size
- 1/2 tsp freshly ground pepper
- 2 TBS extra virgin olive oil
- 1/2 tsp garlic powder
- 1/2 tsp sea salt

Instructions

- Rinse the broccoli under cold running water for a few minutes in a strainer. In a microwave-safe bowl, place the damp broccoli. Then microwave for 1-1/2 minutes on high. Then microwave for an extra minute after stirring the broccoli. Remove the broccoli from the bowl and drain any excess water.

- Heat the air fryer for 3 minutes at 350°F.
- Toss the broccoli with olive oil, garlic powder, salt, and pepper. Toss to coat evenly.
- Cook the broccoli for 3 minutes in the air fryer basket. Continue to roast for 3 to 5 minutes more, shaking the air fryer bucket to rotate the broccoli until the florets are just crispy on the outside. It's possible that you'll have to perform this in two batches.
- Transfer the broccoli to a serving plate & serve plain or with parmesan cheese on top.

Roasted Curried Cauliflower Bites

Preparation and Cooking Time

35 minutes

Servings

2 persons

Nutritional facts

110 calories, 5g fat ,3g fiber ,11g carbs ,4g protein

Ingredients

- 1-1/2 cups whole milk yogurt
- 1/2 large head of cauliflower, washed and core removed
- Pinch of cayenne pepper (optional)
- Lemon wedge for serving
- 1-1/2 TBS extra virgin olive oil or untoasted sesame oil
- 1-1/2 tsps. curry powder
- 1/2 tsp sea salt
- 1/4 tsp freshly ground black pepper
- 1/2 medium cucumber, peeled, seeds removed, and grated
- Juice of 1/2 a lemon
- 1/2 tsp ground cumin
- Sea salt and freshly ground pepper to taste
- 1 TBS chopped flat-leaf parsley for garnish

Instructions

- Combine the yogurt, cucumber, lemon, & cumin in a medium mixing bowl. Then season to taste with salt and pepper. While preparing the cauliflower, cover the bowl and place it in the refrigerator.
- Combine the olive oil, curry powder, cayenne pepper, salt, and pepper in a large mixing bowl. Cauliflower should be broken or sliced into bite-size pieces. Toss the cauliflower in the bowl with the oil mixture until it is well coated.
- Preheat the air fryer to 350 degrees Fahrenheit. Arrange the seasoned cauliflower in a single layer in the fryer basket or dish. Preheat the oven to 350°F and set the timer for 15 minutes.
- Cook the cauliflower for five minutes, rotating the florets with a shake of the basket. Cook for another 5 minutes, or until a sharp knife pierces the meat and reveals a golden brown exterior & tender interior. If necessary, continue to cook for another 5 minutes.
- With a spoon, transfer the raita to a serving bowl. In a separate serving bowl, place the cauliflower. Fresh lemon juice should be squeezed over the cauliflower. Serve with parsley as a garnish.
- The cauliflower should be served with the raita.

Buffalo-Style Cauliflower "Wings" with Blue Cheese Dip

Preparation and Cooking Time

35 minutes

Servings

2 persons

Nutritional facts

110 calories, 13g fat ,3g fiber ,22g carbs ,7g protein

Ingredients

- 1/4 cup sour cream
- 1 scallion, minced
- 3/4 cup panko bread crumbs (gluten-free for Paleo)
- 1/2 tsp sea salt
- 1/2 tsp freshly ground black pepper
- Sea salt and freshly ground pepper to taste
- 1/2 large head of cauliflower, washed and core removed
- 4 TBS melted butter
- 1/4 cup mayonnaise
- 1/4 crumbled blue cheese, such as Maytag
- 1-1/2 TBS fresh lemon juice
- 1 TBS half and half
- 1/4 cup your favorite hot pepper sauce
- Celery and carrot sticks for serving

Instructions

- Combine the sour cream, mayonnaise, blue cheese, half-and-half, lemon juice, and scallions in a small mixing bowl. Then season to taste with salt and pepper.
- Refrigerate the dip till ready to serve by covering it with plastic wrap.
- Combine the butter and spicy sauce in a large mixing bowl. Combine the bread crumbs, salt, and pepper in a separate bowl.
- Cauliflower should be broken or sliced into bite-size pieces. Toss the cauliflower in the sauce until it is well coated. To evenly coat the cauliflower, dip it in the bread crumbs.
- Preheat the air fryer to 350 degrees Fahrenheit. Arrange the prepared cauliflower in a single layer in the fryer basket or dish. Preheat the oven to 350°F and set the timer for 15 minutes.
- Cook the cauliflower for 5 minutes, rotating the florets with a shake of the basket. Cook for another 5 minutes, or until a sharp knife pierces the meat and reveals a golden brown exterior & tender interior. If necessary, continue to cook for another 5 minutes.
- Fill individual ramekins with the blue cheese dip. Put the cauliflower in a parchment-lined serving basket. Serve the cauliflower with celery & carrot sticks.

Air Fryer Honey Glazed Carrots

Preparation and Cooking Time

15 minutes

Servings

4 persons

Nutritional facts

95 calories, 9g fat ,2g fiber ,25g carbs ,4g protein

Ingredients

- 6 whole medium carrots, washed and trimmed
- 1-1/2 tsps. balsamic vinegar
- 1/4 to 1/2 tsp sea salt to taste
- 1-1/2 TBS extra virgin olive oil
- 2 tsp honey
- 1/4 tsp freshly ground pepper

Instructions

- Preheat the air fryer for 3 minutes at 375°F.

- Carrots should be cut into 1/2-inch-thick rounds. In a large mixing bowl, combine the carrots.
- Combine the oil, honey, vinegar, salt, & pepper in a mixing bowl. Toss the carrots with the mixture to coat them evenly.
- Set a timer for 10 minutes and place the prepared carrots in a single layer in the air fryer basket using a slotted spoon. Any remaining dressing in the bowl should be set aside. Carrots should be cooked for 4 minutes. To rotate the carrots, shake the bucket. Cook for another four minutes, then test with a fork to see soft potatoes. If the texture isn't just right, cook for a couple of minutes more.
- Return the heated carrots to the bowl with any remaining dressing and toss once more. Serve right away with your main course. Carrots are a tasty side dish for breaded pork chops.

Easy Air Fryer Zucchini Chips

Preparation and Cooking Time

20 minutes

Servings

2 persons

Nutritional facts

120 calories, 8g fat ,1g fiber ,15g carbs ,2g protein

Ingredients

- 1 medium zucchini, cut into 3/8-inch-thick rounds
- 1/4 tsp sea salt
- Sea salt
- 2 whole eggs, beaten
- 1 cup panko breadcrumbs
- 1/4 tsp freshly ground pepper

Instructions

- Using paper towels, cover a plate. Sprinkle liberally with salt and put the zucchini slices on the towels. Allow the zucchini to sit for 5–10 minutes to allow the moisture to evaporate.
- Prepare two shallow bowls: the first will hold the beaten eggs, and the second will hold the mashed potatoes. The breadcrumbs, salt, & pepper will be in the second bowl.
- Heat the air fryer for 3 to 5 minutes at 390°F.
- Remove any excess moisture from the zucchini rounds by patting them dry. After dipping the rounds in the eggs, coat them in breadcrumbs. Set the timer for 4 minutes and place the chips in a single layer in the fryer basket. Flip the chips after 4 minutes and cook for another 4 to 6 minutes, till golden brown and crispy. You'll probably have to perform this in two or three batches.
- If desired, season the chips with pepper and salt. Serve as an appetizer or snack with ketchup or Russian dressing.

Zucchini Fries with Garlic Aioli

Preparation and Cooking Time

25 minutes

Servings

2 persons

Nutritional facts

120 calories, 6g fat ,2g fiber ,18g carbs ,2g protein

Ingredients

- 1/4 cup of mayonnaise
- 1/4 tsp of sea salt
- 1/2 cup of all-purpose flour
- 2 eggs, beaten
- 3/4 cup of panko bread crumbs

- 1/4 cup of cornmeal
- 2 TBS of grated parmesan cheese
- 1/4 tsp of garlic powder
- 1/4 tsp of freshly ground pepper
- 1 medium zucchini
- Sea salt
- 1/4 cup of plain Greek yogurt
- 1 garlic clove, minced finely
- 1 tsp of minced chives
- 2 tsp of lemon juice
- 1/4 tsp of sea salt
- 1/4 tsp of pepper

Instructions

- Combine the mayonnaise, yogurt, garlic, chives, & lemon juice in a small mixing bowl and whisk until smooth. Then season with salt and pepper, then mix one more time. Cover and keep refrigerated till ready to serve.
- Remove the zucchini's tops and bottoms. Use a sharp knife to cut zucchini into 2-1/2-inch-long sections. These should be cut into 1/2-inch thick fries. Using paper towels, cover a plate. Sprinkle liberally with salt and put the zucchini slices on the towels. Allow the zucchini to rest for 5–10 minutes to allow the moisture to evaporate.
- Prepare three shallow bowls: the first will hold the flour; the second will hold the eggs. The eggs or almond milk mixture will be in the second. Breadcrumbs, cornmeal, cheese or yeast, garlic, salt, & pepper will be in the third.
- Heat the air fryer for 3 to 5 minutes at 390°F.
- Blot any extra liquid from the zucchini slices. Fries should be floured first, then dipped in eggs or milk, and finally in the breadcrumb mixture. Set the timer for 4 minutes and place the zucchini in a single layer in the fryer basket. Flip the fries after 4 minutes and cook for another 4 to 6 minutes, till golden brown and crispy.
- If desired, season the fries with pepper and salt. Serve the aioli in individual ramekins or in a serving bowl. Serve as an appetizer or a light snack.

Brussels Sprouts Salad

Preparation and Cooking Time

25 minutes

Servings

2 persons

Nutritional facts

110 calories, 15g fat ,2g fiber ,20g carbs ,4g protein

Ingredients

- Air fried Brussels sprouts with pancetta
- Freshly ground black pepper
- 2 ounces' feta cheese
- 6 grape tomatoes
- 2 TBS extra virgin olive oil
- 2 tsp balsamic vinegar
- 1/4 cup toasted raw pumpkin seeds (pepitas)

Instructions

- Prepare the Brussels sprouts. Set them aside to cool in a serving bowl.
- Grape tomatoes should be cut in half. Combine this with the sprouts that have been allowed to cool. Over the salad, drizzle the olive oil and vinegar, and gently toss to coat. Then to taste, season with freshly ground black pepper.

- Scatter the feta cheese crumbles on top of the salad. To keep the feta from discoloring from the balsamic, don't toss it. Toasted pumpkin seeds should be sprinkled over the entire salad.
- Serve the salad alongside air-fried proteins like Cornish Game Hens or Rib Eye Steaks.

Air Fryer Baked Whole Sweet Potatoes

Preparation and Cooking Time

43 minutes

Servings

3 persons

Nutritional facts

105 calories, 8g fat ,1g fiber ,17g carbs ,2g protein

Ingredients

- 2 whole sweet potatoes, approximately 6 ounces each, washed well
- Salt and pepper for serving
- 2 tsp extra virgin olive oil
- 1 tsp coarse sea salt
- 1/2 tsp freshly ground black pepper
- Butter and Greek yogurt for serving

Instructions

- The sweet potatoes should be well washed and dried with paper towels. With the tines of a fork, make 6 to 8 holes in the skin of the potatoes, rotating to hit all surfaces.
- Heat the air fryer for 3 minutes at 390°F.
- Olive oil should be rubbed all over the potatoes, and it should be seasoned with salt & pepper to taste.
- In the air fryer basket, place the whole potatoes. Preheat the oven to 350°F and set the timer for forty minutes. Sweet potatoes should be cooked for 20 minutes. Cook for an additional 15 to 20 minutes, rotating the potatoes halfway through, till the skin is browned as well as the flesh is fork-tender.
- Cook the potatoes and cut them in half lengthwise. With a fork, loosen up the flesh a little. Using a pinch of salt and pepper, season the potato halves. It should be topped with butter and Greek yogurt or sour cream. Serve while the dish is still steaming.

Hassel back Potatoes with Parmesan Cheese and Thyme

Preparation and Cooking Time

25 minutes

Servings

4 persons

Nutritional facts

118 calories,10g fat ,1g fiber ,21g carbs ,2g protein

Ingredients

- 4 to 6 medium Yukon Gold potatoes, washed, skins intact
- 1/4 tsp sea salt
- 1/4 tsp freshly ground pepper
- 1-1/2 TBS butter (use all olive oil if vegan)
- 1-1/2 TBS extra virgin olive oil
- 2 tsp dried thyme leaves
- 3 TBS finely grated parmesan cheese, divided

Instructions

- Heat the air fryer to 350°F for 5 minutes.
- Melt the butter in a small saucepan over low heat.

- Slice the potatoes into 1/8 to 1/4-inch thick slices through the center, only going 3/4 of the way through.
- Warm the thyme, salt, & pepper in the melted butter for about 30 seconds, or until the thyme becomes aromatic. Add the olive oil and mix well.
- Spread the butter & oil mixture over the potatoes with a spoon or a brush. Get some in between the slices if you can. Half of the cheese should go on top of each potato.
- Put the potatoes on the crisper plate of the preheated air fryer, or in the basket. Cook for 16 to 20 minutes after closing the drawer or bucket.
- Open the air fryer & top the potatoes with the remaining cheese. Cook for another 2 minutes, or until the cheese has melted.
- Serve the potatoes immediately after they have been removed from the air fryer.

Classic Blooming Onion Recipe with Dipping Sauce

Preparation and Cooking Time

30 minutes

Servings

2 persons

Nutritional facts

102 calories, 11g fat ,1.5g fiber ,19g carbs ,2g protein

Ingredients

- 1 large sweet onion
- 1/2 tsp dried oregano
- 1/2 tsp Worcestershire sauce
- 2 tsp jarred horseradish or pickle relish
- 1/4 tsp sea salt
- 1/4 tsp freshly ground pepper
- 1/2 tsp dried thyme
- 1/2 tsp kosher salt
- 1/2 tsp freshly ground black pepper
- 1/8 to 1/4 tsp cayenne pepper
- Grapeseed or canola oil in a pump bottle (you can use a spoon)
- 2 TBS sour cream
- 2 TBS mayonnaise
- 1 whole egg
- 1/2 cup whole milk
- 1 cup all-purpose flour
- 1-1/2 tsp paprika
- 1-1/2 tsp tomato ketchup
- Pinch of cayenne pepper

Instructions

- Remove 1/2 inch of the onion's pointed top end. Remove and discard the outer skin. On a clean cutting board, place the onion cut side down. Beginning 1/2 inch from the root end, make a downward incision through to the board using a sharp knife. Make four more cuts around the onion, evenly spaced. Cut in between each part till you have 16 evenly spaced sections. Turn the onion over again and carefully separate the parts with your fingertips.
- Whisk the egg and milk together in a large mixing bowl. Combine the paprika, flour, thyme, oregano, salt, pepper, & cayenne in a separate bowl.
- Submerge the onion, cut side up in the liquid mixture, and ladle the liquid over the onion to coat all segments. Allow any surplus liquid to drain. Place the onion, cut side up, in the flour mixture. Using the flour, fully coat the onion. Shake any extra

flour back into the bowl after tossing the onion. Remove the onion and set it aside.

- Preheat the air fryer to 370 degrees Fahrenheit. To lightly coat the onion, just enough oil can be sprayed or drizzled on it. Place the onion in the fryer basket, root side down. Check after 10 minutes to see whether it has crisped up and seems delicate. Cook for an additional 5 minutes until the crispy texture is attained.
- Serve the blooming onions with the dipping sauce in individual ramekins and many napkins.
- Stir together the sour cream, mayonnaise, ketchup, & Worcestershire sauce in a small bowl. Combine the horseradish or relish, salt, pepper, & cayenne pepper in a mixing bowl.
- Refrigerate till ready to serve, covered.

Gluten-Free and Egg-Free Blooming Onion with Ranch Dipping Sauce

Preparation and Cooking Time

1 hour 15 minutes

Servings

2 persons

Nutritional facts

120 calories, 9g fat ,1g fiber ,21g carbs ,2g protein

Ingredients

- 1/2 cup egg-free mayonnaise
- 1/2 cup sour cream (or vegan sour cream)
- 1/4 cup buttermilk (or almond milk with a 1/2 tsp apple cider vinegar)
- 2 tsp fresh chives, minced
- 1 tsp dried dill
- 1/2 tsp sea salt
- 1 large sweet onion
- 1 cup whole milk (or almond milk)
- 3 TBS Greek yogurt (or vegan yogurt)
- 1 cup gluten-free flour mix
- 1 cup gluten-free breadcrumbs
- 1 tsp kosher salt
- 1 tsp Creole or Cajun seasoning
- 1/2 tsp freshly ground black pepper
- Olive or avocado oil in a pump bottle (you can use a spoon)

Instructions

- Whisk together the mayonnaise, sour cream, and buttermilk in a small bowl. Stir in the herbs, salt, and pepper.
- Cover and place in the refrigerator until ready to serve. This will make enough to also use on a side salad and keep in your refrigerator for a few days.
- In a large bowl, whisk together the milk and yogurt until smooth. Set aside.
- Prepare your onion: Cut off 1/2 inch from the pointy top end of the onion. Peel the outer skin off and discard. Place the onion cut-side down on a clean cutting board. Starting 1/2 inch from the base end, make a descending incision all the way through to the board using a sharp knife. Make four more slices around the onion, equally spaced. Cut in between each part until you have 16 portions that are equally spaced. Turn the onion over and carefully separate the parts with your fingertips. Submerge the onion, cut side facing up, in the bowl of milk. Spoon the milk over it to coat. Place in the refrigerator for 1 hour.
- Remove the basket from the air fryer to a counter or cutting board. Place the flour in another large bowl. Remove the onion from the milk and allow the liquid to drip off. Place the onion

in the flour mixture and coat lightly to avoid clumps. Shake off any excess flour. Remove the onion to the fryer basket, root side down, and set aside for a few minutes.

- Discard the excess flour from the bowl. Mix the breadcrumbs, salt, and seasoning blend in the same bowl.

- Preheat your air fryer to 370°F. Coat the onion completely with the breadcrumb mixture. Coat the breadcrumbs lightly with oil. Place the onion in the air fryer and cook for 10 minutes. Check to see if it has crisped up and is tender. Continue to cook for approximately 5 more minutes until the crispy texture is achieved.

- Serve the blooming onion in a large bowl with the ranch dipping sauce in individual ramekins with plenty of napkins.

Air Fryer Asparagus Recipe

Preparation and Cooking Time

11 minutes

Servings

2 persons

Nutritional facts

155 calories, 12g fat ,1g fiber ,31g carbs ,4g protein

Ingredients

- 400 g (14 oz.) Asparagus
- 1 Tbsp. Lemon Juice
- 1/2 Tsp Salt
- 30 g (1 oz.) Butter
- 1 Clove Garlic
- 1/4 Tsp Pepper

Instructions

- Remove the asparagus's woody base.
- Put the spears on a shallow tray that will fit in the air fryer, or make a tray out of foil.
- Then season to taste with salt & pepper.
- Sliced as finely as possible, garlic should be tossed over the asparagus.
- Sprinkle the lemon juice over the asparagus and dot the butter afterward.
- Put in the air fryer & cook for 3 minutes at 200°C or 400°F.
  - Cook for another 3 minutes after flipping the asparagus.

Quick and Crunchy Air Fryer Fried Pickles Recipe

Preparation and Cooking Time

20 minutes

Servings

3 persons

Nutritional facts

120 calories, 21g fat ,1g fiber ,23g carbs ,2g protein

Ingredients

- 1 jar of pickles (Kosher dill)
- 1 container of seasoned bread crumbs
- ½ cup milk
- 1 egg
- 1 tbsp. of oil

Instructions

- First, take the pickles out of the jar and dry them with a dishtowel. Slice the pickles into 1/4- to 1/2-inch pieces.

- Next, make the egg wash by whisking together ½ cup milk & 1 egg. Then, put 1/4 to 1/2 tablespoons of bread crumbs in a bowl.

- Dip the pickle slices or spears into the egg wash, making sure to coat both sides. Put the pickle in the bread crumbs now, and flip to coat the second side once the first side has been coated.

- Use the oil to coat the basket to keep it from sticking, then fill it with all of the breaded pickles and place it into the cooker.

- Preheat the oven to 390°F & set the timer for 10 minutes. Always read the fryer instructions before using and flip the pickles halfway through.

- When the timer goes off, carefully remove the basket and set it aside to cool for five minutes before serving.

Cajun Air Fryer Diced Potatoes Recipe

Preparation and Cooking Time

30 minutes

Servings

6 persons

Nutritional facts

80 calories, 6g fat ,1g fiber ,18g carbs ,2g protein

Ingredients

- 6 White Potatoes
- 1/2 cup (1 stick) Melted Butter
- 1 TBS Cajun Seasoning
- Dice the 6 potatoes

Instructions

- Coat the diced potatoes with butter and place them on an air fryer rack.
- To taste, adjust the amount of Cajun seasoning.
- Preheat the oven to 375°F and air fry for fifteen minutes.
- Flip the potatoes with a spatula.
- Cook for an extra five minutes in the air fryer.
- Serve and have pleasure.

Air Fryer Spaghetti Squash

Preparation and Cooking Time

30 minutes

Servings

4 persons

Nutritional facts

117 calories, 10g fat ,1g fiber ,22g carbs ,3g protein

Ingredients

- 1 spaghetti squash
- salt and pepper to taste
- Half cup grated Parmesan cheese

Instructions

- Preheat the air fryer to 360 degrees Fahrenheit.
- Cut the spaghetti squash in half lengthwise after removing the ends. Using a spoon or melon baller, remove the seeds.
- Put the spaghetti squash side by side in the air fryer, trimming the long edges down if necessary to fit.
- Remove the spaghetti squash from the air fryer after 25-30 minutes of cooking.
- Then season with salt and pepper. Mix in the Parmesan cheese and serve.

Broccoli with Parmesan Cheese

Preparation and Cooking Time

11 minutes

Servings

4 persons

Nutritional facts

87 calories, 8g fat ,1g fiber ,15g carbs ,2g protein

Ingredients

- 1 head of broccoli
- 1/4 cup Parmesan cheese (freshly grated)
- additional parmesan cheese for serving
- 2 tablespoons butter, melted
- 1 clove garlic, minced
- salt and pepper to taste
- pinch of red pepper flakes (optional)

Instructions

- Preheat the air fryer to 400 degrees Fahrenheit.
- Broccoli should be cut into florets and kept aside.
- Melted butter, minced garlic, salt, pepper, & red pepper flakes are combined in a bowl.
- Mix in the broccoli until everything is well combined.
- Mix in the Parmesan cheese, making sure it is evenly coated.
- Cook the broccoli for 6-8 minutes in the air fryer, shaking the basket halfway through.
- Take the broccoli out of the air fryer & serve right away.
- When serving, sprinkle with more Parmesan cheese.

Healthy Vegetables Recipe

Preparation and Cooking Time

35 minutes

Servings

2 persons

Nutritional facts

80 calories, 6g fat ,1g fiber ,11g carbs ,1g protein

Ingredients

- 1 Tbsp. olive oil
- 1 cup cauliflower florets
- 1/4 cup balsamic vinegar
- 1 tsp sea salt
- 1 tsp black pepper
- 1/2 cup baby carrots
- 1 tsp red pepper flakes
- 1/2 cup yellow squash sliced
- 1 Tbsp. of minced garlic
- 1/2 cup of baby zucchini sliced
- 1/2 cup of sliced mushrooms
- 1 cup of broccoli florets
- 1 small onion, sliced
- 1/4 cup of parmesan cheese

Instructions

- Preheat the Air Fryer to 400 degrees Fahrenheit for 3 minutes.
- Mix the olive oil, balsamic vinegar, garlic, salt, and pepper, & red pepper flakes in a large mixing bowl. Combine all ingredients in a mixing bowl.
- Toss in the vegetables to coat.

- Fill the Air Fryer basket with the vegetables.
- Cook for an additional 8 minutes. Cook for an additional 6-8 minutes after shaking the vegetables.
- Bake for 1-two minutes after adding the cheese.

Crispy Air Fryer Vegetables

Preparation and Cooking Time

20 minutes

Servings

4 persons

Nutritional facts

58 calories, 4g fat ,0g fiber ,13g carbs ,1g protein

Ingredients

- 1 red bell pepper chopped
- 1 tablespoon olive oil
- ½ teaspoon Italian seasoning
- 1 cup mushrooms halved
- 1 small zucchini cut into ½" moons
- 2 cloves garlic minced
- salt & pepper to taste
- One tablespoon parmesan cheese grated

Instructions

- Preheat the air fryer to 380 degrees Fahrenheit.
- Toss all ingredients except the parmesan cheese in a large mixing bowl.
- Place in the air fryer in a single layer.
- Cook for 6 minutes and then stir with Parmesan cheese.
- Cook for another 3-5 minutes or until crisp and tender.

Delicious Air Fryer Roasted Vegetables

Preparation and Cooking Time

35 minutes

Servings

6 persons

Nutritional facts

61 calories,6g fat ,1g fiber ,18g carbs ,2g protein

Ingredients

- 1 cup broccoli florets
- 1 teaspoon sea salt
- 1 teaspoon black pepper
- 1 teaspoon red pepper flakes
- 1/2 cup sliced mushrooms
- 1 small onion, sliced
- 1/4 cup balsamic vinegar
- 1 tablespoon olive oil
- 1 cup cauliflower florets
- 1/2 cup baby carrots
- 1/2 cup yellow squash, sliced
- 1/2 cup baby zucchini, sliced
- 1 tablespoon minced garlic
- 1/4 cup parmesan cheese

Instructions

- Mix all of the seasonings. Then drizzle over the vegetables.
- Roast and serve.

Air Fryer Okra (Fresh and Frozen Breaded)

Preparation and Cooking Time

17 minutes

Servings

4 persons

Nutritional facts

184 calories, 10g fat ,1g fiber ,31g carbs ,2g protein

Ingredients

- 12 ounces' okra, cut into 1/2-inch slices and tops and bottoms removed
- 1/2 teaspoon paprika
- sea salt or table salt, to taste
- 1/2 cup flour
- 2 eggs
- 1/3 cup cornmeal
- 1/3 cup breadcrumbs
- Pinch of cayenne pepper

Instructions

- Preheat the air fryer to 380 degrees Fahrenheit.
- Two medium bowls and 1 tiny bowl should be set on the table. Fill a medium mixing bowl with flour, a small mixing bowl with eggs, and a medium mixing bowl with cornmeal, breadcrumbs, paprika, & cayenne pepper (if using).
- Each piece of okra should be dipped in the flour mixture, then the eggs, and finally the cornmeal mixture, covering it on all sides each time.
- In the air fryer, spray the breaded okra with a little oil and cook for 7 to 8 minutes, or till golden brown on the outside.
- Take the okra out of the air fryer and eat it.

Air Fryer Avocado Fries with Sriracha-Ranch Dip

Preparation and Cooking Time

15 minutes

Servings

4 persons

Nutritional facts

533 calories, 21g fat ,2g fiber ,34g carbs ,4g protein

Ingredients

- 4 avocados
- 1/2 teaspoon garlic powder
- 1/2 teaspoon salt
- 3/4 cup panko breadcrumbs
- 1/4 cup flour
- 2 eggs
- 1/4 cup ranch dressing
- teaspoon sriracha sauce

Instructions

- Preheat the air fryer to 400 degrees Fahrenheit.
- To clean the avocados, wash them.
- Each avocado should be cut in half and afterward sliced into wedges. Use a large spoon to scoop the wedges out to keep the wedges intact. Arrange three bowls. Combine the panko breadcrumbs, garlic powder, and salt in the first bowl. To blend, stir everything together.
- Separate the flour and eggs into two separate bowls. The eggs should be whisked together.
- In this order, dip each avocado wedge into the breading: egg, flour, egg, panko.
- Cook the breaded avocado wedges in a single layer in the air fryer basket for 4 to 6 minutes, flipping halfway through.
- Prepare the dipping sauce while cooking. Mix the sriracha & ranch dressing together thoroughly.
- Enjoy right away.

Air Fryer Cinnamon Sugar Dessert Fries

Preparation and Cooking Time

20 minutes

Servings

4 persons

Nutritional facts

110 calories,10g fat ,1g fiber ,21g carbs ,2g protein

Ingredients

- 2 sweet potatoes
- 2 tablespoons sugar
- 1/2 teaspoon cinnamon
- 1 tablespoon butter, melted
- 1 teaspoon butter, melted and separated from the above

Instructions

- Preheat the air fryer to 380 degrees Fahrenheit.
- Sweet potatoes should be peeled and chopped into thin fries.
- Using 1 tablespoon of butter, coat the fries.
- Cook fries for 15-18 minutes in a preheated air fryer.
- Place the sweet potato fries in a bowl after removing them from the air fryer.
- Add the sugar and cinnamon to the remaining butter & coat. To coat, mix everything.
- Enjoy right away.

Air Fried Asparagus with Garlic and Parmesan

Preparation and Cooking Time

10 minutes

Servings

4 persons

Nutritional facts

18 calories, 5g fat ,1g fiber ,14g carbs ,1g protein

Ingredients

- 1 bundle asparagus
- 1/8 teaspoon garlic salt
- 1 Tablespoon Parmesan cheese (powdered or grated)
- 1 teaspoon olive oil
- pepper to taste

Instructions

- Clean the asparagus and dry it. To remove the woody stalks, cut one inch off the bottom.
- In an air fryer, arrange asparagus in a single layer and spray with oil.
- On top of the asparagus, evenly sprinkle garlic salt. Then season with salt and pepper. Then sprinkle with Parmesan cheese.
- Cook for 7-10 minutes at 400 degrees F. Asparagus that is thinner cooks faster.
- Remove the asparagus from the air fryer and top with a little extra Parmesan cheese to finish.
- Enjoy right away.

Air Fryer Twice Baked Potatoes

Preparation and Cooking Time

15 minutes

Servings

4 persons

Nutritional facts

208 calories, 10g fat ,1g fiber ,21g carbs ,5g protein

Ingredients

- 2 cooked baked potatoes
- Two Tablespoon sour cream
- Half cup cheddar cheese
- 1 Tablespoon butter
- Two slices bacon, cooked

Instructions

- Cut the baked potatoes in half and scoop out the insides in a bowl.
- Toss the potatoes with the sour cream, ¼ cup cheddar cheese, and butter in a mixing bowl.
- With a potato masher, mash the potatoes and other ingredients together until they achieve the required consistency.
- Return the contents to the potato shells, mounding it as needed to fit.
- Place in the refrigerator till ready to serve.
- Place the potatoes in an air fryer basket when you're ready to bake them. Cook for 8 minutes at 400 degrees Fahrenheit.
- Finish with the remaining ¼ cup of cheddar cheese on the potatoes. While doing this, be careful not to contact the hot surfaces of the air fryer basket.
- To melt the cheese, return the potatoes to the air fryer & cook for another 2 minutes at 400 F.

Vegan eggplant parmesan in the air fryer

Preparation and Cooking Time

27 minutes

Servings

4 persons

Nutritional facts

276 calories, 9g fat ,2g fiber ,31g carbs ,2g protein

Ingredients

- ½ cup vegan mayonnaise
- 1 teaspoon grated vegan parmesan
- Pinch salt
- Dash black pepper
- 1 medium-sized eggplant cut into ½ inch slices, top & bottom removed
- ½ cup panko breadcrumbs
- 1 teaspoon dried oregano
- 1 teaspoon dried basil
- 1 teaspoon granulated onion
- Spritz Oil spray
- ½ to ¾ cup marinara sauce
- Half cup grated vegan mozzarella cheese

Instructions

- Begin by setting two plates. On one plate, spread the vegan mayonnaise. Mix dried oregano, panko breadcrumbs, granulated onion, dried basil, shredded vegan parmesan, a pinch of salt, and a dash of pepper on a separate plate.

- Apply mayonnaise to each eggplant slice. This should be the lightest possible layer, and it's simply a thin layer to allow the breadcrumb mixture to stick to the slices.
- After that, roll each slice in the breadcrumb mixture. Make sure it's breadcrumb-coated on all sides.
- Fill the air fryer basket with a uniform layer of slices. However, do not overfill the basket with slices on top of each other for optimal browning. Air should be able to circulate freely around each slice. You'll likely be able to put 4 to 6 slices in the basket, depending on the eggplant slices' size and the basket's size. Using an oil spray, spritz the tops of the eggplant slices.
- In the air fryer, place the basket. Preheat the oven to 400 degrees Fahrenheit and bake for 12 minutes. Halfway through, you need to take a break to flip the slices. Spritz the slices one more with the oil spray. You should continue air frying for four minutes and wait till the slices are nutty brown on the other side. Add a tablespoon of marinara sauce as well as a pinch of mozzarella cheese to each slice after 10 minutes. Cook for an additional 2 minutes. Take the eggplant slices out of the air fryer and set them aside.
- Continue to air fry the eggplant in batches till all of it is done.

Air Fryer Frozen Vegetables

Preparation and Cooking Time

16 minutes

Servings

4 persons

Nutritional facts

45 calories, 6g fat ,0.5g fiber ,11g carbs ,2g protein

Ingredients

- 2 (10 oz.) bags frozen mixed vegetables
- 1 teaspoon garlic powder
- 1/2 teaspoon onion powder
- 1/2 teaspoon salt
- 1/2 teaspoon pepper
- olive oil spray

Instructions

- After spraying the air fryer basket with olive oil, place the frozen mixed vegetables in it. Don't let the vegetables thaw first; add them right from the
- freezer to the air fryer to achieve the greatest results.
- Spray the tops of the vegetables with olive oil spray, then season with salt, pepper, garlic powder, and onion powder, shaking to distribute them evenly.
- Then air fry for 10 minutes at 400 degrees. Stir & shake the vegetables, then air fry for a further 5 to 10 minutes, or until crispy. Because different models of air fryers cook at different rates, make careful to check frequently near the finish to avoid burning.
- Serve with a sprinkling of Parmesan, if desired.

Crispy and Tender Air Fryer Vegetables Recipe

Preparation and Cooking Time

35 minutes

Servings

6 persons

Nutritional facts

63 calories,8g fat ,0g fiber ,16g carbs ,3g protein

Ingredients

- 1 cup broccoli florets
- 1/2 cup sliced mushrooms

- 1 tbsp. minced garlic
- 1 tsp sea salt
- 1 tsp black pepper
- 1 tsp red pepper flakes
- 1 onion, sliced
- 1/4 cup balsamic vinegar
- 1 tbsp. olive oil
- 1 cup cauliflower florets
- 1/2 cup baby carrots
- 1/2 cup yellow squash, sliced
- 1/2 cup baby zucchini, sliced
- 1/4 cup parmesan cheese

Instructions
- Heat the Air Fryer for 3 minutes at 400°F.
- Put olive oil, balsamic vinegar, garlic, salt & pepper, and red pepper flakes in a large mixing bowl. Combine all ingredients in a mixing bowl.
- Toss in the vegetables to coat.
- Fill the Air Fryer basket with vegetables. Cook for an additional 8 minutes. Cook for an additional 6-8 minutes after shaking the vegetables.
- Bake for 1-two minutes after adding the cheese.

Air Fryer Vegetable Biriyani

Preparation and Cooking Time

55 minutes

Servings

6 persons

Nutritional facts

480 calories, 23g fat ,1g fiber ,40g carbs ,8g protein

Ingredients
- 1 cup Basmati Rice
- 1 block of paneer cut into cubes
- 1 tbsp. chopped green chilies
- 1 tbsp. ginger paste
- 1 tbsp. garlic paste
- Salt and Pepper to taste
- 1 tbsp. cumin seeds
  - 1/2 tbsp. ground coriander seeds
- 1 tsp turmeric
- 1/2 tbsp. Gram Masala
- 1 onion chopped
- 5 mushrooms sliced
- 1 pepper sliced
- 2 small carrots chopped
- 1/2 tbsp. red chili powder
- Coriander to garnish
- Pomegranate to top optional

Instructions
- Boil the rice for 10 minutes in a pot of water. Drain the rice and set it aside after the 10 minutes are up.
- Caramelise the chopped onions, cumin seeds, green chilies, garlic, & ginger paste in some oil in a pan. Then mix in the chopped vegetables.

- Combine the paneer cubes and all of the additional spices in a mixing bowl. After a few minutes, you need to season with salt and pepper.
- Remove the vegetables from the fire when they are softer but not fully cooked, and set them aside.
- Place one layer of rice in an air fryer-safe dish. After that, put a layer of the veggie mixture on top. Carry on in this manner till the mixture is spent.
- The rice should be the last layer, and it should be garnished with coriander.
- Sprinkle a splash of water on top of the rice to prevent it from crisping, then cook for 15 minutes at 180°C in the Air Fryer.

Air Fryer Vegetable and Cheese Quesadillas

Preparation and Cooking Time

18 minutes

Servings

2 persons

Nutritional facts

291 calories,15g fat ,2g fiber ,19g carbs ,4g protein

Ingredients
- 2 (6 inches) flour tortillas
- 1/2 red bell pepper, sliced
- cooking spray
- 1/2 cup shredded Cheddar cheese
- 1/2 zucchini, sliced

Instructions
- Preheat the air fryer to 400 degrees Fahrenheit (200 degrees Celsius).
- One side of a single tortilla should be generously sprayed with cooking spray before being placed flat in the air fryer basket.
- Half of the Cheddar cheese should be spread over the tortilla. Add bell pepper and zucchini to the top of the cheese layer. Cover with the remaining Cheddar cheese.
- Spray the top of the second tortilla with cooking spray and place it over the fillings.
- It should be air-fried for eight to nine minutes in the air fryer till cheese is melted & tortillas are crunchy.

Air Fryer Eggplant Pizza

Preparation and Cooking Time

30 minutes

Servings

2 persons

Nutritional facts

134 calories,12g fat ,2g fiber ,28g carbs ,5g protein

Ingredients
- 1 medium eggplant, sliced into 1/2" thick rounds
- 1/2 cup shredded mozzarella cheese
- Parmesan, oregano, red pepper, salt, etc. (optional)
- 1/2 cup pizza sauce

Instructions
- Preheat your air fryer to 400 degrees Fahrenheit.
- Sprinkle salt on the sliced eggplant and place it on a paper towel.
- Allow sitting for 5 minutes before blotting excess moisture with a paper towel.

- Cook the eggplant for 5 minutes in a single layer in the air fryer. Cook for another 2-3 minutes, or until the eggplant is browned. It's possible that you'll have to perform this in batches.
- Pizza sauce & cheese should be spread on each piece.
- Cook for another 4-5 minutes, or until the cheese has browned and is bubbly.
- If desired, garnish with basil & shredded Parmesan cheese.

Air Fryer Smoked Sausage and Vegetables

Preparation and Cooking Time

20 minutes

Servings

4 persons

Nutritional facts

423 calories, 20g fat ,3g fiber ,41g carbs ,2g protein

Ingredients

- 2 whole sweet potatoes, peeled and cubed
- 2 teaspoons Cajun seasoning, divided
- 14 ounces smoked sausage
- 1 tablespoon oil, divided
- 1 head broccoli, chopped into florets

Instructions

- Drizzle half of the oil over the potatoes in a mixing bowl. Toss half of the Cajun seasoning on top and toss to coat.
- In your air fryer basket, put the sweet potato cubes.
- Preheat the air fryer to 390°F & cook for 10 minutes.
- Slice the smoked sausage into rounds while the potatoes are cooking. Add the broccoli florets to the mixing bowl as well.
- Then season with the leftover Cajun seasoning and drizzle with the remaining oil.
- When the air fryer has cooled down, put the smoked sausage & broccoli with the potatoes in the basket and stir well to blend.
- Cook for another 5 minutes at 390 degrees.
- Serve immediately.

Air Fryer Cauliflower & Broccoli Bites

Preparation and Cooking Time

25 minutes

Servings

6 persons

Nutritional facts

130 calories, 9g fat ,1g fiber ,16g carbs ,4g protein

Ingredients

- Cooking spray
- 2 cups broccoli florets
- ½ cup whole wheat flour
- 2 large eggs
- 1 cup panko bread crumbs
- ¼ cup grated Parmesan
- 1 Tbsp. creole seasoning
- 2 cups cauliflower florets
- 1 Tbsp. fresh parsley, finely chopped, optional
- Marinara sauce for serving, optional

Instructions

- Preheat the air fryer to 400 degrees Fahrenheit.
- Using a light spray of oil, lightly coat the frying basket.

- Combine panko, Parmesan, and creole spice in a large mixing bowl.
- Set aside the flour in a shallow bowl. Stir in two eggs and set aside in a separate dish
- Dip cauliflower & broccoli florets in flour & gently shake off excess in small batches. Dip into the egg, then into the breadcrumb mixture.
- Put florets in the basket and heat for 5-6 minutes, or until golden and crispy. Remove the fryer basket from the pan and top with parsley.
- Serve with marinara sauce right away.

Air Fried Tempura Veggies

Preparation and Cooking Time

25 minutes

Servings

4 persons

Nutritional facts

179 calories, 10g fat ,1g fiber ,23g carbs ,2g protein

Ingredients

- ½ cup flour
- 2 teaspoons vegetable oil
- ¼ teaspoon Seasoning, or more to taste
- 2 cups vegetable pieces (whole green beans, sweet pepper rings, zucchini slices, whole asparagus spears, red onion rings, or avocado wedges), cut 1/2 inch thick
- ½ teaspoon salt, plus more to taste
- ½ teaspoon black pepper
- 2 eggs
- 1 cup panko bread crumbs
- Dipping sauce

Instructions

- Combine flour, 1/4 teaspoon salt, and pepper in a shallow dish. In a separate shallow dish, whisk together the eggs and water. In a third shallow dish, combine panko and oil. Then season panko & flour mixture with appropriate seasoning.
- Add the remaining 1/4 teaspoon of salt to the vegetables. To coat, dip in the flour mixture, then the egg mixture, and finally the panko mixture.
- Preheat the oven to 200°F and the air fryer to 400°F. Half of the vegetables should be arranged in a single layer in the fryer basket. Cook for about 10 minutes, or until golden brown. If desired, season with a little more salt. To keep the vegetables warm, place them in the oven. Continue with the remaining vegetables. Serve with dipping sauce on the side.

Air Fryer Veggie Sandwich

Preparation and Cooking Time

15 minutes

Servings

1 person

Nutritional facts

491 calories ,16g fat ,4g fiber ,32g carbs ,8g protein

Ingredients

- A handful of grated cheese
- 1 cherry tomato, quartered
- 2 slices of bread
- A few mushroom slices
- A few red bell pepper slices

- A large spoonful of pesto
- A little olive oil for spritzing the bread

Instructions

- Spray the mushrooms & peppers with a little oil & air fry for 5 minutes at 200°C/390°F.
- Assemble the ingredients of your sandwich. On both sides of the bread, spread pesto and then stuff with cheese, mushrooms, pepper, and tomato.
- Spritz or brush the bread on both sides with olive oil. On top of the sandwich, spread a bit of additional cheese.
- Then you need to air-fry the bread for 5 minutes at 200°C/390°F or until brown and crispy.

Air-Fried Crispy Vegetables (Chinese Style)

Preparation and Cooking Time

25 minutes

Servings

2 persons

Nutritional facts

240 calories,10g fat ,2g fiber ,33g carbs ,7g protein

Ingredients

- 2 Cups Mixed Vegetables (Bell Peppers, Cauliflower, Mushrooms, Zucchini, Baby Corn)
- ½-1 tsp Black Pepper Powder
- 1 tbsp. Tomato Ketchup
- 1 tbsp. Vinegar (Rice/Synthetic or Apple Cider)
- 1 tsp Brown Sugar/Coconut Sugar
- 1 tbsp. Sesame Oil or any plant-based oil
- 1 tsp Sesame Seeds
- 1 tsp Salt or as per taste
- 1 tsp Oil
- ½ Cup Water or as required
- 2 tbsp. Soy Sauce
- 1/4 Cup Cornstarch
- 1/4 Cup All-Purpose Flour/Maida
- ½ tsp Garlic Powder
- ½-1 tsp Red Chili Powder
- 1 tbsp. Chili Sauce/
- Spring Onion Greens for Garnish

Instructions

- Cauliflower should be cut into small florets; bell peppers should be cubed, Mushrooms should be cut in half, while carrots and zucchini should be sliced into
- circles. Cut slices that aren't too thin.
- All-purpose flour, corn starch, garlic powder, bell pepper powder, red chili powder, and salt are combined to make the batter.
- To prepare a lump-free batter, you need to start with around 1/2 cup water and add 1-2 tbsp. (if needed) at a time. The batter must be thick enough to coat the vegetables completely. Make sure the batter isn't too runny. It should be similar to the batter for pakoras or fritters.
- Make a smooth, lump-free batter with a tsp of oil. Add all of the vegetables to the batter and coat them well.
- Preheat the air fryer to 350 degrees Fahrenheit, then add the vegetables as directed, and it takes 10 minutes to air fry the vegetables.

- Prepare the sauce mix. Heat a tbsp. of oil in a heavy-bottomed skillet, add finely chopped garlic, sauté until fragrant, and afterward add the sauce mix & freshly ground black pepper.
- Cook for a minute, then add the air-fried veggies and toss gently to combine. Coat all of the vegetables in the sauce.
- Serve immediately with Sesame Seeds and freshly chopped spring onion greens.

Crispy Air Fryer Broccoli

Preparation and Cooking Time

9 minutes

Servings

2 persons

Nutritional facts

201 calories,11g fat ,1g fiber ,28g carbs ,5g protein

Ingredients

- 1 head of broccoli
- 0.5 lemon juice only
- 1 pinch sea salt and black pepper
- 1 tbsp. olive oil
- 3 garlic cloves crushed
- 20 g grated Parmesan

Instructions

- Combine the olive oil, garlic, lemon juice, salt, pepper, and parmesan in a bowl.
- Insert the broccoli and toss everything together until every last bit of broccoli is covered.
- Pour it into an air fryer basket & cook for 7 minutes at 180°C, or until crispy.

Air Fryer Zucchini Chips

Preparation and Cooking Time

20 minutes

Servings

4 persons

Nutritional facts

117 calories,12g fat ,1g fiber ,22g carbs ,2g protein

Ingredients

- 2 zucchinis, thinly sliced
- 1.5 tablespoons paprika
- cooking oil spray
- 3/4 cup panko bread crumbs
- 3 eggs
- 1/2 cup all-purpose flour
- salt
- spicy mayo for dipping

Instructions

- Thinly slice the zucchini, whisk the eggs in a small dish, then add the flour, panko, paprika, and salt in another small bowl.
- Each zucchini slice should be floured first, then dipped in the egg, and afterward floured again.
- Working in batches, set the zucchini chips in a single layer in the air fryer, lightly spritz both sides with cooking spray, cook for 8 minutes at 400 F, flip & spray again, and cook for another 4 minutes. If desired, season with salt after cooking.

Homemade Air Fryer Veggie Tots

Preparation and Cooking Time

15 minutes

Servings

2 persons

Nutritional facts

176 calories, 20g fat ,2g fiber ,19g carbs ,2g protein

Ingredients

- 1 zucchini, peeled
- ¼ cup breadcrumbs
- ¼ cup Parmesan cheese, low sodium
- 1 carrot, peeled
- 1 large egg
- ¼ tsp. black pepper

Instructions

- Preheat the air fryer to 400 degrees Fahrenheit.
- Zucchini and carrots should be grated. Remove any extra water by wringing it out.
- Combine all of the above ingredients in a medium mixing bowl.
- To make the tots, form them into a single layer and place them in the air fryer.
- It should be cooked for ten minutes.

Broccoli Florets with vegetable broth Parmesan

Preparation and Cooking Time

12 minutes

Servings

2 persons

Nutritional facts

126 calories, 8g fat ,1g fiber ,25g carbs ,3g protein

Ingredients

- 4 cups broccoli florets approx. 1 small head of broccoli
- 1/4 tsp chili flakes optional, but recommended
- Vegan Parmesan Cheese optional
- 1 tbsp. avocado oil, or your choice sub for vegetable broth for no oil
- 1/4 tsp sea salt
- 1/4 tsp garlic powder
- lemon wedges optional

Instructions

- Cut the broccoli florets into small pieces and place them in a bowl. Drizzle with oil or vegetable broth & season with salt and pepper. To evenly coat the broccoli, combine all ingredients in a large mixing bowl.
- Fill the bottom of the air fryer with a quarter cup of water, just below the basket. This will prevent the broccoli from smoking as well as from becoming bitter. Then, place the broccoli in the air fryer basket and air fry for 7-9 minutes or till desired brownness is achieved. Give your broccoli a good stir, or shake the basket halfway through.
- If preferred, garnish the broccoli with lemon slices or vegan Parmesan cheese.

Air Fryer Vegetable Omelet

Preparation and Cooking Time

20 minutes

Servings

2 persons

Nutritional facts

380 calories, 10g fat ,2g fiber ,34g carbs ,6g protein

Ingredients

- 2 eggs
- 2 tablespoons red, green, or yellow bell peppers, diced
- 2 tablespoons red onion, diced
- 2 tablespoons cream
- 1/2 teaspoon salt
- 1/4 teaspoon white or black pepper
- 1/4 cup shredded Cheddar cheese, divided

Instructions

- Combine the eggs, cream, salt, & black pepper in a small mixing bowl.
- Mix the diced vegetables and 2 tbsp. of shredded cheese until thoroughly combined.
- Use cooking spray to coat the ramekin or casserole dish.
- Fill the prepared dish with the egg mixture.
- Place the dish in the air fryer basket and cook for 10-15 minutes on the air fryer, setting at 350 degrees F. Spread the remaining cheese on top in the last few minutes.

Air Fryer Spiced Chicken and Vegetables

Preparation and Cooking Time

35 minutes

Servings

2 persons

Nutritional facts

344 calories, 19g fat ,2g fiber ,45g carbs ,8g protein

Ingredients

- 2 boneless skinless chicken breasts
- 1/2 tsp. salt
- 1/2 tsp. pepper
- 1/4 tsp. cumin
- 1 red onion
- 1/2 Tbsp. olive oil
- 1 tsp. chili powder
- 1/2 tsp. paprika
- 1/2 tsp. onion powder
- 1/2 tsp. garlic powder
- 1 large potato
- 2-3 large carrots
- 1/2 Tbsp. olive oil
- 1 pinch salt

Instructions

- Preheat the air fryer to 325 degrees F.
- To make a spice rub, put all of the chicken ingredients in a small bowl (chili powder, onion powder, garlic powder, salt, pepper, cumin, and paprika). Apply 1/2 tbsp. Olive oil to the chicken breasts before applying the spice rub.
- Peel the potatoes and carrots (optional). Carrots should be cut into 1/2" - 1" pieces, while potatoes should be cut into 1/2" - 1" cubes. Remove the outer layer of the onion after cutting it in half. Then cut each piece in half again. Make sure to separate all of the onion's layers. In a mixing bowl, combine all of the vegetables. Using 1/2 tablespoon olive oil and a bit of salt, coat the chicken.

- Place the vegetables in the air fryer basket that has been warmed. Close the air fryer and put the chicken breasts on the vegetables. Allow 35 minutes for cooking. Flip the chicken halfway through cooking and give the vegetables a thorough shake.

Air Fryer Potato Pancakes

Preparation and Cooking Time

45 minutes

Servings

6 persons

Nutritional facts

197 calories, 14g fat ,2g fiber ,31g carbs ,2g protein

Ingredients

- 4 cups mashed potatoes, skin removed, About 6-7 potatoes
- 1 tbsp. olive oil
- 1/2 cup diced green bell pepper
- 1 small zucchini, peeled and diced
- 2 tbsp. Parmesan cheese, grated
- 1/2 tsp salt
- 1 tbsp. olive oil
- 1/2 cup diced onion
- 1/3 cup traditional bread crumbs
- 2 large eggs
- 1/2 tsp salt
- 1/2 tsp ground pepper
- 1/2 cup diced red bell pepper
- 1/2 tsp ground pepper

Instructions

- Boil potatoes until tender, about 20 minutes after peeling and chopping them. Drain the water from the potatoes and place them in a mixing bowl. Using a potato masher, mash the potatoes. Allow cooling before serving.
- Onion, red pepper, green pepper, and zucchini should all be diced.
- Heat olive oil in a medium skillet over medium heat. Add the vegetables and cook for 5 minutes, or until they are cooked. Remove the pan from the heat. Stir in the Parmesan cheese, salt, and pepper to the sautéed vegetables.
- Toss the mashed potatoes with salt, pepper, breadcrumbs, and eggs until thoroughly combined.
- Form the mashed potatoes into balls, lightly press down, and form into 1/4-inch thick flat patties. The patties will be around 5 inches in diameter. Continue until all of the patties are formed. You'll need a total of 12 patties, which should be an even number.
- Place about 2 tablespoons of the veggie mixture on top of one of the patties. Form a sandwich by adding another patty on top. So that no seams are visible, press all of the sides together.
- Brush the tops and bottoms of the patties with olive oil using a pastry brush.
- Remove the air fryer basket and coat it lightly with nonstick cooking spray. Place patties in the basket gently.
- Preheat oven to 400°F and bake for 15 minutes, flipping halfway through. Continue until all of the potato patties are done.

Get Crispy Veggie Quesadillas in an Air Fryer

Preparation and Cooking Time

40 minutes

Servings

4 persons

Nutritional facts

291 calories, 10g fat ,1g fiber ,23g carbs ,2g protein

Ingredients

- 4 whole-grain flour tortillas
- Cooking spray
- 2 ounces of plain 2% Greek yogurt
- 1 teaspoon of lime zest
- 1/4 teaspoon of ground cumin
- 4 oz. of sharp Cheddar cheese
- 1 cup of sliced red bell pepper
- 1 cup of sliced zucchini
- 1 cup of no-salt-added canned black beans
- 2 tablespoons of chopped cilantro
- 1/2 cup of refrigerated pico de gallo

Instructions

- To make the tortillas, place them on a work surface. Half of each tortilla should be topped with 2 tablespoons of shredded cheese. Place 1/4 cup red pepper slices, zucchini slices, & black beans on top of the cheese. The remaining 1/2 cup of cheese should be evenly distributed. Fold the tortillas in half to make half-moon quesadillas. Secure them with toothpicks.
- Apply cooking spray to the basket. Place 2 quesadillas in the basket and bake at 400°F for 10 minutes, turning halfway through cooking, until tortillas are golden brown and a little crispy, cheese is melted, & vegetables are slightly softened. Repeat with the rest of the quesadillas.
- In a small bowl, combine yogurt, lime zest, lime juice, & cumin while the quesadillas are cooking. Cut each quesadilla into wedges & top with cilantro to serve. It should be served with one tablespoon cumin cream and 2 tablespoons pico de gallo per person.

Amazing Air Fryer Vegetables

Preparation and Cooking Time

35 minutes

Servings

2 persons

Nutritional facts

264 calories, 16g fat ,1g fiber ,29g carbs ,2g protein

Ingredients

- 1 Tbsp. olive oil
- 1 cup cauliflower florets
- 1/2 cup baby carrots
- 1 tsp red pepper flakes
- 1/2 cup yellow squash sliced
- 1 small onion sliced
- 1 Tbsp. minced garlic
- 1/2 cup baby zucchini sliced
- 1/2 cup sliced mushrooms
- 1 cup broccoli florets
- 1/4 cup balsamic vinegar
- 1 tsp sea salt
- 1 tsp black pepper
- 1/4 cup freshly grated parmesan cheese optional

Instructions

- Preheat the Air Fryer to 400 degrees Fahrenheit for 3 minutes.

- Mix the olive oil, balsamic vinegar, garlic, salt, and pepper, & red pepper flakes in a large mixing bowl. Combine all ingredients in a mixing bowl.
- Toss in the vegetables to coat.
- Fill the Air Fryer basket with the vegetables. Cook for an additional 8 minutes. Cook for an additional 6-8 minutes after shaking the vegetables.
- Bake for 1-two minutes after adding the cheese.

Air Fryer Roasted Broccoli (low carb + keto)

Preparation and Cooking Time

8 minutes

Servings

4 persons

Nutritional facts

178 calories, 11g fat ,1g fiber ,21g carbs ,5g protein

Ingredients

- 5 cups broccoli florets
- 1/3 cup shredded parmesan cheese
- salt and pepper to taste
- 2 tablespoons butter
- 2 teaspoons minced garlic
- Lemon slices (optional)

Instructions

- Melt the butter with the minced garlic and keep it aside for later.
- Preheat the air fryer to 350 degrees Fahrenheit, as directed by the manufacturer.
- Spray the chopped broccoli florets in the air fryer basket with a light coating of cooking oil.
- Broccoli should be roasted for a total of 8 minutes.
- The broccoli must be fork tender in the thickest section of the stem and crisp on the outside at this time.
- Remove the broccoli from the basket & toss with the garlic butter, parmesan, and then season to taste with salt and pepper.

Air fryer veg Manchurian recipe, Vegetable Manchurian

Preparation and Cooking Time

40 minutes

Servings

4 persons

Nutritional facts

398 calories,12g fat ,1g fiber ,28g carbs ,2g protein

Ingredients

- Carrot – 1 cup
- Ginger – ½ tsp
- Garlic – ½ tsp
- Maida – ¼ cup
- Corn flour – ¼ cup
- Cabbage – 1 cup
- Capsicum – ½ cup
- Beans – ¼ cup
- White stalk of spring onion – 2 tbsp.
- Salt – to taste

- Ginger – ½ tsp
- Sugar – ½ tsp
- Corn flour – 1 tbsp.
- Water – ½ cup
- Red chili sauce - 1 tsp
- Garlic – ½ tsp
- White stalk of spring onion – 2 tbsp.
- Green stalk of spring onion – 1 tbsp.
- Ketchup/ Tomato sauce – 2 tbsp.
- Soy sauce – 1 tbsp.
- Salt – to taste
- Vinegar - ½ tsp
- Oil – 1 tbsp.

Instructions

- Preheat the air fryer to 360 degrees F. Depending on the air fryer, it should take 10 minutes. Grated carrot, chopped capsicum, cabbage, finely chopped beans, ginger, white stem of spring onion, garlic, maize flour, maida, and salt should all be combined in a large mixing bowl. Combine thoroughly, and as you continue to mix, the water from the vegetables will aid in the formation of a dough-like consistency. Take 2 tbsp. of the ingredients and roll it into balls with your fingers. Prepare the balls ahead of time.
- Brush a tbsp. oil on the baking rack (to prevent Manchurian balls from sticking) and arrange the Manchurian balls one by one, evenly spaced, in the air fryer. Do not use very large chunks because the insides may not be thoroughly cooked in the time allotted. Brush the Manchurian balls with a tbsp. of oil as well. Cook for another 10 minutes.
- Remove the rack from the air fryer after 10 minutes, flip the Manchurian balls, and cook for another 10 minutes. After 10 minutes, the Manchurian should be evenly browned and crisp. If the inside does not appear to be cooked, fry for another two minutes. Take the Manchurian balls out of the air fryer and set them aside.
- In a frying pan, heat the oil and put the Manchurian balls one by one into the hot oil. Fry until golden brown on a medium flame. Remove it from the oil when golden brown and drain excess oil on a plate lined with paper towels. Set it aside for now.
- Heat a tablespoon of oil in a pan and add finely chopped ginger and garlic. In a high-flame skillet, brown thoroughly.
- Add the spring onion white stalks, diced. Cook for a few seconds. Toss in the tomato sauce/ketchup, red chili sauce, vinegar, and dark soy sauce at this point. Mix thoroughly. Now gradually add the corn flour mixture, stirring constantly. Toss in the Manchurian balls now. Toss the balls in the sauce thoroughly. Add the chopped green stalk of spring onion when the mixture begins to boil. Remove from the heat and serve immediately with noodles or fried rice.

Chicken Steak with Stir-Fried Vegetables

Preparation and Cooking Time

35 minutes

Servings

2 persons

Nutritional facts

248 calories, 11g fat ,2g fiber ,31g carbs ,2g protein

Ingredients

- Chicken Breast   500 g
- Salt 1/4 tsp or as required
- Garlic paste 1/2 tsp

- Corn flour 1 tbsp.
- Mix vegetables 1 cup
- Dark soy sauce 1 tbsp.
- Sriracha sauce 1-1/2 tbsp.
- Oyster sauce 1 tbsp.
- Rice vinegar 1 tbsp.
- Oil 2 tbsp.
- Spring onion 2-3
- Dark soy sauce 1 tbsp.
- Rice vinegar 1/2 tbsp.
- Salt as required
- Black pepper as required

Instructions

- Take a boneless chicken breast and cut it into the size you want.
- Marinate for 10-15 minutes.
- Preheat the Air Fryer for 5 minutes at 180 degrees Celsius.
- Cook for about 10 minutes, then flip it and cook for another 5 minutes.
- Alternatively, fry it until it gets somewhat crispy.
- Now heat a pan, add 1 tbsp. oil and 1 cup frozen vegetables, and cook for 1 minute on high heat.
- Add the other items and whisk for a few seconds. Turn the heat off.

Air Fryer Chinese Vegetables Buns Recipe

Preparation and Cooking Time

1 hour 25 minutes

Servings

16 persons

Nutritional facts

77 calories, 8g fat ,2g fiber ,17g carbs ,3g protein

Ingredients

- 85 ml Warm Water
- 1½ tsp Ginger Paste
- 1 tsp Cumin Powder
- 2 tsp Hoisin Sauce
- 2 tsp Light Soy Sauce
- 1 tsp Sesame Oil plus more for brushing
- Spring Onions chopped
- Chili Oil for serving
- 1 tsp Salt
- 1 tsp Black Pepper
- 1 tsp Instant Yeast
- 250 g Plain Flour
- 1 tsp Sugar
- 30 g Dried Shiitake Mushrooms soak in hot water for 30 minutes to rehydrate, finely diced
- 1½ tsp Garlic Paste
- 1 tsp Red Chili Flakes
- 120 g Chinese chives chopped
- 120 g Leeks chopped
- Chinese Black Vinegar for serving

Instructions

- Preheat the air fryer to 180 degrees Celsius.

- Apply sesame oil to the bottom of the air fryer basket. Brush each of the vegetable buns with sesame oil before placing them in the basket. It should be cooked for five minutes.
- Cook for another 5 minutes, until golden and crispy, with another layer of sesame oil on top. Serve with Chinese black vinegar and/or chili oil right away.

Moroccan chicken with vegetables

Preparation and Cooking Time

25 minutes

Servings

2 persons

Nutritional facts

415 calories, 20g fat ,1g fiber ,38g carbs ,6g protein

Ingredients

- 2 lbs. boneless chicken thighs
- 1 tsp coriander, ground
- 1 tsp ground cinnamon
- 1 tsp turmeric, ground
- ½ tsp ground ginger
- ¼ tsp cayenne pepper or harissa paste (optional)
- 1 tbsp. olive oil
- ½ lb. red bell peppers, seeded and cut into large slices
- 3 oz. (½ cup) shallots, peeled and halved
- 1 tbsp. paprika powder
- 2 tsp ground cumin
- 1 tsp salt
- 1 cup Greek yogurt
- Salt
- 3 oz. cucumber, grated
- 1 tbsp. fresh mint, finely chopped or ground black pepper, to taste
- 2 garlic cloves, finely chopped

Instructions

- Preheat the air fryer to 380 degrees Fahrenheit (190 degrees Celsius).
- In a large mixing bowl, combine the chicken and vegetables. Combine the cumin, salt, paprika, coriander, turmeric, cinnamon, ginger, cayenne, & olive oil in a large mixing bowl. Coat the chicken and vegetables thoroughly. Set aside for at least ten minutes and up to 3 to 4 hours to marinate.
- Cook for 15-20 minutes, flipping midway through, or till chicken & veggies are slightly charred, and the chicken is cooked through in the prepared air fryer. If your air fryer isn't big enough, you might have to cook them in two or three batches.
- Place the grated cucumber in a colander and season with salt while the chicken is cooking. Allow 5 minutes for the liquid to drain after mixing thoroughly. Wrap a tea towel around the cucumber and squeeze off any extra juice.
- Combine the cucumber, garlic, oil, & fresh mint.
- Toss in the yogurt and season to taste with black pepper and salt.
- Refrigerate the sauce for at least ten minutes to allow the flavors to blend. It will stay in the fridge for about 3 days.
- With a generous dollop of Tzatziki on top, serve the chicken and vegetables.

Homemade Air Fryer Vegetable Egg Roll Recipe

Preparation and Cooking Time

18 minutes

Servings

4 persons

Nutritional facts

159 calories,8g fat ,1g fiber ,21g carbs ,2g protein

Ingredients

- 1 Tbsp. olive oil
- 1 8 ounces can water chestnuts diced
- 1/4 cup coconut aminos or soy sauce
- 1 tsp. sesame oil
- 1/2-1 tsp. chili flakes depending on heat preference
- 1 1/2-ounce bag Broccoli Slaw
- 8 white mushrooms diced
- 1 Tbsp. garlic minced
- 1 Tbsp. fresh ginger finely minced
- 8 full-size wonton wrappers
    - 1/4 cup water for sealing the edges

Instructions

- Pour olive oil into a large skillet. When the pan is hot, add the broccoli slaw & cook for a few minutes until the broccoli has wilted. Diced mushrooms, garlic, ginger, and diced water chestnuts are added to the mix.
- Add in the aminos or soy sauce, sesame oil, and chili flakes once all vegetables have wilted and become tender. Taste and season with salt and pepper as needed. Remove from the heat and put aside.
- This mixture should have very little liquid. If the liquid is too much, make a slurry with 1 tablespoon cornstarch and 1 tablespoon water and stir it into the vegetable mixture to thicken it and remove the moisture.
- Preheat your air fryer to 400 degrees Fahrenheit. Meanwhile, arrange the egg roll wrapper in a diamond shape with the points (corners) on the bottom and top. Moisten all of the edges of the egg roll wrapper with water with your finger.
- In the center of the wrapper, spread a spoonful of filling in a horizontal line. Fold the bottom corner of the egg roll wrapper up and then over the filling, pressing the filling into the wrapper tightly.
- Then, one by one, fold each side over on itself, moistening each edge with water, so it sticks closed. Close the roll thoroughly & moisten any open edges to keep them closed. Repeat with the remaining egg rolls, spraying each side with frying spray.
- Put egg rolls in an Air Fryer basket that has been preheated. Fry for 4 minutes at 400 degrees F, then flip them over in the air fryer. Cook for an additional 4 minutes. Carefully remove the air fryer basket from the air fryer and cut it in half. Serve immediately with soy sauce or coconut aminos.

Chinese Stir Fry Veg & Noodles

Preparation and Cooking Time

20 minutes

Servings

2 persons

Nutritional facts

380 calories,13g fat ,2g fiber ,31g carbs ,4g protein

Ingredients

- 250 gm Noodles / Spaghetti (uncooked) (½ pound)
- 1 count Green Capsicum / Bell Pepper
- as per taste, Salt
- 1 tablespoon Soy sauce (as per taste)
- 1 tablespoon Dry Chili Flakes / Powder
- 1 count Yellow Capsicum / Bell Pepper
- 2 count Fresh Green Chilies
- 3 tablespoons Olive Oil
- 2 tablespoons Whole Black Pepper (crushed)
- 10 count Baby Corn (frozen / fresh)
- 15 count Cherry / Plum Tomatoes
- 1 Red Onion (large size)
- 1 cup Broccoli florets (fresh / frozen)
- 1 count Red Capsicum / Bell Pepper
- 1 teaspoon Garlic Powder / Crushed Garlic (optional)
- 3 twigs Fresh Coriander leaves (optional)

Instructions

- Fill the air fryer basket with all of the vegetable pieces. One tbsp. oil / 1 tbsp. oil-spray & salt is to be used.
- Toss everything together thoroughly.
- Preheat the air fryer to 200 degrees Celsius (390 degrees Fahrenheit) for 8 to 10 minutes. It all depends on how raw you like your vegetables.
- Serve the stir-fried vegetables alongside boiled noodles or steamed rice.

Air Fryer Tempura Veggies

Preparation and Cooking Time

35 minutes

Servings

4 persons

Nutritional facts

247 calories,10g fat ,1g fiber ,28g carbs ,4g protein

Ingredients

- 1/2 cup all-purpose flour
- 2 teaspoons vegetable oil
- 1/2 cup whole green beans
- 1/2 cup whole asparagus spears
- 1/2 cup red onion rings
- 1/2 teaspoon salt, divided, or more to taste
- 1/2 teaspoon ground black pepper
- 2 eggs
- 2 tablespoons water
- 1 cup panko bread crumbs
- 1/2 cup sweet pepper rings
- 1/2 cup avocado wedges
- 1/2 cup zucchini slices

Instructions

- In a shallow dish, combine flour, .25 teaspoons salt, and pepper. In a separate shallow dish, whisk together the eggs and water. In a third shallow dish, combine panko and oil. Then season panko and/or flour mixture with appropriate seasoning.
- Add the remaining 1/4 teaspoon of salt to the vegetables. To coat, dip in the flour mixture, then the egg mixture, & finally the panko mixture.
- Preheat the oven to 200 degrees F (400 degrees C) and the air fryer to 400 degrees F (200 degrees C) (95 degrees C).

- In the air fryer basket, arrange half of the vegetables in a single layer. Cook for about 10 minutes, or until golden brown. If desired, season with a little more salt. To keep the vegetables warm, place them in the oven. Continue with the remaining vegetables.

Air Fryer garlic parmesan broccoli

Preparation and Cooking Time

15 minutes

Servings

4 persons

Nutritional facts

143 calories, 12g fat ,1g fiber ,20g carbs ,2.3g protein

Ingredients

- 1 Broccoli head, cut into bite-sized florets
- 2 tablespoon Parmesan Cheese, finely grated (or more to taste)
- 2 tablespoon Olive Oil
- 2 Garlic Cloves, minced
- 1 teaspoon Chili Flakes
- Wedge of Lemon
- Salt & Pepper, to taste

Instructions

- Stir together the olive oil, garlic, and chili flakes in a mixing bowl. Toss in the broccoli florets and toss thoroughly. Place the broccoli in the air fryer basket and cook for 5-7 minutes on 180C / 350F, shaking the basket every few minutes, till fork soft and gently browned with crisp edges.
- Then season with salt and pepper on a serving plate, then drizzle with lemon juice and finely grated Parmesan.

Honey Roasted Peanuts

Preparation and Cooking Time

20 minutes

Servings

2 persons

Nutritional facts

25 calories,17g fat ,1g fiber ,28g carbs ,2g protein

Ingredients

- 2 cups Peanuts, raw
- Salt, to taste (1-2 teaspoons)
- 2 tablespoon butter
- 2 tablespoon Honey
- 1 teaspoon Cinnamon
- Sugar, to taste (1-2 tablespoons)

Instructions

- Heat the air fryer to 180C / 350F using the preheat setting or operate the air fryer at that temperature for a few minutes.
- Melt the butter and honey together in a small saucepan over medium heat. Stir in the peanuts and cinnamon until everything is well combined.
- Fill the air fryer basket halfway with peanuts and spread them out into a single layer. If your basket is small, fry the peanuts in two batches to avoid overlapping too much.
- Cook for 8 to 10 minutes, or until golden brown, shaking the basket every few minutes, ensuring that the peanuts are evenly cooked.
- Spread the peanuts out in a single layer on a baking sheet lined with foil. Allow it to cool on the tray for the next few minutes

before adding sugar and salt to taste and mix well. As the peanuts cool, keep mixing them every few minutes to keep them from sticking together, then serve or move to an airtight jar or container.

Vegemite and Cheese Pinwheels

Preparation and Cooking Time

20 minutes

Servings

8 persons

Nutritional facts

132 calories, 20g fat ,2g fiber ,31g carbs ,4g protein

Ingredients

- One Frozen Puff Pastry Sheet, defrosted
- Three to four tablespoon Vegemite (or more, to taste)
- 1 cup Cheese, grated (or more, to taste)

Instructions

- Heat the oven to 180 degrees Celsius (350 degrees Fahrenheit) and line a baking tray with parchment paper.
- Vegemite should be spread over the puff pastry sheet; then shredded cheese should be sprinkled on top. Roll the puff pastry tightly into a log, then cut into eight even pieces.
- Bake for 15-twenty minutes, just until the cheese is melted as well as the crust is golden and flaky, on the preheated baking tray.
- You can also use an air fryer to make these pinwheels. Cook the pinwheels in the air fryer basket for 10-15 minutes, just until the cheese is melted and the dough is golden and crispy.

Spinach and Feta Pizza

Preparation and Cooking Time

20 minutes

Servings

2 persons

Nutritional facts

440 calories, 21g fat ,3g fiber ,34g carbs ,5g protein

Ingredients

- 2 large Pizza Bases
- ½ cups Shredded Mozzarella Cheese (or more, to taste)
- ½ cup Tomato Paste
- ½ Brown / Yellow Onion, finely diced
- 4 White Mushrooms, thinly sliced
- ½ Red Capsicum
- / Bell Pepper, finely diced
- 100g / 3.5 oz. Baby Spinach, roughly chopped
- ½ cup Feta Cheese, crumbled

Instructions

- Heat the oven to 200 degrees Celsius (390 degrees Fahrenheit) and line two baking sheets with parchment paper. Put a pizza base on each tray and sprinkle tomato paste over the top afterward. Then, in the following order: mozzarella, spinach, onion, bell pepper/capsicum, mushrooms, and feta, layer toppings evenly across the bases.
- Bake for fifteen minutes, until the cheese is golden brown and the base is crisp. Serve each pizza hot after being cut into even slices.

Vegetarian Pizza Rolls

Preparation and Cooking Time

20 minutes

Servings

10 persons

Nutritional facts

162 calories, 12g fat ,2g fiber ,32g carbs ,4g protein

Ingredients

- 1 cup Greek Yogurt
- ¼ Red Capsicum / Bell Pepper, finely diced
- 2 White Mushrooms, finely diced
- 4 Kalamata Olives, finely diced
- 1 cup Shredded Mozzarella / Cheddar Cheese
- 1 ½ cups Self-Raising / Self-Rising Flour
- 2 tablespoons Tomato Paste
- ¼ Brown / Yellow Onion, finely diced
- 2 tablespoon Tinned Pineapple Pieces, finely diced

Instructions

- In a mixing bowl, whisk together Greek yogurt and honey. Stir in one cup of flour until everything is well combined. Add more flour gradually until the dough begins to form a ball.
- Place the dough on a well-floured surface & knead for a minute or two with your hands. If the dough is still sticky, add more flour and knead it some more. It is ready when the dough holds its shape and does not stick to the hands or the surface.
- Roll out the dough into a rectangle, spread tomato paste on top, then top with the remaining ingredients. Cut the dough into eight equal pieces after rolling it up tightly. Spread the pieces out in the air fryer basket or trays, leaving enough room between each one for them to rise. Top each roll with a sprinkling of cheese.
- Cook for 10-15 minutes at 180°C/350°F, or until golden & cooked through. You may need to cook in 2 batches if you have a smaller air fryer. Cool the rolls fully on a wire rack.

Air Fryer Mushrooms with Parmesan Cheese

Preparation and Cooking Time

15 minutes

Servings

2-3 persons

Nutritional facts

186 calories, 13g fat ,2g fiber ,26g carbs ,6g protein

Ingredients

- 1 tablespoon Olive Oil
- 1 teaspoon Extra Virgin Olive Oil (can sub for Olive Oil if needed)
- ¼ lemon, juiced
- 8 White Button Mushrooms, wiped clean and cut in half
- ½ teaspoon Garlic Powder
- Salt & Pepper, to taste
- 2 tablespoon of grated Parmesan Cheese

Instructions

- Heat the air fryer to 180C / 350F using the preheat setting or operate it at that temperature for 5 minutes.
- Combine the olive oil, mushrooms, salt, garlic powder, and pepper in a bowl.
- Cook for 10 minutes or until mushrooms is cooked in the air fryer basket, shaking the air fryer basket every few minutes.
- Combine sautéed mushrooms, fresh lemon juice, extra virgin olive oil, and parmesan cheese in a mixing bowl. Serve right away.

Air Fryer Carrot Fries

Preparation and Cooking Time

25 minutes

Servings

4 persons

Nutritional facts

31 calories, 9g fat ,1g fiber ,11g carbs ,1g protein

Ingredients

- 4 Carrots, peeled & cut into fries
- 1 tablespoon Olive Oil
- 1 teaspoon Corn Flour / Corn Starch
- 1 teaspoon Paprika
- ½ teaspoon Garlic Powder
- Salt, to taste

Instructions

- Heat your air fryer to 200°C/390°F by using the preheat setting or running it at that temperature for 5 minutes.
- In a mixing bowl, combine all ingredients except the salt and stir well to blend.
- Ensure the carrots are in a single layer& not touching in the air fryer basket or tray. This aids in keeping them crisp. If you have a smaller air fryer, you might have to cook in batches.
- Cook for 15-20 minutes until the carrots are crisp on the outside and tender on the inside, flipping halfway through.
- If desired, serve with a sprinkling of salt on top and a dipping sauce of spicy mayo or sriracha aioli.

Air Fryer French Toast Sticks

Preparation and Cooking Time

12 minutes

Servings

10-12 persons

Nutritional facts

143 calories, 11g fat ,1g fiber ,24g carbs ,2g protein

Ingredients

- 2 slices of bread cut into sticks (1 slice is about 4-5 sticks)
- 1/2 tsp vanilla
- 1 tbsp. coconut sugar
- 1 egg
- 1/2 cup unsweetened almond milk
- 1/2 tsp cinnamon
- 1/2 tsp cinnamon

Instructions

- Mix the egg, milk, cinnamon, & vanilla in a mixing bowl. Dip the stick in the egg, then roll it in the cinnamon-sugar mixture. Repeat with each stick.
- Heat the air fryer to 350 degrees Fahrenheit.
- Toss in the sticks.
- It should be air fried for eight minutes in the air, flipping halfway through.
- Powdered sugar is sprinkled on top, and a variety of sides can be used for dipping.

Crispy Air Fryer Roasted Brussels Sprouts with Balsamic

Preparation and Cooking Time

25 minutes

Servings

4 persons

Nutritional facts

83 calories, 8g fat ,2g fiber ,18g carbs ,3g protein

Ingredients

- 1 pound (454 g) Brussels sprouts, ends removed and cut into bite-sized pieces
- 1 Tablespoon (15 ml) balsamic vinegar
- kosher salt, to taste
- 2 Tablespoons (15 ml) olive oil, or more if needed
- black pepper, to taste

Instructions

- Toss in the sliced Brussels sprouts in a mixing bowl. Drizzle the oil & balsamic vinegar over the Brussels sprouts in an even layer. If you combine the oil and vinegar all at once, it will only coat one Brussels sprout. Make certain that all of the Brussels sprouts are coated.
- Season the Brussels sprouts evenly with salt and pepper. Stir everything together for a long enough time, so the Brussels sprouts absorb all of the marinades. The marinade should not be left at the bottom of the bowl.
- Toss the Brussels sprouts into the air fryer basket. Then air fry for 15-20 minutes at 360°F. Halfway through cooking, roughly 8 minutes in, shake and lightly stir. You don't want your food to be cooked unevenly. If necessary, shake & toss to ensure that everything cooks evenly.
- Continue air-frying the Brussels for the remaining time, or until they are golden brown & cooked through. If necessary, check sooner to ensure that nothing burns. If necessary, you can also add more time to ensure that it is fully cooked.
- If desired, season the Brussels sprouts with more salt and pepper, and serve.

Air Fryer Butternut Squash

Preparation and Cooking Time

35 minutes

Servings

4 persons

Nutritional facts

57 calories, 6g fat ,1g fiber ,16g carbs ,2g protein

Ingredients

- Four cups Cubed Butternut Squash
- 1 Tsp Ground Cinnamon
- Olive Oil Cooking Spray

Instructions

- Spray the air fryer basket with olive oil cooking spray.
- In the basket, place the butternut squash.
- Coat with olive oil spray and sprinkle with cinnamon.
- Cook for 20 minutes at 390 degrees F. After 10 minutes, check on it, mix, coat, and continue to cook. You could also add additional cinnamon at this point if you want

Air Fryer Spanish Spicy Potatoes

Preparation and Cooking Time

27 minutes

Servings

2 persons

Nutritional facts

385 calories, 15g fat ,2g fiber ,31g carbs ,4g protein

Ingredients

- 4 Large Potatoes
- 2 Tsp Coriander
- 2 Tsp Thyme
- 1 Tsp Mixed Spice
- 1 Tsp Oregano
- Salt & Pepper
- ½ Small Onion peeled and diced
- 100 ml Homemade Tomato Sauce get my recipe here
- 1 Tomato thinly diced
- 1 Tbsp. Extra Virgin Olive Oil
- 2 Tsp Paprika
    - 2 Tsp Dried Garlic
- 1 Tsp Barbacoa Seasoning
- 1 Tbsp. Red Wine Vinegar
- 1 Tsp Paprika
- 1 Tsp Chili Powder
- 1 Tsp Rosemary

Instructions

- Cut your potatoes into wedges and combine them with the extra virgin olive oil & dried seasonings in a mixing bowl. In a mixing bowl, combine all of the ingredients & place them in the air fryer.
- Cook for twenty minutes at 160°C/320°F in an air fryer.
- Cook for another 3 minutes at 200°C/400°F after shaking.
- Combine the spicy bravas sauce ingredients while the potatoes are frying in the air fryer.
- Once it beeps, serve the bravas over the patatas

Buffalo Cauliflower

Preparation and Cooking Time

25 minutes

Servings

4 persons

Nutritional facts

191 calories, 8g fat ,1g fiber ,23g carbs ,2g protein

Ingredients

- 1 head cauliflower
- ¼ teaspoon of paprika
- ¼ teaspoon of dried chipotle chili flakes
- 1 cup of soy milk
- 2 tablespoons of non-dairy butter
- ½ cup of Frank's Red-hot Original Cayenne Pepper Sauce
- canola oil spray
- 1 cup of unbleached all-purpose flour
- 1 teaspoon of chicken bouillon granules
- ¼ teaspoon of cayenne pepper
- ¼ teaspoon of chili powder
- 2 cloves of garlic, minced

Instructions

- Cauliflower should be cut into bite-size pieces. Cauliflower should be rinsed and drained.
- Mix the bouillon granules, flour, cayenne, paprika, chili powder, and chipotle flakes in a large mixing bowl. Whisk in the milk slowly till a thick batter forms.

- Heat the air fryer to 390°F for ten minutes after spraying the basket with canola oil.
- Toss the cauliflower in the batter while the air fryer is heating up. In the air fryer basket, place the battered cauliflower. Preheat oven to about 390°F and bake for 20 minutes. After 10 minutes, flip the cauliflower pieces with tongs.
- Heat the butter, spicy sauce, & garlic in a small pot over medium-high heat after turning the cauliflower. Bring the water to a boil and then lower to low heat and cover.
- Transfer the cauliflower to a big mixing bowl once it's done cooking. Toss the cauliflower with tongs after pouring the sauce over it. Serve right away.

Air Fryer Corn on the Cob

Preparation and Cooking Time

21 minutes

Servings

2 persons

Nutritional facts

177 calories, 9g fat ,5g fiber ,40g carbs ,9g protein

Ingredients

- Two (2) ears corn, shucked and cleaned
- salt
- black pepper, to taste
- oil spray or olive oil
- Two tbsp. (30 ml) butter for spreading

Instructions

- To fit the corn in the air fryer basket, cut the end off. Cut the corn in half if using a smaller air fryer.
- Coat the corn on all sides with oil spray or olive oil. Season the whole corn with salt and pepper.
- Air fry for 12-16 minutes at 370°F, flipping halfway through. Cook, occasionally stirring, until the kernels are soft and lightly browned. (Cooking time varies depending on corn size, air fryer basket filling, and air fryer model/size.) Enjoy with a pat of butter.

Air Fried Blooming Onion

Preparation and Cooking Time

25 minutes

Servings

12 persons

Nutritional facts

117 calories, 7g fat ,3g fiber ,22g carbs ,5g protein

Ingredients

- 2.5 cups Flour
- Onion
- 4 tsp Old Bay Seasoning
- ½ Cup Milk
- Eggs Beaten

Instructions

- The onion should be prepared first.
- Preheat the air fryer to 400 degrees Fahrenheit.
- Whisk together the flour and spices in a mixing bowl.
- Whip the milk and eggs together in a separate bowl.
- To begin, evenly coat the onion with the flour mixture. To help coat the onion, it's a good idea to get your hands involved & stir it around in the bowl. Lift the onion out of the bowl and shake off the excess flour mixture.

- Transfer the onion to the second bowl with the egg & milk and coat completely. To coat the entire onion, use a spoon or ladle. The additional flour mixture should be sprinkled on top. This should be air-fried for 8-ten minutes or until crisp.

Fried Garlic Chips

Preparation and Cooking Time

15 minutes

Servings

4 persons

Nutritional facts

45 calories, 9g fat ,2g fiber ,30g carbs ,4g protein

Ingredients

- Ten cloves of garlic
- One teaspoon of olive oil
- pinch of salt

Instructions

- Slice the garlic cloves thinly and combine with olive oil as well as a pinch of salt.
- Air fry for about 6-7 minutes in a lightly greased cake barrel at 380F (190C), stirring about 2-3 times in between, till they turn light golden brown.
- Place the garlic chips on a paper towel to absorb any excess oil and keep them crispy for longer.

Crispy Air Fryer Tofu

Preparation and Cooking Time

40 minutes

Servings

4 persons

Nutritional facts

110 calories, 8g fat ,2g fiber ,32 carbs ,4g protein

Ingredients

- 1 lb. of extra firm tofu cut into 1" cubes
- 2 teaspoons of cornstarch
- ½ tablespoon of light soy sauce
- 1 teaspoon of garlic powder
- ½ teaspoon of onion powder
- 1 teaspoon of paprika
- ½ teaspoon of sea salt
- ½ teaspoon of sesame oil
- ¼ teaspoon of ground black pepper

Instructions

- Put the pressed and diced tofu in a medium mixing bowl. Toss in the liquid aminos to coat. Mix in the remaining seasoning ingredients & toss well to mix.
- Place the tofu in a single row in the air fryer, leaving a little space between each piece. Preheat the air fryer to 400 degrees Fahrenheit. Cook for ten minutes, shake the basket every 5 minutes for the first five minutes and then cook for another 10 minutes.
- When the tofu is done, remove it. Allow for a few minutes of cooling before serving.

Air Fryer Toast

Preparation and Cooking Time

4 minutes

Servings

2 persons

Nutritional facts

100 calories, 22g fat ,2g fiber ,65g carbs ,16g protein

Ingredients

- Two slices Bread

Instructions

- There's no need to preheat the oven.

- In the air fryer basket, place your bread. Preheat the oven to 400 degrees F (204 degrees C) & air fry for four minutes. Your toast will probably be done in 3 minutes if you have extremely thinly sliced bread. Add 30 seconds extra if you prefer your toast dark.

- Butter, avocado, jelly, or peanut butter could be added to the top.

Air Fryer Potato Chips Recipe

Preparation and Cooking Time

40 minutes

Servings

4 persons

Nutritional facts

154 calories, 22g fat ,2g fiber ,65g carbs ,16g protein

Ingredients

- 4 medium yellow potatoes

- One tbsp. oil

- salt to taste

Instructions

- Using a sharp knife, cut potatoes into thin slices. Soak the potatoes for at least 20 minutes in a dish filled with cold water.

- Using a colander, drain the water from the potatoes. Use paper towels to dry the area thoroughly.

- Season the potato chips with a pinch of salt and a drizzle of olive oil. Cook for 20 minutes at 200°F with two layers of potatoes in the air fryer tray.

- Toss the potato chips. Increase the heat to 400°F & continue to cook for another 5 minutes.

Air Fryer Eggplant

Preparation and Cooking Time

25 minutes

Servings

4 persons

Nutritional facts

66 calories, 24g fat ,0g fiber ,10g carbs ,12g protein

Ingredients

- 2 tbsp. olive oil

- 1/2 tsp Italian seasoning

- 1 tsp garlic powder

- 1/2 tsp red pepper

- 1 tsp sweet paprika optional

- 1 eggplant cut into 1-inch pieces

Instructions

- Toss all of the items together until the eggplant chunks are well coated with olive oil & seasonings. In the air fryer basket, place the eggplant.

- Air-fry, the eggplant for 20 minutes at 375 degrees Fahrenheit, shaking the basket halfway through.

The best air fried churros

Preparation and Cooking Time

23 minutes

Servings

22 three-inch churros

Nutritional facts

60 calories, 2g fat ,3g fiber ,6 carbs ,14g protein

Ingredients

- 3/4 cup plus 2 tbsp. water

- 2 medium eggs

- 1/2 cup sugar

- 1/4 cup butter or 1/2 a stick

- 1 tbsp. sugar

- a pinch of salt

- 3/4 cup flour

- 1 tsp cinnamon

Instructions

- Bring the water, butter, sugar, and a pinch of salt to a boil in a medium saucepan over medium heat. Reduce the heat to low and quickly stir in the flour with a wooden spatula after the mixture has reached a boil. Continue to whisk the mixture until it thickens and no longer sticks to the pot's sides.

- Use a paddle attachment to stir the mixture in a stand mixer bowl or a heatproof bowl. This procedure will take approximately 3-5 minutes.

- Once the churro dough has cooled slightly, add the eggs one at a time, mixing constantly. The mixture would become sticky as time went on. Move the churro mixture to a piping bag fitted with a star tip at this point.

- You have to pipe 3-four-inch-long churros onto a parchment-lined baking sheet. Using a pair of scissors or a knife, cut the end. Freeze the baking sheet for at least 30 minutes.

- Heat the air fryer to 360°F three minutes before you're ready to bake your churros. Remove the frozen churros from the parchment paper & carefully set them in the air fryer basket, baking for 13-14 minutes. Place them in the freezer to keep the leftover churros from becoming soggy.

- Mix the sugar and cinnamon in a small bowl or plastic bag. As soon as the baked churros are removed from the air fryer, immediately place them in the sugar mixture. Toss them in the cinnamon-sugar mixture, making sure they are evenly coated.

- It can be served with dulce de leche, sweetened condensed milk, or Nutella.

Air Fryer Apple Chips

Preparation and Cooking Time

30 minutes

Servings

2 persons

Nutritional facts

48 calories ,16g fat ,0.2g fiber ,6g carbs ,11g protein

Ingredients

- 1 apple

- Quarter teaspoon ground cinnamon

- A pinch of salt

Instructions

- Heat the air fryer to 350 degrees Fahrenheit (180 degrees Celsius).

- Using a mandolin, slice the apples into thin, even slices. Place the slices in a big mixing dish.

- Sprinkle the cinnamon & salt over the apples and toss well.
- Place half of the apple slices in a single layer in the air fryer basket.
- Cook, flipping & flatten the apples every 4 minutes, for 8 to 10 minutes.
- Allow 10 to 20 minutes for the apples to cool & crisp on a wire rack.
- Carry on with the other apple slices in the same manner.

Air Fryer Apple Fries

Preparation and Cooking Time

32 minutes

Servings

8 persons

Nutritional facts

185 calories, 43g fat ,2g fiber ,9g carbs ,32 protein

Ingredients

- 3 Gala apples
- 1/4 C of sugar
- 1 C of flour
- 3 beaten eggs
- One cup of graham cracker crumbs
- 1 container of caramel sauce

Instructions

- Preheat the air fryer to 380 degrees Fahrenheit.
- Using parchment paper, line a cookie sheet.
- Peel and core the apples, then cut them into 8 wedges.
- In a medium-sized mixing bowl, place the flour.
- Pour the eggs into a shallow dish after beating them.
- Mix the crushed graham crackers & sugar in a second shallow dish. To combine the ingredients, stir them together.
- First, line the flour bowl, add the beaten eggs, crumbled graham crackers, & sugar mixture.
- Toss each apple wedge in the flour to start.
- Dredge the floured apple slices in the beaten eggs in a separate bowl.
- In the third step, roll the apple pieces in the sugar or crushed graham cracker mixture. Arrange each apple slice on the cookie sheet.
- Combine the apple slices and flour in a large mixing basin. To create a dredging station, dip each apple slice in the egg, then in the graham cracker crumbs. Place the coated slices on a cookie sheet and coat all sides with the sauce.
- Using oil, coat the bottom of the air fryer basket.
- In the air fryer, do not overlap the apple slices. Apply a little oil to the apple pieces. Air fry for 5 minutes at 380°F, then flip the apple chunks and cook for 2 minutes.
- In a serving bowl, pour the caramel sauce. Place the bowl in the microwave. Warm the caramel sauce until it's ready to use with the apple fries.

Crispy Hassel back Potatoes

Preparation and Cooking Time

55 minutes

Servings

4 persons

Nutritional facts

359 calories, 4g fat ,3g fiber ,14g carbs ,9 protein

Ingredients

- 2 pounds Yukon Gold potatoes
- 1/4 cup fresh chopped parsley
- 1 teaspoon salt
- 4 tablespoons olive oil for brushing
- 1 tablespoon minced fresh garlic (approximately 3 large garlic cloves)
- 2 tablespoons olive oil

Instructions

- The potatoes should be washed and dried with paper towels.
- Hold one end of potato down and cut it two-thirds through with a sharp, large knife, slicing it into 1/8-inch fans.
- Brush the potatoes with olive oil all over (even between the folds).
- If using an air fryer, warm to 400°F, then arrange the potatoes cut-side-up on a baking sheet & roast for 35–40 minutes on the middle rack, coating them with extra oil halfway through, until crispy on the exterior and tender on the inside.
- Mix the parsley, garlic, and salt with 2 tbsp. of olive oil and stir thoroughly while the potatoes are cooking.
- When the potatoes are done, spread the garlic-parsley mixture all over them, even between the folds. Serve immediately.

Crispy Buffalo Tofu

Preparation and Cooking Time

18 minutes

Servings

2 persons

Nutritional facts

158 calories, 15g fat ,4g fiber ,26g carbs ,19g protein

Ingredients

- 1 - 14- ounce package extra-firm tofu pressed and drained well
- 6 tablespoons arrowroot flour
- 1/4 cup unsweetened almond milk
- 1 cup Panko breadcrumbs
- 2 tablespoons olive oil
- 1/2 teaspoon paprika
- 1/2 teaspoon sea salt
- 1/2 teaspoon ground black pepper
- 2/3 cup prepared Buffalo-style sauce

Instructions

- Tofu should be cut into six pieces lengthwise. After that, slice vertically and then horizontally to make 12 pieces.
- Add arrowroot powder to a small bowl.
- Add the almond milk to a second small bowl.
- Add olive oil, Panko breadcrumbs, sea salt, paprika, & black pepper to a third medium bowl.
- Dredge each piece in the arrowroot flour, then the milk, & finally the breadcrumb mixture one at a time, coating well on each step.
- Preheat the air fryer to 350 degrees Fahrenheit. Make a uniform layer of tofu. It should be cooked for eight minutes in the air fryer.
- Toss the tofu with the Buffalo sauce until it is evenly coated.
- Return to the air fryer in a single layer. Cook for an additional five minutes or till desired crispiness is reached.

Air Fryer Spinach

Preparation and Cooking Time

7 minutes

Servings

2 persons

Nutritional facts

80 calories, 8g fat ,2g fiber ,13g carbs ,8g protein

Ingredients

- 300 g Fresh Spinach
- Two tsp Garlic Powder
- Salt & Pepper
- 2 tsp Butter

Instructions

- In a colander, rinse the spinach under cold water. Squeeze out any excess water to keep your spinach from becoming too moist.
- Layer the spinach, butter, and seasonings on the spinach in the air fryer cake pan.
- Set the timer for five minutes and the temperature to 180 degrees Celsius (360 degrees Fahrenheit).
- After it beeps, give it a quick stir with a fork & cook for another 2 minutes at the same temperature.
- Serve after a quick stir.

Popcorn Tofu Nuggets

Preparation and Cooking Time

27 minutes

Servings

4 persons

Nutritional facts

261 calories, 9g fat ,1g fiber ,2g carbs ,5g protein

Ingredients

- 14 oz. extra firm tofu in water drained and pressed
- 1 Tablespoon Dijon mustard
- 2 teaspoon garlic powder
- ¾ cup unsweetened dairy-free milk more if needed
- 1.5 cup panko bread crumbs gluten-free if needed
- ½ cup vegan mayo
- 2 teaspoon onion powder
- ½ teaspoon salt
- ½ cup quinoa flour
- ½ cup cornmeal
- 3 Tablespoons nutritional yeast
- 2 Tablespoons Better Than Bouillon Vegetarian No Chicken Base
- ½ teaspoon pepper
- 2 Tablespoon sriracha

Instructions

- Cut the tofu into bite-size pieces once it has been squeezed.
- In a large mixing bowl, combine flour, cornmeal, nutritional yeast, better than bouillon, mustard, garlic, onion, salt, pepper, & milk. It should have the consistency of pancake batter. If it needs to be thinned out, add additional milk.
- In a separate bowl, combine the panko breadcrumbs.
- Toss the tofu in the batter, then in the breadcrumbs.

- Fill the air fryer basket with as many nuggets as it will hold. You'll have to do this in several batches because you don't want the basket to become too crowded. Preheat the air fryer to 350°F and cook for 12 minutes. Halfway through, you need to shake the basket.
- Serve with popcorn tofu and a mixture of vegan mayo and sriracha.

Air Fryer Crumble with Blueberries and Apple

Preparation and Cooking Time

20 minutes

Servings

2 persons

Nutritional facts

310 calories, 15g fat ,2g fiber ,26g carbs ,19g protein

Ingredients

- 1 medium apple, finely diced
- 1/2 cup frozen blueberries, strawberries, or peaches
- 1/4 cup plus 1 tablespoon brown rice flour
- 2 tablespoons sugar
- 1/2 teaspoon ground cinnamon
- 2 tablespoons nondairy butter

Instructions

- Heat the air fryer for 5 minutes at 350°F. In an air fryer-safe baking pan or ramekin, mix the apple & frozen blueberries.
- Mix the flour, sugar, cinnamon, & butter in a small mixing bowl. Using a spoon, smear the flour mixture all over the fruit. To cover any exposed fruit, sprinkle a little additional flour on top. Cook for 15 minutes at 350°F.

Buttermilk Fried Mushrooms

Preparation and Cooking Time

45 minutes

Servings

2 persons

Nutritional facts

355 calories, 10g fat ,1g fiber ,16g carbs ,5g protein

Ingredients

- 2 heaping cups oyster mushrooms 125 g
- 1 tsp of each pepper, salt, garlic powder, smoked paprika, onion powder, cumin
- 1 Tbsp. of oil
- 1 cup of buttermilk
- 1 ½ cups of all-purpose flour

Instructions

- Preheat the air fryer to 375°F (190 C). Clean the mushrooms and combine them with the buttermilk in a large mixing bowl. Allow 15 minutes for marinating.
- Mix flour & spices in a large mixing bowl. Remove the mushrooms from the buttermilk with a spoon (save the buttermilk). In a nutshell, dip the mushroom in the flour mixture, brush off excess flour, then dip again in the buttermilk, then again in the flour (in other words, wet > dry > wet > dry).
- Place mushrooms in a single layer on the bottom of the air fry pan, leaving space between mushrooms. Cook for 5 minutes and then brush with a little oil to facilitate browning on all sides. Cook for 5 to 10 minutes more, or till golden brown and crispy.

Crispy Avocado Tacos

Preparation and Cooking Time

30 minutes

Servings

4 persons

Nutritional facts

624 calories, 6g fat ,1g fiber ,10g carbs ,2g protein

Ingredients

- 1 cup finely chopped or crushed pineapple 240 g
- 1/2 jalapeno finely chopped
- Pinch each cumin and salt
- 2 Tbsp. mayonnaise 30 g
- 1/4 tsp lime juice
- 1 Tbsp. adobo sauce from a jar of chipotle peppers
- 1 avocado
- 1/4 cup all-purpose flour 35 g
- 1 large egg whisked
- 1/2 cup panko crumbs 65 g
- Pinch each salt and pepper
- 1 Roma tomato finely chopped
- 1/2 red bell pepper finely chopped
- 1/2 of a medium red onion 1/2 cup, finely chopped
- 1 clove garlic minced
- 4 flour tortillas click for recipe
- 1/4 cup plain yogurt 60 g

Instructions

- Combine all of the ingredients for the salsa, cover, and refrigerate.
- Remove the pit from the avocado by cutting it in half lengthwise. Place the avocado skin side down to cut each half into four equal pieces, gently peeling away the skin.
- Preheat the oven to 450 degrees Fahrenheit (230 degrees Celsius) or the air fryer to 375 degrees Fahrenheit (190 C). Arrange a bowl of flour, a bowl of whisked egg, a bowl of panko with S&P mixed in, as well as a parchment-lined baking sheet at the end of your workspace.
- Each avocado slice should be floured first, then dipped in the egg, and then the panko. Put on the prepared baking sheet and bake or air fry for 10 minutes, until lightly browned, flipping halfway through.
- Mix all Sauce ingredients while the avocados are frying.
- Top a tortilla with salsa, 2 slices of avocado, and a drizzle of sauce. Serve right away and enjoy.

Baked General Tso's Cauliflower

Preparation and Cooking Time

30 minutes

Servings

3 persons

Nutritional facts

420 calories, 1g fat ,2g fiber ,35g carbs ,4g protein

Ingredients

- ½ head cauliflower
- 1 Tbsp. sesame oil 15 ml
- ¼ cup rice vinegar 60 mL
- ¼ cup brown sugar 50 g
- 2 Tbsp. tomato paste 30 g
- 2 cloves garlic minced
- 1 Tbsp. fresh grated ginger
- ½ cup vegetable broth 120 mL
- ½ cup flour 60g
- 2 large eggs whisked
- 1 cup panko breadcrumbs 50 g
- ¼ tsp each salt and pepper
- ¼ cup soy sauce 60 mL
- 2 Tbsp. cornstarch dissolved in 2 Tbsp. (30 ml) cold water 15 g

Instructions

- Preheat the oven to 400 degrees Fahrenheit (204 degrees Celsius). Set up your workspace by separating the flour, egg, and panko into separate bowls. Season panko with salt and pepper. Cauliflower should be cut into bite-sized florets. Coat the florets in flour, then egg breadcrumbs in batches. Place on a baking sheet lined with parchment paper. Bake for 15–20 minutes, or until golden brown.
- Place the sesame oil, garlic, & ginger in a small saucepan over medium heat. Cook for 2 minutes, or until fragrant, then add the remaining sauce ingredients, excluding the cornstarch mixture, and cook for 2 minutes. Stir everything together and bring to a low simmer. Slowly add in the cornstarch mixture while whisking. If it does not thicken fast, continue it simmer until it does.
- Drizzle the sauce over the baked cauliflower & toss to coat evenly. Cauliflower should be served over warm rice or quinoa.

Air Fryer Hash Browns

Preparation and Cooking Time

55 minutes

Servings

2 persons

Nutritional facts

123 calories, 35g fat ,1g fiber ,1g carbs ,16g protein

Ingredients

- 4 – 5 potatoes
- 1 tsp onion powder
- salt to taste
- chili flakes (optional)
- 2 tbsp. olive oil
- 2 tbsp. corn starch
- 1 tsp garlic powder
- seasoning (optional)

Instructions

- Clean and wash the potatoes.
- Remove the skin by peeling it.
- Shred the potatoes with a box grater.
- Place the grated potatoes in a large colander & rinse them under cold running water.
- This will help remove excess starch from the potatoes and ensure that they do not become soggy.
- Pour ice-cold water over the shredded potatoes in the mixing bowl.
- Soak them in water for at least 30 minutes.
- Remove them from the water once more.
- Dry the shredded potatoes with a clean kitchen towel.
- In a large mixing bowl, place the wiped & dry grated potatoes.

- In a large mixing bowl, corn starch, grated potatoes, garlic powder, salt, onion powder, and oil should all be combined.
- Toss them together well.
- Spray or brush the basket lightly with cooking oil.
- Two tbsp. mixture should now be placed in the basket.
- Make a tiny disc out of it.
- Use a cookie cutter to produce a perfect disc.
- Start the air fryer at 380 degrees Fahrenheit for 20 minutes.
- After about 10 minutes, check for doneness and flip if necessary.
- Then reapply a light coat of oil to the top layer.
- Cook for another ten minutes or till golden brown.

Air Fryer Zucchini Fritters

Preparation and Cooking Time

32 minutes

Servings

6 persons

Nutritional facts

158 calories, 13g fat ,3g fiber ,14g carbs ,7g protein

Ingredients

- 1 large zucchini
- 1 tsp of garlic powder
- 1 tsp of onion powder or onion flakes
- 1 tsp of cayenne pepper optional
- 1 onion shredded
- 1/4 cup of chickpea flour
- 1 tsp of rice flour or corn starch
- 1 tsp of salt
- 2 tbsp. of nutritional yeast
- 2 tbsp. of oil

Instructions

- Using a cheese grater, grate the zucchini.
- Place the zucchini on a muslin towel or cotton napkin and set it aside.
- Mix in 1 teaspoon of salt.
- Allow for 15–20 minutes of resting time. This will aid in the removal of surplus water.
- Using a cotton cloth, squeeze off the juice from the zucchini.
- Squeezed zucchini, onions, green onions, spices, salt (if needed) (previously added for releasing water), and nutritional yeast into a mixing dish (optional).
- All of the ingredients should be well combined. Check to see if the mixture is too moist.
- After that, take a scoopful of the dough and roll it into little discs, which you should arrange on parchment paper.
- If you have a basket-type air fryer, repeat the process and make 6–7 discs because it can only hold this amount.
- Don't overcrowd the basket and keep the layers to a single layer.
- Heat the air fryer for 4 minutes at 400 degrees F or 200 degrees C.
- Place the perforated parchment paper on top.
- Place the fritters on the parchment paper once they've been shaped.
- A small amount of oil should be sprayed on the fritters and kept within the air fryer.

- Preheat the air fryer to 360 degrees Fahrenheit or 180 degrees Celsius for 8 minutes.
- After that, take the basket out of the oven & flip the cakes.
- Start the air fryer at 375 degrees Fahrenheit or 190 degrees Celsius for another 4 minutes.
- Brush or spray a little oil on the patties. The fritters will become brown and crispy as a result of this.
- After 10 minutes, keep an eye on it.
- Remove when the outside is fully done and crispy.
- Serve immediately with a variety of dips and sauces.

Air Fryer Frozen Hash Browns

Preparation and Cooking Time

17 minutes

Servings

5 persons

Nutritional facts

43 calories, 11g fat ,2g fiber ,22g carbs ,4g protein

Ingredients

- Six hash brown patties

Instructions

- Heat the air fryer to 400 degrees Fahrenheit (200 degrees Celsius) for 5 minutes.
- Put the patties in the air fryer basket at this point.
- Put the basket inside the air fryer & set the temperature to 400 degrees Fahrenheit for 12 minutes.
- Around the 6-minute mark, flip the patties.
- Set timer for another 4–5 minutes if you think it needs extra browning after 12 minutes.
- In the meantime, keep checking.
- And when it's done, remove it.

Cauliflower Hash Browns

Preparation and Cooking Time

40 minutes

Servings

8 persons

Nutritional facts

64 calories, 10g fat ,1g fiber ,19g carbs ,6g protein

Ingredients

- 1 large cauliflower head
- 1 onion finely chopped
- 1/4 cup cilantro leaves finely chopped
- 2 green chilies finely chopped
- 1/4 cup chickpea flour
- 1 tbsp. corn starch (optional)
- 1/4 cup nutritional yeast
- 1/4 cup vegan parmesan cheese
- Salt to taste
- 2 Garlic pods finely minced or garlic powder

Instructions

- The cauliflower head should be washed and cleaned before breaking into large florets.
- Using a food processor or a cheese grater, grate the cheese.
- Squeeze out the liquid with a cheesecloth after adding a bit of salt.

- Combine the cauliflower rice, flour, chopped onion, cilantro, green chilies, garlic, salt, pepper, nutritional yeast, and vegan cheese in a large mixing bowl.
- Make a dough-like substance by mixing everything thoroughly.
- Take a small quantity of the mixture and grease your palms.
- Flatten it with your palms and form it into an oval shape like hash browns.
- Heat the air fryer to 375 degrees Fahrenheit for 4–5 minutes.
- To keep the hash browns from sticking, lightly grease the basket.
- In the basket, place the shaped patties.
- Preheat the air fryer to 380 degrees Fahrenheit for 20 minutes.
- After around 15 minutes, flip the patties.
- If necessary, spray some oil on top.
- Cook for an additional 4–5 minutes at 400°F for added crispiness (200C).

Buffalo Broccoli Wings

Preparation and Cooking Time

30 minutes

Servings

4 persons

Nutritional facts

170 calories, 5g fat ,1g fiber ,9g carbs ,2g protein

Ingredients

- 6 cups broccoli florets (2 medium heads)
- 1 tsp hot sauce optional for extra hot
- 1 tsp garlic powder
- 1 tsp onion powder
- 2 tbsp. olive oil or vegan butter or coconut oil
- 1 cup Panko Bread Crumbs
- 1 pinch salt
- 1 pinch cayenne pepper
- 1 cup hot sauce
- 1 cup gram flour or all-purpose flour + cornstarch
- salt to taste
- 1/2 tsp black pepper
- 1/2 – 3/4 cup almond milk as required to make a smooth batter
- 1 tsp vinegar
- 2 tbsp. maple syrup to balance the hot sauce
- 1/2 tsp salt (to taste)
- 1/2 tsp pepper (to taste)

Instructions

- Heat the air fryer to 375 degrees Fahrenheit (180 degrees Celsius) for 4 minutes.
- Put the coated broccoli in the air fryer basket and cook for 5–6 minutes at 375°F.
- Remove the basket & brush the florets with the buffalo sauce.
- Continue to fry at the same temperature for another 4 minutes.
- If you want it crispy, cook it for an additional 2 minutes at 400°F.
- After 3 minutes, you must check on the broccoli. Furthermore, each air fryer cooks differently. Make the necessary adjustments to your time.

Air Fryer Smashed Potatoes

Preparation and Cooking Time

25 minutes

Servings

4 persons

Nutritional facts

135 calories, 3g fat ,9g fiber ,221g carbs ,61g protein

Ingredients

- 1 1/2 lb. baby potatoes
- 1 tsp of onion powder
- 1 tsp of cayenne pepper
- 1 tsp of dried herbs of your choice
- 2 tsp of parsley leaves
- 1 tsp of garlic butter
- grated parmesan cheese
- 1 tsp of salt
- 2 cup of water
- 2 tbsp. of olive oil
- 1 tsp of garlic powder
- 1/2 tsp of rock salt

Instructions

- The potatoes should be washed and cleaned well.
- Do not remove the skin.
- Put the potatoes in the instant pot's inner pot.
- To the water, add two cups of water & 1 teaspoon of salt.
- Seal the vent and close the lid.
- Preheat the instant pot to high pressure for 6 minutes.
- After 6 minutes of cooking, quickly lower the pressure and remove the potatoes.
- Add olive oil to a small mixing bowl.
- Combine all of the spices listed in the ingredients list.
- All of the ingredients should be thoroughly mixed.
- Heat the air fryer to 400 degrees Fahrenheit (200 degrees Celsius) for 5 minutes.
- Place the potatoes on a platter that has been cleaned.
- Smash potatoes softly with a spoon, the bottom of a drinking glass, or a dish.
- Brush the seasoning mixture over the mashed potatoes.
- Put the potatoes in the basket with care.
- Preheat the air fryer to 400 degrees Fahrenheit for 12 minutes.
- Around 7–8 minutes into the cooking time, carefully flip the potatoes with a tong
- Cook until the timer goes off
- Increase the timer for 3 minutes if you like it a little crispier.
- Remove the inside basket from the air fryer once it's finished air frying.
- On top, grate some parmesan (or vegan cheese/ spread) and scatter some fresh parsley leaves.
- Sprinkle some red chili flakes on top if you like things spicy.
- Serve immediately with your preferred dip.

Air Fryer Hassel back Potatoes

Preparation and Cooking Time

25 minutes

Servings

2 persons

Nutritional facts

340 calories, 3g fat ,1g fiber ,23g carbs ,13g protein

Ingredients

- 4 Potatoes Russet
- 1/2 tsp of chili powder
- 3 – 4 tbsp. of olive oil
- 1 tsp of salt
- 1/2 tsp of garlic powder
- 1 tbsp. of herbs, finely chopped

Instructions

- Combine the olive oil/melted butter and all of the spices listed above in a small bowl.
- Thoroughly wash & clean the potatoes.
- Thinly slice the potatoes, leaving a half-inch border at the base.
- Use seasoned oil to brush the potatoes.
- Heat the air fryer to 360 degrees Fahrenheit (180 C).
- Then, in the same air fryer, add the potatoes to the basket & cook for 15 minutes, or until they are soft.
- Set the air fryer to 390 F or 200 C for another 5 minutes to crisp up the skin.
- If you don't want crispy skins on your potatoes, reduce the cooking time to 20 minutes at 360°F (180°C).
- Once done, remove from the oven and serve immediately.
- Brush them with slightly more butter or herbed garlic butter if desired.

Garlic Knots

Preparation and Cooking Time

18 minutes

Servings

16 persons

Nutritional facts

98 calories, 11g fat ,1g fiber ,1g carbs ,6g protein

Ingredients

- 2 cups flour
- 2 tbsp. olive oil
- 1 tsp salt to taste
- 1/2 – 1 tsp chili flakes optional
- 2 – 3 tbsp. olive oil or melted butter/ vegan butter
- 1 tsp Italian seasoning mix
- 2 tsp parsley leaves finely chopped
- 1 tsp yeast
- 1 tsp granulated sugar
- 1/2 cup + 2Tbsp water (as required to make dough)
- 1/2 tsp salt (or as per taste)
- 1/2 tsp garlic powder or 2 small cloves minced
- 1/2 tsp parsley
- Instructions
- In a small bowl, combine yeast and sugar.
- To activate the yeast, add warm water.
- Allow it to sit for 6–7 minutes or until a frothy layer forms on top.
- This indicates that the yeast has been properly activated.
- Add the flour and salt now. With a spatula, combine the flour the yeast water until thoroughly combined.

- If necessary, add a little water a little at a time until the dough is ideal.
- Then gently knead it for 3–4 minutes.
- Now grease the bowl and a small amount of oil on the dough.
- Remove the dough once it has doubled in size.
- Dust the surface with flour & knead the dough for 4–5 minutes.
- Depending on the size you want, divide it into 12–16 equal pieces.
- Take one portion and place it on top of the others.
- This recipe can also be made with store-bought pizza dough.
- Take a ball & roll it into a log form or 1/4-inch thick strands.
- Only use your palms & fingers to smooth it out. Form a knot in the log.
- Add olive oil, vegan butter, or butter to a small mixing bowl. Season with salt, garlic powder, and other seasonings as desired. Stir thoroughly and set away for later use.
- Heat the air fryer to 400 degrees Fahrenheit for 4 minutes.
- In the air fryer basket, place the formed knots.
- Using the seasonings and oil mixture, lightly coat them.
- Preheat the air fryer to 355 degrees Fahrenheit (180 degrees Celsius) for 10 minutes, or until golden brown.
- Check it halfway through. You can also season here with a little salt and pepper, and however, it is optional.
- Brush it again with the seasoning & herb mix with butter/vegan butter/olive oil combination after the knots are finished. It's optional, but it adds flavor to the knots.
- Garlic knots made with vegan ingredients are ready to eat. Serve with your choice of dips.

Air Fryer Fajita Vegetables

Preparation and Cooking Time

32 minutes

Servings

3 persons

Nutritional facts

183 calories, 7g fat ,2g fiber ,14g carbs ,1g protein

Ingredients

- 1 red onion
- 6 – 8 Roma tomatoes
- 1/2 tsp cumin powder
- 1/2 tsp onion powder
- 1/2 – 3/4 tsp salt or as per taste
- 1 tbsp. olive oil
- 2 tbsp. vegan broth or water
- 1/4 tsp paprika
- 1/4 tsp chili powder
- 1/4 tsp cayenne pepper
- 1 red pepper
- 1 yellow pepper
- 1 green pepper
- 200 grams' mushrooms
- 1/4 tsp ground coriander
- 1/2 tsp garlic powder

Instructions

- Combine all of the spices listed in the ingredients list in a small bowl.
- Combine the spices, broth, and oil in a large mixing bowl.

- Vegetables should be cut into stripes.
- On a big platter, arrange the vegetables.
- Pour the sauce over the vegetables.
- The vegetables should be an hour of marinating the vegetables, allowing the vegetables to absorb the taste well.
- Otherwise, leave the vegetables to marinate for at least 15 minutes.
- Meanwhile, preheat the air fryer to 195 degrees Celsius (390 degrees Fahrenheit) for 3 minutes.
- In the air fryer basket, place the marinated vegetables.
- If there is any leftover marinade after transferring the vegetables, add it to the veggies, and this will keep the vegetables moist and prevent them from drying out too much.
- Preheat the oven to 390°F and set the timer for 12 minutes (195C).
- For consistent cooking, pause and stir the vegetables every 5 minutes.
- Remove the vegetables from the air fryer once they appear to be cooked and browned.
- Cook for another 2 minutes if you want additional browned vegetables.

Air Fryer Arancini

Preparation and Cooking Time

25 minutes

Servings

3 persons

Nutritional facts

385 calories, 17g fat ,4g fiber ,31g carbs ,6g protein

Ingredients

We have listed below the ingredients that would be required by you for cooking this healthy and tasty food in the air fryer:

- 2 cups of cooked rice, cold or leftover, is better
- 1/2 cup shredded Mozzarella or vegan cheese
- 2 tbsp. corn starch
- 4 tbsp. water
- 2 tsp Italian herb mix oregano, basil, parsley, chili flakes
- 1/2 tsp garlic powder
- 1 tsp salt or as per taste
- 2 — 3 tbsp. olive oil or avocado oil spray
- 1 cup bread crumbs GF or a mix of 1/2 regular crumbs + 1/2 panko crumbs
- 1 tsp herb mix
- 1/2 tsp salt

Instructions

- Take the rice and place it in a large mixing bowl.
- With the help of a masher, mash it roughly.
- Season with salt and pepper.
- Combine them with the mashed rice and mix well.
- Take one scoop of the mixture and press it flat with your palms.
- Cover the cheese cube (or a little bit) from all sides, forming a ball.
- Don't press too hard; otherwise, it will break apart while cooking.
- Make a slurry using corn starch & water in a bowl.

- Drop the ball into the slurry & roll it in seasoned bread crumbs to finish.
- Repeat with the remaining balls.
- Heat the air fryer to 400 degrees Fahrenheit for 4 minutes.
- Brush the pan lightly with oil to grease it.
- Spray the tops and sides of the coated balls with oil.
- Preheat the air fryer to 375 degrees Fahrenheit (190 degrees Celsius) for 12 minutes.
- Then bake for 3–4 minutes at 400°F (203°C). The crispy balls will turn golden as a result of this.

Air Fryer Egg Rolls

Preparation and Cooking Time

14 minutes

Servings

3 persons

Nutritional facts

78 calories, 8g fat ,1g fiber ,22g carbs ,2g protein

Ingredients

- 6 egg roll wrappers
- 1/4 cup shredded carrot {if not using coleslaw mix}
- 1.5 tsp toasted sesame oil
- 2 tsp ginger grated
- 1 tsp reduced-sodium soy sauce
- 1/4 tsp black pepper
- 2 cloves of minced garlic
- 3 cups cabbage shredded
- 2 green onions sliced
- 1 tsp olive oil

Instructions

- Heat a frying pan over medium heat for a few minutes. Combine the sesame oil, ginger, garlic, cabbage, & shredded carrot in a large mixing bowl. Reduce the heat to low and cook for 2-3 minutes, just until the cabbage has wilted. Combine the green onions, soy sauce, & black pepper in a mixing bowl. Remove from heat after stirring.
- Put together your egg rolls. Brush the tops of the egg rolls with olive oil. You may also use Misto to spray olive oil.
- Brush the basket of the air fryer with olive oil. Put the egg rolls in the basket seam side down, ensuring they don't touch.
- Preheat oven to 360°F and bake for 7 minutes. Bake for another 2 minutes on the other side.

Air Fryer Stuffed Mushrooms

Preparation and Cooking Time

27 minutes

Servings

16 persons

Nutritional facts

44 calories, 6g fat ,1g fiber ,23g carbs ,13g protein

Ingredients

- 16 large mushrooms
- ¼ teaspoon thyme leaves
- 1 teaspoon Worcestershire sauce
- 1 tablespoon fresh parsley chopped
- 1 Tablespoon salted butter
- 2 cloves garlic minced

- ½ cup onion minced
- 4 oz. cream cheese
- ¼ cup parmesan cheese divided
- pepper to taste

Instructions

- Remove the stems and clean the mushrooms. Stems should be diced finely.
- Combine the stems, garlic, onion, and butter in a small saucepan. Cook until the onion is soft. Allow the mixture to cool fully.
- Combine the onion mixture, cream cheese, thyme, Worcestershire sauce, parsley, salt & pepper to taste, and 3 tablespoons parmesan cheese in a mixing bowl.
- Fill mushroom caps halfway with cream cheese mixture, then top with parmesan cheese.
- Cook the caps in the air fryer for 7-9 minutes at 380°F.

Air-Fryer Asian BBQ Cauliflower Wing Recipe

Preparation and Cooking Time

30 minutes

Servings

4 persons

Nutritional facts

305 calories ,24g fat, 1g fiber, 43g carbs, 5g protein

Ingredients

- 1 head cauliflower medium
- 1 tbsp. soy sauce
- 1 tbsp. rice vinegar
- 1 tbsp. ketchup
- 1 tsp sesame oil
- 2 cups panko bread crumbs
- 3 eggs large
- 1/4 cup hoisin sauce
- 1/3 cup honey
- 1/4 tsp ground ginger
- 2 cloves garlic minced
- 1/4 cup water cold
- 2 tsp corn starch

Instructions

- Preheat the air fryer to 400 degrees Fahrenheit.
- A medium head of cauliflower should be washed and dried. Remove any stems from the cauliflower crown and cut them into bite-size pieces.
- Eggs should be beaten in a small bowl, and two cups panko bread. Every piece of cauliflower should be dipped in the egg mixture first and then the panko bread crumbs. Make sure to shake off any excess egg before dipping each piece in the panko bread crumbs. Place the cauliflower on a wire rack that will sit on top of the baking sheet and toss in the panko bread crumbs. Make sure the cauliflower pieces aren't touching or crowded so that air can circulate freely around each one. Cook for 15 minutes in the air fryer or the oven. Turn the cauliflower pieces halfway through the cooking process if you're using a convection oven.
- Meanwhile, combine 1/4 cup hoisin sauce, 1/3 cup honey, 1 tablespoon soy sauce, 1 tablespoon ketchup, 1 tablespoon rice vinegar, 1 teaspoon sesame oil, 1/4 tsp ground ginger, and 2 minced garlic cloves in a small pot over medium-high heat. Stir everything together and bring it to a low boil.

- Insert quarter cup cold water and 2 teaspoons of cornstarch in a small bowl. Mix thoroughly until the cornstarch is completely dissolved. Pour into the BBQ sauce mixture & thoroughly combine. Reduce the heat to medium & continue to cook until the sauce thickens. Approximately 2-3 minutes.
- Add the sauce to the cooked cauliflower pieces in a large mixing bowl. Toss until all of the cauliflower wings are coated. Serve right away.

Air Fryer Parmesan Cauliflower Gnocchi Dippers

Preparation and Cooking Time

22 minutes

Servings

4 persons

Nutritional facts

63 calories, 0.7g fat, 3.1g fiber, 27g carbs,1.3g protein

Ingredients

- bag of Trader Joe's frozen cauliflower gnocchi
- Salt to taste
- Fresh chopped parsley for topping, optional
- 1 & 1/2 tbsp. olive oil
- 1/2 – 1 tsp garlic powder3 tbsp.
- grated parmesan, divided
- 1/2 tsp dried basil
- Trader Joe's romesco dip for dipping

Instructions

- Mix the frozen olive oil, cauliflower gnocchi, salt, dried basil, garlic powder, & 1 tablespoon parmesan cheese in a large mixing bowl. Combine all ingredients in a mixing bowl and place in an air fryer basket.
- Air fry for 10 minutes at 400 degrees F. Give the gnocchi a brisk shake to keep them from sticking together.
- Two tablespoons of grated parmesan cheese should be sprayed.
- Then air fry for another 5-7 minutes at 400 degrees F, just until the gnocchi is crispy to your preference.
- Serve with romesco sauce as a dip.

Air Fryer Curly Zucchini Fries

Preparation and Cooking Time

25 minutes

Servings

4 persons

Nutritional facts

211 calories,10g fat ,1g fiber, 19g carbs, 10g protein

Ingredients

- 2 Spiralized Zucchinis
- 1 tsp black pepper
- 1 tsp salt
- 1 cup flour
- 2 tbsp. paprika
- 1 tsp cayenne pepper
- 1 tsp garlic powder
- 2 eggs
- olive oil or cooking spray

Instructions

- Preheat the Air Fryer to 400 degrees Fahrenheit.

- Combine flour and seasonings in a large mixing bowl.
- In a separate bowl, whisk the eggs.
- Zucchini is dipped in flour, then egg, and then back into the flour.
- Place in the air fryer to cook.
- Oil is sprayed over the surface.
- Cook for ten minutes.
- Cook for an additional ten minutes or until golden brown on the other side.

Air Fryer Sweet Potatoes with Hot Honey Butter

Preparation and Cooking Time

40 minutes

Servings

3 persons

Nutritional facts

237 calories, 9g fat ,8g fiber,10g carbs ,3g protein

Ingredients

- 1-4 sweet potatoes scrubbed clean and patted dry
- 2 teaspoons hot sauce
- ¼ teaspoon salt
- 1 teaspoon oil
- 4 Tablespoon unsalted butter
- 1 Tablespoon Honey

Instructions

- Place sweet potatoes in the air fryer basket after coating them with oil.
- Cook for 35-40 minutes at 400 degrees Fahrenheit, just until the sweet potatoes are tender on the inside.
- While the sweet potatoes are cooking, whisk together the butter, honey, spicy sauce, and salt in a mixing bowl until smooth.
- Cut the sweet potato in half, fluff the insides with a fork, and top it with butter.

Chapter 12: Air Fryer Desserts Recipes

Air Fried Oreos with Crescent Rolls

Preparation and Cooking Time

10 minutes

Servings

8 persons

Nutritional facts

172 calories,11g fat ,1g fiber ,21g carbs ,2g protein

Ingredients

- Eight Oreo cookies or other brand sandwich cookies
- One package of Pillsbury Crescents Rolls (or crescent dough sheet)
- Powdered sugar for dusting (optional)

Instructions

- On a counter, spread out the crescent dough.
- Press down into each perforated line with your finger to make one large sheet.
- Eighths should be cut out of the dough.
- In the center of each crescent roll square, place one Oreo cookie and roll each corner up.
- Bunch up the remaining crescent roll to completely cover the Oreo cookie. The crescent roll should not be stretched too thinly, or it will break.
- Preheat the air fryer for around 2-3 minutes at 320 degrees F.
- Put the Air Fried Oreos in one even row inside the air fryer, making sure they don't touch.
- Cook Oreos for 5-6 minutes at 320 degrees or golden brown outside.
- Take out the Air Fryer Oreos from the air fryer with care and, if preferred, immediately coat them with powdered sugar.
- Allow cooling for 2 minutes before serving.

Air Fryer Lava Cakes

Preparation and Cooking Time

20 minutes

Servings

2 persons

Nutritional facts

776 calories, 14g fat ,2g fiber ,31g carbs ,2g protein

Ingredients

- 1/2 cup semi-sweet chocolate chips

- 3 tablespoons all-purpose flour
- 1/2 cup powdered sugar
- 2 tablespoons Nutella
- 4 tablespoons butter
- 2 eggs
- 1 teaspoon vanilla extract
- 1/4 teaspoon salt
- 1 tablespoon butter, softened
- One tablespoon powdered sugar

Instructions

- Preheat the air fryer to 350 degrees Fahrenheit.
- Cook for 10-12 minutes in an oven-safe ramekin with the frozen lava cake.
- Turn the lava cake onto a dish, set it aside to cool for another few minutes before adding toppings and serving.

Air Fryer Cookie

Preparation and Cooking Time

25 minutes

Servings

2 persons

Nutritional facts

673 calories, 10g fat ,1.2g fiber ,23g carbs ,2g protein

Ingredients

- 1 stick butter, softened (8 tablespoons)
- 1 1/2 cups all-purpose flour
- 1/2 teaspoon baking soda
- 1/2 cup plus 2 tablespoons brown sugar, packed
- 1/4 cup sugar
- 1 cup of semi-sweet chocolate chips
- 1 egg
- 1 teaspoon vanilla extract
- 1/2 teaspoon salt

Instructions

- Preheat the air fryer to 370 degrees Fahrenheit.
- Cream together the butter, brown sugar, and sugar in a large mixing basin.
- Mix in the vanilla & eggs until everything is well mixed.
- Slowly stir in the flour, baking soda, & salt until just combined. Next, stir in chocolate chips until evenly distributed throughout the batter.
- After spraying a 6-inch pan with oil, pour half the batter into the pan and then press it down to fill it evenly. Refrigerate or freeze the other half for later use.
- Cook for ten minutes in the air fryer with the cookie.
- Remove it from the air fryer and set it aside for 5 minutes to cool. Remove the cookie from the pan and serve with vanilla ice cream and your favorite toppings.

Air Fryer Pumpkin Pie Twists

Preparation and Cooking Time

13 minutes

Servings

8 persons

Nutritional facts

219 calories, 12g fat ,2g fiber ,25g carbs ,2g protein

Ingredients

- 1 can Pillsbury crescent rolls
- 1/2 cup confectionery sugar
- 2 tablespoons melted butter
- 1/2 cup pumpkin puree
- 2 teaspoons pumpkin pie spice
- 1/8 teaspoon salt
- 3 tablespoons unsalted butter, melted
- 2 and 1/4 teaspoons milk

Instructions

- Roll out the crescent roll dough and press any perforated lines down.
- Make a lengthwise incision and then a widthwise cut to divide the dough into quarters. If using in a smaller air fryer, cut into eighths.
- Mix the pumpkin puree, ½ of the pumpkin pie spice, and the salt.
- On top of the crescent roll dough, spread the pumpkin puree.
- Place two crescent dough sheets, pumpkin side down, on top of the other two. Ensure the corners and sides are as close as possible to one other.
- Cut each pumpkin twist sheet into four long strips using a dough or pizza cutter, for a total of eight.
- Preheat the air fryer for 2-3 minutes at 320 degrees F.
- Twist each strip a couple of times on the bottom and a couple of times on top.
- Brush the pumpkin pie, twist with melted butter and sprinkle with the additional pumpkin pie spice.
- Put the pumpkin twists in the air fryer in a single layer, not touching, in the air fryer. 6 minutes in the oven
- In a separate bowl, whisk the confectionery sugar, melted butter, & milk to make the icing.
- Remove the Air Fryer Pumpkin Pie Twists from the air fryer and ice them.
- Enjoy right away or keep refrigerated for up to three days.

Easy Air Fryer Apples

Preparation and Cooking Time

15 minutes

Servings

6 persons

Nutritional facts

237 calories, 2g fat ,3g fiber ,10g carbs ,4g protein

Ingredients

- 3 Granny Smith Apples
- 1/4 cup sugar
- 1 cup flour
- 3 eggs, whisked
- 1 cup graham cracker crumbs
- 1 teaspoon ground cinnamon

Instructions

- Preheat the air fryer to 380 degrees Fahrenheit.
- Remove the core from the apples and cut them into wedges.
- Put the flour in the first bowl, the egg in the second bowl, and the graham cracker crumbs, sugar, & cinnamon in the third bowl, using three bowls.

- Dip an apple wedge into the flour. Next, dip the egg and finally the graham cracker mixture, coating the apple as thoroughly as possible each time.
- Repeat with the rest of the apple slices.
- Place the apples in a single layer in the air fryer & cook for 5 to 6 minutes, flipping after one minute.
- Take the apples out of the air fryer and eat them. If preferred, serve with a caramel sauce.

Air Fryer S'mores

Preparation and Cooking Time

10 minutes

Servings

4 persons

Nutritional facts

141 calories, 11g fat ,1g fiber ,20g carbs ,2g protein

Ingredients

- 4 graham crackers broken in half
- Four large marshmallows
- One milk chocolate bar, divided

Instructions

- In the air fryer basket, put four graham cracker halves.
- Cook for 7-8 minutes at 375 degrees or when the marshmallow is golden brown.
- Top with the remaining graham cracker and desired amount of Hershey's chocolate.
- Return to the air fryer for another 2 minutes, or until the chocolate melts.

Domino's Cinnamon Bread Twists

Preparation and Cooking Time

30 minutes

Servings

6 persons

Nutritional facts

105 calories, 12g fat ,4g fiber ,30g carbs ,4g protein

Ingredients

- 1 C (120g) All-Purpose Flour
- 2 Tbsp. (24g) Granulated Sugar
- 1 tsp. Baking Powder
- 1/4 tsp. Kosher Salt (1/8 tsp. table salt)
- 2/3 C (150g) Fat-Free Greek Yogurt
- 2 Tbsp. (28g) Light Butter
- 1-2 tsp. Ground Cinnamon, to taste

Instructions

- Before adding the Greek yogurt, combine the flour, baking powder, and salt. Stir everything together with a fork until crumbly dough forms. There should be some dry flour left in the bowl.
- Move the crumbly dough to a flat surface and knead it into a single smooth ball. Make six 45-gram pieces out of the dough. Roll the dough into thin strips, about 8 inches long, between your palms or on a flat surface.
- Move to an air fryer basket sprayed with cooking spray and fold one end of each strip over to make a ribbon shape. Spray the top of the basket with cooking spray and seal the lid once all six bread twists are in it.
- You need to air fry for 15 minutes at 350°F.

- Microwave the light butter and add the granulated sugar & cinnamon near the end of the cooking time. As soon as the bread twists come out of the air fryer, brush them with the cinnamon-sugar butter. Warm the dish before serving.

Air Fryer Donuts with Chocolate Glaze Recipe

Preparation and Cooking Time

10 minutes

Servings

8 persons

Nutritional facts

276 calories, 20g fat ,2g fiber ,31g carbs ,3g protein

Ingredients

- 1 package Grand Flakey Biscuits
- 3 1/2 tablespoons Water
- 1 cup Powdered Sugar
- 3 1/2 tablespoons Cocoa Powder
- 1 teaspoon Vanilla
- Sprinkles optional

Instructions

- To make a hole in the biscuits, open them up and use a small donut cutter.
- Cook the biscuit donuts in the air fryer on the lower rack for 3-4 minutes at 350 degrees F.
- Flip the donuts and cook for another minute in the air fryer.
- When the donuts are cool enough to handle, dip them in the chocolate glaze & decorate as desired.
- Mix the chocolate glaze ingredients in a bowl and mix till combined.
- If it's too thick, you could add 1 tsp. of water at a time till it reaches the required consistency.

Strawberry Nutella hand pies

Preparation and Cooking Time

30 minutes

Servings

8 persons

Nutritional facts

205 calories, 11g fat ,2g fiber ,23 carbs ,4g protein

Ingredients

- One Pillsbury refrigerated pie crust
- Three to four strawberries
- Nutella
- sugar
- coconut oil cooking spray
- Three-inch heart cookie cutter

Instructions

- Roll out the pie dough and place it on a baking sheet. Cut out hearts as precisely as possible with the cutter. Make a ball out of the scraps. To make a few additional heart shapes, roll out the ball thinly.
- Set aside a baking tray lined with parchment paper.
- Set aside the strawberries, which have been finely chopped. Spread a dollop of Nutella (approximately 1 teaspoon) on one of the hearts. Add a few strawberry pieces to the mix. Add a pinch of sugar to the top.

- Put the second heart on top and use a fork to crimp the edges tightly. Lightly poke holes in the top of the pie with a fork. Place on a baking sheet.
- All of the pies on the tray should be sprayed with coconut oil. Rather than turning the pies, rotate them around the tray to get more coconut oil.
- Heat the air fryer for three minutes at 400 degrees F to bake in the air fryer. Put pie hearts in the basket, making sure they don't touch. You should be able to fit four of them in at once. Let them bake for 5–7 minutes in the oven or until beautifully browned. There's no need to turn the hearts over.
- Preheat the oven to 400 degrees F before baking. You must bake for 10 to 12 minutes on the baking tray or until well-browned

Air Fryer Apple Hand Pies Recipe

Preparation and Cooking Time

25 minutes

Servings

8 persons

Nutritional facts

220 calories, 8g fat ,1g fiber ,19g carbs ,3g protein

Ingredients

- 2 Pre-Made Pie Crusts
- Five ounces Can Apple Pie Filling
- One Egg

Instructions

- Roll out the pie crust and cut out circles with a cookie cutter.
- Half a teaspoon of apple pie filling should be placed in the center of half of the circles.
- Roll out the remaining circles with a rolling pin to make a slightly larger tab than the apple rounds.
- Put the larger circle on top and mend the two circles together with a fork.
- Each apple pie should be egg-washed.
- Preheat the air fryer to 350°F and cook for 12-15 minutes.
- Serve and take pleasure in it.

Air Fryer Beignets

Preparation and Cooking Time

35 minutes

Servings

9 persons

Nutritional facts

123 calories, 5g fat ,2g fiber ,30g carbs ,2g protein

Ingredients

- One Cup Self-Rising Flour
- 1 Cup Plain Greek Yogurt
- Two TBSP Sugar
- One TSP Vanilla
- 2 TBSP Melted unsalted butter
- Half Cup Powdered Sugar

Instructions

- Combine the yogurt, sugar, and vanilla extract in a mixing bowl.
- Stir in the flour until it forms a dough-like consistency.
- Place the dough on a floured surface and roll it out.
- Fold the dough in half a couple of times.

- Make a 1" thick rectangle out of the dough. It should be cut into 9 parts. Using a light dusting of flour, lightly coat each piece.
- Allow 15 minutes for resting.
- Preheat the air fryer to 350 degrees Fahrenheit.
- Spray the tray/basket of your air fryer with canola spray.
- Using melted butter, brush the tops of the dough.
- Place the tray or basket with the butter side down. Brush the dough's tops with butter.
- Air fry for about 6-7 minutes or until the edges brown.
- Cook for another six to seven minutes on the other side.
- Powdered sugar can be used as a finishing touch.

Air Fryer Mini S'mores Pie

Preparation and Cooking Time

8 minutes

Servings

6 persons

Nutritional facts

562 calories, 6g fat ,1g fiber ,15g carbs ,3g protein

Ingredients

- Six Mini Graham Ready Crust
- Twelve Snack Sized Hershey's Bars (broken in half)
- 1 Cup Mini Marshmallows

Instructions

- Preheat the Air Fryer to 320 degrees Fahrenheit.
- Fill each tiny crust with 4 broken Hershey bar pieces.
- You'll need enough small marshmallows to cover the Hershey bars fully.
- Based on how toasty you want the marshmallows, air fry at 320 degrees F for 5-10 mins.
- Serve right away and enjoy.

Air Fryer Churro Apple Pie Bombs

Preparation and Cooking Time

21 minutes

Servings

16 persons

Nutritional facts

124 calories, 9g fat ,3g fiber ,17g carbs ,4g protein

Ingredients

- 1 cup apple pie filling
- One can Grands canned biscuits
- Half cup butter
- ¾ cup sugar
- Three teaspoons ground cinnamon

Instructions

- Use a knife and a fork to cut the pie filling into small pieces.
- Separate the biscuits into two layers and arrange them on a clean surface. You need to roll to a 4-inch circle with a rolling pin.
- Preheat the air fryer to 350 degrees Fahrenheit for 5 minutes.
- Fill each dough with filling and then squeeze the sides together to seal. Make balls out of the dough.
- Place apple pie bombs about 2 inches apart in an air fryer basket, cooking in batches based on how many you can accommodate.

- Cook occasionally, stirring for 8 minutes or till golden brown.
- Melt the butter as the first batch bakes.
- Combine the sugar and cinnamon in a medium mixing basin.
- Cooked apple pie bombs are dipped in melted butter on all sides and drained.
- Place on a wire rack after rolling in the cinnamon-sugar mixture.
- Repeat with the rest of the ingredients.
- Serve hot or cold, depending on your preference.

Air Fryer Twix Cheesecake

Preparation and Cooking Time

1 hour 46 minutes

Servings

12 persons

Nutritional facts

632 calories,10g fat ,2g fiber ,31g carbs ,8g protein

Ingredients

- 1 ½ cups Flour
- 2 Eggs
- ¼ cup Heavy Cream
- ½ package Jello Instant Cheesecake Pudding 3 oz. size
- 1 cup Powdered Sugar
- 1 jar Caramel Ice Cream Topping
- 3 squares Chocolate Almond Bark Melting Chocolate
- 1 ½ sticks Butter melted
- 32 oz. Cream Cheese softened
- 1 tsp. Lemon Juice
- 1 ½ cup Powdered Sugar
- ⅓ cup Heavy Cream

Instructions

- In a mixing bowl, combine the flour & powdered sugar. Microwave the butter until it melts, then pour it into the flour/powdered sugar mixture. In a mixing bowl, combine the flour, butter, and salt.
- Line the bottom of a 7-inch spring form pan using parchment paper and press the flour mixture firmly into the pan.
- Preheat the Air Fryer to 350 degrees Fahrenheit and cook the pan for six minutes.
- Put the softened cream cheese in the mixing bowl of a stand mixer and blend until smooth while the crust is baking.
- Mix in the lemon juice and eggs till the eggs are fully combined. Mix in the heavy cream until the Instant pudding is completely smooth.
- In a mixing bowl, combine the pudding and the milk. Mix in the powdered sugar at low speed until smooth.
- Scrape down the sides of the basin and stir until everything is well combined. Remove the cheesecake mixture from the Air Fryer and pour it into the spring form pan. Preheat the oven to 350 degrees F & bake the cheesecake for 55 minutes.
- After around 10 minutes, remove the cheesecake from the Air Fryer and cover it loosely with foil. Return it to the Air Fryer to complete cooking.
- When the cheesecake is done, remove it from the Air Fryer and set it aside for 30 minutes (with the Air Fryer switched off). Allow cooling on a wire rack.
- Cover the cheesecake with foil and leave it in the refrigerator overnight to achieve the best results. Take out the cheesecake from the refrigerator the next day, spoon the caramel topping on top, and return it to the fridge.

- Put the heavy cream in a microwave-safe dish and heat until hot. Boiling is not recommended. Add 3 squares of Chocolate Almond Bark to the hot cream and swirl to combine to melt the chocolate. If the chocolate doesn't entirely melt, return it to the microwave for another 15 seconds and mix until it's smooth and melted.
- Remove the spring form pan from the pan and remove the cheesecake from the refrigerator. Put the cheesecake on a dish for serving.
- Allow the hot Ganache in the form of melted chocolate to trickle down the sides of the cheesecake and onto the serving platter. Return the cheesecake to the refrigerator until ready to serve to allow the chocolate to set. It can be served right away on dessert plates.

Air Fryer Bread Pudding

Preparation and Cooking Time

25 minutes

Servings

6 persons

Nutritional facts

375 calories,11g fat ,2g fiber ,18g carbs ,2g protein

Ingredients

- 2 cups bread cubed
- 1/2 tsp. vanilla extract
- 1/4 cup sugar
- 1 egg
- 2/3 cup heavy cream
- Quarter cup chocolate chips optional

Instructions

- Apply cooking spray to the inside of a baking dish that fits into the air fryer.
- In a baking dish, place bread cubes. Sprinkle chocolate chips on top of the bread if using.
- Combine the egg, whipped cream, vanilla, and sugar in a separate bowl.
- Allow 5 minutes for the egg mixture to soak into the bread cubes.
- In the air fryer basket, place the baking dish. Cook for 15 minutes in the air fryer at 350°F, or till the bread pudding is cooked through.

Strawberry Cheesecake Chimichangas

Preparation and Cooking Time

14 minutes

Servings

6 persons

Nutritional facts

360 calories,18g fat ,1g fiber ,21g carbs ,3g protein

Ingredients

- 1 package cream cheese (room temperature)
- 1 teaspoon vanilla extract
- 1/2 teaspoon fresh lemon zest
- 6 (8-inch) soft flour tortillas
- 1/4 C sour cream
- 1 TBSP sugar
- 1/4 cup sugar
- One 3/4 cup sliced strawberries
- 1 Tablespoon cinnamon

Instructions

- Cream the cream cheese with the sour cream, 1 tbsp. sugar, vanilla extract, and lemon zest in the bowl of a stand mixer fitted with the paddle attachment, scraping down the sides of the bowl as needed.
- Three-quarter cup sliced strawberries should be folded in.
- Warming the tortillas in the microwave will make them easier to bend. Leave them in the package for 30-45 seconds in the microwave.
- Distribute the mixture evenly among the tortillas, slathering each portion on the lower third.
- After that, fold the 2 sides of each tortilla toward the center and roll it up like a burrito, securing it with a toothpick.
- Roll out the remaining tortillas in the same manner.
- Mix the remaining ¼ cup sugar with the cinnamon in a shallow bowl and set aside.
- Preheat the air fryer to 400 degrees Fahrenheit.
- In the air fryer basket, place the chimichangas.
- Cooking spray should be sprayed on the chimichanga.
- Preheat the oven to 350°F and set the timer for six minutes.
- Take out the chimichangas from the basket after 6 minutes.
- Roll them in a mixture of cinnamon and sugar.
- Place the chimichangas on the serving plates after removing all toothpicks.
- Serve immediately with strawberry slices on top of each chimichanga.

Air Fryer Angel Food Cake

Preparation and Cooking Time

25 minutes

Servings

6 persons

Nutritional facts

246 calories,10g fat ,2g fiber ,31g carbs ,3g protein

Ingredients

- 2 eggs
- 1/2 tsp. cream of tartar
- 8 oz. Cool Whipped, divided
- 6 tbsp. sugar
- 1/4 tsp. vanilla
- 1/4 cup flour
- 1/4 tsp. baking soda
- 1 cup sliced strawberries, divided

Instructions

- To make the first layer of cake, whisk together the eggs and sugar for 6 minutes on high.
- Mix in the vanilla, flour, baking soda, and cream of tartar for 1 minute on medium.
- Pour the batter into an air fryer cake pan that has been oiled.
- Preheat oven to 325°F and bake for 15 minutes.
- Remove the cake from the pan and place it on a plate to cool.
- Repeat for the second layer.
- Half of the container of Cool Whip should be placed on top of the first layer.
- Place the second layer of cake on top of the first.
- On top of the cake, spread the leftover Cool Whip.
- To serve, evenly divide the strawberries as a garnish.

Blueberry Mini Pies in the Air Fryer

Preparation and Cooking Time

1 hour 8 minutes

Servings

12 persons

Nutritional facts

185 calories, 9g fat ,1g fiber ,21g carbs ,2g protein

Ingredients

- 2 tbsp. Cornstarch
- 1 tsp. Cinnamon Optional
- 2 Pillsbury Pie Crusts thawed and at room temperature
- 1 container Cooking spray
- 2 cups Confectioner's sugar
- ½ cup White sugar (granulated)
- 2 cups Blueberries, Fresh or Frozen If frozen, thaw and drain a bit before use.
- Half cup Water
- 1 tsp. Lemon juice Optional
- 3 tbsp. Milk
- 1 tsp. Vanilla

Instructions

- Cornstarch and sugar should be whisked together in a large saucepan.
- Cook over medium heat with the remaining ingredients.
- Stir often, squeezing the blueberries as you do so.
- Remove the pan from the heat once the mixture has thickened noticeably, and let it cool while the dough is being prepared.
- Allow two store-bought refrigerated or frozen pie crusts to come to room temperature as directed on the packaging.
- Roll out the dough on a clean surface once it has reached room temperature.
- Cut circles out of the dough with a four-inch round cookie cutter.
- Scoop one leveled scoop into the center of one dough circle with a small to medium-sized cookie scoop.
- Fold the top half of the dough circle in half to create a flawless half-moon-shaped pie.
- Crimp the edges using a fork.
- Fill the remaining pies, fold the dough over, and crimp the edges.
- Using a cooking oil spray like Pam, lightly coat both sides of the dough.
- Put 4 pies into the basket of the air fryer with care.
- Make sure the pies don't touch or overlap.
- Preheat the air fryer to 375°F and cook for 6 minutes.
- Cook for six minutes more on the other side or until the pies are beautifully browned.
- Continue with the remaining pies.
- Then mix two cups of powdered sugar, 3 tablespoons milk, and 1 teaspoon vanilla extract in a mixing bowl.
- Blend until the glaze is thin enough to pour but not too runny. As needed, add more sugar to thicken the mixture or more milk to thin it down.
- Uniformly drizzle glaze over each cooled pie with a spoon.
- Allow 15 minutes for the glaze to set before serving.
- Keeping leftover pies in an airtight container is a good idea.

Air Fryer Churros

Preparation and Cooking Time

20 minutes

Servings

8 persons

Nutritional facts

204 calories, 22g fat ,1g fiber ,33g carbs ,4g protein

Ingredients

- 1 cup water
- 2 large eggs
- 1 tsp. vanilla extract
- oil spray
- 1/3 cup unsalted butter, cut into cubes
- 2 Tbsp. granulated sugar
- 1/4 tsp. salt
- 1 cup all-purpose flour
- Half cup granulated sugar
- 3/4 tsp. ground cinnamon

Instruction

- Spray a silicone baking mat with oil spray and place it on a baking sheet.
- Insert butter, water, sugar, and salt into a medium pot. Over medium-high heat, bring to a boil.
- Reduce the heat to medium-low and stir in the flour. Cook constantly, whisking with a rubber spatula until the dough is smooth and comes together.
- Remove the dough from the heat and place it in a mixing bowl. Allow 4 minutes for cooling.
- In a mixing basin, beat the eggs and vanilla extract with an electric hand mixer until the dough comes together. The finished product will resemble gluey mashed potatoes. Press the lumps together into a ball with your hands and then move to a large piping bag with a large star-shaped tip.
- Pipe churros into 4-inch lengths onto a greased baking mat and cut with scissors at the end.
- Refrigerate the piped churros for 1 hour on the baking sheet.
- With a cookie spatula, carefully move churros to the Air Fryer basket, allowing about 1/2-inch between churros. Using an oil spray, coat the churros. You may need to fry them in batches based on the size of your Air Fryer.
- You need to air fry for 10-12 minutes at 375°F until golden brown.
- Combine the granulated sugar & cinnamon in a small bowl.
- Toss the baked churros in the bowl with the sugar mixture right away to coat. Serve with Nutella and chocolate dipping sauce while still heated.

Air Fryer Apple Fritters

Preparation and Cooking Time

20 minutes

Servings

14 persons

Nutritional facts

221 calories, 14g fat ,1g fiber ,26g carbs ,2g protein

Ingredients

- 2 large apples
- 1 teaspoons cinnamon
- 1/2 teaspoon ground nutmeg

- 2 cups powdered sugar
- 1/4 cup apple cider or apple juice
- 1/2 teaspoon cinnamon
- 1/4 teaspoon ground cloves
- 3/4 cup apple cider or apple juice
- 2 eggs
- 3 tablespoons butter, melted
- 2 cups all-purpose flour
- 1/2 cup granulated sugar
- 1 tablespoon baking powder
- 1 teaspoon salt
- 1 teaspoon vanilla
- 1/4 teaspoon nutmeg

Instructions

- Apples should be peeled and cored. Cut into 1/4-inch cubes. Spread the apple chunks out on a kitchen towel to absorb excess moisture.
- Mix the flour, sugar, baking powder, salt, and spices in a mixing bowl. Combine the apples and flour in a mixing bowl.
- Whisk together the apple cider, eggs, melted butter, & vanilla in a small bowl. Combine the wet and dry ingredients in a mixing bowl.
- Heat the air fryer to 390 degrees Fahrenheit. In the bottom of the air fryer basket, put a parchment paper.
- Scoop three to four dollops of fritter dough into the air fryer with an ice cream scooper.
- Using a spray bottle, coat the tops of the fritters in oil. It should be cooked for 6 minutes. Cook for another four minutes on the other side.
- Combine the powdered sugar, apple cider, and spices in a mixing bowl and whisk until smooth. Drizzle the apple fritters with the glaze. Allow 10 minutes for the glaze to set.

Air Fryer Apple Hand Pies

Preparation and Cooking Time

18 minutes

Servings

6 persons

Nutritional facts

376 calories, 10g fat ,2g fiber ,29g carbs ,2g protein

Ingredients

- 14.1-ounce refrigerated package pie crust (2 crusts)
- Half can (21 ounces) apple pie filling
- One large egg
- water
- 3 tsp. turbinado sugar
- Caramel sauce for dipping, optional

Instructions

- Remove pie crusts from their packaging and set them aside to come to room temperature, as directed on the package.
- Using a cookie cutter, slice the pie crusts into five-inch circles.
- Place two apple slices from the apple pie filling on the bottom half of the pie crusts. Moisten the outside edges of the pie crust with a little water. To make half-moons, fold the dough over the filling, pinch the sides together, and crimp the corners with a fork to seal.
- Stir together the egg and a splash of water in a small bowl. Brush the egg wash over the tops of the pies.

- Half teaspoon coarse sugar should be sprinkled over each pie.
- Make 3 slits in the top crust of each pie.
- Heat the air fryer for 5 minutes at 350 degrees F. Use nonstick cooking spray to coat the air fryer basket.
- Place 2 pies in the basket at a time in the air fryer and cook for about 10 minutes, or until golden brown. Carefully take the pan from the oven and place it on a wire rack to cool. Continue with the remaining pies.
- Serve with caramel sauce.

Special Scones

Preparation and Cooking Time

25 minutes

Servings

5 persons

Nutritional facts

360 calories, 9g fat ,1g fiber ,30g carbs ,4g protein

Ingredients

- 2 cups Self Raising Flour
- Half cup Lemonade
- Half cup Thickened Cream / Heavy Cream
- Quarter cup Caster Sugar
- 1 tablespoon Milk for brushing

Instructions

- Sift the flour in a large mixing bowl and then add the sugar, cream, and lemonade. Gently combine all ingredients with a butter knife until a soft, sticky dough forms.
- Pour the dough onto a floured surface & lightly knead to bring it together. Next, you need to shape into a 3cm/1-inch-thick disc. Cut dough into rounds with a 6cm / 2.5inch scone cutter. Flour the cutter between each round and press it straight up and down (don't twist it). Fill the air fryer basket halfway with the rounds, leaving a tiny gap between each one.
- Brush the tops of the scones lightly with milk. Next, you need to bake for 15-20 minutes, or until brown on top, at 180°C/350°F. Transfer to a wire rack to cool and cover with a clean tea towel to keep the tops from being crusty.
- Serve with a dollop of cream and a dollop of jam.

Honey Roasted Almonds in Air Fryer

Preparation and Cooking Time

20 minutes

Servings

4 persons

Nutritional facts

179 calories,11g fat ,1g fiber ,18g carbs ,2g protein

Ingredients

- One cup Raw Almonds
- 1 heaped tablespoon Honey
- Half teaspoon Salt
- 1 teaspoon White Sugar

Instructions

- Pour the honey over the almonds in a mixing dish and stir well to mix.
- Spread almonds out in a single layer on the parchment paper in the bottom of the air fryer basket, and then sprinkle salt on top.
- Cook for 7-10 minutes at 180°C/350°F, shaking the nuts every few minutes till they are a few shades darker as well as fragrant. Make sure to keep an eye on them, so they don't burn.

- Immediately transfer to a baking sheet. Allow it to cool completely after sprinkling with white sugar.

Puff Pastry with Nutella

Preparation and Cooking Time

20 minutes

Servings

8 persons

Nutritional facts

175 calories,16g fat ,1g fiber ,21g carbs ,1g protein

Ingredients

- 1 Frozen Puff Pastry Sheet, thawed
- Quarter cup Nutella, or more to taste
- Icing Sugar / Powdered Sugar

Instructions

- Spread Nutella all over the puff pastry sheet, roll it up tightly and cut it into 8 even pieces.
- Cook the pinwheels in the air fryer basket for 10 minutes at 180°C/350°F, or until brown and flaky.
- Allow fried pinwheels to cool completely on a wire rack before sifting icing sugar on top.

Glazed Rolls

Preparation and Cooking Time

20 minutes

Servings

10 persons

Nutritional facts

75 calories,11g fat ,1g fiber ,18g carbs ,2g protein

Ingredients

- 1 Frozen Puff Pastry Sheet, partially thawed
- Quarter cup Brown Sugar
- 1 tablespoon Cinnamon
- One tablespoon Butter, melted

Instructions

- Preheat your air fryer to 180°C/350°F by running it for 5 minutes at that temperature.
- In a small bowl, combine the cinnamon and sugar.
- Place a clean, flat surface on which to lay the pastry sheet. Butter the baking sheet, then evenly sprinkle the cinnamon-sugar mixture on top.
- The pastry sheet should be tightly rolled. Brush the pastry with butter and then cut it into 8 even pieces with a sharp knife.
- Cook the rolls for 10 minutes in the air fryer basket or till golden & cooked through.
- Allow it to cool on a wire rack.
- To prepare the optional glaze, combine the icing sugar & vanilla in a mixing bowl and gradually add the milk, stirring until smooth. Drizzle the cinnamon rolls with the glaze.

Cinnamon Sugar Pretzel Bites

Preparation and Cooking Time

20 minutes

Servings

32 persons

Nutritional facts

44 calories, 3g fat ,0.5g fiber ,10g carbs ,2g protein

Ingredients

- 1 cup Greek Yoghurt
- One and a half cup Self-Raising / Self-Rising Flour (+ extra for flouring surface etc.)
- 2 tablespoon Butter, melted
- Half cup Granulated / White Sugar
- 1 tablespoon Cinnamon

Instructions

- In a mixing bowl, whisk together one cup of Greek yogurt. Then stir in one cup of flour until everything is well combined.
- At this point, continue to mix while gradually adding more flour to the bowl till the dough holds together in a ball shape. This will usually be between 1/2 and 3/4 cup extra, depending on how wet the yogurt was, to begin with.
- Knead your dough ball on a well-floured surface until it is thoroughly combined. If it's still too sticky, keep adding flour till you reach the desired consistency. The dough should keep its shape yet not stick to the work surface.
- Cut the dough into four pieces that are all the same size. Each piece should be rolled out into a long rope shape and then cut into equal bite-sized pieces.
- Arrange the pretzel bites in a single layer in the air fryer basket. If you're using a smaller air frying basket, do them in batches to not overlap and cook evenly. Cook for 7-ten min at 180 degrees Celsius / 350 degrees Fahrenheit, stirring the basket every few minutes, till golden brown.
- In a mixing bowl, combine the cinnamon and sugar. Brush the melted butter over the pretzel bits on a dish. Toss the bites in the cinnamon sugar to evenly coat them. Serve right away.

Apple with cinnamon and oats

Preparation and Cooking Time

30 minutes

Servings

2 persons

Nutritional facts

243 calories,13g fat ,2g fiber ,26g carbs ,5g protein

Ingredients

- 1 Apple, diced
- 1 tablespoon Butter, melted
- 1 tablespoon Maple Syrup
- ½ teaspoon Cinnamon
- ½ tablespoon Maple Syrup
- ½ tablespoon Lemon Juice
- ⅓ cup Old Fashioned / Rolled Oats
- 1 teaspoon Whole Wheat Flour
- ½ teaspoon Cinnamon

Instructions

- Combine the filling ingredients in a mixing bowl and distribute equally between two ramekins. On top of the filling ingredients, pour one tablespoon of water into each ramekin.
- Combine the topping ingredients and distribute them equally over the filling.
- Cover with foil and then put in the air fryer basket. You need to cook for fifteen minutes at 180 degrees Celsius / 350 degrees Fahrenheit.
- Remove the foil and bake for another 5-10 minutes at 180°C/350°F, or until the topping is crisp & golden, and the filling is fork soft.
- Serve warm with Greek yogurt, ice cream, or whipped cream if desired.

Air Fryer Pigs in a Blanket

Preparation and Cooking Time

15 minutes

Servings

9 persons

Nutritional facts

207 calories, 25g fat ,2g fiber ,18g carbs ,2g protein

Ingredients

- 1 Frozen Puff Pastry Sheet, thawed
- Nine Mini Hotdogs / Cocktail Frankfurts
- Egg

Instructions

- The Puff pastry sheet should be cut into nine even squares. Place a tiny hotdog/cocktail Frankfurt diagonally across a puff pastry square and then roll to wrap the hotdog. You need to egg-wash the puff pastry. Repeat with the rest of the ingredients.
- Cook the pigs in a blanket in the air fryer basket for 7-10 minutes, or till the puff pastry is golden brown & cooked through, at 200C / 390F. Serve immediately with a sauce of your choice.

Banana Bread

Preparation and Cooking Time

45 minutes

Servings

4 persons

Nutritional facts

353 calories ,13g fat ,2g fiber ,31g carbs ,3g protein

Ingredients

- 2 Very Ripe Bananas
- ¼ cup Milk
- 1 cup All Purpose / Plain Flour, sifted
- ½ teaspoon Cinnamon
- Pinch of Salt
- ½ teaspoon Baking Soda
- ¼ cup Unsalted Butter, melted
- ⅓ cup Brown Sugar
- 1 Egg
- ½ teaspoon Vanilla Extract
- ½ teaspoon Baking Powder

Instructions

- Heat the air fryer to 180C / 350F using the preheat setting for 5 minutes. Bake for 15 minutes with bananas in the basket. Remove it from the oven and set it aside to cool. Reduce the temperature of the air fryer to 160°C / 320°F and leave it empty for another 5 minutes to keep it warm while you prepare the loaves. Preheat oven to 350°F. Grease loaf pans.
- In a large mixing bowl, combine the butter and sugar. Continue to whisk in the egg, vanilla, and milk.
- Bananas should be peeled and mashed on a platter. Add the mashed potatoes to the mixing bowl and whisk until everything is well combined.
- Combine the flour, baking powder, baking soda, cinnamon, and a pinch of salt in a separate bowl. Pour in the wet ingredients and whisk until everything is well blended.
- Place the mixture in two small loaf pans and cook for 20 minutes in the air fryer basket, or till the bread is cooked through as well as a skewer comes out clean.

- Allow cooling for 10 minutes in the pan before transferring to a cooling rack to cool completely. Serve with butter lashings.

Air Fryer Banana Muffins

Preparation and Cooking Time

20 minutes

Servings

10 persons

Nutritional facts

161 calories,11g fat ,1g fiber ,21g carbs ,3g protein

Ingredients

- 2 very ripe Bananas
- 1 teaspoon Vanilla Extract
- 1 teaspoon Cinnamon
- ⅓ cup of Olive Oil
- ½ cup of Brown Sugar
- 1 Egg
- ¾ cup of Self Raising Flour

Instructions

- Preheat the air fryer to 160C / 320F by running it at that temperature for 5 minutes.
- In a large mixing bowl, mash the bananas and add the egg, brown sugar, olive oil, and vanilla essence. To blend, stir everything together thoroughly.
- Fold in the flour and cinnamon until everything is just blended.
- Divide the batter equally between the muffin tins and carefully place them in the air fryer basket.
- Place the muffin basket in the air fryer & bake for 15 minutes, or until brown.
- Let the muffins cool in their cases on a wire rack.

No Yeast Cinnamon Rolls

Preparation and Cooking Time

25 minutes

Servings

8 persons

Nutritional facts

161 calories, 4g fat ,1g fiber ,12g carbs ,2g protein

Ingredients

- 1 cup Greek Yoghurt
- ½ cup Brown Sugar
- 1 ½ cups Self-Rising Flour + more for dusting
- 1 tablespoon Unsalted Butter, melted
- 1 ½ tablespoon Cinnamon

Instructions

- In a mixing bowl, combine Greek yogurt and stir well. Stir in one cup of flour until everything is well combined. Add more flour gradually until the dough begins to form a ball.
- Place the dough on a well-floured surface & knead for a minute or two with your hands. If the dough is still sticky, add more flour and knead it some more. When the dough holds its shape and does not adhere to the hands or the surface, it is ready.
- Roll the dough into a rectangle, brush with butter, and then sprinkle with brown sugar and cinnamon.
- Cut the dough into eight equal pieces after rolling it up tightly. In the bottom of the air fryer basket, place a sheet of baking paper. Spread the rolls on top of the baking paper, leaving enough space between each one for them to rise. You might have to cook in two batches if you have a smaller air fryer.

- Cook for 10-15 minutes at 180°C/350°F or till the dough is golden & cooked through. Allow cooling completely on a wire rack.

Air Fryer Apple Turnovers

Preparation and Cooking Time

35 minutes

Servings

4 persons

Nutritional facts

154 calories, 11g fat ,2g fiber ,22g carbs ,4g protein

Ingredients

- 2 Apples (I use Pink Lady), skin removed and diced
- 1 sheet Frozen Puff Pastry
- 1 teaspoon Cinnamon
- 1 teaspoon Maple Syrup
- 2 tablespoon Water
- 1 Egg, lightly whisked into an egg wash

Instructions

- Put on a plate and set aside to cool for a few minutes.
- Remove the puff pastry sheet from the freezer, and then let it thaw for a few minutes. Then cut the sheet into four squares and use the egg to brush the edges of each square.
- Fill each puff pastry square with apples and then fold the crust over from corner to corner to form a triangular shape and seal the edges with a fork.
- The tops of each turnover are to be brushed with the egg. Then put 2 turnovers in the air fryer basket as well as cook for 15 minutes at 180 degrees Celsius / 350 degrees Fahrenheit, or until golden brown. Cook the other turnovers in the same manner.
- Serve plain or with a dollop of thickened cream.

Sausage on A Stick and Jimmy Dean Pancake and

Preparation and Cooking Time

15 minutes

Servings

2 persons

Nutritional facts

123 calories, 5g fat ,1g fiber ,16g carbs ,4g protein

Ingredients

- Four frozen pancakes and sausage on a stick

Instructions

- Place frozen pancakes and sausage on the air fryer's stick in a single layer.
- Air fry at 360F for fifteen minutes.

Air Fryer Apple Slices

Preparation and Cooking Time

20 minutes

Servings

2 persons

Nutritional facts

96 calories, 8g fat ,1g fiber ,26g carbs ,2g protein

Ingredients

- Two apples
- Half tsp. cinnamon

Instructions

- Use a nonstick cooking spray to coat the inside of the air fryer basket.
- Apple slices should be cut into slices and sprinkled with cinnamon.
- Cook apple slices in the air fryer for 18 minutes at 390°F, flipping the basket halfway through the cooking period.

Air Fryer Mardi Gras King Cake with Canned Cinnamon Rolls

Preparation and Cooking Time

25 minutes

Servings

8 persons

Nutritional facts

148 calories,15g fat ,1g fiber ,20g carbs ,2g protein

Ingredients

- One can of cinnamon rolls
- purple, green and gold sprinkles

Instructions

- Use a nonstick cooking spray to coat the air fryer basket.
- Place cinnamon rolls in a ring configuration in the air fryer basket.
- Pinch the edges of the cinnamon rolls together to keep them together.
- Cook cinnamon rolls in an air fryer at 300 degrees Fahrenheit for twenty minutes or until done.
- Cautiously invert the cinnamon rolls cake onto a dish and then flip it over to the browned side using another plate.
- Using the frosting, frost the cinnamon rolls cake.
- To make a Mardi Gras King Cake, sprinkle the colored sprinkles on top of the cinnamon rolls cake in alternate stripes of green, gold, and purple colors.

Air Fryer Pillsbury Cinnamon Rolls

Preparation and Cooking Time

15 minutes

Servings

8 persons

Nutritional facts

160 calories,13g fat ,1g fiber ,21g carbs ,3g protein

Ingredients

- One package canned cinnamon rolls

Instructions

- Use a nonstick cooking spray to coat the air fryer basket.
- Remove the icing package from the cinnamon roll packaging and set it aside.
- Place cinnamon rolls in a single layer in the air fryer basket.
- Cook cinnamon rolls in an air fryer for 10 minutes at 350°F.
- Place the baked cinnamon buns on a serving tray after removing them from the air fryer.
- Using a pastry brush, apply the icing all over the cinnamon rolls.

Air Fryer Berry Hand Pies

Preparation and Cooking Time

22 minutes

Servings

8 persons

Nutritional facts

172 calories, 9g fat ,1g fiber ,18g carbs ,2g protein

Ingredients

- 1 box store-bought or homemade pie crust
- 2 tablespoons Caster sugar
- 1/2 cup berry jam
- 1/2 cup berries
- 1 egg white
- Optional: Ice cream and additional berries for serving

Instructions

- Begin by lightly flouring a work area and rolling out 2 pie crusts. Cut 14 circles with a 4-inch circle cutter. Roll the dough leftovers into balls. Cut out two more circles from the rolled-out dough ball.
- Place roughly 2 teaspoons of jam on eight of the sixteen circles and top with a piece of fresh fruit.
- Apply a thin coat of egg white to the filled circles' edges. Use a fork to pinch the edges of the unfilled dough circles. To enable steam to escape during baking, pierce the top with a fork once.
- Brush the tops of the cupcakes with more egg white wash and caster sugar.
- Heat the air fryer to 375 degrees Fahrenheit (190 degrees Celsius). Four of the prepared pies should be placed in the basket tray.
- Bake the pies for 12 minutes or till the dough has browned.
- Serve with ice cream & fresh berries on the side.

Air Fryer Chocolate Chip Skillet Cookie

Preparation and Cooking Time

35 minutes

Servings

2 persons

Nutritional facts

165 calories,17g fat ,4g fiber ,34g carbs ,7g protein

Ingredients

- 1 cup + 2 tablespoons all-purpose flour
- ¼ cup light brown sugar
- 1 egg
- ½ tsp. baking soda
- ½ tsp. salt
- 6 tbsp. butter room temperature
- ⅓ cup granulated sugar
- Half tsp. vanilla extract
- 1 cup semisweet chocolate chips

Instructions

- Mix the flour, baking soda, and salt in a large mixing bowl. To combine the ingredients, whisk them together.
- Mix the butter, sugar, brown sugar, egg, and vanilla extract until smooth.
- Combine the chocolate chips and fold them in.
- Using a light oil spray, lightly coat a shallow 6 to 7" pie pan.

- Bake at 340 degrees F for 11 minutes after pressing the cookie batter onto the prepared pan.
- Reduce the heat to 310°F and bake for another five minutes, until golden brown and well cooked.

Strawberry Pop-Tarts

Preparation and Cooking Time

21minutes

Servings

6 persons

Nutritional facts

588 calories, 6g fat ,2g fiber ,21g carbs ,3g protein

Ingredients

- 1 (15 oz.) pkg of refrigerated pie crusts
- 1 teaspoon vanilla extract
- 6 tablespoons of strawberry jam/preserves
- 2 cups of powdered sugar
- 2-4 tablespoons of heavy cream plus more if necessary
- 2 tablespoons of melted butter
- Sprinkles

Instructions

- Cut each crust into four equal-sized rectangles with a pizza cutter.
- Combine the remaining dough, re-roll it, and cut four additional rectangles. There will be a total of 12 rectangles.
- In the center of 6 rectangles, spread one tablespoon of strawberry jam.
- Spread the jam within a quarter-inch of the edge of the pan.
- Moisten the outside of each pie crust round with water using your finger.
- Each filling rectangle should be topped with a pastry rectangle.
- Use your fingers to push the seams together and then crimp the edges with a fork.
- Make a few slits in the top with a knife.
- Preheat the oven to 350°F & set the timer for 11 minutes.
- Two pop tarts should be placed in the basket.
- Mix the powdered sugar, heavy cream, butter, and vanilla extract in a small bowl until thoroughly blended.
- Spread icing on the cooled tarts and top with sprinkles.
- Before serving, allow the frosting to harden in the refrigerator.

Air Fryer Cherry Hand Pies

Preparation and Cooking Time

13 minutes

Servings

10-12 persons

Nutritional facts

43 calories, 20g fat ,1g fiber ,27g carbs ,4g protein

Ingredients

- One (2-count package) refrigerated pie crusts nearly to room temperature
- One (21-ounce can) cherry pie filling
- Two and a quarter cup confectioners' sugar
- Quarter cup milk

Instructions

- If your air fryer has a preheat function, set it to 370 degrees F.

- Using a round biscuit cutter, cut off 4-4.5" rounds from the unrolled pie crusts one at a time. Place a heaping tbsp. of cherry pie filling in the center of each circle of dough. Moisten the circle's sides with a little water and then fold one side of the circle over the other to make a half-moon shape, pressing the edges to close. It's fine if some of the fillings leak out the sides. With a fork, crimp the edges as well as poke a couple of holes in the top.
- Spritz 3-5 hand pies with butter-flavored frying spray before placing them in the air fryer basket. Preheat oven to 370°F and bake pies for 8 minutes, or until golden brown and firm.
- Mix the confectioners' sugar & milk in a medium mixing bowl until a thick glaze forms. Dip each pie in the glaze, one at a time, coat all sides. Remove with a fork and place on a cooling rack lined with wax paper. Allow 15 minutes for the glaze to set before serving. Bake and glaze the remaining pies as directed.

Lemon Pound Cake Dessert

Preparation and Cooking Time

50 minutes

Servings

6 persons

Nutritional facts

171 calories, 9g fat ,3g fiber ,22g carbs ,2g protein

Ingredients

- 1 1/2 cups all-purpose flour
- 4 eggs
- 1 tablespoon lemon zest
- 2/3 cup plain Greek yogurt or sour cream
- 1 tablespoon Confectioner's Sweetener Optional for dusting
- 2 tablespoons fresh-squeezed lemon juice
- 1 teaspoon baking powder
- 1/2 teaspoon salt
- 1/2 cup softened unsalted butter at room temperature
- 1 cup sweetener
- 1 teaspoon vanilla extract

Instructions

- A six-cup bundt pan can be greased, floured, or sprayed with Pam Baking Spray.
- Mix the flour, salt, and baking powder in a medium mixing bowl.
- In a mixing dish, combine the butter and sweetener. To cream, the butter, use a hand mixer (or a standing mixer). Blend until smooth and creamy.
- Insert two eggs and combine with a hand mixer. You need to combine the remaining eggs in a mixing bowl.
  - Combine the dry flour mix, lemon zest, lemon juice, yogurt, and vanilla extract in a mixing dish. Blend the batter until it is completely smooth.
  - Fill the bundt pan halfway with batter.
  - Wrap foil around the bundt pan. Preheat the oven to 320°F and air fry for fifteen minutes.
- Remove the foil from the air fryer and open it. Cook for an additional 15-twenty minutes in the air fryer. Insert a toothpick into the cake to see whether it's done.
- Permit 10 minutes for the cake to cool.
- To release the cake, put a cake stand over the bundt pan & flip it over.

Chocolate Chip Cookies

Preparation and Cooking Time

38 minutes

Servings

10 persons

Nutritional facts

300 calories,14g fat ,2g fiber ,32g carbs ,2g protein

Ingredients

- 1 1/2 cups semi-sweet chocolate chips
- 8 tablespoons of softened butter
- 1/2 cup of chopped walnuts
- sea salt for sprinkling
- 1/8 teaspoon of lemon juice
- 1 cup of flour
- 1/4 cup of rolled oats
- 1/2 teaspoon of baking soda
- 1/2 teaspoon of salt
- 1/3 cup of granulated sugar or any sweetener
- 1/3 cup of brown sugar or any sweetener
- 1 large egg
- 1 teaspoon vanilla extract
- 1/4 teaspoon cinnamon

Instructions

- For two minutes on medium speed with a stand or hand mixer, sugar, cream butter, & brown sugar in a mixing dish.
- Combine the egg, vanilla extract, and lemon juice in a mixing bowl. Blend on low for thirty seconds with an electric mixer. Then, scrape down the sides of the bowl as needed, blend on medium for a few minutes or till light and fluffy.
- Blend flour, oats, baking soda, salt, and cinnamon for about 45 seconds on low speed with an electric mixer.
- Chocolate chips, as well as walnuts, should be folded in at this point.
- Air fryer parchment paper should be used to line the basket. Scoop about 2 tablespoons of cookie dough into balls and set them 1 1/2 to 2 inches apart in the basket. Flatten the cookies' tops using wet palms.
- You need to air fry for six to eight minutes at 300 degrees F.
- It should be removed from the air fryer basket, and cookies should be allowed to cool for 5 minutes. Shift the cookies to a wire rack to cool for another ten minutes.

Honey Glazed Baked Ham

Preparation and Cooking Time

50 minutes

Servings

12 persons

Nutritional facts

213 calories,12g fat ,2g fiber ,31g carbs ,10g protein

Ingredients

- 1/3 cup honey
- Quarter cup brown sweetener Brown sugar can be used if preferred.
- Quarter teaspoon ground cloves
- 3-4 pound boneless fully cooked ham

Instructions

- Mix the honey, brown sweetener, as well as ground cloves in a saucepan on medium-high heat. Mix till the sweetener has dissolved. Then it should be removed from heat.
- Ham should be glazed using a cooking brush with a quarter of the honey glaze mixture. Then ham should be tightly wrapped in foil.
- Put the foil-wrapped ham in the air fryer basket. Air fry for 40 minutes at 300 degrees F.
- Then remove the foil and the netting from around the ham. The ham should be glazed again.
- Air-fry the ham for yet another five minutes at 400 degrees F.
- The ham should be removed from the air fryer. Let the ham rest for ten minutes before slicing.

Favorite Monkey Bread Recipe in the Air Fryer

Preparation and Cooking Time

30 minutes

Servings

6 persons

Nutritional facts

2411 calories,14g fat ,3g fiber ,21g carbs ,4g protein

Ingredients

- 12 Rhodes White Dinner Rolls
- ½ cup of powdered sugar
- 1-2 tablespoons of milk
- ½ cup of brown sugar
- 1 teaspoon of cinnamon
- 4 tablespoons of butter melted
- ½ teaspoon of vanilla

Instructions

- Combine brown sugar & cinnamon in a small bowl.
- Melt a half stick of butter in a separate bowl.
- Brush the inside of an oven-safe pan that fits in the air fryer with melted butter.
- When the rolls have thawed to room temperature, break them in half as well as roll each half in butter before dipping it in the sugar mixture and placing it on the pan. Repeat!
- Pour any leftover sugar and butter on top of the rolls once they've all been placed in the pan.
- Allow rolls to rise in a hot air fryer that is turned off for 30 minutes or until they have risen to the top of the pan.
- Cover rolls with foil to keep them from burning and bake for 10-20 minutes at 340°F/171°C. When an instant-read thermometer registers around 180°F/82°C, you know the bread is done.
- Make the glaze by mixing powdered sugar, vanilla, and milk until slightly runny while the cake is baking.
- Remove the foil and continue baking for another 1-3 minutes to brown the top lightly. Remove the pan from the oven with care (with oven mitts).
- Allow for a minute of cooling before inverting the pan onto a dish.
- Finish with a glaze and serve.

Apple Pie Air Fryer Egg Rolls

Preparation and Cooking Time

20 minutes

Servings

6 persons

Nutritional facts

186 calories, 8g fat ,1g fiber ,12g carbs ,6g protein

Ingredients

- 21 ounces can apple pie filling
- 1/8 tsp. ground cinnamon
- 1/2 tsp. lemon juice
- 1/4 tsp. apple pie spice
- 1 Tbsp. all-purpose flour
- 4-6 full-size egg roll wrappers

Instructions

- Combine the lemon juice, apple pie filling, apple pie spice, cinnamon, and flour in a mixing bowl.
- Divide the mixture into sections. Place a scoop of apple pie filling in the center of an egg roll wrapper, forming a triangular shape with one point facing the bottom.
- Moisten the four outside borders with a small bit of water.
- Fold the bottom corners up and over the filling, then fold each side over on itself, moistening each edge with water, so it sticks closed.
- Close the roll completely, as well as moisten any open edges to keep them closed. After you've completed all of the egg rolls, spray each side with cooking spray.
- Heat the air fryer to 400 degrees Fahrenheit. Pull off the tray and insert the sprayed egg rolls into the air fryer pan when ready.
- Cook for 8 minutes at 400°F, flipping halfway through.
- Remove from the air fryer and sprinkle with powdered sugar. Serve and have fun.

Air Fryer Shortbread

Preparation and Cooking Time

20 minutes

Servings

4 persons

Nutritional facts

635 calories,14g fat ,2g fiber ,30g carbs ,2g protein

Ingredients

- 250 grams Self Raising Flour
- 175 grams Butter
- 75 grams Caster Sugar

Instructions

- Combine the self-rising flour, butter, and caster sugar in a mixing bowl.
- To make thick breadcrumbs, rub the butter into the flour.
- Knead the dough until it forms a ball, then roll it out with the rolling pin.
- Cut out your preferred shapes with cookie cutters.
- Cook your shortbread in an air fryer using either an air fryer grill plate or an air fryer baking mat. Preheat the oven to 180°C/360°F and set the timer for 10 minutes.
- Allow for some cooling time before serving.

Air Fried Banana

Preparation and Cooking Time

15 minutes

Servings

2 persons

Nutritional facts

113 calories, 9g fat ,1g fiber ,22g carbs ,4g protein

Ingredients

- 1 ripe banana cut into 1/2 inch slices
- Quarter tsp. cinnamon
- Half tsp. brown sugar
- 1 tbsp. Granola to taste
- One tbsp. Chopped toasted nuts to taste

Instructions

- Combine the cinnamon as well as brown sugar in a small bowl and put it aside.
- Grease a shallow baking pan lightly. In the pan, place the banana slices. Spray the banana with oil and then sprinkle it with cinnamon sugar. You need to air fry for 4-5 minutes at 400°F (200°C).
- To serve, sprinkle granola & nuts on top of the banana.

Easy Sweet Potato Biscuits

Preparation and Cooking Time

35 minutes

Servings

8 persons

Nutritional facts

155 calories,11g fat ,1g fiber ,23g carbs ,3g protein

Ingredients

- 2 cups all-purpose flour
- 2 tablespoons unsalted butter
- 1/4 cup plain non-fat Greek yogurt
- 1/2 cup cooked mashed sweet potato
- 1/2 tablespoon baking powder
- 1/2 teaspoon salt
- 2 tablespoons sweetener or sugar
- 1 teaspoon cinnamon
- 1 egg
- 1 tablespoon water

Instructions

- Mix baking powder, flour, cinnamon, sweetener, and salt in a mixing bowl.
- Combine the mashed sweet potatoes, Greek yogurt, & butter in a large mixing bowl.
- To combine, use a fork. Do not over-mix the ingredients. Using a fork, knead the butter into the mixture. You'll note that the dough has turned flaky, and some flour has remained in the bowl, and that's OK. If you over-mix the dough, you'll end up with tough and hard biscuits.
- On a floured surface, you need to roll out the dough. Roll the dough out to 7 by 7 and 1/2-inch height with your hands or a rolling pin. Roll out the dough to a height of 1 inch if you want thick biscuits. As a result, there will be fewer biscuits. Make sure the dough isn't overworked.
- Cut biscuits with a biscuit cutter. If you're using a biscuit cutter, repurpose the dough as well as roll it out again to make more biscuits using the leftover dough.
- In a small bowl, whisk the egg and add it to the water, stirring constantly. Brush the egg wash over the top of each biscuit.
- Air fryer parchment paper should be used to line the air fryer basket.
- Preheat the oven to 300°F and air fry for four minutes.

- Preheat the oven to 400 degrees Fahrenheit and bake the biscuits for 2–5 minutes, or until golden brown.

Easy Air Fryer Loaded Baked Sweet Potatoes

Preparation and Cooking Time

40 minutes

Servings

2 persons

Nutritional facts

166 calories, 8g fat ,4g fiber ,20g carbs ,2g protein

Ingredients

- 2 medium-large sweet potatoes
- 2 teaspoons honey
- 1 teaspoon olive oil
- 2 teaspoons butter
- 1/2 teaspoon cinnamon

Instructions

- Olive oil should be rubbed on the sweet potatoes.
- In the air fryer, place the sweet potatoes. Preheat oven to 400°F and bake for 40 minutes.
- Allow the sweet potatoes to cool after removing them from the air fryer.
- Slice them open & stuff them with 1 teaspoon butter, honey, and 1/4 teaspoon cinnamon.
- Because each air fryer manufacturer is different, cooking times may vary. To see if the potatoes are done, poke them with a knife. The sweet potato ought to be tender on the inside.

Air Fryer Cinnamon Sugar Donuts

Preparation and Cooking Time

21 minutes

Servings

8 persons

Nutritional facts

186 calories, 9g fat ,2g fiber ,21g carbs ,4g protein

Ingredients

- 8 oz. can of biscuits
- One teaspoon ground cinnamon
- One to two teaspoons stevia 1/4 cup of table sugar can be substituted
- cooking oil spray

Instructions

- Place the biscuits on a flat surface and set them aside. Cut holes in the center of the biscuits with a tiny circular biscuit cutter.
- Using a spray bottle, coat the air fryer basket in oil.
- In the air fryer, place the donuts. Using a spray bottle, coat the doughnuts in oil. Donuts should not be stacked. If necessary, cook in two batches.
- Preheat the oven to 360°F and cook for 4 minutes.
- Flip the doughnuts after opening the air fryer. Cook for a further 4 minutes.
- Continue with the remaining donuts.
- Spritz the doughnuts again with oil.
- Distribute the cinnamon and sugar into two dishes.
- Using the cinnamon and sugar, coat the donuts.

Air Fryer Roasted Oranges

Preparation and Cooking Time

4 minutes

Servings

4 persons

Nutritional facts

43 calories, 5g fat ,2g fiber ,19g carbs ,3g protein

Ingredients

- 2 oranges
- Two tsp. honey
- One tsp. cinnamon

Instructions

- Oranges should be cut in half.
- Heat an air fryer to 200 degrees Celsius (395 degrees Fahrenheit).
- Put the oranges in the hot air fryer with cinnamon and honey drizzled on top.
- You need to air-fry the oranges for 3-6 minutes, or until golden on top. While they're still warm, serve them right away.

Air Fryer Apple Pies

Preparation and Cooking Time

45 minutes

Servings

4 persons

Nutritional facts

497 calories, 12g fat ,1g fiber ,16g carbs ,2g protein

Ingredients

- 4 tablespoons butter
- 6 tablespoons brown sugar
- Quarter cup powdered sugar
- 1 teaspoon milk, or more as needed
- 1 teaspoon ground cinnamon
- 2 medium Granny Smith apples, diced
- 1 teaspoon cornstarch
- 2 teaspoons cold water
- Half (14 ounces) package pastry for a 9-inch double-crust pie
- cooking spray
- Half tablespoon grape seed oil

Instructions

- In a non-stick skillet, blend the brown sugar, apples, butter and cinnamon. Cook until the apples have softened, around 5 minutes, over medium heat.
- In cold water, dissolve cornstarch. Stir in the apple mixture and boil for about 1 minute before the sauce thickens. Remove the apple pie from the heat and put it aside to cool while the crust is prepared. On a finely floured board, unroll the pie crust and roll out gently to smooth the surface of the dough. Break the dough into small enough rectangles such that 2 can fit at one time in your air fryer. Repeat with the leftover crust until you have 8 fair rectangles and, if necessary, re-roll any of the dough scraps. Wet the outside edges of four rectangles with water and put some apple filling about 1/2-inch from the edges in the middle. The remaining 4 rectangles are rolled out so that they are marginally wider than the filled ones. On top of the filling, crimp the edges with a fork to cover. Cut the tops of the pies into 4 small slits.

- Use cooking spray to spray the basket of an air fryer. Brush the 2-pie tops with grape-seed oil and use a spatula to move the pies to the air fryer basket.
- Insert and set the temperature of the basket to 385 degrees F (195 degrees C). Bake for approximately 8 minutes, until golden brown. Remove the pies and repeat for the remaining 2 pies from the basket.
- In a small cup, mix the powdered sugar and milk. Brush the glaze and allow it to dry on warm pies. Serve the pies at room temperature.

Cinnamon Churros

Preparation and Cooking Time

25 minutes

Servings

6 persons

Nutritional facts

173 calories, 9g fat ,2g fiber ,22g carbs ,4g protein

Ingredients

- Quarter cup butter
- half cup milk
- 1 pinch salt
- half cup all-purpose flour
- Two eggs
- Quarter cup white sugar
- Half teaspoon ground cinnamon

Instructions

- Melt butter over medium to high heat in a saucepan. Sprinkle with milk and add salt. Lower the heat to medium and bring it to a boil, stirring vigorously with a wooden spoon. Add flour easily, all at once. Keep stirring until it comes along with the dough.
- Remove from the heat and leave for 5 to 7 minutes to cool. Mix with the wooden spoon the eggs until the pastry is mixed. Spoon the dough into a pastry bag with a big star tip. Pipe the dough into strips directly into the basket of the air fryer.
- Air-fry the churros for 5 minutes at 340 degrees F (175 degrees C).
- Meanwhile, add sugar and cinnamon in a little cup and pour on a shallow plate.
- Remove the fried churros and roll in the cinnamon-sugar mixture from the air fryer.

Pound Cake Bites with Bailey's Fudge Sauce

Preparation and Cooking Time

55 minutes

Servings

4 persons

Nutritional facts

295 calories, 20g fat ,3g fiber ,21g carbs ,2g protein

Ingredients

We have listed below the ingredients that you would require for cooking this healthy and tasty food in the air fryer:

- 2/3 cup heavy cream
- 7 ounces baking chocolate
- 2 Tablespoon butter
- 1 teaspoon vanilla extract
- 1/2 cup Light Corn Syrup
- 1/3 cup brown sugar

- 1/4 cup cocoa powder
- 1/2 teaspoon salt
- 5 ounces Bailey's Irish Cream
- 1 Pound Cake

Instructions

- Over medium heat, combine the cream, corn syrup, sugar, cocoa powder, salt, and 4 ounces of chocolate.
- Bring to a low boil, then reduce to low heat and cook for 5 mins, stirring regularly.
- Remove the chocolate from the heat and stir in the remaining chocolate, butter, vanilla extract, and Irish Cream.
- Allow cooling for 20-half an hour.
- Keep refrigerated in an airtight container. Warm for 25-30 seconds when ready to use.
- Cut the pound cake into 1.5" cubes while the fudge sauce cools. Spray liberally with oil and place in the air fryer.
- Cook for 6 minutes on the first side and 4-5 minutes on the second side in an air fryer until the cake is crispy & slightly crunchy.
- Combine the two and dip and eat.

Air Fryer Roasted Bananas

Preparation and Cooking Time

9 minutes

Servings

1 person

Nutritional facts

107 calories, 11g fat ,1g fiber ,31g carbs ,3g protein

Ingredients

- One banana, cut into 1/8-inch thick diagonals
- avocado oil cooking spray

Instructions

- The Air-fryer basket is to be lined with parchment paper.
- Preheat at 375 degrees F the air fryer (190 degrees C).
- Place banana slices in the basket to ensure they do not touch; roast, if necessary, in batches. Mist the slices of the banana with avocado oil.
- Cook for 5 minutes in an air fryer. Break the basket and gently rotate the banana slices (they will be soft). Cook for an extra 2 to 3 minutes before the banana slices have been browned and caramelized. Remove it gently from the basket.

Air Fryer Cake

Preparation and Cooking Time

45 minutes

Servings

12 persons

Nutritional facts

269 calories, 20g fat ,2g fiber ,30g carbs ,4g protein

Ingredients

- Cake batter of some sorts
- Shortening for pan
- Frosting
- Other toppings
- Ingredients for the cake batter

Instructions

- Make your cake batter according to a handmade recipe or the directions on the back of the cake mix box.

- Grease the sides and bottom of a cake pan small enough to fit in the air fryer basket with shortening. Flour the bottom and sides of the pan, tapping out any excess flour. Add a round piece of parchment paper to the bottom of the pan if desired.
- Fill the pan a little more than halfway. If you have any leftover cake batter, you can make cupcakes. Soak the cake strips in water, wring them out, and wrap them around the cake pan afterward. This will help the cake bake evenly and avoid doming.
- Preheat the air fryer to 350 degrees Fahrenheit (176 C) and set the timer for 20 minutes. Allow for a minute or two for it to warm up. Take the basket out of the oven and place it in the cake pan. Place the basket back into the air fryer and turn it on. The cake will take 18-19 minutes to bake.
- Check it with a toothpick once the timer has gone off. Make a hole in the center of the cake with a toothpick; if the toothpick comes out clean, the cake is ready to eat. Cook the cake for another 3 to 5 minutes if there is still some cake batter.
- Allow the cake to cool in the pan for 10 - 15 minutes after baking. After that, remove it from the pan and cool fully on a wire rack. You can frost & decorate the cake in any way you choose.

Air fryer apple and cinnamon fritters

Preparation and Cooking Time

30 minutes

Servings

10 persons

Nutritional facts

243 calories, 6g fat ,1g fiber ,18g carbs ,5g protein

Ingredients

- 225g (1 1/2 cups) self-rising flour
- 2 eggs
- 2 pink lady apples, unpeeled, coarsely grated
- 100g (1/2 cup) caster sugar
- 1 tsp. ground cinnamon
- 125ml (1/2 cup) apple juice
- 1 tsp. vanilla extract
- 50g butter, melted
- Vanilla custard, to serve

Instructions

- In a large mixing bowl, mix the flour, milk, salt, 50g sugar, and 1/2 teaspoon cinnamon. Create a well in the middle. Whisk together the juice, vanilla, and eggs in a jug until well blended. Combine the egg and flour mixture in a mixing bowl. Stir until everything is well blended.
- Add the apple and mix well.
- The baking paper should line the bottom of an air fryer basket. Pour a quarter cup of the batter onto the baking paper (you may be able to accommodate 2 or 3 fritters at a time, depending on the size of your basket). Overcrowding the pan will cause them to expand while cooking). Oil is sprayed over the surface. Preheat oven to 200°C and bake for 5 minutes. Turn the fritters over. Cook for another 5 minutes, or until golden brown and cooked through. Continue with the remaining batter.
- In a shallow bowl, mix the remaining 50g sugar and ½ teaspoon cinnamon while the fritters are frying. Take the fritters out of the air fryer and set them aside. Using melted butter, coat the entire surface. One at a time, roll fritters in cinnamon sugar. You need to coat on the other side.
- Serve the fritters with custard to dip them in right away.

Air fryer lemonade scones

Preparation and Cooking Time

45 minutes

Servings

14 persons

Nutritional facts

275 calories, 9g fat ,2g fiber ,22g carbs ,2g protein

Ingredients

- 525g (3 1/2 cups) self-rising flour
- Milk, for brushing
- Raspberry jam, to serve
- 70g (1/3 cup) caster sugar
- 300ml thickened cream
- 185ml (3/4 cup) lemonade
- 1 tsp. vanilla extract
- Whipped cream, to serve

Instructions

- In a large mixing bowl, combine flour and sugar. Make a hole. Combine the cream, lemonade, and vanilla extract in a mixing bowl. Gently mix with a flat-bladed knife till dough just comes together.
- On a floured surface, roll out the dough. Knead for 30 seconds, or until the mixture is just smooth. Form a 2.5cm thick round out of the dough. Using flour, coat a 5.5cm round cutter. Scones should be cut out. Repeat to make 16 scones by gently pressing leftover dough pieces together.
- To allow air to circulate, put a sheet of baking paper in the air fryer basket 1cm smaller than the basket. Place 5 or 6 scones in a basket, almost touching, on paper. Using a pastry brush, lightly coat the tops with milk. Cook for 15 minutes at 160°C, or till golden and hollow when tapped on the top. Move to a wire rack with care. Repeat with the remaining scones & milk two more times.
    - It can be served with jam and whipped cream.

Air fryer celebration bites

Preparation and Cooking Time

25 minutes

Servings

24 persons

Nutritional facts

213 calories, 8g fat ,1g fiber ,18g carbs ,2g protein

Ingredients

- 4 sheets frozen short crust pastry, partially thawed
- Icing sugar for dusting
- 1 egg, lightly beaten
- 24 Mars Celebrations chocolates, unwrapped
- Cinnamon sugar, for dusting
- Whipped cream, to serve

Instructions

- Each sheet of puff pastry should be cut into six rectangles. Using an egg, softly brush the surface. In the center of each slice of pastry, place 1 chocolate. To enclose the chocolate, fold the pastry over. Trim the pastry and seal the edges. Put on a baking sheet lined with parchment paper. Using a pastry brush, lightly coat the tops with egg. Cinnamon sugar should be liberally applied.
- To allow air to circulate, put a sheet of baking paper in the air-fryer basket 1cm smaller than the basket. Fill the basket with 6

pockets, making sure they don't overlap. Cook for 8-9 minutes at 190°C, or until golden brown and pastry is cooked through. Place on a plate to cool. Carry on with the remaining pockets.

- Using icing sugar, dust the cake. Warm whipped cream is served on top.

Air fryer donuts

Preparation and Cooking Time

50 minutes

Servings

15 persons

Nutritional facts

259 calories, 7g fat ,3g fiber ,22g carbs ,4g protein

Ingredients

- 250ml (1 cup) milk
- 1 egg
- 50g butter, melted
- 70g (1/3 cup) caster sugar
- 3 tsp. dried yeast
- 70g (1/3 cup) caster sugar
- 450g (3 cups) plain flour
- 1/2 tsp. salt
- 380g (2 1/2 cups) pure icing sugar, sifted
- 3 tsp. vanilla extract
- 60ml (1/4 cup) milk
- 3/4 tsp. ground cinnamon

Instructions

- Heat the milk over low heat in a small saucepan until it becomes warm. Remove from the heat and transfer to a large mixing bowl. Combine yeast and 1 tbsp. of sugar in a mixing bowl. Whisk everything together with a fork until everything is well blended. Set aside for 10 minutes, or until foamy, covered.
- Toss the yeast mixture with the flour, salt, egg, butter, and remaining sugar. Knead on low speed in a stand mixer with the dough hook attachment until mixed. Increase the speed to medium and continue to beat for 5 minutes or till the dough is smooth & elastic. Cover dough with plastic wrap after transferring it to a lightly greased basin. Place the dough in a warm, draft-free location for 45 minutes or until it has doubled in size.
- Punch the dough down. Roll out the dough to a thickness of 1.5cm on a lightly floured surface with a lightly floured rolling pin. Cut 15 circles out of the dough with a 7cm pastry cutter. Cut the centers out of each circle with a 3.5cm circular pastry cutter (see tip). Place doughnuts on baking pans lined with parchment paper. Allow 30 minutes or till doughnuts have somewhat risen.
- Preheat an air fryer with a 7-liter capacity to 180°C for 3 minutes. In batches, carefully arrange doughnuts in the basket. Cook for 5 minutes or until golden brown and well cooked.
- Mix the sugar and cinnamon for the cinnamon sugar doughnuts on a shallow plate. After the doughnuts have been fried, brush them with oil and then roll them in cinnamon sugar, one at a time.
- Over a baking tray, place a wire rack. In a medium mixing dish, combine the icing sugar & vanilla extract. Gradually drizzle in the milk to make a thin frosting. Dip the doughnuts in the glaze one at a time with a fork. You need to coat on the other side. Place the doughnuts on a wire rack to cool. Allow for fifteen minutes or until the glaze has hardened.

Air fryer nuts and bolts

Preparation and Cooking Time

35 minutes

Servings

4 persons

Nutritional facts

149 calories,15g fat, 3g fiber ,16g carbs ,6g protein

Ingredients

- 2 cups dried farfalle pasta
- 1/2 tsp. garlic powder
- 1 cup Kellogg's Nutri-grain cereal
- 1 tsp. sea salt
- 1/2 tsp. chili powder
- 1 cup pretzels
- 80g (1/2 cup) raw macadamias
- 60ml (1/4 cup) extra virgin olive oil
- 2 tbsp. brown sugar
- 2 tsp. smoked paprika
- 1 tsp. onion powder
- 80g (1/2 cup) raw cashews

Instructions

- In a big saucepan of boiling salted water, cook pasta until tender. Drain thoroughly. Place on a serving tray. Use a paper towel to pat dry. Place in a large mixing bowl.
- Combine the oil, sugar, paprika, onion, garlic, and chili powders in a small mixing bowl. Half of the mixture should be spooned over the pasta and tossed to coat evenly.
- Preheat the air fryer to 200 degrees Celsius. In the air fryer basket, place the spaghetti. It should be cooked for five minutes in the oven Basket should be shaken. Cook for 5-6 minutes longer, or until brown and crisp. Place in a large mixing bowl.
- In a mixing dish, combine pretzels and nuts. Add the rest of the spice combination. Toss to coat evenly. Place in the basket of an air fryer. Cook for 3 minutes at 180°C. The basket should be shaken. Cook for an additional 2-3 minutes, or until golden brown. After that, add the cereal to the pasta. You can season with salt. Toss everything together. Allow cooling completely. Serve.

Air fryer lemon drizzle cake

Preparation and Cooking Time

45 minutes

Servings

8 persons

Nutritional facts

324 calories, 9g fat, 1g fiber ,23g carbs ,4g protein

Ingredients

- 150g butter, softened
- 1 1/2 cups of self-rising flour
- 3/4 cup of honey-flavored yogurt
- Lemon zest, to serve
- 2/3 cup of caster sugar
- 1 cup of icing sugar mixture
- 1 1/2 tbsp. of lemon juice
- 2 tsp. of finely grated lemon rind
- 1 tsp. of ground cardamom
- 3 Coles of Australian Free Range Eggs
- 10g of softened butter
- 1 cup of icing sugar mixture
- 1 1/2 tbsp. of lemon juice

Instructions

- Grease a 20cm (base measurement) round cake pan with baking paper. Mix the butter, sugar, lemon rind, and cardamom with the electric mixer until pale and creamy. One at a time, add eggs, beating them well after each addition. Combine the flour and yogurt in a mixing bowl. Pour into the pan that has been prepared. Make the surface as smooth as possible.
- Preheat the air fryer to 180 degrees Celsius. Place the pan in the air fryer's basket. Preheat the oven to 350°F and bake for 35 minutes, till a skewer inserted in the middle comes out clean. Allow cooling for 5 minutes in the pan before actually transferring to a wire rack to cool fully.
- Put the butter & icing sugar in a mixing dish to make the lemon icing. To form a smooth paste, add enough lemon juice.
- Place the cake on a serving plate and serve. To serve, drizzle with lemon icing and top with lemon zest.

Four ingredient Nutella

Preparation and Cooking Time

75 minutes

Servings

8 persons

Nutritional facts

267 calories, 7g fat ,3g fiber ,22g carbs ,3g protein

Ingredients

- 150g (1 cup) plain flour
- 3 eggs, lightly whisked
- 225g (1 cup) white sugar
- 300g (1 cup) Nutella

Instructions

- Grease a 20cm circular cake pan lightly. The baking paper should be used to line the base.
- Mix the sugar and flour with a balloon whisk in a mixing bowl. Create a well in the middle. Combine the egg & Nutella in a mixing bowl. Stir everything together with a large metal spoon until everything is well blended. Smooth the top of the dish in the prepared pan.
- Heat the air fryer to 160 degrees Celsius. Bake for 40 minutes, till a skewer inserted in the middle, emerges with a few crumbs stuck to it. Allow cooling completely before serving.
- If used, dust with cocoa powder & cut into pieces to serve.

Cinnamon nut scrolls

Preparation and Cooking Time

40 minutes

Servings

12 persons

Nutritional facts

197 calories,11g fat ,1g fiber ,20g carbs ,3g protein

Ingredients

- Two and a quarter cup self-rising flour
- 2/3 cup finely chopped walnuts
- 1/3 cup of toasted slivered almond
- 1/4 cup of brown sugar

- 1 tbsp. of caster sugar
- 100g butter, finely chopped
- 2/3 of cup milk
- 1 egg
- One tsp. of ground cinnamon
- 2 tbsp. of golden syrup

Instructions

- Preheat the oven to 200 degrees Celsius/180 degrees Celsius. Grease a 19cm × 29cm (base) slice pan with a 3cm depth.
- In a mixing bowl, sift the flour and caster sugar. Half of the butter should be mixed until the mixture resembles rough breadcrumbs. In a jug, whisk together the milk and the egg. Stir until a soft, sticky dough forms in the flour mixture. Turn the dough out onto a floured surface. Knead for 30 seconds or until the mixture is smooth.
- Make a 30cm × 40cm rectangle out of the dough. Walnuts and almonds should be sprinkled. Brown sugar and cinnamon are sprinkled on top. Dot the remaining butter on top. From one long side, tightly roll up the dough. Trim the ends using a serrated knife. Use a knife to cut the roll into twelve slices. Place the pieces in the pan that has been prepared. Preheat oven to 200°F and bake for 22-25 minutes, or until golden brown. Warm scrolls should be served with golden syrup.

Air Fryer Reese's Peanut Butter Cup Treats

Preparation and Cooking Time

20 minutes

Servings

8 persons

Nutritional facts

43 calories, 3g fat ,1g fiber ,14g carbs ,7g protein

Ingredients

- 8 Reese's Peanut Butter Cups FROZEN
- non-stick cooking spray
- Eight Crescent Rolls
- powdered sugar

Instructions

- Place the crescent rolls on the work surface and unroll them.
- In the middle of each crescent roll, put 1 frozen Reese's cup.
- The crescent roll should be wrapped around the Reese's cup.
- Using nonstick cooking spray, coat the air fryer rack.
- Cook for 10 to 12 minutes at 320°F in an air fryer.
- Lastly, dust with powdered sugar.
- Serve and enjoy right away.

Air Fryer Yummy Bread

Preparation and Cooking Time

30 minutes

Servings

6 persons

Nutritional facts

163 calories, 6g fat ,2g fiber ,17g carbs ,3g protein

Ingredients

- 1 1/3 cups of flour
- 1 teaspoon of salt
- 2/3 cups of sugar
- 1/2 cups of milk
- 1 teaspoon of baking powder

- 1 teaspoon of baking soda
- 1 teaspoon of cinnamon
- 1/2 cup of oil
- 3 overripe bananas

Instructions

- In a mixer or a large mixing basin, combine all ingredients.
- Then use nonstick cooking spray to coat your pan (or use olive oil)
- Cook for 20-30 minutes in an Air Fryer @ 330°F (air fryer setting). Do you have a toothpick that comes out clean in your air fryer? If so, you're done; if not, add a few minutes to your time.
- Allow cooling before slicing and serving.

Air Fryer Crème Brûlée

Preparation and Cooking Time

50 minutes

Servings

2 persons

Nutritional facts

201 calories, 4g fat ,1g fiber ,16g carbs ,4g protein

Ingredients

- 100 milliliters Milk
- 30 grams Sugar
- 2 Egg yolks
- 150 milliliters Light cream
- 1 dash Vanilla extract

Instructions

- In a mixing bowl, combine the milk, light cream, egg yolks, and a few drops of vanilla essence. Whip until smooth.
- In a pan over low heat, bring to a simmer and stir in 20g sugar to dissolve.
- Pour into ramekins once the sugar has dissolved. Heat the air fryer to 180-200 degrees Celsius, depending on the ramekins' size. Cook for around 25-30 minutes. Shake it gently with an oven mitt to see if it's set.
- Allow them to cool completely before evenly sprinkling sugar on top. Using a small blowtorch, caramelize the sugar layer.

Air Fryer Grilled Peaches

Preparation and Cooking Time

19 minutes

Servings

2 persons

Nutritional facts

188 calories, 5g fat ,1g fiber ,5g carbs ,2g protein

Ingredients

- 4 Fresh Peaches
- 1 Tsp. Ground Ginger
- Leftover peach cobbler
- 1 Tbsp. Honey
- 2 Tsp. Butter
- Extra Virgin Olive Oil Spray
- Squirty Cream optional

Instructions

- Slice your peaches and spritz them with extra virgin olive oil before placing them in the air fryer basket. At 200°C/400°F, air fry for 10 min.

- In a dish, crumble up the leftover cobbler topping with your hands until it resembles breadcrumbs.
- Place the peaches on foil after removing them from the air fryer.
- Drizzle honey over the peaches and sprinkle with ground ginger. Then add some butter that has been carefully cut. Place your crumbled cobbler layer on top and return to the air fryer. Cook for another 6 minutes at 200°C/400°F in the air fryer.
- Serve with cream when the air fryer beeps.

Healthy Air Fryer Apple Crisp (Gluten-Free)

Preparation and Cooking Time

30 minutes

Servings

4 persons

Nutritional facts

192 calories, 10g fat ,0.5g fiber ,12g carbs ,3g protein

Ingredients

- 3 cups apples chopped
- 1/4 cup brown sugar
- 2 tbsp. light butter melted
- 1 tbsp. pure maple syrup
- 2 tsp. lemon juice
- 3 tbsp. almond flour
- 1/3 cup quick oats
- 1/2 tsp. cinnamon

Instructions

- In a mixing bowl, combine the diced apples, lemon juice, one tablespoon almond flour, maple syrup, and cinnamon. Stir until everything is evenly covered.
- Layer the apple mixture in the bottom of your air fryer's baking dish.
- Combine the brown sugar, oats, and leftover almond flour in a separate bowl. After these ingredients have been thoroughly combined, add the melted butter, coating as much of the mixture as possible.
- Cover the apple layer with the brown sugar topping mix in the air fryer baking dish.
- Preheat the air fryer to 350°F and cook for 20 minutes.
- Allow for some cooling time before serving. Serve with vanilla ice cream or frozen yogurt, if desired.

Air Fryer Blueberry Hand Pies

Preparation and Cooking Time

45 minutes

Servings

4 persons

Nutritional facts

436 calories, 11g fat ,1.1g fiber ,33g carbs ,7g protein

Ingredients

- 1 box Store-Bought Pie Dough
- 1 egg white
- 4 scoops of vanilla ice cream
- Quarter cup (60 ml) blueberry jam
- 16 Fresh Blueberries
- 1 teaspoon (5 ml) lemon zest
- ¼ cup (40 g) raw, sliced almonds

Instructions

- Roll out the dough to a thickness of 1/4 inch (6 cm). Cut eight 3-inch (7.6-cm) circles out of the paper. Apply egg white to the bottom circle.
- One tablespoon (15 ml) jam should be inserted in the center of each circle, and four blueberries should be placed on top of the jam. Place the second dough round on top. To keep the pieces together, press them together. Then, using a flour-dusted fork, you should press down all the way around the circle to make a beautiful circle. More egg white should be brushed on the tops.
- On the top of each pie, cut two slits. Using a floured spatula, move to the air fryer.
- Fry for 10 minutes at 350°F (175°C). Serve with raw sliced almonds and vanilla ice cream

Air-Fryer Cannoli

Preparation and Cooking Time

- 16 minutes

Servings

12 persons

Nutritional facts

243 calories,7g fat ,2g fiber ,14g carbs ,10 protein

Ingredients

- 12 ounces whole-milk ricotta
- 1 package refrigerated pie crust
- 1 egg white, beaten
- 1/4 cup powdered sugar
- 1/2 teaspoon orange zest
- 1/4 teaspoon salt
- flour for working surface
- 1/4 cup mini chocolate chips, optional

Instructions

- Place the ricotta in a sieve lined with cheese cloth (or paper towels) & squeeze until all of the extra liquid has been drained. Combine the strained ricotta, sugar, zest, and salt in a mixing bowl. Mix well and transfer to a piping bag or a zip-top plastic bag. Place in the refrigerator.
- On a lightly floured board, roll out the pie crust to a thickness of 1/16 inch. Twelve molds should be taken out (3.5-inch circles). Wrap rings around cannoli molds, sealing the borders with egg white. Brush the entire wrapper with egg white and then roll it in turbinado sugar to coat it.
- Add a few at a time, not touching, to a lightly oiled air fryer basket. Cook for 5-7 minutes at 400 degrees F. Remove with tongs and set aside to cool for 1 minute before removing cannoli molds. Allow cooling completely before serving. Continue with the remaining shells.
- Pipe ricotta filling into cannoli shells on either end, dipping in chocolate chips if desired. Serve with a sugar dusting.

Air-Fryer Chocolate Chip Oatmeal Cookies

Preparation and Cooking Time

30 minutes

Servings

6 dozen

Nutritional facts

102 calories/1 cookies, 7g fat ,1g fiber ,26g carbs ,34g protein

Ingredients

- 1 cup of butter
- 3 cups of quick-cooking oats

- 1 teaspoon of baking soda
- 1 teaspoon of salt
- 2 cups of semisweet chocolate chips
- 1-1/2 cups of all-purpose flour
- 1 package of (3.4 ounces) instant vanilla pudding mix
- 3/4 cup of sugar
- 3/4 cup of packed brown sugar
- 2 large eggs, room temperature
- 1 teaspoon of vanilla extract
- 1 cup of chopped nuts

Instructions

- Preheat the air fryer to 325 degrees F. Cream the butter and sugars in a large mixing bowl till light and fluffy, about 5-7 minutes. In a separate bowl, whisk together vanilla extract and eggs. Whisk together the flour, oats, baking soda, dry pudding mix, and salt in a separate bowl; gradually fold into the creamed mixture. Combine the chocolate chips & nuts in a mixing bowl.
- Drop tablespoonful of dough onto baking sheets and flatten slightly. Place 1 inch apart on a greased tray in an air-fryer basket in batches. Cook for 8-10 minutes, or until lightly browned. Allow cooling on wire racks.

Air Fried Cinnamon Apple Chips

Preparation and Cooking Time

32 minutes

Servings

8 persons

Nutritional facts

62 calories,1g fat ,5g fiber ,5g carbs ,3g protein

Ingredients

- 5 Apples
- One tbsp. Cinnamon
- Two tbsp. Monk Fruit

Instructions

- Make your apples as thin as possible by slicing them. Then, while you're working, place the apples on a baking sheet or a flat surface coated with parchment paper.
- Blend the cinnamon & sugar substitute in a small bowl using a fork or a whisk. Using the oil spray, lightly coat the apples & then sprinkle the cinnamon and sugar on top. Then repeat with the other apple pieces.
- Put the apple slices in the air fryer basket to air fried them. Cook your apple slices in an air fryer for 20 minutes at 300 degrees, shaking the basket every 5 minutes or as needed. Increase the temperature to 325 degrees Fahrenheit and air fry the apple slices for an additional two minutes. Allow time for the chips to cool.

Air Fryer Cinnamon and Cream Bread Pudding

Preparation and Cooking Time

19 minutes

Servings

2 persons

Nutritional facts

237 calories, 21g fat ,1g fiber ,7g carbs ,9g protein

Ingredients

- Bread
- 1 Tbsp. Sugar
- Cinnamon (optional)

- Chocolate Chips
- 1 Egg
- ⅓ Cup of Milk or Heavy Cream
- ¼ Tsp. Vanilla
- Non-stick cooking spray

Instructions

- Spray the inside of the air fryer pan with nonstick cooking spray.
- Toss in the bread pieces & chocolate chips.
- Mix up one egg, milk or heavy cream, vanilla, sugar, and cinnamon for every three bread slices.
- Allow 5 minutes for the bread to soak in the mixture.
- You need to air fry for 10-12 minutes @ 350°F.

Air Fryer Cheesecake Chimichangas with Cinnamon Sugar

Preparation and Cooking Time

16 minutes

Servings

4 persons

Nutritional facts

491 calories, 1g fat ,2g fiber ,19g carbs ,3g protein

Ingredients

- 4 tortillas
- 1 tbsp. cinnamon
- 8 oz. cream cheese softened
- 1 tsp. vanilla extract
- 1/2 cup granulated sugar
- 1/4 cup unsalted butter melted

Instructions

- Combine the cream cheese, 3 tbsp. sugar, and vanilla in a mixing bowl.
- In the middle of one of the tortillas, spread the cream cheese mixture. Fold the sides inwards a little and roll it up. For each tortilla, repeat the process.
- Place each rolled tortilla in the air fryer & cook for 6 minutes at 400° F.
- Each chimichanga should be rolled in melted butter first and then in the cinnamon-sugar mixture. If desired, drizzle with caramel or chocolate sauce.

Air fryer Valentine's Day Homemade Strawberry Pop-Tarts

Preparation and Cooking Time

21 minutes

Servings

8 persons

Nutritional facts

43 calories, 20g fat ,1g fiber ,14g carbs ,2g protein

Ingredients

- 15 oz. Pie crusts (equivalent to 2 crusts)
- 4 tablespoons valentine day sprinkles
- 4 ounces' strawberry preserves total (reserve 1 oz. for the frosting)
- 1 cup powdered sugar
- 1 egg, whisked
- 1 heart cookie cutter

Instructions

- Cut out as many heart-shaped shapes as you can in the pie crust with the heart cookie cutter, which should be set out flat on a lightly floured surface.
- Spread 1 spoonful of jelly preserves on one of the heart-shaped crusts. Ensure there's enough area around the borders for the top crust to be attached.
- To make an egg wash, whisk your egg in a small bowl. Then, evenly distribute the egg wash along the rims around the jelly using your finger.
- Place a second heart-shaped pie crust on top of the jelly-covered heart. With a fork, push down the corners to seal them.
- Cover the top of the pop tart with the egg wash using a kitchen brush.
- Poke around 6-8 holes in the top layer pastry with a fork or a toothpick.
- Place as many pastry hearts as will fit in your air fryer without touching each other, depending on the size of your air fryer.
- Preheat the oven to 370°F and bake the pop tarts for 7 minutes. Open the air fryer and turn your pop tarts once the timer has finished. Cook for an additional 3-4 minutes at 370° F, or until a soft brown color is achieved.
- Move to a cooling rack after removing from the air fryer.
- While the pastries are cooling, combine the powdered sugar & jelly preserves in a mixing bowl. If you prefer a thicker frosting, you can use extra powdered sugar.
- While the frosting is still wet, drizzle it over the pop tart and cover it with sprinkles.
- Allow for cooling and hardening of the frosting before serving.

Air Fryer Cookie for One

Preparation and Cooking Time

15 minutes

Servings

1 person

Nutritional facts

706 calories, 3g fat ,2g fiber ,30g carbs ,6g protein

Ingredients

- 2 tablespoons melted butter
- ⅓ cup + 1 tablespoon flour
- 1/8 teaspoon baking soda
- 2 tablespoons brown sugar
- 1 tablespoon granulated sugar
- 1 large egg yolk
- ½ teaspoon vanilla
- ⅛ teaspoon salt
- ¼ cup chocolate chips

Instructions

- Preheat the air fryer to 350 degrees Fahrenheit.
- Toss together the butter, brown sugar, and granulated sugar in a mixing bowl with a spoon.
- Stir in the egg yolk & vanilla extract well.
- To make the dough, combine the flour, baking soda, & salt.
- Add the chocolate chips and mix well.
- Form the dough into a large ball and lightly flatten it to make a cookie dough ball about 4 inches in diameter.
- Arrange a piece of parchment paper in the middle of the preheated air fryer basket, as well as carefully place the cookie dough on top. Because the dough will spread, make sure the parchment is large enough to accommodate this.

- Air fry for five minutes in the air fryer
- Allow 5 minutes to cool before serving.

Air Fryer Triple-Chocolate Oatmeal Cookies

Preparation and Cooking Time

25 minutes

Servings

36 persons

Nutritional facts

199 calories, 2g fat ,1g fiber ,14g carbs ,2g protein

Ingredients

- Three cups of oatmeal
- 2 cups of chocolate chips
- 1 cup of chopped walnuts (Optional)
- nonstick cooking spray
- One and a half cup of all-purpose flour
- Quarter cup of cocoa powder
- One (3.4 ounces) package of chocolate pudding mix
- 1 teaspoon of baking soda
- 1 teaspoon of salt
- 1 cup butter, softened
- Three-quarter cup of brown sugar
- Three-quarter cup of white sugar
- 2 eggs
- 1 teaspoon of vanilla extract

Instructions

- Heat an air fryer at 350 degrees F. Spray with nonstick cooking spray in the air fryer basket.
- In a bowl, add the pudding mix, flour, cocoa powder, oatmeal, baking soda, and salt until well mixed. And put aside.
- Mix white sugar, butter and brown sugar using an electronic blender in another bowl. Add the vanilla extract and eggs. Add the mixture of oatmeal and combine properly. Stir in the walnuts and chocolate chips.
- Use a large cookie scoop to drop dough into the air fryer; flatten out and leave roughly 1 inch between each cookie.
- Cook 6 to 10 minutes until finely browned. Before eating, cool on a wire rack.

Air-Fried Banana Cake

Preparation and Cooking Time

40 minutes

Servings

4 persons

Nutritional facts

347 calories,10g fat ,1g fiber ,22g carbs ,3g protein

Ingredients

- Cooking spray
- One-third cup brown sugar
- Three and a half tablespoons butter, at room temperature
- One banana, mashed
- One egg
- Two tablespoons honey
- One cup self-rising flour
- Half teaspoon ground cinnamon
- One pinch salt

Instructions

- Preheat to 320 degrees F an air fryer (160 degrees C). Use cooking spray to spray a tiny fluted tube pan.
- Use an electric mixer to pound the sugar and butter together in a bowl until smooth. Mix the pineapple, potato, and honey in a separate dish. Whisk the banana mixture smoothly into the butter mixture.
- Sift the mixed banana-butter mixture with flour, cinnamon, and salt. The batter is mixed until smooth. Shift to the pan prepared; using the back of a spoon, level the top.
- Place the cake pan in the basket of the air fryer. Set the time for 30 minutes by sliding the basket into the air fryer. Bake until the toothpick comes out of the cake clean.

Air Fryer Butter Cake

Preparation and Cooking Time

30 minutes

Servings

4 persons

Nutritional facts

470 calories, 7g fat ,2g fiber ,17g carbs ,1g protein

Ingredients

- Quarter cup white sugar
- Two tablespoons white sugar
- 1 egg
- 1 ⅔ cups all-purpose flour
- cooking spray
- 7 tablespoons butter, at room temperature
- 1 pinch salt, or to taste
- Six tablespoons milk

Instructions

- Preheat to 350 degrees F an air fryer (180 degrees C). Now use cooking spray to spray the tiny fluted tube pan.
- Just use an electric mixer to beat 1/4 cup plus two tablespoons of sugar and butter together in a bowl until light and smooth. Connect the egg and combine until soft and creamy. Stir in the salt and flour. Attach milk and thoroughly mix the batter. Move the batter to the prepared pan; level the surface using the back of a spoon.
- Place the pan in the basket of the air fryer. Set a 15-minute timer. Bake until the toothpick inserted comes out clean.
- Turn the cake out of the pan and give about 5 minutes to cool.

Gluten-Free Fresh Cherry Crumble

Preparation and Cooking Time

1 hour 10 minutes

Servings

4 persons

Nutritional facts

459 calories, 2g fat ,1g fiber ,21g carbs ,4g protein

Ingredients

- One third cup butter
- Three cups pitted cherries
- 1 teaspoon ground nutmeg
- 1 teaspoon ground cinnamon
- Ten tablespoons white sugar, divided
- 2 teaspoons lemon juice
- One cup gluten-free all-purpose baking flour

- One teaspoon vanilla powder

Instructions

- Cube the butter and put it until solid, around 15 minutes, in the freezer.
- Preheat to 325 degrees F air fryer (165 degrees C).
- Combine two teaspoons of sugar, pitted cherries, and lemon juice in a bowl; blend well. Apply the cherry mixture to the baking bowl.
- In a bowl, mix the flour and 6 tablespoons of sugar. Use fingers to cut the butter until the particles are pea-size. Distribute over the cherries and gently force down.
- Whisk together two teaspoons of sugar, vanilla extract, nutmeg, and cinnamon in a bowl. Dust the sugar topping over the flour and the cherries.
- Bake in an air fryer that is preheated. Check at 30 min; if not yet browned, resume cooking and check until slightly browned at 5-minute intervals. Lock the drawer and turn the air fryer off. Leave it inside to crumble for 10 minutes. Stir and allow it to cool slightly for 5 minutes or so.

Chocolate Cake in an Air Fryer

Preparation and Cooking Time

25 minutes

Servings

4 persons

Nutritional facts

214 calories, 5g fat ,1g fiber ,22g carbs ,2g protein

Ingredients

- Three and a half tablespoons butter softened
- One egg
- 1 tablespoon apricot jam
- Six tablespoons all-purpose flour
- One tablespoon unsweetened cocoa powder
- cooking spray
- Quarter cup white sugar
- salt to taste

Instructions

- Preheat to 320 degrees F an air fryer (160 degrees C). Use cooking spray to spray a tiny fluted tube pan.
- Use an electric mixer to pound the sugar and butter together in a bowl until light and smooth. Insert the jam and egg; blend until mixed. Season with flour, cocoa powder, and salt; blend properly. Pour the batter into the pan. With the back of a spoon, level the top of the batter.
- Place the pan in the basket of the air fryer. Cook for about 15 minutes until a toothpick inserted into the middle of the cake comes out clean.

Conclusion

Air fryers help fry healthy foods. Air-fried foods surprisingly attain a similar taste and texture as that of deep-fried foods. Air-fried foods are healthier than deep-fried foods because they need less oil. Air-fried foods can help decrease calorie consumption, encourage weight loss, and are low in fat compared to deep-fried foods. Air-fried foods are lower in calories, fat, and acrylamide. Air-fried foods are better because they have a low-fat content than deep-fried foods. An air fryer functions by circulating hot air around the cooked food. There is a mechanical fan that, at high intensity, circulates hot air around the food. It makes the meal and renders it crispy. Any other food, including chicken, fries, pastries, or fish, can be fried in an air fryer. Most air fryers have regulated temperatures and times that assist in cooking the food well. Food cooked in the air fryer is best in the smell, taste, color, oiliness, hardness, crispness, etc., then the conventional French fries. The air fryer is quick. It takes less than twenty minutes to cook most foods in the air fryer. Air fryers help you save time and assist you in leading a healthy and safe life.

Printed in Great Britain
by Amazon

COSORI®

User Manual

Pro LE 4.7-Litre Air Fryer

Pro LE Series
Model: CAF-L501-KUK

Questions or Concerns?
support.eu@cosori.com

Thank you for your purchase!

(We hope you love your new air fryer as much as we do.)

 join the Cosori Cooks Community on Facebook
facebook.com/groups/cosoricooks

 explore our recipe gallery
www.cosori.com/recipes

 enjoy weekly, featured recipes
made exclusively by our in-house chefs

CONTACT OUR CHEFS

Our helpful, in-house chefs are ready to assist you with any questions you might have!

Email: recipes@cosori.com

On behalf of all of us at Cosori,

Happy cooking!

Table of Contents

Package Contents

1 x Pro LE 4.7-Litre Air Fryer
1 x Recipe Book
1 x User Manual

Specifications

Power Supply	AC 220-240V, 50/60Hz
Rated Power	1500W
Capacity	4.7 L / 5.0 qt (serves 3–5 people)
Temperature Range	75°–230°C
Time Range	1–60 min
Dimensions	27.2 x 27.5 x 30.3 cm / 10.7 x 10.8 x 11.9 in
Weight	4.54 kg / 10 lb
Standby power	<0.5W

READ AND SAVE THESE INSTRUCTIONS

IMPORTANT SAFEGUARDS

Follow basic safety precautions when using your air fryer.
Read all instructions.

Key Safety Points

- **Do not** touch hot surfaces. Use handle.
- Use caution when turning the basket over after cooking, as the hot crisper plate may fall out and create a safety hazard.
- **Do not** block any ventilation openings. Hot steam is released through openings. Keep your hands and face clear of openings.

General Safety

- **Do not** immerse the air fryer housing, cord, or plug in water or liquid.
- Closely supervise children near your air fryer.
- Unplug when not in use, and before cleaning. Allow to cool before putting on or taking off parts.
- **Do not** use your air fryer if it is damaged, not working, or if the cord or plug is damaged. Contact **Customer Support** (see page 15).
- **Do not** use third-party replacement parts or accessories, as this may cause injuries.
- **Do not** use outdoors.
- **Do not** place the air fryer or any of its parts on a stove, near gas or electric burners, or in a heated oven.

- Be extremely cautious when moving your air fryer (or removing the basket) if it contains hot oil or other hot liquids.
- **Do not** clean with metal scouring pads. Metal fragments can break off the pad and touch electrical parts, creating a risk of electric shock.
- **Do not** place anything on top of your air fryer. **Do not** store anything inside your air fryer.
- **Do not** strike or hit the top of the air fryer with hard objects, as this may cause the tempered glass to crack. Tempered glass is stronger and fractures more safely than ordinary glass, but it may shatter unexpectedly after being cracked. If you see a crack, contact **Customer Support** (see page 15).
- This air fryer can be used by children 8 years and older as well as persons with reduced physical, sensory, or mental capabilities or lack of experience and knowledge if they have been given supervision or instruction concerning use of the air purifier in a safe way and understand the hazards involved.
- Children should not play with the air fryer.
- Cleaning and user maintenance should not be made by children without supervision.
- This air fryer is not intended to be operated by means of an external timer or separate remote-control system.

- **Only** use your air fryer as directed in this manual.
- Not for commercial use. Household use **only**.

While Air Frying

- An air fryer works with hot air **only**. **Never** fill the baskets with oil or fat.
- **Never** use your air fryer without the basket in place.
- **Do not** place oversized foods or metal utensils into your air fryer.
- **Do not** overfill the air fryer basket. Heaping amounts of food may touch the heating coils and cause a fire hazard.
- **Do not** touch accessories during or immediately after air frying.
- **Do not** place paper, cardboard, non-heat-resistant plastic, or similar materials, into your air fryer. You may use parchment paper or foil.
- **Never** put baking or parchment paper into the air fryer without food on top. Air circulation can cause paper to lift and touch heating coils.
- **Always** use heat-safe containers. Be extremely cautious if using containers that aren't metal or glass.
- Keep your air fryer away from flammable materials (curtains, tablecloths, etc). Use on a flat, stable, heat-resistant surface away from heat sources or liquids.
- Immediately turn off and unplug your air fryer if you see dark smoke coming out. White smoke is normal, caused by heating fat or food splashing, but dark smoke means that food is burning or there is a circuit problem. Wait for smoke to clear before pulling the basket out. If the cause was not burnt food, contact **Customer Support** (page 15).

- **Do not** leave your air fryer unattended while in use.

Plug & Cord

- **Do not** let the power cord (or any extension cord) hang over the edge of a table or counter, or touch hot surfaces.
- Remove and discard the protective cover fitted over the power plug of the air fryer to prevent choking hazards.
- **Never** use an outlet below the counter when plugging in your air fryer.
- Keep the air fryer and its cord out of reach of children less than 8 years old.

Electromagnetic Fields (EMF)

The Cosori Air Fryer complies with all standards regarding electromagnetic fields (EMF). If handled properly and according to the instructions in this user manual, the appliance is safe to use based on scientific evidence available today.

This symbol means the product must not be discarded as household waste, and should be delivered to an appropriate collection facility for recycling. Proper disposal and recycling helps protect natural resources, human health and the environment.

For more information on disposal and recycling of this product, contact your local municipality, disposal service, or the shop where you bought this product.

GETTING TO KNOW YOUR AIR FRYER

Your Cosori Air Fryer uses rapid 360° air circulation technology to cook with little to no oil for quick, crispy, delicious food with up to 85% fewer calories than deep fryers. With user-friendly, one-touch controls, a nonstick basket, and an intuitive, safe design, the Cosori Air Fryer is the star of your kitchen.

Note:

- **Do not** *try to open the top of the air fryer. This is not a lid.*
- *The basket and crisper plate are made of aluminium metal with nonstick coating. They are PFOA -free and BPA free.*

Air Fryer Diagram

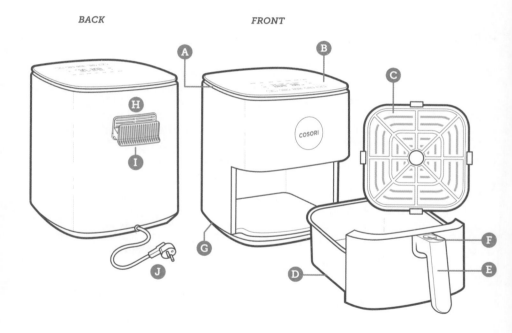

BACK   FRONT

A. Air Inlet	**E.** Basket Handle	**I.** Air Outlet Spacer
B. Control Screen	**F.** Basket Release Button	**J.** Power Cord
C. Crisper Plate	**G.** Housing Handles	
D. Basket	**H.** Air Outlet	

Display Diagram

Note: When you press a button to use a function or program, it will turn white to show that it's active.

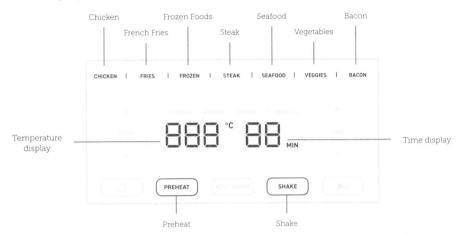

Chicken Frozen Foods Seafood Bacon
French Fries Steak Vegetables

Temperature display — Time display

Preheat Shake

Note: This turns the Shake Reminder on/off.

Control Panel

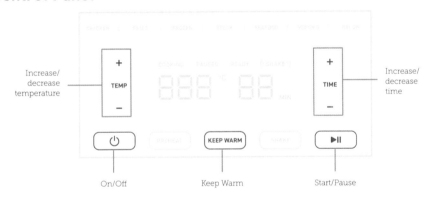

Increase/decrease temperature Increase/decrease time

On/Off Keep Warm Start/Pause

Display Messages

Reminder to shake or flip food

Air fryer is preheated and ready to start cooking

Air fryer is cooking

Cooking is paused

Cooking program has ended

BEFORE FIRST USE

Setting Up

1. Remove all packaging from the air fryer, including any temporary stickers.

2. Place the air fryer on a stable, level, heat-resistant surface. Keep away from areas that can be damaged by steam (such as walls or cupboards).

Note: *Leave 13 cm / 5 inches of space behind and above the air fryer. [**Figure 1.1**] Leave enough room in front of the air fryer to remove the basket.*

3. Hold down the basket release button, and pull the handle to remove the basket. Remove all plastic from the basket.

4. Wash both the basket and crisper plate thoroughly, using either a dishwasher or a non-abrasive sponge.

5. Wipe the inside and outside of the air fryer with a slightly moist cloth. Dry with a towel.

6. Insert the crisper plate back into the basket, and place the basket inside the air fryer.

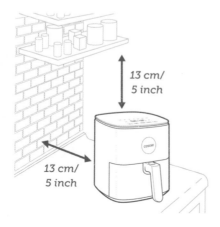

Figure 1.1

Test Run

A test run will help you become familiar with your air fryer, make sure it's working correctly, and clean it of possible residues in the process.

1. Make sure the air fryer basket is empty and plug in the air fryer.

2. Press **PREHEAT**. The display will show "**205°C**" and "**4 MIN**".

3. Press ▶❚❚ to begin preheating. When preheating is done, the air fryer will beep.

4. Pull out the basket and let it cool for 4 minutes. Then place the basket back into the air fryer.

5. Press **STEAK** to select the **Steak** function. The display will show "**230°C**" and "**6 MIN**".

6. Press **TIME** once. The time will change to 5 minutes.

7. Press ▶❚❚ to begin. When finished, the air fryer will beep.

8. Remove the basket. This time, let the basket cool completely for 10–30 minutes.

Note:

- *Use caution when turning the basket over after cooking, as the hot crisper plate may fall out and create a safety hazard.*

- ***Do not*** *unscrew the basket handle from the basket.*

Rubber Stoppers

- The crisper plate contains 4 rubber stoppers made of safe, FDA-approved material. These stoppers keep the crisper plate fitted to the bottom of the basket, prevent the crisper plate from directly touching the basket, and in rare cases, damaging the nonstick coating on the basket.

- **Only** remove the rubber stoppers for cleaning purposes. For easy removal, start from the bottom of the crisper plate and pull out one side of the stopper at a time. [*Figure 1.2*]

- To place the rubber stoppers back onto the crisper plate, first soak them in water. Then, push each stopper back in through the bottom of the crisper plate. Push in one side of the stopper at a time.

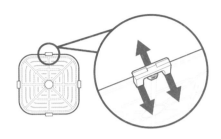

Figure 1.2

USING YOUR AIR FRYER

Preheating

We recommend preheating before placing food inside the air fryer, unless your air fryer is already hot. Food will not cook thoroughly without preheating.

1. Plug in. Press ⏻ to turn on the air fryer display.

2. Press **PREHEAT**. The display will show "**205°C**" and "**4 MIN**".

3. Optionally, press the + or − buttons to change the temperature. The time will adjust automatically.

4. Press ▶‖ to begin preheating.

5. When preheating is done, the air fryer will beep 3 times. The display will show the set preheat temperature. [*Figure 2.1*]

Note: If no buttons are pressed for 3 minutes, the air fryer will clear all settings and go into standby.

Temperature	Time
205°–230°C	4 minutes
145°–200°C	3 minutes
75°–140°C	2 minutes

Figure 2.1

Air Frying

Note:

- **Do not** place anything on top of your air fryer. This may interfere with your cooking program or cause cracks in the glass on the display. *[Figure 2.1]*

- An air fryer is not a deep fryer. **Do not** fill the basket with oil, frying fat, or any liquid.

- When taking the basket out of the air fryer, be careful of hot steam.

Figure 2.1

Cooking Functions

Using a cooking function is the easiest way to air fry. Cooking functions are programmed with an ideal time and temperature for cooking certain foods.

1. Press the function's button to select the function. The air fryer will automatically change to the function's default settings.

2. You can change a function's time (1–60 minutes), temperature (75°–230°C), and Shake Reminder.

3. Press and hold the + or – button to rapidly increase or decrease the time or temperature.

4. Add or remove a Shake Reminder by pressing **SHAKE**.

5. To go back to a function's default settings, press the function's button again.

Note: Results may vary. Check out our Recipe Book for a guide to using cooking functions for perfect results.

Function	Default Temperature	Default Time (minutes)	Shake Reminder?*
Chicken	190°C	20 minutes	-
French Fries**	195°C	25 minutes	((SHAKE))
Frozen Foods	175°C	10 minutes	-
Steak	230°C	6 minutes	-
Seafood	175°C	8 minutes	((SHAKE))
Veggies	170°C	10 minutes	((SHAKE))
Bacon	160°C	8 minutes	-
Preheat	205°C	4 minutes	-
Keep Warm	75°C	5 minutes	-

* See **Shaking Food** (page 11).

** See **Cooking Guide** (page 12) for more tips on air frying French fries.

10

Air Frying

1. **Preheat your air fryer** (see page 9).

2. When your air fryer displays **READY**, add food to the basket.

   - For the best results, add the crisper plate into the basket to allow excess oil to drip down to the bottom of the basket.

3. Select a cooking function (see page 10).

Note: Cooking functions are programmed with an ideal time and temperature for cooking certain foods. You can also set a custom time and temperature without choosing a cooking function.

4. Optionally, change the temperature and time, and add a Shake Reminder. You can do this anytime during cooking.

   a. Press the + or − buttons to change the temperature (75°–230°C) or time (1–60 minutes).

   Note:

   - *To rapidly increase or decrease time or temperature, press and hold the + or − buttons.*

   - *Press **SHAKE** to add or remove a Shake Reminder during cooking.*

5. Press ▶❚❚ to begin air frying.

6. When the Shake Reminder is turned on, it will appear halfway through cooking time. The air fryer will beep 5 times, and **(Shake)** will blink on the display.

   a. Press the basket release button to take the basket out of the air fryer, being careful of hot steam. The air fryer will pause cooking automatically, and the display will turn off until the basket is replaced.

   b. Shake or flip the food.

   c. Put the basket back into the air fryer.

Note: See **Shaking Food** (page 11)

7. The air fryer will beep 3 times when finished. The display will show:

8. Optionally, press **Keep Warm**. Press the + or − buttons to change the time (1–60 minutes).

9. Press the basket release button to take the basket out of the air fryer, being careful of hot steam.

10. Allow to cool before cleaning.

Shaking Food

How to Shake

- During cooking, press and hold the basket release button to take the basket out of the air fryer, and shake, mix, or flip the food.

   A. To shake food:

   1. Hold the basket just above a heat-resistant surface for safety purposes.

   2. Shake the basket.

   Note: Do not *use this method if there is a risk of hot liquids splashing.*

   B. If the basket is too heavy to shake and there are hot liquids present:

   1. Place the basket on a heat-resistant holder or surface.

   2. Use tongs to mix or flip the food.

- When you take the basket out, the air fryer will pause cooking automatically. As a safety feature, the display will turn off until the basket is replaced.

- When you replace the basket, cooking will automatically resume.

- Avoid shaking longer than 30 seconds, as the air fryer may start to cool down.

What to Shake

- Small foods that are stacked will usually need shaking, such as fries or nuggets.
- Without shaking, foods may not be crispy or evenly cooked.
- You can flip other foods, such as steak, to ensure even browning.

When to Shake

- Shake or flip food once halfway through cooking, or more if desired.
- The Shake Reminder is designed to remind you to check on your food. Tap **SHAKE** to turn on the Shake Reminder. Certain cooking functions use the Shake Reminder automatically (see **Cooking Functions**, page 10).

Shake Reminder

- The Shake Reminder will alert you with 5 beeps, and **(Shake)** will blink on the display.
- If you do not remove the basket, the Shake Reminder will beep again after 1 minute and the display will show a solid **(Shake)**.
- The Shake Reminder will go away once you take out the basket.

Cooking Guide

Overfilling

- If the basket is overfilled, food will cook unevenly.

Using Oil

- Adding a small amount of oil to your food will make it crispier. Use no more than 30 mL / 2 US tbsp of oil.
- Oil sprays are excellent for applying small amounts of oil evenly to all food items.

Food Tips

- You can air fry any frozen foods or goods that can be baked in an oven.
- To make cakes, hand pies, or any food with filling or batter, place food in a heat-safe container before placing in the basket.
- Air frying high-fat foods will cause fat to drip to the bottom of the baskets. To avoid excess smoke while cooking, pour out fat drippings after cooking.
- Liquid-marinated foods create splatter and excess smoke. Pat these foods dry before air frying.

French Fries

- Add 8–15 mL / ½–1 US tbsp oil for crispiness.
- When making fries from raw potatoes, soak uncooked fries in water for 15 minutes to remove starch prior to frying. Pat dry with a towel before adding oil.
- Cut uncooked fries smaller for crispier results. Try cutting fries into 0.6- by 7.6-cm / ¼- by 3-inch strips.

Note: For more from the Cosori Kitchen, check out our Recipe Book and Tips from the Chef.

More Functions

Pausing

1. Press ▶II to pause cooking. The air fryer will stop heating, and ▶II will turn blue until you press ▶II to resume cooking.
2. After 30 minutes of inactivity, the air fryer will turn off.
3. This function allows you to pause the cooking program without removing the basket from the air fryer.

Automatically Resume Cooking

- If you pull out the basket, the air fryer will pause cooking automatically. The display will turn off temporarily as a safety feature.

- When you return the basket, the air fryer will automatically resume cooking based on your previous settings.

Automatically Shutoff

- If the air fryer has no active cooking programs, the air fryer will clear all settings and turn off after 3 minutes of inactivity.

Overheat Protection

- If the air fryer overheats, it will automatically shut down as a safety feature.

- Let the air fryer cool down completely before using it again.

CARE & MAINTENANCE

Note:

- **Always** *clean the air fryer basket and crisper plate after every use.*

- *Lining the basket with foil (except the crisper plate) may make cleanup easier.*

1. Turn off and unplug the air fryer. Allow it to cool completely before cleaning. Pull out the basket for faster cooling.

2. Wipe the outside of the air fryer with a moist cloth, if necessary.

3. The basket and crisper plate are dishwasher safe. You can also wash the basket and crisper plate with hot, soapy water and a non-abrasive sponge. Soak if necessary.

Note: The basket and crisper plate have a nonstick coating. Avoid using metal utensils and abrasive cleaning materials.

4. For stubborn grease:

    a. In a small bowl, mix 30 mL / 2 US tbsp of baking soda and 15 mL / 1 US tbsp of water to form a spreadable paste.

    b. Use a sponge to spread the paste on the basket and crisper plate and scrub. Let the basket and crisper plate sit for 15 minutes before rinsing.

    c. Wash basket with soap and water before using.

5. Clean the inside of the air fryer with a slightly moist, non-abrasive sponge or cloth. **Do not** immerse in water. [*Figure 3.1*] If needed, clean the heating coil to remove food debris.

6. Dry before using.

Note: Make sure the heating coil is completely dry before turning on the air fryer.

Figure 3.1

TROUBLESHOOTING

Problem	Possible Solution
The air fryer will not turn on.	Make sure the air fryer is plugged in.
	Push the basket securely into the air fryer.
Foods are not completely cooked.	Place smaller batches of ingredients into the inner basket. If the basket is overstuffed, then ingredients will be undercooked.
	Increase cooking temperature or time.
Foods are cooked unevenly.	Foods that are stacked on top of each other or close to each other need to be shaken or flipped during cooking (see **Shaking Food**, page 11).
Foods are not crispy after air frying.	Spraying or brushing a small amount of oil on foods can increase crispiness (see **Cooking Guide**, page 12).
French fries are not fried correctly.	See **French Fries**, page 14.
Basket will not slide into the air fryer securely.	Make sure the basket is not overfilled with food.
White smoke or steam is coming out of the air fryer.	The air fryer may produce some white smoke or steam when you use it for the first time or during cooking. This is normal.
	Make sure the basket and the inside of the air fryer are cleaned properly and not greasy.
	Cooking greasy foods will cause oil to collect beneath the crisper plate. This oil will produce white smoke, and the basket may be hotter than usual. This is normal, and should not affect cooking. Handle the basket with care.
Dark smoke is coming out of the air fryer.	Immediately unplug your air fryer. Dark smoke means that food is burning or there is a circuit problem. Wait for smoke to clear before pulling the basket out. If the cause was not burnt food, contact **Customer Support** (page 15).
The air fryer has a plastic smell.	Any air fryer may have a plastic smell from the manufacturing process. This is normal. Follow the instructions for a **Test Run** (page 8) to get rid of the plastic smell. If a plastic smell is still present, please contact **Customer Support** (see page 15).
Display shows Error Code "E1".	There is an open circuit in the temperature monitor. Contact **Customer Support** (see page 15).
Display shows Error Code "E2".	There is a short circuit in the temperature monitor. Contact **Customer Support** (see page 15).
Display shows Error Code "E3".	Turn off and unplug the air fryer and allow it to cool completely. If the display continues to show "**E3**", contact **Customer Support** (see page 15).

If your problem is not listed, please contact **Customer Support** (see page 15).

WARRANTY INFORMATION

Product Name	Pro LE 4.7-Litre Air Fryer
Model	CAF-L501-KUK
For your own reference, we strongly recommend that you record your order ID and date of purchase.	
Order ID	
Date of Purchase	

TERMS & POLICY

Arovast Corporation warrants all products to be of the highest quality in material, craftsmanship, and service for 2 years, effective from the date of purchase to the end of the warranty period. Warranty lengths may vary between product categories.

If you have any questions or concerns about your new product, please contact our helpful Customer Support Team.

CUSTOMER SUPPORT

Arovast Corporation
1202 N. Miller St., Suite A
Anaheim, CA 92806
USA

Email: support.eu@cosori.com

*Please have your order invoice and order ID ready before contacting Customer Support.

COSORI®